Frommer's®
Boston 2012

by Marie Morris

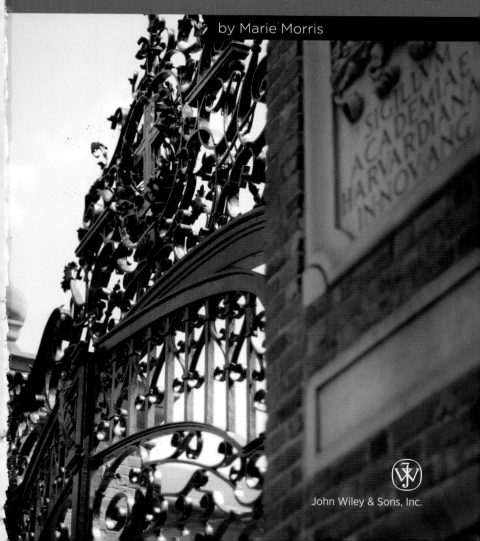

John Wiley & Sons, Inc.

Published by:
John Wiley & Sons, Inc.
111 River St.
Hoboken, NJ 07030-5774

ISBN 978-1-118-01721-0 (paper); ISBN 978-1-118-07482-4 (paper); ISBN 978-1-118-11519-0 (ebk); ISBN 978-1-118-11518-3 (ebk); ISBN 978-1-118-11520-6 (ebk)

Editor: Ian Skinnari
Production Editor: Heather Wilcox
Cartographer: Andrew Dolan
Photo Editors: Alden Gewirtz, Cherie Cincilla
Cover Photo Editor: Richard Fox
Design and Layout by Vertigo Design
Graphics and Prepress by Wiley Indianapolis Composition Services
Front cover photo: Aerial view of Old State House, Boston © John Coletti/Jon Arnold Images Ltd./ Alamy Images
Back cover photos, left to right: Lobster dinner with corn on the cob, in Boston © Richard Nowitz/ National Geographic/Getty Images; Boston, view from Charles river © SIME/eStock Photo; George Washington Statue and tulip beds in the Boston Public Garden © Frank Vetere/Alamy Images

For information on our other products and services or to obtain technical support, please contact our Customer Care Department within the U.S. at 877/762-2974, outside the U.S. at 317/572-3993 or fax 317/572-4002.
Wiley also publishes its books in a variety of electronic formats. Some content that appears in print may not be available in electronic formats.
Manufactured in China
5 4 3 2 1

CONTENTS

List of Maps vi

1 THE BEST OF BOSTON 1

The Most Unforgettable Travel Experiences 3

The Best Splurge Hotels 3

The Best Moderately Priced Hotels 5

The Most Unforgettable Dining Experiences 6

The Best Free (or Almost Free) Things to Do 7

The Best Outdoor Activities 8

The Best Museums 10

The Best Activities for Families 12

The Best Shopping 13

2 BOSTON IN DEPTH 16

Boston Today 18

Looking Back at Boston 19

Boston in Pop Culture 27

Eating & Drinking 31

When to Go 32

BOSTON CALENDAR OF EVENTS 33

Responsible Travel 39

Tours 40

3 SUGGESTED BOSTON ITINERARIES 42

THE NEIGHBORHOODS IN BRIEF 43

THE BEST OF BOSTON IN 1 DAY 50

THE BEST OF BOSTON IN 2 DAYS 55

SUGGESTED EVENING ITINERARIES 56

THE BEST OF BOSTON IN 3 DAYS 58

4 WHERE TO STAY 60

Best Hotel Bets 61

PRICE CATEGORIES 61

WHAT YOU'LL REALLY PAY 62

Downtown 63

Beacon Hill/North Station 70

Charlestown 73

South Boston Waterfront (Seaport District) 73

Chinatown/Theater District 75

The South End 77

The Back Bay 77

FAMILY-FRIENDLY HOTELS 80

Outskirts & Brookline 86

Cambridge 89

At & near the Airport 94

Practical Information 96

Getting the Best Deal 97

5 WHERE TO EAT 99

Best Restaurant Bets 100
PRICE CATEGORIES 101
The Waterfront 101
The North End 104
WEEKDAY BREAKFAST & WEEKEND BRUNCH 109
Faneuil Hall Marketplace & the Financial District 109
Downtown Crossing 111
Beacon Hill 112
Chinatown/Theater District 112
YUM, YUM, DIM SUM 113

The South End 115
The Back Bay 117
FAMILY-FRIENDLY RESTAURANTS 118
QUICK BITES & PICNIC PROVISIONS 120
Kenmore Square, the Fenway & Brookline 122
THE GREAT OUTDOORS: ALFRESCO DINING 123
Cambridge 124
Practical Information 132
Restaurants by Cuisine 133

6 WHAT TO SEE & DO IN BOSTON 135

The Top Attractions 136
LET'S MAKE A DEAL 140
ON TOP OF THE WORLD 146
The Freedom Trail 150
More Museums & Attractions 166
Historic Houses 169
African-American History 172
Parks & Gardens 173
Cambridge 174
CELEBRITY CEMETERY 176

Boston Neighborhoods to Explore 180
WELCOME TO THE NORTH END 181
Especially for Kids 184
Organized Tours 188
MISSING THIS WOULD BE A CRIME 195
Outdoor Pursuits 196
A VACATION IN THE ISLANDS 199
Spectator Sports 202

7 BOSTON STROLLS 207

WALKING TOUR 1: THE BACK BAY 208
WALKING TOUR 2: THE WATERFRONT 214
WALKING TOUR 3: HARVARD SQUARE 219

8 SHOPPING 230

The Shopping Scene 231
Shopping A to Z 234

*AN ARTSY STROLL ALONG NEWBURY
STREET* 235

9 BOSTON AFTER DARK 255

Getting Tickets 256
The Performing Arts 257
The Club & Music Scene 267

The Bar Scene 274
More Entertainment Options 280
Late-Night Bites 283

10 SIDE TRIPS FROM BOSTON 284

Lexington & Concord 285
The North Shore & Cape Ann 299
A WHALE OF AN ADVENTURE 312
NORTH SHORE BEACHES 320

Plymouth 327
THE ADAMS FAMILY 328

11 PLANNING YOUR TRIP TO BOSTON 337

Getting There 338
LET'S MAKE A DEAL 340

Getting Around 343
FAST FACTS: BOSTON 349

Index 362

LIST OF MAPS

Boston's Changing Shoreline   21

Boston Orientation   44

Boston Transit   47

The Best of Boston in 1, 2 and 3 Days   52

Boston Hotels   64

Cambridge Hotels   91

Boston Restaurants   102

North End Restaurants   105

Cambridge Restaurants   125

Boston Attractions   138

Walking Tour 1: The Back Bay   209

Walking Tour 2: The Waterfront   215

Walking Tour 3: Harvard Square   221

Back Bay Shopping   233

Boston After Dark   258

Cambridge After Dark   261

Boston and Surrounding Areas   287

Lexington   289

Concord   293

Marblehead   301

Salem   305

Gloucester   315

Rockport   323

Plymouth   329

ABOUT THE AUTHOR

MARIE MORRIS grew up in New York and graduated from Harvard, where she studied history. She has worked for *Newser.com*, *02138* magazine, the *Boston Herald*, *Boston* magazine, and the *New York Times*. She's the author of *Frommer's Boston Day by Day* and *Boston For Dummies*, and she covers Boston for *Frommer's New England* and *Frommer's New England Day by Day*. She lives in Boston, not far from Paul Revere.

ACKNOWLEDGMENTS

To Kelly Regan, Ian Skinnari, Linda Barth, Maureen Clarke, and the rest of the miracle workers at Frommer's, a world of thanks. Thank you also to Kristin Goss, Michael Dobler, Andrea Rasmussen, Susan Steinway, Jim McCormack, David Wallace, Lauren Goldberg, Alex Moot, Nancy Roosa, Michelle Samplin-Salgado, Diego Salgado, and Tim Naimi. And a warm welcome to future research assistants Amya Naimi and Sonia Naimi.

—Marie Morris

HOW TO CONTACT US

In researching this book, we discovered many wonderful places—hotels, restaurants, shops, and more. We're sure you'll find others. Please tell us about them, so we can share the information with your fellow travelers in upcoming editions. If you were disappointed with a recommendation, we'd love to know that, too. Please write to:

Frommer's Boston 2012
Wiley Publishing, Inc. • 111 River St. • Hoboken, NJ 07030-5774
frommersfeedback@wiley.com

ADVISORY & DISCLAIMER

FROMMER'S STAR RATINGS, ICONS & ABBREVIATIONS

Every hotel, restaurant, and attraction listing in this guide has been ranked for quality, value, service, amenities, and special features using a star-rating system. In country, state, and regional guides, we also rate towns and regions to help you narrow down your choices and budget your time accordingly. Hotels and restaurants are rated on a scale of zero (recommended) to three stars (exceptional). Attractions, shopping, nightlife, towns, and regions are rated according to the following scale: zero stars (recommended), one star (highly recommended), two stars (very highly recommended), and three stars (must-see).

In addition to the star-rating system, we also use seven feature icons that point you to the great deals, in-the-know advice, and unique experiences that separate travelers from tourists. Throughout the book, look for:

Special finds—those places only insiders know about

Fun facts—details that make travelers more informed and their trips more fun

Kids—best bets for kids and advice for the whole family

Special moments—those experiences that memories are made of

Overrated—places or experiences not worth your time or money

Insider tips—great ways to save time and money

Great values—where to get the best deals

The following abbreviations are used for credit cards:

| **AE** | American Express | **DISC** | Discover | **V** | Visa |
| **DC** | Diners Club | **MC** | MasterCard | | |

TRAVEL RESOURCES AT FROMMERS.COM

Frommer's travel resources don't end with this guide. Frommer's website, **www.frommers.com**, has travel information on more than 4,000 destinations. We update features regularly, giving you access to the most current trip-planning information and the best airfare, lodging, and car-rental bargains. You can also listen to podcasts, connect with other Frommers.com members through our active-reader forums, share your travel photos, read blogs from guidebook editors and fellow travelers, and much more.

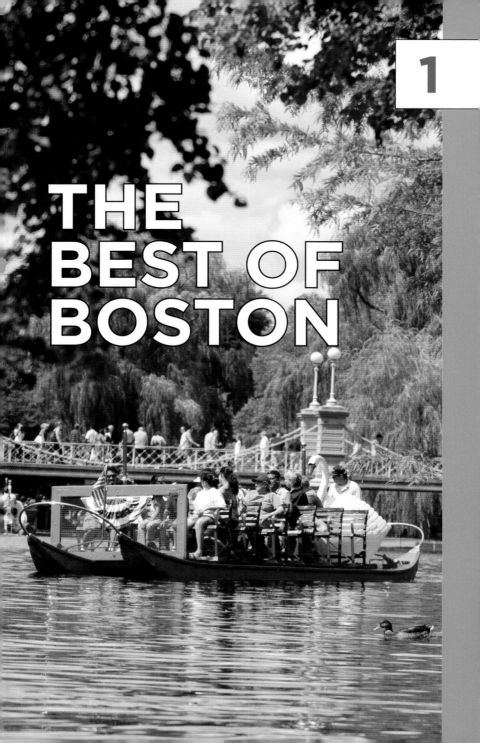

THE
BEST OF
BOSTON

Boston offers residents and visitors an irresistible blend of past, present, and future. History and innovation combine to create a small-scale destination that's easy to explore yet always surprising. One of the oldest American cities, Boston is known around the world for high tech and hospitals, arts and music, and dozens of excellent colleges. With its fascinating attractions, excellent shopping, lovely scenery, and terrific restaurants, the Boston area is perfect for both a quick visit and a longer stay.

Things to Do Bostonians walk everywhere. One top historic attraction is a walking tour—the Freedom Trail—and two favorite neighborhoods are pedestrian-friendly **Beacon Hill** and the **North End**. They walk the galleries of the **Museum of Fine Arts** and the **Institute of Contemporary Art**, the banks of the **Charles River**, and the lively streets of **Harvard Square**. Then they take a break in the **Public Garden** for a ride on a **Swan Boat**, at **Fenway Park** for a Red Sox game, or at a restaurant for local seafood.

Shopping The most interesting shopping in New England is the shops, boutiques, galleries, markets, and malls of the Boston area. **Newbury Street** is a walkable destination that's perfect for window-shopping as well as the real thing; it's the heart of the **Back Bay,** where high-profile chains thrive alongside only-in-Boston merchandise. **Faneuil Hall Marketplace** boasts a similar blend, but the real gems are the neighborhoods, including **Beacon Hill** and the **South End** in Boston, and **Harvard Square** and **Porter Square** in **Cambridge.**

Restaurants & Dining Familiar favorites such as New England clam chowder, Boston baked beans, Boston cream pie, and Samuel Adams beer are just part of the dynamic dining scene. Trends are less significant than seafood from nearby waters, local produce (organic more often than not), and price points fit for both students and special occasions. Head to **the North End** for Italian, to **the South End** for the hottest bistros, and to **Cambridge** for a mix of upscale, ethnic, and budget-friendly options.

Nightlife & Entertainment Classical music is the headliner, but Boston and Cambridge are also famed for rock, folk, and jazz. The legendary Boston Symphony Orchestra and beloved Boston Pops play at landmark **Symphony Hall;** across the river, Cambridge's **Central Square** boasts the best live-music scene in New England. Add top-notch comedy and improv, throw in the wild variety of student performances, and you may not even notice that local nightlife—thanks largely to the 2am curfew for clubs—leaves something to be desired.

PREVIOUS PAGE: **A Swan Boat in the Public Garden.**

THE most unforgettable
TRAVEL EXPERIENCES

o **A Sky Full of Fireworks:** The Fourth of July fireworks flash over the Charles River; Boston greets the New Year with First Night pyrotechnics that flare above the Common in the early evening and the Inner Harbor at midnight. See "Boston Calendar of Events," in chapter 2.

o **A Ride on a Duck:** Board a reconditioned amphibious World War II landing craft (on Huntington Ave. near the Prudential Center, at the Museum of Science, or near the New England Aquarium) for a sightseeing ride that includes a dip in the river—for the Duck boat, not for you. See p. 188.

o **An Afternoon Red Sox Game:** Since 1912, baseball fans have made pilgrimages to Fenway Park, the "lyric little bandbox of a ball park" (in John Updike's words) off Kenmore Square. Soak up the atmosphere and bask in the sun. See p. 202.

Boston's famous Fourth of July fireworks.

o **A Walk Around the North End:** Boston's Little Italy (but don't call it that!) has an old-world flavor you won't want to miss. Explore the shops on Salem Street, and be sure to stop for coffee and a pastry at a Hanover Street *caffè*. See "Welcome to the North End," on p. 181.

o **A Visit to Beacon Hill:** The quintessential Boston neighborhood comes complete with Federal-style homes lining cobblestone streets and overlooking stately parks. Wear good walking shoes, and let your imagination run wild. See "Boston Neighborhoods to Explore," p. 180.

THE best SPLURGE HOTELS

o **Boston Harbor Hotel,** Rowes Wharf, Waterfront (℃ 800/752-7077). Dazzling architecture, a great location between the waterfront and the Rose Kennedy Greenway, and maniacal attention to detail add up to pampering on a suitably dramatic scale. See p. 63.

o **Charles Hotel,** 1 Bennett St., Cambridge (℃ 800/882-1818). Steps from the hubbub of Harvard Square, the unfailingly elegant Charles is a sanctuary of contemporary design and traditional hospitality. See p. 89.

Boston Harbor Hotel.

- **Eliot Hotel,** 370 Commonwealth Ave., Back Bay (✆ **800/443-5468**). Location and layout give the Eliot the feel of a luxury apartment building. Business amenities and elegant traditional furnishings contribute to its seamless blend of commerce and comfort. See p. 78.
- **Four Seasons Hotel,** 200 Boylston St., Back Bay (✆ **800/819-5053**). The best hotel in New England has everything—and what it doesn't have on the premises, the incredible staff will track down. Superb service, plush accommodations, and lavish amenities make a stay here unforgettable. See p. 79.
- **Mandarin Oriental, Boston,** 776 Boylston St., Back Bay (✆ **866/526-6567**). The legendary service, residential atmosphere, and East-meets-West vibe combine to create a can't-miss destination. See p. 80.

The Mandarin Oriental, Boston.

THE best MODERATELY PRICED HOTELS

- **Charlesmark Hotel,** 655 Boylston St. (℡617/247-1212). The Charlesmark's thoughtful features—plush bedding, free local phone calls, friendly service, custom-designed everything—more than make up for the modest size of the rooms. **Bonus:** Units at the front of the building overlook the Boston Marathon finish line. See p. 84.

- **Doubletree Guest Suites,** 400 Soldiers Field Rd., Brighton (℡800/222-8733). Every unit here is a spacious two-room suite. The location, straddling Boston and Cambridge, is especially good if you're driving to Boston. See p. 87.

- **Harborside Inn,** 185 State St., downtown (℡888/723-7565). Exposed-brick walls give this updated 19th-century warehouse a residential feel. Close to downtown attractions, it's convenient to the nearby Financial District. See p. 67.

- **The MidTown Hotel,** 220 Huntington Ave., Back Bay (℡800/343-1177). A unique combination of comfortable, no-frills rooms and a handy location makes this hotel the most motel-like lodging in central Boston. And the cheapest guest parking in the Back Bay can save you as much as $25 per day. See p. 85.

- **Newbury Guest House,** 261 Newbury St., Back Bay (℡800/437-7668). This place would be a bargain even if it weren't ideally situated in the heart of Boston's best shopping. Room prices even include continental breakfast. See p. 85.

The Harborside Inn.

The Newbury Guest House.

THE most unforgettable
DINING EXPERIENCES

- **Durgin-Park,** 340 Faneuil Hall Marketplace (© 617/227-2038). This Boston institution has packed 'em in since 1827. It serves classic New England fare in abundant portions at communal tables, delighting everyone from local tycoons to visiting toddlers. Well, almost everyone: The famously crotchety staff is so much a part of the legend that some people are disappointed when—quite often—the waitresses are courteous and pleasant. See p. 110.

- **Hamersley's Bistro,** 553 Tremont St. (© 617/423-2700). Established and innovative, adventurous and comfortable, Hamersley's is both a neighborhood favorite and a can't-miss special-occasion place. Julia Child encouraged chef-owner Gordon Hamersley to open the restaurant and became a loyal customer—need I say more? See p. 115.

- **Legal Sea Foods,** 255 State St. (© 617/742-5300), and other locations. Like the culinary equivalent of a medical specialist, Legal's does one thing and does it exceptionally well. It's a chain for a great reason: People can't get enough of the freshest seafood around. See p. 101.

- **Mr. Bartley's Burger Cottage,** 1246 Massachusetts Ave., Cambridge (© 617/354-6559). Trends in food and fashion come and go, and Harvard Square sees them all. Luckily, the neighborhood has a place that puts the "comfort" in comfort food. Bartley's is famous for its juicy burgers, incredible onion rings, and a down-to-earth atmosphere that's increasingly rare in these parts. See p. 127.

Legal Sea Foods.

Pizzeria Regina.

- **Pizzeria Regina,** 11½ Thacher St. (©**617/227-0765**). With its red-and-white-checked tablecloths and fiery oven, Regina's looks like Hollywood's idea of a pizza joint. After one bite of slightly smoky crust, you'll be sending Martin Scorsese to the back of the line. See p. 108.
- **Ye Olde Union Oyster House,** 41 Union St. (©**617/227-2750**). Wise guys sneer about all the tourists, but the Union Oyster House is popular with both visitors and locals for a reason—the unbeatable combination of historic atmosphere and traditional food that's drawn crowds since 1826. See p. 109.

THE best FREE (OR ALMOST FREE) THINGS TO DO

- **Picnic by the Water:** Head for the harbor or river, relax on a park bench or patch of grass, turn off your phone, and enjoy the spectacular scene. Whether it's sailboats or ocean liners, sea gulls or scullers, there's always something worth watching. My favorite spot is Sargent's Wharf, on the edge of the North End, but it's just one of thousands of pleasant spots. See chapter 6.
- **Visit a Museum:** Schedule your visit to take advantage of free or reduced admission at certain times. The **USS *Constitution* Museum** is free all the time; the **Museum of Fine Arts** is free after 4pm Wednesday; the **Institute of Contemporary Art** is free after 5pm Thursday; and the **Children's Museum** costs just $1 after 5pm on Friday. See chapter 6.
- **Ride on a Swan:** A Swan *Boat,* that is. The engagingly low-tech vessels ply the waters of the Public Garden lagoon at a stately pace, allowing an up-close view of the barely wild wildlife that flourishes in the heart of the city. For a family of four, a ride costs all of 8 bucks. See p. 173.

Sargent's Wharf.

○ **Take a Ranger-Led Tour:** The National Park Service is such a good use of tax money. Free and cheap tours of historic attractions all over eastern Massachusetts elevate a visit to a park, a house, a neighborhood, or even a government installation (the Charlestown Navy Yard) from good to great. See chapters 6 and 10.

○ **Relish a Vicarious Thrill:** Without so much as lacing up a sneaker, you can participate in the world-famous Boston Marathon. Stretch a little. Drink plenty of fluids. Claim a piece of sidewalk with a front-row view of the course. Cheer as the runners thunder past. Then put your feet up—you must be exhausted. See p. 205.

○ **Prowl Newbury Street:** From the genteel Arlington Street end to the cutting-edge Massachusetts Avenue end, Boston's legendary shopping destination is 8 blocks of pure temptation: galleries, boutiques, jewelry and gift shops, and more. Fortunately, window-shopping is free. See chapter 8.

○ **Check Out a College Concert or Show:** Countless student groups just want an attentive audience, and the free or minimal admission can pay off in the long run. Imagine the credit card commercial: "Ability to say you recognized the talent of [insert name of big star] in a student production? Priceless." See chapter 9.

THE best OUTDOOR ACTIVITIES

○ **A Ride Across the Harbor:** The ferry that connects Long Wharf and the Charlestown Navy Yard is a treasure concealed in plain sight. You might notice the boat traffic on the Inner Harbor as you make your way around downtown; for just $1.70, you can be part of it. See chapter 3.

○ **An Island Excursion:** The Boston Harbor Islands National Recreation Area is something of a hidden secret, just offshore but a world away. Magnificent views combine with natural and man-made features to create a destination so accessible and interesting that you won't believe how uncrowded it is. See chapter 6.

The ferry ride connecting Long Wharf and the Charlestown Navy Yard.

o **An Interlude at a Cafe:** Outdoor seating in a place with great people-watching is a good idea, right up there with fire and the wheel. A passing parade of shoppers and students (on Newbury St. and in Harvard Sq.) is more interesting than suits and ties (downtown and the rest of the Back Bay), but if the breeze and the iced cappuccino are cool, what's not to like? See chapter 7.

o **A Free Concert:** The Boston area's cultural scene has no real off season. During the summer, many musicians and musical groups take their acts outside—to parks, plazas, and even a barge (behind the Boston Harbor Hotel). Plan well and you can enjoy music alfresco almost every night. See chapter 9.

o **A Stroll (or Jog) Along the River:** The bike path that hugs both shores of the Charles accommodates pedestrians, runners, and

Sidewalk dining along Newbury street.

Jogging on the Esplanade.

in-line skaters, as well as cyclists. The Esplanade (adjacent to the Back Bay) offers both people-watching and gorgeous trees and shrubs; the Cambridge side has abundant seating and fabulous views of the Boston skyline. See chapters 6 and 7.

○ **A Walk Back in Time:** Head for Concord to experience nature as Henry David Thoreau did in the mid–19th century. Through a nearly magical combination of circumstances, Walden Pond looks much as it did when the author and naturalist lived there from July 1845 through September 1847. See chapter 10.

○ **A Seaside Saunter:** Gorgeous Marblehead is a quintessential New England town, with crooked lanes leading down to a broad harbor jammed with yachts, sailboats, and fishing vessels. Great shopping, good food, interesting architecture, arresting scenery, and plenty of places to sit and watch the waterborne action make it one of my favorite destinations anywhere. See chapter 10.

THE best MUSEUMS

○ **Concord Museum:** Always informative, never overwhelming, this thoughtfully organized museum shows and tells visitors enough about the town's history to help them make the most of a visit here. See p. 294.

○ **The Institute of Contemporary Art:** Literally and figuratively a trip—it's on the South Boston waterfront and unlike any other cultural institution in Boston—the ICA is a blast. The architecture is amazing; be sure you walk around to the back of the building, which juts out *above* Boston Harbor. See p. 140.

One of the many works on display at the Institute of Contemporary Art.

- **Isabella Stewart Gardner Museum:** The Gardner is a magnificent repository of art and nature in a building that's as impressive as anything hanging on the walls. Modeled on a Venetian *palazzo*, it centers on a glorious plant-filled atrium. See p. 141.

- **John F. Kennedy Presidential Library and Museum:** The exhibits here capture the personality of the library's charismatic namesake through video, artifacts, photos, documents, and more. A visit will help you understand why the Camelot era remains so compelling half a century later. See p. 142.

- **Museum of Fine Arts:** The MFA made headlines when the Art of the Americas wing opened in 2010—but it's a great destination even if you never set foot in the new galleries. The whole place overflows with masterpieces so

The atrium at the Isabella Stewart Gardner Museum.

familiar that seeing them is like running into an old friend on the street. See p. 144.

o **Peabody Essex Museum:** Yes, it's possible to spend a day in Salem and not give witches more than a passing thought. All by itself, the Peabody Essex is worth a trip to the North Shore. Check ahead for information about special exhibitions, or just take in the marvels of the permanent collections. See p. 307.

THE best ACTIVITIES FOR FAMILIES

o **A Visit to Faneuil Hall Marketplace:** Street performers, crowds from all over the world, the food court, restaurants, bars, and shops make Faneuil Hall Marketplace (you'll also hear it called Quincy Market) Boston's most popular destination. It's conveniently located across the street from the harbor, where a stroll along the water can help your crew decompress. See p. 137.

o **An Exploration of the Museum of Science:** Your kids will revel in the displays and exhibits that cram every branch of science and inquiry into this enormous and child-accessible institution. See p. 146.

o **An Excursion to the Public Garden:** A perfect retreat during or after a busy day of sightseeing. Ride a Swan Boat, visit with the Mallard family of *Make Way for Ducklings* fame, admire the real birds, and marvel as the whole family starts to chill out. See p. 173.

The Van de Graaff generator at the Museum of Science.

Fenway Park.

o **A Trip to the Boston Children's Museum:** The hands-on exhibits, noisy galleries, and overall air of discovery and excitement make this excursion catnip for the elementary-school set. See p. 186.

o **A Thrill "Ride":** The Mugar Omni Theater (at the Museum of Science) and the 3-D Simons IMAX Theatre (at the New England Aquarium) offer intrepid visitors hair-raising experiences in the safety of a comfortable auditorium. Most of the large-format films concentrate on the natural world. See p. 147 for the Mugar Omni Theater and p. 149 for the Simons IMAX Theatre.

o **A Tour of Fenway Park:** The creaky, cramped home of the Boston Red Sox, which opened in 1912, is a baseball shrine that entrances visitors. Adolescents too cool to admit that they're having fun at other attractions tend to drop any pretense of boredom here, and younger kids unabashedly love it. The parents saving a bundle by not paying for game tickets tend to agree. See p. 203.

o **A Spell in Salem:** A 12-year-old of my acquaintance—now a college graduate who still cringes when I tell this story—returned from a visit to Salem proclaiming that he wanted to become a witch. Manageable size, interesting attractions, and plenty of space for running around make the Witch City a great choice for an all-ages day trip. See chapter 10.

THE best SHOPPING

o **Every Bookstore in the Boston Area:** Talk about a rising tide lifting all boats—bookworms from around the world flock to Boston and Cambridge, which boast exceptionally well-stocked chain outlets, award-winning

The International Poster Gallery.

independent shops, and special-interest businesses for every appetite. See chapter 8.

o **Barbara Krakow Gallery,** 10 Newbury St., 5th floor, Back Bay (✆617/262-4490). With a handful of notable exceptions, the refrain that haunts the Boston arts scene is "nice, but it's better in New York." Barbara Krakow runs one of the few galleries that gives New Yorkers the inferiority complex. See p. 236.

o **Black Ink,** 101 Charles St., Beacon Hill (✆617/723-3883), and 5 Brattle St., Cambridge (✆617/497-1221). A funky desktop trinket, a retro toy, a beautifully designed kitchen gadget, a gorgeous card—you may not come out of these little treasure chests with what you went in looking for, but you'll almost certainly find something you love. See p. 245.

o **Converse,** 348 Newbury St., Back Bay (✆617/424-5400). Founded in suburban Malden in 1908, the athletic-shoe manufacturer is a local brand with an international presence. If you don't see exactly the right pair of sneakers, head upstairs and create your own. See p. 241.

o **Galería Cubana,** 460 Harrison Ave., South End (✆617/292-2822). It's not the easiest place to find, but this amazing gallery captures the experience of visiting Cuba without a single bit of red tape. See p. 236.

o **International Poster Gallery,** 205 Newbury St., Back Bay (✆617/375-0076). One of the high points of a visit to Newbury Street is a stop here. If you have any interest in graphic design or contemporary art—heck, if you've ever taped a magazine cover to the wall over your desk—you'll find something wonderful here. See p. 236.

○ **John Lewis, Inc.,** 97 Newbury St., Back Bay (✆ **617/266-6665**). The exquisite craftsmanship—executed on the premises by John Lewis himself—makes this jewelry store a favorite with several generations of in-the-know Bostonians. If you see nose prints on the front window, they might be mine. See p. 248.

○ **Joie de Vivre,** 1792 Massachusetts Ave., Cambridge (✆ **617/864-8188**). Just stepping in here puts me at ease. Somewhere in the thoughtful selection of inventive gifts, toys, cards, jewelry, and inspiring tchotchkes is just the right gift (for someone else or for me), and finding it is more than half the fun. See p. 246.

○ **Upstairs Downstairs Antiques,** 93 Charles St., Beacon Hill (✆ **617/367-1950**). Even when I don't wind up buying something here, I come away inspired by the layout of the well-edited merchandise and the knowledge of the helpful staff. See p. 234.

Upstairs Downstairs Antiques.

BOSTON IN DEPTH

Boston embodies contrasts and contradictions—blue blood and blue collar, Yankee and Irish, Brahmin banker and budget-conscious student. The city is home to the country's first public school and to a problematic educational system. A one-time hotbed of abolitionism, it retains an intractable reputation for racism; a proud seaport, it faces a harbor recently reclaimed from crippling pollution. Boston is a famously parochial, insular city whose traditional obsessions are "sports, politics, and revenge," but it's also a magnet for students and intellectuals from all over the world and is the capital of the first U.S. state to make same-sex marriage legal.

Compact in size yet boasting a virtually inexhaustible supply of interesting activities and diversions, Boston is a magnet for history buffs, art lovers, sports fans, shoppers, families, and convention-goers. Whether you fit into one or more or none of those categories, you're still in for an enjoyable time. The interests that draw you here can monopolize your schedule, but you'll have a better experience if you make some room for serendipity—on your schedule and in your attitude.

Boston is a living landmark that bears many marks of its colonial heritage, but where it's theoretically possible (this is just an observation) to spend days without going near anything built before 1960, or even going outdoors. Pick out a suitcase that has room for your walking shoes and get ready for your own adventure.

○ Written in Stone

All over Boston, you'll see plaques commemorating long-gone people, events, and even places ("On this site stood . . ."). Each one tells a little story, in both its text and its context. A plaque commemorating the first Catholic Mass in Boston (on School St. near Washington St., across the street from the Freedom Trail) doesn't seem like a big deal now, but in a Puritan city, toleration of "popery" couldn't have come easily. On Commercial Street near Hull Street, a marker (pictured here) describes the Molasses Flood of 1919, during which 2 million gallons of raw molasses spilled out of a ruptured storage tank into the streets, killing 21 people. The story recalls the days when manufacturing and industry dominated the area that's now the residential North End and scenic waterfront. Look around as you walk around—history is everywhere, just waiting for you to discover it.

FACING PAGE: **The Rose Fitzgerald Kennedy Greenway.**

17

BOSTON TODAY

Twenty-first century Boston is a hot destination. The city has nearly shaken off the well-deserved reputation for stodginess that dogged it for most of its first 4 centuries of existence; the Boston area enjoys a reputation as a hotbed of innovation, its economy slowed but not crippled by the recession that started in 2008. Thanks to a massive highway-construction project that formally wrapped up in 2007, downtown Boston looks better than it has in decades. The parks of the mile-long Rose Kennedy Greenway parallel the waterfront, driving private development and drawing the public with its still-evolving recreational offerings. The "new" convention center—it opened in 2004—has spurred the ongoing transformation of an industrial neighborhood into a tourist magnet, and the triumphs and travails of the local sports teams help keep Boston in back-page headlines around the country.

Today you'll find a metropolis of some 645,000 at the heart of the Greater Boston area, which encompasses 83 cities and towns that are home to 4.4 million people. The hospitals and medical centers are among the best in the world, and healthcare was a hot topic long before the state took a leading role in the country's ongoing debate on the issue. Education and tourism are pillars of the local economy, which has mirrored national trends (positive and negative) in unemployment statistics. The ongoing real-estate downturn has put a damper on the red-hot Boston market, but the city remains one of the most expensive places in the country to live—and to visit, if you don't budget carefully.

As they have for more than a century, immigrants—Irish, eastern European Jewish, Italian, Portuguese, African American, Latino, and West Indian—flock to the Boston area. In the last quarter-century, the Asian and Latino populations have soared.

Whatever their origins, most Bostonians share at least a passing interest in sports. ("How about those Red Sox?" is a favorite conversational gambit all over town.) The New England Patriots, who play in a distant suburb, triumphed in the Super Bowl in 2002, 2004, and 2005—only to find that their third title was

The pre–Big Dig Central Artery slicing through the city.

The Rose Fitzgerald Kennedy Greenway.

virtually a footnote. Three months earlier, in October 2004, the Red Sox won the World Series for the first time since 1918. Many Sox fans believe that victory ended a curse, and they point to the Sox's 2007 Series crown as evidence.

Impressions

For we must consider that we shall be as a city upon a hill. The eyes of all people are upon us . . .
—John Winthrop, sermon, "A Model of Christian Charity," 1630

Pro sports are only part of the story, though: In a region with an enormous student population, college athletics are a big deal, too. You may have heard that Boston is a college town, but you may not realize just how true that is until you're out and about, tripping over chattering post-adolescents nearly everywhere.

To get a sense of what present-day Boston is and isn't like, hit the streets. All over town, you'll find traces of the groups, institutions, and events that shaped Boston's history and created the complex city you see today.

LOOKING BACK AT BOSTON

Permanently settled in 1630, Boston was named for the hometown of some of the Puritans who left England to seek religious freedom in the New World. They met with little of the usual strife with the natives, members of the small, Algonquian-speaking Massachuset tribe that roamed the area. The natives grew corn on some harbor islands but made their homes farther inland.

In 1632, the little peninsula known to the Indians as Shawmut became the capital of the Massachusetts Bay Colony, and the population soon increased rapidly because of the great Puritan migration. Thanks to its excellent location on a deep, sheltered harbor, Boston quickly became a center of shipbuilding, fishing, and trading.

The only thing more important than commerce was religion, and the Puritans exerted such a strong influence that their legacy survives to this day. A concrete reminder is Harvard College's original (1636) mission: preparing young men to be ministers. In 1659, Boston's town fathers officially banned Christmas (the town children apparently had second thoughts—records show that the holiday was back in favor by the 1680s). Another early example of Puritanical stuffiness was recorded in 1673. One Captain Kemble was sentenced to confinement in the stocks for 2 hours because he kissed his wife on their front steps—on a Sunday. He had been away for 3 years.

The indigenous Algonquians.

The Road to Revolution

England began exerting tighter control over its colonies as early as the 1680s. Over the years, laws increasing taxes and restricting trading activities led to trouble. The situation came to a head after the French and Indian War (known in Europe as the Seven Years' War) ended in 1763.

Having helped fight for the British, the colonists were outraged when the Crown expected them to help pay off the war debt. The Sugar Act of 1764 imposed tariffs on sugar, wine, and coffee, mostly affecting those engaged in

The Boston Massacre.

trade; the 1765 Stamp Act taxed everything printed, from legal documents to playing cards, affecting virtually everyone. Boycotts, demonstrations, and riots ensued. The repeal of the Stamp Act in 1766 was no solution—the revolutionary slogan "No taxation without representation" had already helped rouse the colonists.

The Townshend Acts of 1767 imposed taxes on paper, glass, and tea, sparking more unrest. The following year, British troops occupied Boston, and rising tension led to violence. In the Boston Massacre of 1770, five colonists were killed in a scuffle with the redcoats. The first to die was a former slave named Crispus Attucks. The site, represented by a circle of cobblestones, sits on what is now State Street, and the colonists' graves are nearby, in the Granary Burying Ground on Tremont Street.

The Boston Tea Party.

Boston's Changing Shoreline

0   1/2 mi
0   1/2 km

CHARLESTOWN

former Prison Point Bay

former Millers River

EAST BOSTON

CAMBRIDGE

NORTH END

former Mill Pond

former West Cove

former Great Cove

Charles River

BEACON HILL

Boston Harbor

FINANCIAL DISTRICT

BACK BAY

former South Cove

former Back Bay

SOUTH BOSTON

former South Bay

SOUTH END

Since the first permanent English settlers arrived in the Boston area in 1630, land reclamation projects have added over 1,000 acres to the city's land area. This map shows the growth of the city from its original shorelines to the present day.

Original land area, 1630
Additions by 1850
Additions by 1900
Present day

—— Modern street network

Parliament repealed the Townshend Acts but kept the tea tax and, in 1773, granted the East India Company a monopoly on the tea trade with the colonies. The idea was to undercut the price of smuggled tea, but the colonists weren't swayed. In December, three British ships laden with tea sat at anchor in Boston Harbor (roughly where present-day Atlantic Ave. meets the Evelyn Moakley Bridge), waiting for their cargo to be unloaded. Before that could happen, the rabble-rousing Sons of Liberty, stirred up after a spirited public meeting at what's now the Old South Meeting House, boarded the ships and dumped 342 chests of tea into the harbor. The "Boston Tea Party" became a rallying point for both sides; the meetinghouse stages a re-creation of the inflammatory rally every December.

The British responded by closing the port until the tea was paid for and forcing Bostonians to house the soldiers who began to flood the community. They soon numbered 4,000 in a town of 16,000. Mutual distrust ran high—Paul Revere wrote of helping form "a committee for the purpose of watching the movements of the British troops." When the royal commander in Boston, Gen. Thomas Gage, learned that the colonists were accumulating arms and ammunition, he dispatched men to destroy the stockpiles. They departed from what's now Charles Street, between Boston Common and the Public Garden, to cross the Charles River. A lantern signal soon illuminated the steeple of the Old North Church, alerting Revere to their route—the "two if by sea" made famous nearly a century later by Cambridge resident Henry Wadsworth Longfellow.

A New World Order

Troops marched from Boston toward Lexington and Concord late on April 18, 1775. On their "midnight ride," William Dawes and Revere alerted the colonists that the British soldiers were on the march. Just north of Harvard Square, horseshoes embedded in the sidewalk show part of Dawes's route. The riders mobilized the local militia companies, or minutemen. The next day, some 700 British soldiers under Maj. John Pitcairn emerged victorious from a skirmish in Lexington. The troops and militia clashed on the town common, a public area that's still known as the "Battle Green." Later that day, the colonists routed the soldiers at Concord near the North Bridge (a replica now stands in its place), forcing them to retreat to Charlestown.

The redcoats took almost an entire day to make the trip, along the route now marked BATTLE ROAD. You can cover it in a car in about a half-hour. Thanks in no small part to Longfellow's 1861 poem "Paul Revere's Ride" ("Listen my children and you shall hear / Of the midnight ride of Paul Revere"), Lexington and Concord are closely associated with the beginning of the Revolution. In the early stages, military activity left its mark all over eastern Massachusetts, particularly in Cambridge. Royalist sympathizers, or Tories, were concentrated so heavily along one stretch of Brattle Street that it was

Paul Revere's famous lantern.

called "Tory Row." When the tide began to turn, George Washington made his headquarters on the same street (in a house later occupied by Longfellow, which is now a National Park Service site). On nearby Cambridge Common is the spot where Washington took command of the Continental Army on July 3, 1775.

The British won the Battle of Bunker Hill in Charlestown on June 17, 1775, but at the cost of half their forces. (Win a trivia contest by knowing that the battle actually took place on Breed's Hill.) The redcoats abandoned Boston the following March 17. On July 4, 1776, the Continental Congress adopted the Declaration of Independence. Although many Bostonians fought in the 6-year war that followed, Boston itself saw no more battles.

Commerce & Culture

After the war, Boston again became a center of business. Fishing, whaling, and trade with the Far East dominated the economy. Exotic spices and fruits, textiles,

The luxurious homes on Beacon Hill.

Walden author and Massachusetts native Henry David Thoreau.

and porcelain from the other side of the world were familiar luxuries in Boston and nearby Salem. The influential merchant families who became known as Boston Brahmins spearheaded a cultural renaissance that flourished even after the War of 1812 ravaged international shipping, ending Boston's commercial heyday. As banking and manufacturing rose in importance, Boston took a back seat to New York and Philadelphia in size and influence. But the "Athens of America" became known for its intellectual community and its fine art and architecture, including the luxurious homes you see today on Beacon Hill.

In 1822, Boston became a city. From 1824 to 1826, Mayor Josiah Quincy oversaw the landfill project that moved the waterfront away from Faneuil Hall. The market building constructed at that time, which still stands, was named in his honor. It's at Dock Square, one of many locations, all over the city, where hilltops were lopped off and deposited in the water, transforming the coastline and skyline. Projects included the filling of the Mill Pond, now the area around North Station, which began in 1807 and in 25 years consumed the summits of Copp's and Beacon hills.

In the 19th century, landfill work tripled the city's area, creating badly needed space. The largest of the projects, started in 1835 and completed in 1882, was the transformation of the Back Bay from mud flats and marshes into the elegant neighborhood you see today.

By the mid-1800s, Ralph Waldo Emerson, Oliver Wendell Holmes, Henry Wadsworth Longfellow, Nathaniel Hawthorne, Bronson Alcott, Louisa May Alcott, John Greenleaf Whittier, Walt Whitman, Henry David Thoreau, and even Charles Dickens (briefly) and Mark Twain (more briefly) had appeared on the local literary scene. William Lloyd Garrison published the weekly *Liberator* newspaper, a powerful voice in the antislavery movement. Boston became an important stop on the Underground Railroad, the secret network the abolitionists developed to smuggle runaway slaves into Canada.

Local Glory

During the Civil War (1861–65), abolitionist sentiment was the order of the day in Boston—to such a degree that only names of members of the Union Army appear on the rolls listing the war dead in Harvard's Memorial Hall, which is open to the public. Massachusetts's contributions to the war effort included enormous quantities of firearms, shoes, blankets, tents, and men.

Black abolitionist Frederick Douglass, a former member of the

> ### Welcome to "the Hub"
>
> *Boston State-house is the hub of the solar system. You couldn't pry that out of a Boston man if you had the tire of all creation straightened out for a crowbar.*
> **—Oliver Wendell Holmes, Sr., *The Autocrat of the Breakfast-Table*, 1858**

We're Number 1!

Boston's list of firsts is a long one. Here are some highlights:

○ America's first public school (Boston Latin School, 1635)

○ America's first printing press (in Cambridge, 1638)

○ America's first post office (1639)

○ America's first regularly published newspaper, the *Boston News Letter* (1704)

○ America's first St. Patrick's Day parade (1737)

○ America's first chocolate factory (1765)

○ First operation under general anesthesia (removal of a jaw tumor, at Massachusetts General Hospital, 1846)

○ America's first subway (1897)

○ First successful human-to-human organ transplant (of a kidney, at Peter Bent Brigham Hospital, 1954)

○ First successful reattachment of a human limb (a 12-year-old boy's right arm, at Mass. General, 1962)

Massachusetts Anti-Slavery Society, helped recruit the 54th and 55th Massachusetts Colored Regiments. The movie *Glory* tells the story of the 54th, the first army unit made up of free black soldiers, and its white commander, Col. Robert Gould Shaw. The regiment's memorial, a gorgeous bas-relief by Augustus Saint-Gaudens, stands on Boston Common opposite the State House.

A Capital City

The railroad boom of the 1820s and 1830s and the flood of immigration that began soon after made New England an industrial center. Then as now, Boston was the region's unofficial capital. Before and after the Civil War, immigrants from Ireland poured into the city, the first ethnic group to do so in great numbers since the French Huguenots in the early 18th century. Signs reading NO IRISH NEED APPLY became scarce as the new arrivals gained political power, and the first Irish mayor was elected in 1885.

By that time, Boston's class split was a chasm, with the influx of immigrants adding to the social tension. The Irish led the way and were followed by Italian, Portuguese, and eastern European Jewish immigrants. Each group had its own neighborhoods, houses of worship, schools, newspapers, and livelihoods that intersected only occasionally with "proper" society. A small but concrete example: The birthplace of Rose Fitzgerald—later Rose Kennedy, matriarch of the political dynasty—is in the North End, an Irish stronghold at her birth in 1890 that soon became a predominantly Italian neighborhood.

Even as the upper crust was sowing cultural seeds that would wind up enriching everyone—the Boston Symphony, the Boston Public Library, and the Museum of Fine Arts were established in the second half of the 19th century—its prudish behavior gained Boston a reputation for making snobbery an art form. In 1878 the censorious Watch and Ward Society was founded (as the New England Society for the Suppression of Vice), and the phrase "banned in Boston" soon became well known. In 1889, the private St. Botolph Club removed John Singer Sargent's portrait of Isabella Stewart Gardner from public view because her dress was too tight. (It's now at the museum that bears her name.)

John Singer Sargent's "scandalous" portrait of Isabella Stewart Gardner.

The Boston Brahmins could keep their new neighbors out of many areas of their lives, but not politics. The forebears of the Kennedy clan had appeared on the scene—John F. "Honey Fitz" Fitzgerald, Rose's father, was elected mayor in 1910—and the city slowly transformed yet again as WASPs and Catholics struck an uneasy truce.

World War II bolstered Boston's Depression-ravaged industrial economy, and the war's end touched off an economic transformation. Shipping declined, along with New England's textile, shoe, and glass industries, at the same time that students on the GI Bill poured into area colleges and universities. The rise of the local high-technology industry led to new construction, changing the look of the city. The 1960s saw the beginning of a building boom that continues to this day.

The Turn of the Century

Still reeling from the international social upheaval of the 1960s, Boston was the center of a school-busing crisis in the mid-1970s. Sparked by a court-ordered school desegregation plan enacted in 1974, it touched off riots, violence, and a white boycott (a fair number of Bostonians who were then in high school have GEDs rather than diplomas because their parents held them out of class). In the years since, the city has battled its reputation for racism with varying degrees of success. The school system has yet to fully recover from the traumatic experience of busing, but every year it sends thousands of students on to the institutions of higher learning that continue to be Boston's greatest claim to fame.

Those colleges are also magnets for international students, just one element of the city's profound transformation in the late 20th and early 21st centuries. Boston has largely shed its reputation for insularity and become known as one of the "most European" American cities. High-tech businesses helped create a worthy rival for Silicon Valley, and the gentrification that emerged as early as the 1960s continues—the rapidly changing South End is just one indicator of the trend.

It's not all restaurants and shopping, of course—for instance, the Catholic Church's sex-abuse scandal came to light in the Boston Archdiocese, a major presence in this predominantly Catholic area. But social divisions are fading. In 2003, the Massachusetts Supreme Judicial Court ruled that not allowing same-sex couples to marry violated the state constitution, institutionalizing an attitude that had already taken hold outside the courtroom. The typical reaction to legal gay marriage was, more or less, "What's the big deal?" The election of Deval Patrick, who in 2006 became the second African American since Reconstruction (after Virginia's Douglas Wilder) elected governor, inspired similar sentiments.

Cambridge City Hall opened its doors early to become the first city in Massachusetts to issue marriage licenses to same-sex couples in May of 2004.

Thanks in no small part to the college students who clog rapid transit and drive property values out of sight—and who stick around after graduation, keeping the cutting edge nice and sharp—Boston continues to grow and change. A time traveler from the 18th or even 17th century would recognize some parts of the physical city. Its attitude and spirit might be unfamiliar to a visitor from as recently as 20 years ago.

BOSTON IN POP CULTURE

A list of authors, screenwriters, and musicians with ties to Boston could fill a book of its own and only scratch the surface. Here are some suggestions:

Books

FOR CHILDREN

The timeless classic *Make Way for Ducklings,* by Robert McCloskey, tells the story of Mrs. Mallard and her babies on the loose in the Back Bay. After your kids fall for this book (and they will), you can thrill them with a trip to the Public Garden, home to bronze statues representing the family.

Slightly older kids might know the Public Garden as the setting of part of *The Trumpet of the Swan,* by E. B. White. After reading it, a turn around the lagoon on a Swan Boat is mandatory.

An excellent historical title is *Johnny Tremain,* by Esther Forbes, a fictional boy's-eye-view account of the Revolutionary War era. The book vividly describes scenes from the Revolution, many of which take place along the Freedom Trail.

We're Off to Harvard Square, by Sage Stossel, is a delight, written in sprightly verse and beautifully illustrated. It's intended for 9- to 12-year-olds, but younger kids and adults will like it, too.

The popular *Make Way for Ducklings* sculpture in the Public Garden.

FOR ADULTS

My favorite introduction to the city's early history is *Paul Revere and the World He Lived In,* Esther Forbes's look at Boston before, during, and after the Revolution. *Common Ground: A Turbulent Decade in the Lives of Three American Families,* by J. Anthony Lukas, is the definitive account of the busing crisis of the 1970s and the attendant social upheaval. Both won the Pulitzer Prize for nonfiction. In the fiction section, Edwin O'Connor captured Boston machine politics in a book many have challenged but none has surpassed, *The Last Hurrah.*

The Proper Bostonians, an entertaining, perceptive nonfiction look at a bygone era that helped earn Boston its longstanding reputation for stuffiness, is an early work by well-known animal-rights activist Cleveland Amory. *The Friends of Eddie Coyle,* by George V. Higgins, is a crime novel famed for its realistic dialogue and unvarnished take on Boston hoods. *Black Mass,* by Dick Lehr and Gerard O'Neill, updates the story of local organized crime with a nonfiction take on the rise of fugitive (at press time) mobster James "Whitey" Bulger. The novels of Dennis Lehane (see "Film," below), are required reading for Boston-bound fans of mysteries and crime fiction.

Architecture buffs will enjoy *Cityscapes of Boston,* by Robert Campbell and Peter Vanderwarker, and *Lost Boston,* by Jane Holtz Kay. If trivia's your thing, check out the treasury of "did you know" items in *Boston A to Z,* by historian Thomas H. O'Connor.

"Paul Revere's Ride," Henry Wadsworth Longfellow's classic but historically outlandish poem about the events of April 18 and 19, 1775, is collected in many anthologies. It's a must if you plan to walk the Freedom Trail or visit Lexington and Concord.

If you're venturing to Gloucester (or even if you're not), Sebastian Junger's *The Perfect Storm* makes an excellent introduction. The story of a fishing boat caught in historically bad weather will change the way you look at fish on a menu for a long time after you finish reading or watching. The movie version, though heavy on the special effects, is a better-than-average effort.

Film

Thanks to the state's production-friendly tax policies, the Boston area is an increasingly popular film location. Don't be surprised to run across a working crew or hear about a location shoot while you're in town. Two of the best efforts of the past decade—***Gone Baby Gone*** (2007) and ***The Town*** (2010)—share a director, Ben Affleck, who grew up in Cambridge and has become something of a one-man film bureau. ***The Fighter,*** which was set and shot in Lowell, and ***Shutter Island*** rounded out a trio of excellent, well-received Boston-area movies in 2010. Also released in 2010, to considerably less acclaim, were ***Knight & Day*** and ***Edge of Darkness.*** At press time, we're reserving judgment on the 2011 movies ***The Company Men*** and ***The Zookeeper.***

One huge potential stumbling block for movies set in Boston is the nearly impossible feat of rendering local accents accurately. The actors in Affleck's films pull it off, as does the cast of ***Good Will Hunting*** (if you ignore Robin Williams's unfortunate brogue). *Good Will Hunting* stars Affleck and Matt Damon, who grew up in Cambridge and wrote the Academy Award–winning screenplay together. This is the Boston movie to see if you have time for just one.

The Departed (2006), ***The Perfect Storm*** (2000), and ***Mystic River*** (2003)—the latter, like ***Shutter Island*** and ***Gone Baby Gone,*** based on a novel by Dennis Lehane—are among the best recent movies with Boston-area backdrops. They have an awful lot of bad company, however (yes, that was Boston in the Matthew McConaughey vehicle ***Ghosts of Girlfriends Past***). Pictures worth checking out for more than just the cheap thrill of recognizing the locations include ***A Civil Action, The Spanish Prisoner, Next Stop Wonderland*** (all Boston),

Matt Damon and Robin Williams in *Good Will Hunting.*

State and Main (Manchester-by-the-Sea), and *The Love Letter* (Rockport).

If you have a high tolerance for sports and sentiment, check out *Fever Pitch,* a 103-minute video valentine to Boston and the Red Sox. Many scenes were filmed at Fenway Park, and the ending had to be reshot after the Sox won the World Series in 2004 for the first time in 86 years. The script is sappy but captures the maniacal-fan persona with alarming accuracy, and the soundtrack is terrific.

 Summer Lovin'

The axiom that you should order **oysters** only in months with an "R" in them originates in biology. Summer is breeding season, when the energy that usually goes into bulking up (and making lots of juicy meat) gets diverted to reproduction. To experience the best the oyster has to offer, wait till the weather turns colder.

Consider setting the DVR for these older movies: *Blown Away* (especially the scenes when the action first shifts to Boston), *The Verdict* and *The Friends of Eddie Coyle* (Boston), *Glory* (a stylish re-creation of 19th-c. Beacon Hill), *The Witches of Eastwick* (Cohasset), and the sentimental favorite, *Love Story* (Cambridge).

Television

Most TV shows set in Boston use an occasional exterior location shot but otherwise don't get anywhere near the city. They include *Rizzoli & Isles, Boston Legal, The Practice, St. Elsewhere,* and *Spenser: For Hire* (if you can find it). But that's not why you're wondering whether everybody knows your name, is it? *Cheers* was based on a local pub called the Bull & Finch, and the show became so popular that the original bar changed its name and a spin-off opened in Faneuil Hall Marketplace. See p. 274.

Music

Highbrow associations abound: The first American performance of Handel's *Messiah* was in Boston, the city is home to one of the best orchestras in the world, and the Boston Symphony even commissioned a recent Pulitzer Prize winner (George Walker's "Lilacs"). The jukebox or MP3 player is where the recent action is. The 1970s and '80s were the heyday of local rock, with Boston (the band), the Cars, and the J. Geils Band leading the pack. But the piece of music perhaps most closely associated with the city is the Standells' "Dirty Water." Released in 1966, it was written by the band's producer after he was mugged on the Massachusetts Avenue bridge, which connects Boston and Cambridge "down by the banks of the river Charles."

The movie soundtrack to seek out is *Fever Pitch* (see "Film," above), a superb collection of recent songs associated with Boston. It includes "Dirty Water" and Neil Diamond's "Sweet Caroline," a random selection that caught on out of superstition and now booms through Fenway Park in the bottom of the eighth inning of every Red Sox home game.

Download the Dropkick Murphys' "Tessie" and Augustana's "Boston," dig through your grandparents' LPs to find the Kingston Trio's "Charlie on the MTA," learn the words to "Where Everybody Knows Your name" (the *Cheers* theme song), and you'll be well on your way to passing for a local, or at least a local college student.

EATING & DRINKING

The days when restaurant snobs sniffed that they had to go to New York to get a decent meal are long gone. Especially in warm weather, when excellent local produce appears on menus in every price range, the Boston area holds its own with any other market in the country. Celebrity chefs and rising stars spice up a dynamic restaurant scene, and traditional favorites occupy an important niche. The huge student population seeks out value, which it often finds at ethnic restaurants.

Seafood is a specialty in Boston, and you'll find it on the menu at almost every restaurant—trendy or classic, expensive or cheap, American (whatever that is) or ethnic. Some pointers: **Scrod** or **schrod** is a generic term for fresh white-fleshed fish, usually served in filets. **Local shellfish** include Ipswich and Essex clams, Atlantic lobsters, Wellfleet oysters, scallops, mussels, and shrimp. If you're worried about overfishing, visit www.montereybayaquarium.org and download the Monterey Bay Aquarium's pocket guide to fish in the Northeast.

Lobster was once so abundant that the Indians showed the Pilgrims how to use the ugly crustaceans as fertilizer. Order lobster boiled or steamed and you'll get a plastic bib, drawn butter (for dipping), a nutcracker (for the claws and tail), and a pick (for the legs). Restaurants price lobsters by the pound; you'll typically pay at least $15 to $20 for a "chicken" (1- to 1¼-lb.) lobster, and more for the bigger specimens. If you want someone else to do the work, lobster is available in a "roll" (lobster-salad sandwich), stuffed and baked or broiled, in or over pasta, in a "pie" (casserole), in salad, and in bisque.

Well-made **New England clam chowder** is studded with fresh clams and thickened with cream. Recipes vary, but they *never* include tomatoes. (Tomatoes go in Manhattan clam chowder.) If you want clams but not soup, many places serve **steamers,** or soft-shell clams cooked in the shell, as an appetizer or main dish. More common are hard-shell clams—**littlenecks** (small) or **cherrystones** (medium-size)—served raw, like oysters.

Traditional **Boston baked beans,** which date from colonial days, when cooking on the Sabbath was forbidden, earned Boston the nickname "Beantown." House-made baked beans can be hard to find; Durgin-Park (p. 110 does an excellent rendition.

To wash it all down, consider a local beer. The Boston Beer Co., which produces the highly regarded **Samuel Adams** brand, has a brewery in Boston, as does **Harpoon.** Numerous bars in the area feature New England microbrews, and some places—including Boston Beer Works (p. 276) and the Cambridge Brewing Company (p. 274)—make their own.

Finally, **Boston cream pie** is golden layer cake sandwiched around custard and topped with chocolate glaze—no cream, no pie.

New England clam chowder.

Fresh oysters.

WHEN TO GO

Boston attracts throngs of visitors year-round. Between April and November, the city sees hardly any slow times. Make reservations as early as possible if you plan to visit during busy periods; at really popular times, all of eastern Massachusetts seems to book up.

The area is especially busy during college graduation season (May and early June) and major events (see "Boston Calendar of Events," below). Spring and fall are popular times for conventions. Families pour into the area in July and August, creating long lines at many attractions. Summer isn't the most expensive time to visit, though: Foliage season, from mid-September to early November, when many leaf-peepers stay in the Boston area or pass through on the way to other New England destinations, is a huge draw. December is less busy but still a convention time—look out for weekend bargains.

The "slow" season is January through March, when many hotels offer great deals, especially on weekends. However, this is when unpredictable weather plagues the Northeast, often affecting travel schedules, and when some suburban attractions close for the winter.

Weather

You've probably heard the saying about New England weather: "If you don't like it, wait 10 minutes." Variations from day to day or morning to afternoon (if not minute to minute) can be enormous. You can roast in March and freeze in June, shiver in July and sweat in November. Dressing in layers is always a good idea.

Spring and fall are the best bets for moderate temperatures, but spring (also known as mud season) is brief. It doesn't usually settle in until early May, and snow sometimes falls in April. Summers are hot, especially in July and August, and can be uncomfortably humid. Fall is when you're most likely to catch a comfortable run of dry, sunny days and cool nights. Winters are cold and usually snowy—bring a warm coat and sturdy boots.

Holidays

Banks, government offices, post offices, schools, and many stores, restaurants, and museums close on the following legal national holidays: January 1 (New Year's Day), the third Monday in January (Martin Luther King, Jr., Day), the third Monday in February (Presidents' Day), the last Monday in May (Memorial Day), July 4 (Independence Day), the first Monday in September (Labor Day), the second Monday in October (Columbus Day), November 11 (Veterans' Day/Armistice Day), the fourth Thursday in November (Thanksgiving Day), and December 25 (Christmas). The Tuesday after the first Monday in November is Election Day, a federal government holiday in presidential-election years (every 4 years, and next in 2012).

In Massachusetts, state offices close for **Patriots' Day** on the third Monday in April, and Suffolk County offices (including Boston City Hall and the city's public libraries) close on March 17 for **Evacuation Day.**

Boston Calendar of Events

The **Greater Boston Convention & Visitors Bureau** (☎ **888/733-2678** or 617/536-4100; www.bostonusa.com) operates a regularly updated hot line that describes ongoing and upcoming events. The **Mayor's Office of Arts, Tourism & Special Events** (☎ **617/635-3911;** www.cityofboston.gov/arts) can provide information about specific happenings. If you're planning at the last minute, the arts sections of the daily *Boston Globe* and *Boston Herald* are always packed with ideas.

For an exhaustive list of events beyond those listed here, check **http://events.frommers.com**, where you'll find a searchable, up-to-the-minute roster of what's happening in cities all over the world.

JANUARY

Martin Luther King, Jr., Birthday Celebration, various locations. Events include musical tributes, gospel concerts, museum displays and programs, readings, speeches, and panel discussions. Check special listings in the *Globe* for specifics. Third Monday in January.

Chinese New Year, Chinatown. The dragon parade (which draws a big crowd no matter how cold it is), fireworks, and raucous festivals are part of the celebration. Special programs take place at the **Children's Museum** (☎ **617/426-8855;** www.bostonkids.org). For more details, visit **www.chinatownmainstreet.org**. Depending on the Chinese lunar calendar, the holiday falls between January 21 and February 19. In 2012, it's January 23.

Boston Wine Festival, Boston Harbor Hotel and other locations. Tastings, classes, lectures, receptions, and meals

Chinese New Year.

provide a lively liquid diversion throughout winter. Check ahead (📞 **888/660-9463;** www.bostonwinefestival.net) for details. January to early April.

FEBRUARY

African-American History Month, various locations. Programs include special museum exhibits, children's activities, concerts, films, lectures, discussions, readings, and tours of the Black Heritage Trail led by National Park Service rangers (📞 **617/742-5415;** www.nps.gov/boaf). All month.

School Vacation Week, various locations. The slate of activities includes special exhibitions and programs, plays, concerts, and tours. Contact individual attractions or check the *Globe* for information on programs and extended hours. Third week of February.

MARCH

St. Patrick's Day Celebrations, various locations. Concerts, talks, special restaurant menus, and other offerings celebrate the heritage of one of the country's most Irish-American cities.

Note that the parade, along Broadway in South Boston, is not a city-sponsored event; the organization that runs it is private and therefore free to bar any group it wants to from marching. That includes gays and, at least once in recent years, antiwar veterans. March 17; parade is on the closest Sunday.

NCAA Men's Basketball Tournament East Regional, TD Garden (📞 **617/624-1000;** www.tdgarden.com). The team that survives the weekend advances to the Final Four in Dayton, Ohio. Expect giddy crowds, sold-out hotels, and packed sports bars. March 22 and 24.

APRIL

Big Apple Circus (📞 **800/922-3772;** www.bigapplecircus.org), City Hall Plaza, Government Center. The New York–based "one-ring wonder" performs in a heated tent with all seating less than 50 feet from the ring. Proceeds support the Boston Children's Museum. Early April to mid-May.

Red Sox Opening Day, Fenway Park. Even if your concierge is a magician,

St. Patrick's Day.

this is an extremely tough ticket. In 2012, the centennial of Fenway Park, even a regular game will be a challenge. Check ahead (© **877/733-7699;** www. redsox.com) when tickets go on sale in December. If you can't get tickets to Opening Day, try to see the 10am game on **Patriots' Day,** the third Monday in April. The early start allows spectators to watch the Boston Marathon afterward. Early and mid-April.

Swan Boats Return to the Public Garden. Since their introduction in 1877, the Swan Boats (© **617/522-1966;** www. swanboats.com) have been a symbol of Boston. Like real swans, they go away for the winter. Saturday before Patriots' Day (April 16, 2012).

Patriots' Day, North End, Lexington, and Concord. Festivities commemorate and reenact the events of April 18 and 19, 1775. Lanterns glow in the steeple of the **Old North Church** (© **617/523-6676;** www.oldnorth.com). Participants dressed as Paul Revere and William Dawes ride from the North End to Lexington and Concord to warn the minutemen that "the regulars are out" (not that "the British are coming"— most colonists considered themselves British). Musket fire rings out on the Battle Green in Lexington and then at the North Bridge in Concord. For information on reenactments and other events, check the websites of the **Paul Revere House** (© **617/523-2338;** www. paulreverehouse.org) and the **Battle Road Committee** (www.battleroad.org). For information about the riders' destinations, where the festivities traditionally include pancake breakfasts, contact the **Lexington Chamber of Commerce Visitor Center** (© **781/862-1450;** www. lexingtonchamber.org) or the **Concord Chamber of Commerce** (© **978/369-3120;** www.concordchamberof commerce.org). See chapter 10 for information on visiting both towns. Third Monday of April (April 16, 2012).

The Boston Marathon.

Boston Marathon, Hopkinton, Massachusetts, to Boston. International stars and local amateurs join in the world's oldest and most famous marathon (www.bostonmarathon.org). Competitors start in stages, with the first setting out at 9:25am. Cheering fans are welcome until the last weekend warriors stagger across the Boylston Street finish line in the late afternoon. Third Monday of the month (April 16, 2012).

Freedom Trail Week, various locations in Boston, Cambridge, Lexington, and Concord. This is another school vacation week, with plenty of crowds and diversions. Family-friendly events include tours, concerts, talks, and other programs related to Patriots' Day, the Freedom Trail, and the American Revolution. Third week of April.

An Evening with Champions, Bright Athletic Center, Allston. World-class ice skaters and promising local students stage two or three performances to benefit the Jimmy Fund, the children's fundraising arm of the Dana-Farber Cancer Institute. Sponsored by Harvard's **Eliot House** (© **617/942-1392;** www. aneveningwithchampions.org). Mid-April (tickets on sale in Jan).

Independent Film Festival of Boston, various locations. Features, shorts, and documentaries by international filmmakers make up the schedule for this increasingly buzz-worthy event. Check ahead (www.iffboston.org) for the schedule. Late April to early May.

MAY

Lilac Sunday, Arnold Arboretum, Jamaica Plain. The arboretum (✆ **617/524-1717;** www.arboretum. harvard.edu) allows picnicking only once a year, on Lilac Sunday. From sunrise to sunset, wander the grounds and enjoy the sensational spring flowers, including more than 400 varieties of lilacs in bloom. Mid-May.

Street Performers Festival, Faneuil Hall Marketplace. Everyone but the pigeons gets into the act as musicians, magicians, jugglers, sword swallowers, and artists strut their stuff. Late May.

JUNE

Boston Pride Parade, South End to Government Center (✆ **617/262-9405;** www.bostonpride.org). The largest gay pride march in New England is the highlight of a weeklong celebration of diversity. The parade, on the second weekend of the month, starts in the South End and ends at City Hall Plaza, where the Boston Pride Festival takes place. Early June.

Dragon Boat Festival, Charles River near Harvard Square, Cambridge (www. bostondragonboat.org). Teams of paddlers synchronized by a drummer propel boats with dragon heads and tails as they race 1,640 feet. The winners go to the national championships; the spectators go to a celebration of Chinese culture and food on the shore. Second or third Sunday of June.

Cambridge River Festival (✆ **617/349-4380;** www.cambridgeartscouncil.org), Memorial Drive from John F. Kennedy Street to Western Avenue. A salute to the arts, the festival incorporates live music, dancing, children's activities, crafts and art exhibits, and international food on the banks of the Charles River. Mid-June.

JULY

Boston Harborfest, downtown, the waterfront, and the Harbor Islands. The city puts on its Sunday best for the Fourth of July, a gigantic weeklong celebration of Boston's maritime history. Events surrounding Boston Harborfest

Boston Pride Parade.

Puerto Rican Festival & Parade.

(📞 **617/227-1528;** www.boston
harborfest.com) include concerts, children's activities, cruises, fireworks, the
Boston Chowderfest, guided tours,
talks, and USS *Constitution*'s turnaround
cruise. In 2012, for the bicentennial of
the War of 1812, the Tall Ships and other
vessels of **Operation Sail** (www.opsail.
org) will visit Boston for the holiday;
make your reservations early. Beginning
of the month.

**Boston Pops Concert & Fireworks
Display,** Hatch Shell, on the Esplanade.
Spectators start showing up at dawn
(overnight camping is not permitted) to
stake out a good spot on the lawn and
spend all day waiting for the sky to get
dark enough for fireworks. Others show
up at the last minute—the Cambridge
side of the river, near Kendall Square,
and the Longfellow Bridge are good
spots to watch the spectacular aerial
show. The program includes the *1812
Overture,* with real cannon fire and
church bells. For details, check the website (www.july4th.org). July 4.

Puerto Rican Festival & Parade, Franklin
Park. This 3-day event, instituted in
1967, is part street fair, part cultural
celebration, with plenty of live music and
traditional food. The highlight of the final
day is a lively parade. For details, search
Festival Puertorriqueño on Facebook.
Late July.

AUGUST

Italian-American Feasts, North End.
These weekend street fairs begin in July
and end in late August with the two
biggest: the Fisherman's Feast and the
Feast of St. Anthony. The sublime (fresh
seafood prepared while you wait, live
music, dancing in the street) mingles
with the ridiculous (carnival games, tacky
T-shirts, fried-dough stands) to leave a
lasting impression of fun and indigestion.
Visit www.fishermansfeast.com or
www.saintanthonysfeast.com for a preview. Weekends throughout August.

August Moon Festival, Chinatown. A
celebration of the harvest and the coming of autumn, the festival includes dragon and lion dances during the parade
through the crowded streets, and demonstrations of crafts and martial arts.
It's also an excuse to stuff yourself with
tasty mooncakes. For details, visit **www.
chinatownmainstreet.org**. Mid-August.

SEPTEMBER

Cambridge Carnival, Kendall Square, Cambridge (✆ **617/863-0476;** www. cambridgecarnival.org). This Caribbean-style celebration of diversity and unity features live music, ethnic food, kids' activities, and a festive parade of costumed revelers. Sunday after Labor Day.

Boston Film Festival (✆ **617/523-8388;** www.bostonfilmfestival.org), various locations. Independent films continue on the festival circuit or make their premieres, sometimes following a lecture by an actor or filmmaker. Most screenings are open to the public without advance tickets. Mid-September.

OCTOBER

Salem Haunted Happenings, various locations. Parades, parties, a special commuter-rail ride from Boston, fortune-telling, cruises, and tours lead up to a ceremony on Halloween. Contact **Destination Salem** (✆ **877/725-3662)** or check the website (www.haunted happenings.org) for specifics. All month.

Oktoberfest, Harvard Square, Cambridge. This immense street fair is a magnet for college students, families, street performers, musicians, and crafts vendors. Sponsored by the Harvard Square Business Association (✆ **617/491-3434;** www.harvardsquare. com). Second Sunday of October.

Head of the Charles Regatta, Boston and Cambridge. High school, college, and postcollegiate rowing teams and individuals—some 4,000 in all—race in front of tens of thousands of fans along the banks of the Charles River and on the bridges spanning it. The Head of the Charles (✆ **617/868-6200;** www.hocr. org) has an uncanny tendency to coincide with a crisp, picturesque weekend. Late October.

NOVEMBER

Thanksgiving Celebration, Plymouth (✆ **800/872-1620;** www.visit-plymouth.com). Plymouth observes the holiday with a "stroll through the ages," highlighting 17th- and 19th-century Thanksgiving preparations in historic homes. Menus at **Plimoth Plantation,** which re-creates the colony's first years, include a buffet and a Victorian Thanksgiving feast. Reservations (✆ **800/262-9356** or 508/746-1622; www.plimoth.org) are accepted beginning in June. Thanksgiving Day.

DECEMBER

The Nutcracker, Opera House, Boston. Boston Ballet's annual holiday extravaganza is one of the country's biggest and best. This is *the* traditional way to expose young Bostonians (and visitors) to culture, and the spectacular sets make it practically painless. Buy tickets (✆ **617/695-6955;** www.bostonballet. org) as soon as you plan your trip, ask whether your hotel offers a *Nutcracker* package, or cross your fingers and check when you arrive. Thanksgiving weekend through late December.

Boston Tea Party Reenactment, Old South Meeting House (✆ **617/482-6439;** www.oldsouthmeetinghouse.org) and Tea Party Ship and Museum, Congress Street Bridge (✆ **617/338-1773;** www. bostonteapartyship.com). Chafing under British rule, American colonists rose up on December 16, 1773, to strike a blow where it would cause real pain—in the pocketbook. A re-creation of the pre-party rally at the meetinghouse is a lively all-ages audience-participation event; call ahead to see whether the ship has reopened during your visit. Mid-December.

Black Nativity, Blackman Auditorium, Northeastern University, 360 Huntington Ave. (✆ **800/514-3849** [tickets] or 617/585-6366; www.blacknativity.org). Poet Langston Hughes wrote the "gospel opera," and a cast of more than 100 brings it to life. Mid- to late December.

Christmas Revels, Sanders Theatre, Cambridge. This multicultural celebration of the winter solstice features the holiday customs of a different culture each year. Themes have included American folk traditions, Victorian England, and

Romany Gypsies. Be ready to sing along. For information and tickets, contact the **Revels** (📞 **617/972-8300;** www.revels.org). Last 2 weeks of the month.

First Night, Back Bay and the waterfront. This is the original arts-oriented, no-alcohol, citywide New Year's Eve celebration. It begins in the early afternoon and includes a parade, ice sculptures, art exhibitions, theatrical performances, and indoor and outdoor entertainment. Some attractions require tickets, but for most you just need a First Night button, available for less than $20 at visitor centers and stores around the city. Fireworks light up the sky above Boston

Poetry 101 (Degrees)

Check the Boston weather forecast by looking up at the short column of lights on top of the old John Hancock building in the Back Bay. (The new Hancock building is the 60-story glass tower next door.) It has its own poem: *Steady blue, clear view / flashing blue, clouds due / steady red, rain ahead / flashing red, snow instead.* **During the summer, flashing red means that the Red Sox game is canceled.**

Common just before 7pm and over Boston Harbor at midnight. For details, contact **First Night** (📞 **617/542-1399;** www.firstnight.org) or check the newspapers when you arrive. December 31.

Boston's Average Temperatures & Rainfall

	JAN	FEB	MAR	APR	MAY	JUNE	JULY	AUG	SEPT	OCT	NOV	DEC
TEMP. (°F)	30	31	38	49	59	68	74	72	65	55	45	34
TEMP. (°C)	−1	−1	3	9	15	20	23	22	18	13	7	1
PRECIP. (IN.)	3.8	3.5	4.0	3.7	3.4	3.0	2.8	3.6	3.3	3.3	4.4	4.2

RESPONSIBLE TRAVEL

The Boston area is a hotbed of eco-awareness. True, it's not Europe, or even California, but residents and visitors have a smaller-than-usual carbon footprint almost by accident—driving in the area is such a headache that ditching the car makes sense for both the environment and your sanity.

Before you leave home, visit the website of the **Greater Boston Convention & Visitors Bureau** (www.bostonusa.com/visit) and click "Boston Insider" to get the latest info about the bureau's Eco-friendly Traveler program. Here you'll find information about eco-aware attractions along with lists of hotels and restaurants that are certified green or working toward that status.

The industry-leading **Lenox Hotel** (p. 79) was one of the first American hotels to offer a towel reuse program and boasts an impressive portfolio of initiatives and awards—in a luxurious property that makes sustainability matter-of-fact rather than inconvenient. The Lenox is part of the Saunders Hotel Group, which has demonstrated and encouraged green awareness in the hospitality business for 2 decades. The **Comfort Inn & Suites Boston/Airport** (p. 95) is the firm's other Boston-area property. They have plenty of company: Virtually all of the chain lodgings in the area and their independent competitors are on the bandwagon. The **Colonnade Hotel Boston** (p. 78) and the **Seaport Hotel** (p. 74) are particularly green.

The **Chefs Collaborative** (📞 **617/236-5200;** www.chefscollaborative. org) is a Boston-based nonprofit dedicated to "changing the sustainable food landscape"; its website has a search function that locates member restaurants.

The **Green Restaurant Association** (www.dinegreen.com) maintains a regularly updated list of members, which includes **Taranta Cucina Meridionale** in the North End (p. 105) and Cambridge's **Upstairs on the Square** (p. 124). Carbon-neutral Taranta even uses corn-based-polymer drinking straws.

Huge proportions of Boston-area commuters get to work on foot or by public transit. Cambridge has been relatively hospitable to bicyclists for years, and Boston is catching up and even planning a bike-share program similar to the arrangements in such cities as Paris and Montreal (visit **www.cityofboston.gov/bikes** for information). Most subway stations and some bus stops have receptacles for recycling the newspaper after you finish reading it. **Zipcar** originated in Cambridge; your membership at home entitles you to use cars all over the Boston area, including locations at the end of most subway lines.

Awareness of the importance of recycling is nothing radical in New England, where one of the best-known sayings is "Use it up, wear it out, make it do, or do without." To take just one example, Massachusetts is among the national leaders in the campaign to reduce the use of disposable shopping bags. To learn more about statewide green initiatives, visit the Department of Environmental Protection's website at **www.mass.gov/dep**. Learn more about Boston's Environmental and Energy Services initiative at **www.cityofboston.gov/environmentalandenergy**.

In addition to the resources for the Boston area listed above, see **www.frommers.com/planning** for more tips on responsible travel.

TOURS

Academic Trips

Enormous college town that it is, Boston abounds with educational opportunities. Two nonprofit organizations—one large, one small—offer participants a chance to get comfortable with a destination or activity rather than trying to cram in as many attractions as possible.

Road Scholar programs offered by Elderhostel (© 800/454-5768; www.exploritas.org) no longer specifically target seniors, which is good news for younger travelers who appreciate their educational focus. Offerings include tours that focus on history, culture, science, and more; they incorporate scheduled activities led by local experts and free time for you to explore on your own.

Boston's beloved public-television station runs **WGBH LearningTours** (© 617/300-3505; www.wgbh.org/support/learningtours), which draw on the know-how of both the station's producers and the experts who appear in PBS series about such topics as the national parks. They're mostly multiple-day excursions to destinations spotlighted in the station's programming, but some offerings are shorter trips to local points of interest.

Adventure Trips

The **Massachusetts Audubon Society** (© 800/283-8266 or 781/259-9500; www.massaudubon.org), the largest conservation organization in New England, owns and operates wildlife sanctuaries across the state and offers programs that help people of all ages connect with nature. Classes, workshops, programs, and special events of all types, many designed specifically for children and families, take place throughout the year. Membership costs $44 per year for an individual, $58 for a family.

A good introduction to New England's diverse terrain is an excursion with the **Appalachian Mountain Club** (℗ **800/372-1758** or 617/523-0636; www. outdoors.org). The recreation and conservation organization is perhaps best known for its indispensable trail guides and maps, but it coordinates volunteer-led activities that range from walking dogs on a beach to multiple-day backpacking tours. Though closely associated with New Hampshire's White Mountains, the AMC has chapters all over the Northeast and offers many activities in the Boston suburbs. First-time membership costs $50 for an individual, $75 for a family, or $25 if you're under 30 or over 69.

Guided Tours

Countless companies offer escorted tours that stop in Boston, especially during foliage season, when 5- to 10-day tours of New England are wildly popular with travelers from around the world. Few spend more than 2 days in Boston, however, meaning that you'll be rushing around trying to cram maximum action into minimum time, or skipping sights and activities you were looking forward to. If you plan to focus exclusively on Boston, most escorted tours won't meet your needs, but if a quick stop is all you can manage, most major tour operators can accommodate you.

Options include **Liberty Travel** (℗ 888/271-1584; www.libertytravel. com), **Collette Vacations** (℗ 800/340-5158; www.collettevacations.com), **Globus and Cosmos** (℗ 866/755-8581 or 800/276-1241; www.globusand cosmos.com), **Insight Vacations** (℗ 888/680-1241; www.insightvacations. com), **Tauck World Discovery** (℗ 800/788-7885; www.tauck.com), and **Trafalgar Tours** (℗ 866/544-4434; www.trafalgar.com).

Gray Line's New England presence is **Brush Hill Tours** (℗ 800/343-1328 or 781/986-6100; www.brushhilltours.com). Brush Hill operates Boston's Beantown Trolley and allows customers to build their own itineraries by choosing from a variety of half- and full-day escorted tours to destinations such as Plymouth, Salem, Cape Cod, and Newport, Rhode Island.

For more information on guided tours, including questions to ask before booking your trip, see **www.frommers.com/planning**.

Volunteer & Working Trips

The Greater Boston chapter of **Habitat for Humanity** (℗ **617/423-2223;** www.habitatboston.org) welcomes individual volunteers as well as groups to help construct and renovate affordable housing for low-income families. Be prepared and dress appropriately for up to 6½ hours of construction work, which can be strenuous. Volunteers are responsible for their own transportation and should bring lunch, drinks, and work gloves. The minimum age is 16 years old, and 16- and 17-year-olds must have an adult with them. There is no maximum age. Note that you must complete a 1-hour orientation before you can start work, and those sessions fill up quickly.

The **Massachusetts Audubon Society** and the **Appalachian Mountain Club** (see "Adventure Trips," above) rely heavily on volunteers. Most Mass Audubon activities are long-term commitments, but some are one-shot deals suitable for out-of-town visitors. AMC opportunities range from a day of trail clearing to leading a longer-term program.

3

SUGGESTED BOSTON ITINERARIES

L iving near the Freedom Trail, I meet my beloved Frommer's Boston readers all the time. After I assure them that I'm not selling anything or trying to enlist them in a cult (why so suspicious, readers?), they usually make one of two comments. They want to know where they can find a public bathroom, or they want to praise the book's suggested itineraries.

Read on for strategies that can help you organize your time. These itineraries include sightseeing destinations, snack and meal suggestions, shopping pointers, and dinner-and-a-movie alternatives. Two tips: Wear comfortable shoes, and don't ignore the breaks built into each itinerary, which can help you feel more like a relaxed insider and less like a crazed participant in a scavenger hunt.

Unless otherwise indicated, turn to chapter 6 for descriptions of the recommended attractions and activities. For an introduction to some of Boston's most interesting **neighborhoods,** see below. And see "Fast Facts," p. 359, for pointers on finding a public toilet.

The Neighborhoods in Brief

These are the areas visitors are most likely to frequent. When Bostonians say **"downtown,"** they usually mean the first six neighborhoods defined here; there's no "midtown" or "uptown." Neighborhoods outside central Boston include South Boston, East Boston, Dorchester, Roxbury, West Roxbury, Hyde Park, Roslindale, and Jamaica Plain. With a couple of exceptions (noted here), Boston is generally safe, but you should still take the precautions you would in any large city, especially at night. **Note:** I include some compass points here to help you read your map, but that's not how the locals will give you directions: They typically just point you on your way.

THE WATERFRONT This narrow area runs along the Inner Harbor, on **Atlantic Avenue** and **Commercial Street** from the Charlestown Bridge (on N. Washington St.) to South Station. Once filled with wharves and warehouses, today it abounds with luxury condos, marinas, restaurants, offices, and hotels. Also here are the New England Aquarium and embarkation points for harbor cruises and whale-watching expeditions. The **Rose Kennedy Greenway** roughly parallels the coast for a mile from South Station to North Station.

THE NORTH END Crossing the Rose Kennedy Greenway as you head east toward the Inner Harbor brings you to one of the city's oldest neighborhoods. Home to waves of immigrants in the course of its history, it was predominantly Italian for most of the 20th century. It's now less than half Italian American; many newcomers are young professionals who walk to work in the Financial District. Nevertheless, you'll hear Italian spoken in the streets and find a wealth of Italian restaurants, *caffès*, and shops. The main streets are **Hanover Street** and **Salem Street.**

FACING PAGE: **Costumed guides lead tours along the Freedom Trail.**

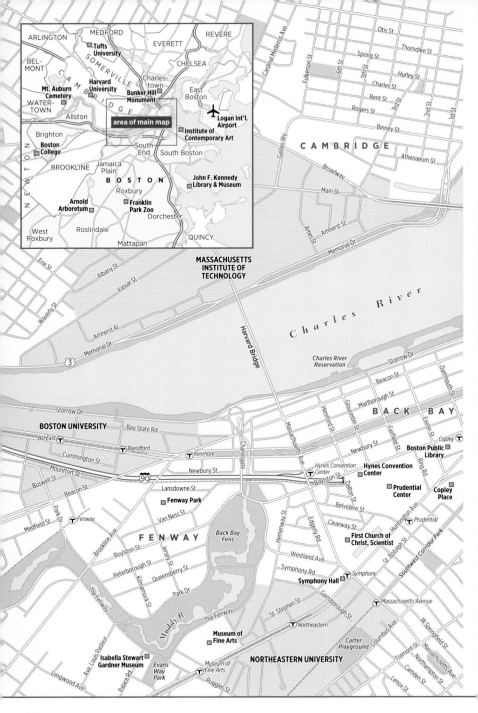

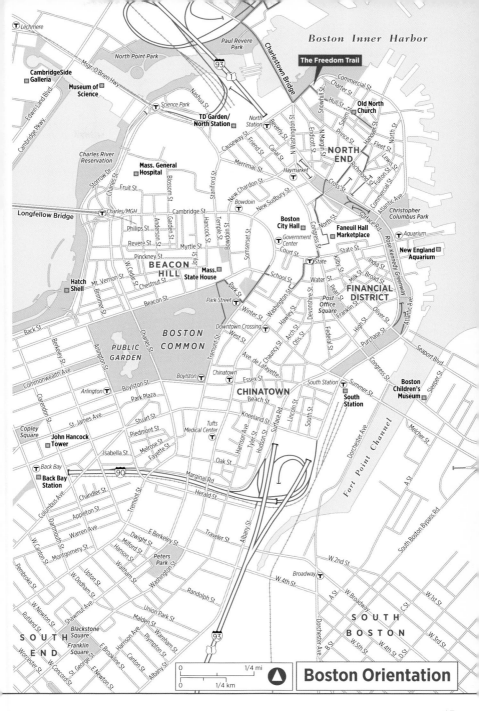

Boston Orientation

NORTH STATION Technically part of the North End but just as close to Beacon Hill, this area around **Causeway Street** is home to the **TD Garden** (sports and performance arena), **North Station,** and many nightspots and restaurants. The neighborhood—sometimes called the West End or the Bulfinch Triangle—gets safer by the day, but wandering alone late at night is not a good idea.

FANEUIL HALL MARKETPLACE Employees aside, Boston residents tend to be scarce at Faneuil Hall Marketplace (also called Quincy Market, after its central building). An irresistible draw for out-of-towners and suburbanites, this cluster of restored market buildings—bounded by the Waterfront, the North End, Government Center, and **State Street**—is the city's most popular attraction. You'll find restaurants, bars, a food court, specialty shops, and Faneuil Hall itself. **Haymarket,** a stone's throw away on **Blackstone Street,** is home to an open-air produce market on Fridays and Saturdays.

GOVERNMENT CENTER Here, stark modern design breaks up Boston's traditional architecture. Flanked by Beacon Hill, Downtown Crossing, and Faneuil Hall Marketplace, Government Center is home to state and federal offices, City Hall, and a major T stop. Its most prominent feature, the red-brick wasteland of City Hall Plaza, lies between **Congress** and **Cambridge streets.**

THE FINANCIAL DISTRICT Bounded loosely by Downtown Crossing, **Summer Street, Atlantic Avenue,** and **State Street,** the Financial District is the banking, insurance, and legal center of the city. Aside from some popular after-work spots, it's generally quiet at night and on weekends.

DOWNTOWN CROSSING The intersection that gives Downtown Crossing its name is at **Washington Street** where **Winter Street** becomes **Summer Street.** The Freedom Trail runs along one edge of this shopping and business district between Boston Common, Chinatown, the Financial District, and Government Center. Most of the neighborhood hops during the day and slows down in the evening, but it's getting livelier thanks to the increasing presence of students from Emerson College and Suffolk University, and theatergoers heading to the Opera House, the Modern Theatre, and the Paramount Center.

BEACON HILL Narrow tree-lined streets, brick and cobblestone alleyways, and architectural showpieces, mostly in Federal style, make up this largely residential area in the shadow of the State House. Two of the loveliest and most exclusive spots in Boston are here: Mount Vernon Street and Louisburg (pronounced "Lewis-burg") Square. Bounded by Government Center, Boston Common, the Back Bay, and the river, Beacon Hill is where you'll find Massachusetts General Hospital. **Charles Street,** which divides the Common from the Public Garden, is the main street of Beacon Hill. Other important thoroughfares are **Beacon Street,** on the north side of the Common, and **Cambridge Street.**

CHARLESTOWN One of the oldest areas of Boston is where you'll see the Bunker Hill Monument and USS *Constitution* ("Old Ironsides"). Yuppification has brought some diversity to what was once an almost entirely white residential neighborhood, but pockets remain that have earned their reputation for insularity.

Boston Transit

Blue Line to Wonderland
Airport

EAST BOSTON

1A

Maverick

Boston Inner Harbor

Silver Line to the airport

0   1/2 mi
0   1/2 km

Seaport Blvd
Summer St.
90

SOUTH BOSTON

Broadway
W. Broadway

Dorchester Ave.

Red Line to JFK/UMass, Ashmont, Braintree

93

Commercial St.
NORTH END
Cross St.
Aquarium
State St.
FINANCIAL DISTRICT
Congress St.
South Station
North Station
Haymarket
Government Center
Downtown Crossing
Chinatown
CHINATOWN
Kneeland St.
Tufts Medical Center
Herald St.
Park Street
Tremont St.
Boylston
Charles St.
Washington St.
Albany St.

CHARLESTOWN
Bunker Hill St.
Main St.
99
93
Community College
Lechmere
Science Park
Charles/MGH
BEACON HILL
Bowdoin

Orange Line to Oak Grove

SOUTH END

W. 4th St.

Berkeley St.
Clarendon St.
Dartmouth St.
Copley
Back Bay
Prudential
Columbus Ave.
Massachusetts Avenue
Tremont St.
Washington St.

Orange Line to Forest Hills

SOMERVILLE
McGrath Hwy.
Cambridge St.
Hampshire St.
28
O'Brien Hwy.
Binney St.
Kendall/MIT
Land Blvd.
Memorial Dr.
Storrow Dr.
3

CAMBRIDGE
Broadway
Central
Massachusetts Ave.
Western Ave.
River St.
Memorial Dr.

Charles River

Beacon St.
Commonwealth Ave.
Boylston St.
Hynes-Convention Center
Mass. Ave.
Symphony
9

BACK BAY

Storrow Dr.
Kenmore
Fenway
Brookline Ave.
Beacon St.

FENWAY

Museum of Fine Arts
Huntington Ave.

Green Line "E" Branch to Heath Street

Longwood

BROOKLINE

Green Line "D" Branch to Riverside

Green Line "C" Branch to Cleveland Circle

Green Line "B" Branch to Boston College

Soldiers Field Rd.
Harvard
J.F.K. St.

Red Line to Alewife

McGrath Hwy.

90
3

SOUTH BOSTON WATERFRONT/SEAPORT DISTRICT Across the Fort Point Channel from the Waterfront neighborhood, this area is home to the convention center, the Seaport Boston World Trade Center, the Institute of Contemporary Art, the Fish Pier, a federal courthouse, the Boston Children's Museum, one end of the Ted Williams Tunnel, and a lot of construction. The ICA and a scattering of restaurants make this area increasingly inviting, but it's still not quite a nonconvention destination. **Seaport Boulevard** and **Northern Avenue** are the main drags. The area closest to the channel, where redevelopment is forcing out artists who live and work in renovated warehouses, is often called simply **Fort Point.**

CHINATOWN One of the largest Chinese communities in the country is a small area jammed with Asian restaurants, groceries, and gift shops. Chinatown takes up the area between Downtown Crossing and the Massachusetts Turnpike extension. The main street is **Beach Street.** The tiny **Theater District** extends about 1½ blocks in each direction from the intersection of Tremont and Stuart streets; be careful there at night after the crowds thin out.

THE SOUTH END Cross **Stuart Street** or **Huntington Avenue** heading south from the Back Bay, and you'll find yourself in a landmark district packed with Victorian row houses and little parks. The South End has a large gay community and some of the city's best restaurants. With the gentrification of the 1980s and '90s, **Tremont Street** (particularly the end closest to downtown) gained a cachet that it hadn't known for almost a century. **Washington Street** and **Harrison Avenue** are up-and-coming destinations for diners and shoppers. Long known for its ethnic, economic, and cultural diversity, the neighborhood is now thoroughly yuppified nearly all the way to Mass. Ave. *Note:* Don't confuse the South End with South Boston, on the other side of I-93.

The Chinatown Gate located at the intersection of Beach Street and Surface Road.

The Back Bay's charming architecture.

THE BACK BAY Fashionable since its creation out of landfill more than a century ago, the Back Bay overflows with gorgeous architecture and chic shops. It lies between the Public Garden, the river, Kenmore Square, and either **Huntington Avenue** or **St. Botolph Street,** depending on who's describing it. Students dominate the area near **Mass. Ave.** but grow scarce as property values soar near the Public Garden. This is one of the best neighborhoods in Boston for aimless wandering. Major thoroughfares include **Boylston Street,** which starts at Boston Common and runs into the Fenway; largely residential **Beacon Street** and **Commonwealth Avenue** (say "Comm. Ave."); and boutique central, **Newbury Street.**

KENMORE SQUARE The landmark white-and-red CITGO sign that dominates the skyline above the intersection of **Commonwealth Avenue, Beacon Street,** and **Brookline Avenue** tells you that you're approaching Kenmore Square. Its shops, bars, restaurants, and clubs attract students from adjacent Boston University, and the Hotel Commonwealth and its high-end retail outlets lend a touch of class. The college-town atmosphere goes out the window when the Red Sox are in town and baseball fans pour into the area on the way to historic Fenway Park, 3 blocks away.

THE FENWAY Between Kenmore Square and the Longwood Medical Area, the Fenway neighborhood encompasses Fenway Park, the Museum of Fine Arts, the Isabella Stewart Gardner Museum, and innumerable students. Boston University, Northeastern University, and Harvard Medical School are just the largest educational institutions in and near the Fenway. The **Fenway** is also the name of a road that winds through the area, at one point bordering a park confusingly named the Back Bay Fens. The area's southern border is **Huntington Av-enue,** the honorary "Avenue

Mass(achusetts) Ave(nue)

One of the most important streets in Boston and Cambridge is Massachusetts Avenue, but almost no one calls it that. Bostonians—who reputedly talk faster than any other Americans (including New Yorkers!)—say "Mass. Ave." You might as well get into the habit now.

of the Arts" (or, with a Boston accent, "Otts"), where you'll find the Christian Science Center, Symphony Hall (at the corner of Mass. Ave.), and the MFA. (Huntington Ave. actually begins in the Back Bay at Copley Sq. and extends into the suburbs.) Parts of Huntington can be a little risky, so if you're leaving the museum at night, stick to a cab or the Green Line, and try to travel in a group.

Cambridge is filled with funky shops.

CAMBRIDGE Boston's neighbor across the Charles River is a separate city. The areas you're likely to visit lie along the MBTA Red Line. **Harvard Square** is a magnet for students, sightseers, and well-heeled shoppers. It's an easy walk along Mass. Ave. southeast to **Central Square,** a gentrifying area dotted with ethnic restaurants and clubs; a short walk away is boho **Inman Square,** a stronghold of independent businesses. North along shop-lined Mass. Ave. from Harvard Square is **Porter Square,** a mostly residential neighborhood with quirky retail outlets of the sort that once characterized Harvard Square. Around **Kendall Square** you'll find MIT and many technology-oriented businesses.

THE BEST OF BOSTON IN 1 DAY

A single day affords the opportunity to sample some experiences unique to Boston. You won't have time for full immersion, but you can touch on several singular attractions and destinations. Your focus will be the downtown area, home to the city's oldest and most historic neighborhoods. *Start: Boston Common (Red or Green Line to Park St.), 15 State St. (Orange or Blue Line to State), or Faneuil Hall (Green or Blue Line to Government Center).*

1 The Freedom Trail ★★★

Boston's signature attraction is a 2.5-mile line of red paint or brick laid out at the suggestion of a local journalist in 1958. Following the whole Freedom Trail (p. 150) can consume the better part of a day, but several options that concentrate on the downtown part of the walk take 2 hours or so. Your goal is to cover—at whatever pace suits you, as carefully or as casually as you like—the first two-thirds of the trail, from **Boston Common** through **Faneuil Hall.** Start at the Boston Common Visitor Information Center with a pamphlet describing the self-guided tour or with the audio tour available from the Freedom Trail Foundation. If you prefer a guided tour, check the schedule of tours with **National Park Service rangers, Boston By Foot,** and the **Freedom Trail Foundation.**

2   Faneuil Hall Marketplace ★★

The retail scene at **Downtown Crossing** is in a down cycle thanks to the temporary closing of the legendary Filene's Basement (for building construction that was on hold at press time); if you need a shopping break early in your excursion, see chapter 8 for pointers. Faneuil Hall Marketplace offers more shopping options, many of which are outlets of national chains. You can give your wallet a workout before, after, or even (this can be our little secret) during your sightseeing.

Guides in period costumes lead tours along Boston's famous Freedom Trail.

3   QUINCY MARKET ▣ ★★

The main level of Faneuil Hall Marketplace's central building, **Quincy Market,** is a gigantic food court. You can eat at the marketplace, but I suggest crossing Atlantic Avenue and enjoying your snack or lunch with a glorious view. Stake out a seat overlooking the marina next to Christopher Columbus Waterfront Park (next to the Marriott, on the side opposite the New England Aquarium). If you'd rather eat indoors, head to **Durgin-Park ★★★**, 340 Faneuil Hall Marketplace (✆ **617/227-2038; p. 110**), or across the street to **Ye Olde Union Oyster House ★**, 41 Union St. (✆ 617/227-2750; p. 109).

4   Paul Revere House ★★★

My favorite Freedom Trail stop is a little 17th-century home overlooking a picturesque cobblestone square. See p. 161.

5   The North End ★★★

The Freedom Trail continues here with another famous Paul Revere hangout, the fascinating **Old North Church ★**. But there's more to this historic neighborhood than just history. The city's "Little Italy" (locals don't call it that) is a great place for wandering around. See p. 162.

6   HANOVER STREET ▣

Coffee outlets throughout the city valiantly attempt to serve good espresso and cappuccino; the shops here always succeed—and if they don't, they don't stay in business very long. Pair your caffeine with a fresh-baked pastry, settle in at a bakery or *caffè*, and take in the scene on the North End's main drag. Top choices: **Caffè Vittoria,** 296 Hanover St. (✆ **617/227-7606**); **Mike's Pastry,** 300 Hanover St. (✆ **617/742-3050**); and **Caffè dello Sport,** 308 Hanover St. (✆ **617/523-5063**). See p. 104.

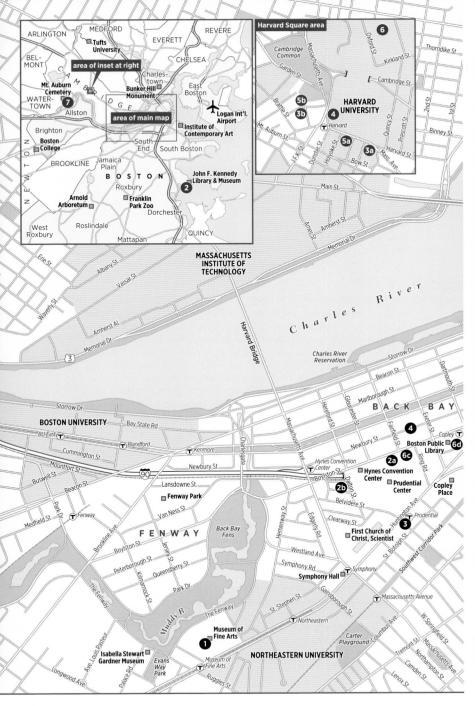

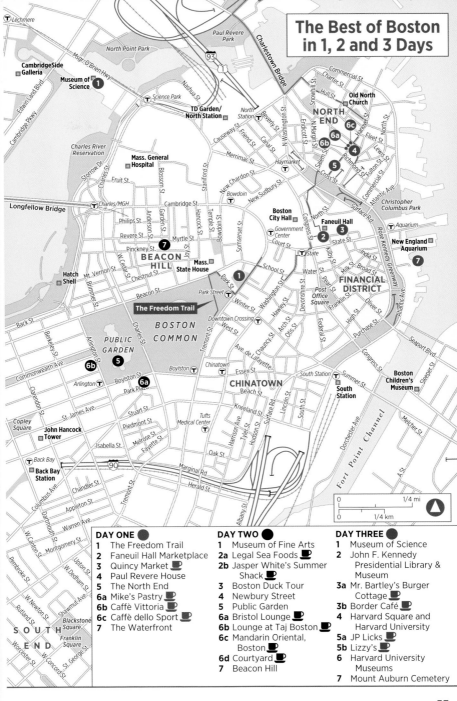

The Best of Boston in 1, 2 and 3 Days

The Freedom Trail

BEACON HILL

BOSTON COMMON

PUBLIC GARDEN

CHINATOWN

FINANCIAL DISTRICT

NORTH END

SOUTH END

DAY ONE
1 The Freedom Trail
2 Faneuil Hall Marketplace
3 Quincy Market
4 Paul Revere House
5 The North End
6a Mike's Pastry
6b Caffè Vittoria
6c Caffè dello Sport
7 The Waterfront

DAY TWO
1 Museum of Fine Arts
2a Legal Sea Foods
2b Jasper White's Summer Shack
3 Boston Duck Tour
4 Newbury Street
5 Public Garden
6a Bristol Lounge
6b Lounge at Taj Boston
6c Mandarin Oriental, Boston
6d Courtyard
7 Beacon Hill

DAY THREE
1 Museum of Science
2 John F. Kennedy Presidential Library & Museum
3a Mr. Bartley's Burger Cottage
3b Border Café
4 Harvard Square and Harvard University
5a JP Licks
5b Lizzy's
6 Harvard University Museums
7 Mount Auburn Cemetery

The interior of the Old North Church.

7 The Waterfront

Now downtown Boston's small size pays off: In almost any direction, the gorgeous harbor is a short stroll from the North End. As the day winds down, you can take a **sightseeing cruise** ★★ (p. 190) from Long Wharf or Rowes Wharf—though a **ferry** ride from Long Wharf to Charlestown and back may be better for your schedule and budget. If cruises aren't for you or are out of season, explore the **New England Aquarium** ★ (p. 148) or the **Boston Children's Museum** ★★ (p. 186). If those don't appeal to you, head for the nearby Seaport District (also known as the South Boston Waterfront) and visit the **Institute of Contemporary Art** ★★ (p. 140). It's a 20- to 30-minute walk or 10-minute cab ride.

Or—it's not the Waterfront, but bear with me— abandon the sightseeing after the Paul Revere House and go **shopping** in the Back Bay, starting with a stroll along Newbury Street (see chapter 8).

Finally, head back to the hotel to wash off the grime of the day, then pick something fun from the "Suggested Evening Itineraries," below.

 One Singular Sensation

On a 1-day visit, consider concentrating on just **one or two things** you're most excited about, plus a good meal or two. If what really gets you going is the Museum of Fine Arts, the Museum of Science, Newbury Street's art galleries and boutiques, or even a day trip (see chapter 10), you have a good excuse for not doing more—and for a return trip to Boston!

THE BEST OF BOSTON IN 2 DAYS

Now that you have a feel for the city, it's time to explore beyond downtown and investigate subjects other than history. The Back Bay, Beacon Hill, and other destinations contrast invitingly with the colonial extravaganza of the Freedom Trail. This itinerary may require some flexibility, because you probably won't have much control over when your Duck Tour starts. Aim for tickets on a tour that starts in the afternoon, when the scene on the river is liveliest, with rowers zipping around and sailboats skimming past. If your tour falls in the morning, the rest of this itinerary easily adjusts to accommodate it. **Start:** *Museum of Fine Arts (Green Line E to Museum of Fine Arts or Orange Line to Ruggles).*

1 Museum of Fine Arts ★★★

Be at the museum when the doors open at 10am. The MFA can easily—and most enjoyably—take up a full day, but it doesn't have to. Check out the website to get some sense of what you want to see. If you prefer not to explore on your own, take the first guided tour of the day, which begins at 10:30am. The museum has a cafeteria, cafe, and restaurant, but I'd suggest saving your appetite for the next stop. See p. 144.

2 SHOPS AT PRUDENTIAL CENTER 🍽

One of my favorite branches of **Legal Sea Foods** ★★★ (p. 101) is here, on the main level off Boylston Street. If you prefer something lighter, the food court is nearby. Or walk 5 minutes to the Back Bay branch of **Jasper White's Summer Shack** ★★. See p. 129.

3 Boston Duck Tour ★★★

This is the most entertaining motorized way to see the city. On a reconditioned World War II amphibious landing vehicle, you see the top attractions, pick up some historical background, and head for the water. Then, thrillingly, the Duck plunges into the Charles River and cruises around the basin. See p. 188.

Duck Tours don't operate from January through March (unless they're needed for a Patriots Super Bowl victory parade) or on weekdays in December. An excellent alternative is a **Boston Symphony Orchestra** ★★★ or **Boston Pops** ★★ concert at Symphony Hall (p. 262), a short walk from either the MFA or the Prudential Center.

One of the amphibious Ducks touring the city.

4 Newbury Street

The commercial heart of the Back Bay, Newbury Street offers the best shopping in New England (see chapter 8). Familiar chains and one-of-a-kind boutiques and galleries make it a can't-miss destination for serious consumerism or just window-shopping. It's also architecturally fascinating (see "Walking Tour 1," in chapter 7). One block away, Boylston Street also offers excellent shopping.

SUGGESTED evening ITINERARIES

If you're traveling as a family, you may be checking the TV listings for your evening plans. If not—or if you had the foresight to book a sitter—here are some suggestions. See chapter 5 for restaurant reviews and chapter 9 for nightlife listings.

- Dinner in the North End, and coffee and dessert at a *caffè*. Afterward, enjoy the view from Copp's Hill Terrace, between Charter and Commercial streets overlooking the harbor, or take in a show at the Improv Asylum. Wind down with a drink at the Cheers bar at Quincy Market.

- Dinner at Legal Sea Foods in the Prudential Center, followed (or preceded) by a visit to the 50th-floor Prudential Center Skywalk or a drink in the lounge at Top of the Hub, on the 52nd floor. If heights aren't your thing, lift a glass at the Oak Bar in the Fairmont Copley Plaza Hotel.

- Summer only: Assemble a picnic and head to the Hatch Shell for music or a movie, to Boston Common for a play, or to City Hall Plaza for a concert.

- Winter only: A Boston Symphony Orchestra or Boston Ballet performance, then a late supper at Brasserie Jo or dessert at Finale.

- Dinner at Sel de la Terre on State Street or around the corner at Legal Sea Foods, then a stroll along the harbor. Hit the North End or the food court at Faneuil Hall Marketplace for dessert.

- Dinner at Brasserie Jo, then a Huntington Theatre Company performance or music at Wally's Cafe (or both).

- Dinner at the Boston location of Jasper White's Summer Shack, a stroll on Newbury Street, and a nightcap at the Bristol Lounge in the Four Seasons Hotel or the Bar at Taj Boston.

- Shopping at the Coop or the Harvard Book Store, then dinner at Mr. Bartley's Burger Cottage. Contemplate Harvard Yard from the Widener Library steps, and finish up with ice cream at JP Licks or Lizzy's, or a show at Club Passim (or both).

- Dinner at the East Coast Grill or Oleana, followed by music at Scullers Jazz Club, the Regattabar, or Ryles Jazz Club.

- Dinner at Baraka Café, ice cream at Toscanini's, and music at the Middle East or T. T. the Bear's Place.

- A movie at the Kendall Square Cinema before or after dinner at Hungry Mother or Oleana, then music at the Cantab Lounge.

- Dinner at Redbones or Johnny D's Uptown Restaurant & Music Club, and a show at Johnny D's or the Somerville Theater.

The Public Garden.

5 Public Garden ★★★

Newbury Street begins across Arlington Street from the most beautiful park in Boston. The Public Garden (p. 173) is lovely year-round—a visit will brighten up even the grayest off-season day—and the **Make Way for Ducklings** sculptures (p. 209) are always delightful. In warm weather, leave time for a **Swan Boat ride** (p. 173).

6 AFTERNOON TEA ☕

All that walking makes a perfect excuse for a hearty meal of pastries, finger sandwiches, and, of course, tea. My favorite afternoon tea is at the **Bristol Lounge,** off the lobby of the Four Seasons. The **Lounge at the Taj Boston** and, on weekends, the **lobby lounge** in the **Mandarin Oriental, Boston,** and the **Courtyard restaurant** at the Boston Public Library also put on a good show. See "Boston Tea Party, Part 2" on p. 121.

7 Beacon Hill ★★★

The most picturesque neighborhood in town is a festival of red brick, cobblestones, and gorgeous architectural details. **Charles Street,** the main thoroughfare, is a lively shopping destination with a refreshing lack of chain stores. Wander on your own (see p. 180 for pointers) or seek out a guide—on summer weekdays, a **Boston By Foot** tour starts at 5:30pm.

"Suggested Evening Itineraries," above, can help you plan the rest of your day.

THE BEST OF BOSTON IN 3 DAYS

You can easily extend the suggestions for the first 2 days to fill a third—for instance, your Museum of Fine Arts admission is good for another visit within 10 days, and you haven't actually completed the Freedom Trail—but you'll probably want to branch out. Today you head for Cambridge, Dorchester, or both. This itinerary may look a little skimpy, but it's packed with interesting destinations and activities. *Start: Museum of Science (Green Line to Science Park) or Kennedy Library (Red Line to JFK/UMass, then free shuttle bus).*

1 Museum of Science ★★★

If you prefer science over history or want to stay close to downtown, head to the museum; if not, you're off to Dorchester to see the:

2 John F. Kennedy Presidential Library and Museum ★★

Although they're very different, both of these museums are well worth a trip and a full morning. The Museum of Science (p. 146), with its wealth of hands-on exhibits, is a great destination for families; adults and older kids who have studied American history can't get enough of the Kennedy Library (p. 142). Both museums open at 9am. Both have cafeterias, but I recommend that you wait to have lunch until you reach Cambridge at midday.

3 EAT LIKE A COLLEGE KID ☕

My favorite Harvard Square lunch destinations are casual places where the sightseer's uniform of jeans or shorts and sneakers fits right in. **Mr. Bartley's Burger Cottage ★★**, 1246 Massachusetts Ave. (✆ **617/354-6559;** p. 127), is my top choice anywhere for onion rings, not to mention great burgers. It's closed Sunday. The **Border Café,** 32 Church St. (✆ **617/864-6100;** p. 126), serves terrific Tex-Mex specialties.

4 Harvard Square & Harvard University

I consider these two entities one big stop because the school couldn't exist without the neighborhood, and vice versa. Allow some time to wander around and enjoy the gentrified-boho atmosphere. Take a tour, which begins at the university's Information Center, or head out on your own (see "Walking Tour 3," in chapter 7). "The Square" is also a fun **shopping** destination (see chapter 8).

5 ICE CREAM ☕

Harvard Square is home to some of the best ice cream shops in this ice-cream-obsessed part of the world. **JP Licks,** 1312 Massachusetts Ave. (✆ **617/492-1001**), and **Lizzy's,** 29 Church St. (✆ **617/354-2911**), are equally delicious, so check the daily specials if you can't decide. Take your treat to Harvard Yard.

6 Harvard University Museums ★

Let your interests be your guide for the rest of the afternoon. If you prefer being indoors, stay on campus to visit the Harvard Museum of Natural History and the adjacent Peabody Museum (p. 177), which are equally welcoming to kids and adults. At the moment, highlights of the collections of the Harvard Art Museums (p. 178) are on display at the Sackler Museum while the institution's other buildings undergo renovation. (That means a relatively short visit, which may suit you just fine.) All of the university museums close at 5pm.

If the weather's fine, you may prefer to point yourself toward:

7 Mount Auburn Cemetery ★

A short distance from Harvard Square, Mount Auburn Cemetery is a gorgeous, fascinating destination. See p. 176.

When you've had enough, head back to the hotel. Stay in and order room service, or dress up for one of the "Suggested Evening Itineraries," above.

Mr. Bartley's Burger Cottage.

One of Mount Auburn Cemetery's eye-catching monuments.

4

WHERE TO STAY

Boston hotels are convenient—the central city is so small that nearly every location is a good one—but generally expensive. Lodgings reflect the city's historic character: Decades- and even century-old properties compete with establishments that opened to meet the demands of the 21st-century tech boom. Rooms vary in size from tiny to enormous. The average room rate flirts with $200, but bargains are available, particularly at slow times; including Cambridge and Brookline in your search increases your options. With enough planning and a little luck, you'll almost certainly find a place that suits your needs, taste, and budget.

BEST HOTEL BETS

- **Best for Families:** The **Doubletree Guest Suites** offers two rooms for the price of one, with two TVs and a refrigerator, and the property has a nice pool. The location, straddling Boston and Cambridge, is especially good if you're driving from the west—you leave the turnpike before downtown traffic shatters the peace in the back of the minivan. See p.87.

- **Best Value:** The **Newbury Guest House** is ideal for travelers who want to take advantage of the Back Bay's excellent shopping. You can't beat the location, right on lively Newbury Street, and room rates even include breakfast. See p. 85.

- **Best Splurge:** The **Boston Harbor Hotel** has it all: Huge rooms, magnificent views, impeccable service, luxurious health club and spa, terrific pool, and a great location adjacent to a marina where you can moor your yacht. Across the river, Cambridge's **Charles Hotel** offers a similar combination of amenities, location, and pampering service (though without the boat accommodations). See p. 63 and p. 89.

- **Most Romantic:** The intimate atmosphere and elegant furnishings make a suite at the **Eliot Hotel** a great spot for a rendezvous. If you and your beloved need some time apart, close the French doors and maintain eye contact while in separate rooms. In Cambridge, the luxurious rooms at the **Hotel Veritas** feel cozy, not cramped—perfect for cuddling. See p. 78 and p. 89.

price CATEGORIES

Very Expensive	$326 and up	Moderate	$151–$225
Expensive	$226–$325	Inexpensive	Under $150

- **Best Service:** The **Four Seasons Hotel** is tops not just in Boston but in all of New England. The hotel's your-wish-is-my-command service—which applies to both humans and their animal companions—isn't the only reason for that status, but it helps. See p. 79.

- **Best for Business Travelers: The Langham, Boston** occupies an unbeatable location in the heart of the Financial District and supplies all the services and amenities a tycoon or would-be tycoon could want. Yes, it's part of a chain, but a small, London-based chain that has a great reputation for a reason. See p. 69.

- **Best for Travelers with Disabilities:** The **Royal Sonesta Hotel** in Cambridge trains its staff in disability awareness and offers 18 rooms (some of which adjoin standard units) equipped for the hearing, ambulatory, and vision impaired. A wheelchair ramp for use in conference rooms is available. See p. 90. The Westin chain is particularly attentive to the needs of travelers with mobility issues; check out the **Westin Copley Place Boston** and the **Westin Boston Waterfront.** See p. 84 and p. 74.

- **Best for Eco-Sensitive Travelers:** Listing hotels that *aren't* on the green bandwagon might be quicker. Every large hotel chain is boosting its environmental awareness, with **Hyatt** and **Kimpton**—parent company of Hotel Marlowe, Nine Zero, and the Onyx Hotel—on the cutting edge. Boston's **Lenox Hotel, Seaport Hotel,** and **Colonnade Hotel** are especially green but by no means the only earth-friendly properties in town.

WHAT YOU'LL really PAY

The prices quoted here are rack rates, the maximum a hotel charges. You will probably not pay that rate in the Boston area unless you arrive at the height of foliage season or during a busy college graduation period. You can typically find discounts when booking through the major discounters (Priceline, Hotels.com, Expedia, and Travelocity). During slow times, it's often possible to land a room at an expensive property for the same rate you'd pay at a less pricey one. Rack rates at the Fairmont Copley Plaza start at $289, but in January 2011, just a cursory search of the usual

Web discount sites revealed that rooms were available for as much as $100 less.

If you're the gambling type, you can bid for a room on Priceline. In late October 2010—the tail end of foliage season—rooms at the Hyatt Regency Cambridge, where rack rates start at $179, were going for about $100.

Sometimes all you have to do is contact the hotel directly and negotiate. Just by asking, you may be able to make a deal with a reservations clerk to match or beat a price that's available through a discount website.

And remember to check hotel websites for special offers. The Colonnade Hotel Boston offers a 2-night winter weekend deal that lets guests pay the Friday evening temperature in dollars for their room that night—in other words, 32ºF at 5pm, $32 for your first night in the room (plus the standard rate for Sat night).

Note: Quoted discount rates almost never include hotel tax. Unless otherwise specified, they don't include breakfast or parking.

- **Best Pool:** The **Sheraton Boston Hotel** has a great indoor-outdoor pool with a re-tractable dome. Cambridge's **Royal Sonesta Hotel** has a similarly enjoyable arrangement. See p. 83 and p. 90.

- **Best Views:** Several hotels offer impressive views of their immediate surroundings, but for a picture-postcard panorama of Boston and Cambridge, head to the upper floors of the **Westin Copley Place Boston.** If you prefer up-close-and-personal views of Boston Harbor, check out the **Fairmont Battery Wharf,** on the edge of the North End, Boston's Italian-American stronghold. See p. 84 and 66.

A Note About Smoking

The city of **Boston bans smoking** in all hotels, inns, and B&Bs, and the **Marriott, Westin,** and **Sheraton** chains forbid smoking in all their properties. Nonsmokers shouldn't assume that they'll get a non-smoking room without requesting one. As hotels squeeze smokers into fewer rooms, the ones they use become saturated with the smell of smoke and air freshener, even in lodgings that are otherwise antiseptic. To avoid this disagreeable situation, be sure that everyone who handles your reservation knows that you need a completely non-smoking room. And if you're a smoker or traveling with one, be sure you understand your hotel's smoking policy—lighting up in a nonsmoking room can subject you to a hefty cleaning fee.

DOWNTOWN

For the purposes of this chapter, "downtown" means most of the **Freedom Trail** and the neighborhoods defined in chapter 3 as the **Waterfront,** the **North End, Faneuil Hall Marketplace,** the **Financial District,** and **Downtown Crossing.** The few accommodations in the moderate price category are mostly bed-and-breakfasts; for information about B&Bs, consult the agencies listed on p. 97.

The Waterfront/North End/Faneuil Hall Marketplace

Businesspeople and sightseers dominate the hotels in these neighborhoods, which become increasingly desirable as the Rose Kennedy Greenway evolves.

BEST FOR Travelers who want easy access to the Financial District and water-front attractions, the airport, and Faneuil Hall Marketplace.

DRAWBACKS Touristy atmosphere, distance from the Back Bay and Cambridge, expense (at most properties).

VERY EXPENSIVE

Boston Harbor Hotel ★★★ Guests at the Boston Harbor Hotel are de-manding—and satisfied—business and leisure travelers drawn to its luxurious accommodations, top-notch service, abundant amenities, and great location. The landmark arch at the center of the 16-story brick complex connects the ma-rina off the lobby to the Rose Kennedy Greenway and the Financial District. The plush guest rooms have residential-style mahogany furnishings, work desks, muted jewel-toned walls and fabrics, pillow-top mattresses, marble bathrooms, and abundant business features. The traditional style distinguishes this hotel from its closest competitor, the nearby InterContinental Boston. Rooms occupy

Ames **46**
Anthony's Town House **4**
The Back Bay Hotel **25**
Best Western Plus Boston/The Inn at Longwood Medical **5**
Boston Harbor Hotel **52**
Boston Marriott Copley Place **17**
Boston Marriott Long Wharf **49**
The Boston Park Plaza Hotel & Towers **29**
Bulfinch Hotel **38**
Chandler Inn Hotel **27**
Charlesmark Hotel **15**
Colonnade Hotel Boston **18**
Comfort Inn & Suites Boston/Airport **61**
Copley Square Hotel **16**
Courtyard Boston Brookline **1**
Doubletree Hotel Boston Downtown **33**
Eliot Hotel **8**
Embassy Suites Hotel Boston at Logan Airport **59**
Fairmont Battery Wharf **42**
The Fairmont Copley Plaza **22**

Fenway Summer Hostel **6**
Fifteen Beacon **43**
40 Berkeley **26**
Four Seasons Hotel **30**
Hampton Inn Boston Logan Airport **60**
Harborside Inn **48**
Hilton Boston Back Bay **10**
Hilton Boston Financial District **51**
Hilton Boston Logan Airport **57**
Holiday Inn Boston at Beacon Hill **37**
Holiday Inn Boston Brookline **2**
Holiday Inn Express Hotel & Suites Boston Garden **40**
Hostelling International—Boston **9**
Hotel Commonwealth **7**
Hotel 140 **24**
Hyatt Harborside **58**
Hyatt Regency Boston Financial District **35**
Inn @ St. Botolph **19**
InterContinental Boston **53**
The John Hancock Hotel & Conference Center **23**
The Langham, Boston **50**

The Lenox Hotel **14**
The Liberty Hotel **36**
Longwood Inn **3**
Mandarin Oriental, Boston **13**
The MidTown Hotel **20**
Millennium Bostonian Hotel **47**
Newbury Guest House **12**
Nine Zero **44**
Omni Parker House **45**
Onyx Hotel **39**
Radisson Hotel Boston **31**
Renaissance Boston Waterfront Hotel **56**
Residence Inn Boston Harbor on Tudor Wharf **41**
The Ritz-Carlton, Boston Common **34**
Seaport Hotel **54**
Sheraton Boston Hotel **11**
Taj Boston **28**
W Boston **32**
The Westin Boston Waterfront **55**
The Westin Copley Place Boston **21**
XV Beacon **43**

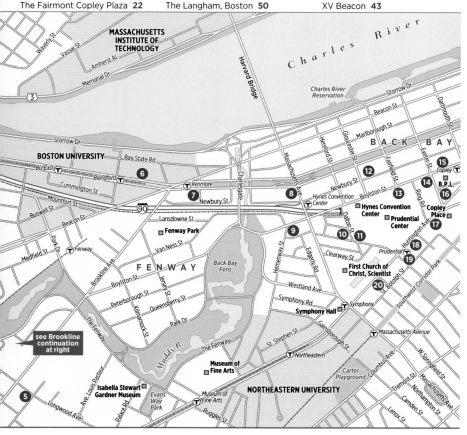

64

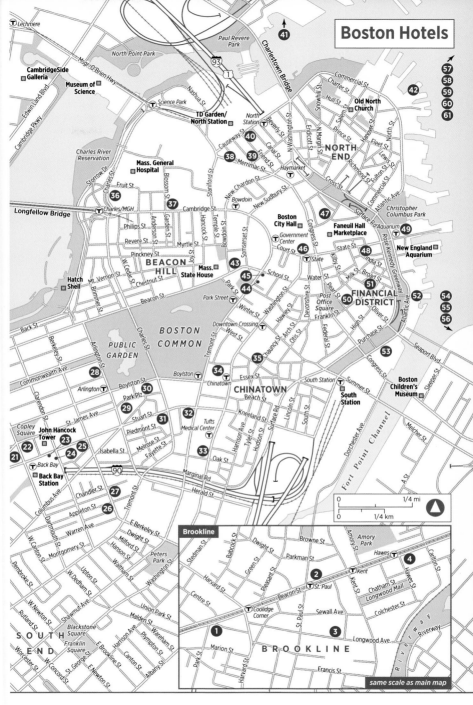

the top nine floors of the 16-story building and offer sensational views of the harbor or of the skyline and Greenway. Rooms with city views are less expensive.

Rowes Wharf (entrance on Atlantic Ave. at High St.), Boston, MA 02110. www.bhh.com. ☎ **800/752-7077** or 617/439-7000. Fax 617/330-9450. 230 units. $345–$795 double; from $685 suite. Extra person $50. Children 17 and under stay free in parent's room. Packages available. AE, DC, DISC, MC, V. Valet parking $44 weekdays, $33 weekends; self-parking $40 weekdays, $29 weekends. T: Red Line to South Station or Blue Line to Aquarium. Pets accepted. **Amenities:** 2 restaurants; bar; babysitting; concierge; well-appointed health club & spa; 60-ft. lap pool; room service. *In room:* A/C, TV, CD player, hair dryer, minibar, Wi-Fi ($15/day).

Boston Marriott Long Wharf ★ In an unbeatable location adjacent to the New England Aquarium, the landmark Marriott attracts business travelers with its proximity to the Financial District and families with its pool and easy access to downtown and waterfront attractions. Rooms surround an airy seven-story atrium. Large and decorated in upscale-chain-hotel style, they hold either one king or two double beds (with pillow-top mattresses and down comforters), and a table and chairs in front of the window. Without any neighbors in the way, the building gets more natural light than any other downtown hotel except perhaps the Boston Harbor Hotel, which offers a more personalized experience but is generally more (often much more) expensive. Rooms close to the water afford good views of the wharves and the waterfront; other units overlook the Rose Kennedy Greenway.

296 State St. (at Atlantic Ave.), Boston, MA 02109. www.marriottlongwharf.com. ☎ **800/228-9290** or 617/227-0800. Fax 617/227-2867. 400 units. Apr–Nov $249–$629 double; Dec–Mar $159–$369 double; year-round $450–$800 suite. Weekend and family packages available. AE, DC, DISC, MC, V. Valet parking $44. T: Blue Line to Aquarium. **Amenities:** Restaurant; lounge; concierge; exercise room; Jacuzzi; indoor pool; room service. *In room:* A/C, TV, fridge, hair dryer, Wi-Fi ($13/day).

Fairmont Battery Wharf ★★ This luxurious boutique hotel is the only large lodging in the North End. Part of a harborfront hotel-condo complex, it has a residential feel, with large and surpassingly comfortable guest rooms. The three low-rise buildings enjoy dazzling water views. Businesspeople can walk to the Financial District or take a water taxi from the hotel dock to locations around the harbor. Water transportation helps make up for the location's only real drawback: the distance from the subway. It's hardly burdensome, but it feels long if you've been on your feet sightseeing all day. The trade-off is that the private wharf is a quiet enclave out of range of traffic and the activity at the adjacent Coast Guard station. *Tip:* Members of Fairmont's frequent-guest program, which is free to join, don't pay for Internet access.

3 Battery Wharf (off Commercial St. at Battery St.), Boston, MA 02109. www.fairmont.com/batterywharf. ☎ **800/441-1414** or 617/994-9000. Fax 617/994-9098. 150 units, 104 with shower only. Apr to mid-Nov from $379 double, from $849 suite; mid-Nov to Mar from $279 double, from $749 suite. Children 17 and under stay free in parent's room. Weekend, spa, and other packages available. AE, DC, DISC, MC, V. Valet parking $42. T: Green Line to North Station, Orange Line to Haymarket, or Blue Line to Aquarium and 10-min. walk. Pets accepted ($25 fee). **Amenities:** Restaurant; bar; babysitting; concierge; well-equipped health club & spa; room service. *In room:* A/C, TV/DVD, CD player, hair dryer, minibar, MP3 docking station, Wi-Fi ($15/day).

InterContinental Boston ★★ With over-the-top amenities and helpful service, InterContinental earns repeat business from its predominantly corporate clientele. The 21-story glass-sheathed building (the hotel occupies the bottom 12 floors) faces the Rose Kennedy Greenway, a block from the Financial District and not far from the convention center. Guest rooms on the east (back) side overlook the harbor, half a block away. All are decorated in polished contemporary style, with plush earth-tone fabrics and pillow-top beds. Rooms are large enough to hold a comfy chaise and oversize work desk, and bathrooms are huge. The spa, health club, dining options, and condos upstairs amplify the residential feel, making the InterContinental a worthy competitor for the nearby Boston Harbor Hotel.

510 Atlantic Ave. (at Pearl St.), Boston, MA 02210. www.intercontinentalboston.com. ℂ **800/424-6835** or 617/747-1000. Fax 617/747-5190. 424 units. $299–$600 double; suites from $800 and way up. Club Lounge access $50. Extra person $35. Children 17 and under stay free in parent's room. Weekend and other packages available. AE, DC, DISC, MC, V. Valet parking $39. T: Red Line to South Station. Pets under 25 lb. accepted ($100 fee). **Amenities:** Restaurant; 2 bars; babysitting; concierge; 24-hr. health club & spa; 45-ft. lap pool; room service. *In room:* A/C, TV, hair dryer, minibar, MP3 docking station, Wi-Fi ($15/day).

EXPENSIVE

Millennium Bostonian Hotel ★ Across the street from Faneuil Hall Marketplace, this relatively small hotel offers excellent service and features that make it competitive with larger rivals such as the nearby Boston Marriott Long Wharf. It's popular with business travelers who want a break from the convention grind and with vacationers who appreciate the boutique atmosphere. Guest rooms fill three brick 19th-century buildings. All cool neutrals and clean lines, they have Frette linens and down comforters on pillow-top beds. Rooms vary in size; in half of them, French doors open onto small private balconies. My favorites overlook the marketplace, which is lively but not noisy, thanks to good soundproofing.

At Faneuil Hall Marketplace, 26 North St. (off Blackstone St.), Boston, MA 02109. www.millennium hotels.com. ℂ **866/866-8086** or 617/523-3600. Fax 617/523-2454. 201 units. $189–$449 double; $229–$489 superior double; suites from $350 and way up. Extra person $20. Children 17 and under stay free in parent's room. Weekend, spa, family, and other packages available. AE, DC, DISC, MC, V. Valet parking $42. T: Green or Blue Line to Government Center, or Green or Orange Line to Haymarket. **Amenities:** Restaurant; lounge; babysitting; concierge; small exercise room; access to nearby health club ($10); room service. *In room:* A/C, TV, hair dryer, high-speed Internet ($10/day), minibar.

MODERATE

Harborside Inn ★★ 🔅 The Harborside Inn offers an unbeatable combination of location and value; at this price point in this neighborhood, it has no competition. Sightseers are near Faneuil Hall Marketplace and the harbor, and business travelers are steps from the heart of the Financial District. Every room is different; each holds a queen- or king-size bed. The decor is modern and unfussy with nautical touches—think models and prints of sailboats, not over-the-top "ahoy, matey." Accommodations on the top floors of the renovated 1858 warehouse have lower ceilings and better views than those on lower floors. Rooms that face the street are more expensive but can be noisier; reserve an interior unit facing the skylit eight-story atrium if that's a concern.

185 State St. (btw. Atlantic Ave. and the Custom House Tower), Boston, MA 02109. www.harborside innboston.com. ℂ **888/723-7565** or 617/723-7500. Fax 617/670-6015. 98 units. $119–$299 double. Extra person $15. Packages and long-term rates available. Rates may be higher during special events. AE, DC, DISC, MC, V. Off-site parking $29; reservation required. T: Blue Line to Aquarium, or Blue or Orange Line to State. **Amenities:** Concierge; access to nearby health club ($15). *In room:* A/C, TV/DVD, hair dryer, Wi-Fi (free).

Financial District & Downtown Crossing

The hotels in this area are closer than their Waterfront competitors to the major shopping areas, the start of the Freedom Trail, and the subway to Cambridge.

BEST FOR Businesspeople and sightseers year-round; winter weekend travelers on a budget.

DRAWBACKS Generally drowsy at night and on weekends; weeknight room rates tend to be high.

VERY EXPENSIVE

Ames ★★ With the most eye-catching interior in town, combining minimalist style and traditional details, the Ames is a hipster magnet—a category that encompasses both business and leisure travelers. The rehab of Boston's first skyscraper, the 1889 Ames Building, created a wide range of room configurations; all units have cushy bedding, work desks, and wood floors, which lend an airy feel even in units that don't have huge windows (the largest windows are on the 3rd, 9th, and 14th floors). The staff is both exceptionally chic and exceptionally welcoming. The Ames is part of Morgans Hotel Group, and it compares favorably with the boutique-hotel pioneer's best-known properties, the Delano in Miami and New York's Hudson. The Ames's closest competitors, XV Beacon and Nine Zero, attract a more traditional crowd and are generally less expensive.

1 Court St. (at Washington and State sts.), Boston, MA 02108. www.ameshotel.com. ✆ **800/697-1791** or 617/979-8100. Fax 617/979-8101. 114 units. Apr–Nov $550 double, $850 suite; Dec–Mar $200 double, $500 suite. Children 17 and under stay free in parent's room. Packages available. AE, DC, DISC, MC, V. Valet parking $42; self-parking $37. T: Green or Blue Line to Government Center or Orange Line to State. **Amenities:** Restaurant; bar; concierge; exercise room; room service. *In room:* A/C, TV, hair dryer, minibar, MP3 docking station, Wi-Fi ($10/day).

Hilton Boston Financial District ★ The meticulously designed Hilton is the closest hotel in this area to the harbor, and the location, except at the height of rush-hour traffic, is surprisingly pleasant—not terribly busy and quite convenient. The spacious guest rooms have 9½-foot ceilings and sleek, sophisticated decor. The 14-story building is near Faneuil Hall Marketplace but not all that close (by Bostonian standards) to the T. The best units, on the upper floors of the renovated 1928 Art Deco building, afford great views of the harbor and downtown. The Hilton's closest competitor, literally and figuratively, is the Langham, which is less convenient to public transit but has a swimming pool.

89 Broad St. (at Franklin St.), Boston, MA 02110. www.bostonfinancial.hilton.com. ✆ **800/445-8667** or 617/556-0006. Fax 617/556-0053. 362 units. $169–$499 double; weekdays $269–$599 suite. Children 17 and under stay free in parent's room. Weekend, holiday, and family packages available. AE, DC, DISC, MC, V. Valet parking $38. T: Blue or Orange Line to State, or Red Line to South Station. Pets accepted ($75 fee). **Amenities:** Restaurant; bar; concierge; 24-hr. exercise room; room service. *In room:* A/C, TV, hair dryer, minibar, MP3 docking station, Wi-Fi ($15/day).

Hyatt Regency Boston Financial District ★ 🍴 Your fellow guests at this 22-story hotel are likely to be other convention-goers during the week, and sightseers and families on weekends. A block or so from Chinatown—home of the nearest competitor, the less expensive Doubletree—it's near the Financial District and a reasonable walk from the Back Bay and Beacon Hill. Rooms are spacious enough to hold sitting areas, desks, and settees, with Hyatt touches such as pillow-top mattresses and good service. Soft earth tones predominate, with cushy upholstery and luxe linens on the king-size or (in about one-quarter of the units) two double beds. Ask to be on a high floor to get away from the construction that's likely to be proceeding on adjacent Washington Street during your visit.

1 Ave. de Lafayette (off Washington St. btw. West and Avery sts.), Boston, MA 02111. www.regency boston.hyatt.com. © **800/233-1234** or 617/912-1234. Fax 617/451-0054. 500 units. $189–$469 double; suites from $350 and way up. Extra person $25. Children 17 and under stay free in parent's room. Weekend, family, and other packages available. AE, DC, DISC, MC, V. Valet parking $43; self-parking $30. T: Red or Orange Line to Downtown Crossing, or Green Line to Park St. or Boylston. **Amenities:** Restaurant; bar; babysitting; concierge; health club; 52-ft. indoor pool; room service; sauna. *In room:* A/C, TV, hair dryer, minibar, MP3 docking station, Wi-Fi ($10/day).

The Langham, Boston ★★ In the heart of the Financial District, the Langham is one of the best business hotels in the city. Leisure travelers who take advantage of weekend discounts will find themselves practically on top of the waterfront and downtown attractions, and perhaps a 10-minute walk from public transit. Elegantly decorated and large enough to hold a generous work area, the luxurious guest rooms have 153 configurations, including loft suites with two bathrooms. The most desirable rooms in the nine-story building overlook the lovely park in Post Office Square. The Langham's views are fine, but they pale in comparison to the vistas from the best units at the hotel's main competitors, the Boston Harbor Hotel and the InterContinental Boston.

250 Franklin St. (at Post Office Sq.), Boston, MA 02110. http://boston.langhamhotels.com. © **800/791-7761** or 617/451-1900. Fax 617/423-2844. 318 units. $185–$495 double; suites from $545 and way up. Extra person $35. Weekend, family, spa, and other packages available. AE, DC, DISC, MC, V. Valet parking $42 Sun–Thurs, $28 Fri–Sat. T: Blue or Orange Line to State, or Red Line to Downtown Crossing or South Station. Pets accepted ($50 fee). **Amenities:** Restaurant and lounge w/DJ on weekends; cafe w/Sun brunch and Sat "Chocolate Bar Buffet" (Sept–June); concierge; state-of-the-art health club & spa; Jacuzzi; 40-ft. indoor pool; room service; sauna. *In room:* A/C, TV, hair dryer, high-speed Internet ($12/day), minibar, MP3 docking station.

Nine Zero ★★ This centrally located boutique hotel offers a sleek, sophisticated atmosphere and service in the old-school customer-is-always-right mold. Guest rooms and oversize bathrooms contain opulent features, including luxurious linens and toiletries, and extensive business amenities. The 19-story hotel, which opened in 2002, is part of the eco-conscious luxury Kimpton chain. Tucked away on a side street, which cuts down on noise, Nine Zero is within easy walking distance of downtown, 2 blocks from Boston Common and the subway. More traditional XV Beacon and the more cutting-edge Ames are the closest competitors. The service at all three is attentive and personal; let style and price guide your choice. *Tip:* Sign up for the frequent-guest program (which is free), and the hotel waives the Internet access fee.

90 Tremont St. (near Bromfield St.), Boston, MA 02108. www.ninezero.com. © **866/906-9090** or 617/772-5800. Fax 617/772-5810. 190 units. $289–$599 double; suites $500 and way up. Packages available. AE, DC, DISC, MC, V. Valet parking $40. T: Red or Green Line to Park St. Pets accepted. **Amenities:** Restaurant; bar; babysitting; concierge; exercise room; access to nearby health club; room service. *In room:* A/C, TV, hair dryer, minibar, MP3 docking station, Wi-Fi ($10/day).

Food for Thought

Yes, this is the Parker House of Parker House roll fame. The rolls (pictured here) were invented (if food is "invented") here, as was Boston cream pie.

That's not the hotel's only claim to fame. Malcolm X and Ho Chi Minh both worked here, and the room that's now Parker's Bar played host to a well-known group: Henry Wadsworth Longfellow, Oliver Wendell Holmes, Ralph Waldo Emerson, Nathaniel Hawthorne, and sometimes Charles Dickens, who made up a literary salon called the Saturday Club.

EXPENSIVE

Omni Parker House ★ ☺ 🍴 The centrally located Parker House offers a huge range of room configurations and prices. In continuous operation longer than any other hotel in America (since 1855), it's in tip-top shape thanks to regular refurbishing and renovation. Many of the 50-plus room layouts aren't large, but even the smallest units are thoughtfully appointed, decorated in traditional style with cherry furnishings. Bathrooms tend to be small. The hotel is especially popular with families (kids receive gifts at check-in) and sightseers, who can economize with a weekend deal or "economy single." The closest competitors are the Ames and Nine Zero, which are boutique properties and considerably pricier. *Tip:* Sign up for the free frequent-guest program, and the hotel waives the in-room Internet access fee.

60 School St. (at Tremont St.), Boston, MA 02108. www.omniparkerhouse.com. ✆ **800/843-6664** or 617/227-8600. Fax 617/742-5729. 551 units, some with shower only. $159–$189 economy room; $189–$289 double; $249–$399 suite. Children 17 and under stay free in parent's room. Weekend packages and AARP discount available. AE, DC, DISC, MC, V. Valet parking $40. T: Green or Blue Line to Government Center, or Red or Green Line to Park St. Pets accepted (deposit required). **Amenities:** Restaurant; 2 bars; concierge; exercise room; room service. *In room:* A/C, TV, hair dryer, high-speed Internet ($10/day), minibar, MP3 docking station.

BEACON HILL/NORTH STATION

These neighborhoods are home to many downtown workers; while they walk to work, visitors can stroll to the waterfront attractions.

BEST FOR Access to public transit. Travelers who prefer the residential feel of Beacon Hill to the more businesslike atmosphere of downtown will be happy here.

DRAWBACKS Generally pricey; check with a B&B agency (p. 97) for more affordable alternatives. The narrow streets around North Station attract rowdy crowds after big events at the TD Garden arena and on weekend nights.

Very Expensive

XV Beacon ★★ Nonstop pampering, high-tech appointments, and outrageously luxurious rooms make this Boston's premier boutique hotel. The meticulously maintained 10-story property has attracted demanding travelers, especially businesspeople and international visitors, since it opened in 2000, and management bends over backward to keep the loyal clientele returning. The guest rooms, individually decorated in an austere but plush style that's more SoHo than Beacon Hill, contain king- and queen-size beds with Frette linens, surround-sound stereo systems, gas fireplaces, 42-inch flatscreens, and 4-inch TVs in the bathroom. "Studio" units have a sitting area. The Ames and Nine Zero, which are part of fancy chains, are the main competition; this smaller independent property gets the nod from its high-maintenance fans.

15 Beacon St. (at Somerset St., 1 block from the State House), Boston, MA 02108. www.xvbeacon. com. © **877/982-3226** or 617/670-1500. Fax 617/670-2525. 62 units, some with shower only. From $295 double; from $1,200 suite. AE, DC, DISC, MC, V. Valet parking $44. T: Red or Green Line to Park St., or Green or Blue Line to Government Center. Dogs accepted ($25 MSPCA donation). **Amenities:** Restaurant; bar; babysitting; concierge; exercise room; access to nearby health club ($15); room service. *In room:* A/C, TV, CD player, hair dryer, minibar, MP3 docking station, Wi-Fi (free).

The Liberty Hotel ★★ A luxury hotel with top-of-the-line furnishings, next-gen tech, and huge bathrooms, the Liberty used to be the Charles Street Jail. The original 1851 hoosegow now holds the public areas (with bars on the windows) and 18 guest rooms that—despite not having been "guest" accommodations before—are in high demand. Other accommodations are in a new building, opened in 2007, between the jail and the adjacent hospital. Rooms that face the Charles River (across the road) are preferable to those with a view of the neighborhood; units on higher floors are best. My favorites are corner rooms with a river view from the bathtub. The Liberty's closest competition, XV Beacon, offers more personal service in a less lively neighborhood with fewer dining options.

215 Charles St. (at Cambridge St.), Boston, MA 02114. www.libertyhotel.com. © **617/224-4000.** Fax 617/399-4259. 298 units. $295–$550 double; $600–$1,000 suite. Children 17 and under stay free in parent's room. Weekend and other packages available. AE, DC, DISC, MC, V. Valet parking $42; self-parking $42. T: Red Line to Charles/MGH. Small pets accepted. **Amenities:** 2 restaurants; bar; concierge; 24-hr. exercise room; room service. *In room:* A/C, TV, hair dryer, minibar, MP3 docking station, Wi-Fi (free).

Expensive

Across the street from the TD Garden and North Station, the **Holiday Inn Express Hotel & Suites Boston Garden,** 280 Friend St. (www.hiexpress. com; © **888/465-4329** or 617/720-5544), consists of 72 units in a five-story building that was previously a hostel. Rates start at $195 for a double, skyrocketing during popular events at the Garden, and include continental breakfast. Valet parking costs $36, and Wi-Fi access costs $10 per day.

Onyx Hotel ★ This plush boutique hotel is the finest property in this evolving neighborhood, which grows more pleasant by the day but is a zoo before and after big events at the nearby TD Garden. Convenient to North Station and the North End, it's an easy walk from downtown and Beacon Hill. The 10-story hotel is contemporary in style, decorated in soothing jewel tones with sleek lines and high ceilings that make the decent-size rooms feel even bigger. Each unit in the eco-friendly Kimpton property holds a large work desk. The best accommodations are the top-floor suites, but any room with a floor-to-ceiling window feels like a mini-palace. The nearby Bulfinch is less expensive and offers correspondingly fewer amenities. *Tip:* Sign up for the (free) frequent-guest program, and the hotel waives the Internet access fee.

155 Portland St. (btw. Causeway St. and Anthony Valenti Way), Boston, MA 02114. www.onyx hotel.com. ⓒ **866/660-6699** or 617/557-9955. Fax 617/557-0005. 112 units. $209–$349 double. Extra person $25. Children 17 and under stay free in parent's room. Rates include evening wine reception. Weekend, family, and other packages, AAA and AARP discounts available. AE, DC, DISC, MC, V. Valet parking $42. T: Green or Orange Line to North Station. Pets accepted. **Amenities:** Lounge; exercise room; access to nearby health club; room service. *In room:* A/C, TV, hair dryer, minibar, MP3 docking station, Wi-Fi ($10).

Moderate

Bulfinch Hotel One block from North Station, the Bulfinch is a leisure-traveler magnet that attracts thrifty businesspeople with its convenient location and reasonable rates. Every room in the 1904 building is different; they're on the small side, but custom furnishings create the illusion of more space. Plush fabrics in cool neutrals, flatscreen TVs, and marble bathrooms set off the contemporary, uncluttered design. The best units in the nine-story hotel are executive kings— oversize doubles—known as "nose rooms" because they're in the pointed end of the triangular building, with windows on three sides of the bed. The Onyx, around the corner, is pricier but offers better amenities and service.

107 Merrimac St. (at Lancaster St., 1 block from Causeway St.), Boston, MA 02114. www.bulfinch hotel.com. ⓒ **877/267-1776** or 617/624-0202. Fax 617/624-0211. 80 units, most with shower only. $169–$399 double; $199–$489 executive king. Children 17 and under stay free in parent's room. Packages, AAA, AARP, and military discounts available. AE, DC, DISC, MC, V. Parking $30 in nearby garage. T: Green or Orange Line to North Station. Pets accepted ($50 fee). **Amenities:** Restaurant; lounge; concierge; exercise room; room service. *In room:* A/C, TV, hair dryer, high-speed Internet (free).

Holiday Inn Boston at Beacon Hill Just off one of Beacon Hill's main streets, this 15-story hotel courts leisure travelers with its easy access to downtown and the Back Bay, the river, and Cambridge. Especially appealing to vacationing families is the seasonal outdoor pool. Guest rooms are quite large, with contemporary furnishings and picture-window views of the city, the State House, or the parking structure—ask for a room on a high floor, facing Blossom Street if possible. The building is part of a small retail complex with a Whole Foods supermarket, a drugstore, and a handful of shops. Because it's adjacent to Massachusetts General Hospital, the hotel books a fair number of patients and relatives, and the staff is sensitive to their needs.

5 Blossom St. (at Cambridge St.), Boston, MA 02114. www.hisboston.com. ⓒ **800/465-4329** or 617/742-7630. Fax 617/742-4192. 303 units, some with shower only. $150–$400 double; from $390 suite. Extra person $15. Rollaway $20. Children 17 and under stay free in parent's room. Weekend and corporate packages available. AE, DC, DISC, MC, V. Valet or self-parking $36. T: Red Line to Charles/MGH. **Amenities:** Restaurant; lounge; concierge; executive-level rooms; small exercise room; access to nearby health club ($20); outdoor heated pool; room service. *In room:* A/C, TV, hair dryer, Wi-Fi (free).

CHARLESTOWN

Charlestown is home to the final stops on the Freedom Trail. Away from the Charlestown Navy Yard (home to "Old Ironsides") and the Bunker Hill Monument, this is a largely residential neighborhood.

BEST FOR Travelers with business in Charlestown or east Cambridge, families who want to be close to the Freedom Trail, and anyone who needs easy access to downtown (by MBTA ferry or water taxi, and on foot).

DRAWBACKS Access to the Back Bay and central Cambridge isn't quick or easy; lodging and nightlife options are limited.

Expensive

Residence Inn Boston Harbor on Tudor Wharf ★★ ✦ The Residence Inn combines the familiar suburban brand and a prime urban location, meaning patrons tend to be business travelers on weeknights and families on weekends. Easy transit access (water taxis stop at the hotel dock) and the included breakfast buffet make this hotel a better deal than many downtown competitors. Adjacent to the Charlestown Navy Yard, it consists of studio and one- and two-bedroom suites with full kitchens and plenty of natural light. Even the smallest units are generous in size. Most rooms in the eight-story building afford impressive views of the harbor or the Charles River and the Zakim Bridge. Prices listed here are for 1 to 4 nights; longer stays mean greater discounts.

34–44 Charles River Ave. (½ block from Chelsea St.), Charlestown, MA 02129. www.marriott. com/bostw. ✆ **866/296-2297,** 800/331-3131 (Marriott), or 617/242-9000. Fax 617/242-5554. 168 units. May–Nov $199–$399 double; Dec–Apr $129–$229 double. Rates include full breakfast. Children stay free in parent's room. Weekend, family, and other packages from $129/night. AAA, government, and long-term discounts available. AE, DC, DISC, MC, V. Valet parking $32. T: Blue Line to Aquarium and ferry from Long Wharf to Navy Yard, then 5-min. walk; Green or Orange Line to North Station, then 10-min. walk; or Orange Line to Community College, then 10-min. walk. Pets accepted ($100 fee). **Amenities:** Indoor lap pool; exercise room; access to nearby YMCA ($8); Jacuzzi. *In room:* A/C, TV, hair dryer, kitchen, Wi-Fi (free).

SOUTH BOSTON WATERFRONT (SEAPORT DISTRICT)

This rapidly evolving neighborhood isn't quite a full-fledged destination yet, but its hotels are magnets for business travelers and conventioneers. The Institute of Contemporary Art and Boston Children's Museum are in this area, which is accessible by Silver Line bus from the airport and South Station.

BEST FOR Access to the Boston Convention and Exhibition Center, Seaport World Trade Center, and Logan Airport. Cambridge is a quick trip from South Station.

DRAWBACKS Downtown is some distance by bus and subway or on foot (Faneuil Hall Marketplace, for instance, is at least a 15-min. walk), and access to the Back Bay isn't great. Dining options are limited, and there's no shopping or entertainment to speak of.

Very Expensive

The Westin Boston Waterfront ★★ The only hotel attached to the Boston Convention and Exhibition Center, the Westin offers the chain's abundant amenities, including Heavenly Beds, in its signature contemporary style. The good-size rooms have plenty of space for oversize work desks, and huge windows show off the city skyline, the water, or nearby office buildings and construction. Northeast-facing units on higher floors of the 16-story building enjoy panoramas of the action on the harbor, which—the hotel's name notwithstanding—is 2 blocks away. Bathrooms hold the nicest mirrors (huge and backlit) I've ever seen in a hotel. Access to the convention center is through a weather-protected skybridge off the enormous lobby, which holds a bar that hops after work on weeknights.

425 Summer St. (at D St.), Boston, MA 02210. www.westin.com. ✆**800/937-8461** or 617/532-4600. Fax 617/532-4630. 793 units. $259–$599 double; $359 and up suite. Children 17 and under stay free in parent's room. Weekend and family packages available. AE, DC, DISC, MC, V. Valet parking $42; self-parking $32. T: Red Line to South Station, then Silver Line SL1/SL2 bus to World Trade Center. Pets accepted. **Amenities:** 2 restaurants; lounge; bar; coffee shop; concierge; state-of-the-art health club; indoor pool; room service. *In room:* A/C, TV, hair dryer, minibar, Wi-Fi ($16/day).

Expensive

Renaissance Boston Waterfront Hotel ★ Ultra-high-tech features make the Renaissance a favorite with business travelers. Lightning-fast DS-3 Internet access makes each guest room a media hub, with the capability to run everything through the 37-inch high-def TV. As you'd expect within walking distance of both the convention center and the World Trade Center, the style is familiar business contemporary, all sleek silhouettes and vibrant colors, with comfy, well-appointed beds. On weekends, expect a predominantly leisure clientele and correspondingly lower prices—which seems only fair, given the distance from most attractions and dining. Higher floors of the glass-clad 21-story building enjoy sensational views of the harbor, a block away, and the downtown skyline.

606 Congress St. (at D St.), Boston, MA 02210. www.renaissanceboston.com. ✆**888/796-4664,** 800/468-3571, or 617/338-4111. Fax 617/338-4138. 471 units. $169–$459 double; from $459 suite. Children 18 and under stay free in parent's room. Weekend, family, and other packages available. AE, DC, DISC, MC, V. Valet parking $42. T: Red Line to South Station, then Silver Line SL1/SL2 bus to World Trade Center or 20-min. walk. Or water taxi to World Trade Center. **Amenities:** Restaurant; lounge; coffee bar; babysitting; concierge; health club; indoor pool; room service. *In room:* A/C, TV, hair dryer, Wi-Fi ($13/day).

Seaport Hotel ★★ ☺ Across the street from and affiliated with the World Trade Center, the independent Seaport Hotel books up unpredictably depending on the schedule there and the nearby convention center. The sophisticated, eco-conscious hotel was designed and built (by Fidelity Investments) to appeal to techno-savvy business travelers. The well-appointed, decent-size rooms have thoughtful features such as pillow-top mattresses, Logan Airport flight information on the TV, and fog-free bathroom mirrors. The views (of the city or harbor) from higher floors of the 18-story building are breathtaking, and the hotel shuttle to downtown destinations comes in handy. The kid-conscious staff, pool, weekend packages, and proximity to the Boston Children's Museum make this a good choice for families, too.

1 Seaport Lane (btw. Seaport Blvd. and Congress St.), Boston, MA 02210. www. seaportboston.com. © **877/732-7678** or 617/385-4000. Fax 617/385-5090. 426 units. $189–$399 double; $450 and way up suite. Children 16 and under stay free in parent's room. Weekend and family packages available. AE, DC, DISC, MC, V. Valet parking $42 (1 night free for hybrid and electric vehicles); self-parking $32. T: Red Line to South Station, then Silver Line SL1/ SL2 bus to World Trade Center or 20-min. walk. Or water taxi to World Trade Center. Pets under 50 lb. accepted. **Amenities:** Well-regarded restaurant; cafe; lounge; concierge; bikes; well-equipped health club; 50-ft. indoor pool; room service; spa. *In room:* A/C, TV, hair dryer, minibar, MP3 docking station, Wi-Fi.

Planning Pointer

If your trip involves a cultural event—for example, a big museum show or *The Nutcracker*—look into a hotel package that includes tickets. Usually offered on weekends, these deals always save time and can save money.

CHINATOWN/THEATER DISTRICT

This lively area—a small part of it was once the red-light district, but the whole neighborhood gets nicer by the day—is near the Public Garden, Boston Common, and the Rose Kennedy Greenway but not very green itself.

BEST FOR A compromise if you need access to both downtown and the Back Bay, often for less than you'd pay in those areas.

DRAWBACKS Narrow, congested streets create a gritty atmosphere; the Theater District is crowded before and after performances but deserted late at night.

Very Expensive

The Ritz-Carlton, Boston Common ★ This plush, ultramodern hotel is a magnet for visiting celebrities—the state-of-the-art Sports Club/LA is a powerful draw—as well as the Ritz-Carlton brand. Let's just say that you don't have to be a movie star for the staff here to treat you like one. The luxurious hotel's guest rooms occupy the 9th through 12th floors of a building a half-block from Boston Common; public spaces are at street level. The good-size guest rooms and huge suites feel more residential than commercial, with indulgent amenities such as Frette linens, feather duvets, and three phones (one in the large bathroom). You'll pay more for a room with a view of the Common. The hotel's chief rivals, the Four Seasons and the Mandarin Oriental, are in the prettier, more interesting Back Bay.

10 Avery St. (btw. Tremont and Washington sts.), Boston, MA 02111. www.ritzcarlton.com. © **800/241-3333** or 617/574-7100. Fax 617/574-7200. 193 units. From $420 double; from $520 Club Level; from $620 suite. Weekend, family, and other packages available. AE, DC, DISC, MC, V. Valet parking $39. T: Green Line to Boylston. Pets accepted. **Amenities:** Restaurant; bar; lounge; babysitting; concierge; club-level rooms; access ($15/day) to adjoining Sports Club/LA (100,000-sq.-ft. facility w/lap pool, complete spa services, salon, regulation basketball court, 10,000-sq.-ft. weight room, steam rooms, saunas, 5 exercise studios, 4 squash courts); room service. *In room:* A/C, TV, CD player, hair dryer, minibar, Wi-Fi ($10/day).

W Boston ★ The W is a favorite with regular guests—mostly corporate travelers drawn to the go-go public spaces and serene accommodations—who seek out the boutique chain and its signature touches. Devotees check them off: compact yet indulgent guest rooms with feather-top mattresses and down comforters, contemporary style with local flair (Thoreau quotes stenciled on the walls of the huge bathrooms), excellent service, and congested lobby with a lounge that roars after work. The hotel occupies the first 15 floors of a 27-story hotel-condo glass tower, which opened in 2009. Views are of the neon marquees and rooftops. Ask to be as high as possible to avoid the chattering scene in the lobby and the traffic that buzzes through the Theater District well into the night.

100 Stuart St. (at Tremont St.), Boston, MA 02116. www.whotels.com. © **877/946-8357** or 617/261-8700. Fax 617/261-8725. 235 units. $259–$579 double; from $439 and way up suite. Weekend, spa, and other packages available. AE, DC, DISC, MC, V. Valet parking $42. T: Green Line to Boylston or Green Line to Tufts Medical Center. Pets accepted ($125 fee for 1st night, then $25/night). **Amenities:** Restaurant (Market; see p. 112); 2 lounges; bike rental; concierge; well-equipped 24-hr. exercise room; room service; Bliss Spa. *In room:* A/C, TV/DVD, CD player, hair dryer, high-speed Internet ($15/day), MP3 docking station.

Expensive

Radisson Hotel Boston ★ Popular with business travelers, tour groups, and vacationers, this is an attractive hotel in a busy neighborhood. It would be a prime property anywhere: The guest rooms are among the largest in the city, and each has a private balcony, with great views from the higher floors. Rooms, decorated in pleasant neutrals and contemporary-chain-hotel style, hold a king or two queen Sleep Number beds and enough space for a sitting area. The best units are on the higher floors of the 24-story building, which enjoy breathtaking views.

200 Stuart St. (at Charles St. S.), Boston, MA 02116. www.radisson.com/bostonma. © **800/395-7046** or 617/482-1800. Fax 617/451-2750. 356 units, some with shower only. $179–$479 double. Extra person $20. Cot $20. Cribs free. Children 17 and under stay free in parent's room. Weekend, theater, and other packages available. AE, DC, DISC, MC, V. Valet parking $39; self-parking $34. T: Green Line to Boylston or Orange Line to Tufts Medical Center. **Amenities:** 2 restaurants; babysitting; concierge; exercise room; indoor pool; room service. *In room:* A/C, TV, hair dryer, Wi-Fi (free).

Moderate

Doubletree Hotel Boston Downtown ★  The Doubletree is a hit with leisure and business travelers as well as people visiting the adjacent medical center. It's cheaper than you might think for such a convenient location. The six-story building is a former high school with high ceilings and compact, well-designed rooms. Ask for a unit facing away from busy Washington Street and you'll have a view of the city rather than Tufts Medical Center, across the street. Nice details include Asian touches in the contemporary decor and features such as a fish tank in the lobby, installed in accordance with the principles of feng shui. Don't confuse this hotel with its all-suite corporate sibling on the Charles River (p. 87).

821 Washington St. (at Oak St., 1 block from Stuart St.), Boston, MA 02111. www.hiltonfamily boston.com/downtown. © **800/222-8733** or 617/956-7900. Fax 617/956-7901. 267 units, some with shower only. $139–$299 double; $189–$359 suite. Extra person $10. Children 17 and under stay free in parent's room. Weekend and other packages, AAA, AARP, and military discounts available. AE, DC, DISC, MC, V. Valet parking $40. T: Orange Line to Tufts Medical Center. **Amenities:** Restaurant; lounge; coffee shop; concierge; executive-level rooms; access to adjoining YMCA w/Olympic-size pool; room service. *In room:* A/C, TV, hair dryer, minibar, Wi-Fi ($13/day).

THE SOUTH END

Berkeley Street runs from the Back Bay across the Massachusetts Turnpike to the most convenient corner of the sprawling South End, where you'll find these two lodgings.

BEST FOR Budget-conscious travelers with business in the Back Bay; easy access to the South End's excellent restaurants.

DRAWBACKS Access to Cambridge isn't easy; Berkeley Street is fairly busy all day and into the evening.

Moderate

Chandler Inn Hotel ★ ✦ Just 2 blocks from the Back Bay, the Chandler Inn was a bargain for its location even before it revamped its guest rooms. The renovations, completed in 2011, transformed the eight-story building from utilitarian to boutique. Rooms are small but well designed, decorated in cool neutrals with splashes of orange and equipped with plasma TVs and marble bathrooms; all have individual climate control. The staff is welcoming and helpful. This gay-friendly hotel books up early for events such as the Boston Marathon and Boston Pride March and for foliage season; off-season rates are excellent.

26 Chandler St. (at Berkeley St.), Boston, MA 02116. www.chandlerinn.com. ✆ **800/842-3450** or 617/482-3450. Fax 617/542-3428. 56 units. $109–$279 double. Children 11 and under stay free in parent's room. AE, DC, DISC, MC, V. Parking $27 at nearby garage. T: Orange Line to Back Bay. Pets under 25 lb. accepted ($50 fee). **Amenities:** Lounge (Fritz; p. 279); access to nearby health club ($10). *In room:* A/C, TV, hair dryer, MP3 docking station, Wi-Fi (free).

Inexpensive

40 Berkeley This pleasant, convenient hostel and residence—it used to be the YWCA—has a dining room, patio garden, piano, and library. Formerly for women only, the seven-story building accommodates both men and women, but not kids. The dorm-style guest rooms are basic, containing little more than beds, but they're well maintained and comfortable—not plush, but not cells, either. The well-kept public areas include a 24-hour TV lounge. That description might not seem to justify the prices, but check around a little before you turn up your nose, especially if you plan to spend most of your time out and about.

40 Berkeley St. (at Appleton St.), Boston, MA 02116. www.40berkeley.com. ✆ **617/375-2524.** Fax 617/375-2525. 200 units, none with bathroom. $65–$80 single; $80–$110 double; $99–$132 triple or quad. Rates include full breakfast. Long-term rates available (5-week minimum). No children accepted. MC, V. Parking $27 at nearby garage. T: Orange Line to Back Bay or Green Line to Arlington. **Amenities:** Cafeteria; computer kiosk w/Internet access ($1/10 min.). *In room:* Wi-Fi (free), no phone.

THE BACK BAY

Boston's widest variety of lodgings is in this neighborhood, which stretches from the area around the Public Garden past the Hynes Convention Center.

BEST FOR Anyone who wants to be where the action is. The Boston area's best shopping and people-watching is here. Budget-conscious travelers have more options here than in any other centrally located part of town. The Esplanade, the recreational area on the Charles River, is a great place for a walk or run.

DRAWBACKS Rates can be extremely high, especially during citywide events such as the Marathon. Tour groups overrun the neighborhood year-round, especially during foliage season. The most convenient T access is on the unreliable Green Line. Reaching Cambridge isn't easy or consistently fast (the subway can be as slow as the pokey No. 1 bus).

Very Expensive

Colonnade Hotel Boston ★★ ☺ Adjacent to Copley Place and the Prudential Center, the independently owned Colonnade caters to an international clientele of businesspeople, sightseers, shoppers, and families. It's a welcome alternative to the chain properties that dominate this neighborhood. The 11-story concrete-and-glass hotel has an attentive, gracious staff and large guest rooms decorated in muted earth tones. The sleek residential-style furnishings include pillow-top beds, marble-clad bathrooms, and a round table with two chairs on casters in place of a desk. Light floods through floor-to-ceiling windows, which open on the bustling Prudential Center or—my preference—the South End's urban patchwork. The seasonal "rooftop resort" and swimming pool are a welcome retreat in warm weather.

120 Huntington Ave. (at Garrison St., 1 block from W. Newton St.), Boston, MA 02116. www.colonnadehotel.com. ✆ **800/962-3030** or 617/424-7000. Fax 617/424-1717. 285 units. $229–$459 double; $575 and way up suite. Children 11 and under stay free in parent's room. Weekend, family, and other packages, winter and other discounts available. AE, DC, DISC, MC, V. Parking $38. T: Green Line E to Prudential. Pets accepted. **Amenities:** Restaurant (Brasserie Jo, p. 119); bar; babysitting; concierge; well-equipped exercise room; heated outdoor rooftop pool; room service. *In room:* A/C, TV/DVD, hair dryer, minibar, MP3 docking station, Wi-Fi ($14/day).

Eliot Hotel ★★ On tree-lined Commonwealth Avenue, this exquisite hotel offers both a romantic atmosphere and top-notch business features. European-style service and abundant amenities keep both leisure and business travelers returning to the traditional-looking red-brick building just a block from the bustle of Newbury Street. Almost every unit is a spacious suite (16 rooms are standard doubles) with a residential feel: subtle geometric and floral patterns on the rugs and upholstery, antique furnishings, down comforters, and marble-clad bathrooms. French doors separate the living rooms and bedrooms in the suites. The hotel is near Boston University and Fenway Park, and just across the river from MIT—convenient, but with a getaway feel that distinguishes the Eliot from its closest rival, the Hotel Commonwealth.

370 Commonwealth Ave. (at Mass. Ave.), Boston, MA 02215. www.eliothotel.com. ✆ **800/443-5468** or 617/267-1607. Fax 617/536-9114. 95 units, some with shower only. $235–$395 double; $355–$545 1-bedroom suite; $580–$890 2-bedroom suite. Extra person $30. Children 17 and under stay free in parent's room. Packages available. AE, DC, MC, V. Valet parking $36. T: Green Line B, C, or D to Hynes Convention Center. Pets accepted. **Amenities:** Restaurant; sashimi bar; babysitting; concierge; free access to nearby health club; room service. *In room:* A/C, TV, hair dryer, minibar, MP3 docking station, Wi-Fi ($5/day).

The Fairmont Copley Plaza ★★ The "grande dame of Boston" is a classic old-fashioned grand hotel, with a clientele of leisure and business travelers who expect luxurious lodgings and superior service. Built in 1912, the seven-story Renaissance-revival building faces beautiful Copley Square. The spacious, painstakingly maintained guest rooms have a residential feel, with plush draperies and upholstery and custom furnishings, including oversize desks and pillow-top mattresses. Rooms that face the square afford better views than those overlooking busy Dartmouth Street, but all beat the views from the hotel's nearest rival, the Lenox. The eco-conscious Copley Plaza boasts countless details (inventive weekend packages, a resident black Lab guests can take for walks) that have made it a favorite with generations of Bostonians and visitors. *Tip:* Members of Fairmont's frequent-guest program, which is free to join, don't pay for Internet access.

138 St. James Ave. (btw. Dartmouth St. and Trinity Place), Boston, MA 02116. www.fairmont.com/copleyplaza. © **800/441-1414** or 617/267-5300. Fax 617/267-7668. 383 units. From $289 double; from $899 suite. Extra person $30. Weekend and other packages available. AE, DC, MC, V. Valet parking $42. T: Green Line to Copley or Orange Line to Back Bay. Pets accepted ($25/day). **Amenities:** Restaurant; lounge (Oak Bar, p. 277); concierge; concierge-level rooms; access to nearby health club ($20); exercise room; room service. *In room:* A/C, TV, hair dryer, minibar, MP3 docking station, Wi-Fi ($15/day).

Four Seasons Hotel ★★★ With its exquisite service, beautiful location, elegant guest rooms and public areas, terrific health club, and wonderful restaurants, the Four Seasons is the best hotel in Boston and perhaps in all of New England. The 16-story brick-and-glass building (the hotel occupies eight floors) overlooks the Public Garden. The spacious accommodations feel more like stylish apartments than hotel rooms, with lots of plush fabrics, elaborate moldings, and marble bathrooms. The best units—which cost as much as the monthly rent on some apartments—overlook the Public Garden; less expensive rooms at the back of the hotel have city views. The welcoming staff is famously sensitive to the needs of businesspeople, families, and celebrities. Compared to its main rivals, the Four Seasons beats the Ritz-Carlton on location and the Mandarin Oriental, which doesn't have a pool, on facilities.

200 Boylston St. (at Hadassah Way, btw. Arlington St. and Charles St. S.), Boston, MA 02116. www.fourseasons.com/boston. © **800/819-5053** or 617/338-4400. Fax 617/423-0154. 273 units. $495 double weekdays, $425 double weekends; from $895 1-bedroom suite; from $1,545 2-bedroom suite. Weekend and family packages available. AE, DC, DISC, MC, V. Valet parking $47. T: Green Line to Arlington. Pets under 25 lb. accepted. **Amenities:** Restaurant and bar (Bristol Lounge, p. 277); babysitting; concierge; health club; Jacuzzi; 24-hr. 44-ft. pool overlooking the Public Garden; room service. *In room:* A/C, TV/DVD, CD player, hair dryer, minibar, MP3 docking station, Wi-Fi ($10/day).

The Lenox Hotel ★★ The central location makes the Lenox popular with business travelers, and its relatively small size and accommodating staff make it a welcome alternative to the huge convention hotels that dominate this neighborhood. As a rule, though, those larger competitors have more extensive fitness facilities. The spacious, luxurious guest rooms have high ceilings and are large enough to contain sitting areas and Aeron chairs. Custom-designed wood furnishings and marble bathrooms add to the anything-but-generic vibe; rooms on the top two floors of the 11-story building enjoy excellent views. My favorites are the 12 corner units with wood-burning fireplaces. The Lenox was one of the first hotels in the country to embrace eco-consciousness, and management's commitment to shrinking the hotel's footprint is truly impressive.

61 Exeter St. (at Boylston St.), Boston, MA 02116. www.lenoxhotel.com. © **800/225-7676** or 617/536-5300. Fax 617/236-0351. 214 units, some with shower only. $215–$425 double; $289–$545 junior suite; from $770 1-bedroom fireplace suite. Children 16 and under stay free in parent's room. Corporate, weekend, and family packages available. AE, DC, DISC, MC, V. Valet parking $43. T: Green Line to Copley. **Amenities:** Restaurant; bar; pub; babysitting; concierge; small exercise room; room service. *In room:* A/C, TV, hair dryer, MP3 docking station, Wi-Fi (free).

Mandarin Oriental, Boston ★★ Mandarin Oriental's first New England property courts both devoted shoppers and international business travelers with its great location, sublime service, and top-notch amenities, including an excellent spa. The hotel, a block from Newbury Street, connects directly to the Prudential Center (and from there to the Hynes Convention Center and Copley Place). Guest rooms are large and luxurious, with Frette linens and color palettes of soft greens and browns that evoke nature. In keeping with the Hong Kong–based luxury chain's philosophy, the elegant, peaceful hotel was designed using the principles of feng shui. It opened in 2008. The Mandarin Oriental's closest competitors— the Four Seasons and the InterContinental—have superior fitness facilities, but better access to shopping and dining here may tip the scales for you.

 ## family-friendly HOTELS

Almost every hotel in the Boston area regularly plays host to children, and many offer special family packages. For more information, see "Family Travel," p. 351. Moderately priced chains have the most experience with youngsters, but their higher-end competitors put on a good show.

Units at the **Doubletree Guest Suites** (p. 87) are a great deal—they have two rooms in which to spread out, and they cost far less than adjoining rooms at any other hotel this nice. Stash breakfast fixings in the in-room refrigerator, then splurge on lunch and dinner.

In the Back Bay, the **Colonnade Hotel Boston** (p. 78) offers a family weekend package that includes parking, breakfast for two adults, up to four passes (for two adults and two children) to an attraction of your choice, and a fanny pack for younger guests that holds sunglasses, a pad and pen, a yo-yo, and a toy duck.

The **Omni Parker House** (p. 70) is on the Freedom Trail and within easy walking distance to the waterfront. Young guests receive a backpack that contains games and toys at check-in, and milk and cookies on the first night of their stay. Parents can request a kit with outlet covers and a night light.

The **Seaport Hotel** (p. 74), near Museum Wharf, offers excellent weekend deals, splendid views of the harbor and airport, underwater music piped into the swimming pool, and even a grandparent-grandchild package.

In Cambridge, the **Royal Sonesta Hotel** (p. 90) is around the corner from the Museum of Science and has a large indoor/outdoor pool. It fills the vacation months with Summerfest, which includes free use of bicycles, ice cream, and boat rides along the Charles River. On off-season weekends, the Family Fun package includes four passes to the Museum of Science.

Across the street, **Hotel Marlowe** (p. 90) boasts an excellent location, the welcoming atmosphere that family travelers have come to expect from the Kimpton chain, and special weekend packages.

The riverfront **Hyatt Regency Cambridge** (p. 90) courts families with its pool, bicycle rentals, easy access to the banks of the Charles, and discounted rates (subject to availability) on a separate room for the kids.

776 Boylston St. (at Fairfield St.), Boston, MA 02199. www.mandarinoriental.com/boston. ℂ **866/526-6567** or 617/535-8888. Fax 617/535-8889. 148 units. Apr–Nov from $495 double, from $1,195 suite; Dec–Mar from $345 double, from $995 suite. Children 16 and under stay free in parent's room. Weekend, spa, and other packages available. AE, DC, DISC, MC, V. Valet parking $45. T: Green Line to Copley or Green Line E to Prudential. Pets accepted. **Amenities:** Restaurant; lounge; airport transfers ($110); babysitting; concierge; exercise room; access to nearby health club ($35); room service; 16,000-sq.-ft. spa. *In room:* A/C, TV/DVD, hair dryer, minibar, MP3 docking station, Wi-Fi ($15/day).

Taj Boston ★ With its luxurious accommodations, wonderful service, and old-Boston atmosphere, Taj Boston appeals to both vacationers and business travelers. In a great location overlooking the Public Garden, the building was completely restored for its 75th anniversary in 2002 and has been considerably spruced up since. The elegantly appointed guest rooms have dark-wood furnishings, feather duvets, Frette linens, three phones (one in the marble bathroom), and windows that open. You'll pay more for a room with a view. The best units are suites, which have wood-burning fireplaces. Taj, an India-based luxury chain, took over the original Ritz-Carlton in 2007, but many people still know this property as "the old Ritz." One of the most traditional lodgings in town, it's competitive with other top-tier hotels on cachet alone. The Mandarin Oriental and archrival Four Seasons have superior fitness facilities—and higher prices.

15 Arlington St. (at Newbury St.), Boston, MA 02116. www.tajhotels.com. ℂ **877/482-5267** or 617/536-5700. Fax 617/536-1335. 273 units. From $249 double; from $399 Club Level or suite. Extra person $20. Children 12 and under stay free in parent's room. Weekend, family, and other packages available. AE, DC, DISC, MC, V. Valet parking $42. T: Green Line to Arlington. Pets under 20 lb. accepted ($150 fee). **Amenities:** Restaurant; bar (p. 277); lounge; babysitting; concierge; club-level rooms; exercise room; room service. *In room:* A/C, TV, hair dryer, minibar, Wi-Fi ($11/day).

Expensive

The 16 units at the **Inn @ St. Botolph,** 99 St. Botolph St. (at W. Newton St.; www.innatstbotolph.com; ℂ **617/236-8099;** T: Green Line E to Prudential), are so popular that they're almost always booked, but I suggest checking anyway. In a residential neighborhood a block from Huntington Avenue and the Prudential Center, guests pretty much fend for themselves, which is perfect if you like the atmosphere of an upscale B&B but not mingling with the staff and other guests. The lavishly decorated suites have self-catering kitchens (management supplies the breakfast fixings) and Wi-Fi but no other services—no parking, bell staff, health club, or restaurant. Rates for a double start at $209.

The Back Bay Hotel ★★ Formerly Boston's police headquarters, this luxurious hotel attracts business (weeknight) and leisure (weekend) travelers with its handy location and excellent service. The 1925 limestone-and-brick building gained a wing and two floors before opening in 2004. Decorated in peaceful, muted colors, the large guest rooms have nice touches such as a work area with an ergonomic chair, down comforters, and windows that open but also do a good job of muffling traffic noise. Still, light sleepers will want to face away from busy Berkeley Street and perhaps request a room on the second floor, where windows are smaller than elsewhere. This is the only New England property of the Doyle Collection, an Irish chain that's giving Boston's corporate giants a run for their money.

350 Stuart St. (at Berkeley St.), Boston, MA 02116. www.doylecollection.com. © **617/266-7200.** Fax 617/266-7203. 225 units, some with shower only. $195–$535 double; $695 jr. suite; $1,265 presidential suite. Extra person $20. Children 12 and under stay free in parent's room. Weekend, family, and other packages available. AE, DC, DISC, MC, V. Valet parking $42. T: Orange Line to Back Bay, or Green Line to Arlington or Copley. **Amenities:** Restaurant; Irish bar; coffee and wine lounge; exercise room; room service. *In room:* A/C, TV, CD player, hair dryer, fridge, Wi-Fi (free).

Boston Marriott Copley Place ★ This 38-story tower with something for everyone—complete business facilities, a good-size pool, and direct access to Boston's shopping wonderland—is extremely popular with convention and meeting planners and is the hotel component of countless package deals. The contemporary-style guest rooms are large enough to hold two armchairs or an armchair and an ottoman; they have the chain's signature Revive bedding and down comforters. As at the Back Bay's other lofty lodgings, ask for the highest possible floor and you'll enjoy excellent views. Besides booking hordes of vacationers, this Marriott and the Sheraton Boston (see below) are New England's biggest convention hotels; the Sheraton has a better pool, but both are reliable and comfortable enough that you can't go wrong by letting price and frequent-traveler points help you distinguish between them.

110 Huntington Ave. (at Harcourt St.), Boston, MA 02116. www.copleymarriott.com. © **800/228-9290** or 617/236-5800. Fax 617/236-5885. 1,147 units. $159–$499 double; $500 and way up suite. Children 17 and under stay free in parent's room. Weekend and other packages available. AE, DC, DISC, MC, V. Valet parking $44; self-parking $35. T: Orange Line to Back Bay, Green Line to Copley, or Green Line E to Prudential. **Amenities:** Restaurant; bar; concierge; recently renovated health club; Jacuzzi; indoor pool; room service. *In room:* A/C, TV, fridge, hair dryer, high-speed Internet ($13/day).

The Boston Park Plaza Hotel & Towers ★ The Park Plaza does a hopping convention and function business and is popular with tour groups. It's in a terrific location a block from the Public Garden, within easy walking distance of the Back Bay, Beacon Hill, and Chinatown. The old-fashioned hotel (built in 1927) offers modern comforts such as pillow-top beds and flatscreen TVs in the guest rooms, which were renovated in 2008. The least expensive units here are tiny; if you're not a crash-and-dash traveler, just asking at the front desk may get you moved into a larger room. Towers units offer upgraded amenities and terrific views, especially from the higher floors of the 15-story building. The Radisson, this hotel's closest competitor, has larger rooms and a pool, but the Park Plaza is more conveniently located and often less expensive.

50 Park Plaza (at Arlington St., 1 block from Boylston St.), Boston, MA 02116. www.bostonparkplaza.com. © **800/225-2008** or 617/426-2000. Fax 617/426-5545. 941 units, some with shower only. $139–$489 double; $279–$3,500 suite. Extra person $25. Children 17 and under stay free in parent's room. Senior discount, weekend, and family packages available. AE, DC, DISC, MC, V. Valet parking $44. T: Green Line to Arlington. **Amenities:** 6 restaurants; cafe; Irish pub; nightclub; concierge; executive-level rooms; exercise room; room service. *In room:* A/C, TV, hair dryer, high-speed Internet ($10/day).

Copley Square Hotel ★ A stone's throw from the Back Bay's convention behemoths, the Copley Square Hotel is an eco-conscious boutique property that primarily courts vacationers. The location and courteous service will also appeal to corporate travelers, who have enough business features to keep them happy.

The seven-story 1891 building was gutted and reopened as a sleek, contemporary hotel in 2009. The 19th-century rooms haven't changed in size—"boutique" units are quite snug—but they're exceedingly comfy, with pillow-top beds and cushy linens and upholstery in grays, taupes, and crisp white. If you can get by without full business features and a tricked-out health club, this is a terrific choice.

47 Huntington Ave. (at Exeter St.), Boston, MA 02116. www.copleysquarehotel.com. © **800/225-7062** or 617/536-9000. Fax 617/421-1402. 143 units, 38 with shower only. Apr–Oct $299–$379 double, $479–$629 suite; Nov–Mar $199 double, $399 suite. Rates include 24-hr. coffee and tea in lobby, evening glass of wine. Children 18 and under stay free in parent's room. Packages available. AE, DC, DISC, MC, V. Valet parking $43. T: Green Line to Copley or Orange Line to Back Bay. Pets under 30 lb. accepted ($40 fee). **Amenities:** Restaurant; lounge; nightclub; concierge; exercise room; access to nearby health club ($15); room service. *In room:* A/C, TV, hair dryer, MP3 docking station, Wi-Fi (free).

Hilton Boston Back Bay ★ Across the street from the Hynes Convention Center, the Hilton is primarily a top-notch business hotel; vacationing families like the convenient location and the pool. The large, well-kept guest rooms are furnished in modern style, with oversize work desks and down comforters. Units on higher floors of the 26-story tower enjoy excellent views. Weekend packages, especially in winter, can be a great deal. The atmosphere tends to be considerably calmer than the scene at the Hilton's main competition, the three mega-hotels attached to the Prudential Center and Copley Place. The closest of those, the Sheraton, is across the street. It's three times the Hilton's size, has a better pool, and books more vacation and function business.

40 Dalton St. (at Belvidere St., off Boylston St.), Boston, MA 02115. www.hiltonfamilyboston.com/bostonbackbay. © **800/445-8667** or 617/236-1100. Fax 617/867-6104. 390 units, 66 with shower only. $179–$399 double; from $450 suite. Extra person $20. Rollaway $25. Children 17 and under stay free in parent's room. Packages and AAA discount available. AE, DC, DISC, MC, V. Self-parking $41. T: Green Line B, C, or D to Hynes Convention Center. Pets accepted ($50 fee). **Amenities:** Restaurant; bar; concierge; well-equipped exercise room; indoor pool; room service. *In room:* A/C, TV, hair dryer, minibar, MP3 docking station, Wi-Fi ($15/day).

Sheraton Boston Hotel ★ Its central location, range of accommodations, extensive convention and function facilities, and huge pool make this 29-story hotel one of the most popular in the city with both business and leisure travelers. It has direct access to the Hynes Convention Center and Prudential Center (which connects to Copley Place). The fairly large guest rooms, decorated in sleek contemporary style, contain the chain's signature sleigh beds with pillow-top mattresses. The top floors hold club-level suites, but even standard accommodations on higher floors afford gorgeous views. Because it's so big, the Sheraton often has available rooms when smaller properties are full. If you're on a budget, shop around before you book; you may land a better deal elsewhere.

39 Dalton St. (at Scotia St., off Boylston St.), Boston, MA 02199. www.sheraton.com/boston. © **800/325-3535** or 617/236-2000. Fax 617/236-1702. 1,220 units. $209–$409 double; $309 and way up suite. Children 17 and under stay free in parent's room. Weekend packages available. AE, DC, DISC, MC, V. Valet parking $44; self-parking $38. T: Green Line E to Prudential, or B, C, or D to Hynes Convention Center. Dogs under 40 lb. accepted with prior approval. **Amenities:** 3 restaurants; concierge; club-level rooms; well-equipped health club; heated indoor/outdoor pool; room service; sauna. *In room:* A/C, TV, hair dryer, high-speed Internet ($10/day).

The Westin Copley Place Boston ★★ Towering 36 stories above Copley Square, the Westin attracts business travelers, convention-goers, sightseers, and shoppers with its great location and solicitous staff. Skybridges connect to Copley Place and the Prudential Center complex. The spacious guest rooms—all on the eighth floor and higher—have traditional oak and mahogany furniture and Westin's beloved pillow-top mattresses. They were renovated in 2010. Junior suites are oversized doubles with generous sitting areas, and one-bedroom suites have one of the most entertaining features around: a queen-size Murphy bed in the living room. You might not notice any of that at first, because the views are so spectacular. Like the other hotels in the Pru complex, this is a reliable chain property; it generally has better packages than the Marriott and Sheraton, but price all three before booking.

10 Huntington Ave. (at Dartmouth St.), Boston, MA 02116. www.westin.com/copleyplace. ℰ **800/937-8461** or 617/262-9600. Fax 617/424-7483. 803 units. $179–$569 double; $239–$599 suite; $999–$3,300 specialty suite. Extra person $25–$50. Weekend packages available. AE, DC, DISC, MC, V. Valet parking $44; self-parking $35. T: Green Line to Copley or Orange Line to Back Bay. Pets accepted. **Amenities:** 3 restaurants; bar; concierge; health club & spa; indoor pool; room service. *In room:* A/C, TV/VCR, hair dryer, minibar, Wi-Fi ($10/day).

Moderate

Charlesmark Hotel ★★ 🍂 In an excellent location overlooking the Boston Marathon finish line, the Charlesmark has a boutique feel and great prices. The amenities don't challenge the perks of the neighborhood's large hotels, but they'll satisfy most business or leisure travelers. The sleek, contemporary design ingeniously uses custom furnishings to maximize the 1892 building's compact spaces. Guest rooms are small but have pillow-top mattresses and enough space to hold a chair. Rates include breakfast, light refreshments such as bottled water and fruit, and local phone calls, all part of management's policy not to pad your bill with incidentals. The only real drawback is that the building has just one elevator—and if that's your biggest problem, you're doing pretty well.

655 Boylston St. (btw. Dartmouth and Exeter sts.), Boston, MA 02116. www.thecharlesmark.com. ℰ **617/247-1212.** Fax 617/247-1224. 40 units, most with shower only. $129–$249 double. Rates include continental breakfast. Children stay free in parent's room. AE, DC, DISC, MC, V. Self-parking $27 in nearby garage. T: Green Line to Copley. Pets accepted with prior approval. **Amenities:** Lounge; access to nearby health club ($10). *In room:* A/C, TV/DVD, CD player, fridge, hair dryer, Wi-Fi (free).

Hotel 140 🍂 Two short blocks from Copley Square, Hotel 140 is a deal in the pricey Back Bay. Contemporary-style rooms and bathrooms are on the small side, but prices are so reasonable that the hotel consistently fills with leisure and thrifty business travelers. It occupies the fifth through eighth floors of the 14-story building; the deli in the lobby serves breakfast and lunch. The hotel opened in 2005 in a renovated former YWCA that dates to 1929. Its main competitor is the John Hancock Hotel, which is roughly comparable but more traditional in style.

140 Clarendon St. (at Stuart St.), Boston, MA 02116. www.hotel140.com. ℰ **800/714-0140** or 617/585-5600. 59 units (all with shower only). $119–$199 double. Rates include continental breakfast. Weekend, theater, and other packages available. AE, MC, V. Self-parking $27 in adjacent garage. T: Orange Line to Back Bay. **Amenities:** Exercise room; access to nearby health club. *In room:* A/C, TV, hair dryer, Wi-Fi (free).

4

WHERE TO STAY | The Back Bay

The John Hancock Hotel & Conference Center ★ 👜 A limited-service lodging with an old-fashioned air and a helpful staff, this eight-story hotel is a hidden jewel. In an unbeatable location on a dead-end street near Back Bay Station, it books many groups that use the abundant meeting space. The compact, comfortable guest rooms aren't fancy, but they're well maintained and big enough not to feel claustrophobic; bathrooms, however, are tiny. Aramark, the national-park and sports-arena concessionaire, manages the hotel for the eponymous insurance firm, which books the whole place in the weeks before the Boston Marathon. The closest competitor, the funkier Hotel 140, sometimes beats this hotel on price; winter rates here are fantastic.

40 Trinity Place (off Stuart St.), Boston, MA 02116. www.jhcenter.com. ℂ **617/933-7700.** Fax 617/933-7709. 64 units. $109–$189 double. Rates include continental breakfast. Extra person $15. Children 17 and under stay free in parent's room. AE, DC, DISC, MC, V. Validated self-parking $27 in nearby garage. Closed to the public 1st 3 weeks of Apr. T: Orange Line to Back Bay or Green Line to Copley. *In room:* A/C, TV, hair dryer, Wi-Fi.

The MidTown Hotel ★ 🍴 This centrally located two-story hotel is a tour-group standby that's popular with families, who like the seasonal pool, and budget-conscious businesspeople. The boxy white building, most recently renovated in 2008, is on a busy street across from the Prudential Center, within walking distance of Symphony Hall and the Museum of Fine Arts. Rooms are large, bright, and attractively outfitted in no-frills contemporary style; bathrooms are small. Some units have connecting doors that allow families to spread out. The best rooms are at the back of the building, away from Huntington Avenue traffic. The hotel is an oddity in this neighborhood of cushy chain and independent accommodations; even if you score a great rate at one of those properties, do the math to see whether the relatively cheap parking here makes the MidTown a better bargain.

220 Huntington Ave. (at Cumberland St., 1 long block from Mass. Ave.), Boston, MA 02445. www.midtownhotel.com. ℂ **800/343-1177** or 617/262-1000. Fax 617/262-8739. 159 units. $119–$259 double; $139–$279 suite. Extra person $15. Children 17 and under stay free in parent's room. Packages and AAA, AARP, and government discounts may be available. AE, DC, DISC, MC, V. Parking $18. T: Green Line E to Prudential or Orange Line to Massachusetts Ave. Dogs accepted ($30 fee). **Amenities:** Concierge; access to nearby health club ($5–$10); heated outdoor pool. *In room:* A/C, TV, hair dryer, Wi-Fi ($10/day).

Newbury Guest House ★★ 🍴 The Newbury Guest House is one of the best bargains in Boston: The well-maintained property offers comfortably furnished, nicely appointed guest rooms at a great price for a terrific location. The largest rooms are the bay-window units, which overlook the lively street; request a room at the back if you're sensitive to traffic noise. Breakfast is served in the restaurant downstairs. The Newbury Guest House, which takes up three 1880s brick town houses, opened in 1991 and operates near capacity year-round, drawing business travelers during the week and sightseers on weekends. Reserve early.

261 Newbury St. (btw. Fairfield and Gloucester sts.), Boston, MA 02116. www.newburyguest house.com. ℂ **800/437-7668** or 617/670-6000. Fax 617/670-6100. 32 units, some with shower only. $139–$279 double. Extra person $20. Off-season discounts available. Rates include continental breakfast. Packages available. Rates may be higher during special events. AE, DC, DISC, MC, V. Parking $20 (reservation required). T: Green Line B, C, or D to Hynes Convention Center. **Amenities:** Access to nearby health club ($25). *In room:* A/C, TV, fridge, hair dryer, Wi-Fi (free).

Inexpensive

Hostelling International–Boston Double-check everything before setting out for this hostel: At press time, a replacement is under construction in the Theater District, and this location is set to close in spring 2012—if Boston's famously baroque permitting process allows. Meanwhile, the modest four-story hostel near the Berklee College of Music and Hynes Convention Center will continue welcoming students, youth groups, and other travelers in search of comfortable, no-frills lodging. Accommodations are dorm-style (all men, all women, or co-ed), with six beds per room. The air-conditioned building has a full kitchen, 29 bathrooms (men and women have separate facilities), a large common room, and meeting and workshop space. It provides linens, or you can bring your own; sleeping bags are not permitted. The enthusiastic staff organizes free and inexpensive cultural, educational, and recreational programs. Hostelling International also operates a summer-only hostel just outside Kenmore Square (below).

12 Hemenway St. (off Boylston St.), Boston, MA 02115. www.bostonhostel.org. *©* **888/999-4678** or 617/536-9455. Fax 617/424-6558. 205 beds. Members of Hostelling International–American Youth Hostels $28–$45 per bed, nonmembers $31–$48 per bed; members $70–$130 per private unit, nonmembers $73–$133 per private unit. Children 3–12 half-price, children under 3 free. Rates include continental breakfast. MC, V. T: Green Line B, C, or D to Hynes Convention Center. **Amenities:** Access to nearby health club ($6); Wi-Fi. *In room:* A/C, lockers, no phone.

OUTSKIRTS & BROOKLINE

What Bostonians consider "outskirts" would be centrally located in many larger cities. Brookline starts about 3 blocks beyond Boston's Kenmore Square.

BEST FOR Travelers who want more room and lower prices than properties in other areas generally offer. For those who must drive, parking is generally (but not always) cheaper than it is elsewhere.

DRAWBACKS Unless they're in town only to visit Fenway Park or the Longwood Medical Area, sightseers staying in this area essentially become commuters to downtown Boston. If you're visiting Cambridge, public transit connections are unwieldy at best.

Very Expensive

Hotel Commonwealth ★★ This five-story boutique hotel in the heart of Kenmore Square draws a lot of business from nearby Boston University and from local cultural institutions. It boasts extensive business features as well as luxurious amenities such as Frette linens and large marble bathrooms. My favorite guest rooms are the huge Commonwealth units; each has a king bed and a heavy curtain that draws across the center of the room, separating the sleeping area and the "parlor." These rooms overlook the bustling street, outdoor restaurant seating, and the bus station (and attendant traffic) at the center of the square. You might prefer a Fenway room—they're smaller, but they face the legendary ballpark, which lies across the Massachusetts Turnpike.

500 Commonwealth Ave. (at Kenmore St.), Boston, MA 02215. www.hotelcommonwealth.com. *©* **866/784-4000** or 617/933-5000. Fax 617/266-6888. 150 units. $235–$415 standard double; $265–$485 minisuite or parlor room. Extra person $20. Children 17 and under stay free in parent's room. Packages and AAA discount available. AE, DC, DISC, MC, V. Valet parking $42. T:

Green Line B, C, or D to Kenmore. Pets accepted ($125 fee). **Amenities:** 2 restaurants; lounge; concierge; exercise room; room service. *In room:* A/C, TV/DVD, hair dryer, minibar, MP3 docking station, Wi-Fi (free).

Expensive

The 188-unit **Courtyard Boston Brookline,** 40 Webster St. (off Beacon St.), Brookline (www.brooklinecourtyard.com; ☎ **866/296-2296,** 800/321-2211, or 617/734-1393; T: Green Line C to Coolidge Corner), is a well-equipped, conveniently located business hotel. It has a breakfast cafe, indoor pool, exercise room, and shuttle service to the nearby Longwood Medical Area. A double in high season goes for $179 to $399, which includes Wi-Fi; parking costs $24.

Doubletree Guest Suites ★★ ☺ ✔ This hotel is one of the best deals in town—almost every unit is a two-room suite with a living room, bedroom, and bathroom. Business travelers can entertain and families can spread out, making this a good choice for both. It's near Cambridge and across the street from the Charles River, but not in an actual neighborhood or near the T; shuttle service is available to local destinations. The well-kept suites surround a 15-story atrium. Rooms are large and attractively furnished in upscale-chain-hotel style. Most bedrooms have a king-size bed (some have two oversize twins) and a writing desk. Each living room contains a full-size sofa bed, dining table, and refrigerator. The Hyatt Regency Cambridge, the hotel's nearest rival, is slightly more convenient but generally more expensive.

400 Soldiers Field Rd. (at Cambridge St.), Boston, MA 02134. www.hiltonfamilyboston.com/boston. ☎ **800/222-8733** or 617/783-0090. Fax 617/783-0897. 308 units. $129–$309 double. Extra person $10. Children 17 and under stay free in parent's room. Packages and AAA and AARP discounts available. AE, DC, DISC, MC, V. Self-parking $35. Pets accepted with prior approval ($250 deposit). **Amenities:** Restaurant; lounge; excellent Scullers Jazz Club (p. 272); concierge; well-equipped exercise room; Jacuzzi; indoor pool; room service. *In room:* A/C, TV, fridge, hair dryer, MP3 docking station, Wi-Fi ($10/day).

Moderate

The Holiday Inn Boston Brookline, 1200 Beacon St. (at St. Paul St.), Brookline (www.holidayinn.com; ☎ **800/465-4329** or 617/277-1200; T: Green Line C to St. Paul St.), overlooks the trolley tracks just outside Coolidge Corner. The six-story hotel has a restaurant, exercise room, small indoor pool, and shuttle service to the nearby hospitals. Rates for a double start at $169, including Wi-Fi; parking costs $21.

Best Western Plus Boston/The Inn at Longwood Medical ★ Next to Children's Hospital in the Longwood Medical Area, this eight-story hotel is a good base for those with business at the hospitals. The helpful staff is sensitive to the needs of patients and their families. Museums, colleges, and Fenway Park are nearby, and downtown Boston is 20 minutes away by T. The well-maintained guest rooms are quite large and furnished in colorful, contemporary style. Try to stay on the highest floor possible, to enjoy the views and to get away from the busy intersection of Longwood and Brookline avenues. Suites have kitchen facilities that make them a good choice for long-term guests. The hotel adjoins the Longwood Galleria business complex, which has a food court (with Boston's only Dairy Queen) and shops, including a drugstore.

342 Longwood Ave. (at Brookline Ave.), Boston, MA 02115. www.innatlongwood.com. © **800/468-2378** or 617/731-4700, TTY 617/731-9088. Fax 617/731-4870. 161 units, 18 with kitchenette. $139–$259 double; from $269 suite. Extra person $15. Children 17 and under stay free in parent's room. Weekend and family packages, hospital and long-term discounts available. AE, DC, DISC, MC, V. Parking $18. T: Green Line D or E to Longwood. **Amenities:** Restaurant; lounge; concierge; access to nearby health club ($8); room service. *In room:* A/C, TV, hair dryer, Wi-Fi (free).

Inexpensive

A summer-only hostel occupies a former Howard Johnson hotel just outside Kenmore Square: The **Fenway Summer Hostel,** 575 Commonwealth Ave. (www.bostonhostel.org; © **617/267-8599;** fax 617/424-6558; T: Green Line B, C, or D to Kenmore). The 485-bed hostel offers well-equipped accommodations in a building that doubles as a Boston University dorm during the school year. Rates are $36 to $45 per bed for members of Hostelling International–American Youth Hostels, $39 to $48 for nonmembers. Private rooms for one to three guests cost $99 to $129.

Anthony's Town House This friendly establishment offers comfortable accommodations with shared bathrooms; it's popular with Europeans and budget-minded Americans. Each floor holds three high-ceilinged rooms furnished in Queen Anne or Victorian style and one bathroom with an enclosed shower. Smaller rooms (one per floor) have twin beds; the large front rooms have bay windows. Two family units hold as many as five comfortably. Guests have the use of two refrigerators and a microwave, and the staff supplies a DVD player, VCR, hair dryer, or iron on request. The four-story brownstone guesthouse, a family business since 1944, is 1 mile from Boston's Kenmore Square and about 15 minutes from downtown by T. It's more convenient than the nearby Longwood Inn, which has private bathrooms. There's no smoking on the premises.

1085 Beacon St. (at Hawes St.), Brookline, MA 02446. www.anthonystownhouse.com. © **617/566-3972.** Fax 617/232-1085. 10 units, none with private bathroom. $78–$108 double; from $125 family room. Extra person $10. Weekly rates and winter discounts available. No credit cards. Limited free parking; off-premises parking $10. T: Green Line C to Hawes St. *In room:* A/C, TV, Wi-Fi (free), no phone.

Longwood Inn In a residential area 3 blocks from the Boston border, this three-story guesthouse offers comfortable accommodations at modest rates. The homey style suits the Victorian architecture of the building, which has been extensively renovated over the past 2 years. Guests have use of a full kitchen, a common dining room, and a patio with tables and chairs. The apartment has a private bathroom, kitchen, and balcony. Tennis courts, a running track, and a playground at the school next door are open to the public. The Longwood Medical Area and Coolidge Corner are within easy walking distance, and public transportation is nearby—not as close as it is to Anthony's Town House, but this property has private bathrooms (one unit's bathroom is across the hall; others are en suite).

123 Longwood Ave. (at Marshall St., 1 block from Kent St.), Brookline, MA 02446. www.longwood-inn.com. © **617/566-8615.** Fax 617/738-1070. 22 units, 4 with shower only. Apr–Nov $129–$154 double; Dec–Mar $94–$129 double. Extra person $5–$10. 1-bedroom apt (sleeps 4-plus) $124–$159. Weekly rates available. AE, DISC, MC, V. Free parking. T: Green Line D to Longwood or C to Coolidge Corner. *In room:* A/C, TV, Wi-Fi (free).

CAMBRIDGE

Across the Charles River from Boston, Cambridge has its own attractions and excellent hotels. Graduation season (May and early June) is especially busy, but campus events can cause high demand at unexpected times, so plan ahead.

BEST FOR Well-heeled visitors to Cambridge, and travelers to downtown Boston and the South Boston waterfront, which are relatively easy to reach on the T from both the Harvard Square area and East Cambridge.

DRAWBACKS Access to most other areas of Boston, notably the Back Bay and South End, can be slow, expensive, or both. Budget accommodations are limited, and parking at most hotels is almost as expensive as parking in Boston.

Very Expensive

The Charles Hotel ★★★ Just a block from Harvard Square, the Charles has been *the* place for business and leisure travelers to Cambridge since it opened in 1985. Vacationing families and visiting parents enjoy the same high level of service as Harvard affiliates, business tycoons, and the odd celebrity. The style in the nine-story brick hotel is luxe contemporary country, with custom adaptations of early American Shaker furniture. The austere design contrasts with the swanky amenities in the good-size guest rooms, which have floor-to-ceiling windows, down quilts, and Bose Wave radios; bathrooms contain telephones and TVs (in the mirrors—cool!). The eco-aware Charles rivals the Four Seasons and Boston Harbor Hotel for cachet and amenities; the only other Cambridge hotel with comparable features and service is the Royal Sonesta, which is less convenient and generally less expensive.

1 Bennett St. (at Eliot St., 1 block from Mount Auburn St.), Cambridge, MA 02138. www.charleshotel.com. ✆ **800/882-1818** or 617/864-1200. Fax 617/864-5715. 294 units. $299–$599 double; $409 and way up suite. Off-season discounts and weekend packages available. AE, DC, MC, V. Valet or self-parking $34. T: Red Line to Harvard. Pets accepted ($50 fee). **Amenities:** 2 restaurants (including Henrietta's Table, p. 124); 2 bars; Regattabar jazz club (p. 271); concierge; free access to adjacent health club w/pool, Jacuzzi, and sauna; room service; adjacent spa. *In room:* A/C, TV/DVD, hair dryer, minibar, Wi-Fi (free).

Hotel Veritas ★ The only boutique hotel in Harvard Square is a lovely property that makes up for potential drawbacks with thoughtful amenities and great service. Rooms are small but luxurious, with high ceilings and plush residential-style appointments. There's no restaurant or room service, but room rates include bottled water as well as coffee, tea, juice, and soda (available in the lobby). Five blocks from the T, the hotel, which opened in 2010, faces busy Mass. Ave. and has a small, low-key lounge in the lobby; ask for a room at the back of the property (numbers that end in "01" and "02") if street noise is a concern, and request a unit away from the lobby if you need quiet before 11pm.

1 Remington St. (at Mass. Ave.), Cambridge, MA 02138. www.thehotelveritas.com. ✆ **888/520-1050** or 617/520-5000. Fax 617/520-5004. 31 units, 26 with shower only. $245–$395 double; $595–$795 suite. Children stay free in parent's room. Weekend and other packages available. AE, DC, DISC, MC, V. Valet parking $34. T: Red Line to Harvard. **Amenities:** Lounge, babysitting, concierge, free access to nearby health club. *In room:* A/C, TV, hair dryer, MP3 docking station, Wi-Fi (free).

Royal Sonesta Hotel ★★ ☺ This luxurious hotel is popular with business travelers and with families, who enjoy the huge pool. The CambridgeSide Galleria mall is across the street, the Museum of Science around the corner, and tech-happy Kendall Square 10 minutes away on foot. Even amid all that activity, the hotel feels serene, thanks in part to the helpful staff. Most of the rooms in the 10-story building look out on the river or the city (higher prices are for better views). Everything is custom designed in modern, comfortable style. The East Tower underwent a $6-million refurbishment in 2011; request a room there if possible. The Sonesta's closest competition is Hotel Marlowe (see below), across the street, which offers less extensive fitness options and fewer river views.

40 Edwin H. Land Blvd. (at CambridgeSide Place), Cambridge, MA 02142. www.sonesta.com/boston. *©* **800/766-3782** or 617/806-4200. Fax 617/806-4232. 400 units, some with shower only. $239–$279 standard double; $259–$299 superior double; $279–$319 deluxe double; $339 and up suite. Extra person $25. Children 17 and under stay free in parent's room. Weekend, family, and other packages available. AE, DC, DISC, MC, V. Valet or self-parking $27. T: Green Line to Lechmere, then a 10-min. walk. **Amenities:** Restaurant; cafe w/seasonal outdoor seating; bike rental (seasonal); concierge; well-equipped 24-hr. health club & spa; heated indoor/outdoor pool w/retractable roof; room service; adjoining standard units are available; staff is trained in disability awareness. *In room:* A/C, TV, hair dryer, minibar, Wi-Fi (free).

Expensive

The **Hampton Inn Boston/Cambridge,** 191 Msgr. O'Brien Hwy., at Water St., Cambridge (www.bostoncambridge.hamptoninn.com; *©* **800/426-7866** or 617/494-5300; T: Green Line to Lechmere), is a 5-minute walk from the T. Rates at the 114-room hotel start at $189 for a double in high season and include parking, buffet breakfast, and high-speed Internet.

Hotel Marlowe ★ ☺ Hotel Marlowe offers abundant amenities for both business and leisure travelers, with easy access to the CambridgeSide Galleria mall, the Museum of Science, the Charles River, and MIT. Rooms in the eight-story building were completely renovated in early 2011; they're elegant yet fun, and large enough to hold a work desk and armchair. All have down comforters and three phones (one in the bathroom), and suites have spa tubs. Views are of the river, a small canal, or the landscaped courtyard/driveway off the lobby. The eco-savvy hotel's closest competitor is the Royal Sonesta Hotel (see above), across the street, which has a pool and health club, better river views, and correspondingly higher prices. *Tip:* Sign up for the (free) frequent-guest program, and the hotel waives the Internet access fee.

25 Edwin H. Land Blvd. (at Cambridge Pkwy., 1 block from Msgr. O'Brien Hwy.), Cambridge, MA 02141. www.hotelmarlowe.com. *©* **800/825-7040,** 800/546-7866, or 617/868-0000. Fax 617/868-8001. 236 units, some with shower only. $199–$449 double; from $409 suite. Extra person $25. Rates include morning coffee and tea, evening wine reception, and use of bikes. Children 17 and under stay free in parent's room. Weekend, family, and other packages, AAA and AARP discounts available. AE, DC, DISC, MC, V. Valet parking $30; self-parking $20. T: Green Line to Lechmere or Red Line to Kendall. Pets accepted. **Amenities:** Restaurant; bar; bikes; concierge; exercise room; room service. *In room:* A/C, TV, hair dryer, MP3 docking station, Wi-Fi (free).

The Hyatt Regency Cambridge ★ ☺ Across the street from the Charles River and 10 minutes by car from downtown Boston, the Hyatt Regency books businesspeople on weeknights and vacationers on weekends. It's convenient to

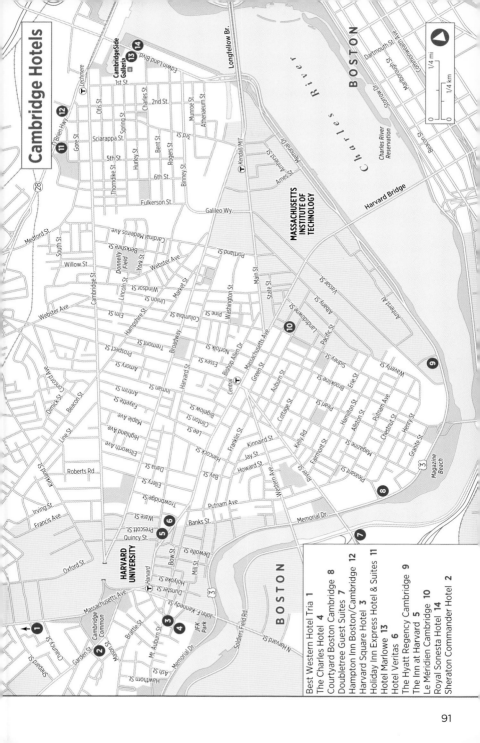

Cambridge Hotels

Best Western Hotel Tria 1
The Charles Hotel 4
Courtyard Boston Cambridge 8
Doubletree Guest Suites 7
Hampton Inn Boston/Cambridge 12
Harvard Square Hotel 3
Holiday Inn Express Hotel & Suites 11
Hotel Marlowe 13
Hotel Veritas 6
The Hyatt Regency Cambridge 9
The Inn at Harvard 5
Le Méridien Cambridge 10
Royal Sonesta Hotel 14
Sheraton Commander Hotel 2

Harvard and Kendall squares and Boston University, though not near the subway. The landmark pyramidal building underwent $15 million in renovations in 2010. The spacious, well-outfitted guest rooms hold pillow-top beds; most face the 16-story atrium, others overlook central Cambridge, and the best enjoy breathtaking views of Boston. Families (see "Family-Friendly Hotels," p. 80) can take advantage of special two-room rates, subject to availability. If you plan to rely on public transit, allow time for the bus or hotel shuttle. The closest competitor is the Doubletree, which is even farther from public transit but consists of all suites.

575 Memorial Dr. (at Amesbury St., 1 block from the BU Bridge), Cambridge, MA 02139. www. cambridge.hyatt.com. © **800/233-1234** or 617/462-1234. Fax 617/491-6906. 470 units, some with shower only. $179–$359 double; $300–$750 suite. Extra person $25. Children 17 and under stay free in parent's room. Weekend packages available. AE, DC, DISC, MC, V. Self-parking $35. T: Red Line to Harvard or Kendall, then shuttle bus (no luggage permitted) or $6 cab ride. Pets under 25 lb. accepted ($50 fee). **Amenities:** Restaurant; lounge; bike rental; concierge; rooftop health club; 75-ft. indoor lap pool; room service; sauna. *In room:* A/C, TV, hair dryer, MP3 docking station, Wi-Fi ($15/day).

The Inn at Harvard ★★ The Georgian-style red-brick Inn at Harvard, adjacent to Harvard Yard, is popular with business travelers and university visitors. Guest rooms are elegantly decorated in subdued neutrals and have pillow-top beds; each holds a work area with an Aeron chair. Some units have dormer windows and window seats; the best rooms are on higher floors facing Harvard Street. The four-story skylit atrium holds the "living room," a huge, well-appointed guest lounge that's suitable (in furnishings and volume level) for meeting with a visitor if you don't want to conduct business in your room.

1201 Massachusetts Ave. (at Quincy St.), Cambridge, MA 02138. www.hotelsinharvardsquare.com. © **800/458-5886** or 617/491-2222. Fax 617/520-3711. 111 units, some with shower only. $159–$269 double; $1,500 presidential suite. AAA and AARP discounts available. AE, DC, DISC, MC, V. Valet parking $30. T: Red Line to Harvard. **Amenities:** Restaurant (breakfast only); dining privileges at the nearby Harvard Faculty Club; exercise room; room service. *In room:* A/C, TV, hair dryer, Wi-Fi (free).

Le Méridien Cambridge ★ The only sizable lodging close to lively Central Square, this hotel primarily attracts visitors to MIT and the tech-oriented businesses nearby. Rooms are large enough to hold small seating areas and oversize desks, with cushy beds that soften the neutrals of the contemporary decor. The eight-story building encloses a lovely courtyard; units facing inward are preferable to those with street views. The closest competitors are the Sonesta and Marlowe, in East Cambridge—about the same distance from the T, but with easier access to the river—and the Hyatt Regency, which is some distance from the subway but has a pool.

20 Sidney St. (at Green St., 1 block from Mass. Ave.), Cambridge, MA 02139. www.lemeridien. com/cambridge. © **800/543-4300** or 617/577-0200. Fax 617/494-8366. 210 units, 8 with shower only. $199–$419 double; $249–$519 suite. Extra person $20. Children 17 and under stay free in parent's room. Weekend, family, and other packages, AAA and AARP discounts available. AE, DC, DISC, MC, V. Valet parking $32; self-parking $28. T: Red Line to Central. Pets under 50 lb. accepted. **Amenities:** Restaurant; bar; concierge; 24-hr. exercise room; access to nearby health club. *In room:* A/C, TV, CD player, hair dryer, Wi-Fi (free).

Sheraton Commander Hotel ★ University guests, visiting parents, and business travelers make up the bulk of the Sheraton Commander's business. In the heart of Cambridge's historic district, the hotel is exactly what you'd expect of a traditional hostelry within sight of the Harvard campus. Many guest rooms have four-poster beds, and all have Sheraton's signature mattresses and plenty of accents in crimson, Harvard's school color. Ask the pleasant front-desk staff for a room facing Cambridge Common; even if you aren't high up in the six-story building, you'll have a pleasant view. The Sheraton Commander doesn't have the Charles Hotel's cachet and amenities, but it doesn't charge the Charles's prices, either. Plan far ahead if you're visiting during a Harvard event.

16 Garden St. (at Berkeley St., 3 blocks from Mass. Ave.), Cambridge, MA 02138. www.sheraton. com/commander. ✆ **800/325-3535** or 617/547-4800. Fax 617/234-1396. 175 units, some with shower only. $159–$479 double; $354 and way up suite. Extra person $20. Children 17 and under stay free in parent's room. Weekend packages, AAA and AARP discounts available. AE, DC, DISC, MC, V. Valet parking $29. T: Red Line to Harvard. Dogs under 80 lb. accepted. **Amenities:** Restaurant; lounge; concierge; small exercise room; room service. *In room:* A/C, TV, hair dryer, Wi-Fi (free).

Moderate

The 112-unit **Holiday Inn Express Hotel & Suites,** 250 Msgr. O'Brien Hwy., at Sciarappa St., Cambridge (www.hiexpress.com/boscambridgema; ✆ **888/887-7690** or 617/577-7600; fax 617/354-1313), is a limited-services property 10 minutes from the Green Line on a busy street. There's no restaurant, but each room has a fridge and microwave, and a supermarket is a block away. Rates for a double in high season start at $160 and include parking—a big plus in Cambridge—Wi-Fi, and breakfast.

Best Western Hotel Tria ★ 🦮 Because of its borderline-suburban location, the Tria usually beats other Cambridge hotels on price and has standard rooms as large as some properties' suites. The property added 55 rooms in a 2009 renovation that overhauled the existing 66 units; all are decorated in muted jewel tones, with comfy contemporary furnishings. The building is set back from the busy road, which cuts down on traffic noise. The walking/jogging path and golf course at Fresh Pond, a shopping center, and Whole Foods and Trader Joe's markets are nearby. The T is about 10 minutes away on foot or 5 minutes on the hotel shuttle. Boston lies a 15-minute drive or a 25-minute T ride away; Lexington and Concord are less than a half-hour by car.

220 Alewife Brook Pkwy. (at Concord Ave.), Cambridge, MA 02138. www.hoteltria.com. ✆ **866/333-8742** or 617/491-8000. Fax 617/491-4932. 121 units. Mid-Mar to Oct $149–$299 double; Nov to mid-Mar $119–$179 double. Rates include breakfast. Rates may be higher during special events. Children 16 and under stay free in parent's room. Packages available. AE, DC, MC, V. Parking $12. T: Red Line to Alewife, then a 12-min. walk. Pets accepted; reservation required ($25 fee and $100 deposit). **Amenities:** Restaurant; bar; coffee shop; bikes; exercise room. *In room:* A/C, TV, fridge, hair dryer, Wi-Fi (free).

Courtyard Boston Cambridge ★ This 16-story hotel is popular with visitors to colleges on both sides of the river. It's across the street from the Charles, meaning the views are great but public-transit access isn't. The tasteful but unremarkable chain-hotel decor—introduced when Marriott took over in 2008—includes super-comfy beds but doesn't compete with the killer views through the floor-to-ceiling windows. Prices vary with room size, floor, and view; units on higher floors facing the river enjoy a panorama of the Boston skyline. Even the priciest units generally undercut rates at the Hyatt Regency and Doubletree, the only nearby competitors. The hotel doesn't offer room service, but Trader Joe's and Starbucks are next door. If you're relying on public transit, allow time for the hotel shuttle.

777 Memorial Dr. (at Pleasant St., 1 block from River St.), Cambridge, MA 02139. www.cambridge courtyard.com. ℂ **800/235-6426,** 888/236-2427 (Marriott), or 617/492-7777. Fax 617/492-6038. 203 units. $169–$329 double; $269–$359 suite. Children stay free in parent's room. Weekend, family, and other packages available. AE, DC, DISC, MC, V. Parking $24. T: Red Line to Kendall/MIT or Central, then hotel shuttle or $10 cab ride. **Amenities:** 2 restaurants; lounge; 24-hr. exercise room; indoor pool; room service. *In room:* A/C, TV, hair dryer, Wi-Fi (free).

Harvard Square Hotel Smack in the middle of "the Square," this six-story brick hotel offers relatively small rooms for relatively low rates—most of the year—that make it a favorite with visiting parents and budget-conscious business travelers. At busy times, including most nights during fall foliage season, rates seem high for the modest accommodations. Still, you can't beat the location, and the unpretentious, well-maintained guest rooms are comfortable and neatly decorated in contemporary style. Each has a flatscreen TV (important when every inch counts), and some overlook Harvard Square.

110 Mount Auburn St. (at Eliot St.), Cambridge, MA 02138. www.hotelsinharvardsquare.com. ℂ **800/458-5886** or 617/864-5200. Fax 617/492-4896. 73 units, some with shower only. $99–$229 double. Extra person $10. Children 16 and under stay free in parent's room. Packages, corporate rates, AAA and AARP discounts available. AE, DC, DISC, MC, V. Parking $30. T: Red Line to Harvard. **Amenities:** Dining privileges at the Harvard Faculty Club; free access to nearby health club. *In room:* A/C, TV, fridge, hair dryer, Wi-Fi (free).

AT & NEAR THE AIRPORT

Accommodations in this neighborhood range from high-end business hotels to budget chain lodgings, but even the least expensive properties aren't the dirt-cheap motels found near airports in many other parts of the country.

BEST FOR Anyone with an early flight. If you're not staying at the Hilton, make sure that you know the shuttle schedule and that the front-desk staff knows you have a plane to catch.

DRAWBACKS Distance from attractions, relying on the hotel shuttle to get to the subway (except at the Hilton).

Very Expensive

Hyatt Harborside ★ Primarily a convention and business destination, this striking waterfront hotel is next to the airport ferry dock, 7 minutes from downtown by water taxi. The sizable guest rooms have oversize work desks and a sophisticated no-frills style that contrasts with luxurious touches like pillow-top beds. Large windows afford dramatic views of the harbor and city skyline, especially from higher floors of the 14-story building. Guests have easy access to the airport and the Airport T stop (a 5-min. ride on the hotel or MBTA shuttle bus) and to downtown Boston by water. The airport Hilton is more centrally located and typically beats this hotel on price, but the views here are better.

101 Harborside Dr., Boston, MA 02128. www.harborside.hyatt.com. ✆ **800/233-1234** or 617/568-1234. Fax 617/567-8856. 270 units, some with shower only. High season $349–$599 double; low season $199–$259 double; year-round from $895 suite. Children 11 and under stay free in parent's room. Family packages available. AE, DC, DISC, MC, V. Valet parking $36; self-parking $32. T: Blue Line to Airport, then take shuttle bus. By car, follow signs to Logan Airport and take Harborside Dr. past car-rental area and tunnel entrance. **Amenities:** Restaurant and lounge w/ seasonal outdoor seating; concierge; exercise room w/harbor view; Jacuzzi; 40-ft. indoor pool; room service; sauna. *In room:* A/C, TV, hair dryer, MP3 docking station, Wi-Fi ($10/day).

Expensive

The **Embassy Suites Hotel Boston at Logan Airport,** 207 Porter St., at Cottage St., Boston, MA 02128 (www.bostonloganairport.embassysuites.com; ✆ **800/362-2779** or 617/567-5000), is a 273-unit hotel with an indoor pool, exercise room, and business center. Each suite in the 10-story hotel has a living room with a pull-out couch. Room rates, which start at $199, include breakfast and shuttle service to the airport and the Airport T stop; Internet access costs $10/night.

Hilton Boston Logan Airport ★ Smack in the middle of the airport, the Hilton draws most of its guests from meetings, conventions, and canceled flights. It's convenient and well equipped for business travelers, and an excellent fallback for vacationers who don't mind commuting to downtown. Guest rooms are large and tastefully furnished in colors that make me think of business suits, with excellent soundproofing. The best units in the 10-story building afford sensational airport and harbor views. A shuttle bus serves all airport locations, including the ferry dock, and walkways link the building to Terminals A (nearby) and E (farther). The Hyatt Harborside (see above) is the closest competition—it's at the edge of the airport, which means less commotion outside and better water views but less convenient access to the T.

1 Hotel Dr., Logan International Airport, Boston, MA 02128. www.hiltonfamilyboston.com/bostonlogan. ✆ **800/445-8667** or 617/568-6700. Fax 617/568-6800. 599 units. $139–$399 double; from $600 suite. Children 17 and under stay free in parent's room. Packages available. AE, DC, DISC, MC, V. Valet parking $38; self-parking $32. T: Blue Line to Airport, then take shuttle bus. Pets accepted ($25 fee). **Amenities:** Restaurant; Irish pub; coffee counter; concierge; health club; Jacuzzi; 40-ft. lap pool; room service; sauna. *In room:* A/C, TV, hair dryer, MP3 docking station, Wi-Fi ($20/day).

Moderate

If the Comfort Inn is booked, consider the **Hampton Inn Boston Logan Airport,** 2300 Lee Burbank Hwy., Revere (www.hamptoninn.com; ✆ **800/426-7866** or 781/286-5665), on a commercial-industrial strip about 3 miles north of the airport. A free shuttle bus serves the 227-room hotel, which has a pool. Rates start at about $129 for a double and include continental breakfast and parking.

Comfort Inn & Suites Boston/Airport ★ 🌿 The airport lies about 3½ miles south of the well-equipped Comfort Inn, which offers a good range of features for business and leisure travelers. The eight-story hotel, part of the environmentally pioneering Saunders Hotel Group, sits on a hill set back from the road near a busy traffic circle. It has an attentive staff, an indoor pool, and round-the-clock shuttle service. Guest rooms are large, with cherrywood furnishings and unassuming beige decor. Suites are oversize rooms that contain sofa beds, and king suites have refrigerators as well. The somewhat inconvenient location translates to reasonable rates, and the North Shore is easily accessible if you plan a day trip. Revere Beach is about 2 minutes away by car.

85 American Legion Hwy. (Rte. 60), Revere, MA 02151. www.comfortinnboston.com. © **877/485-3600** or 781/485-3600. Fax 781/485-3601. 208 units. $109–$239 double; $139–$279 suite. Rates include continental breakfast. Children 17 and under stay free in parent's room. Senior and AAA discounts available. AE, DC, DISC, MC, V. Free parking. T: Blue Line to Airport; then hotel shuttle. Pets accepted ($25/night). **Amenities:** Restaurant; lounge; exercise room; indoor pool; room service. *In room:* A/C, TV, hair dryer, Wi-Fi (free).

PRACTICAL INFORMATION
The Big Picture

As you evaluate Boston hotels, keep the city's relatively small size in mind, and check a map before you rule out a location. Especially downtown, the neighborhoods are so small and close together that the borders are somewhat arbitrary. The division to consider is **downtown vs. the Back Bay vs. Cambridge**—not, for example, the Waterfront vs. the adjacent Financial District.

Year-round, it's always a good idea to **make a reservation,** and the earlier you book, the better your chances of landing a (relative) bargain. Definitely reserve ahead for travel between April and November, when conventions, college graduations, and vacations increase demand. During foliage season, the busiest and priciest time of year—even more expensive than the summer—plan early. If you don't, you risk staying far from Boston, paying dearly, or both.

Thanks to the mix of new construction and repurposed buildings, strict zoning laws and building codes, and varying market conditions at the time of construction, Boston hotels offer wildly **varying room sizes and amenities.** Don't assume that a certain hotel, even one that's part of your favorite chain, has every option you expect. If you must swim a mile every day, order food at 4am, or hold a meeting in a room with a T1 line, always check to see whether your hotel can accommodate you. If it can't, a comparable property almost certainly can.

Major chains operating in and around Boston include leisure-oriented Best Western, Holiday Inn, Radisson, and Ramada; business-traveler magnets Hilton, Hyatt, Marriott (in all its incarnations), Sheraton, and Westin; boutique-hotel trendsetters Kimpton, Morgans, and W; and luxury operators Doyle Collection, Fairmont, Four Seasons, InterContinental, Le Méridien, Mandarin Oriental, Ritz-Carlton, and Sonesta. The scarcest lodging option in the immediate Boston area is the moderately priced chain motel, a category almost completely driven out by soaring real estate prices. And especially at busy times, brands that are bargains elsewhere may be pricey here—twice what you're used to paying, if not more.

Rates in this chapter are for a **double room** (except where noted); if you're traveling alone, single rates are almost always lower. The rates given here do not include the 5.7% state hotel tax. Boston and Cambridge add a 2.75% convention center tax on top of the 6% city tax, making the total tax 14.45%. Not all suburbs impose a local tax, so some towns charge only the state tax. These listings cover Boston, Cambridge, and Brookline. If you plan to visit a suburban town and want to stay overnight, see chapter 10 for suggestions.

GETTING THE BEST DEAL

The **rack rate** is the maximum rate that a hotel charges for a room. Hardly anybody pays it, however, except sometimes in high season. To cut costs:

- **Ask for a rate, then ask about special rates or other discounts.** You may qualify for corporate, student, military, senior/AARP, AAA, or other discounts. Nail down the standard rate before you ask for your discount.

- **Book online.** Many hotels offer Internet-only discounts or supply discounted rooms to Priceline, Hotwire, or Expedia at rates much lower than the ones you can get through the hotel or chain. Some chains guarantee that the price on their websites is the lowest available; check anyway.

- **Dial direct.** When booking a room in a chain hotel, you'll often get a better deal from the hotel's reservation desk than from the chain's main number.

- **Remember the law of supply & demand.** Business-oriented hotels are busiest during the week, so you can expect weekend discounts. Leisure hotels are most crowded and expensive on weekends, so discounts may be available midweek.

- **Visit in the winter.** Boston-bound bargain hunters who don't mind cold and snow (sometimes *lots* of snow) aim for January through March, when hotels offer great deals, especially on weekends.

- **Avoid excess charges & hidden costs.** When you book a room, ask whether the hotel charges for parking—almost every hotel in Boston and Cambridge does—and whether there's a charge for staying in the garage past room checkout time on the last day of your stay. Use your cellphone, prepaid phone cards, or pay phones instead of making expensive calls from hotel phones. If you know you'll be online a lot, seek out a hotel that includes Internet access in the room rate (many older properties and hotels that do a lot of expense-account business don't). And don't be tempted by the minibar: Most hotels charge through the nose for water, soda, and snacks. Finally, ask about local taxes, service charges, and energy surcharges, which can increase the cost of a room by 15% or more.

- **Book an efficiency.** A room with a kitchenette allows you to shop for groceries and even cook. This is a big money saver, especially for families on long stays.

- **Enroll in "frequent guest" programs,** which court repeat customers. Guests can accumulate points or credits to earn free hotel nights, airline miles, in-room amenities, merchandise, concert and event tickets, and more. Fairmont, Kimpton, and Omni frequent guests enjoy free Wi-Fi access, saving as much as $15 a day. Many chains partner with other hotel chains, car-rental firms, airlines, and credit card companies to encourage repeat business.

For tips on surfing for hotel deals online, visit **www.frommers.com**.

Bed & Breakfasts

A bed-and-breakfast can be a good alternative to a chain hotel. B&Bs are usually less expensive than hotels and often more comfortable. Most are near public transportation. Because most B&Bs are small, they fill quickly. An agency can save you a lot of calling around and can match you with a lodging that accommodates your likes and dislikes, allergies, dietary restrictions, tolerance for noise and morning chitchat, and anything else you consider important. Reserve as soon as you start planning, especially for a visit during fall foliage season.

Expect to pay at least $85 a night for a double in the summer and fall, and more during special events. The room rate usually

Planning Pointer

When you've narrowed down the list of hotels you find appealing, follow them on Twitter and friend them on Facebook. You may learn about special offers and receive early notification of events taking place during your trip.

includes breakfast and often includes parking, but be sure to ask. Many lodgings require a minimum stay of at least 2 nights, and most offer good winter specials (discounts or 1-night-free deals).

The following organizations can help you find your ideal B&B in Boston, Cambridge, or the greater Boston area:

- **B&B Agency of Boston** (✆ **800/248-9262** or 617/720-3540, 0800/89-5128 from the U.K.; www.boston-bnbagency.com)

- **Bed and Breakfast Associates Bay Colony,** P.O. Box 57166, Babson Park Branch, Boston, MA 02457 (✆ **888/486-6018** or 617/720-0522; www.bnbboston.com)

- **Bed & Breakfast Reservations North Shore/Greater Boston/Cape Cod** (✆ **617/964-1606** or 978/281-9505; www.bbreserve.com)

- **Host Homes of Boston** (✆ **800/600-1308** outside MA or 617/244-1308; www.hosthomesofboston.com)

- **Inn Boston Reservations** (✆ **617/236-2227;** www.innbostonreservations.com)

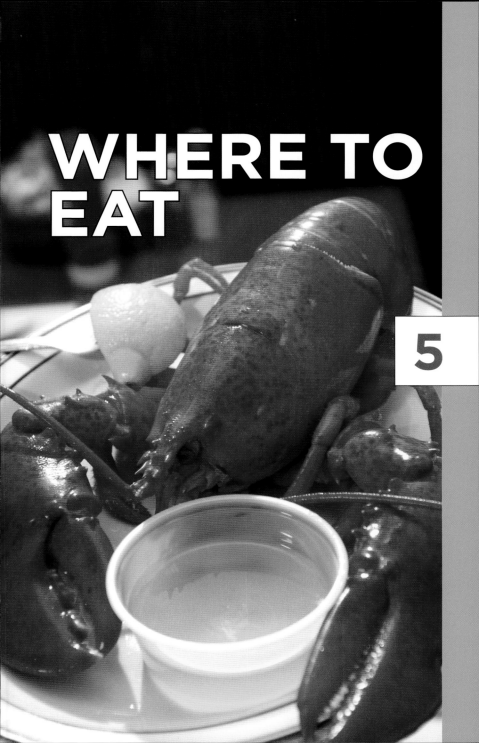

WHERE TO EAT

5

The days when restaurant snobs in Boston sniffed that they had to go to New York to get a decent meal are long gone. Especially in warm weather, when excellent local produce appears on menus in every price range, Boston-area restaurants hold their own. Celebrity chefs and rising stars spice up the dynamic scene, students seek out good value at countless ethnic restaurants, and traditional favorites—notably seafood—occupy an important niche. And year-round, many visitors just want to know where they can get a lobster. This chapter aims to help every visitor find something that hits the spot.

BEST RESTAURANT BETS

- **Best Seafood: Legal Sea Foods** does one thing and does it exceptionally well. It's a chain for a great reason: People can't get enough of the freshest seafood around. See p. 101.
- **Best for Romance:** Soaring ceilings, colorful decor, and (seasonally) a roaring fire make the atmosphere in the Monday Club Bar at **Upstairs on the Square** perfect for a rendezvous. See p. 124.
- **Best for Kids:** The wood-fired brick ovens of the **Bertucci's** chain are magnets for little eyes, and the pizza that comes out of them is equally enthralling. Picky parents will be happy here, too. See p. 118.
- **Best for a Business Lunch:** Plenty of deals go down at private clubs and formal restaurants, but that can take hours. Show your local savvy by joining the line at the **Sultan's Kitchen.** See p. 110.
- **Best American Cuisine:** It's not precisely "cuisine," but what's more American than a burger? **Mr. Bartley's Burger Cottage** is famous for its burgers, its onion rings, and a down-to-earth atmosphere that's increasingly rare in Harvard Square. See p. 127.
- **Best French Cuisine:** The bistro craze that has Boston in its grip started at **Brasserie Jo,** and all of the copycats fall short. The long hours make it a good respite during a Back Bay shopping spree. See p. 119.
- **Best Italian Cuisine:** The best restaurant in the North End, **Mamma Maria,** is one of the best in town. In a lovely setting, it offers remarkable regional Italian fare in a spaghetti-and-meatballs neighborhood. See p. 104.
- **Best Wine List:** A wine list that suits the tricky cuisine and doesn't break the bank is just one of many things to love about **Market.** See p. 112.
- **Best Value:** You'll do a double-take when the check arrives after dinner at the **Helmand.** Yes, you're really that satisfied for that little money. See p. 130.

PREVIOUS PAGE: **Fresh lobster is a local specialty.**

price CATEGORIES

Very Expensive	$41 and up	Moderate	$20–$30
Expensive	$31–$40	Inexpensive	Under $20

○ **Best for Vegetarians:** The ideal middle ground for herbivores dining with omnivores, the **Elephant Walk** serves sublime French and Cambodian cuisine. Both vegetarians and vegans will find dishes that address their needs without compromising on flavor. See p. 122.

○ **Best Reason to Visit Cambridge:** The **East Coast Grill & Raw Bar** is a colorful blur of a place that deserves its national acclaim. When Frank Bruni, then the *New York Times* food critic, wanted "a taste of what servers go through," he spent a week working here. See p. 128.

THE WATERFRONT
Expensive

Legal Sea Foods ★★★ SEAFOOD This family-owned chain enjoys a well-deserved international reputation for serving only the freshest, best-quality fish and shellfish, processed at its own state-of-the-art plant. No, it's not a secret insider tip—it's better. The menu includes regular selections (haddock, salmon, shrimp, calamari, and lobster, among others) plus whatever looked good that morning, and it's all splendid. The chowders—both clam and fish—are justly famous. Entrees run from grilled fish served plain or with Cajun spices (try the arctic char) to cioppino, an aquarium's worth of seafood in tomato broth. Or splurge on a mammoth lobster. For dessert, the Boston cream pie is so good that you might come back just for that. And the wine list is exceptional—a wine journalist friend tells me it's the best restaurant-chain list in the country. At press time, Legal's was about to open a new flagship location on the waterfront at Liberty Wharf, off Northern Avenue (at D St.) in the Seaport District, South Boston.

255 State St. (1 block from Atlantic Ave.). ✆ **617/742-5300.** www.legalseafoods.com. Reservations recommended. Main courses $11–$19 at lunch, $14–$35 at dinner; lobster market price. AE, DC, DISC, MC, V. Mon–Thurs 11am–10pm; Fri–Sun 11am–11pm. T: Blue Line to Aquarium. Also at the Prudential Center, 800 Boylston St., btw. Fairfield and Gloucester sts. (✆ **617/266-6800;** T: Green Line B, C, or D to Hynes Convention Center, or E to Prudential); 26 Park Sq., btw. Columbus Ave. and Stuart St. (✆ **617/426-4444;** T: Green Line to Arlington); Copley Place, 2nd level (✆ **617/266-7775;** T: Orange Line to Back Bay or Green Line to Copley); in the courtyard of the Charles Hotel, 20 University Rd., off Bennett St., Cambridge (✆ **617/491-9400;** T: Red Line to Harvard); 5 Cambridge Center, off Main St., Cambridge (✆ **617/864-3400;** T: Red Line to Kendall/MIT); and in the 3 domestic terminals at Logan Airport.

Sel de la Terre ★★ FRENCH PROVENÇAL A stone's throw from Boston Harbor, Sel de la Terre is a peaceful slice of southern France. Popular with out-of-towners because of its location, it also draws a go-go business-lunch crowd (dinner is calmer). The kitchen uses fresh local ingredients in its subtly flavorful food: scallops handled so gently that they're still sweet, tender beef short ribs with buttery *pommes purée*. The classic steak frites comes with a rich red-wine

Abe & Louie's **21**
Artú **70**
Bangkok City **8**
Barking Crab **61**
Ben & Jerry's **17, 25, 44**
Bertucci's **5, 73**
Bond Restaurant & Lounge **63**
Boston Public Library **26**
Brasserie Jo **29**
The Bristol Lounge **49**
Café Jaffa **13**
The Capital Grille **9**
Chacarero **66**
Charlie's Sandwich Shoppe **30**
Chau Chow City **57**
China Pearl **54**
Citizen Public House & Oyster Bar **4**
Clover Food Truck **59**
Daily Catch **73**
Davio's Northern Italian Steakhouse **41**
Durgin-Park **72**
The Elephant Walk **3**
Emack & Bolio's **11, 70**
Fajitas & 'Ritas **67**

Figs **72**
Finale **2, 45**
Fleming's Prime Steakhouse & Wine Bar **46**
Great Taste Bakery & Restaurant **54**
Grill 23 & Bar **39**
Grotto **68**
Hamersley's Bistro **34**
Hei La Moon **58**
Jacob Wirth Company **52**
Jasper White's Summer Shack **15**
JP Licks **10**
La Verdad Taqueria Mexicana **6**
Legal Sea Foods **19, 28, 48, 84**
The Lounge at Taj Boston **37**
Lobby Lounge at Mandarin Oriental, Boston **20**
Maggiano's Little Italy **47**
Market **51**
McCormick & Schmick's **43, 74**
Miel **60**
Milk Street Cafe **64**
Morton's of Chicago **24, 74**
Nebo **76**
The Oak Room **36**

Orinoco **32**
The Other Side Cafe **7**
P. F. Chang's China Bistro **16, 50**
The Palm **27**
The Paramount **71**
Parish Café and Bar **38**
Peach Farm **56**
Picco Restaurant **35**
Rowes Wharf Sea Grille **62**
Ruth's Chris Steak House **65**
Savenor's Market **69**
Sel de la Terre **21, 69**
Smith & Wollensky **40**
South End Buttery **33**
Stephanie's on Newbury **23**
Sultan's Kitchen **71**
Swans **42**
Tapéo **14**
Teranga **31**
Trader Joe's **12**
Wagamama **18, 72**
Winsor Dim Sum Cafe **55**
Xinh Xinh **53**
Ye Olde Union Oyster House **75**
Zaftigs Delicatessen **1**

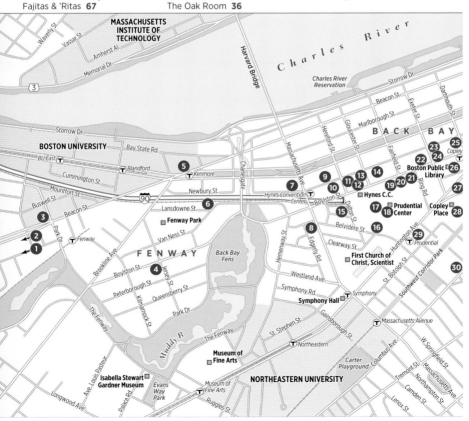

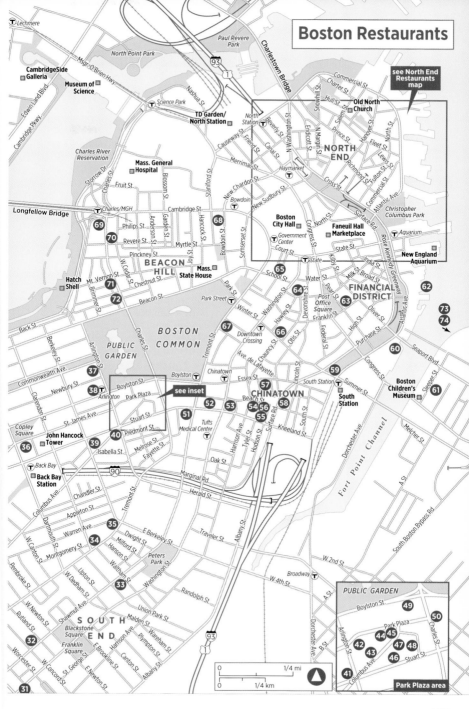

Boston Restaurants

see North End Restaurants map

reduction and *pommes frites*. Those sublime rosemary french fries are also available with the fabulous burger; a friend on a fact-finding mission proclaimed Sel de la Terre's the best in the city. There's seasonal outdoor seating, and the *boulangerie* (bakery) at the entrance sells out-of-this-world breads, pastries, salads, and sandwiches; it's a great place to load up for a picnic.

255 State St. (at Atlantic Ave.). ℂ **617/720-1300.** www.seldelaterre.com. Reservations recommended. Lunch main courses $14–$16, sandwiches $10–$14; dinner main courses $25–$32; children's menu $7–$10. AE, DISC, MC, V. Daily 11am–10pm; late-night menu Wed–Sat 10pm–12:30am. Valet parking available at dinner. T: Blue Line to Aquarium. Also at 774 Boylston St. (at Fairfield St.), adjacent to the Mandarin Oriental, Boston hotel (ℂ **617/266-8800;** daily 11am–11pm; bar menu Sun–Tues 4pm–midnight, Wed–Sat 4pm–1am; T: Green Line to Copley).

Moderate

Barking Crab ★ ☺ SEAFOOD The Barking Crab is a clam shack overlooking the water. That wouldn't be a big deal on the Maine coast or the shores of the Chesapeake Bay, but in downtown Boston, it's beyond cool. This extremely casual restaurant has a lively bar scene and a clientele of local office workers and families visiting the Boston Children's Museum. The place to be in the summer is at a picnic table on the deck, which might require a wait at busy times; in the off season, the dining room is a cozy oasis. The menu includes the usual clam chowder, fried-seafood plates, and lobsters, with a handful of creative options (such as a yummy crab-cake sandwich) and enough non-seafood dishes to keep vegetarians from starving. The food is fine, and overall quite good, but that's not really the point. This is a *downtown* clam shack—what a concept.

88 Sleeper St. (btw. Northern Ave. and Seaport Blvd.). ℂ **617/426-2722.** www.barkingcrab.com. Reservations accepted only for parties of 6 or more. Main courses $10–$25; sandwiches $7–$21 (most less than $15); fresh seafood market price. AE, DC, MC, V. Sun–Wed 11:30am–11pm; Thurs–Sat 11:30am–1am. Closed 3 weeks in Jan. T: Red Line to South Station and 10-min. walk or Silver Line to Courthouse; or Blue Line to Aquarium and 10-min. walk.

THE NORTH END

Boston's Italian-American enclave has dozens of restaurants; many are tiny and don't serve dessert and coffee. Hit the *caffès* for an espresso or cappuccino and fresh pastry in an atmosphere where lingering is welcome. My favorite dessert destinations are **Caffè Vittoria,** 296 Hanover St. (ℂ 617/227-7606; www. vittoriacaffe.com), and **Caffè dello Sport,** 308 Hanover St. (ℂ 617/523-5063; www.caffedellosport.us). **Mike's Pastry,** 300 Hanover St. (ℂ 617/742-3050; www.mikespastry.com), is a bakery that's famous for its bustling takeout business and its cannoli. If you plan to eat in, find what you want in the cases first, then take a seat and order from the server. For gelato, head to **GiGi Gelateria,** 272 Hanover St. (ℂ 617/720-4243; www.gelateriacorp.com), which serves at least two dozen flavors of the Italian version of ice cream as well as pastries, coffee, and Italian soft drinks.

Very Expensive

Mamma Maria ★★★ NORTHERN ITALIAN In a town house overlooking the Paul Revere House, the best restaurant in the North End offers innovative cuisine in a sophisticated yet comfortable setting. Upscale restaurants have been

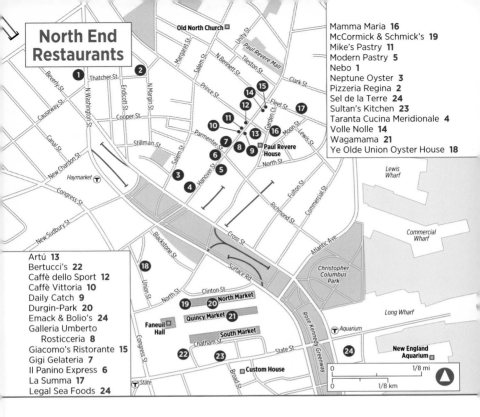

North End Restaurants

- ❶
- ❷
  Old North Church 🔲
- ❶❹
- ❶❺
- ❶❷
- ❶❶
- ❶❼
- ❶❻
- ❶❸
- ❶❷
- ❼
- ❽
- ❾
  Paul Revere House
- ❻
- ❸
- ❺
- ❹

Mamma Maria **16**
McCormick & Schmick's **19**
Mike's Pastry **11**
Modern Pastry **5**
Nebo **1**
Neptune Oyster **3**
Pizzeria Regina **2**
Sel de la Terre **24**
Sultan's Kitchen **23**
Taranta Cucina Meridionale **4**
Volle Nolle **14**
Wagamama **21**
Ye Olde Union Oyster House **18**

Lewis Wharf

Commercial Wharf

- ❶❽
  North Market
- ❶❾
- ❷❶
  Quincy Market
- ❷❶
  South Market
- ❷❷
- ❷❸
  Custom House
- ❷❹

Christopher Columbus Park

Long Wharf

🄣 Aquarium

New England Aquarium 🔲

0   1/8 mi
0   1/8 km

Artú **13**
Bertucci's **22**
Caffè dello Sport **12**
Caffè Vittoria **10**
Daily Catch **9**
Durgin-Park **20**
Emack & Bolio's **24**
Galleria Umberto
   Rosticceria **8**
Giacomo's Ristorante **15**
Gigi Gelateria **7**
Il Panino Express **6**
La Summa **17**
Legal Sea Foods **24**

colonizing the neighborhood for a few years now, with their fashionable bars and noisy dining rooms—and every time someone with a generous budget requests a recommendation, this is it. The menu changes seasonally, featuring superb entrees that are unlike anything else in this neighborhood, except in size—portions are more than generous. Fork-tender *osso buco,* a limited-quantity nightly special, is almost enough for two, but you'll want it all for yourself. You can't go wrong with main-course pastas, either, and the steaks, chops, and fresh seafood specials (say, risotto with Maine crabmeat, Nantucket Bay scallops, and Ipswich clams), are uniformly marvelous. The pasta, bread, and desserts are homemade, and the wine list is excellent.

3 North Sq. (at Prince and Garden Court sts.). ✆ **617/523-0077.** www.mammamaria.com. Reservations recommended. Main courses $26–$36. AE, DC, DISC, MC, V. Sun–Thurs 5–10pm; Fri–Sat 5–11pm. Valet parking available. T: Green or Orange Line to Haymarket.

Taranta Cucina Meridionale ★★ SOUTHERN ITALIAN/PERUVIAN
Taranta's unlikely sounding menu incorporates the flavors of the chef-owner's native Peru, ingredients you won't see on other Boston menus, and classic Italian preparations. The dining room is a typical upscale North End space, with an open kitchen and closely spaced tables. Servers are friendly and eager to explain the unusual cuisine. The risk-averse can opt for pasta with tomato sauce—a good rendition, but not the reason to come here. Dishes like espresso-crusted

filet mignon and grilled trout with Peruvian potatoes and giant lima beans make Taranta a standout. The signature main course is a Flintstones-esque pork chop with a sweet-hot glaze of sugar cane and *rocoto* pepper; it's not unusual to see a whole table of businessmen who resemble NFL linemen ordering it. Desserts are as accomplished as everything else, so try to save room.

210 Hanover St. (btw. Cross and Parmenter sts.). © **617/720-0052.** www.tarantarist.com. Reservations recommended. Main courses $19–$36. AE, DC, MC, V. Daily 5:30–10pm. T: Green or Orange Line to Haymarket.

Expensive

Daily Catch ★ SOUTHERN ITALIAN/SEAFOOD The Daily Catch offers excellent food, chummy service, and very little elbow room. About the size of a large kitchen (it seats just 20), the storefront restaurant packs a wallop—of garlic. The surprisingly varied menu includes an impressive variety of calamari (try it fried, in squid-ink pasta *puttanesca,* or stuffed with bread crumbs, parsley, and garlic) and a tempting selection of broiled, fried, and sautéed fish and shellfish. One of the pickiest eaters I know comes from New York just for the monkfish Marsala. All food is prepared to order, and some dishes arrive still in the frying pan. This isn't fine dining—wine is served in plastic cups—but it's been a favorite since 1973 for a reason.

323 Hanover St. (btw. Richmond and Prince sts.). © **617/523-8567.** www.dailycatch.com. Reservations not accepted. Main courses $17–$27. No credit cards. Sun–Thurs 11:30am–9:30pm; Fri–Sat 11:30am–10:30pm. T: Green or Orange Line to Haymarket. Also at the Moakley Federal Courthouse, 2 Northern Ave., across the bridge from Atlantic Ave. (© **617/772-4402;** reservations recommended at dinner; Mon–Thurs 11am–9:30pm, Fri–Sat 11am–10:30pm, Sun 1–9pm; AE, MC, V; T: Red Line to South Station and 10-min. walk or Silver Line SL1/SL2 bus to Courthouse, or Blue Line to Aquarium and 10-min. walk), and 441 Harvard St. (btw. Thorndike and Coolidge sts.), Brookline Village (© **617/734-2700;** reservations not accepted; Mon–Thurs 4–10pm, Fri–Sat 4–11pm, Sun 2–10pm; AE, MC, V; T: Green Line D to Brookline Village).

Neptune Oyster ★ SEAFOOD Tiny and cramped, Neptune feels like a secret place—or it would, if it weren't so crowded. Super-fresh, inventively prepared seafood keeps it busy and loud, and not just with North Enders sick of chicken parm; even in the winter, plan for lunch or an early dinner on a weekday. Check out the daily specials, then start comparing oysters from both coasts; Pacific Northwest Kumamotos are my favorite. Main courses include some standards, at least two of which aren't seafood (the burger is excellent), and dishes that use whatever's freshest. You might find something unfamiliar like cod cheeks, exotic like sea urchin, or familiar, like a lobster roll (cold with mayonnaise or hot with butter—quite the dilemma). Neptune is just off the Freedom Trail and easy to find: Look for the oysters on ice in the window and the crowd inside.

63 Salem St. (off Cross St.). © **617/742-3474.** www.neptuneoyster.com. Reservations not accepted. Main courses $14–$34; lobster market price. AE, MC, V. Sun–Thurs 11:30am–9:30pm; Fri–Sat 11:30am–10:30pm. Raw bar closes 1 hr. after kitchen. T: Green or Orange Line to Haymarket.

Moderate

Artú ITALIAN A neighborhood favorite and a good stop for Freedom Trail walkers, Artú specializes in roasted meats and veggies, bounteous home-style pasta dishes, and (at lunch) tasty sandwiches. Roast lamb, *penne alla puttanesca,* and

The tiramisu at many North End restaurants comes from **Modern Pastry**, 257 Hanover St. (© **617/523-3783**). The surreally good concoction ($3.50 a slice at the shop) makes an excellent picnic dessert in the summer. Head 4 blocks down Richmond Street to eat in Christopher Columbus Waterfront Park, off Atlantic Avenue.

chicken stuffed with ham and cheese are all terrific. Panini (sandwiches) are big in size and flavor—the prosciutto, mozzarella, and tomato is sublime, and chicken parmigiana is tender and filling. Originally a little takeout place, Artú now fills three storefronts, one of which holds a marble-topped bar. It isn't a great place for quiet conversation, especially during dinner in the noisy main room, but it's one of the most reliably satisfying restaurants in the North End.

6 Prince St. (btw. Hanover St. and North Sq.). © **617/742-4336.** www.artuboston.com. Reservations recommended at dinner. Main courses $8–$14 at lunch, $14–$23 at dinner; sandwiches $6–$8. AE, MC, V. Daily 11am–11pm; bar menu until 1am. T: Green or Orange Line to Haymarket. Also at 89 Charles St. (off Pinckney St.), Beacon Hill (© **617/227-9023;** Mon 5–11pm, Tues–Sat 11am–11pm, Sun noon–11pm; T: Red Line to Charles/MGH).

Giacomo's Ristorante ★★ ITALIAN/SEAFOOD The line outside Giacomo's forms early and grows long, especially on weekends. No reservations, cash only, tiny dining room, open kitchen—what's the attraction? Terrific food, generous portions, and the we're-all-in-this-together atmosphere. My dad is a New York ethnic-dining snob, and this is his favorite Boston restaurant. Start with fried calamari, then check out the specials and either take the chef's advice or put together your own main dish from the list of ingredients on the wall. The best suggestion is salmon and sun-dried tomatoes in tomato cream sauce over fettuccine; any dish with shrimp is delectable, too. Non-seafood offerings such as butternut squash ravioli in mascarpone cheese sauce are equally appetizing. Service is friendly but incredibly swift, and lingering is not encouraged. Have a heart—people are waiting outside whether it's freezing, sweltering, or pouring.

355 Hanover St. (off Fleet St.). © **617/523-9026.** Reservations not accepted. Main courses $14–$18; specials market price. No credit cards. Mon–Thurs 5–10pm; Fri–Sat 5–10:30pm; Sun 4–10pm. T: Green or Orange Line to Haymarket.

La Summa ★ SOUTHERN ITALIAN Because La Summa isn't on a main drag, it maintains a cozy neighborhood atmosphere. Unlike some neighborhood places, it's friendly to outsiders—you'll feel welcome even if your server doesn't greet you by name. La Summa is worth seeking out just for the wonderful homemade pasta and desserts, and the more elaborate entrees are scrumptious, too. You might start with salad, ravioli, or soup (our waitress one night didn't know exactly what was in the excellent butternut squash soup because, and I quote, "My mother made it"). Then try any seafood special, *pappardelle e melanzane* (strips of eggplant tossed with ethereal fresh pasta in marinara sauce), shrimp over linguini, or the house special—veal, chicken, sausage, shrimp, artichokes, *pepperoncini* (pickled hot peppers), olives, and mushrooms in white-wine sauce. Desserts, especially ricotta cheesecake, are terrific.

30 Fleet St. (btw. Garden Court and Moon sts., 1 block from Hanover St.). © **617/523-9503.** www.lasumma.com. Reservations recommended on weekends. Main courses $12–$24. AE, DC, DISC, MC, V. Mon–Wed 4–10:30pm; Thurs–Sat noon–10:30pm; Sun noon–9:30pm. T: Green or Orange Line to Haymarket.

Inexpensive

Galleria Umberto Rosticceria 🦑 ITALIAN The long, fast-moving line snaking toward the door is your first clue that this cafeteria-style spot just off the Freedom Trail is a bargain. Then you notice that most of the customers are locals and businesspeople. They're on to something. You can fill up on a couple of slices of pizza, but for the true experience, try *arancini* (a deep-fried rice ball filled with ground beef, peas, and cheese). Calzones filled with various combinations of meats, vegetables, and cheese are wonderful—mmm, salami—and *panzarotti* (mozzarella-stuffed potato croquettes) are tasty and satisfying. Study the cases of food while you wait, and be ready to order when you reach the head of the line. Enjoy a quick lunch and get on with your sightseeing.

289 Hanover St. (btw. Richmond and Prince sts.). © **617/227-5709.** All items less than $5. No credit cards. Mon–Sat 10:45am–2:30pm. Closed July. T: Green or Orange Line to Haymarket.

Pizzeria Regina ★★ PIZZA Regina's opened in 1926, and the only recent change was the end of the cash-only policy. As it has for decades, the line stretches up the street on busy nights, but even at off hours, business is seldom slow. Locals often call for takeout; if you do that, though, you'll miss the full experience. Busy waitresses who might call you "dear" weave through the boisterous dining room, shouting orders and questions as they deliver peerless pizza steaming hot from the brick oven. (You can also drop in for a slice, weekdays at lunch only.) Let it cool a little before you dig in. Topping options include nouveau ingredients such as sun-dried tomatoes, but that's not authentic. House-made sausage, maybe some pepperoni, and a couple of beers—now, *that's* authentic.

11½ Thacher St. (at N. Margin St.). © **617/227-0765.** www.pizzeriaregina.com. Reservations not accepted. Pizza $13–$19. AE, MC, V. Mon–Thurs 11:30am–10pm; Fri–Sat 11:30am–11pm; Sun noon–10pm. T: Green or Orange Line to Haymarket.

Volle Nolle ★ 🥪 SANDWICHES This little shop is a textbook example of doing one thing and doing it exactly right. The menu—written on the chalkboard-painted back wall—focuses on pressed gourmet sandwiches grilled to crispy perfection. The amazing Cubano (pork, ham, Swiss) was my favorite, until I tried the pesto chicken. And the pastrami and Swiss, the tuna with lemon mayonnaise, and the portabello mushroom with mozzarella and roasted red peppers. Too fancy? There's a kids' grilled cheese as well as salads and a daily soup. Mostly a takeout operation, Volle Nolle has about a dozen seats; grab one and enjoy the parade of neighborhood regulars drawn here by the amazing food, friendly service, selection of gourmet chips and soft drinks, and phenomenal chocolate chip cookies.

351 Hanover St. (near Fleet St.). © **617/523-0003.** All items less than $11 (most less than $9). No credit cards. Mon–Sat 11am–4pm. T: Green or Orange Line to Haymarket.

WEEKDAY breakfast & WEEKEND BRUNCH

Several top hotels serve Sunday brunch buffets of monstrous proportions—outrageous displays that are outrageously expensive. They're worth the investment for a special occasion, but you can have a less incapacitating a la carte experience for considerably less money. Dine on a weekday to get a sense of the neighborhood and mingle with the regulars.

My top choice is in Cambridge: the **S&S Restaurant** (p. 131), a family-run operation that never sends anyone away hungry. In Boston, the **Elephant Walk** (p. 122) and **Hamersley's Bistro** (p. 115) are excellent Sunday brunch destinations. **Charlie's Sandwich Shoppe,** 429 Columbus Ave. (© **617/536-7669**), is a longtime South End favorite not far from the Back Bay—just the right distance to walk off some blueberry-waffle calories—that's closed Sunday

and doesn't accept credit cards. The **Paramount,** 44 Charles St., Beacon Hill (© **617/720-1152;** www.paramount boston.com), is a classic for pancakes and eggs with a side of neighborhood gossip. At the **Centre Street Café,** 669 Centre St., Jamaica Plain (© **617/524-9217;** www.centrestcafe.com), locals tough out long weekend waits for strong coffee and delicious specials made (when possible) with local and organic ingredients.

FANEUIL HALL MARKETPLACE & THE FINANCIAL DISTRICT

Expensive

The national chain **McCormick & Schmick's Seafood Restaurant** has a branch at Faneuil Hall Marketplace in the North Market Building (© **617/720-5522**).

Ye Olde Union Oyster House ★ SEAFOOD/NEW ENGLAND America's oldest restaurant in continuous service (since 1826), the Union Oyster House serves tasty, traditional New England fare to visitors following the adjacent Freedom Trail and savvy locals. They're not looking for anything fancy, and you shouldn't, either—classic preparations account for the restaurant's staying power. At the oyster bar on the lower level of the antique building (a National Historic Landmark "where Daniel Webster drank many a toddy in his day"), try excellent fish chowder, oyster stew, or the cold shellfish sampler to start. Follow with a broiled or grilled dish such as scrod or salmon, or perhaps fried seafood or grilled pork loin. A "shore dinner" of chowder, steamers or mussels, lobster, corn, and potatoes is an excellent introduction to local favorites. For dessert, try gingerbread with whipped cream. A plaque marks John F. Kennedy's favorite booth (no. 18), where he often sat to read the Sunday papers.

41 Union St. (btw. North and Hanover sts.). © **617/227-2750.** www.unionoysterhouse.com. Reservations recommended. Main courses $10–$24 (most under $17) at lunch, $17–$29 at dinner; lobster market price; children's menu $5–$12. AE, DC, DISC, MC, V. Sun–Thurs 11am–9:30pm (lunch menu until 5pm); Fri–Sat 11am–10pm (lunch until 6pm). Union Bar daily 11am–midnight (lunch until 3pm, late supper until 11pm). Validated and valet parking available. T: Green or Orange Line to Haymarket.

Moderate

Durgin-Park ★★ ☺ NEW ENGLAND For huge portions of delicious food and a rowdy atmosphere where CEOs share tables with students, people have poured into Durgin-Park since 1827. If you don't have a reservation, join the quickly moving line that stretches down the stairs to the first floor of Faneuil Hall Marketplace's North Market building; you may wind up at a long table with other people (smaller tables are available). The food is wonderful—prime rib the size of a hubcap, lamb chops, fried seafood, huge salads, broiled-to-order fish, and juicy roast turkey are sure bets. Boston baked beans are a signature dish, and this is the best place to try them. For dessert, Indian pudding (molasses and cornmeal baked for hours and served with ice cream) is a New England classic. Long known for backtalk from cranky waitresses, Durgin-Park now has friendly, professional service—to the disappointment of some regulars.

340 Faneuil Hall Marketplace. ℰ **617/227-2038.** www.durgin-park.com. Reservations recommended at dinner. Main courses $8–$16 at lunch, $11–$40 at dinner; lobster market price; children's menu $8–$9. AE, DC, DISC, MC, V. Mon–Sat 11:30am–10pm; Sun 11:30am–9pm. Validated parking available. T: Green or Blue Line to Government Center, Green or Orange Line to Haymarket, or Blue Line to Aquarium.

Inexpensive

Milk Street Cafe ☙ VEGETARIAN/KOSHER A cafeteria-style restaurant on the ground floor of an office building probably sounds like something you're trying to get away from. Ignore your instincts and follow the corporate crowds. They're here for fresh and delicious soups, salads, quiches, and sandwiches (panini and wraps); a few dishes have fish, but otherwise the Milk Street Cafe is vegetarian. I'm not a fan of the pizza here, but the fresh-baked cookies hit the spot. To beat the crowds, come for breakfast or early for lunch, or opt for takeout—the lovely park at Post Office Square is just a couple of blocks away.

50 Milk St. (at Arch St., 2 short blocks from Washington St.). ℰ **617/542-3663.** www.milkstreet cafe.com. Breakfast items $6 or less; lunch items $4–$9. AE, MC, V. Mon–Thurs 7am–3pm; Fri 7am–2:30pm. T: Orange or Blue Line to State, or Red Line to Downtown Crossing.

Sultan's Kitchen ★ TURKISH/MIDDLE EASTERN Both novel and familiar, the flavorful, reasonably priced food accounts for the long lunchtime lines at the Sultan's Kitchen. The Turkish dishes filling the display case are like nothing else in downtown Boston, and the Middle Eastern options have unusual twists (orange zest in the tabbouleh, fava beans in the falafel). I recommend ordering a combination of *meze* (appetizers) and salads—they include *kabak mucveri* (zucchini patties), *saksuka* (roasted spiced eggplant, zucchini, and green peppers), *zeytinyagli enginar* (braised artichoke hearts), just to name a few—and kebabs, available in sandwiches and as part of a plate with rice pilaf and salads. Most of the businesspeople who flock here are either heading back to the office or eating in the small table area. Lucky you can have everything packed up for a picnic on the Rose Kennedy Greenway or at Christopher Columbus Waterfront Park.

116 State St. (at Broad St.). ℰ **617/570-9009.** www.sultans-kitchen.com. Sandwiches $6–$9; main courses $9–$12. AE, DC, MC, V. Mon–Fri 11am–8:30pm; Sat 11am–4pm. T: Orange or Blue Line to State.

Boston Restaurant Weeks

During Boston Restaurant Week, dozens of places serve a three-course prix-fixe lunch for the decimal equivalent of the year—in 2012, $20.12—and many offer dinner for an additional $10 to $13. The third week of August was the original Restaurant Week; it's now 2 weeks, as is the March incarnation. I find the latter less enjoyable because late winter's seasonal ingredients are dull, but the price is right. Popular restaurants book up quickly, so plan accordingly.

The Convention & Visitors Bureau (✆ 888/733-2678; www.bostonusa.com/restaurantweek) lists names of participating restaurants and individual numbers to call for reservations. Ask whether the menu is set yet, and seek out restaurants that really get into the spirit by offering more than just a couple of choices for each course. If you don't, you're going to experience more chicken, salmon, and begrudging service than anyone deserves.

DOWNTOWN CROSSING

Inexpensive

Clover Food Lab (p. 127) operates Clover Food Truck, which parks near Dewey Square, on the Rose Kennedy Greenway across from South Station (Atlantic Ave. and Summer St.) weekdays from 8am to 6pm.

Fajitas & 'Ritas ★ TEX-MEX This colorful, entertaining restaurant is one of the most fun places around. It serves nachos, quesadillas, burritos, and, of course, fajitas, exactly the way you want them. You mark your food and drink selections on a checklist, and a member of the busy staff quickly returns with big portions of tasty food. You can also try barbecue items, such as smoked brisket or pulled pork, or tequila-marinated chicken wings. There's nothing particularly exotic—beef, chicken, shrimp, beans, and so forth—but it's all super-fresh, because this place is too busy to let anything sit around for very long. As the name indicates, 'ritas (margaritas) are a house specialty. Primarily a casual business destination at lunch, it's livelier at dinner (probably thanks to the 'ritas) and a perfect stop before or after a movie at the nearby AMC Loews Boston Common theater.

25 West St. (btw. Washington and Tremont sts.). ✆ **617/426-1222.** www.fajitasandritas.com. Reservations accepted only for parties of 8 or more. Main courses $5-$9 at lunch, $6-$14 at dinner. AE, DC, DISC, MC, V. Mon-Tues 11:30am-9pm; Wed-Thurs 11:30am-10pm; Fri-Sat 11:30am-11pm; Sun noon-8pm. T: Red or Green Line to Park St., or Red or Orange Line to Downtown Crossing.

The Lunch Line

Try to be near Downtown Crossing at lunchtime at least once during your visit and seek out **Chacarero**, 101 Arch St., off Summer Street (✆ 617/542-0392; www.chacarero.com). It serves other things, but the lines are so long because of the scrumptious Chilean sandwiches, served on house-made bread. Order chicken, beef, or vegetarian, ask for it "with everything"—tomatoes, cheese, avocado, hot sauce, and (unexpected but delicious) green beans—and dig in. The lines are long but move fairly quickly, and for less than $9, you feel like a savvy Bostonian.

BEACON HILL
Moderate

Artú (p. 106) has a branch at 89 Charles St. (© 617/227-9023). It's open Sunday and Monday from 4 to 11pm, Tuesday through Saturday from 11am to 11pm.

Grotto ★★ ✦ ITALIAN Grotto's subterranean dining room is a cozy retreat, with contemporary art on the exposed-brick walls and busy servers bustling around the small, crowded space. Chef-owner Scott Herritt has fun with seasonal local ingredients, beginning his regularly changing menu with imaginative soups and ending with fruit desserts, and his three-course fixed-price dinner is one of the best deals around. You might see crab ravioli with asparagus, almonds, and saffron in the spring; apple-stuffed duck breast in the winter; or spaghetti and meatballs "with Grotto's insanely fabulous tomato sauce" anytime. Hearty gnocchi with braised short ribs, Gorgonzola cheese, and mushrooms is one of the best dishes in Boston. Desserts are indulgent but not overwhelming: A friend who's usually indifferent to sweets devoured banana bread pudding with caramel ice cream. Great—more chocolate cake for me.

37 Bowdoin St. (at Derne St., btw. Cambridge St. and the State House). © **617/227-3434.** www. grottorestaurant.com. Reservations recommended at dinner. Main courses $8–$14 at lunch, $21–$29 at dinner; 3-course fixed-price dinner $35. AE, DC, MC, V. Mon–Fri 11:30am–3pm; daily 5–10pm. T: Green or Red Line to Park St., Green or Blue Line to Government Center, or Blue Line to Bowdoin (weekdays only).

CHINATOWN/THEATER DISTRICT

The most entertaining and delicious introduction to Chinatown's cuisine is **dim sum** (see "Yum, Yum, Dim Sum," below). At lunch and dinner, many restaurants have a second menu for Chinese patrons (often written in Chinese). You can ask for it or tell your waiter that you want your meal Chinese-style.

If you're serious about sweets, consider ending—or even beginning—your meal at **Finale** (p. 266), 1 Columbus Ave. (© 617/423-3184; www.finale desserts.com).

The area around Park Square (near Stuart St. and Charles St. S.), between the Theater District and the Public Garden, is a hotbed of upscale national chain restaurants. None of these places offers a unique or even unusual experience, but they're all reliable destinations if you're feeling unadventurous. They include **Fleming's Prime Steakhouse & Wine Bar,** 217 Stuart St. (© 617/292-0808); **Maggiano's Little Italy,** 4 Columbus Ave. (© 617/542-3456); **McCormick & Schmick's Seafood Restaurant,** 34 Columbus Ave., in the Boston Park Plaza Hotel (© 617/482-3999); and **P. F. Chang's China Bistro,** 8 Park Plaza (© 617/573-0821).

Very Expensive

Market ★★★ FUSION Before Jean-Georges Vongerichten was a culinary megastar, he briefly worked in Boston. A quarter-century later, in 2009, he returned in triumph to open Market. It's the creation of a mature talent with an adventuresome spirit: inventive menu, exotic and local ingredients, impeccable service, exceptional wine list, even a superb burger. The food demonstrates why chefs have groupies. Start with foie gras brûlée, a disc of pure richness with a crackly, almost-burnt caramel crust, or a perfectly balanced salad. Main courses show off those local ingredients, with seafood from New England waters bathing in emulsions of Asian spice, citrus, and soy alongside seasonal vegetables, and expertly prepared meat dishes reminding you that you're in a hotel restaurant. I enlisted the pickiest diners I know to help me evaluate Market, and their biggest criticism was that the glass-walled dining room gets somewhat noisy—it's the buzz of happy, satisfied diners.

In the W Boston hotel, 100 Stuart St. (at Tremont St.). ℂ **617/310-6790.** www.marketbyjg boston.com. Reservations recommended. Lunch main courses $21–$24, pizzas and sandwiches $9–$16, 3-course prix fixe $22–$26; dinner main courses $16–$39 (most $19–$29), 5-course prix fixe $58 (whole tables only). AE, DC, DISC, MC, V. Mon–Fri 7–11am, Sat–Sun 8–11am; Mon–Fri 11:30am–2:30pm, Sat–Sun brunch 11:45am–2:30pm; Sun–Thurs 5–10pm, Fri–Sat 5–11pm. Valet parking available. T: Green Line to Boylston.

Expensive

There's a branch of **Legal Sea Foods** (p. 101) at 26 Park Sq., between Columbus Avenue and Stuart Street (ℂ **617/426-4444;** www.legalseafoods.com).

 YUM, YUM, dim sum

Many Chinatown restaurants offer **dim sum,** the traditional midday meal featuring appetizer-style dishes. You'll see steamed buns (*bao*) filled with pork or bean paste; meat, shrimp, and vegetable dumplings; sticky rice dotted with sausage and vegetables; shrimp-stuffed eggplant; spring rolls; sweets such as sesame balls and coconut gelatin; and more. Waitresses wheel carts laden with tempting dishes to your table, and you order by pointing (unless you know Chinese). The waitress then stamps your check with the symbol of the dish, adding about $2 to $3 to your tab

for each selection. Unless you order a la carte items from the regular menu or the steam table off to the side in most dining rooms, the total usually won't be more than about $10 to $12 per person. On weekends, the selection is wider than on weekdays, the turnover is faster (which means fresher food), and you'll often see three generations of families sharing large tables.

Looking to confirm a hunch, I asked a Hong Kong native to name Boston's best dim sum restaurant, and we agreed: **Hei La Moon ★★**, 88 Beach St. (ℂ **617/338-8813**). It opened in 2004 and has since eclipsed a pair of solid competitors: **China Pearl ★**, 9 Tyler St., 2nd floor (ℂ **617/426-4338**), and **Chau Chow City ★**, 83 Essex St. (ℂ **617/338-8158**). To order off a

sushi-style menu and have dim sum prepared just for you—a good tactic on weekdays—head to **Great Taste Bakery & Restaurant,** 61–63 Beach St. (ℂ **617/426-8899**), or **Winsor Dim Sum Cafe,** 10 Tyler St. (ℂ **617/338-1688**).

I turned to the parents of young acquaintances who have celiac disease in search of suggestions for Frommer's readers who are in the same boat. Perhaps most important is not forgetting to do what you do at home: Be sure your server knows that a diner or diners at the table can't eat gluten. Check out the **Elephant Walk** (p. 122); **Davio's** (p. 117); **Nebo**, 90 N. Washington St. (© **617/723-6326; www.nebo restaurant.com**), an Italian restaurant on the edge of the North End; and the funky **Other Side Cafe,** 407 Newbury St., off Mass. Ave. (© **617/536-8437; www.theothersidecafe.com**), which also has numerous vegan options, outdoor seating in fine weather, and deafeningly loud music inside at night. The **Legal Sea Foods** (p. 101) and **Bertucci's** (p. 118) chains have gluten-free menus. Other dependable choices are branches of two national chains: **P.F. Chang's China Bistro** (www.pfchangs.com), 8 Park Plaza (© **617/573-0821**), and in the Prudential Center, 800 Boylston St. (© **617/378-9961**); and **Wagamama** (www.wagamama.us), Quincy Market, Faneuil Hall Marketplace (© **617/742-9242**); in the Prudential Center, 800 Boylston St. (© **617/778-2344**); and 57 John F. Kennedy St., Cambridge (© **617/499-0930**).

Moderate

Jacob Wirth Company GERMAN/AMERICAN In the heart of the Theater District, "Jake's" has been serving Bostonians since 1868—even before there were theaters here. The wood floor and brass accents give the spacious room the feeling of a saloon, and the menu incorporates traditional pub grub and more contemporary fare. Hearty German specialties include Wiener schnitzel, mixed grills, bratwurst, knockwurst, and potato pancakes; check out the wine-snob-style beer pairings. Daily specials, comfort-food favorites like chicken pot pie, and a large variety of sandwiches and salads round out the menu. Service at lunchtime is snappy, but if you want to be on time for the theater, be ready to remind your server. On Friday after 8pm, a live pianist leads singalong night, which has something of a chicken-and-egg connection to the enormous beer selection (20-plus in bottles, even more on tap).

31–37 Stuart St. (btw. Tremont and Washington sts.). © **617/338-8586.** www.jacobwirth.com. Reservations recommended at dinner. Main courses $7–$14 at lunch, $9–$23 (most items less than $20) at dinner; children's menu $6–$7. AE, DC, DISC, MC, V. Sun–Mon 11:30am–9pm; Tues–Thurs 11:30am–11pm; Fri–Sat 11:30am–midnight. Validated parking available. T: Green Line to Boylston or Orange Line to Tufts Medical Center.

Peach Farm ★ SEAFOOD/CANTONESE/SZECHUAN Chinatown's go-to place for fresh seafood is a subterranean hideaway with no notable decor. You won't be looking around much anyway—the service is so fast that just saying "calamari" seems to make spicy dry-fried salted squid materialize. Main courses follow almost instantly: messy clams with black-bean sauce, Cantonese-style lobster, braised chicken or beef hot pot, an emerald-green pile of stir-fried pea-pod stems. Spicy salt shrimp is a specialty; it's not on the menu, but you can ask to have that same spicy salt preparation applied to tender scallops. Both are fantastic. Fair warning to the soft-hearted: Order the Cantonese classic fresh fish steamed with ginger and scallions, and the waiter brings the poor creature to your table thrashing in a plastic bucket; it reappears moments later, perfectly cooked.

Peach Farm is virtually indistinguishable from the other little restaurants that dot Chinatown's narrow streets, except that it's so crowded—savvy locals and celebratory groups fill both dining rooms every night.

4 Tyler St. (off Beach St.). © **617/482-3332.** Reservations recommended for large groups at dinner. Main courses $5–$34 (most items less than $15); fresh seafood market price. MC, V. Daily 11am–3am. T: Orange Line to Chinatown.

Inexpensive

Xinh Xinh ★★ VIETNAMESE One of the best Vietnamese restaurants in the Boston area is this cheery little storefront with an encyclopedic menu and welcoming service. Xinh Xinh (say "sin sin") lists close to 200 dishes, from fresh spring rolls to specialties that include beef tripe, pork skin, and various other animal parts. It also offers wonderful appetizers (try the fried spring rolls), numerous vegetarian options, and an extensive beverage menu. My favorite options are *bun*—shredded lettuce, cooked vermicelli, fresh mint, and other toppings with your choice of hot protein, all mixed together—anything with lemongrass chicken, and an exceptional version of traditional beef noodle soup, or *pho*. You can also check the specials board. Best of all, if you can't find something appealing or need help deciding, the helpful staff will step in.

7 Beach St. (at Knapp St., 1 block from Washington St.). © **617/422-0501.** Main courses $6–$14 (most less than $11). MC, V. Daily 10am–10pm. T: Orange Line to Chinatown.

THE SOUTH END

Very Expensive

Hamersley's Bistro ★★★ FRENCH/AMERICAN A beloved special-occasion restaurant and neighborhood favorite, Hamersley's put the South End on Boston's culinary map. It opened in 1987 but feels as fresh as the local ingredients all over the menu, which changes seasonally. The dining room has an open kitchen (the tall guy in the Red Sox cap is owner Gordon Hamersley) and lots of sound-muffling soft surfaces, a perfect combination of showy and comfortable—which also describes the vegetarian-friendly food. Deceptively simple roast chicken with garlic, lemon, and parsley is deservedly famous, and I'd cheerfully eat New England bouillabaisse—clams, mussels, scallops, shrimp, and haddock in out-of-this-world broth—every night. For meat-eaters, veal *osso buco* braised in white wine with celery root, mushrooms, lemon, and rosemary is a gorgeous combination of flavors. Desserts are among the best in town—try the lemon custard soufflé. The enthusiastic, professional staff can help navigate the excellent wine list. There's seasonal outdoor seating.

553 Tremont St. (at Clarendon St.). © **617/423-2700.** www.hamersleysbistro.com. Reservations recommended. Main courses $24–$39; 3-course prix-fixe dinner $39–$42. AE, DISC, MC, V. Sun–Thurs 5:30–9:30pm; Fri–Sat 5:30–10pm; Sun brunch 11am–2pm. Closed 1st week. of Jan. Valet parking available. T: Orange Line to Back Bay.

Moderate

Orinoco ★ 🏠 VENEZUELAN Little Orinoco is a magnet for adventurous diners. The intensely flavorful food isn't necessarily spicy, but it's complex and satisfying. To start, try a delectable *arepa*—a corn patty stuffed with meat, cheese, or both, then grilled—or an empanada (I like the *verde* version, enclosing a savory mushroom mixture). The signature main course is *pabellón criollo*, the national dish of black beans and rice, which Venezuelans serve with shredded beef and plantains. The lunch menu includes salads and sandwiches; the dinner specials change regularly, and if you're lucky, your meal will coincide with beef tenderloin *churrasquito* (with crab *picadillo* and salsa *chimi*). Portions are generous, and sauces inventive and flavorful. If you can't get here for lunch, when it's less crowded than at dinner, consider arriving shortly after 6pm to avoid a long wait. Heading to the Brookline location is no shortcut—it's larger but equally crowded.

477 Shawmut Ave. (at W. Concord St.). ✆ **617/369-7075.** www.orinocokitchen.com. Reservations recommended at lunch (accepted only for parties of 4 or more), not accepted at dinner. Main courses $5–$14 (most dishes less than $9) at lunch, $13–$19 at dinner. DISC, MC, V. Tues–Sat noon–2:30pm; Tues–Wed 6–10pm; Thurs–Sat 6–11pm; Sun brunch 11am–3pm. T: Orange Line to Massachusetts Ave, then 10-min. walk, or Silver Line bus to Worcester St. Also at 22 Harvard St., Brookline (✆ **617/232-9505;** Tues–Sat noon–2:30pm, Tues–Wed 5:30–10pm, Thurs–Sat 5:30–11pm, Sun 5:30–9:30pm, Sun brunch 11am–3pm; T: Green Line D to Brookline Village).

South End Buttery AMERICAN A neighborhood hangout on a not-too-busy corner, South End Buttery is primarily a casual cafe and bakery. Scones, croissants, muffins, and other pastries are fresh and wonderful, and the amazing cupcakes put this little place on the map. It's exceedingly popular at breakfast, with long lines of commuters hustling in and out. Lunch—big sandwiches on fantastic bread (try the turkey club), house-made soups that include rib-sticking chili, abundant salads—is a treat, especially if there's room on the sidewalk patio. The counter staff has a reputation for being standoffish, but I've almost always found the service friendly and helpful. At night and during weekend brunch, the back dining room transforms South End Buttery into a full-service comfort-food restaurant that serves bistro favorites to stay or (a popular option in this gentrified neighborhood) to go.

314 Shawmut Ave. (at Union Park St.). ✆ **617/482-1015.** www.southendbuttery.com. Reservations recommended at dinner. Cafe items $2.25–$9 (most under $7); soups, sandwiches and salads $6–$10; brunch items $4–14; dinner main courses $13–$29 (most under $21). AE, MC, V. Cafe daily 6:30am–8pm. Dinner Sun–Wed 5:30–10pm, Thurs–Sat 5:30–11pm; Sat–Sun brunch 10am–3pm. T: Orange Line to Back Bay or Silver Line bus to Union Park.

Teranga ★★ ◢ SENEGALESE The unusual food and beverages, reasonable prices, elegant dining room, and friendly service make Teranga ("hospitality" in the Wolof language) one of the best deals in Boston. Chef-owner Marie-Claude Mendy's Senegalese cuisine, with its French and Vietnamese influences, is a marvel. Start with *croquettes de poisson* (fish cakes) or *fataya* (spiced-fish turnovers) rather than *nems* (spring rolls), which are on the doughy side. Main courses are richly spiced but not spicy; any dish with caramelized onions is amazing. My favorites are *thiébou yap* (lamb with mixed vegetables) and *thiou guinar* (chicken stew); vegetarian versions are available. The only thing I've tried that wasn't sublime was the "national dish," *thiébou djeun.* Our server warned that the whitefish at the center of the fragrant stew is well done, and she wasn't kidding.

1746 Washington St. (btw. Mass. Ave. and E. Springfield St.). ✆ **617/266-0003.** www.teranga boston.com. Reservations not accepted. Main courses $12–$13 at lunch; $14–$17 at dinner. DC, DISC, MC, V, Mon–Sat 11:30am–2:30pm and 5–10:30pm; Sun brunch 11am–2:30pm, dinner 5–10pm. T: Silver Line SL4/SL5 bus to Mass. Ave.

Where's the Beef?

Say "Boston," think "seafood," right? Apparently not. Branches of most of the national steakhouse chains dot the city, and they're all at the top of their game—a rising tide lifts all boats, as the seafood folks say. Make a reservation, and have a light lunch.

The local favorites are **Grill 23 & Bar** (p. 118); the **Oak Room**, in the Fairmont Copley Plaza hotel, 138 St. James Ave. (© 617/267-5300; www.theoakroom.com); and **Abe & Louie's**, 793 Boylston St. (© 617/536-6300; www.abeandlouies.com). Devotees of the national chains can choose from the **Palm**, in the Westin Copley Place Boston, 200 Dartmouth St. (© 617/867-9292; www.thepalm.com); the **Capital Grille,** 359 Newbury St. (© 617/262-8900; www.thecapitalgrille.com); **Fleming's Prime Steakhouse & Wine Bar,** 217 Stuart St. (© 617/292-0808; www.flemingssteakhouse.com); **Morton's of Chicago** (www.mortons.com), 1 Exeter Plaza, Boylston St. at Exeter Street (© 617/266-5858), and World Trade Center East, 2 Seaport Lane (© 617/526-0410); **Ruth's Chris Steak House** (© 800/544-0808; www.ruthschris.com), in Old City Hall, 45 School St.; and **Smith & Wollensky,** 101 Arlington St. (© 617/432-1112; www.smithandwollensky.com).

Inexpensive

Picco Restaurant ★ PIZZA This upscale pizzeria serves traditional and gentrified pizza and phenomenal ice cream in an airy space up the street from the Boston Center for the Arts. The pizza menu ranges from Neapolitan (tomato, basil, and cheese) to the "Alsatian variation," topped with a lip-smacking combo of caramelized onions, shallots, bacon, sour cream, roasted garlic, and Gruyère cheese. The crust—a little smoky from the oven, blistered in spots, thin but not crackery—is as good as the toppings. The menu also includes calzones, pastas, soups, salads, and sandwiches; fish tacos, often available as a special, are phenomenal. Somewhat unexpectedly, Picco also has a fantastic wine list. And the ice cream? Some people are here just for that, and everything—including a huge brownie sundae, ice cream sodas, even a dish of plain old vanilla—is scrumptious. There's outdoor seating in good weather.

513 Tremont St. (btw. Clarendon and Berkeley sts.). © 617/927-0066. www.piccorestaurant.com. Reservations accepted only for parties of 8 or more. Pizza $10 and up; main courses $8–$13. MC, V. Sun–Wed 11am–10pm; Thurs–Sat 11am–11pm. T: Orange Line to Back Bay.

THE BACK BAY

Very Expensive

Davio's Northern Italian Steakhouse ★★★ STEAKS/NORTHERN ITALIAN A cavernous space with a surprisingly comfortable vibe, Davio's offers robust cuisine in a business-chic setting. It's stylish but not trendy: Owner-chef Steve DiFillippo built the restaurant's excellent reputation on its top-notch kitchen and dedicated staff. Northern Italian cuisine shares the menu with picture-perfect steakhouse offerings and inventive-comfort-food sides. The traditional dishes—pasta, homemade sausage, savory soups, out-of-this-world risotto (I'd walk a mile for the lobster version)—are equally superb, making Davio's a great compromise for hard-core carnivores dining with Italophiles. And this is the place to credit (or blame) for the Philly-cheese-steak-spring-roll phenomenon.

The exceptional wine list includes some rare and expensive Italian vintages. Despite the open kitchen, the noise level allows for conversation, even at busy times. Bonus, if you're into this: When the New York Yankees are in town, at least a few of them often turn up here.

75 Arlington St. (at Stuart St., 2 blocks from the Public Garden). ℭ **617/357-4810.** www.davios. com. Reservations recommended. Main courses $9–$43 at lunch (most less than $25), $17–$51 at dinner; 4-course tasting menu $75. AE, DC, DISC, MC, V. Mon–Fri 11:30am–3pm; Sun–Tues 5–10pm (lounge menu until 11pm), Wed–Sat 5–11pm (lounge menu until midnight). Validated and valet parking available. T: Green Line to Arlington.

Grill 23 & Bar ★ STEAKS/AMERICAN The best steakhouse in town, Grill 23 is a wood-paneled, glass-walled place with a businesslike air. A briefcase-toting crowd fills its two levels—the dining rooms get *very* noisy—and chows down on traditional slabs of beef and chops, traditional steakhouse side dishes, and sophisticated yet traditional desserts. The meat is of the highest quality, humanely raised and expertly prepared. Steak au poivre and lamb chops are perfectly grilled, crusty, juicy, and tender. Fish dishes aren't quite as memorable as the meat offerings, but hey, it's a steakhouse. The bountiful a la carte sides include out-of-this-world mashed potatoes, mushrooms with pesto, and "Tater Tots." Desserts are toothsome but (this is *not* your father's steakhouse) don't always include cheesecake. The service is exactly right for the setting, helpful but not familiar.

161 Berkeley St. (at Stuart St.). ℭ **617/542-2255.** www.grill23.com. Reservations recommended. Main courses $22–$49 (most more than $33); Kobe beef $59. AE, DC, DISC, MC, V. Mon–Thurs 5:30–10:30pm; Fri 5:30–11pm; Sat 5–11pm; Sun 5:30–10pm. Valet parking available. T: Green Line to Arlington.

 family-friendly **RESTAURANTS**

Like chocolate and champagne, well-behaved children are welcome almost every-where. Most Boston-area restaurants can accommodate families, and many young-sters can be stunned into tranquillity if a place is fancy enough. If your kids can't or won't sign a good-conduct pledge, here are some suggestions.

The nonstop activity and lively crowds at **Durgin-Park** (p. 110) will entrance any child, and parents of picky eaters appreciate the straightforward New England fare. Other good non-chain choices are **Redbones** (p. 131), the **Barking Crab** (p. 104), and the Cambridge location of **Jasper White's Summer Shack** (p. 129), which has a giant lobster tank.

The **Bertucci's** chain of pizzerias (www.bertuccis.com) appeals to chil-dren and adults equally, with wood-fired brick ovens that are visible from many tables, great rolls made from pizza dough, and pizzas and pastas that range from basic to sophisticated. There are convenient branches at Faneuil Hall Marketplace, on Merchants Row off State Street (ℭ **617/227-7889**); at 533 Commonwealth Ave., Kenmore Square (ℭ **617/236-1030**); and in Cambridge at 21 Brattle St., Harvard Square (ℭ **617/864-4748**), and 799 Main St. (ℭ **617/661-8356**), a short walk from Central Square.

Expensive

For seafood of all sorts, **Jasper White's Summer Shack** (p. 129) has a branch at 50 Dalton St. (✆ 617/867-9955), across the street from the Sheraton Boston and the Hynes Convention Center. The excellent tapas restaurant **Tapéo,** 266 Newbury St. (✆ 617/267-4799), is owned by the same family as **Dalí** (p. 129).

Brasserie Jo ★★ REGIONAL FRENCH   One of the most discriminating diners I know lit up like a marquee upon hearing that Boston has a branch of this Chicago favorite. The food is classic—house-made pâtés, fresh baguettes, superb shellfish, *salade Niçoise,* Alsatian onion tart, *choucroute,* coq au vin—but never boring. The house beer, an Alsace-style draft, is a good accompaniment. The casual, all-day French brasserie and bar fits well in this neighborhood, where shoppers can always use a break. It's also a good bet before or after a Symphony or Pops performance, and it's popular for business lunches. The noise level can be high when the spacious room is full—have your tête-à-tête near the bar.

In the Colonnade Hotel, 120 Huntington Ave. (at Garrison St., 1 block from W. Newton St.). ✆ **617/425-3240.** www.brasseriejoboston.com. Reservations recommended at dinner. Main courses $10–$23 (most under $17) at lunch, $17–$33 at dinner; *plats du jour* $18–$32. AE, DC, DISC, MC, V. Mon–Fri 6:30am–11pm; Sat 7am–11pm; Sun 7am–10pm; Sat–Sun brunch noon–3pm; late-night menu daily until 1am. Valet and garage parking available. T: Green Line E to Prudential.

The Bristol Lounge ★★ AMERICAN   The Bristol Lounge is to a regular restaurant as the Four Seasons is to a regular hotel: It looks about the same, but everything is just *better.* Columns and cushy banquettes break up a large space with floor-to-ceiling windows, red-leather accents, and plenty of wood paneling; there's seating in the lively bar and the stylish dining area. The all-day menu extends from pricey breakfast items to tasty bar bites to sophisticated versions of classic dishes. The juicy burgers are famous, the soups and salads depend on what's fresh and seasonal, and the main courses are top-of-the-line comfort food (grilled salmon, roasted chicken, hand-rolled pastas). Desserts are inventive versions of bread pudding, Boston cream pie, and other traditional favorites. In keeping with every other element of a meal here, the service is fantastic.

In the Four Seasons Hotel, 200 Boylston St. (at Hadassah Way, btw. Arlington St. and Charles St. S.). ✆ **617/338-4400.** www.fourseasons.com/boston/dining. Reservations recommended. Main courses $18–$33 at lunch, $20–$35 at dinner; bar menu $8–$27. AE, DC, DISC, MC, V. Mon–Thurs 6:30am–10:30pm; Fri 6:30am–11:30pm; Sat 7am–11:30pm; Sun 7am–10:30pm. Valet parking available. T: Green Line to Arlington.

Moderate

P. F. Chang's China Bistro has a branch in the Prudential Center, 800 Boylston St. (✆ 617/378-9961).

Bangkok City ★ THAI   In a neighborhood loaded with Thai restaurants, this is my top choice. Tempting aromas and cordial employees greet you as you check out the exotic decor and lengthy menu. Appetizers are the usual dumplings and satays, plus unique items like "Boston triangles" (tasty fried pork-and-shrimp patties). Entrees range from mild pad thai to blow-your-hair-back curries, with many vegetarian options. The mix-and-match selection of proteins and sauces is larger than at many other Thai restaurants, so you can let your palate's imagination run wild. (Oh, great—now I want some tamarind duck.) *Hot tip:* The friend who steered me to this place comes here just for the zesty salt-and-pepper squid.

167 Massachusetts Ave. (btw. Belvidere and St. Germain sts.). © **617/266-8884.** www.bkk cityboston.com. Reservations recommended before Symphony and Pops performances. Main courses $7–$10 at lunch, $10–$18 at dinner; whole fish market price. AE, DC, DISC, MC, V. Mon-Sat 11:30am–3pm; Mon–Thurs 5–10pm; Fri 5–10:30pm; Sat 3–10:30pm; Sun 5–10pm. T: Green Line B, C, or D to Hynes Convention Center.

Inexpensive

The Boston Public Library, 700 Boylston St., offers two dining options (© **617/859-2251;** www.thecateredaffair.com/bpl). The **Courtyard** restaurant serves lunch on weekdays and afternoon tea Wednesday through Friday, and the self-service **Map Room Café** serves meals and snacks Monday through Saturday from 9am to 5pm.

Café Jaffa ✦ MIDDLE EASTERN/MEDITERRANEAN A long, narrow brick room with a glass front, Café Jaffa looks more like a snazzy pizza place than the excellent Middle Eastern restaurant it is. The reasonable prices, high quality, and large portions draw hordes of students and other thrifty diners for traditional Middle Eastern offerings. I'm a fan of the combo plates and sandwiches—mix-and-match falafel, baba ghanouj, hummus, grape leaves, and more—and the chicken kabobs, available in a sandwich, a salad, or a full dinner (with Greek salad, rice pilaf, and pita bread). Burgers and steak tips are popular, too. For dessert, try the baklava if it's fresh; give it a pass if not.

48 Gloucester St. (btw. Boylston and Newbury sts.). © **617/536-0230.** www.cafejaffa.net. Main courses $8–$19; sandwiches and salads $6–$10. AE, DC, DISC, MC, V. Mon–Thurs 11am–10:30pm; Fri–Sat 11am–11pm; Sun noon–10pm. T: Green Line B, C, or D to Hynes Convention Center.

QUICK BITES & picnic PROVISIONS

If you're walking the Freedom Trail, pick up food at **Faneuil Hall Marketplace** and stake out a bench. Or buy a tasty sandwich in the North End at **Volle Nolle** (p. 108) or **Il Panino Express,** 266 Hanover St. (© **617/720-5720**), and stroll down Fleet or Richmond street toward the harbor. Eat at the park on Sargent's Wharf, behind 2 Atlantic Ave., or in Christopher Columbus Waterfront Park, overlooking the marina (which is also an option if you stocked up at Faneuil Hall Marketplace).

Two neighborhoods abut the Charles River Esplanade, a great destination for a picnic, concert, or movie. In the **Back Bay,** stop at **Trader Joe's,** 899 Boylston St. (© **617/262-6505**), for prepared food. At the foot of **Beacon Hill,** pick up all you need for a do-it-yourself feast at **Savenor's Market,** 160 Charles St. (© **617/723-6328**). Or call ahead for gourmet thin-crust pizza from **Figs,** 42 Charles St. (© **617/742-3447**).

On the Cambridge side of the river, **Harvard Square** is close enough to the water to allow a riverside repast. About 5 minutes from the heart of the Square and well worth the walk, **Darwin's Ltd.,** 148 Mount Auburn St. (© **617/354-5233;** www.darwinsltd. com), serves excellent gourmet sandwiches and salads. Take yours to John F. Kennedy Park, on Memorial Drive and Kennedy Street, or right to the riverbank, a block away. Nowhere near the Charles, there's a branch at 1629 Cambridge St. (© **617/491-2999**), between Harvard and Inman squares.

In Boston, the only city that has a tea party named after it, the tradition of afternoon tea is alive and well. Reservations are strongly recommended; at the Four Seasons and Taj Boston hotels, they're pretty much mandatory.

The best afternoon tea in town is at the **Bristol Lounge** in the Four Seasons Hotel, 200 Boylston St. (✆ **617/351-2037**). The gorgeous room, lovely view, and courtly ritual elevate scones, pastries, tea sandwiches, and nut bread from delicious to unforgettable. The Bristol serves tea ($28) every day from 3 to 4:15pm.

Taj Boston, 15 Arlington St. (✆ **617/598-5255**), serves tea in the celebrated **Lounge** at 2 and 4pm; it's available Saturday and Sunday in the winter, Friday through Sunday the rest of the year. The price is $25 for tea and pastries, $33 to add sandwiches.

The Langham, Boston, 250 Franklin St. (✆ **617/956-8751**), serves afternoon tea ($31) daily from 3 to 5pm in **Bond Restaurant & Lounge.** The chain's flagship is in London, and as you'd expect, this is a proper British experience. The **Rowes Wharf Sea Grille,** in the Boston Harbor Hotel, 70 Rowes Wharf (✆ **617/856-7744**), serves tea daily from 2:30 to 4pm in a lovely room overlooking the hotel marina. It costs $19 to $30. The Mandarin Oriental, Boston, 776 Boylston St. (✆ **617/535-8800**), serves tea in the **Lobby Lounge** Thursday through Sunday from 2:30 to 4pm. It prices food ($27) and drinks ($6–$9) separately. **Swans** at the Boston Park Plaza Hotel & Towers, 50 Park Plaza (✆ **617/654-1906**), serves tea Friday through Sunday from 3 to 5pm and offers meatless and dairy-free options. The price is $30 to $32 for adults, $17 for children.

Two non-hotel destinations are worth considering. The **Courtyard** restaurant at the Boston Public Library, 700 Boylston St. (✆ **617/859-2251**), serves tea ($23) Wednesday through Friday from 2 to 4pm. And across the river, beloved Cambridge restaurant **Upstairs on the Square** (p. 124), shown here, makes a wonderful destination. Zebra Tea ($28) is a three-tiered wonder that lets the inventive kitchen cut loose on a small scale. Food and drinks are also available a la carte, and the Grand Peppermint Tea ($18) combines minty sweets and a pot of the headliner. Tea is served Saturday and Sunday (Thurs–Sun in Dec) from 2 to 4pm.

And if you just want a well-prepared cuppa, head to Harvard Square, where **Tealuxe,** Zero Brattle St., Cambridge (✆ **617/441-0077;** www.tealuxe.com), has been delighting tea aficionados since 1996. It serves and sells more than 100 varieties and serves light fare and desserts.

5

WHERE TO EAT | The Back Bay

121

KENMORE SQUARE, THE FENWAY & BROOKLINE

Expensive

Citizen Public House & Oyster Bar ★★ AMERICAN The neighborhood behind Fenway Park has taken off as a culinary destination in the past couple of years, and this welcoming gastropub is one very good reason. A cozy space with a long bar, Citizen serves comfort food so good that I almost don't care how loud it is. (Very.) Start with feather-light *canederli* meatballs or roasted-tomato soup served with a cute little grilled-cheese sandwich. Main courses are high-end homey, with a lot of seafood and pork options (the logo is a pig); the tuna burger is perfectly dressed up with Asian accents and served almost raw. Vegetarians have their own equally appealing menu. As for the name, Citizen is more public house than oyster bar; the alcohol selection dwarfs the shellfish variety. Options include 75 whiskeys, artisan cocktails, over a dozen beers, and the cult-favorite *digestif* Fernet Branca on tap.

1310 Boylston St. (at Jersey St.), Boston. ✆ **617/450-9000.** www.citizenpub.com. Reservations accepted only for parties of 6 or more. Main courses $17–$22. AE, DC, DISC, MC, V. Daily 5pm–1am. T: Green Line B, C, or D to Kenmore, then 10-min. walk. Validated parking available.

The Elephant Walk ★★ FRENCH/CAMBODIAN The menu at this madly popular spot 4 blocks from Kenmore Square is French on one side and Cambodian on the other, but the boundary is porous. Many Cambodian dishes have part-French names, such as *curry de crevettes* (wonderful shrimp curry with vegetables) and *mee siem au poulet*, a tangle of rice noodles, sliced omelet, tofu, chicken, and picture-perfect vegetables. I'd come here just for *loc lac*, fork-tender beef in addictively spicy-hot sauce. On the French side, you'll find *poulet rôti* (roasted chicken) and top-notch pan-seared tuna. The pleasant staff will help if you need guidance. Many dishes are vegetarian, and this is one of the best destinations in the Boston area if you can't have gluten. *Tip:* Sunday brunch, which includes the prettiest omelets I've ever seen, is worth checking out.

900 Beacon St. (at Park Dr.), Boston. ✆ **617/247-1500.** www.elephantwalk.com. Reservations recommended. Main courses $8–$20 at lunch (most items less than $13), $15–$23 at dinner; dinner tasting menu $30 for 3 courses, $34 for 4 courses. AE, DC, DISC, MC, V. Mon–Fri 11:30am–2:30pm; Sun–Thurs 5–10pm; Fri–Sat 5–11pm; Sun brunch 11:30am–2:30pm. Valet parking available at dinner. T: Green Line C to St. Mary's St. Also at 2067 Massachusetts Ave., Porter Sq., Cambridge (✆ **617/492-6900,** Mon–Fri 11:30am–10pm, Sat–Sun 5–10pm, Sun brunch 11:30am–2:30pm; T: Red Line to Porter).

Moderate

For after-dinner dessert and coffee, head to **Finale** (p. 266), 1306 Beacon St., Coolidge Corner, Brookline (✆ **617/232-3233;** www.finaledesserts.com).

La Verdad Taqueria Mexicana MEXICAN Let's cut to the chase: The dining room here is a noisy eyesore, the service far from polished, the food a bit pricey (five bucks for chips and salsa, really?), and I couldn't care less. La Verdad serves the best fish tacos in Boston, one of 12 outstanding taco options that include grilled skirt steak, *carnitas* (pork), pork adobo, chorizo and sweet potato, and duck with fig marmalade. To start, skip the pricey chips and opt for incredible grilled corn coated in garlic mayonnaise, chile powder, and crumbled *cotija* cheese. To finish, skip dessert—I honestly can't recommend any of them—and order another margarita. Try not to come here before or after a Red Sox game or a big show at the House of Blues, when it's painfully crowded and loud, even in the outdoor seating area.

1 Lansdowne St. (at. Ipswich St.). 📞 **617/421-9595** (restaurant) or 617/351-2580 (taqueria). www.laverdadtaqueria.com. Reservations recommended at dinner. Main courses $9–$19 (most under $13). AE, DISC, MC, V. Restaurant Tues–Thurs 4–11pm; Fri 4pm–midnight; Sat 11am–midnight. Taqueria Tues–Thurs 11am–1am; Fri–Sat 11am–2am. T: Green Line B, C, or D to Kenmore, 10-min. walk.

Inexpensive

Zaftigs Delicatessen DELI/AMERICAN The magical phrase "breakfast served all day" might be enough to lure you to this bustling restaurant, but even breakfast haters will be happy at Zaftigs. The name, Yiddish for "pleasingly plump," is no joke—portions are more than generous. Try fluffy pancakes, challah French toast, or a terrific omelet. They share the menu with wonderful overstuffed deli sandwiches as well as entrees that seem basic but demonstrate a certain flair. Roasted chicken is juicy and flavorful, meatloaf and gravy equally enjoyable. The knock on Boston-area deli food is that it's not New York (well, duh), but the deli items here are more than acceptable. The gefilte fish is light, citrus twinkles in the blintz filling, and—the true test—the chicken soup is excellent. Weekend lunch here is comically crowded; be early or late, or expect to wait a while.

335 Harvard St. (btw. Babcock and Stedman sts.), Brookline. 📞 **617/975-0075.** www.zaftigs. com. Reservations recommended at dinner; limited number accepted. Main courses $8–$17; sandwiches and burgers $8–$17; breakfast items $4–$17 (most under $12). AE, DISC, MC, V. Daily 8am–10pm. T: Green Line C to Coolidge Corner.

THE GREAT OUTDOORS: alfresco DINING

Cambridge is a better destination for outdoor dining than Boston, where an alarming number of tables sit unpleasantly close to busy traffic, but both cities offer agreeable spots to lounge under the sun or stars.

Across the street from the Charles River near Kendall Square, both restaurant patios at the **Royal Sonesta Hotel,** 5 Cambridge Pkwy. (📞 **617/491-3600**), have great views. The hotel's **ArtBar** is casual; **Dante** is fancier. On one of Harvard Square's main drags, **Shay's Pub & Wine Bar,** 58 John F. Kennedy St. (📞 **617/864-9161**), has a small, lively seating area. More peaceful are the patios at **Henrietta's Table** (p. 124) and **Oleana** (p. 128).

On the other side of the river, try the airy terrace at **Miel** (📞 **617/217-**

5151), in the InterContinental Boston hotel, which overlooks Fort Point Channel. Most bars and restaurants in **Faneuil Hall Marketplace** offer outdoor seating and great people-watching. In the Back Bay, Newbury Street is similarly diverting; a good vantage point is **Stephanie's on Newbury,** 190 Newbury St. (📞 **617/236-0990**). A popular shopping stop and after-work hangout is the **Parish Cafe and Bar,** 361 Boylston St. (📞 **617/247-4777**), where the sandwich menu is a "greatest hits" roster of top local chefs' creations.

CAMBRIDGE

The dining scene in Cambridge, as in Boston, offers something for everyone, from penny-pinching students to the tycoons many of them aspire to become. The Red Line runs from Boston to Harvard Square, and many of the restaurants listed here are within walking distance of the square; others (including a couple of real finds over the Somerville border) are under the heading "Outside Harvard Square."

Harvard Square & Vicinity

A brilliant idea cooked up by a pair of Harvard Business School students, **Finale** (p. 266), 30 Dunster St. (© **617/441-9797**), specializes in dessert.

VERY EXPENSIVE

Upstairs on the Square ★★ AMERICAN Overlooking a little park, Upstairs on the Square is the perfect combination of comfort food and fine dining. It consists of two lovely spaces. The second-floor Monday Club Bar dining room is a relaxed yet romantic space where firelight flickers on jewel-toned walls. The food—unusual salads and sandwiches, pizza (at lunch), fried chicken, inventive pastas, steak with ever-changing versions of potatoey goodness—is homey and satisfying, and the bar is a tweedy Cambridge scene. The top-floor Soirée Room, all pinks and golds under a low, mirrored ceiling, is the place for that big anniversary dinner. The menu is enjoyably old-fashioned, with inventive starters and straightforward main courses (olive oil–poached salmon, pork loin with caraway-roasted bacon). Tasting menus, for vegetarians and carnivores, let the kitchen show off. In both rooms, you'll find outstanding wine selections and desserts.

91 Winthrop St. (at John F. Kennedy St.). © **617/864-1933.** www.upstairsonthesquare.com. Reservations recommended. Monday Club Bar main courses $13–$29; prix-fixe lunch $20. Soirée Room main courses $23–$34; tasting menus $72–$95. AE, DC, DISC, MC, V. Monday Club Bar Mon–Sat 11am–3pm, Sun–Thurs 5–10pm, Fri–Sat 5–11pm (bar open until 1am); Sun brunch 10am–3pm; afternoon tea Sat 2–4pm. Soirée Room Tues–Thurs 5–10pm; Fri–Sat 5:30–11pm. Validated and valet parking available. T: Red Line to Harvard.

EXPENSIVE

There's a **Legal Sea Foods** (p. 101) in the Charles Hotel courtyard, 20 University Rd. (© **617/491-9400**).

Henrietta's Table ★★ NEW ENGLAND Before it was a cliché, "sophisticated comfort food" was a great idea, and Henrietta's Table does it exactly right. Decorated in upscale farmhouse style, the restaurant serves deceptively simple food—baked scrod, roasted chicken, Yankee pot roast, and so on—made with fresh, usually local, often organic provisions. Complementing top-of-the-line meats, fish, and poultry are terrific breads and an impressive variety of gorgeous produce, prepared to let the quality of the ingredients take center stage. I especially enjoy the bounteous salads and tasty desserts, but try any dish with ingredients you like: Mysterious additions aren't a problem here. Given a choice, go for lunch over "supper," when service can be scattered and a la carte side dishes can run up the bill. There's seasonal outdoor seating in the pleasant courtyard.

In the Charles Hotel, 1 Bennett St. (at Eliot St.). © **617/661-5005.** www.henriettastable.com. Reservations recommended. Main courses $13–$20 at lunch, $15–$23 at dinner; "yard sale" dinner (Sun–Thurs) $25 for 2 courses, $32 for 3 courses. AE, DC, MC, V. Mon–Fri 6:30–11am; Sat 7–11am;

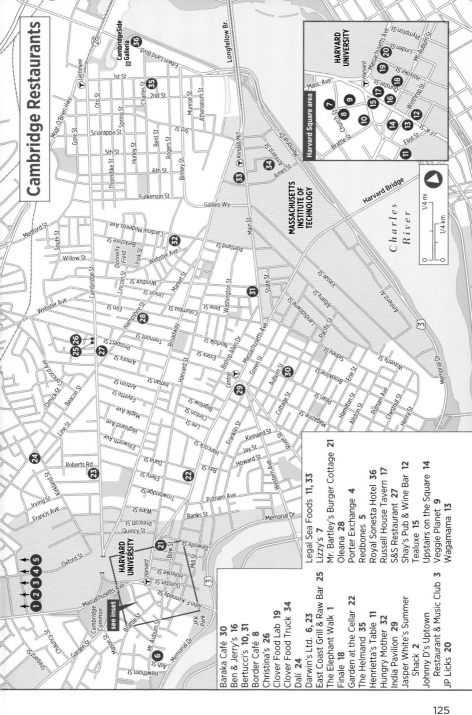

Cambridge Restaurants

CambridgeSide Galleria

HARVARD UNIVERSITY

Harvard Square area

MASSACHUSETTS INSTITUTE OF TECHNOLOGY

Charles River

Harvard Bridge

1/4 mi
1/4 km

see inset

HARVARD UNIVERSITY

Baraka Café **30**
Ben & Jerry's **16**
Bertucci's **10, 31**
Border Café **8**
Christina's **26**
Clover Food Lab **19**
Clover Food Truck **34**
Dalí **24**
Darwin's Ltd. **6, 23**
East Coast Grill & Raw Bar **25**
The Elephant Walk **1**
Finale **18**
Garden at the Cellar **22**
The Helmand **35**
Henrietta's Table **11**
Hungry Mother **32**
India Pavilion **29**
Jasper White's Summer Shack **2**
Johnny D's Uptown Restaurant & Music Club **3**
JP Licks **20**

Legal Sea Foods **11, 33**
Lizzy's **7**
Mr. Bartley's Burger Cottage **21**
Oleana **28**
Porter Exchange **4**
Redbones **5**
Royal Sonesta Hotel **36**
Russell House Tavern **17**
S&S Restaurant **27**
Shay's Pub & Wine Bar **12**
Tealuxe **15**
Upstairs on the Square **14**
Veggie Planet **9**
Wagamama **13**

Sun 7–10:30am; daily noon–3pm (Sat a la carte brunch; Sun buffet brunch); daily 5:30–10pm. Valet and validated parking available. T: Red Line to Harvard.

Russell House Tavern ★ NEW AMERICAN This cavernous gastropub seems to be trying to be all things to (almost) all people, and somewhat improbably succeeding. In the heart of Harvard Square, Russell House Tavern is popular with everyone from starving students to picky parents to committed locavores. Try a craft cocktail and some perfect oysters. Split a pizza topped with fantastic house-made sausage. Savor a locally sourced salad or the signature poached-and-deep-fried egg (much better than it sounds). Then dig into short rib "Wellington," a potpie with a lid of puff pastry covering luscious beef, apples, and mushrooms, or simple grilled fish with yummy garlic-herb mayonnaise. If the menu has a weak spot, it's heavy desserts; the trio of sprightly fruit sorbets is a perky exception. Seating is in the street-level bar, on the patio, or in the huge downstairs dining room. All are loud at busy times.

14 John F. Kennedy St. (at Brattle St.). ✆ **617/500-3055.** www.russellhousecambridge.com. Reservations recommended at dinner. Main courses $9–$14 at lunch, $11–$39 (most less than $25) at dinner; pizzas $10–$13. AE, DC, MC, V. Daily 11am–11pm (late-night menu Sun–Wed until midnight, Thurs–Sat until 1am); brunch Sat–Sun until 4pm. T: Red Line to Harvard.

MODERATE

Border Café TEX-MEX/CAJUN This Harvard Square hangout has been packing 'em in since 1987 with generous portions of tasty food that goes well with beer and margaritas. Patrons loiter at the bar for hours, enhancing the festival atmosphere. Finally seated, you'll probably have to shout your order. Try an excellent chorizo appetizer, quesadillas (shrimp and crawfish is delectable), tacos, or popcorn shrimp. Fajitas for one or two, sizzling noisily, are a popular choice. The menu features plenty of vegetarian options, and the staff keeps the chips—fried after you order them—and fresh house-made salsa coming. Set aside a couple of

 The Scoop on Ice Cream

No less an expert than Ben Cohen of Ben & Jerry's has described Boston as "a great place for ice cream." That goes for Cambridge, too—residents of both cities famously defy even the most frigid weather to get their fix. I like Cambridge better: Try **JP Licks,** 1312 Massachusetts Ave. (✆ 617/492-1001; www.jplicks. com); **Ben & Jerry's,** in the Garage mall, 36 John F. Kennedy St. (✆ 617/864-2828; www.benjerry.com); or **Lizzy's,** 29 Church St. (✆ 617/354-2911; www. lizzysicecream.com)—all in Harvard Square—or **Christina's,** 1255 Cambridge St., Inman Square (✆ 617/492-7021; www.christinasicecream.com). Favorite Boston destinations include **Emack &**

Bolio's, 290 Newbury St., Back Bay (✆ 617/536-7127; www.emackand bolios.com), and 255 State St., across from the New England Aquarium (✆ 617/367-0220); and **JP Licks,** 352 Newbury St., Back Bay (✆ 617/236-1666), and 659 Centre St., Jamaica Plain (✆ 617/524-6740). **Ben & Jerry's** also has stores in Boston at the Prudential Center, 800 Boylston St. (✆ 617/266-0767); 174 Newbury St., Back Bay (✆ 617/536-5456); and 20 Park Plaza, a block from the Public Garden (✆ 617/426-0890). Check the JP Licks and Emack & Bolio's websites for addresses of locations in Somerville and Brookline.

5

Cambridge

WHERE TO EAT

126

hours, get into a party mood, and ask to be seated downstairs if you want to be able to hear your companions. *Tip for parents:* Although there's no children's menu, this place is great for kids, but only if you eat early. (You do that anyway, right?)

32 Church St. (at Palmer St.). ☏ **617/864-6100.** www.bordercafe.com. Reservations not accepted. Main courses $7–$18. AE, MC, V. Daily 11am–11pm. T: Red Line to Harvard.

Garden at the Cellar ★★ AMERICAN The Boston area's first gastropub is a tiny place with a huge following. Local, sustainable ingredients and the bounty of his family's herb farm go into Chef Will Gilson's seasonal cuisine, which is perfect for sharing. Try chickpea fries, split a plain or fancy flatbread, divide a couple of crackling-fresh salads with some of those family herbs, and you might not have room for an entree; let the friendly servers help you decide how much food is enough. Eating here is a bit of an ordeal—you'll probably have to wait at the bar for one of the dozen tables along one wall of a slightly dressed-up bar, and you can't have dessert because the restaurant doesn't serve it—but don't be surprised if you find yourself trying to figure out how to get back here again as soon as possible.

991 Massachusetts Ave. (at Dana St.). ☏ **617/230-5880.** www.gardenatthecellar.com. Reservations not accepted. Main courses $9–$13 at lunch, $17–$25 at dinner; small plates, appetizers, and flatbreads $5–$13. MC, V. Tues–Sat 11:30am–2:30pm; Sun–Mon 5–10pm; Tues–Sat 5–11pm; Sun brunch 11am–2:30pm. T: Red Line to Central or Harvard, 10-min. walk.

INEXPENSIVE

Clover Food Lab ★ VEGETARIAN/VEGAN Clover specializes in local, organic-when-possible vegetarian and vegan-friendly food, but you might not notice. This cheery place lets you feel virtuous without sacrificing flavor or spending a fortune. The regularly changing menu includes soups, salads, rosemary fries, and sandwiches on whole-wheat pita. Chickpea fritter (falafel, basically) is the signature sandwich, but consider barbecued seitan—wheat gluten dressed up with sauce so good, you won't miss the meat. Besides terrific coffee and tea, the drinks menu features delicious fresh-squeezed juices, lemonades, and housemade soda. The brainchild of an MIT and Harvard grad who gave up management consulting to work at Burger King (as research), Clover started as a food truck; it now has two, at MIT and in Boston. Visit the website or check Twitter (@cloverfoodtruck) to learn more about this eco-conscious, employee-empowering phenomenon. Or just worry about whether there are any cookies left.

7 Holyoke St. (off Mass. Ave.). ☏ **617/640-1884.** www.cloverfoodtruck.com. All items $5 or less. MC, V. Daily 7am–10pm. T: Red Line to Harvard.

Mr. Bartley's Burger Cottage ★★ AMERICAN Great burgers and incomparable onion rings make Bartley's a perennial favorite with a cross-section of Cambridge. In increasingly generic Harvard Square, it's a beacon of originality. Founded in 1960, this family business is a crowded, high-ceilinged room (there's also a small outdoor seating area) plastered with signs, posters, and memorabilia. Burgers bear the names of local and national celebrities, notably political figures; the names change, but the ingredients stay the same.

Anything you can think of to put on your personal 7 ounces of house-ground beef is available, from American cheese to grilled pineapple. Good meatless dishes include veggie burgers, huge salads, and creamy, garlicky hummus. Bartley's also serves sandwiches and comfort-food dinners, and it's one of the only places around that still serves a real raspberry lime rickey (raspberry syrup, lime juice, lime wedges, and club soda).

1246 Massachusetts Ave. (btw. Plympton and Bow sts.). ☎ **617/354-6559.** www.bartleys
burgers.com. Burgers $10–$14; main courses, salads, and sandwiches $5–$9; children's menu
$4–$5. No credit cards. Mon–Sat 11am–9pm. Closed Memorial Day, July 4, Labor Day, Dec 25–
Jan 1. T: Red Line to Harvard.

Veggie Planet ★ PIZZA/VEGETARIAN/VEGAN Don't let the virtuous slant
of Veggie Planet's menu put you off—this is tasty, flavorful food that happens
to be (mostly) good for you. The subterranean restaurant in the legendary coffeehouse and folk club has an unusual specialty: your choice of organic pizza
dough, brown rice, or coconut rice, topped with combinations of ingredients.
Some—tomatoes, spinach, and cheese—you'd expect to see on pizza; others, like
zesty peanut curry or black beans, salsa, and pepper jack cheese, you might not.
There's no meat, and dairy only if you want it. Salads, soups, and tasty desserts
round out the menu, which features natural and fair-trade soft drinks in addition
to beer and wine.

In Club Passim, 47 Palmer St. (at Church St., 1 block from Mass. Ave.). ☎ **617/661-1513.** www.
veggieplanet.net. Main courses $7–$11; children's menu $3–$6. No credit cards. Mon–Sat
11:30am–10:30pm; Sun 11am–10:30pm (brunch until 3pm). T: Red Line to Harvard.

Outside Harvard Square

VERY EXPENSIVE

East Coast Grill & Raw Bar ★★★ SEAFOOD/BARBECUE Huge portions, a
dizzying menu, and funky decor have made the East Coast Grill madly popular since
1985. Just walking into the colorful, noisy restaurant is exciting. The kitchen handles fresh seafood (an encyclopedic variety), barbecue, and grilled fish and meats
with equal authority and imagination, and no wonder: Founder Chris Schlesinger is
a nationally recognized expert on grilling and spicy food. To start, consider the raw-
bar offerings, or try the sublime fried oysters. The seafood entrees are exceptional—
always check the specials board, but consider shrimp and scallops over ginger-garlic
noodles with perfect sesame-chile spinach. Barbecue comes on abundant platters in
three styles: Texas beef, Memphis spareribs, and North Carolina pork. Vegetarians
can opt for the "all-vegetable experience of the day." Desserts are above average, but
if you've played your cards right, you won't have room.

1271 Cambridge St. (off Prospect St.), Inman Sq. ☎ **617/491-6568.** www.eastcoastgrill.net. Reservations accepted only Sun–Thurs for parties of 5 or more. Main courses $16–$30; fresh seafood
market price. AE, DISC, MC, V. Sun–Thurs 5:30–10pm; Fri–Sat 5:30–10:30pm; Sun brunch 11am–
2:30pm. Validated parking available. T: Red Line to Central, then a 10-min. walk on Prospect St.,
or Red Line to Harvard, then no. 69 (Harvard-Lechmere) bus to Inman Sq.

Oleana ★★ MEDITERRANEAN The wonderful food and welcoming atmosphere make Oleana, a casual neighborhood place outside Inman Square, one of
the best restaurants in the Boston area. The seasonal menu, which features cuisine typical of and inspired by the Mediterranean—not just the usual suspects;
Turkey and Armenia figure in—relies on fresh ingredients and unusual flavors.
Tempting aromas signal the arrival of striped bass with black garlic–tahini sauce,
which might land next to a plate of veal sausage with beans, pumpkin, and feta.
A signature offering is the vegetarian tasting menu, which leaves even carnivores
happy. Portions are generous, and the dessert menu is heavy on house-made ice
cream. In warm weather, there's seating on the peaceful patio; it can't be reserved, so try to eat early.

134 Hampshire St. (off Elm St.), Inman Sq. ℂ **617/661-0505.** www.oleanarestaurant.com. Reservations recommended; not accepted for patio. Main courses $22–$30; vegetable tasting menu $40. AE, MC, V. Sun–Thurs 5:30–10pm; Fri–Sat 5:30–11pm. Free parking. T: Red Line to Central, then a 10-min. walk.

EXPENSIVE

There's a **Legal Sea Foods** (p. 101) at 5 Cambridge Center, Kendall Sq. (ℂ **617/864-3400**). The **Elephant Walk** (p. 122) has a branch outside Porter Square, at 2067 Massachusetts Ave. (ℂ **617/492-6900**).

Dalí ★★ TAPAS/SPANISH This festive restaurant is noisy and inconvenient, accepts only limited reservations, and still fills nightly with people cheerfully waiting for a table. The payoff is authentic tapas—little plates of hot or cold creations that burst with flavor. Entrees include excellent paella, but most diners come with friends and explore the tapas offerings. Each is enough for three or four people to have a good-sized taste. They include *patatas ali-oli* (garlic potatoes), *albóndigas de salmón* (salmon balls with caper sauce), and *lomito al cabrales* (pork tenderloin with blue cheese), plus monthly specials. The helpful staff sometimes seems rushed but supplies plenty of bread for sopping up juices and sangria for washing it all down. Finish with "ubiquitous flan" or luscious *tarta de chocolates.*

415 Washington St. (at Beacon St.), Somerville. ℂ **617/661-3254.** www.dalirestaurant.com. Reservations recommended; accepted Sun–Thurs until 6:30pm, Fri until 6pm, Sat at 5:30pm. Tapas $4.50–$16 (most less than $10); main courses $24–$26; late-night menu $4.50–$9. AE, DC, MC, V. Mon–Sat 5:30–11pm; Sun noon–11pm. Bar serves food until 12:30am. T: Red Line to Harvard, then follow Kirkland St. to intersection of Washington and Beacon sts. (20-min. walk or $6 cab ride).

Hungry Mother ★ SOUTHERN/CONTEMPORARY AMERICAN Seasonal produce, top-quality pork, plenty of butter—Southern food and French technique are made for each other. They meet at this casual little place, one of the Boston area's most reliable neighborhood restaurants. Hungry Mother's menu changes with the season, emphasizing local and sustainable ingredients. That translates to an unforgettable appetizer of Maine shrimp and grits with chunks of house-made tasso ham, super-crispy cornmeal crusts on green tomatoes and delectable catfish, pork shoulder stewed in bourbon and served with one chewy rib. Desserts are more Southern than French; if sweets aren't your thing, you might be better off with something from the inventive drinks menu. As for the name, it's a happy coincidence—chef and co-owner Barry Maiden is from Virginia, near the state park of the same name.

233 Cardinal Medeiros Ave. (at Bristol St., 1 block from Hampshire St.), Kendall Sq. ℂ **617/499-0090.** www.hungrymothercambridge.com. Reservations recommended. Main courses $19–$25; late-night menu $3–$11. AE, DC, DISC, MC, V. Tues–Sun 5–10pm; late-night menu 10pm–12:30am. Validated parking available. T: Red Line to Kendall/MIT, then 10-min. walk.

Jasper White's Summer Shack ★★ ☺ SEAFOOD An enormous space with a giant lobster tank, the Summer Shack feels like an overgrown seaside clam shack—but nationally renowned chef Jasper White makes it something more. All the basics are here: raw bar, excellent fries, lobster rolls, corn dogs, fantastic tuna burgers, and much more. Turn to the specials and the aptly named "big bucks lobster" section of the menu for foodie favorites like wok-seared lobster with ginger and scallions or steamed mussels in wine-and-herb broth. When it's full, this is one of the loudest restaurants in the Boston area. Arrive early, and ask to sit on the second level; it's just a few steps up, but much quieter.

The Summer Shack in Boston's **Back Bay** is especially popular before and after Red Sox games and Symphony performances.

149 Alewife Brook Pkwy. (at Cambridgepark Dr., opposite Alewife Station). ✆ **617/520-9500.** www.summershackrestaurant.com. Reservations recommended at dinner. Main courses $8–$36 (most $25 or less); sandwiches $5–$15; lobster and specials market price. AE, DISC, MC, V. Mon–Thurs 11:30am–9:30pm (lunch menu until 5pm); Fri 11:30am–10:30pm (lunch menu until 5pm); Sat noon–10:30pm; Sun noon–9pm. Free parking. T: Red Line to Alewife. Also at 50 Dalton St. (at Scotia St., 1 block from Boylston St.), Boston (✆ **617/867-9955**), Apr–Oct Sun–Wed 11:30am–10pm, Thurs–Sat 11:30am–11pm; Nov–Mar Mon–Wed 5–10pm, Thurs–Fri 5–11pm, Sat 11:30am–11pm, Sun 11:30am–10pm.

MODERATE

Besides being a magnet for music fans, **Johnny D's Uptown Restaurant & Music Club** (p. 270), in Somerville's Davis Square, is a good stop for a meal, especially if you're a vegetarian or want to keep one happy.

Baraka Café ★ ALGERIAN/TUNISIAN/MEDITERRANEAN On a run-down side street off Central Square, Baraka Café is a tiny, aromatic destination for adventurous diners. Flavorful, highly spiced (not necessarily hot) food served in an elaborately decorated dining room makes it a favorite with local foodies. They talk about it as though it's a secret, but one look at the line that forms on weekend evenings tells you it's not. The quality of the food outweighs the drawbacks—no alcohol, cash only, tiny dining room, deliberate service. Start with house-made breads and appetizers such as spicy *merguez* sausage and *bedenjal mechoui* (Algerian baba ghanouj, more or less). Main courses include fantastic couscous, fork-tender lamb chops, and eggplant stuffed with a tasty concoction of olives, spinach, scallions, and two cheeses. Be sure to ask about daily specials, which show off the kitchen's considerable abilities better than the limited regular menu.

80½ Pearl St. (at William St., 3½ blocks from Massachusetts Ave.), Central Sq. ✆ **617/868-3951.** www.barakacafe.com. Reservations not accepted. Main courses $5–$9 at lunch, $9–$16 at dinner. No credit cards. Tues–Sat 11:30am–3pm; Tues–Sun 5:30–10pm. T: Red Line to Central.

The Helmand ★★ 🍴 AFGHAN The Helmand, named for the region and river in Afghanistan, is low-profile yet always crowded. The elegant setting near the CambridgeSide Galleria mall belies the reasonable prices. Afghan food has elements of Middle Eastern, Indian, and Pakistani cuisine, with many vegetarian options; meat is often one element rather than the centerpiece of a dish. To start, try baked pumpkin topped with spicy ground meat sauce or *aushak*, "Afghan ravioli" filled with leeks or potatoes with a sauce of either meat or split peas and carrots. The grilled entrees are fine, but I prefer homier dishes such as a larger portion of those irresistible *aushak* or *kourma challow*, an excellent mélange of lamb, potatoes, onion, tomatoes, and green beans. Every meal comes with fluffy bread made fresh in the wood-fired brick oven. Service could be more attentive, but with food this good, that's a minor quibble.

143 First St. (at Bent St.). ✆ **617/492-4646.** www.helmandrestaurant.com. Reservations recommended. Main courses $13–$23. AE, MC, V. Sun–Thurs 5–10pm; Fri–Sat 5–11pm. T: Green Line to Lechmere.

Redbones ★ ☺ BARBECUE Geographically, this raucous restaurant is in Somerville, but in spirit it's on a Southern back road. Barbecued ribs (Memphis-, Texas-, and Arkansas-style), smoked beef brisket, fried Louisiana catfish, and grilled chicken come with traditional side dishes such as coleslaw and beans. The chummy staff can help you choose sweet, hot, mild, or vinegar sauce. The best non-barbecue dish is succulent buffalo shrimp, swimming in hot sauce. Portions are large, so pace yourself. Don't miss the appetizers and sides—catfish "catfingers," succotash, corn pudding, and collard greens, just to name a few; if you're with enough other people, the appetizer samplers are a good deal. The only less-than-tasty dish I've ever had here was watery broccoli. The beer selection is huge, and there's valet bike parking. Given a choice, sit upstairs—Underbones, downstairs, is a noisy bar.

55 Chester St. (off Elm St.), Somerville. ✆ **617/628-2200.** www.redbones.com. Reservations accepted only Sun–Thurs before 7pm for parties of 10 or more. Main courses $9–$21; sandwiches $6–$11; children's menu $5. AE, MC, V. Mon–Thurs 11:30am–10:30pm; Fri–Sat 11:30am–11pm; Sun 11am–10:30pm (brunch until 4pm); late-night menu daily until 12:30am. T: Red Line to Davis.

INEXPENSIVE

Clover Food Lab (p. 127) sends a **Clover Food Truck** to MIT, where it parks at 20 Carleton St. (btw. Amherst and Main sts.), weekdays from 8am to 7pm.

The food court on the lower level of the **Porter Exchange mall,** 1815 Massachusetts Ave., Porter Square, is home to half a dozen or so Japanese businesses that attract expats from all over the Boston area. The super-authentic dining options are mostly fast-food counters with small seating areas in front; wander around until you see a dish that strikes your fancy. All open in the late morning and close by 9pm. Start at **Cafe Mami** (✆ 617/547-9130), but also check out—in rough order of preference—**Sapporo Ramen** (✆ 617/876-4805), **Tampopo** (✆ 617/868-5457), and **Ittyo Restaurant** (✆ 617/354-5944; www.ittyo.com). Afterward, hit **Japonaise Bakery** (✆ 617/547-5531; www.japonaisebakery.com) for French- and Japanese-style pastries, notably the items that incorporate *azuki* (red bean) cream.

India Pavilion 🍴 INDIAN The oldest Indian restaurant in the Boston area opened in 1979 and remains a favorite for its flavorful cuisine, lunch buffet, and reasonable prices. Among excellent renditions of now-familiar northern Indian favorites—*rogan josh* (lamb in spiced tomato sauce), chicken tikka masala (in tomato cream sauce), *saag paneer* (spinach with cheese)—are less common options such as eggplant-based *baingan bharta* and Peshwari nan (stuffed with coconut, almonds, raisins, and apricots). If that actually doesn't sound familiar, the house dinners for two and the *thali* (literally, "plate") selections make good introductions. As at most Indian restaurants, vegetarians will be happy, and so will their carnivore friends.

17 Central Sq. (at Green St.). ✆ **617/547-7463.** www.royalbharatinc.com. Lunch buffet $8; main courses $8–$19 (most less than $14). AE, DC, MC, V. Daily noon–11pm (lunch until 3pm). T: Red Line to Central.

S&S Restaurant ★★ DELI *Es* is Yiddish for "eat," and this Cambridge classic is as straightforward as its name ("eat and eat"). Founded in 1919 by the great-grandmother of the current owners, it draws huge weekend brunch crowds, and it's worth a visit during the week, too. With lots of light wood and plants, it looks contemporary, but the brunch offerings are huge portions of traditional dishes such as pancakes, waffles, and omelets. The bagels and cinnamon rolls are among the best in the area; you'll also find traditional deli items (corned beef, pastrami, tongue, potato pancakes, and blintzes), yummy house-made corned beef hash, and breakfast anytime. At dinner, comfort food—barbecue, fresh seafood, chicken parmigiana—prevails. Be early for brunch, or plan to spend part of your Saturday or Sunday standing around people-watching and getting hungry—I'll be right there with you.

1334 Cambridge St. (at Oak St.; back entrance off Hampshire St.), Inman Sq. ✆ **617/354-0777.** www.sandsrestaurant.com. Main courses $4–$19; brunch main courses $10–$16. AE, MC, V. Mon–Wed 7am–10pm; Thurs–Fri 7am–11pm; Sat 8am–11pm; Sun 8am–10pm; brunch Sat–Sun until 4pm. Free parking; ask cashier for token on weekends. T: Red Line to Harvard, then bus 69 (Harvard-Lechmere) to Inman Sq.; or Red Line to Central, then a 10-min. walk on Prospect St.

PRACTICAL INFORMATION

RESERVATIONS At restaurants that take reservations, it's always a good idea to make them, particularly for dinner. To make reservations at any hour, visit **www.opentable.com**, which handles many local restaurants. If you strike out, consider eating at the bar. It won't be as comfortable as the dining room, but the food and service tend to be roughly comparable.

WHEN TO DINE Boston-area restaurants are far less busy early in the week than they are Friday through Sunday. If you're flexible about when you indulge in fine cuisine and when you go for pizza and a movie, choose the low-budget option on the weekend and pamper yourself on a weeknight. Note that many chefs have Sunday or Monday (or both) off. If you plan to eat at a particular restaurant to check out a specific chef, call ahead to make sure he or she is working that night.

BARGAINS **Lunch** is an excellent, economical way to check out a fancy restaurant. At higher-end restaurants that offer it (many don't), you can get a sense of the dinner menu without breaking the bank. To get a bargain at dinner, investigate **group-buying sites** such as Groupon (www.groupon.com), Living Social (www.livingsocial.com), and BuyWithMe (www.buywithme. com). Sign up for Boston alerts when you start planning your trip, and you may land a great deal.

DRESS CODES As you might expect in a city overrun with college students and tourists, just about anything goes. Even at pricier establishments, being clean and neat suffices, but you—and the couple at the next table who just got engaged—will probably feel more comfortable if you change out of the shorts and sneakers you wore for a day of sightseeing.

INGREDIENTS At almost every restaurant—trendy or classic, expensive or cheap, American (whatever that is) or ethnic—you'll find seafood on the menu. A quick introduction: **Scrod** or **schrod** is a generic term for fresh white-fleshed fish, usually served in filets. Local shellfish includes Ipswich and Essex **clams,** Atlantic (usually Maine) **lobsters,** Wellfleet and Island Creek **oysters, scallops, mussels,** and **shrimp.** If you're worried about overfishing, visit www.montereybayaquarium.org and download the Monterey Bay Aquarium's pocket guide to buying and eating fish in the Northeast.

    Lobster ordered boiled or steamed usually comes with a plastic bib, drawn butter (for dipping), a nutcracker (for the claws and tail), and a pick (for the legs). Restaurants price lobsters by the pound; you'll typically pay at least $15 to $20 for a "chicken" (1- to 1¼-lb.) lobster, and more for the bigger specimens. If you want someone else to do the work, lobster is available in a "roll" (lobster-salad sandwich), stuffed and baked or broiled, in or over pasta, in a "pie" (casserole), in salad, and in bisque.

Well-made **New England clam chowder** is studded with fresh clams and thickened with cream. Recipes vary, but they *never* include tomatoes. (Tomatoes go in Manhattan clam chowder.) If you want clams but not soup, many places serve **steamers,** or soft-shell clams cooked in the shell, as an appetizer or main dish. More common are hard-shell clams—**littlenecks** (small) or **cherrystones** (medium-size)—served raw, like oysters.

Traditional **Boston baked beans,** which date from colonial days, when cooking on the Sabbath was forbidden, earned Boston the nickname "Beantown." Durgin-Park (p. 110) does an excellent rendition.

Finally, **Boston cream pie** is golden layer cake sandwiched around custard and topped with chocolate glaze—no cream, no pie.

RESTAURANTS BY CUISINE

AFGHAN
The Helmand ★★ ($$, p. 130)

ALGERIAN
Baraka Café ★ ($$, p. 130)

AMERICAN
The Bristol Lounge ★★ ($$$, p. 119)
Citizen Public House & Oyster
    Bar ★★ ($$$, p. 122)
Garden at the Cellar ★★ ($$, p. 127)
Grill 23 & Bar ★ ($$$$, p. 118)
Hamersley's Bistro ★★★ ($$$$,
    p. 115)
Hungry Mother ★ ($$$, p. 129)
Jacob Wirth Company ($$, p. 114)
Mr. Bartley's Burger Cottage ★★ ($,
    p. 127)
Russell House Tavern ★ ($$$, p. 126)
South End Buttery ($$, p. 116)
Upstairs on the Square ★★ ($$$$,
    p. 124)
Zaftigs Delicatessen ($, p. 123)

BARBECUE
East Coast Grill & Raw Bar ★★★
    ($$$$, p. 128)
Redbones ★ ($$, p. 131)

CAJUN
Border Café ($$, p. 126)

CAMBODIAN
The Elephant Walk ★★ ($$$,
    p. 122)

CANTONESE/SZECHUAN
Peach Farm ★ ($$, p. 114)

DELI
S&S Restaurant ★★ ($, p. 131)
Zaftigs Delicatessen ($, p. 123)

FRENCH
Brasserie Jo ★★ ($$$, p. 119)
The Elephant Walk ★★ ($$$,
    p. 122)
Hamersley's Bistro ★★★ ($$$$,
    p. 115)
Sel de la Terre ★★ ($$$, p. 101)

FUSION
Market ★★★ ($$$$, p. 112)

GERMAN
Jacob Wirth Company ($$, p. 114)

INDIAN
India Pavilion ($, p. 131)

ITALIAN

Artú ($$, p. 106)
Daily Catch ★ ($$$, p. 106)
Davio's Northern Italian
  Steakhouse ★★★ ($$$$, p. 117)
Galleria Umberto Rosticceria ($,
  p. 108)
Giacomo's Ristorante ★★ ($$,
  p. 107)
Grotto ★★ ($$, p. 112)
La Summa ★ ($$, p. 107)
Mamma Maria ★★★ ($$$$, p. 104)
Taranta Cucina Meridionale ★★
  ($$$$, p. 105)

MEDITERRANEAN

Baraka Café ★ ($$, p. 130)
Café Jaffa ($, p. 120)
Oleana ★★ ($$$, p. 128)

MEXICAN

La Verdad Taqueria Mexicana ($$,
  p. 122)

MIDDLE EASTERN

Café Jaffa ($, p. 120)
Sultan's Kitchen ★ ($, p. 110)

NEW ENGLAND

Durgin-Park ★★ ($$, p. 110)
Henrietta's Table ★★ ($$$, p. 124)
Ye Olde Union Oyster House ★ ($$$,
  p. 109)

PERUVIAN

Taranta Cucina Meridionale ★★
  ($$$$, p. 105)

PIZZA

Picco Restaurant ★ ($, p. 117)
Pizzeria Regina ★★ ($, p. 108)
Veggie Planet ★ ($, p. 128)

SANDWICHES

Volle Nolle ★ ($, p. 108)

SEAFOOD

Barking Crab ★ ($$, p. 104)
Daily Catch ★ ($$$, p. 106)
East Coast Grill & Raw Bar ★★★
  ($$$, p. 128)

Giacomo's Ristorante ★★ ($$,
  p. 107)
Jasper White's Summer Shack ★★
  (Cambridge, $$$, p. 129)
Legal Sea Foods ★★★ ($$$,
  p. 101)
Neptune Oyster ★ ($$$, p. 106)
Peach Farm ★ ($$, p. 114)
Ye Olde Union Oyster House ★ ($$$,
  p. 109)

SENEGALESE

Teranga ★★ ($$, p. 116)

SOUTHERN

Hungry Mother ★ ($$$, p. 129)

SPANISH

Dalí ★★ ($$$, p. 129)

STEAKS

Davio's Northern Italian Steakhouse
  ★★★ ($$$$, p. 117)
Grill 23 & Bar ★ ($$$$, p. 118)

TAPAS

Dalí ★★ ($$$, p. 129)

TEX-MEX

Border Café ($$, p. 126)
Fajitas & 'Ritas ★ ($, p. 111)

THAI

Bangkok City ★ ($$, p. 119)

TUNISIAN

Baraka Café ★ ($$, p. 130)

TURKISH

Sultan's Kitchen ★ ($, p. 110)

VEGETARIAN

Clover Food Lab ★ ($, p. 127)
Milk Street Cafe ($, p. 110)
Veggie Planet ★ ($, p. 128)

VENEZUELAN

Orinoco ★ ($$, p. 115)

VIETNAMESE

Xinh Xinh ★★ ($, p. 115)

WHAT TO SEE & DO IN BOSTON

Whether you want to immerse yourself in the colonial era or just cruise around the harbor, you can do it—and plenty more—in Boston. Throw out your preconceptions of the city as an open-air history museum (although that's certainly one of the guises it can assume), and allow your interests to dictate where you go.

It's possible but not advisable to take in most of the major attractions in 2 or 3 days if you don't linger anywhere too long. For a more enjoyable, less rushed visit, plan fewer activities and spend more time on them. For descriptions of suggested itineraries, see p. 42.

The recent economic climate has taken a toll on many cultural institutions. Admissions fees and hours in this chapter are current at press time, but by the time you visit, establishments that rely heavily on corporate and government support may cost a bit more or close a little earlier. Prices for attractions that use fuel, such as tours and cruises, are subject to changes or surcharges depending on the fluctuating energy market. If you're on a tight schedule or budget, check ahead.

Visitors in 2012 will be able to visit a new wing at the **Isabella Stewart Gardner Museum** (p. 141), the museum's first major physical change since 1924. It has a tough act to follow: The neighboring **Museum of Fine Arts** (p. 144) scored a major success with the 2010 opening of its Art of the Americas wing. Renzo Piano designed the new wing of the Gardner as well as the major renovation project that's under way at the **Harvard Art Museums** (p. 178). Two of the three Harvard museums are closed through 2013. *Re-View,* the changing exhibit featuring highlights of all three collections, is up at the one that remains open, the Arthur M. Sackler Museum.

Downtown Boston gained not one but two new visitor centers in 2011. The **Rose Kennedy Greenway Boston Harbor Islands Visitor Center Pavilion** is on the Greenway near the New England Aquarium, not far from the National Park Service's **Faneuil Hall Visitor Center,** on the first floor of the historic building.

At press time, the **Boston Tea Party Ship & Museum** (© 617/269-7150; www.bostonteapartyship.com), which closed after a fire in 2001, was scheduled to reopen in 2012. Chronically delayed plans in place since shortly after the fire called for the construction of two more ships, doubling the size of the museum, and addition of a tearoom. Check at your hotel or call ahead before setting out.

THE TOP ATTRACTIONS

The attractions in this section are easily accessible by **public transportation;** given the difficulty and expense of parking, it's preferable to take the T everywhere. Even the Kennedy Library, which has a large free parking lot, operates a free shuttle bus to and from the Red Line. To maximize your enjoyment, try to

PREVIOUS PAGE: **A bell on the USS *Constitution*.**

Street performers at Faneuil Hall Marketplace.

visit these attractions during relatively slow times. If possible, especially in the summer, sightsee on weekdays; if you're traveling without children, aim for times when school is in session. And if you're in town on a July or August weekend, resign yourself to lines and crowds.

Faneuil Hall Marketplace ★★ ☺ Since Boston's most popular attraction opened in 1976, cities all over the country have imitated the "festival market" concept. Each complex of shops, food counters, restaurants, bars, and public spaces reflects its city, and Faneuil Hall Marketplace is no exception. Its popularity with visitors and suburbanites is so great that you might understandably think the only Bostonians here are employees.

The marketplace includes five buildings—the central three-building complex is on the National Register of Historic Places—set on brick and stone plazas that teem with crowds shopping, eating, performing, cheering for performers, and people-watching. In warm weather, it's busy from early morning until well past dark. **Quincy Market** (you'll also hear the whole complex called by that name) is the three-level Greek revival–style building at the center of the marketplace. It reopened after extensive renovations on August 26, 1976, 150 years after Mayor Josiah Quincy opened the original market. The **South Market building** reopened on August 26, 1977, the **North Market building** on August 26, 1978.

The central corridor of Quincy Market is the food court, where you can find anything from a fresh-shucked oyster to a full Greek dinner to sweets of all sorts. On either side of this building, under glass canopies, are full-service restaurants as well as pushcarts that sell everything from crafts created by New England artisans to hokey souvenirs. Here you'll find a bar that exactly replicates the set of the TV show *Cheers.* In the plaza between the **South Canopy** and the South Market building is an **information kiosk,** and throughout the complex you'll

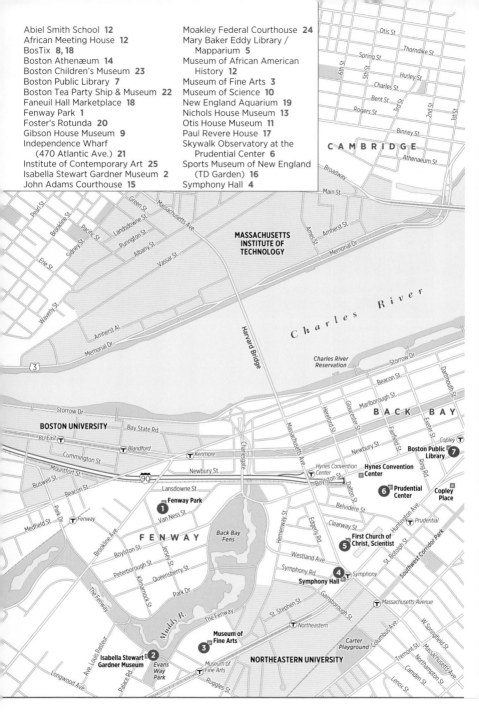

Abiel Smith School **12**
African Meeting House **12**
BosTix **8, 18**
Boston Athenæum **14**
Boston Children's Museum **23**
Boston Public Library **7**
Boston Tea Party Ship & Museum **22**
Faneuil Hall Marketplace **18**
Fenway Park **1**
Foster's Rotunda **20**
Gibson House Museum **9**
Independence Wharf
(470 Atlantic Ave.) **21**
Institute of Contemporary Art **25**
Isabella Stewart Gardner Museum **2**
John Adams Courthouse **15**

Moakley Federal Courthouse **24**
Mary Baker Eddy Library /
Mapparium **5**
Museum of African American
History **12**
Museum of Fine Arts **3**
Museum of Science **10**
New England Aquarium **19**
Nichols House Museum **13**
Otis House Museum **11**
Paul Revere House **17**
Skywalk Observatory at the
Prudential Center **6**
Sports Museum of New England
(TD Garden) **16**
Symphony Hall **4**

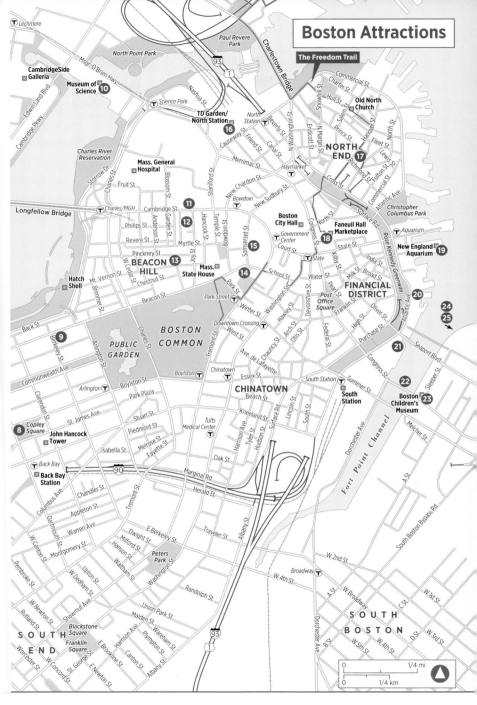

Boston Attractions

The Freedom Trail

find a mix of predictable chain stores and unique shops (see chapter 8). On warm evenings, the tables that spill outdoors from the restaurants and bars fill with people. One constant since the year after the market—the *original* market—opened is **Durgin-Park ★★★** (p. 110), a traditional New England restaurant.

The original **Faneuil Hall ★** sometimes gets lost in the shuffle, but it's well worth a visit. At press time, the first floor was closed for construction of a new National Park Service Visitor Center. See p. 360 for a full description.

Btw. North, Congress, and State sts. and John F. Fitzgerald Surface Rd. ℰ **617/523-1300.** www. faneuilhallmarketplace.com. Marketplace Mon–Sat 10am–9pm; Sun noon–6pm. Food court opens earlier; bars and some restaurants close later. T: Green Line to Government Center, Orange Line to Haymarket or State, or Blue Line to Aquarium or State.

Institute of Contemporary Art ★★ The city's first new art museum in nearly a century, the endlessly fascinating ICA is a work of art in its own right. The cantilevered building—designed by the New York firm Diller Scofidio + Renfro,

LET'S MAKE A deal

As you plan your sightseeing, consider these money-saving options. Check their respective websites for info about buying each pass.

If you concentrate on the included attractions, a **Boston CityPass** (ℰ **888/330-5008;** www.citypass. com) offers great savings. It's a booklet of tickets (so you can go straight to the entrance) to the Museum of Fine Arts, Museum of Science, New England Aquarium, Skywalk Observatory at the Prudential Center, and either the Harvard Museum of Natural History or the John F. Kennedy Library. The price represents a 46% savings for adults who visit all five, and it feels like an even better deal on a steamy day when the line at the aquarium is long. At press time, the cost was $46 for adults, $29 for children 3 to 11, subject to change as admission prices rise. The passes, good for 9 days from first use, also include discounts at other local businesses.

The main competition for CityPass is the **Go Boston Card** (ℰ **800/887-9103;** www.gobostoncard.com). The original Go Boston Card includes admission to 70 Boston-area and New England attractions, plus dining and shopping discounts, a guidebook, and a 2-day trolley pass. If you strategize wisely, this card can be a great value, but make sure you understand the logistics. It costs $50 for 1 day, $75 for 2 days, $96 for 3 days, $135 for 5 days, and $165 for 7 days, with discounts for children and winter travelers (some of the included businesses close in the winter). The **Boston Explorer Pass** lets you select three of the 26 included attractions and is good for 30 days. It costs $45 for adults and $29 for children.

If you're a Bank of America credit or debit card holder, the **Museums on Us** program gets you into cultural institutions around the country free on the first full weekend of each month. Participating establishments in eastern Massachusetts are the Museum of Fine Arts, the Harvard Museum of Natural History, and deCordova Sculpture Park and Museum (p. 297). Visit http://museums.bankofamerica.com for details.

The MBTA's 7-day **LinkPass** (ℰ **877/927-7277** or 617/222-4545; www.mbta.com) can be a bargain—but only if you plan to use public transit often enough. See p. 345.

The Institute of Contemporary Art.

whose work on this landmark project helped boost its growing reputation—juts out above the harbor, affording dizzying views of the water, the waterfront, and the airport. Besides making the museum an instant landmark, the architecture reflects the institution's curatorial philosophy that art is inseparable from everyday life, rather than a singular experience reserved for special occasions and field trips. The ICA showcases 20th- and 21st-century art in every imaginable medium, including film and video, music, literature, and dance. Opened in 2006, the 65,000-square-foot museum gives the institution the space it needs to create a permanent collection for the first time since its founding (under a different name) in 1936. Visitors have already enjoyed works by Louise Bourgeois and Anish Kapoor that wouldn't have fit in (literally or figuratively) elsewhere in Boston, and the schedule of events, concerts, films, and other activities is a joy for anyone with even a passing interest. The cafe overlooks the water and offers outdoor seating in fine weather. The gift shop, the **ICA Store,** stocks a good mix of souvenirs and creative designs.

100 Northern Ave. (off Seaport Blvd. at E. Service Rd.). © **617/478-3100.** www.icaboston.org. Admission $15 adults, $13 seniors, $10 students, free for children 17 and under and those visiting only the cafe. Free to all Thurs after 5pm and to families (up to 2 adults with children 12 and under) last Sat of month Jan–Nov. Sat–Sun, Tues–Wed, and some Mon holidays 10am–5pm; Thurs–Fri 10am–9pm. T: Silver Line SL1/SL2 bus to World Trade Center.

Isabella Stewart Gardner Museum ★★ In early 2012, the Gardner Museum is scheduled to open a gorgeous new wing designed by internationally renowned architect Renzo Piano. Because founder Isabella Stewart Gardner's will forbids changing the arrangement of the museum's content, this is the most significant physical change the institution has ever experienced.

Gardner (1840–1924) was a fascinating character. She was an incorrigible individualist long before strong-willed behavior was acceptable for women in polite Boston society, and her legacy is a treasure for art lovers. "Mrs. Jack" designed this exquisite building in the style of a 15th-century Venetian palace and filled it with

 A Note on Online Ticketing

Many museums and other attractions sell tickets online, subject to a service charge, through their websites or an agency. This can be handy, but it can also cost you some flexibility and perhaps some money. If there's any chance that your plans will change, make sure you **understand the refund policy** before you enter your credit card info—you may not be able to return or exchange prepaid tickets.

The Isabella Stewart Gardner Museum.

European, American, and Asian paintings and sculptures, many chosen with the help of her friend and protégé Bernard Berenson. You'll see works by Titian, Botticelli, Raphael, Rembrandt, Matisse, and Mrs. Gardner's friends James McNeill Whistler and John Singer Sargent. Titian's magnificent **Europa,** which many scholars consider his finest work, is one of the most important Renaissance paintings in the United States.

The original 1903 building, which opened to the public after Mrs. Gardner's death, also holds a glorious hodgepodge of furniture and architectural details imported from European churches and palaces. The *pièce de résistance* is the magnificent skylit courtyard, filled year-round with fresh flowers grown by the museum's horticultural staff. The new wing not only adds gallery space and a concert hall but also gives visitors a closer look at the greenhouses. It will contain the excellent cafe and gift shop.

The celebrated **concert series** (p. 264) will return to the premises after the addition opens; check ahead for information and tickets. For updates, visit **www. buildingproject.gardnermuseum.org**.

280 the Fenway. (© **617/566-1401.** www.gardnermuseum.org. Admission $12 adults, $10 seniors, $5 college students with ID. Free for children 17 and under, adults named Isabella with ID, and adults on their birthdays. Tues–Sun (and some Mon holidays) 11am–5pm. Closed July 4, Thanksgiving, and Dec 25. T: Green Line E to Museum of Fine Arts.

John F. Kennedy Presidential Library and Museum ★★ ☺ The Kennedy era springs to life at this dramatic library, museum, and educational research complex overlooking Dorchester Bay. It captures the 35th president's accomplishments and legacy in video and sound recordings and fascinating displays of memorabilia and photos. Far from being a static experience, it changes regularly,

The John F. Kennedy Presidential Library and Museum.

with temporary shows and reinterpreted displays that highlight and complement the permanent installations. Every day from November 8, 2010, through November 25, 2013, is the 50th anniversary of an event that occurred during the Kennedy administration; check ahead for observances during your visit.

You begin with a 17-minute film narrated by John F. Kennedy—it's eerie for a moment, then perfectly natural. Through skillfully edited audio clips, he discusses his childhood, education, war experience, and early political career. Then you enter the museum to spend as much time as you like on each exhibit. Starting with the 1960 presidential campaign, the displays immerse you in the era. The galleries hold campaign souvenirs, film of Kennedy debating Richard Nixon and delivering his inaugural address, a replica of the Oval Office, gifts from foreign dignitaries, letters, documents, and keepsakes. There's a film about the Cuban Missile Crisis and displays on Attorney General Robert F. Kennedy, First Lady Jacqueline Bouvier Kennedy, the civil rights movement, the Peace Corps, the space program, and the Kennedy family. As the tour winds down, you pass through a darkened chamber where news reports of John Kennedy's assassination and funeral play. The final room, the soaring glass-enclosed pavilion that is the heart of the I. M. Pei design, affords a glorious view of the water and the Boston skyline.

Columbia Point. ⓒ **866/JFK-1960** or 617/514-1600. www.jfklibrary.org. Admission $12 adults, $10 seniors and students with ID, $9 youths 13–17, free for children 12 and under. Surcharges may apply for special exhibitions. Daily 9am–5pm (last film begins at 3:55pm). Closed Jan 1, Thanksgiving, and Dec 25. T: Red Line to JFK/UMass, then take free shuttle bus (every 20 min.). By

More JFK

For details about visiting President Kennedy's birthplace in suburban Brookline, see p. 170.

car, take Southeast Expressway (I-93/Rte. 3) south to exit 15 (Morrissey Blvd./JFK Library), turn left onto Columbia Rd., and follow signs to free parking lot.

Museum of Fine Arts ★★★ ☺ One of the world's great art museums, the MFA works nonstop to become even more accessible and interesting. It earned international headlines in 2010 with the opening of the **Art of the Americas Wing ★★★**, the heart of a quarter-million-square-foot expansion project that transformed the experience of visiting. The design, by Sir Norman Foster of Foster + Partners, incorporates the dramatic 62-foot-high glass-enclosed Shapiro Courtyard and four floors holding 53 galleries. If that sounds overwhelming, even a little planning before you set out will be time well spent. Take advantage of the excellent website to preview the collections, noting pieces and periods that especially interest you.

The Art of the Americas Wing is home to some of the museum's highest-profile works, including Childe Hassam's *Boston Common at Twilight;* Gilbert Stuart's 1796 portrait of George Washington; John Singleton Copley's 1768 portrait of Paul Revere (which looks suspiciously like the Samuel Adams beer logo); several Luminist masterpieces by Fitz Henry Lane; and *The Passage of the Delaware,* an enormous, dramatic painting by Thomas Sully, in a 17-foot-wide frame that had been in storage for over a century before being installed here. The wing holds works from the pre-Columbian period through the mid-1970s, from both North and South America.

To focus exclusively on American art would be to miss out on some of the museum's most magnificent holdings. The MFA is known for its **Impressionist ★★★** paintings (including one of the largest collections of Monets outside of Paris), Asian and Old Kingdom Egyptian collections, classical art, Buddhist temple, and fashion arts. Favorites include Renoir's *Dance at Bougival,* a bronze casting of Edgar Degas's sculpture *Little Dancer,* and Gauguin's *Where Do We Come From? What Are We? Where Are We Going?* There are also outstanding holdings of prints, photographs, furnishings, and decorative arts.

The museum is particularly welcoming to children, who can launch a scavenger hunt, admire the mummies, or participate in family-friendly programs scheduled year-round (and extra offerings during school vacations).

 Spotlight on Sargent

One of the signature installations in the Museum of Fine Arts' new Art of the Americas Wing is a beloved portrait by John Singer Sargent, ***The Daughters of Edward Darley Boit.*** The four little girls—their mother was Mary Louisa Cushing Boit, the subject of her own Sargent portrait, hanging nearby—are depicted in the family apartment in Paris, alongside two huge Japanese vases. The painting hangs on Level 2 of the new wing, next to those very same vases.

Sargent (1856–1925) is a significant presence at the MFA. He created the murals in the **Ruth and Carl J. Shapiro Rotunda,** at the top of the grand staircase inside the Huntington Avenue entrance. Installed in 1921, the mythology-themed work proved so popular that the museum commissioned Sargent to create the adjacent **Colonnade Murals.** In 1925, the night before he was to sail from London to Boston to supervise the installation of the final section, Sargent died in his sleep.

The MFA's new Art of the Americas Wing.

John Singleton Copley's portrait of Paul Revere.

None of this comes cheap: The MFA's adult admission fee (which covers two visits within 10 days) is among the highest in the country. A Boston CityPass or Go Boston Card (see the "Let's Make a Deal" box on p. 140) is a bargain if you plan to visit enough of the other included attractions.

The grand entrances from Huntington Avenue and the Fenway are the main points of public access; after disembarking from the Green Line, walk back about half a block to begin your visit. Pick up a floor plan (available in eight languages) at the Sharf Information Center or take a free **guided tour** (daily except Mon holidays 10:30am and 1:30pm, Wed 6:15pm). For more in-depth information about selected topics, download a multimedia guide ($6) to your smartphone. The sprawling complex encompasses four dining options—cafeteria, two cafes, and fine-dining restaurant—two excellent gift shops, two auditoriums.

Special exhibitions scheduled to coincide with the lifespan of this book include *Jewels, Gems and Treasures: Ancient to Modern* (through Nov 12, 2012), *Degas and the Nude* (through Jan 29, 2012), and *Ellsworth Kelly: Wood Sculpture* (Sept 18, 2011–Mar 4, 2012).

465 Huntington Ave. © **617/267-9300.** www.mfa.org. Admission $20 adults, $18 students and seniors, $7.50 children 7-17 on school days 10am-3pm (otherwise free), free for children 6 and under. Admission good for 2 visits within 10 days. Voluntary contribution ($20 suggested) Wed 4-9:45pm. Free admission to Museum Shop, library, and restaurants. Sat-Tues 10am-4:45pm; Wed-Fri 10am-9:45pm. Closed Jan 1, Patriots' Day, July 4, Thanksgiving, and Dec 25. T: Green Line E to Museum of Fine Arts or Orange Line to Ruggles.

ON top OF THE WORLD

The **Skywalk Observatory at the Prudential Center (pictured below)** ★★, 800 Boylston St. (℃ **617/859-0648;** www.topofthehub.net/sky walk_home.html), offers a 360-degree view of Boston and far beyond. From the enclosed observation deck on the 50th floor of the Prudential Tower, you can see for miles, even (when it's clear) as far as the mountains of New Hampshire to the north and the beaches of Cape Cod to the south. Away from the windows, interactive audiovisual exhibits chronicle the city's history. The admission price includes a narrated audio tour, available in versions targeted to adults and children. *Wings Over Boston,* a dramatic aerial video tour of the city, screens in the on-site theater. Also here are fascinating exhibits, including video presentations about refugees, on the history of immigration to Boston. Call before visiting, because the space sometimes closes for private events. Hours are 10am to 10pm daily (until 8pm Nov–Mar). Admission is $13 for adults, $11 for seniors and college students with ID, and $9 for children 12 and under.

Museum of Science ★★★ ☺ For the ultimate pain-free educational experience, head to the Museum of Science. The demonstrations, experiments, and interactive displays introduce facts and concepts so effortlessly that everyone winds up learning something. Take a couple of hours or a whole day to explore the permanent and temporary exhibits, most of them hands-on and all of them great fun.

Among the 700-plus exhibits, you might meet a dinosaur or a live butterfly, find out how much you'd weigh on the moon, or climb into a space module. Activity centers and exhibits focus on fields of interest—natural history (with live animals), computers, the human body—while others take an interdisciplinary approach. **Investigate!** teaches visitors to think like scientists, formulating questions, finding evidence, and drawing conclusions through activities such as strapping on a skin sensor to measure reactions to stimuli or sifting through an

The Museum of Science.

archaeological site. **Beyond the X-Ray** explores medical-imaging techniques and allows would-be diagnosticians to try to figure out what's ailing their "patients." The **Science in the Park** exhibit introduces the concepts of Newtonian physics through familiar objects such as playground equipment and skateboards. Temporary exhibits change regularly, and just about any **major touring show** (national or international) that focuses on a scientific topic stops here; *A Day in Pompeii*, which includes a dramatic re-creation of the eruption of Mount Vesuvius, opens Oct 2, 2011.

The separate-admission **theaters** are worth planning for. Even if you're skipping the exhibits, try to see a show. If you're making a day of it, buy all your tickets at once, because shows sometimes sell out. The **Mugar Omni Theater ★★★**, which shows IMAX movies, is an intense experience, bombarding

you with images on a five-story domed screen and digital sound. The engulfing sensations and steep pitch of the seating area will have you hanging on for dear life, whether the film is about (for example) tornadoes, whales, or risk-taking. Features change every 4 to 6 months. The **Charles Hayden Planetarium** ★★, which reopened in 2011 after extensive renovations, is now a high-def theater capable of "immersive video" in addition to a great introduction to astronomy. The domed venue has a state-of-the-art digital optics system that allows visitors to see thousands of stars in configurations as much as 10,000 years old, and to experience an astronaut's-eye-view of the earth.

 Network, Socially

Just about every attraction in the Boston area communicates with visitors on **Facebook** and **Twitter**. Friend and follow the establishments that interest you as soon as you start planning your visit—amid schedule changes and other humdrum announcements, you may find information about the exhibition, tour, event, or other offering that winds up being a high point of your trip.

The museum has a terrific gift shop, with toys and games that promote learning without lecturing. The ground-floor Riverview Cafe offers spectacular views of the skyline and the Charles River. There's a parking garage on the premises, but it's on a busy street, and entering and exiting can be harrowing; take the T.

Science Park, off O'Brien Hwy. on bridge btw. Boston and Cambridge. ⓒ **617/723-2500.** www. mos.org. Admission to exhibit halls $21 adults, $19 seniors, $18 children 3–11, free for children 2 and under; to Butterfly Garden or 3-D Digital Cinema (available only with exhibit hall admission) $5 adults, $4.50 seniors, $4 children 3–11. Admission to Mugar Omni Theater or planetarium $9 adults, $8 seniors, $7 children 3–11, free for children 2 and under. Discounted combination tickets available. July 5–Labor Day Sat–Thurs 9am–7pm, Fri 9am–9pm; day after Labor Day–July 4 Sat–Thurs 9am–5pm, Fri 9am–9pm. Check ahead for extended hours during school vacations. Closed Thanksgiving and Dec 25. T: Green Line to Science Park.

New England Aquarium ★ ☺ This complex is home to more than 30,000 fish and aquatic mammals, and at busy times, it seems to contain at least that many people—in July and August, try to make this your first stop of the morning, especially on weekends. Pause as you enter to visit with the **Atlantic harbor seals,** who frolic in a free outdoor enclosure just past the ticket booth.

Inside, **penguins** from three continents greet visitors as they enter. The focal point of the aquarium is the four-story, 200,000-gallon **Giant Ocean Tank.** A four-story spiral ramp encircles the tank, which contains a replica of a Caribbean coral reef and an assortment of sea creatures that seem to coexist amazingly well. Part of the reason for the peace might be that scuba divers feed the sharks twice a day. The new **Shark and Ray Touch Tank** will be open by the time you visit; the 25,000-gallon enclosure lets visitors get up close and personal with the animals. At the **Edge of the Sea** exhibit, visitors can touch the sea stars, sea urchins, and horseshoe crabs in the tide pool. Other exhibits show off tropical sea creatures, freshwater specimens, denizens of the Amazon, and marine life in the Gulf of Maine. The **Medical Center** is especially involving: It's a working veterinary hospital where you can sometimes see marine animals that ran into trouble in New England waters and had to be rescued. (The aquarium is one of the most important facilities on the East Coast for marine-animal rescue; visit the team blog at **http://rescue.neaq.org** for information about recent activities.)

The four-story aquarium at the heart of the New England Aquarium.

Behind the building, fronting the harbor, the sheltered, open-air **New Balance Foundation Marine Mammal Center** is home to lively, curious fur seals.

The **Simons IMAX Theatre ★★★**, which has its own building, hours, and admission fees, is worth planning for, too. Its 85×65-foot screen shows 3-D films with digital sound that concentrate on the natural world as well as 3-D versions of recent Hollywood releases. It's an impressive experience.

 The Harborwalk and Walk to the Sea

The **Harborwalk ★★** is a path that traces 47 miles of Boston's shoreline, allowing public access to multimillion-dollar views of the water. In theory, it extends from East Boston to Dorchester; in practice, the pathway isn't continuous. Distinctive royal blue signs with a white logo and text point the way along the Harborwalk, which is an ideal route to take from downtown to the Institute of Contemporary Art, on the South Boston waterfront. The ambitious project has been in the works since 1984 and is more than three-quarters complete. Learn more by visiting the website, **www.bostonharborwalk.com**, which

features a map and a free downloadable audio tour.

Intersecting the Harborwalk is the 1-mile **Norman B. Leventhal Walk to the Sea ★** (www.walktothesea.com), which begins on Beacon Street in front of the State House and ends at the tip of Long Wharf. It tracks 4 centuries of Boston history with compelling narration on freestanding trail markers; visit the website to download a map and get more information. The Walk to the Sea makes an excellent compromise if you don't have the time or energy to tackle the whole Freedom Trail or Black Heritage Trail, both of which it intersects.

I suggest starting your day here because you'll want to spend at least half a day, and huge afternoon crowds can make getting around painfully slow. Discounts are available when you combine a visit to the aquarium with an IMAX film or a **whale watch** (p. 193). Also consider investing in a Boston CityPass or Go Boston Card (see the "Let's Make a Deal" box on p. 140). They allow you to skip the ticket line, which can be uncomfortably long, and the price may represent a savings on the steep admission charge.

Central Wharf (Milk St. and Old Atlantic Ave.). ✆ **617/973-5200.** www.neaq.org. Admission $23 adults, $21 seniors, $16 children 3–11, free for children 2 and under and for those visiting only the outdoor exhibits, cafe, and gift shop. July–Labor Day Sun–Thurs 9am–6pm, Fri–Sat and holidays 9am–7pm; day after Labor Day–June Mon–Fri 9am–5pm, Sat–Sun and holidays 9am–6pm. Simons IMAX Theatre: ✆ **866/815-4629.** Tickets $10–$13 adults, $8–$11 seniors and children 3–11. Daily from 9:30am. Closed Thanksgiving and Dec 25 and until noon Jan 1. T: Blue Line to Aquarium.

THE FREEDOM TRAIL

A line of red paint or red brick on the sidewalk, the 2.5-mile **Freedom Trail ★★★** links 16 historic sites, many of them associated with the Revolution and the early days of the United States. The route cuts across downtown, passing through Downtown Crossing, the Financial District, and the North End, on the way to Charlestown. Markers identify the stops, and plaques point the way

Informative costumed guides lead visitors along the historic Freedom Trail.

from one to the next. For a map of the Freedom Trail, see the inside front cover of this book.

This section lists the stops on the trail in the customary order, from Boston Common to the Bunker Hill Monument. It's important to remember that this is the *suggested* route, and nobody's checking up on you. You don't have to visit every stop or even go in order—you can skip around, start in Charlestown and work backward, visit different sights on different days, or even omit some sights. Here's a suggestion: If you find yourself sighing and saying "should" a lot, take a break. That goes double if you're traveling with children.

A hard-core history fiend who peers at every artifact and reads every plaque can easily spend 4 hours along the trail. A family with restless kids will probably appreciate the enforced efficiency of a free 90-minute ranger-led tour. At press time, tours are leaving from the **Boston National Historical Park Visitor Center,** 15 State St. (© **617/242-5642;** www.nps.gov/bost). Check before you set out to see whether the new visitor center on the first floor of **Faneuil Hall,** about a block away, is open.

The excursions cover the "heart" of the trail, from the Old South Meeting House to the Old North Church. From Patriots' Day through mid-June and September through November, they begin weekends at 10am and 2 and 3pm, weekdays at 2pm only. From mid-June through August, starting times are daily at 10am and 2 and 3pm. The first-come, first-served tours are limited to 30 people (rangers distribute stickers starting 30 min. before tour time) and not available in bad weather. No tours December through mid-April.

The nonprofit **Freedom Trail Foundation** (© **617/357-8300;** www.the freedomtrail.org) is an excellent resource as you plan your visit. The foundation's costumed **Freedom Trail Players** lead 90-minute tours ($13 adults, $11 seniors and students, $7 children 6–12, with a discount for buying online) of the trail. Buy tickets online, allowing time to explore the interactive website. It lists a plethora of other activities, including a pub crawl (participants must be 21 or older) and holiday stroll.

The best time to start on the trail is in the morning. During the summer and fall, aim for a weekday if possible. Try not to set out later than midafternoon, because attractions will be closing and you'll run into the evening rush hour.

Boston Common In 1634, when their settlement was just 4 years old, the town fathers paid the Rev. William Blackstone £30 for this property. In 1640 it was set aside as common land. The 45 or so acres of the country's oldest public park have served as a cow pasture, a military camp, and the site of hangings, protest marches, and visits by dignitaries. Today the Common buzzes with activity all day. You might see a demonstration, a musical performance, a picnic lunch—almost anything other than a cow. Cows have been banned since 1830, which seems to be one of the few events related to the Common that isn't commemorated with a plaque.

One of the loveliest markers is on this route; head up the hill inside the fence, walking parallel to Park Street. At Beacon Street is a **memorial ★★★** designed by Augustus Saint-Gaudens to celebrate the deeds (indeed, the very existence) of Col. Robert Gould Shaw and the Union Army's **54th Massachusetts Colored Regiment,** who fought in the Civil War. You might remember the story of the first American army unit made up of free black soldiers from the movie *Glory.*

To continue on the Freedom Trail: Cross Beacon Street.

Boston Common.

Btw. Beacon, Park, Tremont, Boylston, and Charles sts. Visitor information center: 148 Tremont St. 📞 **888/733-2678** or 617/536-4100. www.bostonusa.com. Mon–Fri 8:30am–5pm; Sat 9am–5pm. Center closed Sun. T: Green or Red Line to Park St.

Massachusetts State House Boston is one of the only American cities where a building whose cornerstone was laid in 1795 (by Gov. Samuel Adams) can be the "new" anything. Nevertheless, this is the new State House, as opposed to the Old State House (see later). The great Federal-era architect Charles Bulfinch designed the central building of the state capitol, and in 1802 copper sheathing manufactured by Paul Revere replaced the shingles on the landmark dome. Gold leaf now covers the dome; during World War II blackouts, it was painted black. The state legislature, or Massachusetts General Court, meets here. The House of Representatives congregates under a wooden fish, the **Sacred Cod,** as a reminder of the importance of fishing to the local economy. Take a self-guided tour, or call ahead to schedule a conducted tour.

Whether or not you go inside, be sure to study some of the many statues outside. Subjects range from **Mary Dyer,** a Quaker hanged on the Common in 1660 for refusing to abandon her religious beliefs, to Pres. **John F. Kennedy.** The 60-foot monument at the rear (off Bowdoin St.) illustrates Beacon Hill's original height, before the top was hacked off to use in 19th-century landfill projects.

To continue on the Freedom Trail: Walk down Park Street (which Bulfinch laid out in 1804) to Tremont Street.

The "new" Massachusetts State House.

Park Street Church.

Beacon St. at Park St. ✆ **617/727-3676.** www.mass.gov/statehouse. Mon–Fri 9am–5pm. Free tours Mon–Fri 10am–3:30pm. T: Green or Red Line to Park St., or Blue Line to Bowdoin (weekdays only).

Park Street Church Famed author Henry James called this 1809 structure with a 217-foot steeple "the most interesting mass of bricks and mortar in America." The church has accumulated an impressive number of firsts: The first Protestant missionaries to Hawaii left from here in 1819; the prominent abolitionist William Lloyd Garrison gave his first antislavery speech here on July 4, 1829; and "America" ("My Country 'Tis of Thee") was first sung here on July 4, 1831. You're standing on **"Brimstone Corner,"** named either for the passion of the Congregational ministers who declaimed from the pulpit or for the fact that

Listen Up:
The Audio Freedom Trail

A 2-hour tour narrative commissioned by the Freedom Trail Foundation (✆ 617/357-8300; www.thefreedomtrail.org) includes interviews, sound effects, and music that help bring the sites to life. It costs $15 (credit cards only); buy it as an MP3 download, or rent a handheld digital audio player, for use with or without headphones, that can be picked up at the Boston Common Visitor Center, 148 Tremont St. (and dropped off there or at several other locations).

gunpowder (made from brimstone) was stored in the basement during the War of 1812. This was part of the site of a huge granary (grain storehouse) that became a public building after the Revolutionary War. In the 1790s, the sails for USS *Constitution* ("Old Ironsides") were manufactured in that building.

To continue on the Freedom Trail: Walk away from the Common on Tremont Street.

1 Park St. ✆ **617/523-3383.** www.parkstreet.org/tours. Tours late June to Aug Tues–Fri 9am–4pm, Sat 9am–3pm, and by appointment. Sun services year-round 8:30 and 11am, 4 and 6pm. T: Green or Red Line to Park St.

Granary Burying Ground ★ This cemetery, established in 1660, was once part of Boston Common. You'll see the graves of patriots **Samuel Adams, Paul Revere, John Hancock,** and **James Otis;** merchant **Peter Faneuil;** and Benjamin Franklin's parents. Also buried here are the victims of the **Boston Massacre** (see below) and the wife of Isaac Vergoose, who is believed to be **"Mother Goose"** of nursery rhyme fame. Note that gravestone rubbing, however tempting, is illegal in Boston's historic cemeteries.

To continue on the Freedom Trail: Turn left as you leave the cemetery and continue 1½ blocks on Tremont Street. En route to King's Chapel, you'll pass a 21st-century phenomenon: Suffolk University's **Studio 73,** in the lobby of 73 Tremont St. and visible from the sidewalk. Local news station NECN conducts live interviews in the high-definition TV facility, which it shares with Suffolk broadcast journalism and communications students.

Tremont St. at Bromfield St. Daily 9am–5pm (until 3pm in winter). T: Green or Red Line to Park St.

The Granary Burying Ground, final resting place of many famous New Englanders.

King's Chapel and Burying Ground Architect Peter Harrison sent the plans for this Georgian-style building from Newport, Rhode Island, in 1749. Rather than replacing the existing wooden chapel, the granite edifice was constructed around it. Completed in 1754, it was the first Anglican church in Boston. George III sent gifts, as did Queen Anne and William and Mary, who presented the communion table and chancel tablets (still in use today) before the church was even built. The Puritan colonists had little use for the royal religion; after the Revolution, this became the first Unitarian church in the new nation. Today, the church conducts Unitarian Universalist services using the Anglican Book of Common Prayer. It schedules public concerts (p. 264) every Tuesday at 12:15pm and some Sundays at 5pm.

The **burying ground ★★**, on Tremont Street, is the oldest in the city; it dates to 1630. Among the scary colonial headstones (winged skulls are a popular decoration) are the graves of **John Winthrop,** the first governor of the Massachusetts Bay Colony; **William Dawes,** who rode with Paul Revere; **Elizabeth Pain,** the model for Hester Prynne in Nathaniel Hawthorne's novel *The Scarlet Letter;* and **Mary Chilton,** the first female colonist to step ashore on Plymouth Rock.

To continue on the Freedom Trail: Follow the trail back along Tremont Street and turn left onto School Street.

58 Tremont St. ℰ **617/523-1749.** www.kings-chapel.org. Chapel: Summer Sun 1:30–4pm; Mon and Thurs–Sat 10am–4pm; Tues–Wed 10–11:15am and 1:30–4pm. Year-round Sat 10am–4pm. Check website for up-to-date spring and fall hours. Closed to casual tourists during religious services. $2 donation suggested. Services Wed 12:15pm, Sun 11am. Burying ground: Daily 8am–5:30pm (until 3pm in winter). T: Green or Blue Line to Government Center.

First Public School/Benjamin Franklin Statue A colorful folk-art **mosaic** embedded in the sidewalk marks the site of the first public school in the country. Founded in 1634, 2 years before Harvard College, the school educated

King's Chapel and Burying Ground.

The Benjamin Franklin statue near the former site of the first public school.

Samuel Adams, Benjamin Franklin, John Hancock, and Cotton Mather. The original building (1645) was demolished to make way for the expansion of King's Chapel, and the school moved across the street. Other alumni include Charles Bulfinch, Ralph Waldo Emerson, George Santayana, Arthur Fiedler, and Leonard Bernstein. Now called Boston Latin School, the prestigious institution later moved to the Fenway neighborhood and started admitting girls.

Behind the fence in the courtyard to your left is the **Benjamin Franklin statue,** the first portrait statue erected in Boston (1856). Franklin was born in Boston in 1706 and was apprenticed to his half-brother James, a printer, but they fought constantly. In 1723, Benjamin ran away to Philadelphia. Plaques on the base of the statue describe Franklin's numerous accomplishments. The lovely granite Second Empire–style building behind the statue is **Old City Hall** (1865), designed

The Old Corner Bookstore was a key component of America's early literary and publishing scene.

by Arthur Gilman (who laid out the Back Bay) and Gridley J. F. Bryant. The administration moved to Government Center in 1969, and the building now houses commercial tenants.

To continue on the Freedom Trail: Follow School Street to Washington Street.

School St. at City Hall Ave. (btw. Tremont and Washington sts.). T: Blue or Orange Line to State.

Old Corner Bookstore Building Built in 1718, this building stands on a plot of land that was once home to the religious reformer Anne Hutchinson, who was excommunicated and expelled from Boston in 1638 for heresy. In the 19th century, the brick building held the publishing house of Ticknor & Fields, which effectively made this the literary center of America. Publisher James Fields, known as "Jamie," counted among his friends Henry Wadsworth Longfellow, James Russell Lowell, Henry David Thoreau, Ralph Waldo Emerson, Nathaniel Hawthorne, and Harriet Beecher Stowe. For many years this was the Globe Corner Bookstore, which is now in Harvard Square (p. 237).

To continue on the Freedom Trail: Turn right and walk 1 block.

3 School St. T: Blue or Orange Line to State.

Old South Meeting House ★ Look for the beautifully restored clock tower that tops this religious and political gathering place, best known as the site of an important event that led to the Revolution. On December 16, 1773, a restive crowd of several thousand, too big to fit into Faneuil Hall, gathered here. They were waiting for word from the governor about whether three ships full

The Old South Meeting House.

of tea—priced to undercut the cost of smuggled tea and force the colonists to trade with merchants approved by the Crown—would be sent back to England from Boston. The ships were not, and revolutionaries haphazardly disguised as Mohawks cast the tea into the harbor. The meetinghouse commemorates that uprising, the **Boston Tea Party.** You can even see a vial of the tea.

Originally built in 1669 and replaced by the current structure in 1729, the building underwent extensive renovations in the 1990s. In 1872, a devastating fire that destroyed most of downtown stopped at Old South, a phenomenon considered evidence of the building's power. The exhibit *Voices of Protest* tells the story of the events that unfolded here.

The meetinghouse frequently schedules speeches, readings, panel discussions, and children's activities, often with a colonial theme. Each December, it stages a reenactment of the debate that led to the tea party—it's especially fun for kids, who can participate in the heated debate. Check ahead for schedules.

To continue on the Freedom Trail: Exit through the gift shop and look across Milk Street to see **Benjamin Franklin's birthplace.** In a little house at 17 Milk St., Franklin was born in 1706, the 15th child of Josiah Franklin. The house is long gone, but look across at the second floor of what's now 1 Milk St. When the building went up after the Great Fire of 1872, the architect guaranteed that the Founding Father wouldn't be forgotten: A bust and the words BIRTHPLACE OF FRANKLIN adorn the facade.

Now backtrack on Washington Street (passing Spring Lane, one of the first streets in Boston and originally the site of a real spring) and follow it to State Street.

310 Washington St. ℂ **617/482-6439.** www.osmh.org. Admission $6 adults, $5 seniors and students with ID, $1 children 6–18, free for children 5 and under. Daily Apr–Oct 9:30am–5pm; Nov–Mar 10am–4pm. Closed Jan 1, Thanksgiving, Dec 24–25. T: Blue or Orange Line to State St.

Old State House Museum ★ Built in 1713, this brick structure served as the seat of colonial government before the Revolution and as the state capitol until 1798. From its balcony, the Declaration of Independence was first read to Bostonians on July 18, 1776. In 1789, Pres. George Washington reviewed a parade from here. The exterior decorations are particularly interesting—the clock was installed in place of a sundial, and the gilded lion and unicorn are reproductions of the original symbols of British rule that were ripped from the facade and burned the day the Declaration of Independence was read.

The Old State House Museum.

The site of the Boston Massacre.

Inside is the **Bostonian Society's museum** ★ of the city's history. The society was founded in 1881 to save this building, which was badly deteriorated and, incredibly, about to be sold and shipped to Chicago. Two floors of exhibits focus on the role of the city and the building in the Revolution and the events that led to it—a Paul Revere print depicting the Boston Massacre and tea from the Boston Tea Party are on view—but this experience is hardly a static history lesson. A multimedia presentation explains the Boston Massacre, an interactive display helps recount the story of the building, and changing exhibits focus on other topics, such as the Great Fire of 1872, using vintage photographs and artifacts from the society's collections.

To continue on the Freedom Trail: Leave the building, turn left, and walk half a block.

206 Washington St. © **617/720-1713,** ext. 21. www.bostonhistory.org. Admission $7.50 adults, $6 seniors and students, $3 children 6-18, free for children 5 and under. July-Aug daily 9am-6pm; Feb-June and Sept-Dec daily 9am-5pm; Jan daily 9am-4pm. Closed Jan 1, Thanksgiving, Dec 25. T: Blue or Orange Line to State.

Boston Massacre Site A ring of cobblestones on a traffic island marks the location of the skirmish that helped consolidate the spirit of rebellion in the colonies. On March 5, 1770, angered at the presence of royal troops in Boston, colonists threw snowballs, garbage, rocks, and other debris at a group of redcoats. The soldiers panicked and fired into the crowd, killing five men. Their graves, including that of Crispus Attucks, the first black man to die in the Revolution, are in the Granary Burying Ground.

To continue on the Freedom Trail: Turn left onto Congress Street and walk down the hill, covering 1 long block. Faneuil Hall will be on your right.

State St. at Devonshire St. T: Blue or Orange Line to State.

Faneuil Hall ★ Built in 1742 (and enlarged using a Charles Bulfinch design in 1805), this building was a gift to Boston, which was then just a town, from prosperous merchant Peter Faneuil. This "Cradle of Liberty" rang with speeches by orators such as Samuel Adams—whose statue stands outside the Congress Street entrance—in the years leading to the Revolution. Abolitionists, temperance advocates, and suffragists also used the hall as a pulpit. The upstairs is still a public meeting and concert hall, and downstairs holds retail space, all according to Faneuil's will. The grasshopper **weather vane,** the sole remaining detail from the original building, is modeled after the weather vane on London's Royal Exchange.

National Park Service rangers give **free historical talks** every half-hour from 9am to 5pm in the second-floor auditorium. On the top floor is a small museum that houses the weapons collection and historical exhibits of the **Ancient and Honorable Artillery Company of Massachusetts.**

In late 2011, the National Park Service will open a new **visitor center** on the first floor. The center will have exhibits focusing on Boston history and—in keeping with the nearly 3-century history of retail in this space—a bookstore.

To continue on the Freedom Trail: Leave Faneuil Hall, cross North Street, and follow the trail through the "Blackstone Block." These buildings, among the oldest in the city, give a sense of the scale of 18th- and 19th-century Boston. In the park at the corner of North and Union streets are two sculptures of legendary Boston mayor (and Congressman, and federal prisoner) **James Michael Curley,** the inspiration for the protagonist of Edwin O'Connor's *The Last Hurrah.* Beyond the sculptures, you'll see six tall glass columns arranged parallel to Union Street. Pause here.

Dock Sq. (Congress St. and North St.). © **617/242-5642.** www.nps.gov/bost. Free admission. Daily 9am–5pm; no public access during special events. T: Green or Blue Line to Government Center, or Orange Line to Haymarket.

Faneuil Hall.

⦿ Trail Mix

Faneuil Hall Marketplace is a great spot for a break. Time your walk right, and it can be the starting point of a picnic lunch. Visit the **Quincy Market** food court for takeout, then head across the Rose Kennedy Greenway toward the water. **Christopher Columbus Waterfront Park** (pictured), on the left-hand side of the Marriott Long Wharf hotel, is a popular place to picnic, watch the action at the marina, and play in the playground. On this section of the Greenway, near the **visitor center pavilion,** a carousel operates in the summer.

Back on the trail, as you walk from Faneuil Hall to the Paul Revere House, you'll find yourself in the midst of **Haymarket.** On Friday and Saturday, the bustling open-air market on North, Blackstone, and Hanover streets consists of stalls piled high with produce, seafood, and flowers. Shoppers aren't allowed to touch anything they haven't bought, a rule you might learn from a hollering vendor or a cutthroat customer. It's a great scene and a favorite with photographers.

The New England Holocaust Memorial ★★ Erected in 1995, these six glass towers designed by Stanley Saitowitz spring up in the midst of attractions that celebrate freedom, reminding us of the consequences of a world without it. The pattern on the glass, which at first appears merely decorative, is actually 6

The New England Holocaust Memorial.

million random numbers, one for each Jew who died during the Holocaust. As you pass through, pause to read the inscriptions.

To continue on the Freedom Trail: Follow Hanover Street across the Rose Kennedy Greenway to reach the North End, which begins at Cross Street. Take Hanover Street 1 block to Richmond Street, passing the post office on your right. Turn right, go 1 block, and turn left.

Union St. btw. North and Hanover sts. ℭ **617/457-8755.** www.nehm.org. T: Orange or Green Line to Haymarket.

Paul Revere House ★★★ One of the most pleasant stops on the Freedom Trail, this 2½-story wood structure presents history on a human scale. Revere (1734–1818) was living here when he set out for Lexington on April 18, 1775, a feat immortalized in Henry Wadsworth Longfellow's poem "Paul Revere's Ride" ("Listen my children and you shall hear / Of the midnight ride of Paul Revere"). It holds neatly arranged and identified 17th- and 18th-century furnishings and artifacts, including the famous Revere silver, considered some of the finest anywhere. The oldest house in downtown Boston, it was built around 1680, bought by Revere in 1770, and put to a number of uses before being turned into a museum in 1908.

The thought-provoking tour is self-guided, with staff members around in case you have questions. The format allows you to linger on the artifacts that hold your interest. Revere and his two wives had a total of 16 children—he called them "my lambs"—and he supported the family with a thriving silversmith's trade. At his home, you'll get a good sense of the risks he took in the events that led to the Revolutionary War. Across the courtyard is the home of Revere's Hichborn cousins, the **Pierce/Hichborn House** ★. The 1711 Georgian-style home is a rare example of 18th-century middle-class architecture. It's suitably furnished and shown only by guided tour (usually twice a day at busy times). Contact the Paul Revere House for schedules and reservations.

A new **Education and Visitor Center** in a 19th-century building adjoining the house should be open by the time you visit. The center will give visitors with

Paul Revere's house.

disabilities access to the second floor of the Revere House for the first time.

Before you leave North Square, look across the cobblestone plaza at **Sacred Heart Church.** It was established in 1833 as the Seamen's Bethel, a church devoted to the needs of the mariners who frequented the area. Wharves ran up almost this far in colonial days; in the 19th century, this was a notorious red-light district.

To continue on the Freedom Trail: The trail leaves the square on Prince Street and runs along Hanover Street past Clark Street. Before turning onto Prince Street, take a few steps down Garden Court Street and look for no. 4, on the right. The private residence was the birthplace of Rose Fitzgerald (later Kennedy).

19 North Sq. ℭ **617/523-2338.** www.paul reverehouse.org. Admission $3.50 adults, $3 seniors and students, $1 children 5–17, free for children 4 and under. Apr 15–Oct daily 9:30am–5:15pm; Apr 1–14 and Nov–Dec daily 9:30am–4:15pm; Jan–Mar Tues–Sun 9:30am–4:15pm. Closed Jan 1, Thanksgiving, and Dec 25. T: Green or Orange Line to Haymarket, Blue Line to Aquarium, or Green or Blue Line to Government Center.

The Paul Revere statue in James Rego Square.

James Rego Square (Paul Revere Mall) A pleasant little brick-paved park also known as "the Prado," the mall holds a famous equestrian statue of Paul Revere—a great photo op. Take time to read some of the **tablets** ★ on the left-hand wall that describe famous people and places in the history of the North End.

To continue on the Freedom Trail: Walk around the fountain and continue to Salem Street, heading toward the steeple of the Old North Church.

Hanover St. at Clark St. T: Green or Orange Line to Haymarket.

Old North Church ★ Look up! In this building's original steeple, sexton Robert Newman hung two lanterns on the night of April 18, 1775, to signal Paul Revere that British troops were setting out for Lexington and Concord in boats across the Charles River, not on foot. We know that part of the story in Longfellow's words: "One if by land, and two if by sea." (*Trivia bonus:* Newman was a great-grandson of George Burroughs, one of the victims of the Salem witch trials of 1692.)

Officially named Christ Church, Old North is the oldest church building in Boston (1723). The design is in the style of Sir Christopher Wren. The steeple fell in hurricanes in 1804 and 1954; the current version is an exact copy of the original. The 190-foot spire, long a reference point for sailors, appears on navigational charts to this day.

Church Chat

One surefire way to announce yourself as an out-of-towner is to pause on Hanover Street between Prince and Fleet streets and proclaim that you see the Old North Church. The first house of worship you see is **St. Stephen's,** the only Charles Bulfinch–designed church still standing in Boston. St. Stephen's is perhaps best known as the church where **Rose Fitzgerald Kennedy,** Pres. John F. Kennedy's mother, was baptized (in 1890), and where her funeral took place (in 1995). The church was Unitarian when it was dedicated in 1804. The next year, the congregation bought a bell from Paul Revere's foundry for $800; it's still in use. The building's design is a paragon of Federal-style symmetry. St. Stephen's became Roman Catholic in 1862. During refurbishment in 1964 and 1965, it regained its original appearance, with clear glass windows, white walls, and gilded organ pipes. It's one of the plainest Catholic churches you'll ever see.

Members of the Revere family attended this church; their plaque is on pew 54. Famous visitors have included presidents James Monroe, Theodore Roosevelt, Calvin Coolidge, Franklin D. Roosevelt, and Gerald R. Ford; and Queen Elizabeth II. Markers and plaques appear throughout; note the bust of George Washington, reputedly the first memorial to the first president. The **gardens** ★ on the north side of the church (dotted with more plaques) are open to the public. On the south side of the church, volunteers maintain an 18th-century garden.

Free presentations that introduce the self-guided tour begin periodically during open hours year-round. For a more complete look at the church, take a **Behind the Scenes tour** ($5 adults, $3 seniors, $4 students and children 16 and under). The tour includes visits to the steeple and the crypt. It's offered on weekends in June, daily from July through October and from December 25 through January 1, and the rest of the year by appointment. Tickets are available in the gift shop.

To continue on the Freedom Trail: Cross Salem Street onto Hull Street and walk uphill toward Copp's Hill Burying Ground. On the left you'll pass 44 Hull St., a fine example of the phenomenon known as the "spite house." The 10-foot-wide private residence is the narrowest house in Boston.

193 Salem St. © **617/523-6676.** www.old-north.com. $3 donation requested. Jan–Feb

The Old North Church (of "one if by land, two if by sea" fame).

Tues–Sun 10am–4pm; Mar–May daily 9am–5pm; June–Oct daily 9am–6pm; Nov–Dec daily 9:30am–4:30pm. Closed to visitors Thanksgiving, Dec 25. Services (Episcopal) Sun 9 and 11am, Thurs 6pm. T: Orange or Green Line to Haymarket.

Copp's Hill Burying Ground ★ The second-oldest cemetery (1659) in the city is the burial place of Cotton Mather and his family, Robert Newman, and Prince Hall. Hall, a prominent member of the free black community that occupied the north slope of the hill in colonial times, fought at Bunker Hill and established the first black Masonic lodge. The highest point in the North End, Copp's Hill was the site of a windmill and of the British batteries that destroyed the village of Charlestown during the Battle of Bunker Hill on June 17, 1775. Charlestown is clearly visible (look for the masts of USS *Constitution*) across the Inner Harbor. No gravestone rubbing is allowed.

Copp's Hill Burying Ground.

To continue on the Freedom Trail: Follow Hull Street down the hill to Commercial Street (be careful crossing Commercial at the dangerous intersection with Hull) and follow the trail to North Washington Street and across the bridge to Charlestown. Signs and the trail lead to the Charlestown Navy Yard.

Off Hull St. near Snowhill St. Daily 9am–5pm (until 3pm in winter). T: Green or Orange Line to North Station.

USS *Constitution* ★★ ☺ "**Old Ironsides,**" one of the U.S. Navy's six original frigates, never lost a battle. The 30-minute tour, led by an active-duty sailor in an 1812 dress uniform, is an excellent introduction to an era when the future of the new nation was anything but certain. The ship was constructed in the North End from 1794 to 1797 at a cost of $302,718, using bolts, spikes, and other fittings from Paul Revere's foundry. As the United States built its naval and military reputation, the *Constitution* played a key role, battling French privateers and Barbary pirates, repelling the British fleet during the War of 1812, participating in 33 engagements, and capturing 20 vessels. The frigate earned its nickname during a battle on August 19, 1812, when shots from HMS *Guerriere* bounced off its thick oak hull as if it were iron.

Retired from combat in 1815, the *Constitution* was rescued from destruction when Oliver Wendell Holmes's poem "Old Ironsides" launched a preservation movement in 1830. The frigate was completely overhauled for its bicentennial in 1997, when it sailed under its own power for the first time since 1881, drawing international attention. Tugs tow the *Constitution* into the harbor every **Fourth of July** for its celebratory "turnaround cruise," and for occasional events around

Trailing Off

If you don't feel like retracing your steps at the end of the Freedom Trail, you have two public transit options. Return to the Charlestown Navy Yard for the **ferry** to Long Wharf, which leaves every half-hour from 6:45am to 8:15pm on weekdays (every 15 min. 6:45–9:15am and 3:45–6:45pm), and every half-hour on the quarter-hour from 10:15am to 6:15pm on weekends. The 10-minute trip costs $1.70 (or show your 7-day LinkPass), and the dock is an easy walk from "Old Ironsides." Alternatively, walk to the foot of the hill; on Main Street, take **bus no. 92 or 93** toward Haymarket (Green or Orange Line).

the harbor. If you see TV helicopters circling over the water, wander down and take a look.

Adjacent to the ship in Building 5, National Park Service rangers staff the **Navy Yard Visitor Center** (✆ 617/242-5601; www.nps.gov/bost) and give free 1-hour guided tours of the base.

To continue on the Freedom Trail: Walk straight ahead to the museum entrance.

Charlestown Navy Yard. ✆ **617/242-7511.** www.history.navy.mil/ussconstitution. Free tours. Apr–Oct Tues–Sun 10am–6pm (closes earlier in late Oct); tours every 30 min. 10am–5:30pm. Nov–Mar Thurs–Sun 10am–4pm; tours every 30 min. 10am–3:30pm. Closed Jan 1, Presidents Day, Thanksgiving, and Dec 25. T: Ferry from Long Wharf (Blue Line to Aquarium); or Green or Orange Line to North Station, then a 10-min. walk.

USS *Constitution* Museum ★ ☺ ✦ Just across from the vessel, the museum features engaging participatory exhibits that allow visitors to hoist a sail, fire a cannon, swing in a hammock, and learn about life onboard the ship during the War of 1812. The interactive computer displays and naval artifacts appeal to visitors of all ages. A favorite exhibit looks at the frigate from a compelling and relevant perspective: that of a sailor. The museum's collections include more than 3,000 items, arranged and interpreted to put them in context, and staff members and volunteers conduct interesting talks (I've seen one every time I've been in the galleries) that expand on the exhibits. In February and March, special displays and activities focus on ship models.

To continue on the Freedom Trail: Follow the trail up Constitution Road, crossing Chelsea Street, and continue to the Bunker Hill Monument. A more interesting, slightly longer route runs from Chelsea Street and Rutherford Avenue (back where you entered Charlestown) across City Square Park and up Main Street to Monument Street.

Off First Ave., Charlestown Navy Yard. ✆ **617/426-1812.** www.ussconstitutionmuseum.org. Free admission; suggested donation $4 adults, $2 children. Apr–Oct daily 9am–6pm; Nov–Mar daily 10am–5pm. Closed Jan 1, Thanksgiving, and Dec 25. T: Ferry from Long Wharf (Blue Line to Aquarium), or Green or Orange Line to North Station, then a 10-min. walk.

Bunker Hill Monument The 221-foot granite obelisk, a landmark that's visible from miles away, honors the memory of the colonists who died in the Battle of Bunker Hill on June 17, 1775. The rebels lost the battle, but nearly half the British troops were killed or wounded, a loss that contributed to their leaders' decision to abandon Boston 9 months later. The Marquis de Lafayette, the celebrated hero

The Bunker Hill Monument.

of the American and French revolutions, helped lay the monument's cornerstone in 1825. He is buried in Paris under soil taken from the hill. A punishing flight of 294 steps—imagine your worst Stairmaster experience, then imagine not being able to quit in the middle—leads to the top of the monument. It's not a can't-miss experience unless you're traveling with children you'd like to tire out. There's no elevator, and although the views of the harbor and the Zakim–Bunker Hill Bridge are good, the windows are quite small.

Across the street is the excellent **Battle of Bunker Hill Museum ★**. The ranger-staffed museum, at the corner where Monument Avenue enters Monument Square, holds dioramas, a cyclorama mural, and other exhibits about the battle and the community.

Monument Sq., Charlestown. ℭ **617/242-5641.** www.nps.gov/bost. Free admission. Monument daily 9am–4:30pm (until 5:30pm July–Aug). Museum daily 9am–5pm (until 6pm July–Aug). T: Orange Line to Community College, 10-min. walk.

MORE MUSEUMS & ATTRACTIONS

Boston Athenæum ★ Both a private library and an art gallery, the Athenæum gives outsiders an insider's perspective on proper Boston society—including the impulse to reach out to the community through arts and culture. In other words, it may sound stuffy, but it isn't. The city's leading families founded the Athenæum in 1807 to make "the great works of learning and science in all languages" available to members. The arts component was added in 1827, and the building is now filled with artwork. Docent-led **tours** (offered twice weekly, by reservation only; ℭ **617/227-0270,** ext. 279) show off the Palladian-inspired

sandstone building, replete with soaring galleries and hideaway nooks, that backs up to the Granary Burying Ground. Completed in 1849 and expanded in 1913–15, it was extensively renovated around the turn of the 21st century. The Athenæum mounts exhibits in the compact **art gallery** on the first floor—the only part of the building regularly open to the public—and schedules lectures, readings, concerts, and, on rare occasions, viewings of the library's most famous holding: an 1847 volume bound in the author's skin.

10½ Beacon St. Ⓒ **617/227-0270.** www.boston athenaeum.org. Free admission. Year-round Mon and Wed 9am–8pm, Tues and Thurs–Fri 9am–5:30pm; Sept–May Sat 9am–4pm. Free tours (reservations required) Tues and Thurs 3pm. Closed Sat June–Aug, Sun, and major holidays year-round. T: Red or Green Line to Park St.

Boston Athenaeum.

Boston Public Library The central branch of the city's library system is an architectural and intellectual monument. The original 1895 building, a National Historic Landmark designed by Charles F. McKim, is an Italian Renaissance–style

Boston Public Library's central branch.

masterpiece that fairly drips with art. The **lobby doors** are the work of Daniel Chester French (who also designed the Abraham Lincoln statue in the memorial in Washington, the *Minute Man* statue in Concord, and the John Harvard statue in Cambridge). The **murals** are by John Singer Sargent and Pierre Puvis de Chavannes, among others. Visit the lovely **courtyard ★** or peek at it from a window on the stairs. The adjoining addition, of the same height and material (pink granite), was designed by Philip Johnson and opened in 1972. Ask the staff at the information desk about changing exhibits. The **Courtyard** restaurant serves lunch Monday through Friday and afternoon tea Wednesday through Friday, and the **Map Room Café** is open Monday through Saturday 9am to 5pm.

Free **Art & Architecture Tours** (www.bpl.org/central/tours.htm) begin Monday at 2:30pm, Tuesday and Thursday at 6pm, Friday and Saturday at 11am, with an additional tour October through May on Sunday at 2pm. Visit the website and click "A Walking Tour of the McKim Building" for more information. Call € **617/536-5400,** ext. 2216, to arrange group tours.

700 Boylston St., Copley Sq. € **617/536-5400.** www.bpl.org. Free admission. Mon–Thurs 9am–9pm; Fri–Sat 9am–5pm; Sun 1–5pm. Closed Sun June–Sept and legal holidays. T: Green Line to Copley.

Mary Baker Eddy Library/Mapparium ☺ The Mary Baker Eddy Library, a research center with two floors of interactive exhibits, aims to explore ideas such as liberty and spirituality through history, with a central role for Mary Baker Eddy, the founder of Christian Science. The most intriguing artifact is the **Mapparium ★**, a unique hollow globe 30 feet across. A work of both art and history, it

The Mapparium at the Mary Baker Eddy Library.

consists of a bronze framework that connects 608 stained-glass panels. Kids especially like the weird acoustics—the nonporous surfaces of the globe distort sound—and the chance to "journey to the center of the earth." As you cross the glass bridge just south of the Equator, you'll see the political divisions of the world from 1932 to 1935, when the three-story-high globe was constructed.

World Headquarters of the First Church of Christ, Scientist, 200 Massachusetts Ave. ℂ **888/222-3711** or 617/450-7000. www.mbelibrary.org. Admission $6 adults; $4 seniors, students, and children 6–17; free for children 5 and under. Tues–Sun 10am–4pm. Closed federal holidays. T: Green Line E to Symphony; Green Line B, C, or D to Hynes Convention Center; or Orange Line to Massachusetts Ave. Parking $7.

Eyes in the Skies

For a smashing view of the airport, the harbor, and the South Boston waterfront, stroll along the harbor or Atlantic Avenue to Northern Avenue. On either side of this intersection are buildings with free observation areas. Be ready to show an ID to gain entrance. The space on the 14th floor of **Independence Wharf**, 470 Atlantic Ave., is open daily from 11am to 5pm. Across the way is **Foster's Rotunda**, on the ninth floor of 30 Rowes Wharf, in the Boston Harbor Hotel complex. It's open Monday to Friday from 11am to 4pm.

Museum of African American History ★★ In Revolutionary War–obsessed New England, the history of the black community that thrived in Boston from early colonial times often gets overlooked, with some notable exceptions. The final stop on the **Black Heritage Trail** (p. 172), this museum is one of those exceptions, presenting a comprehensive look at the history and contributions of blacks in Boston and Massachusetts. It occupies the **Abiel Smith School** (1834), the first American public grammar school for African-American children, and the **African Meeting House,** 8 Smith Court. Changing and permanent exhibits use art, artifacts, documents, historic photographs, and other objects—including many family heirlooms—to explore an important era in the country's history. The oldest standing black church in the United States, the meetinghouse opened in 1806. William Lloyd Garrison founded the New England Anti-Slavery Society in this building, where Frederick Douglass made some of his great abolitionist speeches. Once known as the "Black Faneuil Hall," it also schedules lectures, concerts, and church meetings.

46 Joy St. ℂ **617/725-0022.** www.maah.org. Admission $5 adults, $3 seniors and youths 13–17, free for children 12 and under. Mon–Sat 10am–4pm. Closed Jan 1, Thanksgiving, and Dec 25. T: Red or Green Line to Park St., Red Line to Charles/MGH, or Blue Line to Bowdoin (weekdays only).

HISTORIC HOUSES

The home in Boston imbued with the most history is the **Paul Revere House** (p. 161). For information on **Longfellow's House,** see p. 175.

On **Beacon Hill,** you'll find houses that are as interesting for their architecture as for their occupants. The south slope, facing Boston Common, has been a fashionable address since the 1620s; excellent tours of two houses (one on the north slope) focus on the late 18th and early 19th centuries. The architect of the homes was Charles Bulfinch; he also designed the State House, which sits at the hill's summit.

The Gibson House Museum's beautiful period pieces.

Historic New England owns and operates the Otis House Museum (see below) and dozens of other historic properties throughout New England. Contact the organization (☎ **617/227-3956;** www.historicnewengland.org) for information on its properties, visiting hours, and admission fees.

Gibson House Museum The Gibson House is an 1859 brownstone that embodies the word "Victorian." Forget you've ever heard the phrase "less is more"—the ornate furnishings and abundant accessories offer a compelling look at the domestic life of a socially prominent family in the then-new Back Bay neighborhood. You'll see decorations of all kinds, including family photos and portraits, petrified-wood hat racks, a sequined red-velvet pagoda for the cat, a Victrola, and an original icebox. Check ahead for the schedule of lectures and other special events.

137 Beacon St. ☎ **617/267-6338.** www.thegibsonhouse.org. Admission $9 adults, $6 seniors and students, $3 children under 12. Tours on the hour Wed–Sun 1–3pm. Closed Jan 1, July 4, Thanksgiving, and Dec 25. T: Green Line to Arlington.

John F. Kennedy National Historic Site The 35th president's birthplace is a modest 1909 house in a quiet residential neighborhood. The president's mother, Rose Fitzgerald Kennedy, collected many of the items on display and helped with the restoration; the current configuration is her recollection of the house's appearance around 1917, when "Jack," her second child, was born. The tour, led by a National Park Service ranger, explores the future president's formative years. If you miss the last guided tour, ask about the self-guided option, which is available in English, French, German, Japanese, and Spanish. Ranger-led walking tours of the neighborhood take place several times each weekend.

83 Beals St., Brookline. ☎ **617/566-7937.** www.nps.gov/jofi. House tours $3 adults, free for children 17 and under. Walking tours free. May to early Oct Wed–Sun 10am–4:30pm; last house tour

The John F. Kennedy National Historic Site.

at 3pm. Call ahead to double-check hours and tour schedules, especially early and late in the season. Closed Nov to Apr. T: Green Line C to Coolidge Corner, then walk 4 blocks north on Harvard St. and turn right.

Nichols House Museum ★ A stroll around Beacon Hill leaves many visitors pining to know what the stately homes look like inside. This grand residence is one of the only places to satisfy that curiosity. The 1804 home holds beautiful antique furnishings, art, carpets, and tapestries collected by several generations of the Nichols family. Its most prominent occupant, Rose Standish Nichols (1872–1960), was a suffragist and a pioneering landscape designer. Her legacy includes not just family heirlooms but objects she brought back from her many travels to the thoroughfare that author Henry James (who lived at no. 131) reputedly called "the only respectable street in America."

55 Mount Vernon St. ✆ **617/227-6993.** www.nicholshousemuseum.org. Admission $7, free for children 12 and under. Apr–Oct Tues–Sat 11am–4pm; Nov–Mar Thurs–Sat 11am–4pm; tours every 30 min. T: Red or Green Line to Park St.

Otis House Museum ★★ Legendary architect Charles Bulfinch designed this gorgeous 1796 mansion for his friends Harrison Gray Otis, an up-and-coming young lawyer who later became mayor of Boston, and his wife, Sally. The restoration was one of the first in the country to use computer analysis of paint, and the result was revolutionary: It revealed that the walls were drab because the paint had faded, not because the colors started out dingy. Furnished in the style to which a wealthy family in the young United States would have been accustomed, the Federal-style building is a colorful, elegant treasure. Guided tours (the only way to see the property) discuss the architecture of the house and post-Revolutionary social, business, and family life, and touch on the history of the neighborhood.

The Otis House Museum.

141 Cambridge St. ℂ **617/994-5920.** www.historicnewengland.org. Guided tour $8 adults, $7 seniors, $4 students. Wed–Sun 11am–4:30pm; tours every 30 min. T: Blue Line to Bowdoin (weekdays only), Green or Blue Line to Government Center, or Red Line to Charles/MGH.

AFRICAN-AMERICAN HISTORY

The 1.5-mile **Black Heritage Trail ★★** covers sites on Beacon Hill that preserve the history of 19th-century Boston. The neighborhood was the center of the free black community, and the trail links stations of the Underground Railroad, homes of famous citizens, and the first integrated public school in the city. You can take a free 2-hour guided tour with a ranger from the National Park Service's **Boston African American National Historic Site** (ℂ **617/742-5415;** www.nps.gov/boaf). Tours start at the **Robert Gould Shaw Memorial,** on Beacon Street across from the State House. They're available Monday through Saturday from Memorial Day to Labor Day, and by request at other times; call ahead for a reservation. Or go on your own, using a brochure (available at the Museum of African American History and the Boston Common and State Street/ Faneuil Hall visitor centers) that includes a map and descriptions of the buildings. The only buildings on the trail that are open to the public are the **African Meeting House** and the **Abiel Smith School,** which make up the **Museum of African American History** (p. 169). Check ahead for special programs year-round.

In February, the **Freedom Trail Foundation** (ℂ **617/357-8300;** www. thefreedomtrail.org) offers the African-American Patriots Tour, which focuses on the black community in 18th-century Boston and its role in the Revolution. Visit the website to make a reservation and buy tickets ($12 adults, $6 children 6–12), or to arrange a private group tour.

Across the river, the **Cambridge African American Heritage Trail** focuses on significant sites in the history of the city's large black community. To buy the guide, visit the office on the second floor of 831 Massachusetts Ave., download an order form from the website, or send a check for $3.50 (includes shipping) to the **Cambridge Historical Commission,** 831 Massachusetts Ave., Cambridge, MA 02139 (© **617/349-4683;** www. cambridgema.gov/historic, click "History and Links").

The Robert Gould Shaw Memorial.

PARKS & GARDENS

Green space is an important part of Boston's appeal, and the public parks are known for their beauty. The world-famous **Emerald Necklace,** Frederick Law Olmsted's vision for a loop of green spaces, runs through the city.

The best-known park, for good reason, is the spectacular **Public Garden ★★★**, bordered by Arlington, Boylston, Charles, and Beacon streets. Something lovely is in bloom at the country's first botanical garden at least half the year. The spring flowers are particularly impressive, especially if your visit happens to coincide with the first really warm days of the year. It's hard not to enjoy yourself when everyone around you seems ecstatic just to be seeing the sun.

For many Bostonians, the official beginning of spring coincides with the return of the **Swan Boats ★★** (© **617/522-1966;** www.swanboats.com). The pedal-powered vessels—the attendants pedal, not the passengers—plunge into the lagoon on the Saturday before Patriots' Day, the third Monday of April. The surrounding greenery and placid water help lend a 19th-century aura to the attraction, which the Paget family has operated since 1877. Although the Swan Boats don't move fast, they'll transport you. They operate daily from 10am to 5pm in the summer, daily from 10am to 4pm in the spring, and weekdays noon to 4pm and weekends 10am to 4pm from the day after Labor Day to mid-September. The cost for the 15-minute ride is $2.75 for adults, $2 for seniors, and $1.50 for children 2 to 15.

Across Charles Street is **Boston Common,** the country's first public park and the first site on the **Freedom Trail** (p. 150). The property was purchased in 1634 and officially set aside as public land in 1640. Although the city refurbished it recently, the Common still seems run-down, especially compared to the gorgeous Public Garden. The **Frog Pond** makes a pleasant spot to splash around in the summer and skate in the winter. At the Boylston Street side of the Common is the **Central Burying Ground,** where you can see the grave of famed portraitist Gilbert Stuart. There's also a bandstand where you might take in a free concert or play, and many beautiful shade trees.

The most spectacular garden in town is the **Arnold Arboretum ★★**, 125 Arborway, Jamaica Plain (✆ **617/524-1718;** www.arboretum.harvard.edu), which Frederick Law Olmsted designed as part of the Emerald Necklace. One of the oldest parks in the United States, founded in 1872, the arboretum is open daily from sunrise to sunset. Its 265 acres contain more than 15,000 ornamental trees, shrubs, and vines from all over the world. In the spring, blossoming dogwood, azaleas, and rhododendrons are everywhere, and the air fills with the dizzying scent of hundreds of varieties of lilacs, for which the arboretum is especially famous. This is definitely a place to take a camera—but not food. Lilac Sunday, in May, is the only time the arboretum allows picnicking.

There is no fee to enter this National Historic Landmark, which Harvard University administers in cooperation with the Boston Department of Parks and Recreation. To get there, take the MBTA Orange Line to the Forest Hills stop and follow signs to the entrance. The visitor center is open weekdays from 9am to 4pm, Saturday 10am to 4pm, and Sunday noon to 4pm (closed major holidays). Call or visit the website for information about educational programs and driving directions.

CAMBRIDGE

Boston and Cambridge are so closely associated that many people believe they're the same place—a notion that both cities' residents and politicians are happy to dispel. Cantabrigians are often considered more liberal and better educated than Bostonians, which is another idea that's sure to get you involved in a lively discussion. Take the Red Line across the river and see for yourself.

For a good overview, begin at the main Harvard T entrance. Follow our Harvard Square walking tour (p. 219), or set out on your own. At the **information booth** (✆ **617/497-1630**) in the middle of Harvard Square at the intersection of Massachusetts Avenue, John F. Kennedy Street, and Brattle Street, trained volunteers dispense maps and brochures and answer questions Monday through Friday from 9am to 5pm, Saturday and Sunday from 1 to 5pm. The website of the **Cambridge Office for Tourism** (www.cambridge-usa.org), which operates the booth, lists organized excursions and features a tour of its own; the narration is available for download for $5.

Whatever you do, spend some time in **Harvard Square.** It's a hodge-podge of college and high school students, professors and instructors,

You never know what you may see when you visit Harvard Square.

The buildings along "Tory Row" have housed many famous Americans.

commuters, street performers, and sightseers. Stores and restaurants line all three streets that spread out from the center of the square and the streets that intersect them. If you follow **Brattle Street** to the residential area just outside the square, you'll arrive at a part of town known as **"Tory Row"** because many residents were loyal to King George during the Revolution.

The yellow mansion at 105 Brattle St. is the **Longfellow House– Washington's Headquarters National Historic Site** ★ (© 617/876-4491; www.nps.gov/long), the longtime home of Henry Wadsworth Longfellow (1807– 82). The poet first lived here as a boarder in 1837. When he and Fanny Appleton married, in 1843, her father made the house a wedding present. The furnishings and books in the stately 1759 home are original to Longfellow, who lived here until his death, and his descendants. During the siege of Boston in 1775–76, the house served as the headquarters of Gen. George Washington, with whom Longfellow was fascinated. On a tour—the only way to see the house—you'll learn about the history of the building and its famous occupants.

The house is usually open June through October Wednesday through Sunday from 10am to 4:30pm, but always check ahead. Tours begin at 10:30 and 11:30am, and 1, 2, 3, and 4pm. Admission is $3 for adults, free for children 15 and under.

Farther west, near where Brattle Street and Mount Auburn Street intersect, is **Mount Auburn Cemetery** (see the box titled "Celebrity Cemetery," below). It's a pleasant but long walk; you might prefer to drive or take a bus from Harvard station.

Harvard University

Our Harvard Square walking tour (p. 219) describes many of the buildings you'll see on the Harvard campus. Free student-led tours leave from the **Events & Information Center** in Holyoke Center, 1350 Massachusetts Ave. (© 617/495-1573; www.harvard.edu/visitors). They operate during the school

celebrity CEMETERY

Three important colonial burying grounds—Granary, King's Chapel, and Copp's Hill—are in Boston on the Freedom Trail (see "The Freedom Trail," earlier in this chapter), but the most famous cemetery in the area is in Cambridge.

Mount Auburn Cemetery ★, 580 Mount Auburn St. ((C) **617/547-7105; www.mountauburn.org**), the final resting place of many well-known people, is also famous simply for existing. Dedicated in 1831, it was the first of America's rural, or garden, cemeteries. The establishment of burying places removed from city centers reflected practical and philosophical concerns: Development was encroaching on urban graveyards, and the ideas associated with Transcendentalism and the Greek revival dictated that communing with nature take precedence over organized religion. Since the day it opened, Mount Auburn has been a popular place to retreat and reflect.

Visitors to this National Historic Landmark find history and horticulture coexisting with celebrity. The graves of Henry Wadsworth Longfellow, Oliver Wendell Holmes, Julia Ward Howe, and Mary Baker Eddy are here, as are those of Charles Bulfinch, James Russell Lowell, Winslow Homer, Transcendentalist leader Margaret Fuller, and abolitionist Charles Sumner. In season you'll see gorgeous flowering trees and shrubs (the Massachusetts Horticultural Society had a hand in the design).

Stop at the **visitor center** in Story Chapel (daily 9am–4pm Apr–Oct; closed Sun Nov–Mar and year-round during burials) for an overview and a look at the changing exhibits, or ask at the office or front gate for brochures and a map. You can rent an audio tour ($7; a $15 deposit is required) and listen in your car or on a portable player; there's a 60-minute driving tour and two

75-minute walking tours. The **Friends of Mount Auburn Cemetery** conducts workshops and lectures and coordinates walking tours; call the main number for topics, schedules, and fees.

The cemetery is open daily from 8am to 7pm May through September, 8am to 5pm October through April (call ahead in autumn to double-check closing time). There is no admission charge. Animals and recreational activities such as jogging, biking, and picnicking are not allowed. MBTA bus nos. 71 and 73 start at Harvard station and stop near the cemetery gates; they run frequently on weekdays and less often on weekends. By car (5 min.) or on foot (30 min.), take Mount Auburn Street or Brattle Street west from Harvard Square; just after the streets intersect, the gate is on the left.

year twice a day on weekdays and once on Saturday, except during vacations, and during the summer four times a day Monday through Saturday. Call or surf ahead for times; reservations aren't necessary. The Information Center is open Monday through Saturday 9am to 5pm and has maps, illustrated booklets, and self-guided walking-tour directions in nine languages, as well as a bulletin board where flyers publicize campus activities.

Also on campus are two engaging museum complexes:

Harvard Museum of Natural History and Peabody Museum of Archaeology & Ethnology ★ ☺ These fascinating museums house the university's collections of items and artifacts related to the natural world. Just about everyone finds something interesting here, be it a 42-foot-long prehistoric marine reptile skeleton, the largest turtle shell in the world, an exploration of climate science, or a Native American artifact.

The natural history museum's best-known collection is the world-famous **Glass Flowers ★★★**, 3,000 models of more than 840 plant species devised between 1887 and 1936 by the German father-and-son team of Leopold and Rudolph Blaschka. You may be skeptical, but it's true: They look real. Children love the museum's **zoological collections ★★**, where dinosaurs share space with preserved and stuffed insects and animals that range in size from butterflies to whales. The evolution exhibition makes a great introduction. Arthropods—insects, centipedes, spiders, and other creepy-crawlies—have their own multimedia installation. The **mineralogical collections** are the most specialized but can be just as compelling as the rest, especially if gemstones hold your interest.

The adjacent **Peabody Museum of Archaeology & Ethnology ★** boasts the **Hall of the North American Indian,** where 500 artifacts representing 10 cultures are on display. Photographs, textiles, pottery, and art and crafts of all ages and descriptions fill the galleries, spanning six continents and countless years.

One of the university's most popular attractions, this complex is also a world-famous academic resource; interdisciplinary programs and exhibitions tie in elements of all the associated fields. Check ahead for special events, including family programs and lectures by celebrated scientists, during your visit.

The incredibly lifelike glass flowers at the Harvard Museum of Natural History.

Spending time in the Harvard Art Museums.

Harvard Museum of Natural History: 26 Oxford St. ✆ **617/495-3045.** www.hmnh.harvard.edu. Peabody Museum: 11 Divinity Ave. ✆ **617/496-1027.** www.peabody.harvard.edu. Admission to both $9 adults, $7 seniors and students, $6 children 3–18, free for children 2 and under; free to MA residents Sun until noon year-round and Wed 3–5pm Sept–May. Daily 9am–5pm. Closed Jan 1, Thanksgiving, Dec 24–25. T: Red Line to Harvard. Cross Harvard Yard, keeping John Harvard statue on right. Before reaching Science Center entrance, turn right and quickly turn left (onto Oxford St.). Check website for parking info.

Harvard Art Museums While two of the three institutions that make up the university's internationally renowned art museum are under renovation, the **Arthur M. Sackler Museum** is showing highlights from all three collections. Special exhibitions complement *Re-View,* an overview of objects drawn from the quarter-million works in the Harvard Art Museums' impressive repository. You'll see pieces from the modern and contemporary, Asian, and Islamic collections. The **Fogg Museum** and the **Busch-Reisinger Museum** are scheduled to reopen in 2013, when the museums reunite in a single state-of-the-art facility; architect Renzo Piano is leading the renovation and expansion.

485 Broadway. ✆ **617/495-9400.** www.harvardartmuseums.org. Admission $9 adults, $7 seniors, $6 students, free for children 18 and under; free to MA residents until noon Sat. Tues–Sat 10am–5pm. Closed major holidays. T: Red Line to Harvard, cross Harvard Yard diagonally from the T station and exit onto Quincy St., turn left, and walk to the next corner. Or turn your back on the Coop and follow Massachusetts Ave. to Quincy St., then turn left and walk 1 long block to Broadway.

Massachusetts Institute of Technology (MIT)

The public is welcome at the Massachusetts Institute of Technology campus, a mile or so from Harvard Square, across the Charles River from Beacon Hill and the Back Bay. Visit the **Information Office**, 77 Massachusetts Ave. (© **617/253-4795**), to take a free guided tour (weekdays at 11am and 3pm) or to pick up a copy of a self-guided walking tour. At the same address, the **Hart Nautical Galleries** (open Tues–Fri 10am–5pm) contain ship and engine models that illustrate the development of marine engineering.

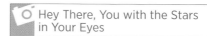

Hey There, You with the Stars in Your Eyes

Two local colleges have on-campus observatories that allow the public a look at the skies above Boston—through a telescope. This is a good evening activity for high school students as well as adults. The Judson B. Coit Observatory at **Boston University**, 725 Commonwealth Ave. (© **617/353-2630;** www.bu.edu/astronomy/events), throws open its doors on most Wednesdays, year-round. The **Harvard College Observatory**, 60 Garden St. (© **617/495-9059;** http://cfa.harvard.edu/events), schedules a lecture and quality time with a telescope on the third Thursday of each month.

MIT's campus is known for its art and architecture. The excellent **outdoor sculpture** collection includes works by Picasso and Alexander Calder, and notable modern buildings include designs by Frank Gehry, Eero Saarinen, and I. M. Pei. Gehry designed the **Stata Center** (http://web.mit.edu/evolving/buildings/stata), a curvilinear landmark that opened on Vassar Street off Main Street in 2004. Fumihiko Maki, a Pritzker Prize winner, designed the **Media Lab** complex, 20 Ames St. (at Amherst St.).

To get to MIT, take the MBTA Red Line to Kendall/MIT. The scenic walk from the Back Bay takes you along Massachusetts Avenue over the river straight to the campus. By car from Boston, cross the river at the Museum of Science, Cambridge Street, or Massachusetts Avenue and follow signs to Memorial Drive, where you can usually find parking during the day.

MIT Museum ☺ Engaging holography displays and robots are the hallmarks of the MIT Museum, where you'll also find works in more conventional media, such as kinetic sculpture. But the focus isn't art—it's the role of science and technology in society, explored through practical applications such as medical devices and gorgeous documents such as historic architectural plans. Little kids aren't the target audience, but middle-schoolers and their older siblings will have a blast with activities and programs geared to them. Be sure to check out the entertaining gift shop.

Tip: The **List Visual Arts Center** (© **617/253-4680;** http://web.mit.edu/lvac), home to MIT's contemporary art collections, is about 5 minutes away—and it's free. Head to the Wiesner Building, 20 Ames St. (btw. Main and Amherst sts.), Tuesday through Sunday from noon to 6pm, until 8pm on Thursday.

265 Massachusetts Ave. (Building N51, at Front St.). © **617/253-5927.** web.mit.edu/museum. Admission $8 adults; $3 seniors, students, and children 5–17; free for children under 5. Closed major holidays. T: Red Line to Central, then 10-min. walk.

BOSTON NEIGHBORHOODS TO EXPLORE

Boston is a city of neighborhoods, some of which I've described in talking about the Freedom Trail (see "The Freedom Trail," earlier in this chapter) and in the walking tours in chapter 7. Here are several other areas that are fun to explore. Bear in mind that many of the buildings you will see are private homes, not tourist attractions. See chapter 5 for dining suggestions and chapter 8 for shopping tips.

Beacon Hill ★★★

The original Boston settlers, clustered around what are now the Old State House and the North End, considered Beacon Hill far away. Today the distance is a matter of atmosphere; climbing "the Hill" is like traveling back in time. Lace up your walking shoes (the brick sidewalks gnaw at anything fancier, and driving is next to impossible), wander the narrow streets, and admire the brick and brownstone architecture.

At Beacon and Park streets is a figurative high point (literally, it's *the* high point): Charles Bulfinch's magnificent **State House.** The 60-foot **monument** at the rear illustrates the hill's original height, before the top was lopped off to use in 19th-century landfill projects. **Beacon and Mount Vernon streets** run downhill to commercially dense **Charles Street,** but if ever there was an area where there's no need to head in a straight line, it's this one. Your travels might take you past the former homes of Louisa May Alcott (10 Louisburg Sq.), Henry Kissinger (1 Chestnut St.), Julia Ward Howe (13 Chestnut St.), Edwin Booth (29A Chestnut St.), and Robert Frost (88 Mount Vernon St.). One of the oldest standing black churches in the country, the **African Meeting House** (p. 169), is at 8 Smith Court.

Strolling around the Back Bay is a great way to spend an afternoon.

These days, Alcott's neighbors on **Louisburg Square** (say "Lewis-burg") would include U.S. Senator John Kerry and his wife, Teresa Heinz Kerry. Twenty-two homes where a struggling writer would more likely be an employee than a resident surround the lovely park. The iron-railed square is open only to residents with keys.

Let your wandering take you down to Charles Street. A great stop for a drink and a pastry or snack is **Cafe Vanille,** 70 Charles St. (© **617/523-9200**).

WELCOME TO THE north end

The Paul Revere House and the Old North Church are the best-known buildings in the **North End ★★★**, Boston's "Little Italy" (although locals *never* call it that). Home to natives of Italy and their assimilated children, numerous Italian restaurants and private social clubs, and many historic sites, this is one of the oldest neighborhoods in the city. It was home in the 17th century to the **Mather family** of Puritan ministers, who certainly would be shocked to see the merry goings-on at the festivals and street fairs that take over different areas of the North End on weekends in July and August.

The Italians and their descendants (and the yuppie neighbors who have crowded many of them out since the 1980s) are only the latest immigrant group to dominate the North End. In the 19th century, this was an Eastern European Jewish enclave and later an Irish stronghold. In 1890, President Kennedy's mother, Rose Fitzgerald, was born on Garden Court Street and baptized at St. Stephen's Church on Hanover Street.

Modern visitors might be more interested in a Hanover Street *caffè,* the perfect place to have coffee or a soft drink and feast on sweets. **Mike's Pastry ★★**, 300 Hanover St. (© **617/742-3050;** www.mikespastry.com), is a bakery that does a frantic takeout business and has tables where you can sit down and order one of the confections on display in the cases. The signature item is cannoli (tubes of crisp-fried pastry filled with sweetened ricotta cheese); the cookies, cakes, and other pastries are excellent, too. You can also sit and relax at **Caffè Vittoria** or **Caffè dello Sport,** on either side of Mike's.

Before you leave the North End, stroll down toward the water and see whether there's a **boccie** game going on at the courts on Commercial Street near Hull Street. The European pastime is both a game of skill and an excuse to hang around and shoot the breeze—in Italian and English—with the locals (mostly men of a certain age). It's so popular that the neighborhood has courts both outdoors, in the Langone Playground at Puopolo Park, and indoors, at the back of the adjacent Steriti Rink, 561 Commercial St.

After you've had your fill of the shops and restaurants there, investigate the architecture of the **"flats,"** between Charles Street and the Charles River. Built on landfill, the buildings here are younger than those higher up, but many are just as eye-catching. MTV fans might recognize the converted firehouse at Mount Vernon and River streets as a former *Real World* location (it's also a one-time S*penser: For Hire* set).

T: Red Line to Charles/MGH, Green Line to Park Street, or Blue Line to Bowdoin (weekdays only).

The South End ★★

One of Boston's most diverse neighborhoods is also one of its largest, but fans of Victorian architecture won't mind the sore feet they'll have after trekking around the South End.

The neighborhood was laid out in the mid–19th century, before the Back Bay. While the newer area's grid echoes the boulevards of Paris, the South End tips its hat to London. The main streets are broad, and pocket parks dot the side streets. Late-20th-century gentrification saw many South End brownstones reclaimed from squalor and converted into luxury condominiums, driving out many longtime residents and making construction materials as widespread as falling leaves. Even on the few remaining run-down buildings, you'll see wonderful details.

Exit Back Bay Station and walk away from Copley Square down **Dartmouth Street,** crossing Columbus Avenue. Proceed on Dartmouth and explore some of the streets that extend to the left, including **Chandler, Lawrence, and Appleton streets.** This area is known as **Clarendon Park.** Turn left on any of these streets and walk to **Clarendon Street.** Its intersection with Tremont Street is the part of the South End you're most likely to see if you're not out exploring. This is the area where businesses and restaurants surround the **Boston Center for the Arts** (p. 257) and **Hamersley's Bistro** (p. 115). The BCA's **Cyclorama** building (the interior is dome-shaped), at 539 Tremont St., is listed on the National Register of Historic Places. Here you can see a show, have a meal, or continue your expedition, perhaps to do a little shopping on Tremont Street, Shawmut Avenue, or Washington Street. The 2 blocks of **Union Park Street** between Tremont and Washington streets are especially pretty, with some interesting shops and a good cafe, **South End Buttery** (p. 116), at the corner of Shawmut Avenue. You can wander and explore all the way to Massachusetts Avenue. From there, take the no. 1 bus to the Back Bay or into Cambridge, or the Orange Line downtown.

T: Orange Line to Back Bay or Green Line to Copley.

The BCA's Cyclorama building.

Jamaica Plain ★

You can combine a visit to the Arnold Arboretum (p. 174) with a stroll around Jamaica Pond or along Centre Street. Culturally diverse Jamaica Plain abounds with interesting architecture and open space. The pond is especially pleasant in good weather, when people walk, run, skate, fish, picnic, and sunbathe. Many of the 19th-century mansions overlooking the pond date to the days when families fled the oppressive heat downtown and moved to the "country" for the summer.

Another popular destination—it's better for contemplation than for sun-worshiping—is **Forest Hills Cemetery,** 95 Forest Hills Ave., off Tower Street (✆ **617/524-0128;** www.foresthillscemetery.com). Consecrated in 1848, the beautifully landscaped cemetery exists in the shadow of Cambridge's Mount Auburn (p. 176), another horticulturally notable institution known for its famous inhabitants. Forest Hills is the final resting place of Eugene O'Neill, e e cummings (whose gravestone reads EDWARD ESTLIN CUMMINGS), and the abolitionist William Lloyd Garrison, among others.

After you've had your fill of nature (or before you set out), Centre Street makes a good destination for wandering and snacking. The AIDS Action Committee's excellent resale shop, **Boomerangs,** 716 Centre St. (✆ **617/524-5120;** www.aac.org), is worth a look for upscale merchandise and reasonable prices. A favorite among the neighborhood's countless dining destinations is **JP Licks Homemade Ice Cream,** 659 Centre St. (✆ **617/524-6740;** www.jplicks.com). The **Centre Street Café,** 669 Centre St. (✆ **617/524-9217;** www.centrestcafe.com), is *the* place for weekend brunch in this neighborhood, and there's a line outside for a reason. Across the street from the Forest Hills T is the **Dogwood Café,** 3712 Washington St. (✆ **617/522-7997;** www.dogwood cafe.com), a family-friendly bar and restaurant with plenty of beers on tap and tasty pizza.

T: Orange Line to Forest Hills or Green Street.

Jamaica Pond.

ESPECIALLY FOR KIDS

What can the children do in Boston? A better question might be "What *can't* the children do in Boston?" Just about every major attraction in the city either is specifically designed to appeal to youngsters or can easily be adapted to do so.

The following attractions are covered extensively elsewhere in this chapter; here's the boiled-down version for busy parents.

Destinations that offer something for every member of the family include **Faneuil Hall Marketplace** (✆ 617/338-2323; p. 137); the **Museum of Fine Arts** (✆ 617/267-9300; p. 144), which offers special weekend and after-school programs; and the **USS Constitution Museum** (✆ 617/426-1812; p. 165).

Hands-on exhibits and large-format films are the headliners at the **New England Aquarium** (✆ 617/973-5200; p. 148), where you'll find the Simons IMAX Theatre, and at the **Museum of Science** (✆ 617/723-2500; p. 146), home to the Mugar Omni Theater as well as the Hayden Planetarium.

You might get your hands on a baseball at a **Red Sox game** (p. 202) or the **Sports Museum of New England** (✆ 617/624-1234; p. 202).

The allure of seeing people the size of ants draws young visitors to the **Prudential Center Skywalk Observatory** (✆ 617/859-0648; p. 146). And they can see actual ants—although they might prefer the dinosaurs—at the **Harvard Museum of Natural History** (✆ 617/495-3045; p. 177).

Older children who have studied modern American history will enjoy a visit to the **John F. Kennedy Presidential Library and Museum** (✆ 617/929-4523; p. 142). Middle-schoolers who enjoyed Esther Forbes's *Johnny Tremain* will probably get a kick out of the **Paul Revere House** (✆ 617/523-2338; p. 161). Young visitors who have read Robert McCloskey's classic *Make Way for Ducklings* will relish a visit to the **Public Garden** (p. 173), and fans of E. B. White's *The Trumpet of the Swan* certainly will want to ride on the **Swan Boats** (✆ 617/522-1966; p. 173). Considerably less tame (and much longer) are **whale watches** (p. 193).

 More Kid Stuff

For more suggestions, check (or let the kids check) elsewhere in this book. Chapter 9 lists nightlife destinations for all ages. Before night falls (and sometimes afterward), the whole family can have a great time at the **Hard Rock Cafe** (food and music), **Club Passim** (folk music), *Shear Madness* (audience-participation theater), **Blue Man Group** (performance art), and the **Puppet Showplace Theater.**

Turn to chapter 8 for shopping recommendations—the **Boston Bead Company,** the **CambridgeSide Galleria** mall, **Curious George & Friends,** and the area's numerous **college bookstores** can be almost as fun as all-toy stores.

Finally, check chapter 10 for information about day trips. Fun destinations include **Salem, Plymouth,** and (for *Little Women* fans) **Concord.**

Boston Harbor Cruises, 1 Long Wharf (☎ **877/733-9425** or 617/227-4321; www.bostonharborcruises.com), offers a cruise called **Codzilla,** which it bills as a "high-speed thrill boat ride." It leaves Long Wharf daily from mid-May through early October; from the shore, you may be able to hear delighted screaming. Tickets cost $25 for adults, $23 for seniors, and $21 for children 4 to 12; reservations are recommended.

Note: At press time, the **Boston Tea Party Ship & Museum** (☎ 617/269-7150; www.bostonteapartyship.com) was under renovation and scheduled to reopen in 2012 as the Boston Tea Party Ships & Museum. The expanded institution will comprise full-size replicas of all three merchant ships that were raided during the colonial uprising in December 1773 (not just the one that was here originally). I've updated some version of this paragraph at least once a year since a devastating fire shuttered the attraction in 2001, so definitely check ahead before heading out.

The walking-tour company **Boston By Foot ★★** (☎ 617/367-2345; www.bostonbyfoot.org) offers **"Boston By Little Feet"** for children 6 to 12 years old. The 1-hour walk gives a child's-eye view of the architecture along the Freedom Trail and of Boston's role in the American Revolution. Children must be accompanied by an adult, and a map is provided. Tours run from May through October and begin at the statue of Samuel Adams on the Congress Street side of Faneuil Hall. They begin Friday and Saturday at 10am and Sunday at 2pm, rain or shine. The cost is $8 per person.

Blue Hills Trailside Museum ☺ At the foot of Great Blue Hill, a 20-minute drive south of Boston, this museum is fun for all ages and especially popular with the under-10 set. Here you'll see replicas of the natural habitats found in the area, displays about Native Americans, and live animal exhibits. Resident animals include a bald eagle, owls, honeybees, otters, snakes, opossum, and turtles. Children can feed the ducks and turkeys. Other activities include climbing the lookout tower and hiking around the 7,500-acre Blue Hills Reservation recreation area. Check ahead for the schedule of weekend programs, which might include a live animal presentation, outdoor excursion, or another activity. Special events and family programs change with the seasons; call ahead to register.

1904 Canton Ave., Milton. ☎ **617/333-0690.** www.massaudubon.org. Admission $3 adults, $2 seniors, $1.50 children 2–12, free for children 1 and under and Mass.Audubon Society members. Museum: Thurs–Sun and Mon holidays 10am–5pm. Trails: Daily dawn–dusk. By car, take I-93 S. to exit 2B (Rte. 138 N.).

The Blue Hills Trailside Museum focuses on the natural world.

Boston Children's Museum ★★ ☺ As you approach this wonderful museum, look for the 40-foot-high red-and-white milk bottle out front—and for children and their chronological-adult companions racing each other to the entrance. The under-11 set is the target audience for this delightful museum, but it appeals to the little kid in everyone.

As they explore, beginning in the glass-enclosed lobby, young visitors can stick with their adults or wander on their own, learning, doing, and role-playing. A three-story-high structure, the **New Balance Climb,** incorporates motor skills and problem-solving; kids work their way through while adults watch from the stairs. Other favorite hands-on exhibits include physical experiments (such as creating giant soap bubbles) in **Science Playground** and getting creative with **Johnny's Workbench,** a souped-up version of puttering in the garage. You can explore **Boston Black,** which celebrates the city's black history and culture, and the **Japanese House,** a 2-story residence from Kyoto, one of Boston's sister cities. Children under 4 and their caregivers have a special room, **PlaySpace,** that's packed with toys and activities; kids 3 to 5 can learn basic science skills in **Peep's World,** based on the PBS program *Peep and the Big Wide World.*

The museum, the second-oldest children's museum in the country (only Brooklyn's is older), is gearing up for its centennial in 2013. It occupies a converted wool warehouse, and is a certified green building right down to the toilets; visit the website to learn more. Check ahead for information about traveling exhibitions and special programs. And be sure to check out the excellent gift shop.

308 Congress St. (Museum Wharf). © **617/426-6500.** www.bostonchildrensmuseum.org. Admission $12 adults, seniors, and children 1–15, free for children under 1; Fri 5–9pm $1 for all. Sat–Thurs 10am–5pm; Fri 10am–9pm. Closed Thanksgiving, Dec 25, and until noon Jan 1. T: Red Line to South Station; from South Station walk north on Atlantic Ave. 1 block (past Federal Reserve Bank), turn right onto Congress St., then walk 2 blocks (across bridge). Or Silver Line to Courthouse; walk toward downtown and turn left at Fort Point Channel. Discounted parking available.

The giant milk bottle out front makes the Boston Children's Museum easy to spot.

Lowland gorillas are just one of the many animals you'll encounter at the Franklin Park Zoo.

Franklin Park Zoo ☺ This enjoyable, engaging attraction is in an outlying neighborhood of Boston; animal-mad families won't mind the cab ride or trek on public transit. The centerpiece is the **Tropical Forest** exhibit, a sprawling complex that houses more than 50 species of animals. Here you might have a close encounter with a Western lowland gorilla (Little Joe, who made international headlines by literally going over the wall in 2003, is secure in a redesigned enclosure) or see a pygmy hippo. Kids find the hands-on **Franklin Farm** both entertaining and educational. **Tigers, lions,** and **giraffes** (with their zebra friends) have their own turf, as do the zoo's 400 budgies (parakeets). The **Serengeti Crossing** and **Outback Trail** exhibits assemble species from their respective continents—African zebras, ibex, and ostriches; and Australian kangaroos, emus, and cockatoos.

Allow at least half a day for a visit, and try to budget for a cab ride in at least one direction. Franklin Park is 40 minutes from downtown by subway and bus, and the walk from the main gate and parking area to the entrance is fairly long.

1 Franklin Park Rd. ✆ **617/541-LION (5466).** www.franklinparkzoo.org. Admission $16 adults, $13 seniors, $10 children 2–12, free for children 1 and under; $10 for all 1st Sat of the month before noon. Apr–Sept Mon–Fri 10am–5pm, Sat–Sun and holidays 10am–6pm; Oct–Mar daily 10am–4pm. T: Orange Line to Forest Hills or Red Line to Andrew, then bus 16 to the main entrance, or a $15 cab ride from central Boston. Check website for driving directions and information about winter discounts.

ORGANIZED TOURS
Orientation Tours

GUIDED WALKING TOURS Even if you usually prefer to explore on your own, I heartily recommend a walking tour with **Boston By Foot ★★** (© 617/367-2345; www.bostonbyfoot.org). From April to October (the full schedule starts in May), the nonprofit educational corporation conducts historical and architectural tours that focus on particular neighborhoods or themes. The rigorously trained guides are volunteers who encourage questions. Buy tickets ($12 adults, $8 children 6–12) from the guide; reservations are not required. The 90-minute tours take place rain or shine. On the last Sunday of each month, a special tour ($15) covers a particular subject or area such as Art Deco design or Harvard Square. In addition, the company offers themed holiday strolls and year-round group tours.

Note: All excursions from Faneuil Hall start at the statue of Samuel Adams on Congress Street.

The **Heart of the Freedom Trail** tour starts at Faneuil Hall daily at 10am and Friday through Monday at 2pm. Tours of **Beacon Hill** begin at the foot of the State House steps on Beacon Street weekdays at 5:30pm, Saturday and Sunday at 2pm. Other tours and meeting places are **Victorian Back Bay,** on the front steps of Trinity Church, Monday at 5:30pm, Friday at 2pm, and Sunday at 10am; the **North End,** at Faneuil Hall, Friday through Sunday at 1pm; **Literary Landmarks,** School and Washington streets, Saturday at 10am; and the **Dark Side of Boston,** Hanover and Cross streets, North End, Saturday at 5:30pm.

Boston Underfoot looks at subterranean technology, including the subway and the relocation of the Central Artery. It starts at Faneuil Hall Sunday at 1pm and costs $14 (including subway fare).

Unofficial Tours (© 617/674-7788; www.unofficialtours.com), the brainchild of some entrepreneurial Harvard grads, offer an insider's perspective on Harvard Square and a separate tour of the Freedom Trail. Two guides lead each of the tours, which cost $10 for adults, $9 for seniors and students, and $6 for children.

For information about other guided walking tours of the **Freedom Trail** (with a costumed Freedom Trail Player, or free with a National Park Service ranger) see the section "The Freedom Trail," on p. 150.

"DUCK" TOURS The most unusual and enjoyable way to see Boston is with **Boston Duck Tours ★★★** (© 800/226-7442 or 617/267-3825; www.bostonducktours.com). The tours, offered from late March through November and on the first 3 weekends of December, are pricey but great fun. Sightseers board a "duck," a reconditioned World War II amphibious landing craft, behind the Prudential Center on Huntington Avenue or at the Museum of Science. The 80-minute narrated tour begins with a quick but comprehensive jaunt around the city. Then the duck lumbers down a ramp, splashes into the Charles River, and goes for a spin around the basin. Fun!

Tickets, available at the Prudential Center, Museum of Science, and New England Aquarium, are $33 for adults, $28 for seniors and students, $23 for children 3 to 11, and $10 for children 2 and under. Tours run every 30 or 60 minutes from 9am to 30 minutes before sunset, and they usually sell out. Discounted (by $2–$4) 55-minute tours leave from the New

The Boston Duck Tours give you a unique perspective on the city.

England Aquarium starting at 3pm daily from June through August and on weekends in April, May, September, and October. Timed tickets go on sale 30 days ahead online, in person, and by phone; same-day in-person sales start at 8:30am (9am at the aquarium). Reservations are accepted only for groups of 20 or more. No tours late December through mid-March.

TROLLEY TOURS The ticket vendors who clamor for your business wherever tourists gather will claim that no visit is complete without a day on a trolley. Sometimes that's true. If you're unable to walk long distances, are short on time, or are traveling with children, a narrated tour on a trolley (actually a bus chassis with a trolley body) can be a good idea. You can get an overview of the city before you focus on specific attractions, or use the all-day pass to hit as many places as possible in 8 hours or so. In some neighborhoods, notably the North End, trolleys stop some distance from the attractions—don't believe a ticket seller who tells you otherwise. Because Boston is so pedestrian-friendly, a trolley tour isn't the best choice for the able-bodied and unencumbered making a long visit, but it can save time and effort. For those who are physically able, I can't say this enough: *Climb down and look around.*

The business is very competitive, with various firms offering different stops

Behind the Scenes at the BSO

From October through early May, free volunteer-led tours of **Symphony Hall,** 301 Massachusetts Ave. (*©* **617/638-9390; www.bso.org**), take visitors all around the landmark building and relate the Boston Symphony Orchestra's fascinating history. The 1-hour tours start on Wednesday at 4pm and on the second Saturday of each month at 2pm, subject to change (always check ahead). E-mail **bsav@bso.org** to request a slot, then meet in the lobby at the Massachusetts Avenue entrance. For information about performances, see p. 262.

Moon River, Moon Harbor

Fire up the camera as you approach the water. Every **bridge** that crosses the river between Boston and Cambridge affords an excellent perspective. If your travels take you to the area around the Esplanade or Kendall Square (T: Red Line to Charles/MGH or Kendall/MIT), wander out onto the **Longfellow Bridge,** especially at twilight—the views of the river are splendid, and if you hit it just right, the moon appears to shine out of the Hancock Tower.

In warm weather, check the time of moonrise and stroll down to the plaza at the end of **Long Wharf** (T: Blue Line to Aquarium). The full moon seems to rise out of the Boston Harbor Islands, and because it's so close to the horizon, it looks huge. For astronomical reasons, this only works in the summer, but boy, is it cool.

and add-ons in an effort to distinguish themselves from the rest. All cover the major attractions and offer informative narratives and anecdotes in their 90- to 120-minute tours; most offer free reboarding if you want to visit the attractions. Each tour is only as good as its guide, and quality varies widely —every few years a TV station or newspaper runs an "exposé" of the wacky information a tour guide is passing off as fact. If you have time, you might chat up guides in the waiting area and choose the one you like best.

Trolley tickets cost $25 to $40 for adults, $16 or less for children. Most companies offer online discounts and reservations, and you may find discount coupons at visitor information centers and hotel-lobby brochure racks. Boarding spots are at hotels, historic sites, and tourist information centers. Busy waiting areas are near the New England Aquarium, the Park Street T stop, and the corner of Boylston Street and Charles Street South, across from Boston Common. Each company paints its cars a different color. They include orange-and-green **Old Town Trolley Tours** (© 617/269-7010; www.trolleytours.com/boston), red **Beantown Trolley** vehicles (© 800/343-1328 or 617/720-6342; www.beantowntrolley.com), silver **CityView Trolleys** (© 617/363-7899; www.cityviewtrolleys.com), and yellow-and-green **Upper Deck Trolley Tours** (© 877/343-8257 or 617/742-1440; www.bostonsupertrolleytours.com).

Sightseeing Cruises

Take to the water for a taste of Boston's rich maritime history or a daylong break from walking and driving. You can cruise around the harbor or go all the way to Provincetown. The **sightseeing cruise ★★** season runs from **April through November,** with spring and fall offerings often restricted to weekends. Check websites for discount coupons before you leave home. If you're traveling in a large group, call ahead for information about reservations and discounted tickets.

And if you're prone to seasickness, check the size of the vessel for your tour before buying tickets; larger boats provide more cushioning and comfort than smaller ones.

Before taking a cruise just for the sake of taking a cruise, weigh the investment of time and money against your group's interests. Especially if kids are along, you might be better off with an excursion that targets a destination—the Charlestown Navy Yard (see the box titled "On the Cheap," below), the Boston Harbor Islands (see the box titled "A Vacation in the Islands" on p. 199), or Boston Light (see the box titled "Trip the Light Fantastic," below)—than with a pricey narrated cruise.

The largest company is **Boston Harbor Cruises,** 1 Long Wharf (© **877/733-9425** or 617/227-4321; www.bostonharborcruises.com). Ninety-minute **historic sightseeing cruises,** which tour the Inner and Outer harbors, depart from Long Wharf May through September daily at 11am, 1pm, and 3pm, with extra excursions at busy times. Tickets are $21 for adults, $19 for seniors, and $17 for children 4 to 12; tickets for the sunset cruise (6 or 7pm) are $1 more. The 45-minute **USS *Constitution* cruise** takes you around the Inner Harbor and docks at the Charlestown Navy Yard so that you can go ashore and visit "Old Ironsides." Tours leave Long Wharf daily April through November hourly from 10:30am to 4:30pm,

---

Trip the Light Fantastic

North America's oldest lighthouse, **Boston Light** ★★, is the only one in the country that's still staffed (by the Coast Guard). Built on **Little Brewster Island** in 1716, it fell to the British in 1776 and was rebuilt in 1783. Excursions to the 102-foot lighthouse include a narrated cruise that passes two other lighthouses, 90 minutes to explore the island, and a chance to climb the spiral stairs to the top (you must be at least 50 in. tall). The 3-hour tours operate on weekends from late June to late September from the

Moakley Courthouse dock at Fan Pier, off Northern Avenue. Tickets cost $41 for adults, $37 for seniors, $31 for children 3 to 11, free for children 2 and under. Only 48 people may take each tour; reservations (© **617/223-8666;** www.boston islands.com/tour-lighthouse) are strongly recommended. Visit the website for information about a tour of Boston Harbor that concentrates on three lighthouses and includes a visit to Little Brewster, but not a lighthouse climb.

and on the hour from the Navy Yard from 11am to 5pm. The cruise is $16 for adults, $14 for seniors, and $12 for children. Check the website for other offerings, including dining cruises and a 5-hour excursion that passes a dozen lighthouses.

The **Charles Riverboat Company** (① 617/621-3001; www.charlesriverboat.com) offers 60-minute narrated cruises from

On the Cheap

You don't have to take a tour to take a cruise. The MBTA runs a **ferry** that connects Long Wharf, next to the New England Aquarium, and the Charlestown Navy Yard. It costs $1.70, is included in the MBTA's 7-day LinkPass, and makes a good final leg of the Freedom Trail.

the CambridgeSide Galleria mall daily May through October. Tours of the **lower Charles River basin** start at 11:30am and 12:45, 2, 3:15, and 4:30pm. A tour of the **Charles River lock system and Boston Harbor** begins at 10am. The **sunset cruise** runs daily from June through August; call to confirm times. Tickets cost $14 to $16 for adults, $12 to $14 for seniors, and $8 to $10 for children 2 to 12.

DAY TRIPS Two companies serve **Provincetown ★★★**, at the tip of Cape Cod. On a day trip, you'll have time for world-class people-watching, strolling around the novelty shops and art galleries, lunching on seafood, and—if you're quick—a trip to the famous beaches. However, you'll have to forgo the hopping gay nightlife scene unless you've planned a longer excursion. (For in-depth coverage of Provincetown and other Cape Cod locales, consult *Frommer's Cape Cod, Nantucket & Martha's Vineyard* or *Frommer's New England*.)

Bay State Cruise Company (① 877/783-3779 or 617/748-1428; www.provincetownfastferry.com) operates high-speed and conventional service to Provincetown. High-speed service takes half as long and costs almost twice as much as the conventional excursion, which is a time-honored New England tradition that's especially popular with families. Trips leave from the Seaport World Trade Center Marine Terminal, 200 Seaport Blvd. To get to the pier, take the Silver Line bus from South Station to the World Trade Center stop, the $10 water taxi (① 617/422-0392; www.citywatertaxi.com) from locations around the harbor, or a regular taxi (when you reserve your cruise, ask the clerk for the best way to reach the pier from your hotel).

Fast ferry service on the *Provincetown III* takes 90 minutes and operates three times a day from mid-May to mid-October. The round-trip fare is $79 for adults, $69 for seniors, and $58 for children 3 to 12, plus $6 each way for your bike. Reservations are recommended. **M/V *Provincetown II*** sails Saturday only from late June through early September. It leaves at 9am for the 3-hour trip to Provincetown, at the tip of Cape Cod. The return leg leaves at 3:30pm, giving you 3½ hours for shopping and sightseeing in P-town. The same-day round-trip fare is $44 for adults, free for children. Bringing a bike costs $6 extra each way.

Boston Harbor Cruises, 1 Long Wharf (① 877/733-9425 or 617/227-4321; www.bostonharborcruises.com), operates catamarans that make the trip in just 90 minutes. They operate from mid-May through Columbus Day, three times a day between early June and Labor Day weekend, and less often early and late in the season. The round-trip fare is $79 for adults, $69 for seniors, and $58 for children 4 to 12.

An up-close-and-personal glimpse of a whale.

Whale-Watching

For info about whale-watching trips from Cape Ann, see the box titled "A Whale of an Adventure" on p. 312.

The **New England Aquarium** (© 617/973-5200 for information, 617/973-5206 for tickets; www.neaq.org; p. 148) runs **whale watches ★★** daily from mid-April through late October and on weekends in early April. You'll travel several miles out to sea to Stellwagen Bank, the feeding ground for the whales as they migrate from Newfoundland to Provincetown. Enthusiastic naturalists narrate and identify the whales, many of which they call by name. Allow 3 to 4 hours. Tickets are $40 for adults, $32 for children 11 and under. Children must be at least 30 inches tall. Reservations are strongly recommended; you can buy tickets online, subject to a service charge.

With its onboard exhibits and vast experience, the aquarium offers the best whale watches in Boston. If they're booked, try **Boston Harbor Cruises** (© 877/733-9425 or 617/227-4321; www.bostonharborcruises.com), which operates up to five trips a day on its two high-speed catamarans, trimming the excursion time to 3 hours total.

Specialty Tours

Two excellent resources to investigate before you leave home are the **Boston Center for Adult Education** (© 617/267-4430; www.bcae.org) and the **Cambridge Center for Adult Education** (© 617/547-6789; www.ccae.org). Multiple-week courses are the norm, but both schools also schedule single-day classes that last 2 hours or longer. The expert-led offerings include walking tours (often with a focus on local architecture), cooking classes and wine tastings, and workshops about everything from poetry to gardening. Prices start at $30, and preregistration is required.

The **French Library Alliance Française** (✆ 617/912-0400; www. frenchlib.org) is a cultural center that offers cooking classes as well as intensive language instruction.

FOR HISTORY BUFFS Historic New England ★ (✆ 617/994-5920; www. historicnewengland.org) offers a 2-hour walking tour of Beacon Hill and other excursions that concentrate on particular areas or topics—surf ahead for specifics and schedules. Most tours begin at the Otis House Museum, 141 Cambridge St. Prices start at $12, which includes a tour of the museum, and reservations are recommended.

A map of the self-guided tour created by the **Boston Irish Tourism Association** (✆ 617/696-9880; www.irishheritagetrail.com) is available at the Boston Common and Prudential Center visitor centers. Check the website for an interactive map with pop-ups describing the sites, and information about guided tours.

FOR ARCHITECTURE BUFFS Check ahead for walking tours and classes with the **Boston Center for Adult Education** or **Cambridge Center for Adult Education** (see above).

FOR CRIMINAL-JUSTICE MAJORS Free guided tours of the **John Joseph Moakley U.S. Courthouse,** 1 Courthouse Way, show off the waterfront building's dramatic architecture and introduce visitors to the workings of the justice system. You may even see part of a trial. Docents from **Discovering Justice** (✆ 617/748-4185; www.discoveringjustice.org) lead the 1-hour tours, which are available to individuals and groups by appointment only Tuesday, Wednesday, and Friday throughout the year (reserve 2 weeks in advance).

The courthouse is on Fan Pier, off Northern Avenue across Fort Point Channel from the Coast Guard building at 408 Atlantic Ave. You can walk from downtown or take the Silver Line bus from South Station to the Courthouse stop, 1 block away. To enter the building, adults must show two forms of ID (one of which must have a photo), and everyone must temporarily surrender his or her cellphone. You don't have to take a tour to enter— local office workers often visit the second-floor cafeteria, which has decent food and a breathtaking view.

FOR PEDAL PUSHERS A group bicycle tour covers more in 2½ to 3 hours than you could ever see on foot. The diverse offerings of **Urban AdvenTours,** 103 Atlantic Ave. (✆ 800/979-3370 for tickets, or 617/670-0637 for info; www.urbanadventours.com), include a tour that focuses on historic neighborhoods and landmarks and another that focuses on the harbor and the Charles River. You can also request a customized special-interest excursion. Prices begin at $50 per person and include bicycle and helmet rental. You can also rent bikes, which can be picked up at the North End shop (across the Rose Kennedy Greenway from Faneuil Hall Marketplace) or delivered to your hotel or any other location.

FOR SHUTTERBUGS The unusual offerings of **PhotoWalks** (✆ 617/851-2273; www.photowalks.com) combine narrated walking tours with photography tips. On a 90-minute stroll around Beacon Hill, the Public Garden, or the Freedom Trail, visitors learn to look at Boston from (literally) a different angle—that of a creative photographer. Adults pay $30, youths 10 to 17 $15.

missing **THIS WOULD BE A CRIME**

A bailiff at the adjacent Suffolk County Courthouse tipped me off to the wonders of the **John Adams Courthouse ★★**, one of the most beautiful buildings in Boston and one of the city's most interesting destinations. Constructed between 1886 and 1894, expanded in 1910, and extensively renovated around the turn of the 21st century, the courthouse recalls an era when public buildings were more like cathedrals.

It is the suitably impressive home of the Supreme Judicial Court, or SJC, the highest court in the Massachusetts system and the oldest (1692) appellate court in the Western Hemisphere. The French Second Empire facade of the courthouse conceals an unbelievably elaborate interior dripping with frescoes, moldings, paintings, and sculptures, all surrounding the soaring central space, the Great Hall, which sits beneath a richly decorated vaulted ceiling. The galleries on either side of the lowest level hold exhibits relating to history and the courts; *John Adams: Architect of American Government* will be on display during your visit.

The public is welcome to look around or to attend a court session if one is going on. The building is open Monday through Friday from 8:30am to 5pm, and you and your bags must be inspected before entering. The entrance is at 1 Pemberton Sq., hidden in plain sight behind the curving Center Plaza complex on Cambridge Street, across from City Hall Plaza and the Government Center T stop. Head to the second floor and ask for a brochure from the helpful staff of the Public Information Office (© **617/557-1114;** www.mass.gov/courts/sjc), or arrange in advance to take a 1-hour tour with **Discovering Justice** (© **617/748-4185;** www.discoveringjustice.org).

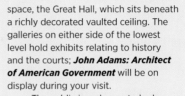

Tours run several times a week from April through October, and by appointment during the winter. Call or surf ahead for reservations.

FOR MOVIE FANS Boston Movie Tours (© **866/668-4345;** www.boston movietours.net) boast that they offer "behind-the-scenes trivia and insider gossip" about the city's incarnations on the silver and small screens—a busy undertaking now that there's film production going on all over the state, but these tours keep up. Guides offer regularly updated info about the local color in *The Departed, Good Will Hunting, Mystic River, Legally Blonde,* and, of course, *Cheers,* among other projects. The 90-minute Boston Movie Mile walking tours ($21 adults, $18 seniors and students, $11 children 6–12) and 2½-hour Theater-on-Wheels bus tours ($37 adults, $34 seniors and students, $28 children) operate April through October daily except Tuesday.

Check start times and locations when you make reservations, which are strongly recommended.

FOR HORROR-MOVIE FANS Ghosts & Gravestones (℃ 888/920-8687 or 617/269-3626; www.ghostsandgravestones.com) covers burial grounds and other shiver-inducing areas in a trolley and on foot, with a guide dressed as a gravedigger. The 90-minute tour starts at dusk on weekends in April, May, and early November, and nightly from Memorial Day weekend through October. It costs $38 for adults, $24 for children 4 to 12. Children 3 and under are not allowed, and the company cautions that the tour might not be suitable for kids 12 and under. Reservations are required.

FOR FOODIES A neighborhood resident offers **North End Market Tours ★** (℃ 617/523-6032; www.foodtoursofboston.com), 3-hour excursions that stop at many of the shops in the legendary Italian-American stronghold. Tours include product tastings, cooking tips, and plenty of local lore. They cost $50 per person. The same company offers a 3½-hour **Chinatown Market Tour;** the $65 fee includes a dim sum lunch. Visit the website to register and pay in advance.

A cooking or wine-tasting class makes an excellent, if pricey, break from shopping and sightseeing. Resources to check out before you leave home include: **Boston University**'s Seminars in the Arts and Culinary Arts (℃ 617/353-9852; www.bu.edu/foodandwine); the **Cambridge School of Culinary Arts** (℃ 617/354-2020; www.cambridgeculinary.com); the **Boston Vegetarian Society** (℃ 617/424-8846; www.bostonveg.org); the **Elephant Walk** restaurant (p. 122; ℃ 617/285-0410; www.elephant walk.com/classes); and the **Bristol Lounge,** in the Four Seasons Hotel, 200 Boylston St. (℃ 617/338-4400; www.fourseasons.com/boston/ dining). Winter visitors can check ahead for classes during the **Boston Wine Festival** (p. 33; ℃ 888/660-9463; www.bostonwinefestival.net). Another resource for wine lovers is the **Boston Wine School** (℃ 617/784-7150; www.bostonwineschool.com).

OUTDOOR PURSUITS

The **Department of Conservation & Recreation,** or DCR (℃ 617/626-1250; www.state.ma.us/dcr), oversees outdoor activities on public lands across the state through its divisions of Urban Parks & Recreation and State Parks & Recreation. (The Division of Urban Parks & Recreation replaced the Metropolitan District Commission, a name that still appears on many signs.) The incredibly helpful website includes descriptions of properties and activities, and has a planning area to help you make the most of your time.

Beaches

The beaches in Boston proper are not worth the trouble. Besides being bone-chilling, Boston Harbor water is subject to being declared unsafe for swimming for health reasons. If you want to swim, book a hotel with a pool. If you want the sand-between-your-toes experience, visit the North Shore or Walden Pond in Concord. See chapter 10 or consult the DCR (see the introduction to this section) for information on suburban beaches.

Biking

Despite Boston's recent push to be more welcoming to cyclists, out-of-towners who are anything other than complete experts will be better off exploring the area's numerous bike paths or visiting Cambridge. If you must stay in Boston, consider taking a tour (see "For Pedal Pushers," above)—the supervision of a guide who's experienced in the city's terrifying traffic is well worth the money. Check **www.cityofboston.gov/bikes** for information about the Boston Bikes initiative, which includes plans for a bike-sharing system.

State law requires that children 11 and under wear helmets. Bicycles are forbidden on buses and the Green Line at all times and during rush hours on the other lines of the subway system.

On summer Sundays from 11am to 7pm, a flat 1½-mile stretch of **Memorial Drive ★** in Cambridge, from Western Avenue to the Eliot Bridge (Central Sq. to west Cambridge), closes to cars. It's also popular with pedestrians and in-line skaters, and can get quite crowded. The **Dr. Paul Dudley White Charles River Bike Path ★★** is an 18-mile circuit that begins at Science Park (near the Museum of Science) and runs along both sides of the river as far as Watertown. Note that there's heavy vehicular traffic at nearly every crosswalk along the way. Bikers share the path with joggers and in-line skaters, especially in Boston near the Esplanade and in Cambridge near Harvard Square. The DCR (see the introduction to this section) maintains this path and the 5-mile **Pierre Lallement Bike Path,** in Southwest Corridor Park. It starts behind the Copley Place mall, on Dartmouth Street between Huntington and Columbus avenues, and runs through the South End and Roxbury along the route of the MBTA Orange Line to Franklin Park. The 11-mile **Minuteman Bikeway ★★** (www.minuteman bikeway.org) starts at Alewife station at the end of the Red Line in Cambridge. It runs through Arlington and Lexington to Bedford along an old railroad bed and is a wonderful way to reach the historic sites in Lexington.

The Dr. Paul Dudley White Charles River Bike Path is popular with both joggers and cyclists.

Rental shops require you to show a driver's license or passport and leave a deposit using a major credit card. Daily flat rates run $30 to $50. Check out **Urban AdvenTours** (see "For Pedal Pushers," above), which will deliver to your hotel; **Back Bay Bicycles,** 366 Commonwealth Ave., near Massachusetts Avenue (© 617/247-2336; www.backbaybicycles.com); **Cambridge Bicycle,** 259 Massachusetts Ave. (© 617/876-6555; www.cambridgebicycle.com), near MIT; and **Landry's Bicycles,** 890 Commonwealth Ave. (© 617/232-0446; www.landrys.com), near Boston University.

For additional information, including a calendar of events, contact **MassBike** (© 617/542-2453; www.massbike.org).

Golf

You won't get far in the suburbs without seeing a golf course, and given the sport's popularity, you won't be the only one looking. If possible, opt for the lower prices and smaller crowds that you'll find on weekdays. The **Massachusetts Golf Association** (© 800/356-2201 or 774/430-9100; www.mgalinks.org) represents more than 400 golf courses around the state and has a searchable online database.

One of the best public courses in the area, **Newton Commonwealth Golf Course,** 212 Kenrick St., Newton (© 617/630-1971; www.sterlinggolf.com), is a challenging 18-hole Donald Ross design. It's 5,305 yards from the blue tees, par is 70, and greens fees are $30 on weekdays, $37 on weekends.

Within the city limits is the legendary 6,009-yard **William J. Devine Golf Course,** in Franklin Park, Dorchester (© 617/265-4084; www.cityofboston golf.com). As a Harvard student, Bobby Jones sharpened his game on the 18-hole, par-70 course, which is managed by the city parks department. Greens fees are $40 on weekdays, $45 on weekends.

Less challenging but with more of a neighborhood feel is the 9-hole, par-35 **Fresh Pond Golf Course,** 691 Huron Ave., Cambridge (© 617/349-6282; www.freshpondgolf.com). The 3,161-yard layout adjoins the Fresh Pond Reservoir, and there's water on four holes. It charges $23, or $33 to go around twice, on weekdays; $26 and $38, respectively, on weekends and holidays.

Gyms

If your hotel doesn't have a health club, your best bet is to ask the concierge or front desk staff to recommend one nearby; you may receive a pass good for free or discounted admission. Guests at the **Ritz-Carlton, Boston Common,** have the use of the over-the-top facilities at the 100,000-square-foot Sports Club/LA, which is otherwise closed to nonmembers. Other hotels with good health clubs (see chapter 4) include the **Boston Harbor Hotel,** the **Charles Hotel,** the **Four Seasons Hotel,** the **Hilton Boston Logan Airport,** the **InterContinental Boston,** and the **Royal Sonesta Hotel.**

The "Y" (www.ymcaboston.org) offers the best combination of facilities and value; each of these locations has a pool, gym, weight room, and fitness center. The **Wang YMCA of Chinatown,** 8 Oak St. W., off Washington Street (© 617/426-2237), is convenient to downtown and charges $15 for a 1-day pass. The **Central Branch YMCA,** 316 Huntington Ave. (© 617/536-7800), near Symphony Hall, charges $10. **Fitcorp** (© 617/375-5600; www.fitcorp. com) charges $20 for a guest pass and offers well-equipped facilities but no pool.

A VACATION IN THE islands

Majestic ocean views, hiking trails, historic sites, rocky beaches, nature walks, campsites, and picnic areas abound in New England. To find them all together, head east (yes, east) of Boston to the **Boston Harbor Islands** (© **617/223-8666;** www.boston harborislands.org). The national park area's unspoiled beauty is a welcome break from the urban landscape, and the islands are not well known, even to many long-time Bostonians. Thirty-four islands dot the Outer Harbor, and at least a half dozen are open for exploring, camping, swimming, and more. Bring a sweater or jacket. Plan a day trip or even an overnight trip, but note that only Georges and Spectacle islands have fresh water, and management strongly suggests bringing your own.

Ferries run to **Georges Island** and **Spectacle Island.** Georges Island has a visitor center, refreshment area, fishing pier, picnic area, and wonderful views of Boston's skyline. It's home to Fort Warren (1833), which held Confederate prisoners during the Civil War. You can investigate on your own or take a ranger-led tour. **Spectacle Island,** which opened to the public in 2006, holds more than 3 million cubic yards of material dug up during the Big Dig—then sealed, covered with topsoil, and landscaped to allow recreational use. It's home to 5 miles of hiking trails, a beach, and an eco-friendly visitor center with a cafe.

Allow at least half a day, longer if you plan to take the water shuttle ($3/day) to **Bumpkin, Grape,** or **Lovells Island,** all of which have picnic areas and campsites. On the largest island, **Peddocks,** you can hike and picnic but not camp.

Admission to the islands is free. To get there, take a ferry run by **Boston's Best Cruises** (© **617/222-6999;** www.bostonsbestcruises.com) to Georges Island (30 min. or less) or Spectacle Island (15 min.) from Long Wharf. Round-trip tickets cost $14 for adults, $10 for seniors, $8 for children 3 to 11, $39 families (two adults, two kids); the water shuttle costs $3/day. Cruises depart daily on the hour from 9am to 5pm (6pm on weekends) from mid-June through Labor Day weekend, with shorter hours in the spring and fall. In the off season, check ahead for winter wildlife excursions (scheduled occasionally).

A public-private National Park Partnership administers the Boston Harbor Islands National Recreation Area (www.nps.gov/boha). For more information, consult the staff at the **Rose Kennedy Greenway Boston Harbor Islands Visitor Center Pavilion,** on the Greenway across from Faneuil Hall Marketplace, or contact the **Friends of the Boston Harbor Islands** (© **617/740-4290;** www.fbhi.org). The Friends coordinate a variety of cruises on and around the harbor throughout the summer and fall; check ahead for details. For information about tours of **Boston Light,** the lighthouse on Little Brewster Island, see the box "Trip the Light Fantastic," p. 191.

It has a dozen area branches, including 1 Beacon St., near Government Center (✆ **617/248-9797**); 125 Summer St., in the Financial District (✆ **617/261-4855**); and 197 Clarendon St. (✆ **617/933-5090**) and 800 Boylston St., in the Prudential Center (✆ **617/262-2050**), both in the Back Bay. A day pass costs $20 at women-only, no-pool **Healthworks** (www.healthworksfitness.com), which has well-equipped facilities in the Back Bay at 441 Stuart St. (✆ **617/859-7700**) and in Cambridge at the Porter Square Shopping Center, 35 White St. (✆ **617/497-4454**).

Hiking

For information about hiking in state parks and forests, visit **www.massparks.org**. The **Boston Harbor Islands** offer great hiking; circling the largest island, Peddocks, takes half a day. See the box, "A Vacation in the Islands," p. 199.

Ice Skating & In-Line Skating

The outdoor ice-skating season runs from mid-November to mid-March, weather permitting. Check ahead for open hours and closures for private events.

The rink at the Boston Common **Frog Pond** ★★ (✆ **617/635-2120**; www.cityofboston.gov/parks) is an extremely popular cold-weather destination. It's an open surface with an ice-making system and a clubhouse. Admission is $4 for adults and free for children 13 and under; skate rental costs $8 for adults, $5 for kids. The rink gets unbelievably crowded on weekend afternoons, so try to go in the morning or on a weekday.

Kendall Square Community Skating, 300 Athenaeum St., East Cambridge (✆ **617/492-0941;** www.kendallsquare.org), is an open rink in a courtyard not far from MIT. It charges $5 for adults, $3 for seniors and students,

Skating on the Frog Pond is a popular winter activity.

$1 for children 13 and under; skate rentals are $8 for adults, $5 for kids. Validated discounted parking is available.

A favorite spot for in-line skaters is the **Esplanade,** between the Back Bay and the Charles River. It continues onto the bike path that runs to Watertown and back (p. 197), but after you leave the Esplanade, the pavement isn't totally smooth, which can lead to mishaps. Your best bet is to wait for a Sunday in the summer, when **Memorial Drive ★** near Harvard Square in Cambridge closes to traffic from 11am to 7pm. It's a perfect surface. Unless you're confident of your ability and your knowledge of Boston traffic, stay off the streets.

To rent skates or blades, visit the **Beacon Hill Skate Shop,** 135 Charles St. S. (© 617/482-7400). It's not on Beacon Hill but near the Theater District, not too far from the Esplanade, and has a knowledgeable staff. Expect to pay about $15 a day. The **InLine Club of Boston**'s website (www.sk8net.com) offers up-to-date event and safety information.

Jogging

The **Dr. Paul Dudley White Charles River Bike Path ★★** is also a jogging route. The 18-mile loop along the water is extremely popular because it's car-free (except at intersections), scenic, and generally safe. The bridges that connect Boston and Cambridge allow for circuits of various lengths. Be careful around abutments, where you can't see far ahead. Don't jog at night, try not to go alone, and keep the headphone volume low. Visit the DCR website (www.state. ma.us/dcr) to view a map that gives distances. If the river's not convenient, the concierge or desk staff at your hotel probably can provide a map with suggested jogging routes. As in any other city, stay out of park areas at night.

Sailing

Sailboats fill the Charles River basin all summer and skim across the Inner Harbor in all but the coldest weather. Your options during a short stay aren't especially cost-effective, but they are fun.

The best deal is with **Community Boating,** 21 David Mugar Way, on the Esplanade (© 617/523-1038; www.community-boating.org). It's on a gorgeous but congested patch of water between the Back Bay and Cambridge's Kendall Square. The oldest public sailing facility in the country offers lessons and boating programs for children and adults from April through November. The fleet includes 13- to 23-foot sailboats as well as windsurfers and kayaks. Experienced visitors pay $75 for a day of sailing or $35 for a day of kayaking.

Tennis

Public courts are available throughout the city at no charge. Well-maintained courts that seldom get busy until after work are at several spots on the Southwest Corridor Park in the **South End** (there's a nice one near **West Newton St.**). The courts on **Boston Common** and in **Charlesbank Park,** overlooking the river next to the bridge to the Museum of Science, are more crowded during the day. To find the court nearest you, ask the concierge or desk staff at your hotel or visit the DCR website (www.state.ma.us/dcr).

SPECTATOR SPORTS

Boston has a well-deserved reputation as a great sports town. The Red Sox, Celtics, and New England Patriots have been more successful and popular than the Bruins recently, but local fans are nothing if not loyal—just ask all those Celtics fans who waited 22 years between NBA championships. Fans are also passionate about college sports, particularly hockey, in which the Division I schools are fierce rivals.

The **TD Garden,** 100 Legends Way (Causeway St.; ✆ **617/624-1000** for events line or 800/745-3000 for Ticketmaster; www.tdgarden.com), is home to the **Sports Museum of New England** (✆ **617/624-1234;** www.sports museum.org), which celebrates local teams and athletes of all ages—especially the Celtics and Bruins, who play in the building. Exhibits, which are on the fifth and sixth floors of the arena, include Red Sox legend Ted Williams's locker and a penalty box from the old Boston Garden. Visit the website to download an audio tour. The museum is open from 10am to 4pm daily, subject to closures depending on the arena schedule. Tickets cost $10 for adults, $5 for seniors and children 10 to 18, free for children 9 and under. Always call ahead; there's no access during events. ***Note:*** Visitors may not bring any bags, including backpacks and briefcases, into the arena.

Beyond the "big four" professional sports and dozens of college options, several lower-profile pro franchises call the Boston area home, including two lacrosse teams. The **New England Revolution** (✆ **877/438-7387;** www.revolutionsoccer.net) of Major League Soccer plays at Gillette Stadium on Route 1 in Foxboro from March through October. Tickets cost $20 to $40 and are available through Ticketmaster (✆ **800/745-3000;** www.ticketmaster.com). The **Boston Blazers** (✆ **888/252-9377;** www.blazerslacrosse.com) of the National Lacrosse League play at the TD Garden from January through late April. Tickets are $16 to $25. The **Boston Cannons** (✆ **888/847-9700** or 617/746-9933; www.bostoncannons.com) of Major League Lacrosse play at Harvard Stadium from mid-May through mid-August; tickets cost $15 and $20. The **Boston Breakers** of Women's Professional Soccer (✆ **877/439-2732** or 781/251-2100; www.womensprosoccer.com/boston) also play at Harvard Stadium, from April through August. Tickets run $15 to $27.

Baseball

Ho-hum, another World Series championship—that's something you'll *never* hear from a true **Boston Red Sox** fan. The baseball world was still pinching itself over the team's 2004 title, which ended an 86-year dry spell, when the Sox brought home the 2007 crown. "Home" is legendary **Fenway Park** ★★★, and no other experience in all of sports matches watching a game there. Fenway was already selling out well before the 2004 Series, and tickets remain a precious commodity, sky-high prices notwithstanding.

The season runs from early April to early October, later if the team makes the playoffs. The quirkiness of the oldest park in the major leagues (1912), rich with history and atmosphere, only adds to the mystique. Most seats are narrow and uncomfortable, but also gratifyingly close to the field. A hand-operated scoreboard fronts the 37-foot left-field wall, or "Green Monster." Watch carefully during a pitching change—the left fielder from either team might suddenly disappear into a door in the wall to get out of the sun.

A Red Sox game at historic Fenway Park.

One of the most imaginative management teams in baseball strives to make visiting Fenway worth the big bucks. New sections of seats keep cropping up in previously unused areas of the ballpark, notably including the section *above* the Green Monster. Just outside the park, Yawkey Way turns into a sort of carnival midway for ticket-holders before games, with concession stands, live music, and other diversions. One good stop is **Comcast Town**—sure, the company is promoting its telecom products, but it's also offering free long-distance phone calls and Internet access, HD TVs showing Red Sox programming, and, best of all on a steamy day, air-conditioning.

Practical concerns: Compared with its modern brethren, Fenway is tiny. Tickets are the most expensive in the majors—a few upper bleacher seats go for $12, but most are in the $25-to-$95 range, with the best dugout boxes topping

Play Ball!

Fenway Park tours (☎ **617/226-6666;** www.redsox.com/tours) take visitors around the legendary ballpark. This is an excellent alternative if your budget or schedule doesn't allow for attending a game. Depending on what's going on at the park, the 50-minute tour may include a walk on the warning track, a stop in the press box, and a visit to the Red Sox Hall of Fame. During the season, tours start on the hour daily from 9am to 4pm (or 3½ hr. before game time, whichever is earlier). There are no tours on holidays or before day games. In the winter, hours are shorter and tours may be truncated because of construction (but also cheaper than in the summer); check ahead to avoid disappointment. Admission is $12 for adults, $11 for seniors, $10 for children 3 to 15. Advance individual sales aren't available.

$300, and that's *if* you pay face value. They go on sale in December; order early. Forced to choose between seats in a low-numbered grandstand section—say, 10 or below—and in the bleachers, go for the bleachers. They can get rowdy during night games, but the view is better from there than from deep right field. "Monster" seats prices top $150, but they're so popular that they're sold by lottery in batches throughout the season; check the website. A limited number of same-day standing-room tickets ($20–$35) are available before each game, and fans sometimes return presold tickets, especially if a rainout causes rescheduling. It can't hurt to check, particularly if the team isn't playing well; visit the website and navigate to "Red Sox Replay." *Tip:* The Game Day Ticket Sales office, near Gate E on Lansdowne Street, offers tickets that went unsold for some reason. The doors open 2 hours before game time; lining up is permitted 3 hours before that (but not earlier).

The **Fenway Park ticket office** (© 888/REDSOX6; www.redsox.com; T: Green Line B, C, or D to Kenmore, or D to Fenway) is at 4 Yawkey Way, near the corner of Brookline Avenue. Tickets for people with disabilities and in no-alcohol sections are available. Smoking is not allowed in the park.

Basketball

The **Boston Celtics** raised their 17th National Basketball Association championship banner to the rafters of the TD Garden in 2008 after a 22-year dry spell. The team's rejuvenation made it madly popular even before Shaquille O'Neal signed a deal that runs through the 2011–12 season. Plan far ahead. The Celtics play from early October until at least mid-April; when a top contender or a star player is visiting, getting tickets is especially tough. Prices are as low as $10 for some games and top out at $278 ($750 for floor seats). For information, call the Garden (© 617/624-1000; www.nba.com/celtics); for tickets, contact Ticketmaster (© 800/745-3000; www.ticketmaster.com). To reach the Garden, take the MBTA Green or Orange Line or commuter rail to North Station. *Note:* Spectators may not bring any bags, including backpacks and briefcases, into the arena.

Football

The **New England Patriots** (© 800/543-1776; www.patriots.com) were playing to standing-room-only crowds even before they won three Super Bowls in 4 years (2002, 2004, and 2005). The Pats play from August through December or January at Gillette Stadium on Route 1 in Foxboro, about a 45-minute drive south of Boston. Tickets ($65–$169) sell out well in advance, often as part of season-ticket packages. Call or check the website for information on individual ticket sales and resales as well as public-transit options.

Boston College is the state's only Division I-A team. The Eagles, who compete in the Atlantic Coast Conference, play at Alumni Stadium in Chestnut Hill (© 617/552-4622; www.bceagles.cstv.com). The area's FCS (formerly Division I-AA) team is Ivy League power **Harvard University,** Harvard Stadium, North Harvard Street, Allston (© 617/495-2211; www.gocrimson.com).

Golf Tournaments

Over Labor Day weekend, the PGA Tour visits the Tournament Players Club of Boston, which is actually in suburban Norton (© 508/285-3200; www.

thetpcofboston.com), for the **Deutsche Bank Championship.** Visit www. deutschebankchampionship.com or www.pgatour.com for more information. The senior women on the **Legends Tour** (www.thelegendstour.com) stop at Plymouth's Pinehills Golf Club (© **508/209-3000;** www.pinehillsgolf.com) in September. Aside from the pro tours, the *Globe* and *Herald* regularly list numerous amateur events for fun and charity.

Hockey

Tickets to see the **Boston Bruins,** one of the NHL's original six teams, are expensive ($25–$296) but worth it for hard-core fans. For information, call the TD Garden (© **617/624-1000;** www.bostonbruins.com); for tickets, contact Ticketmaster (© **800/745-3000;** www.ticketmaster.com). To reach the Garden, take the MBTA Green or Orange Line or commuter rail to North Station. **Note:** Spectators may not bring any bags, including backpacks and briefcases, into the arena.

Budget-minded fans who don't have their hearts set on seeing a pro game will be pleasantly surprised by the quality of local **college hockey ★.** Even for sold-out games, standing-room tickets are usually available the night of the game. The local teams regularly hit the national rankings; they include **Boston College,** Conte Forum, Chestnut Hill (© **617/552-4622;** www. bceagles.cstv.com); **Boston University,** Agganis Arena, 928 Commonwealth Ave. (© **617/353-4628** or 800/745-3000 [Ticketmaster]; www.goterriers.com); **Harvard University,** Bright Hockey Center, North Harvard Street, Allston (© **617/495-2211;** www.gocrimson.com); and **Northeastern University,** Matthews Arena, St. Botolph Street (© **617/373-4700;** www.gonu.com). These four are the Beanpot schools, whose men's teams play a tradition-steeped tournament on the first two Mondays of February at the TD Garden. Women's games don't normally sell out.

Horse Racing

Suffolk Downs ★, 111 Waldemar Ave., off Route 1A, East Boston (© **617/567-3900;** www.suffolkdowns.com; T: Blue Line to Suffolk Down, then take shuttle bus or walk 10 min.), is one of the best-run smaller tracks in the country. The legendary Seabiscuit raced here; a marker commemorates his storied career. The live racing season runs from May to November; post time is 12:45pm. The track offers extensive simulcasting options day and night year-round. General admission for live racing costs $2, and general parking is free.

The Marathon

Every year on Patriots' Day—the third Monday in April—the **Boston Marathon ★★★** rules the roads from suburban Hopkinton to Copley Square in Boston. Cheering fans line the entire route. An especially nice place to watch is tree-shaded Commonwealth Avenue between Kenmore Square and Mass. Ave., but you'll be in a crowd wherever you stand. The finish line is on Boylston Street in front of the Boston Public Library. For information about watching, ask the staff at your hotel or check the daily papers. For information about qualifying, contact the **Boston Athletic Association** (© **617/236-1652;** www.boston marathon.org).

Rowing

On the third or fourth weekend of October, the **Head of the Charles Regatta** ★ (☎ 617/868-6200; www.hocr.org) attracts more rowers than any other crew event in the country. Some 4,000 oarsmen and women race against the clock for 3 miles from the Charles River basin to the Eliot Bridge in west Cambridge. Hundreds of thousands of spectators line the riverbanks, socializing—it's hard to overstate just how preppy the whole event is—and occasionally watching the action.

The Head of the Charles Regatta.

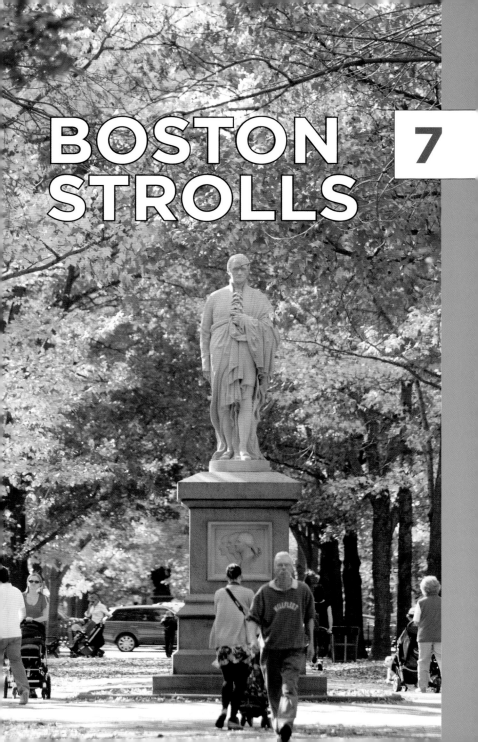

BOSTON STROLLS

7

W alking is the best way to see Boston. The narrow, twisting streets that make driving such a headache are a treat for pedestrians, who are always close to something worth seeing. The central city is compact—walking quickly from one end to the other takes about an hour—and abounds with historically and architecturally interesting buildings and neighborhoods.

In this chapter you'll find a tour of **Boston's Back Bay**, a walk along **Boston's Waterfront**, and an excursion around **Harvard Square** in Cambridge. For information on Boston's most famous walking tour, the 2.5-mile **Freedom Trail ★★★**, see chapter 6.

Be sure to wear comfortable shoes, and if you're not inclined to pay designer prices for designer water, bring your own bottle and fill it at your hotel.

WALKING TOUR 1: THE BACK BAY

START:	**The Public Garden (T: Green Line to Arlington).**
FINISH:	**Copley Square.**
TIME:	**2 hours if you make good time, 3 hours if you detour to the Esplanade, and longer if you do a lot of shopping.**
BEST TIME:	**Any time before late afternoon.**
WORST TIME:	**Late afternoon, when people and cars pack the streets. And don't attempt the detour on July 4th, when concertgoers jam the neighborhood. This walk is mostly outdoors, so if the weather is bad, you may find yourself in lots of shops. You decide whether that makes an overcast day a "best" or "worst" time.**

The Back Bay is the youngest neighborhood in central Boston, the product of a massive landfill project that transformed the city from 1835 to 1882. It's flat, symmetrical, logically designed—the names of the cross streets go in alphabetical order—and a refreshing contrast to downtown Boston's tangled geography.

Begin your walk in the:

1 Public Garden

Before the Back Bay was filled in, the Charles River flowed right up to Charles Street, which separates Boston Common from the Public Garden. On the night of April 18, 1775, British troops bound for Lexington and Concord boarded boats at the edge of the Common ("two if by sea") and set off for Cambridge across what's now the Public Garden.

PREVIOUS PAGE: **The Commonwealth Avenue Mall.**

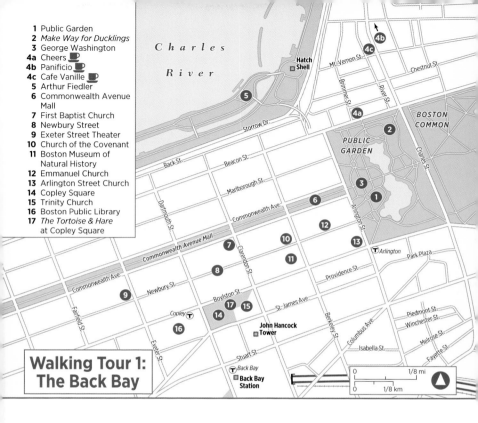

1 Public Garden
2 *Make Way for Ducklings*
3 George Washington
4a Cheers
4b Panificio
4c Cafe Vanille
5 Arthur Fiedler
6 Commonwealth Avenue Mall
7 First Baptist Church
8 Newbury Street
9 Exeter Street Theater
10 Church of the Covenant
11 Boston Museum of Natural History
12 Emmanuel Church
13 Arlington Street Church
14 Copley Square
15 Trinity Church
16 Boston Public Library
17 *The Tortoise & Hare* at Copley Square

Walking Tour 1: The Back Bay

Explore the lagoon, the trees and other flora, and the statuary. Take a ride on the **Swan Boats** (mid-Apr to mid-Sept), and then make your way toward the corner of Charles and Beacon streets, staying inside the Public Garden (follow the sound of delighted children).

Here you'll see a 35-foot strip of cobblestones topped with the bronze figures that immortalize Robert McCloskey's book:

2 Make Way for Ducklings

Installed in 1987 and wildly popular since the moment they were unveiled, Nancy Schön's renderings of Mrs. Mallard and her eight babies are irresistible. Mrs. Mallard is just 38 inches tall, but that doesn't keep people of all ages from climbing on. If you don't know the story of the family's perilous trip to meet Mr. Mallard at the lagoon, ask one of the parents or children you'll find here.

The city bought the site of the Public Garden from private interests in 1824. Planting began in 1837, but it wasn't until the late 1850s that Arlington Street was built and the land permanently set aside. George F. Meacham executed the design.

Cross the lagoon using the tiny suspension bridge—reputedly the smallest in the world—and look for the statue of:

3 George Washington

Unveiled in 1875, this was Boston's first equestrian statue. It stands 38 feet tall and is considered an excellent likeness of the first president of the United States, an outstanding horseman. The artist, Thomas Ball, was a Charlestown native who worked in Italy. Among his students was noted sculptor Daniel Chester French. Pass through the gate onto Arlington Street. Before you begin exploring in earnest, this is a good place to detour.

The George Washington equestrian statue.

4 TAKE A BREAK 🍽

Turn right and walk up Arlington Street to Beacon Street. On your right, across the busy intersection, is **Cheers,** 84 Beacon St. (𝄢 **617/227-9605;** www.cheersboston.com), originally the Bull & Finch Pub. The food at this tourist magnet is tasty enough, and the bar looks enough like its TV offspring to satisfy all but the most devoted fans (you'll find a replica of the set at the Faneuil Hall Marketplace spin-off).

Alternatively, turn right on Beacon Street and walk 1 long block to Charles Street. You can pick up food to go at **Panificio,** 144 Charles St. (𝄢 **617/227-4340**), or indulge in a delicious French-style pastry at **Cafe Vanille,** 70 Charles St. (𝄢 **617/523-9200**). This street is also a promising place for a shopping break (see chapter 8).

After you've picked up something to eat, backtrack along Beacon Street past Arlington Street to Embankment Road and turn right. Take the Arthur Fiedler Footbridge across Storrow Drive to the Esplanade, proceed forward across another (smaller) bridge, and unpack your food near the giant head of:

5 Arthur Fiedler

Installed in 1985, this sculpture by Ralph Helmick consists of sheets of aluminum that eerily capture the countenance of the legendary conductor of the Boston Pops, who died in 1979. The amphitheater that's visible from all over the Esplanade is the **Hatch Shell,** where the Pops perform free in early July. The July 3 performance is a dress rehearsal for the legendary Fourth of July concert.

When you're ready, retrace your steps to the corner of Arlington Street and Commonwealth Avenue. You're looking down the:

6 Commonwealth Avenue Mall

The 8-block mall is the centerpiece of architect Arthur Gilman's design of the Back Bay. The graceful promenade is 100 feet wide (the entire street is 240 ft.) and stretches to Kenmore Square. Elegant Victorian mansions, almost all divided into apartments or in commercial or educational use, line the street. One of the great delights of being a pedestrian in Boston is taking in the details that adorn these buildings, which superficially look very much alike and up close resemble the members of a large, stylish, exceedingly eccentric family. Down the center of the boulevard, an apparently random collection of sculptures adorns the mall. They begin with **Alexander Hamilton,** across Arlington Street from **George Washington.** The most moving sculpture is at Dartmouth Street: The **Vendome Memorial** honors the memory of the nine firefighters who lost their lives in a blaze at the Hotel Vendome in 1972.

The Shape of Things to Come

The **First Baptist Church** on Commonwealth Avenue is a fine building, but the design is notable mainly because its creators went on to much more famous projects. The architect, **H. H. Richardson,** is best known for nearby **Trinity Church.** The artist who created the frieze, which represents the sacraments, was **Frédéric Auguste Bartholdi,** who designed the **Statue of Liberty.**

Two blocks from the Public Garden, at 110 Commonwealth Ave., at the corner of Clarendon Street, is the:

7 First Baptist Church

Built from 1870 to 1872 of Roxbury puddingstone, it originally housed the congregation of the Brattle Street Church (Unitarian), which had been downtown, near Faneuil Hall.

At Clarendon Street or Dartmouth Street, turn left and walk 1 block to:

8 Newbury Street

Commonwealth Avenue is the architectural heart of the Back Bay, and Newbury Street is the commercial center. Take some time to roam around here (see chapter 8 for pointers), browsing in the galleries, window-shopping at the boutiques, and watching the chic shoppers.

Walk down Newbury Street to Exeter Street. At 26 Exeter St. is the building that was once the:

9 Exeter Street Theater

Designed in 1884 as the First Spiritualist Temple, it was a movie house from 1914 to 1984. Once known for the crowds flocking to *The Rocky Horror Picture Show,* it now houses offices and a restaurant.

When you're ready to continue your stroll (or when your credit cards cry for mercy), turn back toward the Public Garden and seek out three of Newbury Street's oldest buildings, starting with the:

10 Church of the Covenant

This Gothic revival edifice at 67 Newbury St. was designed by Richard Upjohn and completed in 1867. The stained-glass windows—which are on view to the public only during Sunday services (10:30am)—are the work of Louis Comfort Tiffany.

Across the street, set back from the sidewalk at 234 Berkeley St., is the original home of the:

11 Boston Museum of Natural History

A forerunner of the Museum of Science, it was built according to William Preston's French Academic design. The 1864 structure, originally two stories high, still has its original roof, preserved when the building gained a third floor.

Cross Newbury Street again and continue walking toward the Public Garden. On your left, at 15 Newbury St., is:

12 Emmanuel Church

The first building completed on Newbury Street, in 1862, this Episcopal church ministers through the arts, so there might be a concert (classical to jazz, solo to orchestral) going on during your visit. Check ahead (© **617/536-3355;** www.emmanuel-boston.org) for schedules.

Now you're almost back at the Public Garden. On your left is the swanky Taj Boston hotel, which until 2007 was known as the original **Ritz-Carlton** (1927).

Turn right onto Arlington Street and walk 1 block. On your right, at 351 Boylston St., is the:

13 Arlington Street Church

This is the oldest church in the Back Bay, completed in 1861. An interesting blend of Georgian and Italianate details, it's the work of architect Arthur Gilman, who laid out this whole neighborhood. Here you'll find more Tiffany stained glass. Step inside (ask at the office for admission to the sanctuary) to see the pulpit that was in use in 1788 when the congregation worshipped downtown on Federal Street.

Follow Boylston Street away from the Public Garden. Two blocks up is:

14 Copley Square

Enjoy the fountain and visit the farmers' market, which operates Tuesday and Friday afternoons from July through November.

Overlooking the square is one of the most famous church buildings in the United States. This is:

15 Trinity Church

H. H. Richardson's Romanesque masterpiece, completed in 1877, is to your left. The church, 206 Clarendon St. (© **617/536-0944;** www.trinity churchboston.org), was built on 4,502 pilings driven into the mud that was once the Back Bay. Brochures and guides are available to help you find your way around a building considered one of the finest examples of church architecture in the country. Tours (check ahead for the schedule) cost $6 for adults, $4 for seniors and students with ID. The building is open daily from 8am to 6pm; self-guided tours are offered weekdays 10am to 3:30pm, Saturday 9am to 4pm, Sunday 1 to 5pm. Friday organ recitals begin at 12:15pm.

Across Dartmouth Street is the:

The Copley Square Farmer's Market

16 Boston Public Library

The work of architect Charles Follen McKim and many others, the Renaissance revival building was completed in 1895 after 10 years of construction. Its design reflects the significant influence of the Bibliothèque Nationale in Paris. Wander up the steps to check out the building's impressive interior (p. 167). **Daniel Chester French** designed the doors.

Head back across the street to Copley Square. In a sense, you've come full circle; as at the Public Garden, you'll see a playful and compelling sculpture by Nancy Schön:

17 The Tortoise & Hare at Copley Square

Designed to signify the end of the **Boston Marathon** (the finish line is on Boylston St. between Exeter and Dartmouth sts.), this work was unveiled for the 100th anniversary of the event in 1996.

From here you're in a good position to set out for any other part of town or walk a little way in any direction and continue exploring. Copley Place and the Shops at Prudential Center are nearby, Newbury Street is 1 block over, and there's a Green Line T station at Boylston and Dartmouth streets.

The Tortoise & Hare at Copley Square.

START:	**Old State House Museum (T: Orange or Blue Line to State).**
FINISH:	**John Joseph Moakley U.S. Courthouse.**
TIME:	**2–5 hours, depending on how much time you spend in shops and museums.**
BEST TIME:	**Mid-morning to early afternoon.**
WORST TIME:	**Mid-afternoon or later. Most attractions will be closing, and you'll be wandering through rush-hour traffic.**

One of America's legendary seaports, Boston draws much of its considerable appeal from its proximity to the water. This tour takes you near and along the shoreline of the colonial town and the modern city.

The same building holds the subway station and your first stop, the:

1 Old State House Museum

The little brick building at 206 Washington St. (© 617/720-1713; www.bostonhistory.org) was erected in 1713, replacing the Boston Town House. Back then, the shore was just a couple of blocks away, and this was a tall building. Exit and turn toward the water (downhill), passing the subway entrance. See p. 157 for details about the museum and the **Boston Massacre Site,** a circle of cobblestones that sits on a triangular traffic island beneath the balcony.

> ### Impressions
>
> *From where he sat on the steps of the Town House, he [Johnny] could look the brief length of King Street which quickly and imperceptibly turned into Long Wharf, running for half a mile into the sea. . . . There was not another wharf in America so large, so famous, so rich.*
>
> **—Esther Forbes, *Johnny Tremain*, 1943**

Down the shallow hill to your left is **Faneuil Hall.** Now landlocked, it stood on the water before the harbor began to fill with silt and garbage. The filling-in was completed (using earth) and new streets laid out as part of the Quincy Market project of 1826. Ahead of you, sloping gently toward Boston Harbor, is **State Street.** This was King Street until 1784 (fairly late considering the antiroyal sentiment that inspired the change), and it ran right out into the harbor.

With the Old State House at your back, follow State Street toward the water. Note that the 40-story glass skyscraper at the corner of Congress Street, Exchange Place, encloses the facade of its predecessor, the Boston Stock Exchange (1891). On State Street just before Kilby Street, a plaque marks the former site of the:

2 Bunch of Grapes Tavern

Constructed in 1712, the tavern entertained both independence-minded colonists and their royalist counterparts before and during the Revolutionary War. After the British symbols (including the lion and unicorn from the Old State House) were removed from most of the public buildings in town in July 1776, they were made into a bonfire here. The Ohio Company, which settled that state, was formed here in 1786.

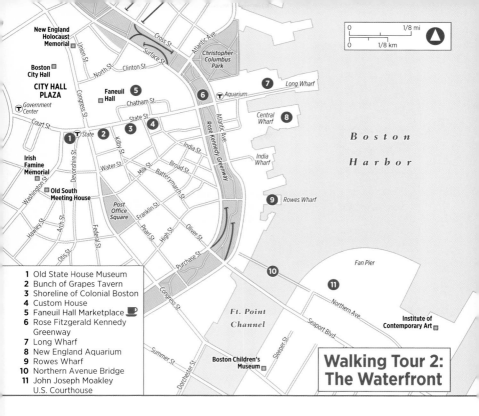

1 Old State House Museum
2 Bunch of Grapes Tavern
3 Shoreline of Colonial Boston
4 Custom House
5 Faneuil Hall Marketplace
6 Rose Fitzgerald Kennedy
  Greenway
7 Long Wharf
8 New England Aquarium
9 Rowes Wharf
10 Northern Avenue Bridge
11 John Joseph Moakley
   U.S. Courthouse

Walking Tour 2: The Waterfront

Where Kilby Street and Merchants Row meet on either side of State Street, pause and step out of the way of other pedestrians. This is the:

3 Shoreline of Colonial Boston

The construction of Long Wharf began here in 1709. At its greatest, Boston's main wharf was 1,743 feet long and 104 feet wide, extending so far into the harbor that the water at the end was 17 feet deep.

Continue on State Street, crossing Broad Street, developed in 1805–07 as part of a plan to improve the waterfront. Charles Bulfinch helped design 60 of the brick warehouses that stood here, some of which survive today. Pause at the corner of State and India streets and look up at the:

4 Custom House

Construction took a full decade, from 1837–47; the foundation alone, which sits on some 3,000 wooden piles resting on bedrock, took 3 years to build. The tower, added in 1911–15, was for many years the tallest structure in town. The building is now a Marriott time-share property. Admire the colorful clocks on all four sides of the tower, but don't count on them to tell the correct time.

The Rose Fitzgerald Kennedy Greenway has replaced the traffic jams of the Central Artery with a greenery-filled escape.

5 TAKE A BREAK 🍵

Faneuil Hall Marketplace is a block away. If the weather is fine, head to the enormous food court inside Quincy Market for a snack or meal to go, then take it across the street to the Greenway (see the next stop).

Leave through the archway at the east end of the complex, in Marketplace Center (look for the Gap). Filling the space between the market and the harbor, where traffic on an ugly interstate highway once roared about 20 feet above street level, is the:

6 Rose Fitzgerald Kennedy Greenway

This lovely park occupies 15 acres of prime real estate, arranged like no park you've ever seen before—it's 1 mile long and a block or less wide. The major legacy of the $15-billion Big Dig highway-construction project, this constantly evolving institution already features gorgeous plants and flowers along with dramatic public art. Check the website, **www.rosekennedy greenway.org**, to see whether any events are scheduled during your visit. Formally opened in 2008, the Greenway consists of four sections: North End, Wharf District, Dewey Square, and Chinatown. You're standing in the Wharf District.

Across the way, to your right as you face the harbor, is the Boston Marriott Long Wharf hotel. Cross the John F. Fitzgerald Surface Road, the Greenway, and Atlantic Avenue and step out of the flow of the crowd to take in:

7 Long Wharf

Boston's principal wharf opened for business in 1710. This is the embarkation point for many sightseeing cruises, as well as the MBTA ferry to Charlestown. Even at its busiest, it's not nearly as crowded and frantic as it was in its 18th- and 19th-century heyday, when Boston was one of the most important ports in the country. Near the end of the wharf is a granite building, dating from 1846, that was used by Customs appraisers. Now it houses offices and residences. At the very end of the wharf is a small plaza that may be covered in construction equipment during your visit. If you're able to gain access to the very end of the wharf, the view is worth the effort.

Return to the Marriott and stand with the lobby behind you. Walk 1 block (with Legal Sea Foods on your right) on Old Atlantic Avenue to the:

8 New England Aquarium

The aquarium opened in 1969. Peter Chermayeff, then with Cambridge Seven Associates, designed the structure, which echoes the waves of the adjacent harbor. You don't have to buy a ticket to check out the harbor seals, who frolic in an exhibit near the entrance. See the listing on p. 148.

Continue to walk along the waterfront for the equivalent of 2 blocks. On your right, you'll pass the residential Harbor Towers, designed by I. M. Pei and opened in 1971. This is India Wharf, which adjoins your next stop:

9 Rowes Wharf

Turn left as you reach the first redbrick building in this complex and follow the walkway that encircles it, along the water. The hotel-office-residential development bears the name of John Rowe (known as "Merchant" Rowe), who donated the Sacred Cod that hangs in the State House. The wharf was constructed after a fire in 1760 and has long been used as a ferry terminal. It's probably better known today for the dramatic arch in the center of the Boston Harbor Hotel (1985), designed by the Chicago architecture firm Skidmore, Owings, and Merrill. Enjoy the peek-a-boo view of the Greenway through the arch as you walk past the hotel and the boats in the marina and at the docks.

At the end of this little promenade is a short staircase that leads up to the:

10 Northern Avenue Bridge

An iron-turntable bridge built in 1908, the pedestrian-only bridge is a favorite with bridge aficionados—if "through truss swing span" means something to you, make sure you have your camera—and makes a good place to pause and look around. Beneath you is Fort Point Channel, which separates downtown from South Boston. A stone's throw away is the Evelyn Moakley Bridge, the vehicular access point to the Seaport District and an important piece of the Big Dig. Behind you, at the corner of Atlantic Avenue, is the First District Headquarters of the U.S. Coast Guard. The *Massachusetts,* the first commissioned revenue cutter, was based here. (Revenue cutters were the forerunners of the U.S. Coast Guard.)

Cross the Northern Avenue Bridge. You're on Old Northern Avenue, but the formal address of your destination is 1 Courthouse Way. This is the:

The striking architecture of the John Joseph Moakley U.S. Courthouse.

11 John Joseph Moakley U.S. Courthouse

Dedicated in 2001, the courthouse bears the name of a longtime Massachusetts congressman who was instrumental in securing funding for the Big Dig. Henry N. Cobb of Pei Cobb Freed & Partners designed the deceptively plain structure. Follow the Harborwalk around to the back to take in the centerpiece of the design, an 88-foot-tall wall of glass that opens the interior of the courthouse to the harbor. During business hours, the public is welcome to enter the building, take in the dramatic views, and even have a meal or snack overlooking the water in the second-floor cafeteria. You can't bring in your cellphone (the guards in the lobby will take it away and return it as you leave), and adults must show two forms of ID to enter.

The park outside the courthouse makes a good place to stop and plan your next stop. From here, both the **Boston Children's Museum** (p. 186) and the **Institute of Contemporary Art** (p. 140) are within easy walking distance. You can return to the Greenway and work up an appetite by following it south to **Chinatown** or north to the **North End.** Or take public transportation— the Silver Line Courthouse stop is nearby, and South Station is about 15 minutes away on foot—to your next destination.

> ### It's All French to Me
>
> As you explore the Boston area, you may hear the name of sculptor **Daniel Chester French.** French (1850–1931) was responsible for the gorgeous doors on the Dartmouth Street side of the **Boston Public Library,** the statue of **John Harvard** in Harvard Yard, and the *Minute Man* statue near the North Bridge in Concord. If you're not a parochial Bostonian, you probably know him best as the sculptor of the seated Abraham Lincoln in the presidential memorial in Washington.

WALKING TOUR 3: **HARVARD SQUARE**

START: | **Harvard Square (T: Red Line to Harvard).**
FINISH: | **John F. Kennedy Park.**
TIME: | **2–4 hours, depending on how much time you spend in shops and museums; allow an hour for the detour to the Longfellow National Historic Site.**
BEST TIME: | **Almost any time during the day. The Harvard Art Museums offer free admission to Massachusetts residents on Saturday morning.**
WORST TIME: | **The last week of May. You might have trouble gaining admission to Harvard Yard during commencement festivities. The ceremony is Thursday morning; without a ticket, you won't be allowed in.**

Popular impressions to the contrary, Cambridge is not exclusively Harvard. In fact, even Harvard Square isn't exclusively Harvard. During a walk around the area, you'll see historic buildings and sights, interesting museums, and notable architecture on and off the university's main campus.

Leave the T station by the main entrance (use the ramp to the turnstiles, then take the escalator) and emerge in the heart of:

1 Harvard Square

Town and gown meet at this lively intersection, where you'll get a taste of the improbable mix of people drawn to the crossroads of Cambridge. To your right is the landmark **Out of Town News** kiosk (✆ **617/354-1441**). It stocks newspapers, magazines, and tons of souvenirs (a selection that reflects the Internet-fueled drop in demand for non-virtual journalism). At the colorful kiosk in front of you, you can request information about the area. Step close to it so that you're out of the flow of pedestrian traffic and look around.

The store across Massachusetts Avenue is the **Harvard Coop.** The name rhymes with *hoop*—say "co-op" and risk being taken for a Yalie. On the far side of the intersection, at the corner of John F. Kennedy and Brattle streets, is a sign reading DEWEY, CHEETHAM & HOWE (say it out loud) on the third floor of the brick building. National Public Radio's "Car Talk" originates here.

Turn around so that the Coop is at your back and walk half a block, crossing Dunster Street. Across the way, at 1341 Massachusetts Ave., you'll see:

2 Wadsworth House

Most of the people waiting for the bus in front of this yellow wood building probably don't know that it was built in 1726 as a residence for Harvard's fourth president—but then, neither do most Harvard students. Its biggest claim to fame is a classic: George Washington slept here.

Cross Mass. Ave., pass through the gate, and continue until you're at the edge of a sweeping lawn crisscrossed with walking paths. This is:

3 Harvard Yard

You're standing in the oldest part of "the Yard." It was a patch of grass with animals grazing on it when Harvard College was established in 1636 to train young men for the ministry, and it wasn't much more when the Continental Army spent the winter of 1775–76 here. Harvard is the oldest college in the country, with the most competitive admissions process, and if you suggest aloud that it's not the best, you might encounter the attitude that inspired the saying "You can always tell a Harvard man, but you can't tell him much."

Walk forward until you see majestic Johnston Gate on your left and take in the classroom and administration buildings and dormitories that make up the:

When school is in session, Harvard Yard fills with students.

4 Old Yard

Just inside the gate stands **Massachusetts Hall.** Built in 1720, this National Historic Landmark is the university's oldest surviving building. First-year students share "Mass. Hall" with the first-floor office of the university president (or perhaps it's the other way around), whom they traditionally invite upstairs for tea once a year. Across the way is **Harvard Hall,** a classroom building constructed in 1765. Walk along the Yard side of Harvard Hall until you reach matching side-by-side buildings, **Hollis** and **Stoughton halls.** Hollis dates to 1763 (Stoughton "only" to 1805) and has been home to many students who went on to great fame, among them Ralph Waldo Emerson, Henry David Thoreau, and Charles Bulfinch. Almost hidden across the tiny lawn between these two buildings is **Holden Chapel,** a Georgian-style gem completed in 1744. It has been an anatomy lab, a classroom building, and, of course, a chapel, and it is now home to the oldest American college choir, the Harvard Glee Club.

Cross the Yard to the building opposite Johnston Gate. This is:

	Impressions
	One emerged, as one still does, from the subway exit in the Square and faced an old red-brick wall behind which stretched, to my fond eye, what remains still the most beautiful campus in America, the Harvard Yard. If there is any one place in all America that mirrors better all American history, I do not know of it.
	—Theodore H. White, ***In Search of History,*** **1978**

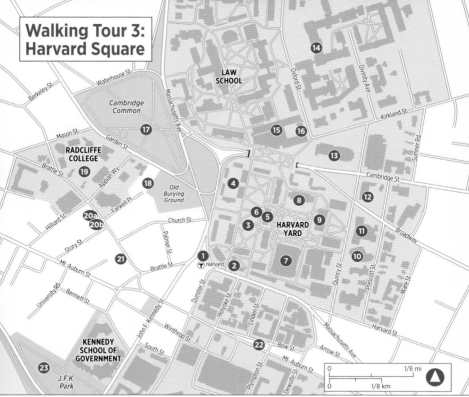

Walking Tour 3: Harvard Square

1 Harvard Square
2 Wadsworth House
3 Harvard Yard
4 Old Yard
5 University Hall
6 John Harvard Statue
7 Widener Library
8 Memorial Church
9 Sever Hall
10 Carpenter Center for the Visual Arts
11 Fogg Museum (closed through 2013)
12 Arthur M. Sackler Museum
13 Memorial Hall
14 Harvard Museum of Natural History
15 Science Center
16 Science Center ☕
17 Cambridge Common
18 Christ Church
19 Radcliffe Yard
20a Hi-Rise at the Blacksmith House ☕
20b L.A. Burdick Chocolates ☕
21 Brattle Theatre
22 Harvard Lampoon Castle
23 John F. Kennedy Park

5 University Hall

Designed by Charles Bulfinch and constructed of granite quarried in sub-urban Chelmsford, the 1813 structure is the college's main administration building. In 1969, students protesting the Vietnam War occupied it.

University Hall is best known as the backdrop of the:

6 John Harvard Statue

This is one of the most photographed objects in the Boston area. Daniel Chester French designed it in 1884.

Walk around University Hall into the adjoining quad. This is still the Yard, but it's the **"New Yard,"** sometimes called **Tercentenary Theater** because the college's 300th-anniversary celebration was held here in 1936. Commencement and other university-wide ceremonies take place here.

On your right is:

7 Widener Library

The centerpiece of the world's largest university library system was built in 1913 as a memorial to Harry Elkins Widener, Harvard class of 1907. Thoroughly debunked legend has it that he died when the *Titanic* sank in 1912 because he was unable to swim 50 yards to a lifeboat, and his mother donated $2 million for the library on the condition that every undergraduate prove his ability to swim 50 yards. Today the library holds more than 3 million volumes, including 3,500 rare volumes collected by Harry Elkins Widener himself, on 50 miles of shelves. Don't even think about swiping Harry's Gutenberg Bible. The last person to try, in 1969, gained access from above but couldn't climb out. With the 70-pound bible in his knapsack, he fell six stories to the courtyard below (and survived).

The famous John Harvard Statue.

Horace Trumbauer of Philadelphia designed the library. His primary design assistant was Julian Francis Abele, a student of architecture at the University of Pennsylvania and the first black graduate of L'Ecole des Beaux

---

💬 Nothing but the Truth

The likeness of **John Harvard** outside University Hall is known as the "Statue of Three Lies" because the inscription reads "John Harvard/Founder/1638." In fact, the college was founded in 1636, and Harvard (one of many benefactors) didn't establish it, but donated money and his library. What's more, this isn't even John Harvard. No portraits of him survive, so the model for the benevolent-looking bronze gentleman was, according to various accounts, either his nephew or a student.

Arts in Paris. The lobby—which sits within view of the locked memorial room that holds Widener's collection—is not open to the public, but you may be able to talk your way in if you're affiliated (student or staff) with another university; visit the office to the left of the main entrance. If you're not allowed to take a peek, pause at the top of the outside staircase and turn around to enjoy the view.

Pssst . . . Check This Out

Climb the front steps of **Sever Hall** and scoot to the side of the entrance, out of the way of passing students. The doorway is set in a "whispering gallery." Stand on one side of the arch, station a friend or willing passerby on the opposite side, and speak softly into the facade. Someone standing next to you can't hear you, but the person at the other side of the arch can.

Walk down the stairs and across the quad. Facing the library is:

8 Memorial Church

Built in 1931, the church is topped with a tower and weather vane 197 feet tall. You're welcome to look around the Georgian revival–style edifice unless services are going on, or to attend them if they are. Morning prayers run daily from 8:45 to 9am, and the Sunday service is at 11am. Weddings and funerals also take place here. The entrance is on the left. Inside, on the south wall (toward the Yard), panels bear the names of Harvard alumni who died in the world wars, Korea, and Vietnam. One is Joseph P. Kennedy, Jr., the president's brother, class of 1938.

Facing Widener Library with Memorial Church behind you, turn left toward:

9 Sever Hall

H. H. Richardson, architect of Boston's Trinity Church, designed this classroom building (1880). Surveys of architects and designers consistently name the deceptively simple structure one of the professionals' favorite buildings in the Boston area. Note the gorgeous brickwork that includes rolled moldings around the doors, the fluted brick chimneys, and the arrangement of the windows.

Facing Sever Hall, turn right and go around to the back. The building on your right is Emerson Hall, which appeared in the movie *Love Story* as Barrett Hall, named after the family of Ryan O'Neal's character. Cross this quad and exit through the gate onto Quincy Street.

Turn right and walk about 300 feet. On the other side of the street, at 24 Quincy St., is the:

10 Carpenter Center for the Visual Arts

Art exhibitions occupy the lobby, the Harvard Film Archive shows movies in the basement (pick up a schedule on the main floor), and the concrete-and-glass building is itself a work of art. Opened in 1963, it was designed by the Swiss-French architect Le Corbusier and the team of Sert, Jackson, and Gourley. It's the only Le Corbusier design in North America.

Sever Hall's whispering gallery.

Backtrack along Quincy Street. Opposite the gate through which you left the Yard is the:

11 Fogg Museum

Founded in 1895, the museum has been at 32 Quincy St. since the building was completed in 1927. The Fogg, the adjacent Busch-Reisinger Museum, and the Sackler Museum (described below) make up the Harvard Art Museums. The Fogg and Busch-Reisinger are closed for extensive renovations through 2013, but highlights of the excellent collections are on display at our next stop. See p. 178 for details.

Continue on Quincy Street and cross the street to 485 Broadway, the:

12 Arthur M. Sackler Museum

The British architect James Stirling designed the Sackler, which he called "the newest animal in Harvard's architectural zoo." It opened in 1984. The Sackler normally houses the university's spectacular collection of Asian art; during your visit, expect to see a selection of work from the Harvard Art Museums' collections.

Continue on Quincy Street. As you cross Cambridge Street, watch out for confused drivers emerging from the underpass to your left. Filling the block between Cambridge and Kirkland streets is:

13 Memorial Hall

This imposing Victorian structure, known to students as "Mem Hall," was completed in 1874. Enter from Cambridge Street and investigate the hall of memorials, a transept where you can read the names of the Harvard men who died fighting for the Union during the Civil War—but not of their Confederate counterparts. (The name of Col. Robert Gould Shaw, Matthew Broderick's character in the movie *Glory*, is halfway down on the right.) To the right is **Sanders Theatre**, prized as a performance space and lecture hall for its excellent acoustics and clear views. To the left is **Annenberg Hall.** It's a dining hall that's closed to visitors, but you may be able to sneak a look at the gorgeous stained-glass windows. Harvard graduates William Ware and Henry Van Brunt won a design competition for Memorial Hall, which was constructed for a total cost of $390,000 (most of it donated by alumni). The colorful tower is a replica of the original, which was destroyed by fire in 1956 and rebuilt in 1999.

Facing in the same direction you were when you entered, walk through the transept and exit onto Kirkland Street. Turn left and quickly right, onto Oxford Street. One block up on the right, at 26 Oxford St., you'll see an entrance to the:

14 Harvard Museum of Natural History

Adjoining the **Peabody Museum of Archaeology & Ethnology** at 11 Divinity Ave., the Museum of Natural History entertainingly presents the university's collections and research relating to the natural world. See p. 177 for a full description.

Leave through the back door of 11 Divinity Ave. and look around. Across the street at 6 Divinity Ave. is the **Semitic Museum** (©617/495-4631; www.semiticmuseum.fas.harvard.edu), where the second- and third-floor galleries hold displays of archaeological artifacts and photographs from the Near and Middle East. Horace Trumbauer, the architect of Widener Library, designed the building next door, 2 Divinity Ave. It's home to the **Harvard-Yenching Library,** a repository of the university's hundreds of thousands of volumes relating to the Far East. For every person who can tell you that, there are several thousand who know this building for the pair of **Chinese stone lions** flanking the front door.

Turn right and return to Kirkland Street, then go right. You'll pass Memorial Hall on your left as you proceed to the intersection of Kirkland and Oxford streets. At 0 Oxford St. is the university's:

15 Science Center

The 10-story monolith is said to resemble a Polaroid camera (Edwin H. Land, founder of the Polaroid Corporation, was one of its main benefactors). The Spanish architect Josep Lluís Sert designed the Science Center, which opened in 1972. Sert, the dean of the university's Graduate School of Design from 1953 to 1969, was a disciple of Le Corbusier (who designed the Carpenter Center for the Visual Arts). On the plaza between the Science Center and the Yard is the **Tanner Rock Fountain,** a group of 159 New England boulders arranged around a small fountain. Since 1985 this

The Science Center is said to resemble a Polaroid camera.

has been a favorite spot for students to relax and watch unsuspecting passersby get wet: The fountain sprays a fine mist, which begins slowly and gradually intensifies.

16 TAKE A BREAK ☕

The **main level of the Science Center** is open to the public and has several options if you want a soft drink, gourmet coffee, or sandwich. Go easy on the sweets, though, in anticipation of the next break.

Leave the Science Center through the doors near the fountain and turn right. Keeping the underpass on your left, follow the walkway for the equivalent of 1½ blocks as it curves around to the right. The Harvard Law School campus is on your right. You're back at Massachusetts Avenue. Cross carefully to:

17 Cambridge Common

Memorials and plaques dot this well-used plot of greenery and bare earth. Follow the sidewalk along Massachusetts Avenue to the left, and after a block or so you'll walk near or over horseshoes embedded in the concrete. This is the path William Dawes, Paul Revere's fellow alarm-sounder, took from Boston to Lexington on April 18, 1775. Turn right onto Garden Street and continue following the Common for 1 block. On your right you'll see a monument marking the place where Gen. George Washington took control of the Continental Army on July 3, 1775.

Cross Garden Street and backtrack to Zero Garden St. This is:

18 Christ Church

Peter Harrison of Newport, Rhode Island (also the architect of King's Chapel in Boston), designed the oldest church in Cambridge, which opened in 1760. Note the square wooden tower. Inside the vestibule you can still see bullet holes made by British muskets. At one time the church was used as the barracks for troops from Connecticut, who melted down the organ pipes to make ammunition. The graveyard on the Massachusetts Avenue side of the building, the **Old Burying Ground,** is the oldest in Cambridge, dating to 1635. It's the final resting place of nine Harvard presidents as well as many early settlers and at least two black Revolutionary War soldiers.

Facing Christ Church, turn right and follow Garden Street to the next intersection. This is Appian Way. Turn left and take the first right into:

19 Radcliffe Yard

Radcliffe College was founded in 1879 as the "Harvard Annex" and named for Ann Radcliffe, Lady Mowlson, Harvard's first female benefactor. Undergraduate classes merged with Harvard's in 1943, Radcliffe graduates first received Harvard degrees in 1963, and Harvard officially assumed responsibility for educating undergraduate women in 1977. Radcliffe was an independent corporation until 1999; it's now the university's Radcliffe Institute for Advanced Study. The institute's first dean, Drew Gilpin Faust, became the university's first female president in 2007.

After you've strolled around, return to Appian Way, turn right, and walk half a block. You'll emerge on Brattle Street.

A visit to the Longfellow National Historic Site, 105 Brattle St. (✆ 617/876-4491; www. nps.gov/long; p. 175), makes an interesting detour and adds about an hour to your walk. If you don't detour, turn left and continue walking along Brattle Street. Excellent shops (see chapter 8) line both sides of the street.

20 TAKE A BREAK ☕

Hi-Rise at the Blacksmith House, 56 Brattle St. (✆ **617/492-3003**), a branch of a well-known local artisan bakery, makes the bread and delectable pastry served here. The Henry Wadsworth Longfellow poem "The Village Smithy" was about this building, which really stood "under the spreading chestnut tree" before the street was widened and the tree removed in 1876. If you're not in the mood for a sandwich or snack, you can sate your sweet tooth with something from the celebrated New Hampshire–based confectioner **L. A. Burdick Chocolates,** 52 Brattle St. (✆ **617/491-4340;** www.burdickchocolate.com).

Down the street, at 40 Brattle St., is the:

21 Brattle Theatre

Opened in 1890 as Brattle Hall, the theater (✆ **617/876-6837;** www.brattlefilm.org) was founded by the Cambridge Social Union and used as a cultural and entertainment venue. It became a movie house in 1953 and gained a reputation as Cambridge's center for art films.

Brattle Theatre.

You're now in the **Brattle Square** part of Harvard Square. You might see street performers, a protest, a speech, or more shopping opportunities. Facing Dickson Brothers Hardware, cross Brattle Street, bear right, and follow the curve of the build-

 Play It, Sam

The **Brattle Theatre,** one of the oldest independent movie houses in the country, started the *Casablanca* revival craze, which explains the name of the restaurant in the basement.

ing all the way around the corner so that you're on Mount Auburn Street. Stay on the left-hand side of the street as you cross John F. Kennedy, Dunster, Holyoke, and Linden streets. On your left between Dunster and Holyoke streets is **Holyoke Center,** an administration building designed by Josep Lluís Sert that has commercial space on the ground floor.

The corner of Mount Auburn and Linden streets offers a good view of the:

22 Harvard Lampoon Castle

Constructed in 1909, designed by Wheelwright & Haven (architects of Boston's Horticultural Hall), and listed on the National Register of Historic Places, this is the home of Harvard's undergraduate humor magazine, the *Lampoon.* The main tower resembles a face, with windows as the eyes, nose, and mouth, topped by what looks like a miner's hat. All five of the building's addresses have been mentioned on "The Simpsons," which draws many of its writers from the staff. The *Lampoon* and the daily student newspaper, the *Crimson,* share a long history of reciprocal pranks and vandalism.

You'll pass the *Crimson* offices on your right if you detour to the **Harvard Book Store** (turn left onto Plympton St. and follow it up the hill to the corner of Mass. Ave.). Otherwise, cross Mount Auburn Street and walk away from Holyoke Center on Holyoke Place, Holyoke Street, or Dunster Street to get a sense of some of the rest of the campus. The tower directly in front of you sits atop Lowell House, one of a dozen residences for upperclassmen. (First-year students live in and around Harvard Yard.)

Turn right on Winthrop Street or South Street, and proceed to John F. Kennedy Street. Turn left and walk toward the Charles River. On your right at Memorial Drive is:

23 John F. Kennedy Park

In the 1970s, when the search was on for a site for the Kennedy Library, this lovely parcel of land was an empty plot near the MBTA train yard (the Red Line then ended at Harvard). Traffic concerns led to the library's being built in Dorchester, but the

The Harvard Lampoon Castle.

Graduate School of Government and this adjacent park bear the president's name. Walk away from the street to enjoy the fountain, which is engraved with excerpts from JFK's speeches. This is a great place to take a break and plan the rest of your day.

8

SHOPPING

f you turned straight to this chapter, you're in good company: Surveys of visitors to Boston consistently show that shopping is their most popular activity, beating museum-going by a comfortable margin.

Boston-area shopping represents a tempting blend of classic and contemporary. Boston and Cambridge teem with tiny boutiques and sprawling malls, esoteric bookshops and national chain stores, exclusive galleries and snazzy secondhand-clothing outlets.

One of the most popular shopping destinations in New England will most likely be closed during your visit: **Filene's Basement** temporarily shuttered its flagship store in 2007 to make way for extensive renovations and construction in the building upstairs, which slowed in 2008 along with the global economy. Ask at your hotel to see whether the retail landmark has reopened, or check out the Back Bay branch (p. 240), which carries an excellent selection of discounted fashion but doesn't offer the original's beloved automatic-markdown policy.

This chapter concentrates on only-in-Boston businesses, and it includes many national (and international) names that are worth a visit. I'll point you to areas that are great for shop-hopping and toward specific destinations that are great for particular items.

THE SHOPPING SCENE

One of the best things about shopping in Massachusetts is that there's **no sales tax** on clothing priced below $175 or on food items. All other items are taxed at 6.25%. Just about every store will ship your purchases home for a fee, but if the store is part of a chain that operates in your home state, you'll probably have to pay that sales tax. Be sure to ask.

In the major shopping areas, stores usually open at 10am and close at 6 or 7pm Monday through Saturday. On Sunday, most open at noon and close at 5 or 6pm, but some don't open at all. Closing time may be later 1 night a week, usually Wednesday or Thursday. Malls keep their own hours (noted below), and some smaller shops open later. Days and hours can vary in winter. Year-round, many art galleries close on Monday. In short, if a store sounds too good to pass up, call to make sure it's open before you head out.

Great Shopping Areas

The area's premier shopping district is Boston's **Back Bay,** where dozens of up-market galleries, shops, and boutiques make **Newbury Street** a world-famous destination. Parallel to Newbury is retail-rich Boylston Street.

Stretching from Boylston Street past Huntington Avenue are two high-end malls, the **Shops at Prudential Center** and **Copley Place** (linked by an enclosed walkway across Huntington Ave.), which bookend a giant retail complex. Here you'll find the posh department stores **Neiman Marcus, Lord & Taylor,** and **Saks Fifth Avenue.** A branch of **Barneys New York,** the luxe fashion

FACING PAGE: **Newbury Street is popular with shoppers.**

Boylston Street, like Newbury Street, is a mecca for shoppers.

wonderland, is in Copley Place. The adjacent **South End,** though less commercially dense, boasts a number of art galleries and quirky shops; it's a great destination for strolling, shopping, and snacking.

Another popular destination is chain-heavy **Faneuil Hall Marketplace.** The shops, boutiques, and pushcarts at Boston's busiest attraction sell everything from candles to costume jewelry, sweaters to souvenirs. Nearby, the **North End** has augmented its dozens of Italian restaurants with a limited but fun retail scene. Venture beyond the main drag, Hanover Street, and you'll find worthwhile stops on Salem, Parmenter, and Richmond streets.

Beacon Hill is a classic shopping destination. Picturesque Charles Street, at the foot of the hill, is a short but retail-heavy street noted for its excellent gift shops and antiques dealers.

Inman Square is a great stop for fans of independent retailers, such Boutique Fabulous.

One of Boston's oldest shopping areas is **Downtown Crossing,** a traffic-free pedestrian mall along Washington, Winter, and Summer streets near Boston Common. With construction ongoing at the site of the old Filene's building (and the century-old Filene's Basement flagship on hiatus), the center of this area can be something of a mess. But you'll still find Macy's, Swedish fashion phenomenon H&M, tons of smaller clothing and shoe stores, food and merchandise pushcarts, and a Borders bookstore.

Harvard Square in Cambridge, with its bookstores, boutiques, and T-shirt shops, is about 15 minutes from downtown Boston by subway. Despite the neighborhood association's efforts, chain stores have swept over "the Square." You'll find a mix of national and regional outlets, and more than a few persistent independent retailers.

For a less generic experience, stroll from Harvard Square along shop-lined **Massachusetts Avenue** toward **Porter Square** to the north or **Central Square**

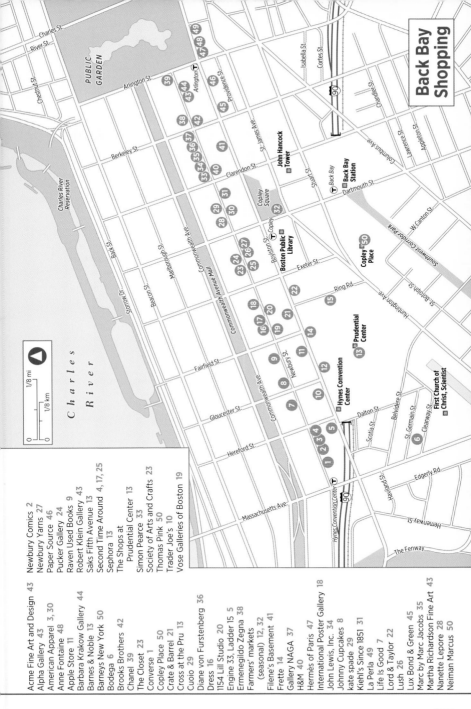

PUBLIC GARDEN

Charles River Reservation

Charles River

Charles St.

River St.

Chestnut St.

Arlington St.

Berkeley St.

Clarendon St.

Dartmouth St.

Exeter St.

Fairfield St.

Gloucester St.

Hereford St.

Massachusetts Ave.

Commonwealth Ave.

Commonwealth Avenue Mall

Marlborough St.

Beacon St.

Back St.

Storrow Dr.

Newbury St.

Boylston St.

Ring Rd.

Stuart St.

St. James Ave.

Providence St.

Columbus Ave.

Isabella St.

Cortes St.

Charles St. S.

Lawrence St.

Appleton St.

Lenox St.

W. Canton St.

Southwest Corridor Park

Huntington Ave.

St. Botolph St.

Belvidere St.

St. Germain St.

Clearway St.

Scotia St.

Dalton St.

Haviland St.

Edgerly Rd.

Hemenway St.

The Fenway

Scotia St.

Providence St.

John Hancock Tower

Back Bay Station

Copley Square

Boston Public Library

Copley Place

Prudential Center

Hynes Convention Center

First Church of Christ, Scientist

Back Bay

Copley

Hynes Convention Center

0   1/8 mi
0   1/8 km

N

Acme Fine Art and Design 43
Alpha Gallery 43
American Apparel 3, 30
Anne Fontaine 48
Apple Store 11
Barbara Krakow Gallery 44
Barnes & Noble 13
Barneys New York 50
Bodega 6
Brooks Brothers 42
Chanel 39
The Closet 23
Converse 1
Copley Place 50
Crate & Barrel 21
Cross at the Pru 13
Cuoio 29
Diane von Furstenberg 36
Dress 16
1154 Lill Studio 20
Engine 33, Ladder 15 5
Ermenegildo Zegna 38
Farmers' markets
  (seasonal) 12, 32
Filene's Basement 41
Frette 14
Gallery NAGA 37
H&M 40
Hermès of Paris 47
International Poster Gallery 18
John Lewis, Inc. 34
Johnny Cupcakes 8
kate spade 29
Kiehl's Since 1851 31
La Perla 49
Life Is Good 7
Lord & Taylor 22
Lush 26
Lux Bond & Green 45
Marc by Marc Jacobs 35
Martha Richardson Fine Art 43
Nanette Lepore 28
Neiman Marcus 50

Newbury Comics 2
Newbury Yarns 27
Paper Source 46
Pucker Gallery 24
Raven Used Books 9
Robert Klein Gallery 43
Saks Fifth Avenue 13
Second Time Around 4, 17, 25
Sephora 13
The Shops at
  Prudential Center 13
Simon Pearce 33
Society of Arts and Crafts 23
Thomas Pink 50
Trader Joe's 10
Vose Galleries of Boston 19

to the southeast. About 10 minutes up Prospect Street from Central Square is **Inman Square,** home to a number of vibrant independent retailers.

Stay on the Red Line subway for one stop beyond Porter Square and you'll come to Somerville's **Davis Square,** where the relatively reasonable rents have helped create a hipster mecca with plenty of retail options. Another neighborhood with a well-deserved reputation for shopping variety is Brookline's **Coolidge Corner,** which is worth a trip (on the Green Line C train).

SHOPPING A TO Z

Here I've singled out establishments that I especially like and neighborhoods that suit shoppers interested in particular types of merchandise. Addresses are in Boston unless otherwise indicated.

Antiques & Collectibles

No antiques hound worthy of the name will leave Boston without an expedition along both sides of **Charles Street ★★**, with a detour to **River Street** (parallel to Charles St., 1 block closer to the river).

Bromfield Pen Shop ★ This shop's selection of antique pens will thrill any collector. Whether you're sick of digital communication or looking for a gift, the knowledgeable staff will help make a good match. The shop also repairs pens and sells new pens—including Montblanc, Pelikan, Waterman, and Omas—Swiss army knives, watches, and business gifts. Closed Sunday. 5 Bromfield St. (off Washington St.). ✆ **617/482-9053.** www.bromfieldpenshop.com. T: Red or Orange Line to Downtown Crossing.

Cambridge Antique Market ★★ 🎁 As you navigate the enormous variety of merchandise spread over five floors (don't forget to check out the basement), you may feel as though you're on a treasure hunt—and really, aren't you? Weekends, especially Saturday, are when most of the 100-plus dealers are likeliest to be open. Prices are better than in Boston, but the selection is more catch-as-catch-can. Closed Monday. 201 Monsignor O'Brien Hwy. (at Third St.), Cambridge. ✆ **617/868-9655.** www.marketantique.com. T: Green Line to Lechmere.

Danish Country European & Asian Antiques ★ Owner James Kilroy specializes in Scandinavian antiques dating from the 1700s onward. In this mahogany-intensive neighborhood, the light woods are a visual treat. You'll also see folk art, lovely Mora clocks, Royal Copenhagen porcelain, and antique Chinese furniture and home accessories. 138 Charles St. (btw. Revere and Cambridge sts.). ✆ **617/227-1804.** www.danishcountry.net. T: Red Line to Charles/MGH.

Upstairs Downstairs Antiques ★★ 🎁 The merchandise in this unexpectedly large store (keep walking toward the back) spans 3 centuries and every price point. You'll find everything from majestic sideboards to delicate teacups to just the right gift—ask a member of the amiable staff for brainstorming help. 93 Charles St. ✆ **617/367-1950.** T: Red Line to Charles/MGH.

Art

Art galleries dot the city and suburbs, with the greatest concentrations in Boston's Back Bay and South End. Time (yours) and space (mine) preclude listing galleries in outlying neighborhoods and suburbs, but if your travels take you off the beaten path, by all means look around—soaring rents have driven savvy proprietors to some unexpected locations. For tips on navigating **Newbury Street,** see the box "An Artsy Stroll Along Newbury Street," below.

The **SoWa district**—short for "south of Washington Street"—centers on 450 Harrison Ave. The **SoWa Artists Guild** (www.sowaartistsguild.com) website makes a good introduction to this thriving community. The best time to visit is the first Friday of the month, when guild members in the building throw open their doors to visitors from 5 to 9pm for **First Friday Open Studios.**

An excellent way to see artists at work is to visit during neighborhood **open studio** days. Artists' communities throughout the Boston area stage the weekend events once or twice a year. You might be asked for a contribution to a charity in exchange for a map of the studios. Check listings in the *Globe, Herald,* and *Improper Bostonian* or visit **www.cityofboston.gov/arts** for information.

Acme Fine Art and Design Twentieth-century American art is Acme's raison d'être, and the gallery represents numerous living artists. That means a lively mix of styles and media, with an emphasis on abstraction over figurative works. Closed Sunday and Monday. 38 Newbury St. (btw. Arlington and Berkeley sts.), 4th floor. ☎ **617/585-9551.** www.acmefineart.com. T: Green Line to Arlington.

Alpha Gallery ★★ The Alpha Gallery specializes in contemporary paintings, sculpture, and works on paper, as well as modern master paintings and prints. Established in 1967, this is a family operation: Director Joanna E. Fink is founder Alan Fink's daughter. Closed Sunday and Monday. 38 Newbury St. (btw. Arlington and Berkeley sts.), 7th floor. ☎ **617/536-4465.** www.alphagallery.com. T: Green Line to Arlington.

 AN artsy **STROLL ALONG NEWBURY STREET**

The Boston area's best-known destination for art lovers is **Newbury Street.** New England's equivalent of New York's Madison Avenue, it's home to galleries of all descriptions. As you explore, don't forget to look up—some great businesses thrive at street level, but their upstairs neighbors who pay lower rents can often afford to be more adventuresome. Most galleries are open Tuesday through Saturday or Sunday from 10 or 11am to 5:30 or 6pm. Exhibitions typically change once a month. For specifics, visit individual websites or pick up a copy of the free monthly *Gallery Guide,* available at many businesses along Newbury Street.

If gallery-hopping isn't a habit for you, here's an observation: Galleries can look intimidating, but remember that each one is a business—and a proprietor who keeps a gallery operating in tough economic times is by definition a good businessperson. Gallery owners aren't selling art because they couldn't break into widget sales; they're in the art business because they love it. They welcome browsers and questions that show you've given the art some thought.

For a good overview, plot a course that starts with **Barbara Krakow Gallery**

at 10 Newbury St. or at 38 Newbury St., where **Robert Klein Gallery** shares a floor with three other worthy establishments (Acme Fine Art and Design, Martha Richardson Fine Art, and Miller Block Gallery). Your ultimate destination is 238 Newbury St., home of **Vose Galleries of Boston,** which is closer to its 300th anniversary than to its 200th. Stop along the way to check out at least a couple of the other galleries listed in this chapter. Now, that's an "only in Boston" experience.

Barbara Krakow Gallery ★★★ This prestigious gallery, founded in 1964, is as cutting-edge as they come. It specializes in paintings, sculptures, drawings, and prints created after 1945. If you're lucky, the delightfully opinionated owner will be on the premises. Closed Sunday and Monday; closed August. 10 Newbury St. (btw. Arlington and Berkeley sts.), 5th floor. ©️ **617/262-4490.** www.barbarakrakow gallery.com. T: Green Line to Arlington.

Galería Cubana ★★ Galería Cubana shows extraordinary work by contemporary Cuban artists—it's not an underground operation, but the holder of one of the scarce licenses permitting Americans to travel to and trade with the island. Owner Michelle Wojcik, who opened the gallery's first location in Provincetown in 2007, visits three times a year on a quest to build up ties between the U.S. and Cuba through culture. Closed Monday and Tuesday fall through spring; call ahead in summer. 460 Harrison Ave. (at Thayer St.). ©️ **617/292-2822.** www.lagaleria cubana.com. T: Orange Line to Tufts Medical Center or Back Bay, then 15-min. walk; or Silver Line SL4/SL5 bus to E. Berkeley St., then 5-min. walk.

Gallery NAGA ★★ In the neo-Gothic Church of the Covenant, Gallery NAGA exhibits contemporary paintings, photography, and studio furniture, often by New England artists. A stop here is a must if you want to see holography (trust me, you do). Closed Sunday and Monday. 67 Newbury St. (at Berkeley St.). ©️ **617/267-9060.** www.gallerynaga.com. T: Green Line to Arlington.

International Poster Gallery ★★★ 🛍 Yes, posters are art—as you'll see before you even cross the threshold of this extraordinary gallery. It features extensive collections of French, Swiss, Soviet, and Italian vintage posters, and thousands of other posters, including originals from around the world. The enthusiastic, accommodating staff will comb its databases (cyber and cerebral) to help you find the exact image you want, and the website is a great resource. The theme of the works on display changes three or four times a year. Prices start at $50, with most between $500 and $2,500. 205 Newbury St. (btw. Exeter and Fairfield sts.). ©️ **617/375-0076.** www.internationalposter.com. T: Green Line to Copley.

Martha Richardson Fine Art ★ Contemporary art often seems to predominate on Newbury Street, but not here—the specialty is 19th- and 20th-century American and European paintings and drawings. You'll see landscapes, still lifes, portraits, and the occasional abstract. Closed Sunday and Monday. 38 Newbury St. (btw. Arlington and Berkeley sts.), 4th floor. ©️ **617/266-3321.** www.martharichardsonfineart. com. T: Green Line to Arlington.

Pucker Gallery ★ The eclectic offerings here include African, Asian, Inuit, and Israeli art; contemporary paintings, prints, drawings, sculpture, and ceramics by regional and international artists; and excellent photographs. The staff is eager to answer questions about the art, which spreads over five floors. 171 Newbury St. (btw. Dartmouth and Exeter sts.). ©️ **617/267-9473.** www.puckergallery.com. T: Green Line to Copley.

Robert Klein Gallery ★★★ For 19th- to 21st-century photography, head here. Among the dozens of artists represented are Diane Arbus, Robert Mapplethorpe, Man Ray, and Ansel Adams. Closed Sunday and Monday. 38 Newbury St. (btw. Arlington and Berkeley sts.), 4th floor. ©️ **617/267-7997.** www.robertkleingallery.com. T: Green Line to Arlington.

Vose Galleries of Boston ★ One of Vose's specialties is Hudson River School paintings—fitting, because the business and the mid-19th-century movement are about the same age. Six generations of Voses have run the oldest family-owned gallery in the United States, which opened in 1841. You'll see works of the Boston School and American Impressionist art among the 18th-, 19th-, and early-20th-century American paintings, as well as contemporary pieces by American realists. Closed Sunday and Monday. 238 Newbury St. (off Fairfield St.). ℂ **617/536-6176.** www.vosegalleries.com. T: Green Line to Copley, or Green Line B, C, or D to Hynes Convention Center.

Books

The Boston area is a book-lover's paradise. It's an important stop on most author tours; check the local papers or stop by any store that sells new books for details on **readings and book signings.**

Barnes & Noble The well-stocked Prudential Center branch of the national chain offers both a cafe and plenty of kids' events. Barnes & Noble runs most of the college bookstore operations around town (see "College Merchandise," below). Shops at Prudential Center, 800 Boylston St. (enter from Huntington Ave. at Belvidere St.). ℂ **617/247-6959.** www.barnesandnoble.com. T: Green Line E to Prudential; Green Line to Copley; or Green Line B, C, or D to Hynes Convention Center.

Borders Both local branches make good places to retreat when you've had enough of the abundant shopping around them. The sprawling Downtown Crossing store contains two levels of books and one of music; the Cambridge Borders is one of the only quiet places in the mall. 10–24 School St. (at Washington St.). ℂ **617/557-7188.** www.borders.com. T: Orange or Blue Line to State. CambridgeSide Galleria, 100 CambridgeSide Place, Cambridge. ℂ **617/679-0887.** T: Green Line to Lechmere.

Brattle Book Shop ★★ Bibliophiles who start here might not get any other shopping done. This marvelous store near Macy's buys and sells used, rare, and out-of-print titles, and second-generation owner Kenneth Gloss does free appraisals. Be sure to check the outdoor carts and shelves for good deals on books of all ages. Closed Sunday. 9 West St. (btw. Washington and Tremont sts.). ℂ **800/447-9595** or 617/542-0210. www.brattlebookshop.com. T: Red or Orange Line to Downtown Crossing, or Green Line to Park St.

Brookline Booksmith ★★★ The huge, varied selection makes this store a polymath's dream. The employees have excellent taste—look for their recommendations. A great gift-and-card section, a small but choice used-book selection in the basement, and tons of events are among the offerings. 279 Harvard St. (btw. Beacon and Green sts.), Brookline. ℂ **617/566-6660.** www.brooklinebooksmith.com. T: Green Line C to Coolidge Corner.

Curious George & Friends In addition to Curious George books and merchandise, this welcoming shop carries a superlative selection of children's books and gifts, including stuffed animals, toys, and games. Check downstairs for items that suit older kids, with an emphasis on old and new classics. 1 John F. Kennedy St. (at Brattle St.). ℂ **617/498-0062.** www.curiousg.com. T: Red Line to Harvard.

Globe Corner Bookstore ★ The offspring of the dear departed original on the Freedom Trail, the Globe Corner carries huge selections of travel guides and essays, maps, atlases, and globes. Check ahead for special events, such as the annual adventure-travel lecture series. 90 Mt. Auburn St. (btw. John F. Kennedy and Dunster sts.), Cambridge. ℂ **617/497-6277.** www.globecorner.com. T: Red Line to Harvard.

Grolier Poetry Book Shop Shelves packed with poetry line this tiny space from floor to high, high ceiling. The shop carries just what the name says: only poetry, and lots of it. Closed Sunday and Monday. 6 Plympton St. (off Mass. Ave.), Cambridge. ℂ **617/547-4648.** www.grolierpoetrybookshop.org. T: Red Line to Harvard.

Harvard Book Store ★★★ On the main level of this shop, readers peruse an excellent scholarly selection and discounted bestsellers. Also here is one of just a few dozen Espresso Book Machines in the country, an amazingly cool device that prints and binds paperback books—you choose, from the 3.6-million-title catalog—to order while you wait. The basement is the draw for those in the know: Prices on remainders are good, and used paperbacks (many bought for classes and hardly opened) are 50% off their original prices. Check ahead for information on readings and other special events. 1256 Mass. Ave. (at Plympton St.), Cambridge. ✆ **800/542-7323** or 617/661-1515. www.harvard.com. T: Red Line to Harvard.

Lorem Ipsum Books A well-edited selection of used titles fills this airy space in the heart of Inman Square. The staff is as helpful or hands-off as you like, and the constantly changing stock includes everything from current bestsellers to "Murder & Mayhem." 1199 Cambridge St. (at Oakland St.), Cambridge. ✆ **617/497-7669.** www.loremipsumbooks.com. T: Red Line to Central, then 10-min. walk on Prospect St.

Porter Square Books ★★ A well-stocked independent bookstore with everything from bestsellers to esoteric academic tomes to a great children's department—it's a dying breed. If they were all run as well as this one, with staffs this helpful and selections this brain-tickling, the species would be anything but endangered. In the Porter Square Shopping Center, 25 White St. (off Mass. Ave.), Cambridge. ✆ **617/491-2220.** www.portersquarebooks.com. T: Red Line to Porter.

Raven Used Books The specialty at these little shops is scholarly titles—an underserved market when the Cambridge location opened, and a niche Raven filled so well that in 2010 it branched out to Boston. Both carry enough general-interest stock to keep casual browsers engaged while their more academic companions explore. 52B John F. Kennedy St. (near Winthrop St.), Cambridge. ✆ **617/441-6999.** www.ravencambridge.com. T: Red Line to Harvard. 263 Newbury St. (btw. Fairfield and Gloucester sts.). ✆ **617/578-9000.** T: Green Line B, C, or D to Haynes Convention Center.

Schoenhof's Foreign Books ★ The oldest foreign-language bookseller in the country stocks volumes for adults and children in more than 50 languages. It also carries dictionaries and language-learning materials for 700-plus languages and dialects, plus quirky gift items (haven't you always wanted a Hannah Arendt T-shirt?) and translations of children's classics. 76A Mt. Auburn St. (at Holyoke St.), Cambridge. ✆ **617/547-8855.** www.schoenhofs.com. T: Red Line to Harvard.

College Merchandise

The big names are Harvard and BU (you'll see Boston College merchandise on pushcarts downtown, too), but you have literally dozens of other options—the Boston area is home to that many schools. Look like an insider with a T-shirt from **Barnes & Noble at Emerson College,** 114 Boylston St. (✆ **617/824-8696;** http://emerson.bncollege.com; T: Green Line to Boylston); the **MIT Coop,** 3 Cambridge Center (✆ **617/499-3200;** www.thecoop.com; T: Red Line to Kendall/MIT) and 84 Massachusetts Ave. (✆ **617/499-3240;** T: Red Line to Kendall/MIT); the **Northeastern University Bookstore,** 360 Huntington Ave. (✆ **617/373-2286;** http://northeastern.bncollege.com; T: Green Line E to Northeastern); or the **Suffolk University Bookstore,** 148 Cambridge St., Beacon Hill (✆ **617/227-4085;** http://suffolk.bkstr.com; T: Blue Line to Bowdoin [closed weekends] or Green Line to Government Center).

Barnes & Noble at Boston University ★ The BU crest, terrier mascot, or name appears on at least a floor's worth of clothing and just about any other item with room for a logo. The book selection is huge, and the author series brings writers to campus year-round. 660 Beacon St. (at Commonwealth Ave.). © **617/267-8484.** http://bu.bncollege.com. T: Green Line B, C, or D to Kenmore.

The Harvard Coop ★★ The Coop (rhymes with *hoop*), or Harvard Cooperative Society, is student-oriented but not a run-of-the-mill college bookstore. You'll find Harvard insignia merchandise, stationery, prints, and posters. As at BU, Barnes & Noble runs the sprawling book operation. 1400 Massachusetts Ave. (at Brattle St.), Cambridge. © **617/499-2000.** www.thecoop.com. T: Red Line to Harvard.

Crafts

Cambridge Artists' Cooperative Craft Gallery ★ Top-notch creations fill this three-level space on a Harvard Square side street. The artist-owned-and-operated gallery carries a huge variety of work by American artisans, including jewelry, home accessories, glassware, clothing, gifts, and other handcrafted treasures. It's not cheap—consider the neighborhood—but prices are reasonable given the quality. 59A Church St. (off Brattle St.), Cambridge. © **617/868-4434.** www.cambridgeartistscoop.com. T: Red Line to Harvard.

Society of Arts and Crafts ★★ Contemporary American work is the focus at the oldest nonprofit craft organization in the country. The exquisite jewelry, furniture, home accessories, glass, ceramics, and fiber art range from practical to purely decorative; the second floor holds a gallery that mounts four shows a year. The society also sponsors **CraftBoston** (www.craftboston.org), a prestigious juried show that takes place in the spring and before the holidays; check the website for dates and locations. 175 Newbury St. (btw. Dartmouth and Exeter sts.). © **617/266-1810.** www.societyofcrafts.org. T: Green Line to Copley.

TistiK 🎁 Artisans from developing countries, mostly in Latin America, create the merchandise in this dazzling gallery. The ever-changing stock varies widely in style and price; it's mostly women's jewelry, with some gifts and home accessories in the mix. TistiK is definitely worth a visit, if only to see how true the name—Maya for "a warm welcome"—is. 54 Church St. (off Brattle St.), Cambridge. © **617/661-0900.** www.shoptistik.com. T: Red Line to Harvard.

Craft Supplies

See "Jewelry," later in this chapter, for information about **Boston Bead Company.**

Newbury Yarns ★ A single large room packed with high-end yarns from all over the globe, Newbury Yarns is a welcoming destination for both experts and beginners. Check ahead for information about classes and workshops, or drop in to browse the impressive selection and ask the patient, helpful staff for advice. 164 Newbury St. (btw. Dartmouth and Exeter sts.). © **617/572-3733.** www.newburyyarns.com. T: Green Line to Copley.

Paper Source ★★ Gorgeous paper (writing and wrapping), cards, pens, ink, stamps, books, stickers, unusual gifts, and custom invitations make these well-organized stores magnets for anyone with a thing for stationery. Be sure to check out the handmade paper from around the world. A crafty friend swears by the Boston location, but all three are delightful. 338 Boylston St. (off Arlington St.). © **617/536-3444.** www.paper-source.com. T: Green Line to Arlington. 1810 Massachusetts Ave. (at Arlington St.), Cambridge. © **617/497-1077.** T: Red Line to Porter. 1361 Beacon St. (at Webster St.), Brookline. © **617/264-2800.** T: Green Line C to Coolidge Corner.

8

Shopping A to Z

Windsor Button The name doesn't come close to telling the whole story of this 70-plus-year-old business. It's known for its impressive range of yarn and knitting and crochet patterns and accessories; except at the busiest times, the staff is a great resource. Also in stock are thousands of buttons, from utilitarian to ultra-fancy, as well as ribbon, trim, notions, and needlework kits. Closed Sunday. 35 Temple Place (btw. Tremont and Washington sts.). © **617/482-4969.** www.windsorbutton. com. T: Red or Green Line to Park St., or Orange Line to Downtown Crossing.

Discount Shopping

City Sports ★ The regional athletic-apparel retailer City Sports carries clothing, footwear, and some sports equipment. The crowded lower level of this store—also a regular retail location—stocks a constantly changing selection of out-of-season merchandise at excellent prices. 11 Bromfield St. (btw. Washington and Province sts.). © **617/423-2015.** www.citysports.com. T: Red or Orange Line to Downtown Crossing.

DSW Shoe Warehouse Here you'll find two large floors of discounted women's and men's shoes, boots, sandals, and sneakers. Check the clearance racks for the real deals. 385 Washington St. (at Bromfield St.). © **617/556-0052.** www.dsw.com. T: Red or Orange Line to Downtown Crossing.

Eddie Bauer Outlet Not what you might expect from an outlet—the prices aren't breathtaking (they're lowest during Jan and Aug end-of-season sales), but the quality and selection of casual, outdoorsy clothes and accessories for men and women are generally excellent. 500 Washington St. (at West St.). © **617/423-4722.** www.eddiebaueroutlet.com. T: Red or Orange Line to Downtown Crossing.

Filene's Basement ★ New England's most famous discount retailer opened at Downtown Crossing in 1908. At press time, that location—the only one where the celebrated automatic-markdown pricing policy applies—was closed for construction. The Back Bay store is many things the original wasn't (well lit and scrubbed clean, just to name two), but I find the merchandise roughly equivalent to the stock at other branches. Still, in this neighborhood, any store that acknowledges the concept of discounts is definitely worth a look. 497 Boylston St. (at Clarendon St.). © **617/424-5520.** www.filenesbasement.com. T: Green Line to Arlington or Copley.

Electronics

Apple Store ★ The glittering glass box across the street from the Prudential Center holds two floors of high-tech toys, with the Genius Bar on the third floor. A madhouse since it opened in 2008, the Boston store is open Monday through Saturday 9am to 10pm, Sunday 11am to 7pm. The Cambridge location is smaller and in a mall—a plus or a minus, depending on your tastes. 815 Boylston St. (btw. Fairfield and Gloucester sts.). © **617/385-9400.** www.apple.com/retail/boylstonstreet. T: Green Line to Copley. CambridgeSide Galleria, 100 CambridgeSide Place, Cambridge. © **617/225-0442.** www.apple.com/retail/cambridgeside. T: Green Line to Lechmere, or Red Line to Kendall/MIT and free shuttle bus (every 20 min.).

Fashion

In addition, see "Shoes & Boots" and "Vintage & Secondhand Clothing" later in this chapter.

ADULTS

The **Back Bay** is New England's top destination for swanky boutiques and if-you-have-to-ask-you-can't-afford-it designer shops. Long considered Boston's answer to Fifth Avenue or Rodeo Drive, **Newbury Street** is in some ways a victim of its own success: Rents are so high that many—though not all—of the quirky independent retailers that give a shopping destination much of its zing have been priced out. Still, you'll want to leave time for some exploring along Newbury, before or after checking out the second level of **Copley Place.**

Bring your platinum card to **Chanel,** 15 Arlington St., in the Taj Boston (✆ 617/859-0055); **Diane von Furstenberg,** 73 Newbury St. (✆ 617/247-7300); **Ermenegildo Zegna,** 39 Newbury St. (✆ 617/424-6657); **kate spade,** 117 Newbury St. (✆ 617/262-2632); **Marc by Marc Jacobs,** 81 Newbury St. (✆ 617/425-0707); and **Nanette Lepore,** 119 Newbury St. (✆ 617/421-9200). In the Heritage on the Garden complex at Boylston and Arlington streets, in addition to Anne Fontaine (see below) are **Hermès of Paris,** 22 Arlington St. (✆ 617/482-8707), and **La Perla,** 250 Boylston St. (✆ 617/423-5709).

American Apparel ★ A leading light of the anti-sweatshop movement, American Apparel sells women's and men's T-shirts, underwear, and other fashionable knits—all manufactured in downtown L.A.—that are fun, gorgeous, or both. Sizes run small; try things on before checking out. www.americanapparel. com. 138 Newbury St. (off Dartmouth St.). ✆ **617/536-4768.** T: Green Line to Arlington. 330 Newbury St. (btw. Hereford St. and Mass. Ave.). ✆ **617/236-1636.** T: Green Line B, C, or D to Hynes Convention Center. 47 Brattle St. (at Church St.), Cambridge. ✆ **617/661-2770.** T: Red Line to Harvard.

Anne Fontaine ★ This was the first U.S. outlet for the designer's "perfect white blouse collection from Paris." I wanted to laugh, but then I saw for myself—almost every item *is* a perfect (for one reason or another) white blouse. Prices start at $80. Closed Sunday. Heritage on the Garden, 318 Boylston St. (at Arlington St.) ✆ **617/423-0366.** www.annefontaine.com. T: Green Line to Arlington.

Bodega ★★ This place gets an extra star for being nearly impossible to find: It's the back room of what appears to be a convenience store (stand in front of the Snapple machine and watch what happens). Vintage and limited-edition sneakers are the headliners; add a discriminating selection of bleeding-edge-trendy streetwear—mostly for guys, with some women's accessories and clothing—and you have a destination for hipsters and wannabes from all over Boston and well beyond. Closed Tuesday. 6 Clearway St. (at Mass. Ave.). ✆ **617/421-1550.** www.bdgastore. com. T: Green Line B, C, or D to Hynes Convention Center or Green Line E to Symphony.

Brooks Brothers Would-be "proper Bostonians" head here for blue blazers, gray flannels, seersucker suits, and less conservative business and casual wear for men and women. Brooks is the only place for exactly the right preppy shade of pink button-down oxford shirts—something I've never seen at the outlet stores. 46 Newbury St. (at Berkeley St.). ✆ **617/267-2600.** www.brooksbrothers.com. T: Green Line to Arlington. 75 State St. (at Kilby St.). ✆ **617/261-9990.** T: Orange or Blue Line to State.

Converse ★★ The Converse store is more than just Chuck Taylors (I was wondering, too). Along with a whole floor of athletic shoes, it carries a good selection of men's and women's sportswear, including jeans. The helpful staff at the second-floor customization bar will trick out your new Chucks just for you. 348 Newbury St. (btw. Hereford St. and Mass. Ave.). ✆ **617/424-5400.** www.converse.com. T: Green Line to B, C, or D to Hynes Convention Center.

Crush Boutique ★ The staff at Crush will help dress you from the skin up. The boutique features up-and-coming designers whose work has caught the sharp eyes of the young owners, and the well-edited stock of women's fashion includes plenty of affordable options. 131 Charles St. (btw. Cambridge and Revere sts.). ✆ **617/720-0010.** www.shopcrushboutique.com. T: Red Line to Charles/MGH.

Dress ★ Think of the verb, not the noun. This airy boutique stocks women's fashion (including dresses), jeans, shoes, and jewelry. Many pieces are the work of designers whose creations aren't available elsewhere in Boston—always the goal on Newbury Street. 221 Newbury St. (btw. Exeter and Fairfield sts.). ✆ **617/424-7125.** www.dressboston.com. T: Green Line to Copley.

1154 Lill Studio ★★ 👜 Shoppers at this adorable design-your-own-handbag shop have a lot of decisions to make, starting with a big one: instant or delayed gratification? Bags of all sizes are on display; if you don't see *exactly* what you want, customize your own using an impressive variety of materials, from fabric to straps to lining. It arrives at your home a month or so later, built from scratch just as you imagined it. This is a branch of the Chicago-based mini-chain. Prices run $28 to $200. 220 Newbury St (btw. Exeter and Fairfield sts.). ✆ **617/247-1154.** www.1154lillstudio.com. T: Green Line B, C, or D to Hynes Convention Center.

H&M The Swedish discount-fashion juggernaut specializes in cheap, stylish clothing and accessories. The Downtown Crossing store outfits women, men, and kids; the Cambridge branch concentrates on fashions for women (including underwear) and teens of both sexes. 350 Washington St. (at Franklin St.). ✆ **617/482-7001.** www.hm.com. T: Red or Orange Line to Downtown Crossing. 100 Newbury St. (at Clarendon St.). ✆ **617/859-3192.** T: Green Line to Copley. CambridgeSide Galleria, 100 CambridgeSide Place, Cambridge. ✆ **617/225-0895.** T: Green Line to Lechmere, or Red Line to Kendall/MIT and free shuttle bus (every 20 min.).

Injeanius ★★ The North End doesn't have a bookstore, but it does have a designer-jean boutique—and it's a really good one. Owner Alison Barnard and her staff will find just the right fit for you in their well-edited selection of high-end denim; the tops, shoes, and bags represent an impressive variety of hard-to-find-in-Boston brands. The nearby sister shop, **Twilight,** 12 Fleet St. (off Hanover St.; ✆ **617/523-8008**), carries a gorgeous, ever-changing selection of party dresses and accessories. 441 Hanover St. (at Salutation St.). ✆ **617/523-5326.** www.injeanius.com. T: Green or Orange Line to Haymarket.

Johnny Cupcakes There's no food in the bakery cases at this adorable shop—just limited-edition, custom-designed T-shirts made in the U.S. Pricey but adorable, they've inspired something of a cult, with clever designs that often play off the cupcake theme. And yes, there really is a Johnny (but his last name is Earle). 279 Newbury St. (off Gloucester St.). ✆ **617/375-0100.** www.johnnycupcakes.com. T: Green Line B, C, or D to Hynes Convention Center.

Life Is Good ★ This popular casual clothing and accessories brand got its start in a Boston suburb with some T-shirts and a van. My sister is a devotee, so I asked her to tell you about it: "Really nice colors, fun designs, very comfortable, wears well, great baby stuff." Prices for adult T-shirts start at $25. The company mascot, a stick figure named Jake, adorns many items, doing everything from snowboarding to just kicking back. 285 Newbury St. (btw. Fairfield and Gloucester sts.). ✆ **617/262-5068.** www.lifeisgood.com. T: Green Line to Hynes Convention Center.

Looc Boutique The retro vibe—don't come here looking for jeans—makes this airy space on a South End side street a magnet for women more interested in book clubs than nightclubs. Don't take that as code for "stodgy," though; think "sophisticated and versatile." Be sure to check out the accessories. 12 Union Park St. (btw. Shawmut Ave. and Washington St.). ✆ **617/357-5333.** www.loocboutique.com. T: Orange Line to Back Bay.

Looks ★★ A picky post-hoodie-and-Chucks clientele has made Looks a favorite in this college town for well over 2 decades. Sophisticated yet comfortable, the women's clothes suit everything from barbecue to boardroom, with an excellent selection of special-occasion fashions. Equally appealing are the eye-catching accessories and jewelry. 11–13 Holyoke St. (btw. Mass. Ave. and Mount Auburn St.), Cambridge. ✆ **617/491-4251.** www.looksclothing.com. T: Red Line to Harvard.

Louis Boston Louis (pronounced "Louie's") enjoys a well-deserved reputation for introducing stuffy Bostonians to cutting-edge New York style. The ultra-prestigious store sells men's designer suits, handmade shirts, silk ties, and Italian shoes; the women's fashions are equally elegant. A longtime Back Bay stalwart, Louis is now one of the few retailers in the Seaport District, where its sleek building overlooks the harbor. On the premises are a full-service salon and a restaurant. Fan Pier, 60 Northern Ave. (off Seaport Blvd.). ✆ **617/262-6100.** www.louisboston.com. T: Silver Line SL1/SL2 bus to Court House.

Thomas Pink The London-based haberdasher carries top-quality men's (mostly) and women's dress shirts, both off the rack and made to order. The merchandise is just as lovely and the prices less tic-inducing during periodic sales. And you get to say "haberdasher." The Downtown Crossing location closes Sunday. Copley Place, 100 Huntington Ave. ✆ **617/267-0447.** www.thomaspink.com. T: Orange Line to Back Bay. 280 Washington St. (at School St.). ✆ **617/426-7859.** T: Blue or Orange Line to State.

Wish The interior is stark, the service chilly, the prices high—and the designer fashions unbeatable. Wish is a default destination for an incredible number of stylish Bostonians and suburbanites, not because the labels are unusual but because the selection is so painstaking. The January and July sales are worth waiting for. 49 Charles St. (btw. Chestnut and Mount Vernon sts.). ✆ **617/227-4441.** www.wishboston.com. T: Red Line to Charles/MGH.

 An Outlet Excursion

If you can't get through a vacation without some outlet shopping, the fact that you left the car at home doesn't have to stop you. **Boston Common Coach** (✆ **877/723-3833** or 617/773-2784; www.bostoncommoncoach.com) and **Brush Hill Tours** (✆ **800/343-1328** or 617/720-6342; www.brushhilltours.com) offer service from Boston to **Wrentham Village Premium Outlets** (✆ **508/384-0600**; www.premiumoutlets.com), a huge complex about 45 minutes south of town. Its dozens of outlet stores include—and this is merely scratching the surface—Anne Klein, Banana Republic, Barneys New York, Juicy Couture, J. Crew, Kenneth Cole, Nike, Polo Ralph Lauren, Reebok, Tommy Hilfiger, and Versace. Shoppers leave Boston between 9 and 10am. The round-trip fare is $42 for adults (Brush Hill charges $23 for children 3 to 11); both companies require reservations.

CHILDREN

Bird by Bird ★ This "urban boutique," the brainchild of two local moms, stocks everything you need to turn your youngster into a teeny-tiny fashionista and offers classes (such as yoga and massage) for kids as well as adults. Closed Monday. 1361 Cambridge St. (off Springfield St.), Inman Sq., Cambridge. ✆ **617/497-1361.** www.mybird bybird.com. T: Red Line to Central; 10-min. walk.

The Red Wagon ★ Just about everything in this boutique is as cute as a kitten. Busy parents cherish this Beacon Hill mainstay for its wide selection of American and European clothing and shoes (newborn to size 8) and the fact that it's also a well-stocked toy shop—two errands in one stop. 69 Charles St. (off Mount Vernon St.). ✆ **617/523-9402.** www.theredwagon.com. T: Red Line to Charles/MGH.

Food & Candy

Beacon Hill Chocolates This shop's artisan creations are a consistently hot topic on the chocoholic grapevine. The special-occasion selections in handmade boxes are as beautiful as they are delicious. Salted caramels are a sublime non-chocolate option, and the gelato, hot chocolate, and coffee drinks are delectable. 91 Charles St. (at Pinckney St.). ✆ **617/725-1900.** www.beaconhillchocolates.com. T: Red Line to Charles/MGH.

Penzeys ★★ The Wisconsin-based purveyor of spices, herbs, flavorings, and rubs attracts delighted cooks and foodies from miles around (the closest branch is in Connecticut) with its huge, reasonably priced selection. Getting here is a pain, but it's absolutely worth the trip. 1293 Massachusetts Ave. (at Davis Rd.), Arlington. ✆ **800/741-7787** or 781/646-7707. www.penzeys.com. T: Red Line to Harvard or Porter, then bus no. 77.

Polcari's Coffee ★ Dozens of varieties of coffee beans, half a dozen types of espresso, and a wide tea selection make Polcari's the North End's go-to place for do-it-yourself caffeine (and decaf). The little shop also stocks bulk candy and nuts, spices and herbs, domestic and imported kitchen staples, and numerous cheeses. Best of all, it's a neighborhood favorite—that means great people-watching—with a knowledgeable, friendly staff. Closed Sunday. 105 Salem St. (at Parmenter St.). ✆ **617/227-0786.** www.northendboston.com/polcaricoffee. T: Green or Orange Line to Haymarket.

Salumeria Italiana ★★ The city's premier Italian grocer caters to picky North Enders and foodies from all over the Boston area. Owner Gaetano Martignetti, the son of the founder, prides himself on his selection of meats, cheeses, olives, olive oils, vinegars, pastas, and more. The store is small, the variety huge. 151 Richmond St. (btw. Hanover and North sts.). ✆ **617/523-8743.** www.salumeriaitaliana.com. T: Green or Orange Line to Haymarket.

Trader Joe's ★ The celebrated California-based retailer stocks a large selection of prepared foods, cheese, nuts, baked goods, natural and organic products, and other edibles, all at excellent prices. Get a preview on the website or just ask devotees—they can't shut up about it. The Cambridge locations are good stops for picnic provisions if you're driving. The Memorial Drive and Brookline stores sell beer and wine. 899 Boylston St. (at Gloucester St.). ✆ **617/262-6505.** www.traderjoes. com. T: Green Line B, C, or D to Hynes Convention Center. 1317 Beacon St. (off Harvard St.), Brookline. ✆ **617/278-9997.** T: Green Line C to Coolidge Corner. 748 Memorial Dr. (at Riverside Rd., 1 block from Magazine St.), Cambridge. ✆ **617/491-8582.** 211 Alewife Brook Pkwy. (at Concord Ave.), Cambridge. ✆ **617/498-3201.** T: Red Line to Alewife, 10-min. walk.

Gifts & Souvenirs

Boston has dozens of shops and pushcarts that sell T-shirts, hats, and other souvenirs. At the stores listed here, you'll find gifts that say Boston without actually *saying* "Boston" all over them. Remember to check out museum shops for unique items, including crafts and games. Particularly good outlets include those at the **Museum of Fine Arts,** the **Museum of Science,** the **Isabella Stewart Gardner Museum,** the **Institute of Contemporary Art,** the **Concord Museum,** and the **Peabody Essex Museum** in Salem. The online-only merchandise of the **Boston Public Library** (www.bpl.org) incorporates images from the library's vast holdings, including historic maps, photos, and even sports memorabilia—and you don't have to take up space in your carry-on to get your souvenirs home.

Aunt Sadie's ★ Brimming with perhaps the most miscellaneous merchandise in the South End (which is saying something), Aunt Sadie's started out as a candle shop, and you'll see its products at high-end stores across the country. The retail location carries inventive gifts and accessories for home, bath, kitchen, adults, children, pets, and maybe even your own Aunt Sadie. 18 Union Park St. (off Washington St.). ☎ **617/357-7117.** www.auntsadiesinc.com. T: Orange Line to Back Bay and 10-min. walk, or Silver Line SL4/SL5 bus to Union Park St.

Black Ink ★★★ The wacky wares here defy categorization, but they all fit comfortably under the umbrella of "oh, cool." Rubber stamps, stuffed animals, and doll figurines from Japan caught my eye recently; greeting cards, desktop accessories, and retro toys are equally appealing. 101 Charles St. (btw. Revere and Pinckney sts.). ☎ **617/723-3883.** www.blackinkboston.com. T: Red Line to Charles/MGH. 5 Brattle St. (off John F. Kennedy St.), Cambridge. ☎ **866/497-1221** or 617/497-1221. T: Red Line to Harvard.

Buckaroo's Mercantile ★ Slightly off the beaten track in Central Square, this place stocks a wild selection of vintage and retro-style contemporary gifts, home accessories, clothing, and gadgets. The wacky stock—there's a nun candle in my living room, and I have my eye on a Wonder Woman clock—changes regularly. 5 Brookline St. (at Mass. Ave.), Cambridge. ☎ **617/492-4792.** www.buckmerc.com. T: Red Line to Central.

Copley Flair Late for a party, unwilling to show up with an unwrapped book and a drugstore card *again*, I realized for the umpteenth time how great this little shop is. It's crammed with high-quality greeting cards, wrapping paper, ribbons

---

 Fired Up

A good souvenir is something you'd never find anywhere else, and a **Boston Fire Department T-shirt** is a great one. They cost about $15 at most neighborhood firehouses. The handiest for out-of-towners are **Engine 8, Ladder 1,** 392 Hanover St. (at Charter St.), in the North End near the Freedom Trail; **Engine 4, Ladder 24,** 200 Cambridge St. (at Joy St.), on the north side of Beacon Hill; and **Engine 33, Ladder 15,** 941 Boylston St. (at Hereford St.), in the Back Bay near the Hynes Convention Center.

and bows, stationery, and unusual gifts and novelty items. Closed weekends. 176 Federal St. (at High St.). ☏ **617/737-2420.** www.copleyflair.com. T: Red Line to South Station.

Cross at the Pru The Rhode Island–based pen company operates just a handful of retail outlets, one of which is this kiosk. It's surprisingly well stocked with stationery and cards, gift items such as journals and picture frames, and office accessories. Oh, right—pens, too. Shops at Prudential Center, 800 Boylston St. ☏ **617/236-4486.** www.cross.com. T: Green Line E to Prudential; Green Line to Copley; or Green Line B, C, or D to Hynes Convention Center.

Joie de Vivre ★★★ 🎁 When I'm stumped for a present for a person who has everything, I head to this delightful little shop, in business since 1984. Joie de Vivre's constantly changing selection of gifts and toys for adults and sophisticated children is beyond compare. The kaleidoscope collection alone is worth the trip; you'll also find jewelry, postcards, puzzles, music boxes, clocks, puppets, and salt and pepper shakers. 1792 Massachusetts Ave. (at Arlington St.), Cambridge. ☏ **617/864-8188.** www.joiedevivre.net. T: Red Line to Porter.

Museum of Fine Arts Gift Shop ★★ For those without the time or inclination to visit the museum, the satellite shop carries posters, prints, cards and stationery, books, educational toys, scarves, mugs, T-shirts, and reproductions of jewelry in the museum's collections. You might even be inspired to pay a call on the real thing. 3 South Market Building, Faneuil Hall Marketplace. ☏ **617/720-1266.** www.mfashop.org. T: Green or Blue Line to Government Center.

St. Francis Gift & Book Store Across the street from the Freedom Trail, St. Leonard of Port Maurice Church has a secular feature: this little gift shop. In addition to religious merchandise, it carries greeting cards, jewelry, and an extensive selection of books. Proceeds benefit the church and its Franciscan missions. Hanover St. at Prince St. ☏ **617/523-2111.** T: Green or Orange Line to Haymarket.

Shake the Tree Tucked in among the North End's innumerable restaurants is this appealing boutique. It's artsier than a lot of gift shops, with an ever-changing stock of handmade jewelry, clothing, handbags, baby presents, home accessories, candles, and soaps. Check ahead for details of the monthly cocktail party. 67 Salem St. (off Cross St.). ☏ **617/742-0484.** www.shakethetreeboston.com. T: Green or Orange Line to Haymarket.

WardMaps LLC ★ A "ward map" shows municipal divisions, usually on a grid and often bound into an atlas. This entrancing shop outside Porter Square carries maps—not just ward maps—and prints in various sizes and conditions, with an especially good selection of 19th-century items. The excellent gift items include posters, coasters, puzzles, mugs, notebooks, and more—printed with (can you guess?) maps. 1735 Massachusetts Ave., Cambridge. ☏ **617/497-0737.** www.wardmaps.com. T: Red Line to Porter.

Home & Garden

The Boston Shaker The cocktail craze is in full swing, and this little shop just outside Davis Square carries everything for the hipster mixologist except the booze. You'll find glassware, bar accessories, books and magazines, and nonalcoholic ingredients, from olives to an encyclopedic selection of bitters (celery—who knew?). Check ahead to see whether a class or workshop is taking place during your visit. 69 Holland St. (at Irving St.), Somerville. ☏ **617/718-2999.** www.thebostonshaker.com. T: Red Line to Davis.

Boutique Fabulous ★ The name, a classic case of truth in advertising, only partly conveys the fun of exploring this jampacked emporium of home accessories, antiques, cosmetics, tableware, memorabilia, greeting cards, vintage fashion, and (in case this isn't implied) offbeat gifts. A visit to Boutique Fabulous is the perfect treat after brunch or dinner in Inman Square—it's open Thursday through Saturday 11am to 10pm, other days until 8pm. 1309 Cambridge St. (at Oak St.), Cambridge. ☎ **617/864-0656.** www.boutiquefabulous.com. T: Red Line to Central, 10-min. walk on Prospect St.

Crate & Barrel ★★ This is wedding-present heaven, packed with contemporary and classic housewares as well as furniture and home accessories. The merchandise, from juice glasses and linen napkins to top-of-the-line knives and roasting pans, includes items to suit any budget. 777 Boylston St. (btw. Exeter and Fairfield sts.). ☎ **617/262-8700.** www.crateandbarrel.com. T: Green Line to Copley. 1045 Massachusetts Ave. (at Trowbridge St.), Cambridge. ☎ **617/547-3994.** T: Red Line to Harvard.

Frette Maybe a night in a luxury hotel is so restful because many of them use Frette bed and bath linens. The legendary Italian retailer also carries plush bathrobes and nightclothes, adorable baby gifts, and home accessories such as throws and pillows. True, some of them cost as much as a car, but there's no harm in looking—and maybe finding something gorgeous on sale. In the Mandarin Oriental, Boston, 776B Boylston St. (at Fairfield St.). ☎ **617/267-0500.** www.frette.com. T: Green Line to Copley.

Greenward A quick glance reveals what appears to be an upscale boutique that may be taking "colorful" a bit too literally, but that's part of what makes Greenward so ingenious. The merchandise—home goods, fashion accessories (including jewelry), cleaning products for your home and yourself, kids' clothing, toys, and more—is both desirable and eco-conscious (organic, handmade, recycled, recyclable, generally virtuous). 1764 Massachusetts Ave. (at Lancaster St.), Cambridge. ☎ **617/395-1338.** www.greenwardshop.com. T: Red Line to Porter.

Koo De Kir ★★ In the heart of 19th-century Beacon Hill, Koo De Kir is a splash of modern style. Creative director Kristine Irving has a great eye, and her selection of contemporary home accessories, furniture, lighting, sculpture, and gifts at every price point—from impulse to investment—ranges from classic to whimsical. 65 Chestnut St. (off Charles St.). ☎ **617/723-8111.** www.koodekir.com. T: Red Line to Charles/MGH.

Lekker *Lekker* is Dutch for "tempting," which this striking store certainly is. A perfect fit for the modish South End, it features contemporary home accessories and furniture. Be sure to check out the delightful selection of gifts for adults and children. Closed Monday. 1317 Washington St. (at Waltham St.). ☎ 877/7-LEKKER or **617/542-6464.** www.lekkerhome.com. T: Orange Line to Back Bay and 10-min. walk, or Silver Line SL4/SL5 bus to Union Park St.

Marimekko Concept Store The Finnish design company—you might recognize the bold, colorful prints from the Crate & Barrel catalogue—operates just four concept stores in North America. This one, in a mostly residential West Cambridge neighborhood, stocks home accessories and linens, textiles, and clothing and accessories for women, children, and men. Closed Sunday except in December. 350 Huron Ave. (at Gurney St.). ☎ **617/354-2800.** www.marimekko cambridge.com. T: Red Line to Harvard, then no. 72 bus or 25-min. walk.

Simon Pearce ★ Dramatic designs make Simon Pearce's hand-blown glass and handmade pottery as much art as tableware. The Vermont-based company originated in Ireland, where Simon Pearce himself learned glassblowing, and has grown into an internationally recognized go-to destination for high-end wedding presents. 103 Newbury St. (at Clarendon St.). 🕿 **617/450-8388.** www.simonpearce.com. T: Green Line to Copley.

Jewelry

Boston Bead Company The jewelry here will suit you exactly—you make it yourself. Prices for the dazzling variety of raw materials start at 5¢ a bead, findings (hardware) are available, and you can assemble your finery at the in-store worktable. Ready-made pieces are in stock, and the store schedules jewelry-making workshops; check ahead for details. 23 Church St. (btw. Mass. Ave. and Palmer St.), Cambridge. 🕿 **617/868-9777.** www.beadworkscambridge.com. T: Red Line to Harvard.

High Gear Jewelry ★★ The biggest jewelry snob I know invents excuses to visit the North End just to stop in here. The eye-catching shop right on the Freedom Trail carries an impressive selection of reasonably priced costume jewelry, watches, and hair accessories. If you don't see what you want, ask the friendly staff for help—the owner recently turned a pair of pierced earrings into clip-ons for my sister in a matter of seconds, for no extra charge. 204 Hanover St. (off Cross St.). 🕿 **617/523-5804.** T: Green or Orange Line to Haymarket.

John Lewis, Inc. ★★★ 📖 John Lewis's imaginative women's and men's jewelry—designed and made on the premises—suits both traditional and avant-garde tastes. The wide selection of silver, gold, and platinum items and unusual colored stones add to the museum-like shop's appeal. The pieces that mark you as a savvy Bostonian are earrings, necklaces, and bracelets made of hammered metal circles. Closed Sunday and Monday. 97 Newbury St. (at Clarendon St.). 🕿 **617/266-6665.** www.johnlewisinc.com. T: Green Line to Arlington.

Lux Bond & Green ★★ A family business founded in 1898, Lux Bond & Green is a full-service jeweler with an "only in Boston" feature: The company is the official Red Sox jeweler. This is the go-to destination for high-end souvenirs (cuff links, Christmas ornaments) as well as memorabilia (autographed baseballs). 416 Boylston St. (at Berkeley St.). 🕿 **617/266-4747.** www.lbgreen.com. T: Green Line to Arlington.

Topaz ★ Inventive jewelry is the headliner here, with sterling silver and semiprecious stones taking precedence over pricier materials—but not at the expense of style. The baubles range widely in price and size, from ladylike to borderline gaudy (not that there's anything wrong with that!). You'll also find funky gifts, a well-edited selection of accessories, including lovely leather goods and scarves, and a lively, helpful staff. 11 Dunster St. (off Mass. Ave.), Cambridge. 🕿 **617/492-3700.** www.topazcambridge.com. T: Red Line to Harvard.

Flying Lobsters

Why go to the trouble of sending a postcard? Send a lobster instead. **James Hook & Co.**, 15 Northern Ave. at Atlantic Avenue (🕿 **617/423-5500;** www.jameshooklobster.com; T: Red Line to South Station), and **Legal Sea Foods**, Logan Airport Terminal B and C (🕿 **800/343-5804,** 617/568-2811, or 617/568-2800; www.sendlegal.com; T: Blue Line to Airport), do overnight shipping.

Malls & Shopping Centers

CambridgeSide Galleria This three-level mall houses two large department stores—**Macy's** (☎ 617/621-3800) and **Sears** (☎ 617/252-3500)—and more than 100 specialty stores. Pleasant but quite generic, it might be the bargaining chip you need to lure your teenager to the nearby Museum of Science. There's trendy sportswear at **Abercrombie & Fitch** (☎ 617/494-1338) and **H&M** (p. 242), electronics at the **Apple Store** (p. 240), casual and dressier clothing at **J. Crew** (☎ 617/225-2739) and **White House Black Market** (☎ 617/374-6180), cosmetics at **Sephora** (p. 252), and music and appliances at **Best Buy** (☎ 617/577-8866). The mall also has a branch of **Borders** (p. 237), two restaurants, a food court, and seating along a pleasant canal.

Strollers and wheelchairs are available. Open Monday through Saturday from 10am to 9pm, Sunday from noon to 7pm. 100 CambridgeSide Place (btw. Edwin H. Land Blvd. and First St.), Cambridge. ☎ **617/621-8666.** www.shopcambridgeside.com. T: Green Line to Lechmere, or Red Line to Kendall/MIT and free shuttle bus (every 20 min.). Garage parking from $2/hr.

Copley Place ★ Copley Place has set the standard for upscale shopping in Boston since 1985. Connected to the Westin and Marriott hotels and the Prudential Center, it's a crossroads for office workers, out-of-towners, and enthusiastic consumers. You can while away a couple of hours or a whole day shopping and dining here and at the adjacent Shops at the Prudential Center (see below) without ever going outdoors.

Some of Copley Place's 70-plus shops will be familiar from the mall at home, but this is emphatically not a suburban shopping complex that happens to be in the city. You'll see designer boutiques that don't have another branch in Boston, including **Christian Dior** (☎ 617/927-7577), **Jimmy Choo** (☎ 617/927-9570), and **Louis Vuitton** (☎ 617/437-6519), as well as the Boston branch of **Tiffany & Co.** (☎ 617/353-0222). The anchor department stores are **Barneys New York** and **Neiman Marcus.** Also here is a branch of **Legal Sea Foods** (p. 101).

Open Monday through Saturday from 10am to 8pm, Sunday from noon to 6pm. Some establishments keep longer or shorter hours. 100 Huntington Ave. (at Dartmouth St.). ☎ **617/262-6600.** www.simon.com. T: Orange Line to Back Bay or Green Line to Copley. Discounted validated parking with purchase.

Faneuil Hall Marketplace ★★ The original festival market hall is both wildly popular and widely imitated, and Faneuil Hall Marketplace changes constantly to appeal to visitors as well as locals wary of its touristy reputation. The original part of **Faneuil Hall** itself dates to 1742 (the first floor was under renovation at press time; check ahead to see whether it's reopened). The **Quincy Market Colonnade,** in the central building, houses a gargantuan selection of food and confections. The bars and restaurants always seem to be crowded, and the shopping is terrific if generic.

In and around the five buildings, the shops tend less toward "only in Boston" than toward "only at every mall in the country." **Marketplace Center** and the ground floors of the **North Market** and **South Market buildings** have lots of chain outlets. Most of the unique offerings are under the Quincy Market canopies, where crafts and gifts cram dozens of **pushcarts,** and upstairs and downstairs in the market buildings.

Shop hours are Monday through Saturday from 10am to 9pm and Sunday from noon to 6pm. The Colonnade opens earlier, and most bars and restaurants close later. If you must drive, many businesses offer a discount at the 75 State St. Garage; there's also parking in the Government Center garage off Congress Street and the marketplace's crowded garage off Atlantic Avenue. Btw. North, Congress, and State sts. and Atlantic Ave. ©️ **617/338-2323.** www.faneuilhallmarketplace. com. T: Green or Blue Line to Government Center or Orange Line to Haymarket.

The Shops at Prudential Center ★ The main level of the city's second-tallest tower holds this sprawling complex. In addition to **Saks Fifth Avenue** (©️ **617/262-8500**), it's home to dozens of shops and boutiques, a large **Barnes & Noble** (p. 237), a food court, a post office, and 10 restaurants, including **Legal Sea Foods** (p. 101) and the **Cheesecake Factory.** Also here are Boston's branches of **Club Monaco** (©️ **617/262-2658**) and **Sephora** (p. 252), and one of a handful of retail outlets for the upscale office and home accessories that **Levenger** (©️ **800/667-8934** or 617/536-3434; www.levenger.com) calls "tools for serious readers." Vendors sell gifts, souvenirs, and novelty items off carts and kiosks in the arcades, and the Greater Boston Convention & Visitors Bureau operates an **information booth.** The complex has outdoor space if you need some fresh air, and a farmers' market on summer and fall Thursdays.

Hours are Monday through Saturday from 10am to 9pm, Sunday from 11am to 6pm. Restaurant hours vary. 800 Boylston St. (btw. Fairfield and Gloucester sts.); back entrance off Huntington Ave. at Belvidere St. ©️ **800/746-7778.** www.prudentialcenter.com. T: Green Line E to Prudential; Green Line to Copley; Orange Line to Back Bay; or Green Line B, C, or D to Hynes Convention Center. Discounted validated parking with purchase.

Markets

Massachusetts farmers and growers under the auspices of the state **Department of Agricultural Resources** (©️ **617/626-1700;** www.mass.gov/massgrown) dispatch trucks filled with whatever's in season to the heart of the city from late spring through October or November. Depending on the time of year, you'll have your pick of berries, herbs, tomatoes, squash, pumpkins, apples, corn, and more, all fresh and reasonably priced. Visit the website for a complete list of state-sponsored markets. In Boston, you can stop by **City Hall Plaza** (Cambridge St. near School St.) on Monday or Wednesday (T: Green or Blue Line to Government Center); **Copley Square** (St. James Ave. at Dartmouth St.) on Tuesday or Friday (T: Green Line to Copley or Orange Line to Back Bay); or the **Shops at Prudential Center** (Boylston St. near Gloucester St.) on Thursday (T: Green Line B, C, or D to Hynes Convention Center). In Cambridge, several locations around **Harvard Square** (T: Red Line to Harvard) play host to relatively small markets throughout the week; to see the full range of local produce, head to Parking Lot 5, Norfolk Street and Bishop Allen Drive (1 block from Mass. Ave.), in **Central Square** on non-holiday Mondays (T: Red Line to Central). For more info, visit **www.massfarmersmarkets.org.**

The **Boston Public Market** (©️ **617/263-3355;** www.bostonpublic market.org) is the first major step in a drive for a permanent public market a la Philadelphia's or Seattle's. Open from late May through late November, it offers a tasty mix of farm products and specialty foods. It takes place Tuesday and Thursday at Dewey Square, on the Rose Kennedy Greenway across Atlantic Avenue from South Station (T: Red Line to South Station).

The funky, fashionable **SoWa Open Market** (©️ **617/481-2257;** www. sowaopenmarket.com) operates most Sundays 10am to 5pm from mid-May through October at 460 Harrison Ave. in the South End (T: Orange Line to Back Bay, then a 10-min. walk, or Silver Line SL4/SL5 bus to E. Berkeley St., then 5-min. walk). It features numerous craftspeople as well as food merchants in a neighborhood you may not have a chance to explore otherwise.

The **Independent Designer's Market** (www.idmboston.com) specializes in women's and men's fashion, accessories, photography, and jewelry by young designers—sort of a three-dimensional Etsy. It's open Saturday from 11am to 5pm. At press time, it had just relocated from Boston to 30 Brattle St. (at Mount Auburn St.), Cambridge (T: Red Line to Harvard); double-check schedule and location details before heading out.

Music

Cheapo Records The specialty here is vinyl, but the selection of other formats is nothing to sneeze at. And sneeze you might, as you search for something specific or let serendipity be your guide. If you need help, the staff members are as friendly as they are knowledgeable. 538 Massachusetts Ave. (at Norfolk St.). © **617/354-4455.** www.cheaporecords.com. T: Red Line B to Central.

In Your Ear Records ★★ Asked to recommend a used-music store, a DJ friend instantly suggested In Your Ear. These stores, adjacent to Boston University and Harvard, carry huge, constantly changing inventories of CDs, vinyl, DVDs, and even cassettes and eight-track tapes, plus turntables and posters. 957 Commonwealth Ave. (at Harry Agganis Way). © **617/787-9755.** www.iye.com. T: Green Line B to Pleasant St. 72 Mount Auburn St. (off Holyoke St.), lower level. © **617/491-5035.** T: Red Line to Harvard.

Newbury Comics ★ A quickly adapting survivor of the format revolution, Newbury Comics is a funky local chain that stocks a wide selection of music, gifts, novelty items, posters, T-shirts—and, of course, comics. You'll find video games, DVDs, and new and used CDs of mainstream and cutting-edge music, with lots of independent labels and imports. 332 Newbury St. (btw. Hereford St. and Mass. Ave.) © **617/236-4930.** www.newburycomics.com. T: Green Line B, C, or D to Hynes Convention Center. North Market Building, Faneuil Hall Marketplace. © **617/248-9992.** T: Orange Line to Haymarket, or Green or Blue Line to Government Center. In the Garage mall, 36 John F. Kennedy St., Cambridge. © **617/491-0337.** T: Red Line to Harvard.

Stereo Jack's ★ I love music; I'm not obsessed, but I can recognize people who are, and the staff here qualifies. If you just can't get enough jazz, blues, and R&B (new and used), you'll feel right at home. 1686 Massachusetts Ave. © **617/497-9447.** www.stereojacks.com. T: Red Line to Porter.

Perfume & Cosmetics

Colonial Drug ★★ 🎁 The perfume counter at this family business puts the "special" in "specialize." You can choose from more than 1,000 fragrances—plus cosmetics, soap, shaving necessities, and countless other body-care products—with the help of the gracious staff members. They remain unflappable even during Harvard Square's equivalent of rush hour, Saturday afternoon. No credit cards; closed Sunday except in December. 49 Brattle St. (off Church St.), Cambridge. © **617/864-2222.** www.colonialdrug.com. T: Red Line to Harvard.

Kiehl's Since 1851 ★ Lots of retail chains originate in New York, but few of them develop this kind of cult following. Customers wax evangelical over the skin, hair, and body products from Kiehl's, which straddle the line between cosmetics and pharmaceuticals. 112 Newbury St. (off Clarendon St.). ☎ **617/247-1777.** www.kiehls.com. T: Green Line to Copley.

Lush ★★★ Of all the lotions-and-potions purveyors in the Boston area, this is my favorite. It smells great, and the enthusiastic staff is entirely attitude-free. U.K.-based Lush specializes in fresh, organic, natural products, notably "bath bombs" (solid bubble bath) and solid shampoo priced by the pound. 166 Newbury St. (btw. Dartmouth and Exeter sts.). ☎ **617/375-5874.** www.lushusa.com. T: Green Line to Copley. 30 John F. Kennedy St. (at Mt. Auburn St.). ☎ **617/497-5874.** T: Red Line to Harvard.

Sephora ★★ This European phenomenon is a fashionista magnet. You'll find an encyclopedic, international selection of manufacturers and products in well-lit, well-organized spaces overflowing with testers. Everything is self-service, and the staff provides as much help as you want. Shops at Prudential Center, 800 Boylston St. (at Fairfield St.). ☎ **617/262-4200.** www.sephora.com. T: Green Line E to Prudential; Green Line to Copley; or Green Line B, C, or D to Hynes Convention Center. CambridgeSide Galleria, 100 CambridgeSide Place, Cambridge. ☎ **617/577-1005.** T: Green Line to Lechmere, or Red Line to Kendall/MIT and free shuttle bus (every 20 min.).

Shoes & Boots

Also see the listing for **DSW Shoe Warehouse** under "Discount Shopping," earlier in this chapter.

Berk's Shoes ★ "Trendy" doesn't adequately describe the wares at this Harvard Square institution. College students and people who want to look like them come here to seek out whatever's fashionable right this red-hot minute. 50 John F. Kennedy St. (at Winthrop St.). ☎ **888/462-3757** or 617/492-9511. www.berkshoes.com. T: Red Line to Harvard.

Cuoio The enormous selections of designer footwear at these compact boutiques are dream fuel for the truly fetishistic (you know who you are). Be sure to check out the dramatically discounted clearance merchandise. 115 Newbury St. (btw. Clarendon and Dartmouth sts.). ☎ **617/859-0636.** T: Green Line to Arlington. 170 Faneuil Hall Marketplace. ☎ **617/742-4486.** T: Blue Line to Aquarium or Green Line to Government Center.

Helen's Leather Shop ★ Homesick Texans visit Helen's just to gaze upon the boots. Many are handmade from exotic leathers, including ostrich, buffalo, and snakeskin. The shop carries brands such as Lucchese and Tony Lama, along with a large selection of Western apparel for adults and children, leather goods, belts and buckles, and Stetson hats. And it smells great. Closed Tuesday. 110 Charles St. (at Pinckney St.). ☎ **617/742-2077.** www.helensleather.com. T: Red Line to Charles/MGH.

Moxie ★★ A chic little shop with an unbelievable selection of designer shoes, Moxie may look like an intimidating boutique, but it really isn't. The welcoming, helpful staff will help you put together an ensemble of accessories (shoes, handbag, jewelry) for any occasion. 51 Charles St. (btw. Chestnut and Mount Vernon sts.). ☎ **617/557-9991.** www.moxieboston.com. T: Red Line to Charles/MGH.

Sudo Shoes You may need a minute to figure out why your fellow shoppers seem so excited, because much of the merchandise here is so fashionable that it's hard to believe it's vegan. The clientele is largely online shoppers thrilled with the opportunity for 3-D browsing—for men's, women's, and kids' footwear—plus the occasional fashionista who doesn't even miss the leather and suede. 1771

Massachusetts Ave. (at Forest St.), Cambridge. ☎ **617/354-1771.** www.sudoshoes.com. T: Red Line to Porter.

Toys & Games

A number of businesses listed earlier in this chapter are good places to look for toys. They include most of the shops under "Gifts & Souvenirs," the children's specialists in the "Fashion" section, and **Curious George & Friends** (see "Books"). Also be sure to check out the gift shops at the **Boston Children's Museum, Museum of Science,** and **New England Aquarium.**

The Games People Play ★ Just outside Harvard Square, this store carries enough board games (foreign as well as domestic) to outfit every country, summer, and beach house in New England. Also check out the wide selection of puzzles (jigsaw and mechanical), playing cards, Steiff toys, and chess, backgammon, and go sets. 1100 Massachusetts Ave. (at Putnam Ave.), Cambridge. ☎ **800/696-0711** or 617/492-0711. www.thegamespeopleplaycambridge.com. T: Red Line to Harvard.

Henry Bear's Park ★★★ This mini-chain is well into its 4th decade of thrilling Boston-area children and the adults who want to keep them delighted. The toys "promote healthy and positive play," which luckily is a concept that knows no age limit (yes, that yo-yo was for me). Staff members are enthusiastic and helpful, and gift-wrapping is free. In the Porter Square Shopping Center, 25 White St. (off Mass. Ave.), Cambridge. ☎ **617/547-8424.** www.henrybear.com. T: Red Line to Porter. 19 Harvard St. (near Webster Place), Brookline. ☎ **617/264-2422.** T: Green Line D to Brookline Village.

Magic Beans ★ A small local chain with a big reputation, Magic Beans is mostly a baby-gear destination, with terrific toy and gift selections. The closest locations to downtown are a bit out of the way, but hey—the 'burbs are where the kids are. 361 Huron Ave. (btw. Chilton and Standish sts.), Cambridge. ☎ **617/300-0171.** www.mbeans.com. T: Red Line to Harvard, then No. 72 bus or 25-minute walk. 321 Harvard St. (at Babcock St.), Brookline. ☎ **617/264-2326.** T: Green Line to Coolidge Corner.

Stellabella Toys ★★ Both retro (lots of wooden toys) and modern (no guns), Stellabella is a welcoming destination for parents and kids alike. It carries everything from baby strollers to craft supplies and costumes for big kids, and the friendly staff can lend a hand if you need help maintaining your status as the cool aunt or uncle. 1967 Massachusetts Ave. (btw. Allen and Beech sts.), Cambridge. ☎ **617/864-6290.** www.stellabellatoys.com. T: Red Line to Porter. 1360 Cambridge St. (btw. Oak and Springfield sts.), Inman Sq., Cambridge. ☎ **617/491-6290.** T: Red Line to Central, then 10-min. walk on Prospect St.

Vintage & Secondhand Clothing

Bobby From Boston ★★ Boston's vintage clothing scene tends to be light on men's options, though not on people whining about it. The perfect rejoinder is this off-the-beaten-track shop—in 2009, *Esquire* proclaimed it the best in the country for men's vintage—run by a veteran dealer who specializes in supplying wardrobe for period films. The focus is the 1940s through '70s. Closed Sunday and Monday. 19 Thayer St. (off Harrison Ave.). ☎ **617/423-9299.** T: Silver Line SL4/SL5 bus to E. Berkeley St. or Orange Line to Tufts Medical Center and 10-min. walk.

Boomerangs ★★ 🎁 The AIDS Action Committee operates this mini-chain of resale stores; the crown jewel is the "Special Edition" in the chic South End, which stocks women's and men's fashion. Some items are new, but the real finds here are vintage and "gently used." Check the website for information about the Jamaica Plain and West Roxbury locations, which also carry furniture and home accessories. 1407 Washington St. (btw. Union Park and Pelham sts.). © **617/456-0996.** www.shopboomerangs.com. T: Silver Line SL4/SL5 bus to Union Park St. or Orange Line to Tufts Medical Center and 10-min. walk.

The Closet ★★★ This is the not-very-secret weapon of many a chic shopper. One of the Boston area's best consignment shops, it opened in 1979 and offers "gently worn" (not vintage) high-end designer clothing and accessories for women and men at drastically reduced prices. Be sure to check out the shoes and bags. 175 Newbury St. (btw. Dartmouth and Exeter sts.). © **617/536-1919.** www.closet boston.com. T: Green Line to Copley.

The Garment District ★ You're hitting the clubs and you want to look cool, but money is tight. Join the shoppers here, paying great prices for a huge selection of contemporary and vintage clothing, costumes, and accessories. "Dollar a pound" merchandise on the first floor actually costs $1.50 a pound. And Boston Costume, which is on the premises, is *the* place for rental, retail, and vintage costumes, which are available year-round. 200 Broadway (at Davis St.), Cambridge. © **617/876-5230.** www.garmentdistrict.com. T: Red Line to Kendall/MIT.

Kulturez 👕 Vintage and vintage-y T-shirts appeal to skater dudes and graffiti artists, who find a well-edited selection of apparel, "urban art supplies" (think spray paint), and a friendly vibe—I'm hardly the target audience, but I always feel welcome. Formerly known as Proletariat, Kulturez caters to the fashion-conscious of both genders. In the Garage mall, 36 John F. Kennedy St. (at Mount Auburn St.), Cambridge. © **617/661-3865.** www.kulturez.com. T: Red Line to Harvard.

Oona's Experienced Clothing ★★★ From funky accessories and costume jewelry to vintage dresses nice enough to get married in, Oona's carries a large but choice selection of women's and men's clothing at good prices. The Harvard Square stalwart, which opened in 1973, changed hands in 2010 and kept its friendly, fashionable vibe. 1210 Massachusetts Ave. (near Bow St.), Cambridge. © **617/491-2654.** T: Red Line to Harvard.

Second Time Around Part of an East Coast chain, these consignment stores have a catch-as-catch-can flavor that entrances some shoppers and drives others nuts. The Closet (see listing above) outshines Second Time Around in every regard, but if you're in a bargain-hunting mood, you might find a keeper. 82 Charles St. (btw. Mount Vernon and Pinckney sts.). © **617/227-0049.** www.secondtimearound.net. T: Red Line to Charles/MGH. 176 Newbury St. (btw. Dartmouth and Exeter sts.). © **617/247-3504.** T: Green Line to Copley. 219 Newbury St. (btw. Exeter and Fairfield sts.). © **617/266-1113.** T: Green Line to Copley. 324 Newbury St. (at Hereford St.). © **617/236-2028.** T: Green Line B, C, or D to Hynes Convention Center.

The Velvet Fly ★★ The merchandise here isn't exclusively vintage, but even the newest pieces share that sensibility—you definitely won't see your outfit on anyone else. Unusual accessories complement the flirty fashions. The Velvet Fly is one of the little boutiques that are helping the North End develop its own quirky fashion sense, and the chic, friendly owners give great advice. 28 Parmenter St. (btw. Hanover and Salem sts.). © **617/557-4359.** www.thevelvetfly.com. T: Green or Orange Line to Haymarket.

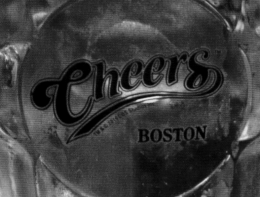

BOSTON AFTER DARK

9

Countless musicians, actors, and comedians went to college or got their start in the Boston area, and it's a great place to check out rising stars and promising unknowns. You might get an early look at the next Branford Marsalis, Matt Damon, Bonnie Raitt, John Mayer, or Yo-Yo Ma. And you can certainly enjoy the work of many established artists who perform at world-renowned Symphony Hall and countless lower-profile venues. Nearly every day of the year, no matter your budget, you'll find someone expressing him- or herself in public, and eager for an audience.

The Boston-area nightlife scene is, to put it mildly, somewhat dull. You can be home from a jampacked night on the town when your friends in New York are still drying their hair. (In fact, flying to New York after work and taking the first shuttle back the next morning isn't unheard of.) Clubs close at 2am, which means cramming a lot into 4 hours or less.

For up-to-date entertainment information online, start at **http://events. frommers.com**. The *Boston Globe* offers suggestions at **www.boston.com/ thingstodo/nightlife** and on Twitter (**@bostoncalendar**), where you'll also find the *Phoenix* (**@BostonPhoenix**). The websites of the agencies listed under "Getting Tickets," below, list events by date and location (don't forget to check Cambridge as well as Boston). To do low-tech research, consult the daily *Boston Globe,* Friday's *Boston Herald,* and the Sunday arts sections of both papers. Four free publications, available at newspaper boxes around town, publish good nightlife listings: the weekly *Boston Phoenix* and *Weekly Dig,* and the biweekly *Stuff@Night* (a *Phoenix* offshoot) and *Improper Bostonian.* The *Phoenix* website (**www.bostonphoenix.com**) archives the paper's season-preview issues; especially before a summer or fall visit, it's a valuable planning tool.

GETTING TICKETS

Some companies and venues sell tickets online or over the phone; many will refer you to a ticket agency. Two major agencies serve Boston: **Ticketmaster** (✆ 800/745-3000; www.ticketmaster.com) and **Telecharge** (✆ 800/432-7250 or TTY 888/889-8587; www.telecharge.com). Many smaller venues use independent companies that charge lower fees than the national companies. One popular firm is **Brown Paper Tickets** (✆ 800/838-3006; www.brown papertickets.com). To avoid fees—and possible losses if your plans change and you can't get your money back—visit the box office in person. *Tip:* If you wait until the day before or day of a performance, you'll sometimes have access to tickets that were held back for some reason and have just gone on sale.

PREVIOUS PAGE: **Everyone at the Faneuil Hall Cheers may not know your name, but if you're a fan of the show, you'll be glad you came.**

Some of the best bargains in town are available at the **BosTix** booths at **Faneuil Hall Marketplace** (T: Green or Blue Line to Government Center, or Orange Line to Haymarket) and in **Copley Square** at the corner of Boylston and Dartmouth streets (T: Green Line to Copley or Orange Line to Back Bay). At press time, the Faneuil Hall location is on the second floor of the **Quincy Market rotunda** while the freestanding kiosk, on the south side of Faneuil Hall, is under renovation.

Both locations sell half-price same-day tickets to musical and theatrical performances, subject to availability.

You must pay cash in person, and there are no refunds or exchanges. Check the board or the website for the day's offerings. The booths are also Ticketmaster outlets. Both are open Tuesday through Saturday from 10am to 6pm, and Sunday from 11am to 4pm. The Copley Square location is also open Monday from 10am to 6pm. BosTix (© **617/262-8632**; www.bostix.org) also offers full-price advance tickets; discounts on more than 100 theater, music, and dance events; and tickets for trolley tours. *Tip:* Sign up for e-mail updates (you can always unsubscribe after you return home).

THE PERFORMING ARTS
Performance Venues

The **Hatch Shell** on the Esplanade (© **617/626-4970**; www.mass.gov/dcr/hatch_events.htm; T: Red Line to Charles/MGH or Green Line to Arlington) is an amphitheater best known as the site of the Boston Pops' Fourth of July concerts. On many summer nights, free music and dance performances and films take over the stage, to the delight of crowds on the lawn.

Agganis Arena at Boston University BU's hockey arena is also a popular midsize concert venue that seats 6,300 to 7,200. It books rock and pop concerts and ice shows, such as Kylie Minogue and Cirque du Soleil (not together), as well as sporting events. 925 Commonwealth Ave. (at Pleasant St.). © **617/353-4628** (ticket office) or 800/745-3000 (Ticketmaster). www.agganisarena.com. T: Green Line B to St. Paul St. or Pleasant St.

Bank of America Pavilion One of the most pleasant venues in the area, this giant white tent encloses a 5,000-seat waterfront pavilion. It schedules pop, rock, country, rap, folk, and jazz on evenings from May through September. Check ahead for information about water transportation. 290 Northern Ave. (at Congress St.), South Boston. © **617/728-1600** or 877/598-8497 (Live Nation). www.livenation.com. T: Waterfront Silver Line bus to Silver Line Way.

Berklee Performance Center The Berklee College of Music's theater features professional artists (many of them former Berklee students, both alumni and dropouts), instructors, and students. Offerings are heavy on jazz and folk, with plenty of other options. 136 Massachusetts Ave. (at Boylston St.). © **617/747-2261.** www.berkleebpc.com. T: Green Line B, C, or D to Hynes Convention Center.

Boston Center for the Arts Multiple performance spaces and an anything-goes booking policy make the BCA a leading venue for contemporary theater, music and dance performances, and visual arts exhibitions. The BCA and the

Agganis Arena **1**
AMC Loews Boston Common **58**
Bank of America Pavilion **91**
The Bar at Taj Boston **40**
The Beehive **35**
Berklee Performance Center **20**
The Black Rose **82**
Bleacher Bar **10**
BosTix **29, 80**
Boston Beer Works **5, 71**
Boston Center for the Arts **35**
Boston Common
　Coffee Co. **63, 75, 87**
Boston Opera House **61**
Brasserie Jo **27**
Bricco **77**
The Bristol Lounge **44**
Cafe 939 **24**
Caffe Pompei **74**
Cask 'n Flagon **7**
Charles Playhouse **51**
Cheers **38, 80**
Citi Wang Theatre **55**
Club Café **33**
Colonial Theatre **46**
Commonwealth Shakespeare
　Company **45**
Cutler Majestic Theatre **46**
Davio's Northern Italian
　Steakhouse **41**
DeLux Cafe **34**
Drink **90**

Eastern Standard **8**
Emmanuel Church **39**
Equal Exchange Cafe **69**
The Estate **47**
Finale **43**
The Fours **70**
Fritz **36**
Game On! Sports Cafe **6**
The Grand Canal **72**
Great Scott **2**
Hard Rock Cafe **79**
Hatch Shell **37**
House of Blues **9**
Huntington Theatre
　Company **18**
Improv Asylum **76**
Isabella Stewart Gardner
　Museum **14**
Jacob Wirth **57**
Jacques Cabaret **50**
Jasper White's Summer
　Shack **22**
Jerry Remy's Sports Bar &
　Grill **12**
Jillian's Boston **11**
Kings **23**
King's Chapel **66**
The Littlest Bar **85**
Lyric Stage **32**
M Bar and Lounge **26**
Machine **13**
Mr. Dooley's Boston Tavern **86**

Modern Theatre **62**
Mottley's Comedy Club **81**
Museum of Fine Arts **15**
New England Conservatory **17**
Oak Bar **31**
Old South Church **28**
Orpheum Theater **64**
Paradise Rock Club **3**
Paramount Center **60**
Pizzeria Regina **73**
The Place **83**
The Purple Shamrock **78**
Radius **88**
Royale Boston **54**
Rumor **52**
Sel de la Terre **26, 84**
Shubert Theatre **53**
Silvertone Bar & Grill **65**
South Street Diner **89**
Stuart Street Playhouse **50**
Symphony Hall **19**
TD Garden **68**
Thinking Cup **59**
Top of the Hub **25**
Trident Booksellers & Café **21**
Trinity Church **30**
21st Amendment **67**
Via Matta **42**
Wally's Cafe **16**
Wheelock Family Theatre **4**
Wilbur Theatre **56**

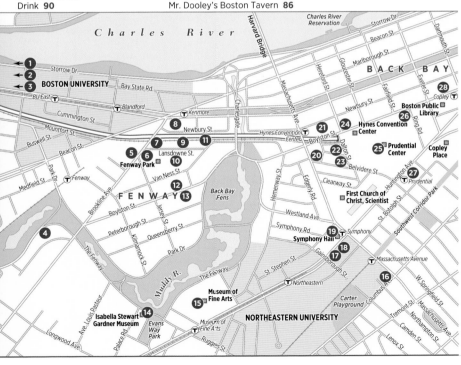

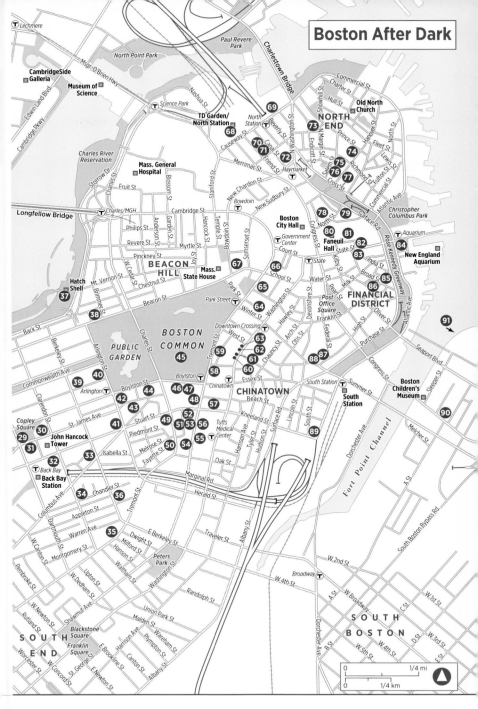

Boston After Dark

Huntington Theatre Company (see "Theater," later in this chapter) are partners in the Calderwood Pavilion, which incorporates 350- and 200-seat theaters. 539 Tremont St. (at Clarendon St.). ✆ **617/426-5000.** www.bcaonline.org. T: Orange Line to Back Bay.

Cambridge Multicultural Arts Center Concerts, plays, art and photography exhibits, dance performances, and films jam the schedule at this renovated courthouse not far from the CambridgeSide Galleria mall. CMAC is also home to the **Jazz Club at the Multicultural Arts Center,** a 200-seat cabaret that books local, national, and international performers. 41 Second St. (at Otis St.), Cambridge. ✆ **617/577-1400.** www.cmacusa.org. T: Green Line to Lechmere.

Citi Wang Theatre This Art Deco palace books numerous and varied national arts companies, including touring Broadway shows, and individuals such as musicians and comedians. Part of Citi Performing Arts Center, it's sometimes still called the Wang Center, its pre-Citicorp name. 270 Tremont St. (½ block from Stuart St.). ✆ **866/348-9738** (box office) or 617/482-9393. www.citicenter.org. T: Green Line to Boylston or Orange Line to Tufts Medical Center.

Comcast Center When a mainstream act's summer schedule says "Boston," that often means this bucolic setting about an hour south of town. A sheltered (it has a roof but no sides) auditorium surrounded by a lawn, the Comcast Center features rock, pop, folk, country, and light classical artists. Shows go on rain or shine. 885 S. Main St. (Rte. 140), Mansfield. ✆ **508/339-2331** or 800/745-3000 (Ticketmaster). www.livenation.com.

Cutler Majestic Theatre A popular music, dance, and opera performance space, the Cutler Majestic is the home stage of several small arts companies. The gorgeous theater also books a diverse slate of touring shows, groups, and companies as well as Emerson College student productions. To schedule a 1-hour tour ($5 per person) of the building, a 1903 Beaux Arts landmark, call the info line. 219 Tremont St. (btw. Boylston and Stuart sts.). ✆ **800/233-3123** (Telecharge) or 617/824-8000 (information). www.artsemerson.org. T: Green Line to Boylston or Orange Line to Chinatown.

Modern Theatre Suffolk University's lovingly restored 1914 performance space seats less than 200 for films, readings, and dramatic and musical performances. 525 Washington St. (at Ave. de Lafayette). ✆ **617/557-6537.** www.moderntheatre.com. T: Green Line to Boylston, or Red or Orange Line to Downtown Crossing.

Orpheum Theater Although it's old (1852) and cramped, the Orpheum offers an intimate setting for big-name music and comedy performers. It books top local acts, popular up-and-coming artists, and international icons, recently including Margaret Cho, the Allman Brothers, and Pink Martini. 1 Hamilton Place (off Tremont St., across from Park Street Church). ✆ **617/482-0106** or 800/745-3000 (Ticketmaster). www.livenation.com. T: Red or Green Line to Park St.

Paramount Center A complete rehab of a 1932 movie theater, the Páramount is a key element of Emerson College's rising profile on the local and national arts scene. Its two performance spaces and screening room feature established and emerging artists. 559 Washington St. (btw. West and Avery sts.). ✆ **617/824-8000.** www.artsemerson.org. T: Green Line to Boylston, or Red or Orange Line to Downtown Crossing.

Sanders Theatre A landmark space in Harvard's Memorial Hall, Sanders Theatre schedules big names in classical, folk, and world music, as well as student performances. 45 Quincy St. (at Cambridge St.), Cambridge. ✆ **617/496-4595.** www.fas.harvard.edu/-memhall. T: Red Line to Harvard.

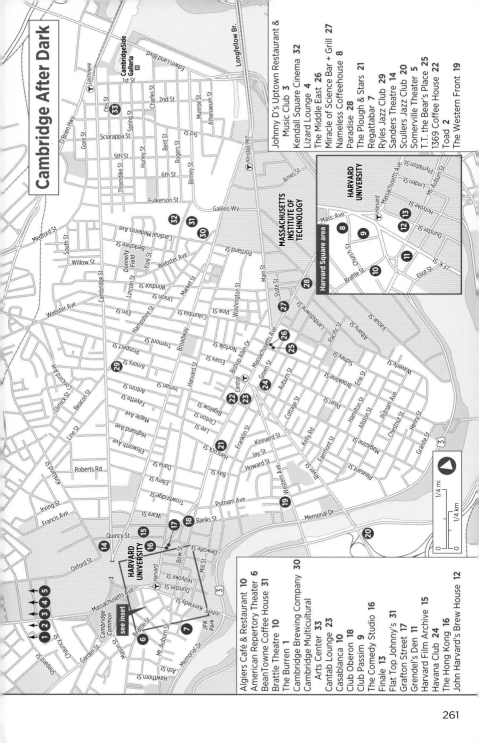

Cambridge After Dark

CambridgeSide Galleria

Johnny D's Uptown Restaurant &
Music Club **3**
Kendall Square Cinema **32**
Lizard Lounge **4**
The Middle East **26**
Miracle of Science Bar + Grill **27**
Nameless Coffeehouse **8**
Paradise **28**
The Plough & Stars **21**
Regattabar **7**
Ryles Jazz Club **29**
Sanders Theatre **14**
Scullers Jazz Club **20**
Somerville Theater **5**
T.T. the Bear's Place **25**
1369 Coffee House **22**
Toad **2**
The Western Front **19**

HARVARD UNIVERSITY

Harvard Square area

MASSACHUSETTS INSTITUTE OF TECHNOLOGY

HARVARD UNIVERSITY

Algiers Café & Restaurant **10**
American Repertory Theater **6**
BeanTowne Coffee House **31**
Brattle Theatre **10**
The Burren **1**
Cambridge Brewing Company **30**
Cambridge Multicultural
Arts Center **33**
Cantab Lounge **23**
Casablanca **10**
Club Oberon **18**
Club Passim **9**
The Comedy Studio **16**
Finale **13**
Flat Top Johnny's **31**
Grafton Street **17**
Grendel's Den **11**
Harvard Film Archive **15**
Havana Club **24**
The Hong Kong **16**
John Harvard's Brew House **12**

261

Symphony Hall Acoustically perfect Symphony Hall, which opened in 1900, is the home of the **Boston Symphony Orchestra** and the **Boston Pops.** When they're away, top-notch classical, chamber, world, and popular music artists from elsewhere take over. For information on free tours of Symphony Hall, see p. 189. 301 Massachusetts Ave. (at Huntington Ave.). © **617/266-1492** or 888/266-1200 (tickets). www.bostonsymphonyhall.org. T: Green Line E to Symphony or Orange Line to Massachusetts Ave.

Music Under the Sky & Stars

The **Boston Landmarks Orchestra** (© **617/520-2200; www.landmarksorchestra.org**) performs at venues around town—often outdoors, always free—on evenings from July through September (and occasionally the rest of the year). A concert is a great excuse to visit a pretty park and hear some excellent music.

TD Garden This 19,600-seat facility is home to the Celtics (basketball), the Bruins (hockey), the circus (in Oct), ice shows (at least twice a year), and touring rock and pop artists of all stripes. Concerts at the Garden—"Gah-den," in Bostonian—are in the round or in the arena stage format. 100 Legends Way (Causeway St.). © **617/624-1000** (event info) or 800/745-3000 (Ticketmaster). www.tdgarden.com. T: Orange or Green Line to North Station.

Wilbur Theatre This historic Theater District venue (it opened in 1914) holds 1,200 for performances by big-name standup comics and touring musical acts. 246 Tremont St. (at Stuart St.). © **617/248-9700** or 800/745-3000 (Ticketmaster). www.thewilburtheatre.com. T: Green Line to Boylston or Orange Line to Tufts Medical Center.

Classical Music

Boston Symphony Orchestra ★★★ The Boston Symphony, one of the world's greatest, was founded in 1881. Its repertoire includes contemporary music, but classical is the BSO's calling card—you might want to schedule your trip to coincide with a particular performance or with a visit by a celebrated guest artist.

The season runs from October to April, with performances most Tuesday, Thursday, and Saturday evenings; Friday afternoons; and some Friday evenings. Thirty-minute explanatory talks (included in the ticket price) begin 1 hour and 15 minutes before the curtain rises. If you can't buy tickets in advance, check at the box office for returns from subscribers 2 hours before show time. A limited number of same-day **rush tickets** (one per person, cash only) are available for Tuesday and Thursday evening and Friday afternoon and evening. Some Wednesday evening and Thursday morning rehearsals are open to the public. Symphony Hall, 301 Massachusetts Ave. (at Huntington Ave.). © **617/266-1492,** 617/266-2378 (concert info), or 888/266-1200 (tickets). www.bso.org. Tickets $29–$118. Rush tickets $9 (cash only; on sale Fri 10am and Tues, Thurs, Fri 5pm). Rehearsal tickets $20. T: Green Line E to Symphony or Orange Line to Massachusetts Ave.

Boston Pops ★★ "It's nice to eat a good hunk of beef," longtime Boston Pops conductor Arthur Fiedler once said, "but you want a light dessert, too." The Pops are the dessert to the BSO's beef. From early May to early July, tables and chairs replace the floor seats at Symphony Hall, and drinks and light refreshments are served. Under the direction of conductor Keith Lockhart, the Pops play a range of music from light classical to show tunes to popular (hence the name), often with

A Major Music Festival in the Bucolic Berkshires

When the Boston Symphony Orchestra goes away for the summer, it heads to **Tanglewood** (© **413/637-1600** or 617/266-1492 out of season; www.tanglewood.org), in Lenox, Massachusetts, a 2½-hour drive from Boston. Weekend concerts sell out in advance, but tickets to weeknight performances and Saturday morning rehearsals are usually available at the box office. If you can't get a seat inside, bring a blanket and picnic on the lawn. Consult *Frommer's New England* for in-depth coverage of western Massachusetts.

celebrity guest stars of both the Broadway and Top 40 variety. Performances are Tuesday through Sunday evenings. Special holiday performances in December ($27–$125) usually sell out well in advance, but it can't hurt to check; tickets go on sale in late October.

The regular season ends with two **free outdoor concerts at the Hatch Shell** on the Esplanade along the Charles River. The traditional **Fourth of July** concert is a mob scene; the rehearsal the night before is merely very crowded. Both are great fun. Performing at Symphony Hall, 301 Massachusetts Ave. (at Huntington Ave.). © **617/266-1492,** 617/266-2378 (concert info), or 888/266-1200 (tickets). www.bso. org. Tickets $40–$99 for tables, $20–$63 for balcony seats. T: Green Line E to Symphony or Orange Line to Massachusetts Ave.

Handel & Haydn Society ★★ The Handel & Haydn Society uses period instruments and techniques in its orchestral, choral, and opera performances, yet it's as cutting-edge as any other ensemble in town. Established in 1815, it's the oldest continuously performing arts organization in the country. The company prides itself on its creative programming of "historically informed" concerts, which it stages from October through May, with most performances at Symphony Hall and New England Conservatory's Jordan Hall. Works by Handel and Haydn predominate but don't take up the entire schedule.

H&H gave the American premiere of Handel's *Messiah,* in 1818, and has made it an annual holiday tradition since 1854. If you'll be in town in December, check for ticket availability as soon as you start planning your trip. 300 Massachusetts Ave. © **617/266-3605.** www.handelandhaydn.org. Tickets $15–$87. Student rush tickets $10 (cash only). T: Green Line E to Symphony or Orange Line to Massachusetts Ave.

ADDITIONAL OFFERINGS

The **Boston Lyric Opera** (© **866/348-9738** or 617/542-6772; www.blo. org) nurtures and showcases emerging talent in its classical and contemporary productions. The season runs from November to May at Citi Performing Arts Center's Shubert Theatre, 265 Tremont St. (½ block from Stuart St.), and the Calderwood Pavilion at the BCA, 527 Tremont St. (at Berkeley St.). Tickets cost $34 to $140, more for opening night.

Less familiar works make up the repertoire of **Opera Boston** (© **617/824-8000** [ArtsEmerson] or 617/451-3388; www.operaboston.org), which performs at the Cutler Majestic Theatre, 219 Tremont St. (btw. Boylston and Stuart sts.). Tickets go for $29 to $171.

Boston Baroque (© **617/484-9200;** www.bostonbaroque.org), a Grammy-nominated period orchestra with a chamber chorus, performs at New England Conservatory's Jordan Hall and Harvard's Sanders Theatre. Tickets cost $25 to $73.

Concert & Performance Series

The starriest names in classical music, dance, theater, jazz, opera, and world music play Boston as part of the **Celebrity Series of Boston** (✆ **617/482-2595** [info] or 617/482-6661 [tickets]; www.celebrityseries.org). It's a subscription series that also offers tickets to individual events, which go on sale in September. Performances take place at Symphony Hall, New England Conservatory's Jordan Hall, the Wang and Shubert theaters, and other venues.

World Music (✆ **617/876-4275**; www.worldmusic.org) showcases top-flight musicians, dance troupes, and other performers from around the globe. Shows (70 a year) are at the Somerville Theater, the Berklee Performance Center, Sanders Theatre, the Cutler Majestic Theatre, and other venues.

The excellent music program at the **Isabella Stewart Gardner Museum** (✆ **617/278-5156**; www.gardnermuseum.org) is in flux while the museum undergoes renovation and expansion. Check ahead for information about the classical series, which at press time had relocated to the nearby Massachusetts College of Art (MassArt), and the jazz series, which was on hiatus. Tickets (including museum admission) cost $23 adults, $18 seniors, $10 students with ID, $5 children 5 to 17 (children under 5 not admitted). Free podcasts are available through the website. See p. 141 for a full museum listing.

FREE (& ALMOST FREE) CONCERTS

Radio stations sponsor free outdoor music all summer. Specifics change frequently, but you can count on hearing oldies, pop, jazz, alternative, rock, and classical music at various venues, including City Hall Plaza, Copley Square, and the Hatch Shell, at lunch, after work, and in the evening. Check the papers when you arrive, listen to a station that sounds good to you, or just follow the crowds.

Students and faculty members at two prestigious musical institutions perform frequently during the academic year; admission is usually free. For information, contact the **New England Conservatory of Music,** 290 Huntington Ave. (at Gainsborough St.; ✆ **617/585-1260**; www.necmusic.edu/concerts-events), or the **Longy School of Music,** 1 Follen St. (at Garden St.), Cambridge (✆ **617/876-0956,** ext. 1500; www.longy.edu, click "Concerts & Events"). Also check listings for free or cheap student performances at other area colleges.

Emmanuel Music ★★ Gorgeous Emmanuel Church fills with equally exquisite music every Sunday from early October through early May. Emmanuel Music's orchestra and chorus perform Bach cantatas during the 10am service. Check ahead for details of evening and chamber performances. Emmanuel Church, 15 Newbury St. (btw. Arlington and Berkeley sts.). ✆ **617/536-3356.** www.emmanuelmusic. org. Free-will offering. T: Green Line to Arlington.

Fridays at Trinity The Copley Square landmark features 30-minute organ recitals by local and visiting artists on Friday at 12:15pm. Trinity Church, 206 Clarendon St. (btw. Boylston St. and St. James Ave.). ✆ **617/536-0944.** www.trinitychurchboston.org. Free-will offering. T: Green Line to Copley or Orange Line to Back Bay.

King's Chapel Noon Hour Recitals Organ, instrumental, and vocal classical, jazz, and folk performers fill this historic building with music, making for a pleasant break along the Freedom Trail. Concerts begin at 12:15pm on Tuesday and last 30 to 40 minutes. 58 Tremont St. (at School St.). ✆ **617/227-2155.** www.kings-chapel. org. $3 donation requested. T: Red or Green Line to Park St.

Old South Church The choir sings or the handbell choir performs at the 11am Sunday service, accompanied by a Skinner organ, and a 1-hour jazz service begins at 6pm every Thursday. The congregation dates to 1669, the elaborate Northern Italian Gothic building to 1875, and the 7,625-pipe organ to 1921. 645 Boylston St. (off Dartmouth St.). © **617/536-1970.** www.oldsouth.org. Free-will offering. T: Green Line to Copley.

Dance

The **Celebrity Series of Boston** and **World Music** (see "Concert & Performance Series," above) schedule numerous touring dance troupes; check ahead when you're planning your trip.

Boston Ballet ★★ Boston Ballet's reputation seems to jump a notch every time someone says, "So it's not just *The Nutcracker.*" One of the top dance companies in the country, Boston Ballet performs the holiday classic from Thanksgiving to New Year's and an eclectic mix of classic story ballets and contemporary works during the rest of the season (Oct–May). *Nutcracker* tickets go on sale in early July; for the rest of the season, in September. Performing at the Boston Opera House, 539 Washington St. (at Ave. de Lafayette). © **617/695-6955.** www.bostonballet.org. Tickets $25–$132. Senior, student, and child rush tickets (2 hr. before curtain) $20, except for Nutcracker. T: Orange Line to Chinatown or Green Line to Boylston.

Theater

Local and national companies, professional and amateur actors, and classic and experimental drama combine to make the local theater scene a lively one. Call or surf ahead, or check the papers or BosTix (see "Let's Make a Deal," on p. 257) after you arrive.

Boston is one of the last cities for pre-Broadway tryouts, allowing an early look at a classic (or a catastrophe) in the making. It's also a popular destination for touring companies of established hits. The promoter is often **Broadway Across America** (© 866/523-7469; www.broadwayacrossamerica.com). You'll find most of the shows headed to or coming from Broadway in the Theater District, at the **Colonial Theatre,** 106 Boylston St. (off Tremont St.; © 617/426-9366; www.bostonscolonialtheatre.com); the **Boston Opera House,** 539 Washington St. (at Ave. de Lafayette; © 617/259-3400; www.bostonoperahouseonline.com); the **Shubert Theatre,** 265 Tremont St. (½ block from Stuart St.; © 617/482-9393); and the **Citi Wang Theatre,** 270 Tremont St. (½ block from Stuart St.; © 617/482-9393). The Citi Performing Arts Center (www.citicenter.org) operates the Shubert and the Wang.

The excellent local theater scene boasts two nationally acclaimed repertory companies that stage classic and contemporary productions. In Boston you'll find the **Huntington Theatre Company,** which performs at the Boston University Theatre, 264 Huntington Ave. (btw. Massachusetts Ave. and Gainsborough St.; © 617/266-0800; www.huntingtontheatre.org).

9

BOSTON AFTER DARK

The Performing Arts

The **American Repertory Theater,** or ART (pronounced A-R-T) makes its home at Harvard University's **Loeb Drama Center,** 64 Brattle St. (at Hilliard St.), Cambridge (© **617/547-8300;** www.american repertorytheater.org). The ART also books **Club Oberon,** a "theatrical club space"—think performance art, cabaret, and liquor—at 2 Arrow St. (at Mass. Ave.; © **617/496-8004;** www. cluboberon.com).

The **Lyric Stage,** 140 Clarendon St. (at Stuart St.; © **617/585-5678;** www.lyricstage.com), mounts contemporary and modern works in an intimate second-floor setting.

College companies and venues are too numerous to list. The following websites can give you a sense of what's on when you're in town at **Boston University** (www.bu.edu/life/

The American Repertory Theater's production of *Alice vs. Wonderland* at the Loeb Drama Center.

arts), **Harvard University** (http://ofa.fas.harvard.edu), **MIT** (http://arts.mit. edu), **Northeastern University** (www.centerforthearts.neu.edu), and **Suffolk University** (www.suffolk.edu/theatre).

FAMILY THEATER/AUDIENCE PARTICIPATION

Charles Playhouse ☺ The off-Broadway sensation **Blue Man Group** ★ began selling out the Charles Playhouse's Stage I as soon as it arrived in 1995. The trio of cobalt-colored entertainers backed by a rock band uses music, percussion, food, and audience members in its performance. It's not recommended for children under 8, but older kids will love it. Shows are usually at 8pm Tuesday through Thursday; 7 and 10pm Friday; 4, 7, and 10pm Saturday; and 2 and 5pm Sunday (with extra days and performances during the holidays and school vacations). Tickets are available at the box office and through Ticketmaster (© **800/982-2787**).

 Dessert Alert

Finale is a little chain of "desserteries"— cafes that serve a mouth-watering variety of glorious desserts in elegant, romantic surroundings. Yes, it's a tad expensive. No, this is not a balanced meal. But the sweet tooths (sweet teeth?) who flock to Finale don't care. The original is in the Theater District at 1 Columbus Ave., in the pointy end of the Park Plaza Building

(© 617/423-3184; www.finaledesserts. com; T: Green Line to Arlington), with branches at 30 Dunster St., Harvard Square (© 617/441-9797; T: Red Line to Harvard), and 1306 Beacon St., Coolidge Corner, Brookline (© 617/232-3233; T: Green Line C to Coolidge Corner). Finale also serves real food, such as salads and pizzas, but the desserts are the real draw.

Shear Madness ★, on Stage II (downstairs), is the longest-running nonmusical play in theater history. Since January 1980, the zany "comic murder mystery" has turned the stage into a unisex hairdressing salon—and crime scene.

The show's never the same twice; one of the original audience-participation productions, the play changes as spectator-investigators question suspects, reconstruct events, and then name the murderer. Performances are Tuesday through Friday at 8pm, Saturday at 6 and 9pm, and Sunday at 3 and 7pm. 74 Warrenton St. (off Stuart St.). ✆ **617/426-6912** (Blue Man Group) and 617/426-5225 (Shear Madness). www. blueman.com and www.shearmadness.com. Blue Man Group $69 and $48; student rush $38 when available. Shear Madness $50, seniors $40, student rush $25 when available. T: Green Line to Boylston.

Le Grand David and His Own Spectacular Magic Company ★ ☺ Three generations of magicians make up this company, a nationally acclaimed troupe of illusionists that has delighted families since 1977. The ever-changing 2-hour shows, directed by master magician Marco the Magi, take place on alternating Sunday afternoons at two historic theaters in Beverly, about 40 minutes from Boston by car. It makes a perfect stop after a sightseeing excursion to the North Shore (see chapter 10). Cabot Street Cinema Theater, 286 Cabot St., Beverly; and Larcom Theatre, 13 Wallis St., Beverly. ✆ **978/927-3677.** www.legranddavid.com. Tickets $26 adults, $15 children 11 and under.

Puppet Showplace Theatre ☺ The Puppet Showplace presents favorite fables, ethnic legends, and folktales and fairy tales from around the world. Professional puppeteers put on creative, engaging shows year-round in a lovely 100-seat theater. The theater displays historic puppets and puppet posters, offers puppet-making workshops and other classes, and sells toy puppets. Family performances take place on weekends, with shows for toddlers on weekdays. Adult-oriented "Puppets at Night" shows play this theater and other local venues. Check ahead for schedules and to buy tickets, which frequently sell out. 32 Station St. (off Washington St.), Brookline. ✆ **617/731-6400.** www.puppetshowplace.org. Tickets $10 for children's shows, $13–$20 for adult shows. T: Green Line D to Brookline Village.

Wheelock Family Theatre ★★ ☺ The company mounts three productions a year—typically a family musical, a children's play, and an adult comedy or drama—with casts that mix professionals and talented amateurs, children and adults. The top-notch performers and the seamless combination of entertainment and education make an afternoon or evening here great fun for everyone. Check ahead for the suggested minimum age for audience members; not appropriate for children under 3. 180 The Riverway (near Short St.). ✆ **617/879-2234.** www. wheelockfamilytheatre.org. Tickets $20–$30 all ages; $15 children in pajamas Fri–Sat evening. T: Green Line D to Fenway.

THE CLUB & MUSIC SCENE

The Boston-area club scene is multifaceted and constantly changing. As a rule, live music is more compelling than the dance-club scene by several orders of magnitude, but somewhere out there is a good time for anyone, regardless of

9

BOSTON AFTER DARK

The Club & Music Scene

age, musical taste, or budget. Check the sources listed in the introduction to this chapter for ideas; if you prefer to wait for inspiration to strike after you reach Boston, find ideas in the daily *Globe,* the Friday *Herald,* the *Phoenix, Stuff@ Night,* or the *Improper Bostonian.* If you run across a venue that shares your taste, follow it on Twitter and friend it on Facebook, and you may get advance notice about special bookings and deals.

Clubs cluster in the Theater District and on nearby **Boylston Place,** off Boylston Street near Boston Common. The center of the local live-music universe is **Central Square** in Cambridge. Rowdy college bars and clubs abound near the intersection of Harvard and Brighton avenues in **Allston** (T: Green Line B to Harvard Ave.). That makes club-hopping easy, but it also means dealing with swarms of teenagers, students, and recent college grads. To steer clear, stick to slightly more upscale and less centrally located nightspots. If you do like teenagers (or you are one), seek out a place where admission is 18- or 19-plus. Policies change regularly, sometimes from night to night, so check ahead.

A night on the town in Boston and Cambridge is brief: Most bars close by 1am, clubs close at 2am, and the T shuts down between 12:30 and 1am. The drinking age is 21; a valid driver's license or passport is required as proof of age, and the law is strictly enforced, especially near college campuses.

Comedy Clubs

The **Wilbur Theatre** (p. 262) books high-profile comics on national tours as well as music acts. The annual **Boston International Comedy & Movie Festival** (✆ 617/499-3380; www.bostoncomedyfestival.com) attracts big-name national performers, local up-and-comers, and films. The popular weeklong event takes place all over town in November; check ahead for schedules and venues.

The Comedy Studio ★★ 🍸 Nobody here is a sitcom star—yet. With a stellar reputation for searching out undiscovered talent, the no-frills Comedy Studio draws a savvy crowd of connoisseurs, college students, and network scouts. It's not just setup–punch line–laugh, either; sketches and improv spice up the standup. Shows are Tuesday ("Mystery Lounge," featuring magicians) through Sunday at 8pm. At the Hong Kong restaurant, 1238 Massachusetts Ave. (at Bow St.), Cambridge. ✆ **617/661-6507.** www.thecomedystudio.com. Cover $8–$10. T: Red Line to Harvard.

Improv Asylum Let the posters that catch your eye on the Freedom Trail draw you back to the North End later for raucous improv and sketch comedy in a subterranean setting. Performances are Tuesday through Saturday evenings, and buying tickets in advance is suggested. Recommended for people over 16; you must be 21 to buy alcohol. 216 Hanover St. (off Cross St.). ✆ **617/263-6887.** www.improvasylum.com. Tickets $15–$25; midnight shows and student performances $5–$10. T: Green or Orange Line to Haymarket. Validated parking available.

ImprovBoston ★ 🍸 Founded in 1982, ImprovBoston presents pros and amateurs in two spaces—mainstage and cabaret—and offers a lengthy list of classes. Standup, storytelling, and student showcases complement the improv and sketch comedy. The 6pm Saturday show is geared for families. Shows run Wednesday through Sunday, and the lobby bar serves beer and wine. 40 Prospect St. (off Massachusetts Ave.). ✆ **617/576-1253.** www.improvboston.com. Tickets $7–$16. T: Red Line to Central.

Mottley's Comedy Club 🍸 The basement of a fratty bar a block from Faneuil Hall Marketplace isn't the most promising venue, but Mottley's rises above its geography. Management makes a point of booking aspiring comics alongside more established names, creating a good mix of familiarity and novelty that keeps the demanding crowds laughing. 61 Chatham St. (off Commercial St., beneath Trinity Bar). © **877/615-2844.** www.mottleyscomedy.com. Tickets $8–$30. T: Blue Line to Aquarium.

Dance Clubs

Most clubs enforce a **dress code** that forbids athletic wear (including game jerseys), sneakers, jeans, Timberland boots, and ball caps—or some combination thereof—on everyone, as well as tank tops on men. Some places require that men wear a shirt with a collar, and a few require a jacket. Check ahead. The *Improper Bostonian* and the *Phoenix* club listings are good resources, but a savvy concierge is even better. *Tip:* While you're visiting websites, note that some clubs will let you put your name on the VIP list online. Can't hurt, might help.

The Estate A cavernous space with a balcony overlooking the large dance floor, the Estate attracts a lively 20-something crowd with well-known local DJs and an excellent sound system. The dress code is "dress like you mean it," which appears to equal collared shirts on men and something tight and black on women. The key to jumping the inevitable line is to reserve a table and look sharp. Open Thursday (gay night) through Saturday; check ahead for specifics. 1 Boylston Place (off Boylston St., near Tremont St.). © **617/351-7000.** www.theestateboston.com. Cover $20–$25. T: Green Line to Boylston.

Royale Boston ★★ This onetime hotel ballroom boasts excellent house and techno DJs, a huge dance floor, and a U-shaped balcony that's perfect for checking out the action below. Live music, booked by a New York–based promoter noted for its rock acts, takes good advantage of the sight lines. Check ahead for the schedule of all-ages shows in the early evening. In the Courtyard Boston Downtown/ Tremont hotel, 279 Tremont St. (½ block from Stuart St.). © **617/338-7699.** www.royale boston.com. Cover $15–$25. T: Green Line to Boylston or Orange Line to Tufts Medical Center.

Eclectic

Cafe 939 ★ 🎵 A certain present-at-the-creation vibe prevails here. Berklee College of Music students run and often perform at the all-ages coffeehouse—in other words, no alcohol—which holds 200 for live music most Wednesday through Saturday nights. The club, also known as the Red Room, books professionals as well as students; popular acts often sell out. To buy advance tickets without a service fee, or to use your student discount, visit the Berklee Performance Center box office at 136 Massachusetts Ave. 939 Boylston St. (off Hereford St.). © **617/747-2261** or 800/745-3000 (Ticketmaster). www.cafe939.com. Tickets free to $20; most $12 or less. T: Green Line B, C, or D to Hynes Convention Center.

Put Some Salsa on That

The hip-shaking party that is **Havana Club** ★ (© 617/312-5550; www.havana clubsalsa.com) makes a great introduction to salsa dancing. Lessons—beginners are welcome—precede 3 hours of nonstop motion accompanied by a DJ or live band. The crowd consists mostly of dance fiends and curious novices of all ages and ethnicities. Havana Club takes place on Friday and Saturday from 10pm to 1am (lessons start at 9pm) at the Greek American Political Club, 288 Green St. (at River St., 1 block from Mass. Ave.), Central Sq., Cambridge. Both nights are 21-plus, admission is $12, and the bar is cash only.

Johnny D's Uptown Restaurant & Music Club ★★★ 🍴 This family-owned and -operated establishment is one of the best places in the area for live music. It draws a congenial, low-key crowd for acts on international tours as well as artists who haven't been out of eastern Massachusetts. The music ranges from zydeco to rock, rockabilly to jazz, blues to ska. The veggie-friendly food's good, too; try the weekend jazz brunch. The club, which opened in 1969, is worth a long trip, but it's only two T stops past Harvard (about 15 min. at night). Most shows are 21-plus; some are all ages. Open Monday at 3pm, Tuesday through Friday at 11am, and weekends at 8:30am (brunch until 2:30pm); food's available Sunday and Monday until 10pm, Tuesday through Saturday until midnight. *Tip:* Make a dinner reservation, and you're guaranteed a seat for the show. 17 Holland St. (½ block from the center of Davis Sq.), Somerville. ☏ **617/776-2004** or 617/776-9667 (concert line). www.johnnyds.com. Cover $3–$30 (usually $8–$12). T: Red Line to Davis.

Lizard Lounge ★★ In the basement of the Cambridge Common restaurant, this way-cool, cozy-but-not-cramped room features well-known local rock, folk, and jazz musicians, who play right out on the floor. It draws a postcollegiate-and-up crowd (Harvard Law School is next door) and serves food until 1am on weekends and midnight on weekdays. Shows take place daily; the doors usually open at 7:30pm. Sunday is poetry night; Monday is open-mic night. 1667 Massachusetts Ave. (at Wendell St.), Cambridge. ☏ **617/547-0759.** www.lizardloungeclub.com. Cover for late show $5–$15. T: Red Line to Harvard.

T.T. the Bear's Place ★★ A mainstay of the Central Square live-music scene since it opened in 1985, "T.T.'s" has an uncanny knack for booking hot new talent. A friendly, no-frills spot, it generally attracts a young, savvy crowd, but 30-somethings will feel comfortable, too (especially at the twice-a-month '80s dance night). Bookings—three or four per night—range from cutting-edge alternative and roots music to up-and-coming indie-rock acts. New bands predominate early in the week, with more established artists on weekends. Open Sunday to Wednesday until 1am, Thursday through Saturday until 2am. 10 Brookline St. (at Massachusetts Ave.), Cambridge. ☏ **617/492-0082** or 617/492-2327 (concert line). www.ttthebears.com. Cover $3–$17. T: Red Line to Central.

The Western Front A 30-ish friend swears by this legendary reggae club because "you're never the oldest one there." Open since 1968, it's a casual, friendly spot on a nondescript street south of Central Square. Integrated crowds flock here for world-beat music, blues, jazz, hip-hop, salsa, soca, and especially reggae. Open Thursday through Saturday from 8pm to 2am; live entertainment usually begins at 9pm. 343 Western Ave. (at Putnam Ave., 2 blocks from the Charles River), Cambridge. ☏ **617/492-7772.** Cover $5–$10. T: Red Line to Central.

Folk

Boston is one of the only cities where folk musicians consistently sell out large venues that usually book rock and pop performers. If an artist you want to see is touring, check ahead for Boston-area dates.

The music listings in Thursday's *Globe* include information about **coffeehouses,** the area's main outlets for folk. Probably the best known of these, the 4-decade-old **Nameless Coffeehouse** (☏ **617/864-1630;** www.namelesscoffeehouse.org), puts on a show every month or so in the First Parish Church, 3 Church St., Harvard Sq., Cambridge. The streets around **Harvard Square** are another promising venue—Tracy Chapman is just one famous graduate of the scene.

The **Boston Folk Festival** (©617/287-6911; www.bostonfolkfestival.
org) takes place at the UMass-Boston campus in Dorchester on a Sunday in
early June; check ahead for the schedule and lineup. Also see the **Lizard Lounge**
(p. 270).

Club Passim ★★★ Passim has launched more careers than the mass production of acoustic guitars—Joan Baez, Shawn Colvin, and Tom Rush started
out here, and this is where you'll find Arlo Guthrie and Ellis Paul when they're
in town. In a basement on a Harvard Square side street, the legendary coffeehouse has nurtured new talent and showcased established musicians since
1958. Patrons who have been regulars since day one mix with college students.
There's live music nightly, vegetarian food from **Veggie Planet** (p. 128) until
10:30pm, plus beer, wine, and, of course, coffee. Tuesdays without other bookings are open-mic nights. Open Sunday through Thursday from 11am to 11pm,
Friday and Saturday from 11am to midnight. Most shows start at 8pm; on two-
show nights, starting times are 7 and 10pm. 47 Palmer St. (at Church St.), Cambridge.
© **617/492-7679.** www.passimcenter.org. Cover $5–$40 (most shows $20 or less). T: Red
Line to Harvard.

Jazz & Blues

Jazz Week (www.jazzboston.org) is a 10-day event in late April and early May at
multiple venues. Surf around the website for an introduction to the local scene.
The 10-day **Berklee Beantown Jazz Festival** (www.beantownjazzfestival.
com), in late September, books top-notch artists into various professional venues
around Boston and draws tens of thousands of aficionados to Columbus Avenue
in the South End for a full weekend afternoon of free music. Check the website
for details.

On summer Thursdays at 6pm, the **Boston Harbor Hotel** (©617/491-
2100; www.bhh.com) sponsors free performances on the "Blues Barge," behind
the hotel.

The theater at the Cambridge Multicultural Arts Center (p. 260) becomes
the **Jazz Club at the Multicultural Arts Center** at least a couple of times a
month, year-round.

Cantab Lounge ★ Follow your ears to this friendly neighborhood bar, which
attracts a lively three-generation crowd. When the door swings open at night,
deafening music—usually blues, bluegrass, rock, or jazz—spills out. Downstairs
is the Cantab Underground, which has its own schedule, including a poetry slam
every Wednesday. 738 Massachusetts Ave. (at Pleasant St.), Cambridge. © **617/354-2685.**
www.cantab-lounge.com. Cover $3–$10. T: Red Line to Central.

House of Blues ★★ The House of Blues chain originated in Cambridge,
and its Boston-area presence is now this enormous space across the street from
Fenway Park. It draws large crowds with a stellar slate of touring blues, rock,
and pop acts and above-average Southern food (Tues–Sat 4pm–midnight). 15
Lansdowne St. (btw. Brookline Ave. and Ipswich St.). © **888/693-2583** or 617/960-8358 (restaurant). www.houseofblues.com. Tickets $23–$55 (most shows $40 or less). T: Green Line
B, C, or D to Kenmore.

Regattabar ★★ The Regattabar's selection of local and international jazz
artists may be the best in the area—I'd give the edge to Scullers Jazz Club
(see below), but check both schedules before you decide. Cassandra Wilson,
Buckwheat Zydeco, and McCoy Tyner have appeared recently. The large third-floor

room holds about 225. Buy tickets in advance or at the door an hour before show time. Open Tuesday through Saturday and some Sundays, with one or two performances per night. In the Charles Hotel, 1 Bennett St. (at Eliot St.), Cambridge. © **617/661-5000** or 617/395-7757 for tickets. www.regattabarjazz.com. Tickets $15–$35. T: Red Line to Harvard.

Ryles Jazz Club ★ This popular spot, which doubles as a barbecue joint, books a wide variety of excellent blues, jazz, R&B, world beat, and Latin in two rooms. Sunday jazz brunch runs from 10am to 3pm. Open Tuesday through Sunday at 5pm; shows start between 9 and 10pm. 212 Hampshire St. (at Inman St.), Inman Square, Cambridge. © **617/876-9330.** www.ryles.com. Cover for music $10–$20 (usually $15 or less). T: Red Line to Central, then a 10-min. walk.

Scullers Jazz Club ★★★ Overlooking the Charles River, Scullers is a lovely, comfortable room with a top-notch sound system. The club, which opened in 1989, books acclaimed singers and instrumentalists—recent notables include Wayne Shorter, Oleta Adams, Nicholas Payton, and Diane Schuur. Patrons tend to be more hard-core than the crowds at the Regattabar (above), but it depends on who's performing. Scullers usually schedules two shows a night Tuesday through Saturday; the box office is open Monday through Saturday from 11am to 6pm. Ask about dinner packages ($58–$88 per person), which include preferred seating and a three-course meal. In the Doubletree Guest Suites hotel, 400 Soldiers Field Rd. (at Cambridge St.). © **617/562-4111.** www.scullersjazz.com. Tickets $20–$50. Validated parking available.

Wally's Cafe ★★ This Boston institution, near a busy corner in the South End, opened in 1947. Its New Orleans–style all-about-the-music atmosphere draws a notably diverse crowd—black, white, straight, gay, affluent, indigent. Live jazz, by local ensembles, students and instructors from the Berklee College of Music, and the occasional regional or international star, starts every night at 9pm. Monday is blues night. Open daily until 2am. *Tip:* I can't promise anything, but big-name performers in town to play bigger venues have been known to turn up at Wally's afterward. 427 Massachusetts Ave. (off Columbus Ave.). © **617/424-1408.** www.wallyscafe.com. No cover; 1-drink minimum. T: Orange Line to Massachusetts Ave.

Rock

Great Scott ★★ Worth the trek to the student mecca of Allston, Great Scott is a friendly neighborhood bar that happens to be an excellent live-music venue. It books mostly rock bands, usually local, plus DJs. On a busy night you might see four different acts. Open daily from noon to 2am; live shows usually start at 9pm. The bar accepts cash only. 1222 Commonwealth Ave. (at Harvard Ave.). © **617/566-9014.** www.greatscottboston.com. Cover $5–$15 (usually $10 or less). T: Green Line B to Harvard Ave.

The Middle East ★★★ The best rock club in the area and one of the best in New England, the Middle East books an impressive variety of progressive and alternative artists in two rooms (upstairs and downstairs) every night.

 Rock of Ages

Bring your driver's license or passport when you go club-hopping, no matter how old you think you look—you must be 21 to drink alcohol, and the law is strictly enforced. Most bouncers won't risk a fine or license suspension, especially at 18-plus shows.

If you love your nightlife raucous, be sure to swing by the Middle East.

Showcasing top local talent as well as bands with local roots and international reputations, it's a popular hangout that gets crowded, hot, and *loud*. The club is the heart of a complex that incorporates the **Corner,** a former bakery that features acoustic artists most of the time and belly dancers on Sunday and Wednesday, and **ZuZu,** a Middle Eastern restaurant that has its own music schedule and gallery space with rotating art exhibits. Most shows are 18-plus (ZuZu is 21-plus); the age of the crowd varies with the performer. 472–480 Massachusetts Ave. (at Brookline St.), Central Sq., Cambridge. ✆ **617/864-3278** or 866/777-8932 (TicketWeb). www.mideastclub.com. Cover $8–$25 (usually $15 or less; ZuZu cover $5 Fri–Sat only). T: Red Line to Central.

Paradise Rock Club ★   Close by the Boston University campus, the medium-size Paradise draws enthusiastic, student-intensive crowds for top local rock and alternative performers. You might also see national names who want a relatively small venue and others who aren't ready to headline a big show on their own (lately, Plain White T's, Travie McCoy, and the Del Fuegos's reunion gig). Most shows are 18-plus. 967–969 Commonwealth Ave. (½ block from Pleasant St.). ✆ **617/562-8800** or 877/598-8497 for tickets. www.thedise.com. T: Green Line B to Pleasant St.

Toad ★★ 🍴 Essentially a bar with a stage, this narrow, high-ceil-inged space draws a savvy three-generation clientele attracted by local big-name performers—rock, rockabilly, and sometimes blues—and the lack of a cover charge. Toad enjoys good acoustics but not much elbow room—a plus when restless performers wander into the crowd. 1912 Massachusetts Ave. (at Porter Rd.), Cambridge. ✆ **617/497-4950** (info line). www.toadcambridge.com. T: Red Line to Porter.

 Theme a Little Theme

The **Hard Rock Cafe,** 24 Clinton St. (at North St.; ✆ 617/424-7625; www.hardrock.com), is a fun link in the fun chain—just ask the other tourists all around you. The memora-bilia that covers the walls of this cavernous space across the street from Faneuil Hall Marketplace celebrates rock musicians, and the kid-friendly menu features salads, burgers, sandwiches, and barbecue.

THE BAR SCENE

Bostonians had some quibbles with the TV show *Cheers,* but no one complained that the concept of a neighborhood bar where everybody knows your name was implausible. This tends to be a fairly insular scene—as a stranger, don't assume that you'll get a warm welcome. This is one area where you can and probably should judge a book by its cover: If you peek in and see people who look like you and your friends, give it a whirl.

The familiar exterior of the Beacon Hills Cheers.

Bars & Lounges

The Beehive This restaurant and lounge takes up a funky two-level space beneath the Boston Center for the Arts (p. 257). The Beehive schedules live music, usually jazz, every night. Early in the week, the crowd tends toward laid-back and local; weekends are more of a see-and-be-seen scene for suburbanites. 541 Tremont St. (at Clarendon St.). ✆ **617/423-0069.** www.beehiveboston. com. T: Orange Line to Back Bay.

Cambridge Brewing Company ★ CBC brews its own excellent beers, offering year-round and seasonal selections. The patio is especially pleasant in fine weather, but this place is popular with the techy neighborhood crowd year-round. 100 Kendall Sq., Building 100 (Hampshire St. and Cardinal Medeiros Ave.), Cambridge. ✆ **617/494-1994.** www.cambrew.com. T: Red Line to Kendall/MIT; 10-min. walk.

Casablanca ★★ Students and professors jam this legendary Harvard Square watering hole, especially on weekends. You'll find an excellent jukebox, excellent Middle Eastern food, and excellent eavesdropping. 40 Brattle St. (btw. Brattle Sq. and Church St.), Cambridge. ✆ **617/876-0999.** T: Red Line to Harvard.

Cheers (Beacon Hill) Originally the Bull & Finch Pub, this one-time neighborhood hangout has embraced its status as a TV icon. A copy of the bar from the set of the long-running sitcom makes a good photo backdrop, and the souvenir selection is impressive. There's food from 11am until late evening. 84 Beacon St. (at Brimmer St.). ✆ **617/227-9605.** www.cheersboston.com/pub. T: Green Line to Arlington.

Cheers (Faneuil Hall Marketplace) Blatantly but good-naturedly courting fans of the sitcom, this bar's interior is an exact replica of the *Cheers* TV set. It serves pub fare starting at noon Monday through Thursday, 11am on weekends, and plays dance music on weekend nights. Memorabilia on display includes Sam Malone's Red Sox jacket. Bring a camera. Quincy Market Building, South Canopy, Faneuil Hall Marketplace. ✆ **617/227-7532.** www.cheersboston.com. T: Green or Blue Line to Government Center, or Orange Line to Haymarket.

DeLux Cafe ★★ One of the coolest places in the increasingly yuppified South End, the DeLux is the epitome of a classy dive. The funky decor, selection of microbrews, and veggie-friendly ethnic menu attract a cross-section of the neighborhood. Part of the appeal is the decor, a scrapbook of 20th-century pop culture (posters, photos, postcards, and such)—check out the Elvis shrine. 100 Chandler St. (at Clarendon St.). ✆ **617/338-5258.** T: Orange Line to Back Bay.

Grafton Street Deftly accommodating party-hearty students and demanding Cantabrigians, this Harvard Square veteran is a classy watering hole with a superb beer selection. It's also a busy restaurant, but I prefer a snack or sandwich at the bar to a meal in the dining room. Open daily until 2am. 1230 Massachusetts Ave. (at Bow St.), Cambridge. ✆ **617/497-0400.** www.graftonstreetcambridge.com. T: Red Line to Harvard.

Grendel's Den ★ A vestige of pre-franchise Harvard Square, this cozy subterranean space is *the* place to celebrate turning 21. Recent grads and grad students dominate, but Grendel's has been so popular for so long that it also attracts Gen Y's parents. The food is tasty, with loads of vegetarian dishes, and the fireplace enhances the comfy atmosphere. 89 Winthrop St. (at John F. Kennedy St.), Cambridge. ✆ **617/491-1160.** www.grendelsden.com. T: Red Line to Harvard.

The Hong Kong This fun hangout is a retro Chinese restaurant on the first floor, a bar on the second floor, and a small dance club (starting at 11pm nightly) on the third floor. It's also the home of the scorpion bowl, a rum-based concoction that has contributed to the destruction of countless Ivy League brain cells. Nevertheless, you might see Harvard football players here. Never mind how I know. 1236 Massachusetts Ave. (at Bow St.), Cambridge. ✆ **617/864-5311.** www.hongkongharvard.com. T: Red Line to Harvard.

Miracle of Science Bar + Grill ★★ A stone's throw from both Central Square and the MIT campus, Miracle of Science is the perfect match for its hipster-geek neighbors. The friendly vibe and decent, if not huge, beer selection make it a popular after-work hangout. The kitchen serves three meals daily—perfect if you've been up all night writing code. The menu is on the chalkboard festooned with what you thought was the periodic table. 321 Massachusetts Ave. (at State St.), Cambridge. ✆ **617/686-ATOM** (2866). www.miracleofscience.us. T: Red Line to Central.

The Place ★ Is it a Financial District hangout? A sports bar on (pardon the expression) steroids, with flatscreen TVs all over? An after-work destination for bankers and lawyers and the men and women who love them? Yes, yes, and yes. 2 Broad St. (off State St.). ✆ **617/523-2081.** www.theplaceboston.com. Cover $5 Thurs–Sat after 9pm. T: Orange or Blue Line to State. Validated parking available.

The Purple Shamrock Across the street from Faneuil Hall Marketplace, the Purple Shamrock packs in wall-to-wall tourists of all ages. This is a rowdy, fun place that schedules DJs and cover bands. 1 Union St. (off North St.). ✆ **617/227-2060.** www.irishconnection.com. Cover $5–$10 Thurs–Sat. T: Green or Blue Line to Government Center, or Orange Line to Haymarket.

Radius The high-tech bar at this hot, *haute* restaurant offers almost everything the dining room does—the chic crowd, the noise, the perfect martinis—without the sky-high food bill. The bar snacks are pricey but worth every penny. 8 High St. (off Summer St.). ✆ **617/426-1234.** www.radiusrestaurant.com. T: Red Line to South Station.

Silvertone Bar & Grill ★ One of the few real hangouts in the Downtown Crossing area, this tiny, subterranean bar attracts a noisy after-work crowd. The dining room is noted for reasonably priced comfort food (try the sublime macaroni and cheese). Closed Sunday. 69 Bromfield St. (off Tremont St.). ✆ **617/338-7887.** www.silvertonedowntown.com. T: Red or Green Line to Park St.

Top of the Hub ★★★ Boasting a panoramic view of greater Boston, Top of the Hub is 52 stories above the city; the view is especially beautiful at sunset. It's an elegant destination and a favorite with couples out on a big date or celebrating a special occasion. Take a turn around the dance floor or just enjoy the live jazz and the late-night menu, which features superb desserts. Dress is casual but neat (no jeans). Open Sunday through Wednesday until 1am, Thursday through Saturday until 2am. Prudential Center, 800 Boylston St. ✆ **617/536-1775.** www.topofthehub.net. T: Green Line E to Prudential. Validated parking available.

21st Amendment A Beacon Hill standby, this tavern looks like a regular old neighborhood bar and restaurant—unless the Massachusetts legislature is in session. Then it turns into an annex of the State House, just across the street, and the entertainment value of the conversation jumps dramatically. (In case you were absent that day, the 21st Amendment repealed Prohibition.) 150 Bowdoin St. (off Beacon St.). ✆ **617/227-7100.** www.21stboston.com. T: Red Line to Park St.

Via Matta This chic Italian restaurant's equally stylish bar and divine wine list make this a perfect place to recharge after an afternoon of hard work or hard shopping—Newbury Street is 3 blocks away. 79 Park Plaza (Arlington St. and St. James Ave.). ✆ **617/422-0008.** www.viamattarestaurant.com. T: Green Line to Arlington.

Brewpubs

Boston Beer Works Across the street from Fenway Park, this cavernous space is frantic before and after Red Sox games. Don't plan to be able to hear anything your friends are saying. It has a full food menu and 16 brews on tap, including excellent bitters and ales. The sweet-potato fries make a terrific snack. The **North Station** branch, near the TD Garden, is equally loud and has 11 pool tables. Open daily from 11:30am to 1am. 61 Brookline Ave. (at Lansdowne St.). ✆ **617/536-BEER.**

 Make Some Noise in a Museum

The **Museum of Fine Arts,** 465 Huntington Ave. (✆ **617/267-9300;** www.mfa.org), becomes a spirited nightlife destination at least once a month. It courts 20- and 30-somethings with live music, cocktails, food, and mingling; a visit is an equally good couple or group activity. "MFA First Fridays" take place on the first Friday of each month—and every Friday in the summer—from 5:30 to 9:30pm. General admission to the museum ($20) includes the evening event. A similar program, the **Isabella Stewart Gardner Museum'**s monthly "Gardner After Hours" series (shown here), is on hold while the museum undergoes expansion. It's expected to return in 2012. See p. 141 for a museum listing.

www.beerworks.net. T: Green Line B, C, or D to Kenmore. 110 Canal St. (btw. Causeway St. and Valenti Way). ℂ 617/896-BEER. T: Green or Orange Line to North Station.

John Harvard's Brew House ★★ This subterranean Harvard Square hangout, the flagship of the regional chain, pumps out terrific English-style brews in a clublike setting and prides itself on its food. The brewed-on-the-premises beer selection changes regularly. Order a sampler if you can't decide, and while you wait, try to find the sports figures in the stained-glass windows. Open Monday through Thursday from 11:30am to 12:30am, Friday and Saturday until 2am, Sunday until midnight, with food service until 11:30pm. 33 Dunster St. (off Mount Auburn St.), Cambridge. ℂ **617/868-3585.** www.johnharvards.com. T: Red Line to Harvard.

Hotel Bars & Lounges

Many popular nightspots are associated with hotels and restaurants (see chapters 4 and 5); as a rule, these are the only watering holes in town where you don't have to shout to be heard. The following are particularly agreeable, albeit expensive, places to while away an hour or three.

The Bar at Taj Boston ★ The Bar at the Ritz, this lovely space's predecessor, established it as *the* place to go for a classic martini. The cushy seating, crackling fire, impeccable service, and view of the Public Garden have made it a favorite with generations of Bostonians. Open Monday through Saturday 11:30am to 12:30am, Sunday noon to 11:30pm. In the Taj Boston hotel, 15 Arlington St. (at Newbury St.). ℂ **617/536-5700.** T: Green Line to Arlington.

The Bristol Lounge ★★★ This is a perfect choice after the theater, after work, or after anything else. An elegant room with soft lounge chairs, a fireplace, and fresh flowers, it features a fabulous Viennese dessert buffet ($25) on Friday and Saturday from 9pm to midnight. There's live music every evening. Food is available until 11:30pm (Fri–Sat until 12:30am). In the Four Seasons Hotel, 200 Boylston St. (at Hadassah Way, btw. Arlington St. and Charles St. S.). ℂ **617/351-2037.** T: Green Line to Arlington.

Eastern Standard A cavernous brasserie with a mile-long marble bar, Eastern Standard is an all-things-to-all-people destination. It serves food from early morning through late night, offers outdoor seating, and has a hopping bar scene every night during the week and almost all day on weekends. The specialty cocktails are numerous and diverse, and the bartenders know their way around the wine list. On Red Sox game nights, be ready to stand. In the Hotel Commonwealth, 528 Commonwealth Ave. (at Kenmore St.). ℂ **617/532-9100.** www.easternstandardboston.com. T: Green Line B, C, or D to Kenmore.

M Bar and Lounge ★ A shadowy hideaway from the Back Bay's retail circus, M Bar is an all-day destination with a lively after-work clientele. A menu of tapas and other light fare complements the inventive mixed drinks. This is also a good stop for a pick-me-up in the middle of an afternoon shopping spree. As you might expect when the home office is in Hong Kong, the tea selection and presentation are perfect. In the Mandarin Oriental, Boston, 776 Boylston St. (at Fairfield St.). ℂ **617/535-8800.** www.mandarinoriental.com. T: Green Line to Copley.

Oak Bar ★★ This paneled, high-ceilinged room feels like an old-fashioned men's club—but one that welcomes women. The lighting is muted, the leather seating soft and welcoming, and the raw bar picture-perfect. There's live entertainment on weekends. Proper dress (no shorts or sneakers) is required. Open Sunday through Thursday until midnight, Friday and Saturday until 1am. In the Fairmont

Copley Plaza hotel, 138 St. James Ave. (btw. Dartmouth St. and Trinity Place). ℭ **617/267-5300.** www.theoakroom.com. T: Green Line to Copley or Orange Line to Back Bay.

Irish Bars

The Black Rose Purists might sneer at the Black Rose's touristy location, but performers don't. Sing along with the authentic entertainment at this jampacked pub and restaurant at the edge of Faneuil Hall Marketplace. You might even be able to make out the tune on a fiddle over the din. 160 State St. (at Commercial St.). ℭ **617/742-2286.** www.irishconnection.com. Cover $3–$8. T: Orange or Blue Line to State.

The Burren ★ The expatriate Irish community has found the Burren an antidote to homesickness since 1996, and you will, too. There's traditional music in the front room, acoustic rock in the large back room, and good food. 247 Elm St. (at Chester St.), Somerville. ℭ **617/776-6896.** www.burren.com. Cover (back room only) $5–$10. T: Red Line to Davis.

The Grand Canal This atmospheric pub and restaurant boasts an excellent beer selection, good food, a 12-foot TV screen, and Irish or rock cover bands or DJs Friday and Saturday nights. French windows that open to the street make it a popular after-work spot in good weather. If you're wondering, the namesake waterway isn't in Venice—it connects Dublin to the Shannon River. 57 Canal St. (btw. New Chardon St. and Valenti Way). ℭ **617/523-1112.** www.grandcanalboston.com. Cover $5 for music. T: Green or Orange Line to Haymarket or North Station.

The Littlest Bar ★ A low-key Financial District hangout with a fine selection of beers and whiskeys, the Littlest Bar is not particularly little. (The original location, however, was minuscule.) Prices are reasonable, the staff is friendly, and one table has a contraption that lets you pour your own beer—though you should really stick to Smithwick's and let the sure-handed bartenders handle the Guinness dispensing. 102 Broad St. (at Wharf St.). ℭ **617/542-8469.** T: Blue Line to Aquarium.

Mr. Dooley's Boston Tavern ★★ Sometimes an expertly poured Guinness is all you need. If one of the nicest bartenders in the city pours it, and you enjoy it in

Cocktail Culture

Like a lot of other trends, the cocktail craze arrived in Boston late and quickly took off. All over town, devoted bartenders and adventuresome drinkers unite to combat the cosmopolitanizing of the American libation. A nationally renowned example of the hard-core cocktail bar is **Drink** ★★, 348 Congress St. (near A St.; ℭ **617/695-1806;** www.drinkfortpoint.com; T: Red Line to South Station). Don't take my word for it—high-profile amateur mixologist Rachel Maddow of MSNBC says it's the best bar in Boston, if not the country. Drink has no menu, just bartenders who chat with you about what you're in the mood for and create something on the spot. Sounds crazy, works perfectly. It's pricey, but you're paying for an evening's entertainment and an enthusiastic guide. Open daily at 4pm. Other destinations where "genever," "elderflower," and "Sazerac" are more than just crossword puzzle answers include **Eastern Standard** (p. 277); **Hungry Mother** (p. 129); and **Green Street,** 280 Green St. (off Magazine St., 1 block from Mass. Ave.; ℭ **617/876-1655;** www.greenstreetgrill.com; T: Red Line to Central).

an authentically decorated room, so much the better. This Financial District spot offers a wide selection of imported beers on tap, live entertainment on weekend nights, and a menu of pub favorites at lunch and dinner. 77 Broad St. (at Custom House St.). © **617/338-5656.** www.somerspubs.com. Cover (Fri–Sat only) $3–$5. T: Orange Line to State or Blue Line to Aquarium.

The Plough & Stars ★ Although it's tiny, the Plough is a huge presence on the local pub scene. A neighborhood hangout during the day, it's a hipster magnet at night. Live music is a regular feature and a big draw, and the kitchen serves lunch, dinner, and weekend brunch. 912 Massachusetts Ave. (at Hancock St.), Cambridge. © **617/576-0032.** www.ploughandstars.com. Cover $6 or less. T: Red Line to Central or Harvard.

Gay & Lesbian Bars & Clubs

In addition to the clubs listed here, some mainstream venues schedule a weekly gay night. The particulars are current at press time, but always check ahead. **Rumor,** 100 Warrenton St. (© **617/422-0045;** www.rumorboston.com), features Latin music and the occasional drag show on Wednesday; the **Estate** (p. 269) plays host to **Glamlife** (www.chrisharrispresents.com) on Thursday; and Saturday is gay night at the **House of Blues** (p. 271).

On the first Friday of each month, the Boston chapter of **Guerrilla Queer Bar** (www.bostonguerrilla.com) stages a flash mob–style takeover of a straight bar just for the night. Visit the website to sign up for a notification e-mail. The first Sunday of the month means a men's dance party at **ZuZu** in Cambridge (p. 273).

For up-to-date listings, check *Bay Windows,* the *Improper Bostonian,* and the *Phoenix.* Worthwhile websites include www.edgeboston.com, www.dyke night.com, and http://boston.lesbiannightlife.com.

Club Café ★★ This fun South End spot draws a chic crowd of men and women for conversation (the noise level is reasonable), dining, live music in the front room, and video entertainment in the back room. Thursday is the busiest night. Open daily until 2am; the restaurant serves Sunday brunch, dinner nightly, and a light lounge menu daily starting at noon. 209 Columbus Ave. (at Berkeley St.). © **617/536-0966.** www.clubcafe.com. T: Green Line to Arlington or Orange Line to Back Bay.

Fritz This popular South End hangout is a neighborhood favorite that serves brunch on weekends. The friendly crowd bonds over sports on the plasma satellite TVs. In the Chandler Inn Hotel, 26 Chandler St. (at Berkeley St.). © **617/482-4428.** T: Orange Line to Back Bay.

Jacques Cabaret ★ The only drag venue in town, Jacques draws a friendly crowd of gay and straight patrons who mix with the "girls" and sometimes engage in a shocking activity—that's right, disco dancing. The eclectic entertainment includes live music (on weekends), performance artists, and, of course, drag shows. Open daily from noon to midnight; no credit cards. 79 Broadway (at Piedmont St.), Bay Village. © **617/426-8902.** www.jacquescabaret.com. Cover $6–$10. T: Green Line to Arlington.

Machine The large dance floor sets Machine apart from the rest of Boston's gay nightlife destinations. Be in the mood to move or to play pool (in a separate room). Thursday is karaoke night, and one Saturday a month is Dyke Night. Upstairs is the **Ramrod** (© **617/266-2986;** www.ramrod-boston.com), a leather bar with a strict dress code for the back room. 1254 Boylston St. (at Ipswich St.).

📞 **617/536-1950.** www.machine-boston.com. Cover $10. T: Green Line B, C, or D to Kenmore, then a 10-min. walk.

Paradise Not to be confused with the Boston rock standby (well, you can, but it won't be quite the same experience), this club near MIT attracts an all-ages male crowd. There's a stripper every evening. Monday is karaoke night. Open Sunday through Wednesday until 1am, Thursday through Saturday until 2am. 180 Massachusetts Ave. (at Albany St.), Cambridge. 📞 **617/868-3000.** www.paradise cambridge.com. T: Red Line to Central, then a 10-min. walk.

Sports Bars

Bleacher Bar ★ This place has an irresistible gimmick: It's *under* the Fenway Park bleachers. The most coveted seats—there's a time limit on game days—are adjacent to a large outfield-facing window that's covered with one-way glass when the Red Sox are playing and otherwise open, weather permitting. (I'm told the urinals in the men's room enjoy the same view.) The unimaginative beer menu and decent food are reasonably priced, all things considered—and look, the outfield! 82A Lansdowne St. (btw. Brookline Ave. and Ipswich St.). 📞 **617/262-2424.** www.bleacherbarboston.com. T: Green Line B, C, or D to Kenmore.

Cask 'n Flagon ★ A long fly ball away from Fenway Park, "the Cask," which opened in 1969, is one of the best-known sports bars in this sports-mad city. It's much bigger than it looks from Brookline Avenue, but lines on game days are still comically long. The crowds watching major events on numerous TVs in the memorabilia-drenched bar are large and enthusiastic year-round. 62 Brookline Ave. (at Lansdowne St.). 📞 **617/536-4840.** www.casknflagon.com. T: Green Line B, C, or D to Kenmore.

The Fours ★★ One of Boston's best and best-known sports bars—*Sports Illustrated* says it's the best in the country—the Fours is across the street from the TD Garden. Festooned with sports memorabilia and TVs, it's a madhouse before Celtics and Bruins games—and a promising place to pick up an extra ticket. 166 Canal St. (off Causeway St.). 📞 **617/720-4455.** www.thefours.com. T: Green or Orange Line to North Station.

Game On! Sports Cafe Yes, it's actually *in* Fenway Park, and no, you can't sneak into the stands. The overgrown sports bar and restaurant boasts the latest techno toys, including high-def TVs and a booming sound system, on two deafeningly loud levels of a onetime bowling alley. On game days, the line stretches out the door. 82 Lansdowne St. (off Brookline Ave.). 📞 **617/351-7001.** www.gameonboston. com. T: Green Line D to Fenway, or B, C, or D to Kenmore.

Jerry Remy's Sports Bar & Grill ★ As a player and a broadcaster, Jerry Remy has made his living at Fenway Park for years. This cavernous establishment across the street proves his talent in yet another line of work. It's on the expensive side, but the food is tasty, and the sheer number of TVs means you won't miss a play. There's seating on the breezy patio in good weather. 1265 Boylston St. (at Ipswich St.). 📞 **617/236-7369.** www.jerryremys.com. T: Green Line B, C, or D to Kenmore, then 10-min. walk.

MORE ENTERTAINMENT OPTIONS
Coffeehouses

As in most other American cities, you won't get far without seeing a Starbucks. I'll seldom say no to a frozen drink, but for coffee and hanging out, there are plenty of less generic options. Many are in the North End (see chapter 5); other favorites are listed here. At all of them, hours are long and loitering is encouraged—these are good places to bring your laptop or journal.

Algiers Café & Restaurant ★ Middle Eastern food and music, plain and flavored coffees, and the legendary atmosphere make this a classic Harvard Square hangout. Your "quick" snack or drink (try the mint coffee) might turn into a longer stay as the sociologist in you studies the would-be intellectuals. This is a good spot to eavesdrop while you sample terrific soups, sandwiches, homemade sausages, falafel, and hummus. 40 Brattle St. (btw. Brattle Sq. and Church St.), Cambridge. ℮ **617/492-1557.** T: Red Line to Harvard.

BeanTowne Coffee House A splash of the bohemian in a buttoned-up office-retail complex, this is a good stop before or after a film at the Kendall Square Cinema. Order from the extensive beverage menu or the tempting selection of soups, salads, and sandwiches. There's only one problem with this little place—it's too popular. If a table empties, move in fast. Closed weekends. 1 Kendall Sq. (off Broadway near Cardinal Medeiros Ave.), Cambridge. ℮ **617/621-7900.** www.beantowne cambridge.com. T: Red Line to Kendall.

Boston Common Coffee Co. ★★ Most of the other coffee places in the North End are right out of a Scorsese movie. This is a yuppier caffeine-delivery system, with free wireless Internet and a menu of delectable baked goods and hearty sandwiches. It seems a bit incongruous at first, but it's always crowded. The **Downtown Crossing** branch, 515 Washington St. (at West St.; ℮ **617/542-0595**), is popular with shoppers and Emerson College students. The **Financial District** location, 10 High St., off Summer Street (℮ **617/695-9700**), is frantic on weekdays and closed on weekends. 97 Salem St. (off Parmenter St.). ℮ **617/725-0040.** www.bostoncommoncoffee.com. T: Green or Orange Line to Haymarket.

Equal Exchange Cafe Virtuous and delicious, this sunny little spot near the TD Garden serves fair-trade coffee, tea, and hot chocolate. The veggie-friendly food and sweets come from several local vendors, and the drinks from the well-known Equal Exchange co-op, which is based in a Boston suburb. Wi-Fi is free, but seating is scarce at busy times. Open weekdays 7am to 7pm, Saturday 9am to 5pm. 226 Causeway St. (off N. Washington St.). ℮ **617/372-8777.** www.equalexchangecafe.com. T: Green or Orange Line to North Station.

Thinking Cup Across the street from Boston Common, Thinking Cup serves cult favorite Stumptown coffee, organic teas, tasty sandwiches, and house-made baked goods. The cozy space, decorated with black-and-white photos and vintage newspaper headlines, is a magnet for students and instructors from nearby Emerson College and Suffolk University. 165 Tremont St. (near Avery St.). ℮ **617/482-5555.** www.thethinkingcup.com. T: Green Line to Boylston.

1369 Coffee House ★ A long, narrow room with a colorful clientele, the 1369 offers excellent baked goods, a dazzling selection of premium teas and coffees, and great people-watching. There's also a light lunch menu and a pleasant outdoor seating area. The equally enjoyable but less convenient original location is at 1369 Cambridge St. (at Springfield St.), Inman Square (℮ **617/576-1369**). 757 Massachusetts Ave. (at Pleasant St.), Central Sq., Cambridge. ℮ **617/576-4600.** www.1369coffeehouse.com. T: Red Line to Central.

Trident Booksellers & Café ★★ This Back Bay institution is more than just a cafe. The veggie-friendly menu (including breakfast served all day) complements the free Wi-Fi access, thoughtful book selection, and casual, New Age-y atmosphere. There's patio seating in fine weather. Open 8am to midnight daily. 338 Newbury St. (btw. Hereford St. and Massachusetts Ave.). ℂ **617/267-8688.** www.trident bookscafe.com. T: Green Line B, C, or D to Hynes Convention Center.

Pool & Bowling

These establishments aren't the divey hangouts you remember from your misspent youth; they're upscale destinations with prices to match. For pool, expect to pay at least $12 an hour on weekend evenings, with weekday and daytime discounts. Bowlers can count on parting with at least $6 per person per game.

Flat Top Johnny's ★★ I blink like a geisha every time I walk in here—I can't believe such a cool, funky spot is this close to MIT. A spacious, loud room with an impressive beer selection and 12 red-topped pool tables, Flat Top Johnny's has a casual neighborhood feel despite being in a rather sterile office-retail complex. Open weekdays noon to 1am, weekends 3pm to 1am. 1 Kendall Sq. (off Broadway near Cardinal Medeircs Ave.), Cambridge. ℂ **617/494-9565.** www.flattopjohnnys.com. T: Red Line to Kendall/MIT.

Jillian's Boston ☺ The 70,000-square-foot Jillian's complex, which anchors the Lansdowne Street strip, offers billiards on 34 tables, an upscale bowling alley (part of the Lucky Strike Lanes chain), a spring break–themed dance club (Tequila Rain), tons of plasma TVs, five full bars, and two restaurants. If you can't scare up some fun here, check your pulse. Open Monday through Saturday from 11am to 2am, Sunday from noon to 2am. Children under 18 accompanied by an adult are admitted before 8pm Sunday through Thursday; on Friday and Saturday, Jillian's is 21-plus after 8pm. 145 Ipswich St. (at Lansdowne St.). ℂ **617/437-0300.** www.jilliansboston.com or www.luckystrikeboston.com. Valet parking available after 6pm, except during Red Sox games. T: Green Line B, C, or D to Kenmore.

Kings ★ In a former movie theater across from the Hynes Convention Center, Kings is a popular date destination that attracts the occasional pro athlete or celebrity. It has 20 bowling lanes (4 of them private) and an eight-table billiards room. It's open Monday 5pm to 2am, Tuesday through Sunday 11:30am to 2am; after 6pm, patrons must be at least 21. 50 Dalton St. (at Scotia St., ½ block from Boylston St.). ℂ **617/266-2695.** www.backbaykings.com. T: Green Line B, C, or D to Hynes Convention Center.

Films

Free Friday Flicks at the Hatch Shell ★★★ (ℂ 617/787-7200) are family-friendly movies that play on a large screen in the amphitheater on the Esplanade. On the lawn in front of the Hatch Shell, hundreds of people picnic until the sky grows dark and the credits roll. The films tend toward recent releases (no big thrill for anyone with a Netflix subscription), but the movie is only part of the experience. *Tip:* Bring sweaters in case the breeze off the river grows chilly.

Two superb local revival houses feature lectures and live performances in addition to foreign and classic films: the **Brattle Theatre,** 40 Brattle St., Cambridge (ℂ 617/876-6837; www.brattlefilm.org; T: Red Line to Harvard), and the **Coolidge Corner Movie Theater,** 290 Harvard St., Brookline (ℂ 617/734-2500; www.coolidge.org; T: Green Line C to Coolidge Corner). The Coolidge also schedules midnight shows. Classic and foreign films are the tip of the iceberg at the quirky **Harvard Film Archive,** 24 Quincy St., Cambridge (✆ **617/495-4700;** http://hcl.harvard.edu/hfa; T: Red Line to Harvard), which also shows student films.

For first-run independent and foreign films, head to the **Kendall Square Cinema,** 1 Kendall Sq., Cambridge (✆ **617/499-1996;** www.landmarktheatres. com; T: Red Line to Kendall/MIT). The best movie theater in the immediate Boston area, it offers discounted parking in the adjoining garage. First- and second-run current releases at discount prices are the usual fare at the **Somerville Theater,** 55 Davis Sq. (✆ **617/625-5700;** www.somervilletheatreonline.com; T: Red Line to Davis), which schedules occasional concerts, too. For mainstream releases, head to the 19-screen **AMC Loews Boston Common,** 175 Tremont St. (at Avery St.; ✆ **888/262-4386** [show times] or 617/423-5801; www. amctheatres.com; T: Green Line to Boylston), which has stadium seating, digital sound, and 3D capability. At press time, the **Stuart Street Playhouse,** 200 Stuart St. (at Charles St. S.), in the Radisson Hotel Boston (✆ **617/426-4499;** www.stuartstreetplayhouse.com), is showing recent art-house releases.

Lectures & Readings

The Thursday *Globe* and the *Improper Bostonian* are the best printed sources for listings of lectures, readings, and talks on a wide variety of subjects, often at colleges, libraries, and museums. Many are free or charge a small fee. Most of the bookstores listed in chapter 8 sponsor author readings; check their websites or in-store displays.

LATE-NIGHT BITES

To be frank, Boston's late-night scene needs to climb a couple of notches to reach pathetic, and Cambridge's wee-hour diversions are even skimpier. The only plus is that just about every working cabdriver knows how to reach the places that are still open. In the late evening, especially on weekends, you have it a bit easier: Hit a restaurant (see chapter 5) that keeps long hours. They include **Brasserie Jo, Davio's, Jacob Wirth, Jasper White's Summer Shack, Pizzeria Regina,** and the bar at **Sel de la Terre.** In the North End, **Bricco,** 241 Hanover St. (btw. Cross and Richmond sts.; ✆ **617/248-6800;** www.bricco.com), serves pizza at the bar until 2am Tuesday through Saturday.

A number of **Chinatown** restaurants (see chapter 5) don't close until 3 or 4am. Asking for "cold tea" might—*might*—get you a teapot full of beer. In the North End, **Caffé Pompei,** 280 Hanover St. (✆ **617/523-9438**), draws club-hoppers and neighborhood shift workers until 3:30am. Or make like a college student and road-trip to the **International House of Pancakes** at 1850 Soldiers Field Rd. in Brighton (✆ **617/787-0533**). It's open 24 hours daily.

Another classic late-night destination is on the edge of Chinatown, not far from South Station. The **South Street Diner,** 178 Kneeland St. (✆ **617/350-0028;** www.southstreetdiner.com), is a '50s-style joint with a wine and beer license and a jukebox; it's open 24 hours and is a popular morning-after destination.

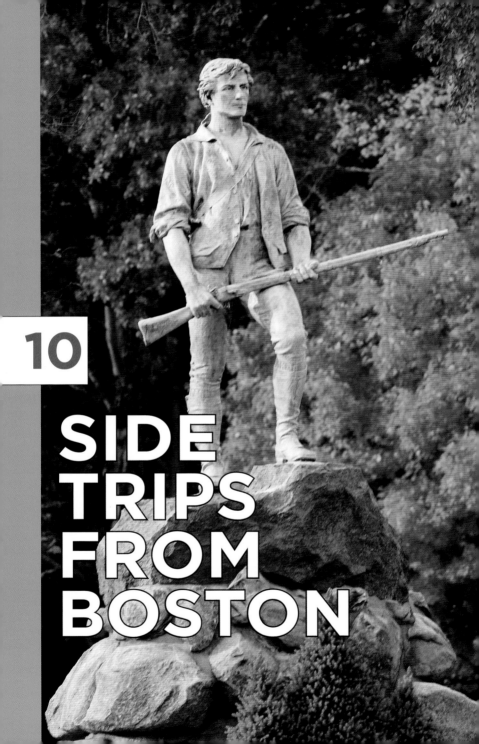

10

SIDE TRIPS FROM BOSTON

n addition to being, in Oliver Wendell Holmes's words, "the hub of the solar system," Boston is the hub of a number of delightful excursions. The destinations in this chapter—Lexington and Concord, the North Shore and Cape Ann, and Plymouth—make fascinating, manageable day trips and offer enough diversions to fill several days.

Like Boston, the suburbs are home to many attractions that rely heavily on aid from outside sources. Admission fees in this chapter are current at press time, but the double whammy of funding cuts and energy prices may have nudged them higher by the time you visit. In addition, some establishments have laid off staff (which means fewer guides), shortened open hours, and even stopped operating on the slowest day of the week, usually Monday. If you're on a tight budget or schedule, check ahead.

LEXINGTON & CONCORD

The shooting stage of the Revolutionary War began here, and parts of the towns still look much as they did in April 1775, when the fight for independence began. Start your visit in **Lexington,** where colonists and British troops first clashed. Spend some time at **Minute Man National Historical Park,** on the border with **Concord,** investigating the battle that raged there. Decide for yourself where the "shot heard round the world" rang out—bearing in mind that **Ralph Waldo Emerson,** who wrote those words, lived in Concord. Emerson's house and **Louisa May Alcott'**s nearby family home are just two of the historic residences in this area that welcome visitors.

Some attractions close from late fall to March, April, or mid-April (opening after **Patriots' Day,** the third Mon in Apr). Information about both towns is available from the **Greater Merrimack Valley Convention & Visitors Bureau,** 40 French St., 2nd floor, Lowell, MA 01852 (© **800/443-3332** or 978/459-6150; www.merrimackvalley.org).

Lexington ★

6 miles NW of Cambridge, 9 miles NW of Boston

A country village turned prosperous suburb, Lexington takes great pride in its history. It's a pleasant town with some engaging destinations, but it lacks the atmosphere and abundant attractions of nearby Concord. Making sure to leave time for a tour of the Buckman Tavern, you can schedule as little as a couple of hours to explore downtown Lexington, possibly en route to Concord; a visit can also fill a half or full day, especially if you visit the **National Heritage Museum.** The town contains part of **Minute Man National Historical Park** (see "Exploring the Area" in the "Concord" section, below), which is definitely worth a visit.

British troops marched from Boston to Lexington late on April 18, 1775. Tipped off, Paul Revere and William Dawes rode ahead to sound the warning to

FACING PAGE: **The Lexington Minute Man statue.**

Minute Man National Historical Park.

their fellow rebellious colonists. Members of the local militia, known as minutemen for their ability to assemble quickly, were waiting at the **Buckman Tavern.** John Hancock and Samuel Adams, leaders of the revolutionary movement, were sleeping (or trying to) at the nearby **Hancock-Clarke House.** The warning came around midnight, followed about 5 hours later by some 700 British troops who stopped in Lexington en route to Concord, where they planned to destroy the rebels' military supplies. Ordered to disperse, the colonists—fewer than 100, and some accounts say 77—stood their ground. Nobody knows who started the shooting, but when it was over, eight militia members lay dead, including a drummer boy, and 10 were wounded.

ESSENTIALS

GETTING THERE From downtown Boston, take Storrow Drive or Memorial Drive to Route 2. Take Route 2 from Cambridge through Belmont, exit at Route 4/225, and follow signs to the center of Lexington. Or take Route 128 (I-95) to exit 31A and follow the signs. Massachusetts Avenue—the same Mass. Ave. you saw in Boston and Cambridge—runs through Lexington. There's metered parking on the street and in several municipal lots, and free parking at the National Heritage Museum and the National Historical Park.

TheMBTA(✆617/222-3200; www.mbta.com) runs

 Poetry in Motion

Before you visit Lexington and Concord, track down **"Paul Revere's Ride,"** Henry Wadsworth Longfellow's classic but historically questionable poem that dramatically chronicles the events of April 18 and 19, 1775.

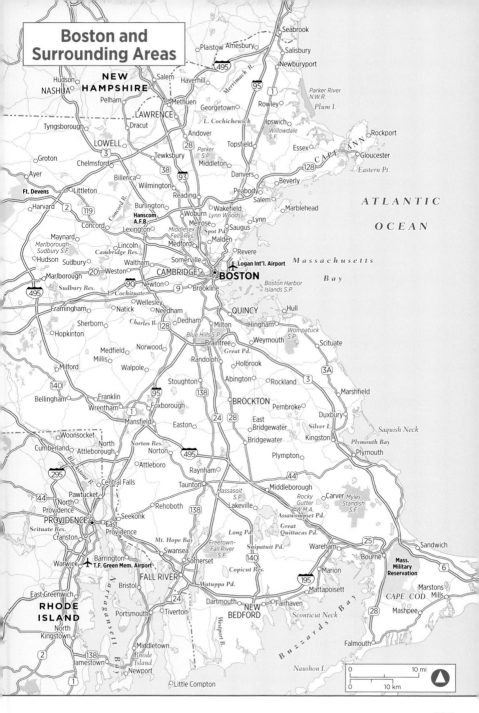

Boston and Surrounding Areas

Touring Lexington & Concord

The **Liberty Ride** (℡ 781/862-0500, ext. 702; www.libertyride.us) is a 90-minute trolley tour, narrated by a costumed guide, that connects the attractions in Lexington and Concord. It operates from 10am to 4pm Saturday and Sunday of Patriots' Day weekend and daily from Memorial Day weekend through late October; check ahead for schedules.

Tickets—$25 for adults, $10 for children 5 to 17, free for children under 5—are good for 24 hours and include admission to all three Lexington Historical Society houses. There's free parking at the National Heritage Museum and the national park, and your ticket entitles you to discounts at local attractions.

bus route nos. 62 (Bedford) and 76 (Hanscom) to Lexington from Alewife station, the last stop on the Red Line. The one-way fare is $1.25 with a CharlieCard or $1.50 with a CharlieTicket, and the trip takes about 25 minutes. Buses leave every hour during the day and every half-hour during rush periods, Monday through Saturday. There's no Sunday service. The bus route passes the Munroe Tavern and the National Heritage Museum, if you prefer not to walk from the center of town. There's no public transit between Lexington and Concord, but the seasonal Liberty Ride tour connects the towns.

VISITOR INFORMATION The **Chamber of Commerce Visitors Center,** 1875 Massachusetts Ave., Lexington, MA 02420 (℡ 781/862-2480; www. lexingtonchamber.org), on the Battle Green, distributes sketch maps and information. It's open daily from 9am to 5pm (Dec–Mar 10am–4pm).

EXPLORING THE TOWN

Minute Man National Historical Park is in Lexington, Concord, and Lincoln. At the Lexington end of the park, less than 10 minutes from the center of town by car, is the **Minute Man Visitor Center ★**, off Route 2A, about ½ mile west of I-95 exit 30B (℡ 781/674-1920; www.nps.gov/mima). This area of the park includes the first 4 miles of the Battle Road, the route the defeated British troops took as they left Concord. Begin your visit by watching "The Road to Revolution," a fascinating multimedia program that explains Paul Revere's ride and the events of April 19, 1775. (It's open Mar–Nov; winter visitors can start in Concord.) Also here are informational displays and a 40-foot mural illustrating the battle. From late May through October, rangers give talks and demonstrations daily; on summer weekends, they lead hiking tours of the park. Surf or call ahead for times. The **Battle Road Trail,** a 5-mile interpretive path, carries pedestrian, wheelchair, and bicycle traffic. Panels and granite markers along the trail display information about the military, social, and natural history of the area. In season (Mar–Nov), this center is open daily from 9am to 4 or 5pm; schedules vary. Check the website or call ahead (try the North Bridge Visitor Center, ℡ 978/369-6993, if there's no answer here) for open days and hours. For more information, see "Concord," below.

Start your visit to downtown Lexington at the **visitor center,** on the town common, better known as the Battle Green. It's open daily from 9am to 5pm (Dec–Mar 10am–4pm). A **diorama** and accompanying narrative illustrate the Battle of Lexington. The *Minuteman* statue on the Green is of Capt. John Parker, who commanded the militia. When the British confronted his troops,

10

SIDE TRIPS FROM BOSTON | Lexington & Concord

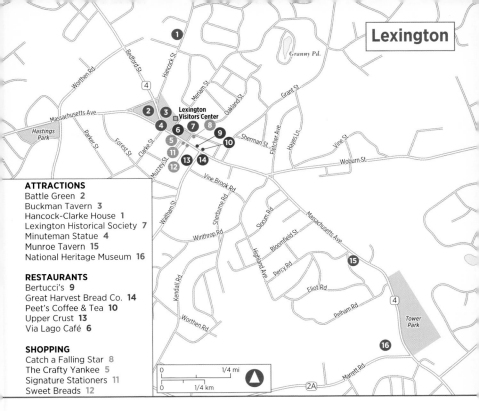

Lexington

Granny Pd.

Lexington
Visitors Center

ATTRACTIONS
Battle Green **2**
Buckman Tavern **3**
Hancock-Clarke House **1**
Lexington Historical Society **7**
Minuteman Statue **4**
Munroe Tavern **15**
National Heritage Museum **16**

RESTAURANTS
Bertucci's **9**
Great Harvest Bread Co. **14**
Peet's Coffee & Tea **10**
Upper Crust **13**
Via Lago Café **6**

SHOPPING
Catch a Falling Star **8**
The Crafty Yankee **5**
Signature Stationers **11**
Sweet Breads **12**

0   1/4 mi
0   1/4 km

Parker called: "Stand your ground. Don't fire unless fired upon, but if they mean to have a war, let it begin here!" Allow about 30 minutes to look around the visitor center and the Green.

Lexington Historical Society ★★ ☺ The historical society's signature properties were among the country's first **historic houses** when restoration of the three buildings began around the turn of the 20th century. A guided tour (30–45 min. each) is the only way to see the houses.

Across from the Battle Green is the **Buckman Tavern** ★★, 1 Bedford St., built around 1710. If time is short and you have to pick just one house to visit, make it this one. The tour of the tavern, by a guide in period dress, is both educational and entertaining. The interior of the tavern has been restored to approximate its appearance on the day of the battle. The colonists gathered here to await word of British troop movements, and they brought their wounded here after the conflict.

Within easy walking distance, the **Hancock-Clarke House,** 36 Hancock St., is where Samuel Adams and John Hancock were staying when Paul Revere arrived. They fled to nearby Woburn. Visit the 1737 house, which contains some original furnishings as well as artifacts of the Battle of Lexington, to see an orientation film about the town.

The British took over the **Munroe Tavern** ★, 1332 Massachusetts Ave. (about 1 mile from the Battle Green), to use as their headquarters and, after the battle, as their field hospital. In this building (1690), you'll learn more about the royal troops and see furniture carefully preserved by the Munroe family, including the table and chair Pres. George Washington used when he dined here in 1789. The historically accurate gardens in the rear (free admission) are beautifully planted and maintained.

The historical society makes its headquarters downtown in the 1846 Lexington Depot, where changing exhibits on local history are open to the public.

Depot Square (off Mass. Ave. near the Battle Green). © **781/862-1703** or 781/862-5598 for information about group tours, offered by appointment only. www.lexingtonhistory.org. Buckman Tavern: Apr–Oct daily 10am–4pm. Tours every 30 min. Hancock-Clarke House: Apr–Oct daily 10am–4pm. Tours on the hour. Munroe Tavern: Apr–Oct daily noon–4pm. Tours on the hour. Houses closed Nov–Mar. Admission to all 3 houses $10 adults, $6 children 6–16; to individual houses, $6 adults, $4 children. Free for children 5 and under.

National Heritage Museum ★★ ☺ ✦ The fascinating exhibits at this unusual museum explore American history and culture. The focus on everyday life makes an entertaining complement to the colonial-history focus of the rest of the town. The installations in the six exhibition spaces change regularly. You can start with another dose of the Revolution, the permanent exhibit **Sowing the Seeds of Liberty,** which tells the story of that tumultuous period through the lives of Lexington residents. Other topics of exhibits have ranged from early-20th-century postcards to Jim Henson and the Muppets to America's national parks. Check ahead for the schedule of lectures, concerts, and family programs. The Scottish Rite of Freemasonry sponsors the museum.

33 Marrett Rd. (Rte. 2A), at Mass. Ave. © **781/861-6559.** www.nationalheritagemuseum.org. Free admission. Wed–Sat 10am–4:30pm; Sun noon–4:30pm. Closed Jan 1, Thanksgiving, and Dec 24–25. From downtown Lexington, follow Mass. Ave. east to intersection with Rte. 2A; enter from Rte. 2A.

SHOPPING

Mass. Ave. near the center of town is a retail hub. Check out **Catch a Falling Star,** 7 Depot Sq. (© **781/674-2432;** www.catchafallingstartoys.com), for toys and games; **Sweet Beads,** 1792 Massachusetts Ave. (© **781/860-7727;** www.sweetbeads.us), which sells jewelry and lets you make your own; high-end paper goods, journals, note cards, and travel accessories at **Signature Stationers,** 1800 Massachusetts Ave. (© **781/863-2777;** www.signaturestationers.com); and jewelry and gifts at the **Crafty Yankee,** 1838 Massachusetts Ave. (© **781/861-1219;** www.craftyyankee.com).

WHERE TO EAT

If you're not continuing to Concord, which has more interesting dining options, Lexington offers some pleasant choices. **Via Lago Café,** 1845 Massachusetts Ave. (© **781/861-6174;** www.vialagocatering.com), is the retail arm of a popular local caterer. Its tasty international specialties, prepared from scratch, are available to stay or go. The town center has two excellent chain pizzerias: The **Upper Crust,** 41 Waltham St. (© **781/247-0089**), and **Bertucci's,** 1777 Massachusetts Ave. (© **781/860-9000**). **Peet's Coffee & Tea,** 1749 Massachusetts Ave. (© **781/357-2090**), is a good place for a pick-me-up. For a muffin or scone and a hot drink, seek out Lexington's branch of **Great Harvest Bread Co.,** 1736 Massachusetts Ave. (© **781/861-9990**).

Concord ★★★

18 miles NW of Boston, 15 miles NW of Cambridge, 6 miles W of Lexington

Concord (say "conquered") revels in its legacy as a center of groundbreaking thought and its role in the country's political and intellectual history. The first official battle of the Revolutionary War took place in 1775 at the North Bridge (now part of Minute Man National Historical Park). In the 19th century, Concord was an important center of literature and philosophy. A visit can easily fill a day; if your interests are specialized or time is short, a half-day excursion is reasonable. For an excellent overview, start at the **Concord Museum.**

After just a little time in this lovely town, you might find yourself adopting the local attitude toward two famous residents: **Ralph Waldo Emerson,** who comes across as a respected uncle figure, and **Henry David Thoreau,** everyone's favorite eccentric cousin. The contemplative writers wandered the countryside and did much of their work in Concord, forming the nucleus of a group of influential writers who called the town home. By the mid–19th century, Concord was the center of the Transcendentalist movement. Sightseers can tour the former **homes of Emerson, Thoreau, Nathaniel Hawthorne,** and **Louisa May Alcott,** and visit their graves at **Sleepy Hollow Cemetery.**

ESSENTIALS

GETTING THERE From Lexington, take Route 2A west from Massachusetts Ave. (Route 4/225) at the National Heritage Museum; follow the BATTLE ROAD signs. From Boston and Cambridge, take Route 2 into Lincoln and stay in the right lane. Where the main road makes a sharp left, go straight onto Cambridge Turnpike. Signs that point to HISTORIC CONCORD lead downtown. To go straight to Walden Pond, stay in the left lane on Route 2, take the main road (Route 2/2A) another mile or so, and turn left onto Route 126. There's parking throughout town and at the attractions.

The **commuter rail** (✆ 617/222-3200; www.mbta.com) takes about 45 minutes from North Station in Boston, with a stop at Porter Square in Cambridge. The round-trip fare is $13. There is no bus service from Boston to Concord, and no public transportation between Lexington and Concord. The **Liberty Ride** tour (p. 288) operates in the summer and fall.

VISITOR INFORMATION The **Concord Chamber of Commerce,** 15 Walden St., Ste. 7, Concord, MA 01742 (✆ 978/369-3120; www.concordchamber ofcommerce.org), maintains a visitor center at 58 Main St., next to Middlesex Savings Bank, 1 block south of Monument Square. It's open daily 10am to 4pm from April through October; public restrooms in the same building are open year-round. Ninety-minute guided walking tours ($20 adults, $12 seniors and students 13–18, $5 children 6–12, free for children under 6, $45 family [two adults, two kids]) are available Friday through Monday from mid-April through October. Tours start at the visitor center. Group tours are available by appointment. The chamber office is open year-round Monday through Friday; hours vary, so call ahead.

The town website, **www.concordma.gov,** has an area with visitor information.

GETTING AROUND The train station is about three-quarters of a mile over flat terrain from the town center. Concord is relatively compact; if you plan to concentrate on attractions near downtown, the commuter rail and your feet

Walden Pond is still a great place to escape the hustle and bustle of the 21st century.

will get you there. If you plan to visit more than a couple of destinations, or if you can't miss the Old Manse, the North Bridge, or Walden Pond, seriously consider driving.

EXPLORING THE AREA

Minute Man National Historical Park ★★ ☺ This 970-acre park preserves the scene of the first Revolutionary War battle at Concord on (all together now) April 19, 1775. After the skirmish at Lexington, royal troops continued to Concord in search of stockpiled arms (which militia members had already moved). Warned of the advance, the colonists prepared for a confrontation. The minutemen crossed the North Bridge, evading the "regulars" (soldiers) standing guard, and waited on a hilltop for reinforcements. The British searched nearby homes and burned any guns they found. The colonials saw the smoke and, mistakenly thinking that the troops were torching the town, mounted an attack at the bridge. The gunfire that ensued is remembered as "the shot heard round the world," the opening salvo of the Revolution.

The park is open daily, year-round. A visit can take as little as half an hour for a jaunt to the North Bridge (a reproduction) or as long as half a day or more, if you stop at both visitor centers and perhaps participate in a ranger-led program. The rangers suggest beginning your visit at the Minute Man Visitor Center (see "Lexington," above), which is closed in the winter. Alternatively, start at the **North Bridge Visitor Center ★**, 174 Liberty St., off Monument Street (✆ **978/369-6993;** www. nps.gov/mima), which overlooks the Concord River and the bridge. A diorama and video program illustrate the battle, and exhibits include uniforms, weapons, and tools of colonial and British soldiers. Park rangers are on duty if you have questions. Outside, picnicking is allowed, and the scenery

> **◎ Row, Row, Row Your Boat**
>
> Pretend you're Henry David Thoreau and take to the Concord River. The **South Bridge Boathouse,** 496–502 Main St. (✆ **978/369-9438;** www.canoeconcord.com), just over half a mile west of the town center, will rent you a canoe for about $17 an hour on weekends, less on weekdays. Single and double kayak rentals are available, too.

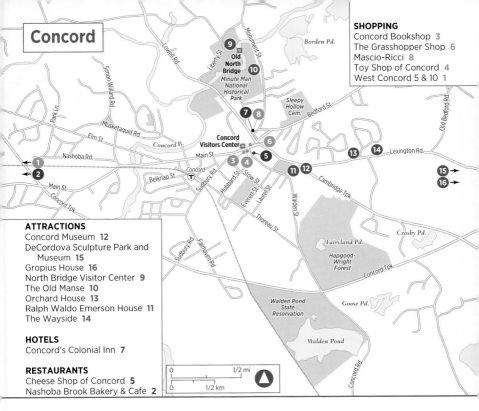

Concord

SHOPPING

Concord Bookshop 3
The Grasshopper Shop 6
Mascio-Ricci 8
Toy Shop of Concord 4
West Concord 5 & 10 1

Borden Pd.

Old North Bridge **9**
Minute Man National Historical Park **10**

Sleepy Hollow Cem.

Concord Visitors Center

7 **8**

6

3 **4** **5**

11 **12**

13 **14** Lexington Rd.

15
16

Fairyland Pd.

Crosby Pd.

Hapgood-Wright Forest

Concord Tpk.

Goose Pd.

Walden Pond State Reservation

Walden Pond

ATTRACTIONS

Concord Museum 12
DeCordova Sculpture Park and Museum 15
Gropius House 16
North Bridge Visitor Center 9
The Old Manse 10
Orchard House 13
Ralph Waldo Emerson House 11
The Wayside 14

HOTELS

Concord's Colonial Inn 7

RESTAURANTS

Cheese Shop of Concord 5
Nashoba Brook Bakery & Cafe 2

0 — 1/2 mi
0 — 1/2 km

is lovely, especially in the fall. The center is open daily from 9am to 5pm (11am–3pm in winter) and is closed January 1 and December 25.

To go straight to the bridge, follow Monument Street out of Concord Center about half a mile until you see the parking lot on the right. Park and walk a short distance to the bridge, stopping along the unpaved path to read the narratives and hear the audio presentations. On one side of the bridge is a plaque marking the grave of the British soldiers who died here; on the other is Daniel Chester French's famed **Minute Man** statue.

Walden Pond State Reservation ★★ The conservation movement started here, in a small wooden structure where a misunderstood social activist moved to "live deliberately." A pile of stones marks the site of the cabin where Henry David Thoreau lived from 1845 to 1847; he captured the experience in the book *Walden*. Today the picturesque park is an extremely popular destination for walking (a path circles the pond), swimming, and fishing. Although crowded, the park's 462 acres are well preserved and insulated from development, making it less difficult than you might expect to imagine Thoreau's experience. Check ahead for the schedule of ranger-led interpretive programs. No dogs or bikes are allowed. In good weather, the parking lot fills early every day—call before setting out, because the rangers turn away visitors after the park reaches capacity (1,000).

Visitors Center: 915 Walden St. (Rte. 126). © **978/369-3254.** www.mass.gov/dcr/parks/walden. Free admission. Parking $5 (cash only). Daily 8am–sunset. From downtown Concord, take Walden St. (Rte. 126) south, cross Rte. 2, and follow signs to the parking lot.

Museums & Literary Sites

Concord Museum ★★ ☺ Just when you're (understandably) suspecting that everything interesting in this area started on April 18, 1775, and ended the next day, this superb museum sets you straight. It's a great place to start your visit to the town.

The **History Galleries** ★★ explore the question "Why Concord?" Artifacts, murals, films, maps, documents, and other exhibits illustrate the town's changing roles. It has been a Native American settlement, Revolutionary War battleground, 19th-century intellectual center, and focal point of the 20th-century historic preservation movement. Items on display include silver from colonial churches, a fascinating collection of embroidery samplers, 19th-century clocks (Concord was a center of clockmaking), and rooms furnished with period furniture and textiles. Explanatory text places the objects in context. One of the **lanterns** immortalized by Longfellow in "Paul Revere's Ride" ("one if by land, two if by sea") is on display. You'll also see the contents of **Ralph Waldo Emerson's study,** arranged the way it was at his death in 1882, and a large collection of **Henry David Thoreau's belongings.**

Pick up a **Family Explorer Kit** ★ as you enter; kids and parents can sketch artifacts and share picture books that give a feel for life in the past. The museum also mounts changing exhibits, offers special events such as living history performances and tea (winter only; call for reservations), and has an outstanding gift shop.

53 Cambridge Tpk. (at Lexington Rd.). © **978/369-9609** (recorded info) or 978/369-9763. www.concordmuseum.org. Admission $10 adults, $8 seniors and students, $5 children 6–17, free for children 5 and under. June–Aug daily 9am–5pm; Apr–May and Sept–Dec Mon–Sat 9am–5pm, Sun noon–5pm; Jan–Mar Mon–Sat 11am–4pm, Sun 1–4pm. Closed Easter, Thanksgiving, and Dec 25. Parking allowed on road. Follow Lexington Rd. out of Concord Center and bear right at museum onto Cambridge Tpk.; entrance is on left.

One of the Concord Museum's diverse exhibits.

The historic Old Manse.

Orchard House is a must-see for fans of *Little Women.*

The Old Manse ★ The engaging history of this home touches on the military and the literary, but it's mostly the story of a family. The Rev. William Emerson built the Old Manse in 1770 and watched the Battle of Concord from the yard. He died during the Revolutionary War, and for almost 170 years the house was home to his widow, her second husband (Rev. Ezra Ripley), their descendants, and two famous friends. Nathaniel Hawthorne and his bride, Sophia Peabody, moved in after marrying in 1842 and stayed for 3 years. As a wedding present, Henry David Thoreau sowed a vegetable garden; today, a re-creation of the garden is part of a self-guided tour of the grounds. William Emerson's grandson Ralph Waldo Emerson wrote the essay "Nature" here, in the same study where Hawthorne later toiled. On the guided tour (the only way to visit the house), you'll see mementos and memorabilia of the Emerson and Ripley families and of the Hawthornes, who scratched notes on two windows with Sophia's diamond ring.

269 Monument St. (at North Bridge). ℂ **978/369-3909.** www.oldmanse.org. Guided tour $8 adults, $7 seniors and students, $5 children 6–12, $25 families. Apr 19–Oct Mon–Sat 10am–5pm, Sun and holidays noon–5pm (last tour at 4:30pm); check ahead for winter hours. From Concord Center, follow Monument St. ½ mile; Old Manse is on left, North Bridge parking lot on right.

Orchard House ★★★ ☺ *Little Women* (1868), Louisa May Alcott's best-known and most popular work, was written and set at Orchard House. Seeing the Alcotts' home brings the author and her family to life for legions of female visitors and their pleasantly surprised male companions. Fans won't want to miss the excellent tour (the only way to explore the house), copiously illustrated with heirlooms. Serious buffs can check ahead for information on the extensive schedule of special events and seasonal and holiday programs, some of which require reservations.

Louisa's father, Amos Bronson Alcott, was a writer, educator, philosopher, and leader of the Transcendentalist movement. He created Orchard House by joining and restoring two homes on 12 acres of land that he bought in 1857. Bronson and his wife, the social activist Abigail May Alcott, and their family lived here from 1858 to 1877, socializing in the same circles as Emerson, Thoreau, and Hawthorne.

Their daughters inspired the characters in *Little Women*. "Jo" was Louisa's alter ego; Anna ("Meg"), the eldest, was an amateur actress; and May ("Amy") was a talented artist. Elizabeth ("Beth"), a gifted musician, died before the family moved to this house, which has been open to the public since 1911.

399 Lexington Rd. 🕿 **978/369-4118.** www.louisamayalcott.org. Guided tours $9 adults, $8 seniors and students, $5 children 6–17, $25 families. Apr–Oct Mon–Sat 10am–4:30pm, Sun 1–4:30pm; Nov–Mar Mon–Fri 11am–3pm, Sat 10am–4:30pm, Sun 1–4:30pm. Closed Jan 1–2, Easter, Thanksgiving, and Dec 25. Follow Lexington Rd. out of Concord Center and bear left at Concord Museum; house is on the left. Overflow parking lot is across the street.

Ralph Waldo Emerson House Emerson's stately home offers an instructive look at the days when a philosopher could attain the status we now associate with rock stars. Emerson, also an essayist and poet, lived here from 1835 until his death, in 1882. He moved in after marrying his second wife, Lydia Jackson, whom he called Lydian; she called him Mr. Emerson, as the staff still does. The tour (the only way to enter the house) gives an affectionate look at Emerson's personal side and at the fashionably ornate interior decoration of the time. You'll see original furnishings and some of Emerson's personal effects. The contents of his study from the time of his death are in the Concord Museum (p. 294).

28 Cambridge Tpk. 🕿 **978/369-2236.** www.rwe.org/emersonhouse. Guided tours $8 adults, $6 seniors and children 7–17, free for children 6 and under. Call to arrange group tours (10 people or more). Patriots' Day weekend to Oct Thurs–Sat 10am–4:30pm, Sun 1–4:30pm. Closed Nov to mid-Apr. Follow Cambridge Tpk. out of Concord Center; just before Concord Museum, house is on right.

Sleepy Hollow Cemetery ★ Follow the signs for AUTHOR'S RIDGE and climb the hill to the graves of some of the town's literary giants, including the Alcotts, Emerson, Hawthorne, and Thoreau. Emerson's bears no religious symbols; the marker is an uncarved quartz boulder. Thoreau is buried nearby; at his funeral, in 1862, his old friend Emerson concluded his eulogy with these words: " . . . wherever there is knowledge, wherever there is virtue, wherever there is beauty, he will find a home."

Entrance on Rte. 62 W. 🕿 **978/318-3233.** www.concordma.gov/pages/concordma_cemetery/sleepy. Daily 7am–dusk, weather permitting. No buses allowed.

The Wayside ★ The Wayside was Nathaniel Hawthorne's home from 1852 until his death, in 1864. The Alcotts also lived here (the girls called it "the yellow house"), as did Harriett Lothrop, who wrote the *Five Little Peppers* books under the pen name Margaret Sidney and owned most of the current furnishings. The Wayside is part of Minute Man National Historical Park, and the fascinating 45-minute ranger tour (the only way to see the house) illuminates the occupants' lives and the house's crazy-quilt architecture. The exhibit in the barn (free admission) consists of audio presentations and figures of Hawthorne, Louisa May and Bronson Alcott, and Sidney. Call ahead to double-check hours, which are subject to change.

455 Lexington Rd. 🕿 **978/318-7863** or 978/369-6993 (park headquarters).

 Military Intelligence

Veterans' graves in Sleepy Hollow Cemetery bear small American flags from Memorial Day until just before Veterans Day. Of the famous occupants of Author's Ridge, only Louisa May Alcott (a Union Army nurse during the Civil War) qualifies.

The Wayside is a local home with a rich literary history.

www.nps.gov/mima. Guided tours $5 adults, free for children 16 and under. Late May to Oct; open days and hours vary. Closed Nov to late May. Follow Lexington Rd. out of Concord Center past Concord Museum and Orchard House. Park across the street.

NEARBY SIGHTS

DeCordova Sculpture Park and Museum ★★ Outdoors and in, this dramatic institution shows the work of American contemporary and modern artists, with an emphasis on living New England residents. The imaginative curatorial staff builds exhibits around themes as well as the work of individual artists. If you're interested in contemporary sculpture, deCordova is a can't-miss destination: The main building, on a leafy hilltop, overlooks the outdoor public sculpture park, and a sculpture terrace displays the work of one sculptor per year.

Allow at least half a day, perhaps including lunch. Year-round, free guided tours of the main galleries start Thursday at 1pm and Sunday at 2pm; sculpture-park tours run May through October on weekends at 1pm. Picnicking is allowed in the sculpture park; bring food or buy it at the cafe (open Tues–Fri 11am–3pm, Sat–Sun 11am–4pm). Be sure to check out the excellent Store @ DeCordova (✆ 781/259-8692; Mon and Fri–Sat 9:30am–5:30pm, Tues–Thurs 9:30am–7:30pm, Sun 10:30am–5:30pm).

51 Sandy Pond Rd., Lincoln. ✆ **781/259-8355.** www.decordova.org. Admission $12 adults; $10 AAA and Zipcar members; $8 seniors, students, and children 6–12. Admission to sculpture park free when museum is closed. Museum: Tues–Sun and some Mon holidays 10am–5pm. Closed Jan 1, July 4, Thanksgiving, and Dec 25. Sculpture park: Daily daylight hours. From Rte. 2 E., take Rte. 126 south to Baker Bridge Rd. (1st left after Walden Pond). When it ends, go right onto Sandy Pond Rd.; museum is on the left. From I-95, take exit 28B, follow Trapelo Rd. 2½ miles to Sandy Pond Rd., then follow signs.

Gropius House ★ Architect Walter Gropius (1883–1969), founder of the Bauhaus school of design, built this hilltop home for his family in 1938 after accepting a job at the Harvard Graduate School of Design. He used traditional materials such as clapboard, brick, and fieldstone, with components then seldom seen in domestic architecture, including glass blocks and chrome (on the banisters). Marcel Breuer designed many of the furnishings, which were made for the family at the Bauhaus. Decorated as it was in the last decade of Gropius's life, the house affords a revealing look at his life, career, and philosophy. Call for information on workshops and special tours; evening tours (reservation required) take place throughout the year.

68 Baker Bridge Rd., Lincoln. ✆ **781/259-8098.** www.historicnewengland.org. Guided tours $10 adults, $9 seniors, $5 students with ID and children. Tours on the hour June–Oct 15 Wed–Sun 11am–4pm; Oct 16–May Sat–Sun 11am–4pm. From Rte. 2 E., take Rte. 126 south to Baker Bridge Rd. (1st left after Walden Pond); house is on the right. From I-95, take exit 28B, follow Trapelo Rd. to Sandy Pond Rd., go left onto Baker Bridge Rd.; house is on the left.

SHOPPING

Downtown Concord, off **Monument Square,** is a terrific shopping destination. Here you'll find the **Toy Shop of Concord,** 4 Walden St. (✆ **978/369-2553;** www.concordtoys.com); the **Grasshopper Shop,** 36 Main St. (✆ **978/369-8295**), which carries women's clothing and accessories; jewelry at **Mascio-Ricci,** at Concord's Colonial Inn, 48 Monument Sq. (✆ **978/371-1191;** www.mascio-ricci.com); and the **Concord Bookshop,** 65 Main St. (✆ **978/369-2405;** www.concordbookshop.com). The compact shopping district in **West Concord,** along Route 62, is worth a side trip just to check out the old-school **West Concord 5 & 10,** 106 Commonwealth Ave. (✆ **978/369-9011**), which carries everything from light bulbs to rubber duckies.

WHERE TO STAY & EAT

Consider taking a **picnic** to the North Bridge, Walden Pond, or another spot that catches your eye. Stock up at **Nashoba Brook Bakery** (see below) or downtown at the **Cheese Shop of Concord,** 29 Walden St. (✆ **978/369-5778;** www.concordcheeseshop.com).

Concord's Colonial Inn ★ The main building of the Colonial Inn has overlooked Monument Square since 1716. Additions since it became a hotel in 1889 have made the inn large enough to offer modern conveniences and small enough to feel friendly. Like many historic inns, it's not luxurious, but it is comfortable, centrally located, and possibly haunted. The 15 original guest rooms are in great demand; the most popular, no. 24, supposedly is home to a ghost. Reserve early if you want to stay in the main inn, which is decorated in colonial style. Rooms in the 1970 Prescott House have country-style decor, as do the one-, two-, and three-bedroom suites (available for long-term stays) in four freestanding buildings. The amenities, variety of rooms, and accommodating staff make the inn popular with business travelers as well as vacationers, especially during foliage season.

The two lounges serve light meals; ask for an outdoor table, and you'll have a front-row seat for the action on Monument Square. The restaurant serves salads, sandwiches, and pasta at lunch and traditional American fare at dinner. Afternoon tea ($16 or $25 per person) is served Saturday and Sunday; reservations (✆ **978/369-2373**) are required.

48 Monument Sq., Concord, MA 01742. www.concordscolonialinn.com. ✆ **800/370-9200** or 978/369-9200. Fax 978/371-1533. 56 units, some with shower only. Apr to early Sept $179–$249 main inn; $149–$199 Prescott House; mid-Sept to Oct $199–$249 main inn; $169–$219 Prescott House; Nov–Mar from $159 main inn, from $129 Prescott House. Long-term rates from $50/day. AAA and AARP discounts available. AE, DC, DISC, MC, V. **Amenities:** Restaurant (American); 2 lounges; bar w/live music on weekends; concierge; executive-level rooms; access to nearby health club ($10). *In room:* A/C, TV/DVD, hair dryer, Wi-Fi (free).

Nashoba Brook Bakery & Café ★★ AMERICAN True story: A friend living in Australia recently returned home on vacation craving two things: a nap and a visit here. The enticing variety of fresh artisan breads, scrumptious baked goods and pastries, and made-from-scratch soups, salads, and sandwiches makes the airy cafe a popular destination throughout the day. It offers a good break from the sightseeing circuit. The industrial-looking building off West Concord's main street backs up to little Nashoba Brook, which is visible through the glass back wall. Order and pick up at the counter, and then grab a seat along the window or near the children's play area. You can also order takeout—this is great picnic food—or a loaf of crusty bread. On weekend mornings, the cafe serves home-made Belgian waffles.

152 Commonwealth Ave., West Concord. ℂ **978/318-1999.** www.slowrise.com. Sandwiches $7; other menu items $2–$8. MC, V. Mon–Fri 7am–5:30pm; Sat 7am–5pm; Sun 8am–5pm. From Concord Center, follow Main St. (Rte. 62) west, across Rte. 2; bear right at traffic light in front of train station and go 3 blocks. To reach overflow parking, turn right onto Commonwealth Ave. and take 1st right into lot on Winthrop St.; walk across bridge over brook.

THE NORTH SHORE & CAPE ANN

The areas north of Boston abound with historic sights and gorgeous ocean vistas. Cape Ann is a rocky peninsula so enchantingly beautiful that when you hear the slogan "Massachusetts's *Other* Cape," you might forget what the first one was. Cape Ann and Cape Cod do share some attributes—scenery, shopping, seafood, and traffic. Cape Ann's proximity to Boston and manageable scale make it a wonderful day trip as well as a good choice for a longer stay.

If possible, explore the North Shore by car. Public transportation in this area is good, but it doesn't go everywhere, and in some towns the train station is some distance from the attractions. For the full day-trip experience, try to visit on a spring, summer, or fall weekday; traffic is brutal on warm weekends. Many areas are practically ghost towns from November through March, but all of the destinations in this chapter have enough of a year-round community to make an off-season excursion worthwhile.

The **North of Boston Convention & Visitors Bureau,** 10 State St., Ste. 309, Newburyport, MA 01950 (ℂ **800/742-5306** or 978/225-1559; www. northofboston.org), publishes a map and a visitor guide that covers 34 munici-palities, including Salem, Marblehead, and all of Cape Ann. It also coordinates

---

 You Do the Math

The **MBTA** (ℂ **800/392-6100** or 617/222-3200; www.mbta.com) serves most of the destinations in this chap-ter, but public transit isn't necessarily cheaper than renting a car for a day. For example, suppose you're visiting Gloucester with three other adults, each paying a total of $15 for the commuter rail. Even with summer gas prices, a good deal on a rental car will likely be cheaper than $60 in train fares. What's more, having a car allows you to make your own schedule instead of being tethered to the train's timetable—and you don't have to leave from North Station. Just make sure that the car-rental company accepts returns at the time you anticipate returning to Boston, so that you don't get stuck paying to park.

Escapes North (www.escapesnorth.com), a clearinghouse for arts- and culture-oriented travel throughout the area. The **Cape Ann Chamber of Commerce** (see "Gloucester," later in this chapter) is another good resource.

Marblehead ★★★

15 miles NE of Boston

Like an attractive person with a great personality, Marblehead has it all. Scenery, history, architecture, and shopping combine to make this one of the area's most popular day trips for both locals and visitors. It's welcoming, manageable in size, and even polite—many speed-limit signs say PLEASE. Allow at least a full morning, but be flexible, because you might want to hang around.

One of the most picturesque neighborhoods in New England is **Old Town ★★★**, where narrow, twisting streets lead down to the magnificent harbor that helps make this Marblehead self-proclaimed "Yachting Capital of America." As you stroll the downtown historic district, you'll see plaques on the houses bearing the construction date and the names of the builder and original occupant—a history lesson without studying. Many of the houses have stood since before the Revolutionary War, when Marblehead was a center of merchant shipping. Two historic homes are open to the public (see "Exploring the Town," below).

ESSENTIALS

GETTING THERE By car, take Route 1A north through Revere and Lynn; bear right at the signs for Nahant and Swampscott. Follow Lynn Shore Drive through Swampscott to Route 129, which runs into town. Or take I-93 or Route 1 to Route 128, then follow Route 114 through Salem into Marblehead. Parking is tough, especially in Old Town—grab the first spot you see.

MBTA (☎ **617/222-3200;** www.mbta.com) bus no. 441/442 runs from Haymarket (Orange or Green Line) to downtown Marblehead on weekdays; on weekends service is from Wonderland station at the end of the Blue Line. During rush periods on weekdays, the no. 448/449 connects Marblehead to Downtown Crossing. The trip takes about an hour, and the one-way fare is $2.80 with a CharlieCard, $3.50 with a CharlieTicket.

VISITOR INFORMATION The **Marblehead Chamber of Commerce,** 62 Pleasant St., Marblehead, MA 01945 (☎ **781/631-2868;** www.visitmarblehead.com), is open weekdays from 9am to 5pm. The **information booth** (☎ **781/639-8469**), on Pleasant Street near Spring Street, is open mid-May through October, Monday to Friday 1 to 5pm, Saturday

Marblehead Harbor has a rich maritime tradition.

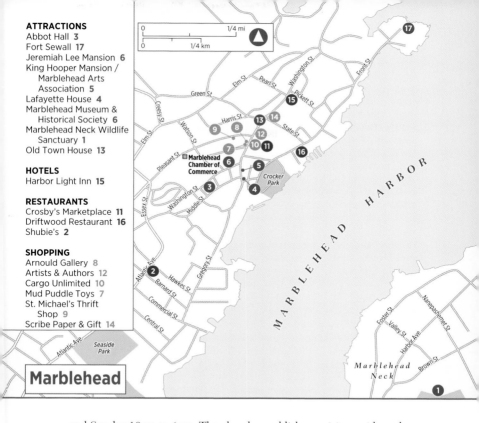

ATTRACTIONS
Abbot Hall **3**
Fort Sewall **17**
Jeremiah Lee Mansion **6**
King Hooper Mansion /
    Marblehead Arts
    Association **5**
Lafayette House **4**
Marblehead Museum &
    Historical Society **6**
Marblehead Neck Wildlife
    Sanctuary **1**
Old Town House **13**

HOTELS
Harbor Light Inn **15**

RESTAURANTS
Crosby's Marketplace **11**
Driftwood Restaurant **16**
Shubie's **2**

SHOPPING
Arnould Gallery **8**
Artists & Authors **12**
Cargo Unlimited **10**
Mud Puddle Toys **7**
St. Michael's Thrift
    Shop **9**
Scribe Paper & Gift **14**

Marblehead

and Sunday 10am to 6pm. The chamber publishes a visitor guide and map that includes a calendar of events; before you visit, download a description of a walking tour as an MP3 file or document.

SPECIAL EVENTS Sailing regattas take place in the outer harbor all summer. The biggie, the **National Offshore One Design (NOOD) Regatta,** better known as Race Week, falls in late July and attracts enthusiasts from all over the country. The **Christmas Walk,** on the first weekend in December, incorporates music, arts and crafts, shopping, and Santa Claus, who arrives by lobster boat.

EXPLORING THE TOWN

Marblehead is a wonderful place for aimless wandering; to add some structure, consult the walking tour available on the chamber of commerce's website. Whatever else you do, be sure to spend some time in **Crocker Park ★★**, on the harbor off Front Street. Especially in the warmer months, when boats jam the water nearly as far as the eye can see, the view is breathtaking. The park has benches and a swing, and it's a great place for a picnic. The view from **Fort Sewall,** at the other end of Front Street, is equally mesmerizing.

Just inland, the **Lafayette House** is at the corner of Hooper and Union streets. A corner of the private home was chopped off to make room for the passage of the Marquis de Lafayette's carriage when he visited the town in 1824. In

For the Birds

Across the causeway from Devereux Beach on Marblehead Neck, one of the ritziest neighborhoods on the North Shore, is the Massachusetts Audubon Society's **Marblehead Neck Wildlife Sanctuary** (✆ 800/283-8266 or 781/259-9500; www.massaudubon. org). Turn east on Ocean Avenue south of downtown and follow it less than a mile until you see a little sign to the left at Risley Avenue. Park in the small lot and follow the path into the sanctuary, where you can see the varied species of birds that use the Atlantic flyway, especially in spring and fall. Admission is free. To return to Marblehead proper, continue on Ocean Avenue, which becomes Harbor Avenue and forms a loop. En route, at the end of "the Neck," you can park near the decommissioned lighthouse and take in a breathtaking view.

Market Square on Washington Street, near the corner of State Street, is the **Old Town House,** in use for meetings and gatherings since 1727. The Marblehead Museum & Historical Society (see the listing for the Jeremiah Lee Mansion, below) maintains a small **Civil War museum** on the second floor. It's open every other Saturday in the summer, starting on Memorial Day weekend.

Abbot Hall A 5-minute stop here (look for the clock tower) is just the ticket if you want to be able to say you did some sightseeing. The town offices and historical commission share Abbot Hall with Archibald M. Willard's famous painting *The Spirit of '76* ★, on display in the Selectmen's Meeting Room. The thrill of recognizing the drummer, drummer boy, and fife player is the main reason to stop here. Cases in the halls contain objects and artifacts from the collections of the Marblehead Historical Society and other organizations. The Maritime Room, which focuses on the town's naval history, is open weekday mornings in the summer.

Washington Sq. ✆ 781/631-0528. www.marblehead.org. Free admission. Mon–Tues and Thurs 8am–5pm, Wed 8am–6pm, Fri 8am–12:30pm; check ahead for open days and hours in summer. From the historic district, follow Washington St. up the hill.

Jeremiah Lee Mansion/Marblehead Museum & Historical Society ★★

Built in 1768 for one of the wealthiest merchants in the colonies, the Lee Mansion is internationally recognized as an extraordinary example of pre-Revolutionary Georgian architecture. The attraction for aficionados is the excitement of seeing original hand-painted wallpaper in an 18th-century home, but the friendly, knowledgeable guides make visitors of all interest levels feel welcome. The tour touches on the history of the town as well as the home. Rococo woodcarving and other details complement historically accurate room arrangements, and ongoing restoration and interpretation by the Marblehead Museum & Historical Society place the 18th- and 19th-century furnishings and artifacts in context. The peaceful gardens are open to the public.

Across the street are two galleries (free admission) and

Architectural Details

On the hill between the Jeremiah Lee Mansion and Abbot Hall, notice the private homes at 185, 181, and 175 Washington St. Like the Lee Mansion—and hundreds of other residences in the tiny downtown area—these are good original examples of the architecture of the colonial and early national period.

administrative offices. One gallery shows paintings by the noted early-20th-century folk artist J.O.J. Frost, a Marblehead native; the other mounts changing exhibits that illustrate town history. Call ahead for the schedule of **summer walking tours** of Marblehead.

161 Washington St. ℂ **781/631-1768.** www.marbleheadmuseum.org. Guided tours $5 adults, $4.50 seniors and students. June–Oct Tues–Sat 10am–4pm. Closed Nov–May. Galleries: 170 Washington St. Free admission; donations appreciated. June–Oct Tues–Sat 10am–4pm; Nov–May Tues–Fri 10am–4pm. From Abbot Hall, follow Washington St. down the hill; mansion is on left, galleries on right.

King Hooper Mansion/Marblehead Arts Association & Gallery Shipping tycoon Robert Hooper got his nickname because he treated his sailors so well, but it's easy to think he was called "King" because he lived like royalty—his house has both a wine cellar and a ballroom. Around the corner from the home of Jeremiah Lee (whose sister-in-law was the second of Hooper's four wives), the 1728 mansion gained a Georgian addition sometime after 1745. The **Marblehead Arts Association** bought the building in 1938 and stages monthly exhibits in four galleries (with a public reception on the first Sunday of every month from 2–4pm), schedules special events, and sells members' work in the gift shop. The mansion has a lovely garden; enter through the gate at the right of the house.

8 Hooper St. ℂ **781/631-2608.** www.marbleheadarts.org. Free admission. Summer Sun and Tues–Wed noon–5pm, Thurs–Sat 10am–5pm; winter Sun and Tues–Fri noon–5pm, Sat 10am–5pm; and by appointment. Where Washington St. curves at the foot of hill near Lee Mansion, look for the colorful sign.

SHOPPING

Marblehead is a legendary (or notorious, if you're on a budget) shopping destination. Shops, boutiques, and galleries abound in **Old Town** and on **Atlantic Avenue** and the east end of **Pleasant Street.** Good stops include **Arnould Gallery & Framery,** 111 Washington St. (ℂ **781/631-6366**); **Artists & Authors,** 108 Washington St. (ℂ **781/639-0400;** www.artists-authors.com), which carries rare books and fine art; **Cargo Unlimited,** 118 Washington St. (ℂ **781/631-1112;** www.cargounlimited.com), for home furnishings and accessories; **Mud Puddle Toys,** 1 Pleasant St. (ℂ **781/631-0814;** www.mudpuddletoys.com); and **Scribe Paper & Gift,** 84 Washington St. (ℂ **781/631-7274;** www.scribepaper.com). One of my favorite stops is the **St. Michael's Thrift Shop,** behind the Episcopal church at 20 Pleasant St. (ℂ **781/631-0657;** www.stmichaels1714.org; no credit cards). The gift shop at the Marblehead Arts Association (see above) sells members' creations.

WHERE TO STAY

This is B&B heaven. Space considerations preclude listing the numerous small inns and bed-and-breakfasts, but the accommodations listings of the **Marblehead Chamber of Commerce** (ℂ **781/631-2868;** www.visitmarblehead.com), include many of them. Check the website, call or write for a visitor guide, or consult one of the B&B agencies listed on p. 97.

Harbor Light Inn ★★ Near the Old Town House, two Federal-era mansions make up this gracious inn, which is much bigger and more luxurious than its austere facade suggests. From the wood floors to the 1729 beams (in a third-floor room) to the swimming pool, it's both historic and relaxing. Rooms are comfortably furnished in period style, with some lovely antiques; most have canopy or four-poster beds. Eleven hold working fireplaces, and five have double Jacuzzis. The best rooms, on the top floor at the back of the building, away from the street, enjoy views of the harbor from a distance. The undeniably romantic inn, a popular honeymoon and weekend-getaway destination, also attracts weekday business travelers.

58 Washington St., Marblehead, MA 01945. www.harborlightinn.com. © **781/631-2186.** Fax 781/631-2216. 21 units, 7 with shower only. $145–$365 double; $195–$365 suite. Rates include breakfast buffet, afternoon refreshments, and use of bikes. Corporate rate available midweek. 2-night minimum stay weekends, 3-night minimum holiday and high-season weekends. AE, MC, V. Free parking. **Amenities:** Tavern; airport shuttle; concierge; access to nearby health club ($5); Jacuzzi; heated outdoor pool. *In room:* A/C, TV/DVD, hair dryer, Wi-Fi (free).

WHERE TO EAT

Marblehead has a number of serviceable dining options, plus a ton of bars that serve decent food. The tavern at the **Harbor Light Inn** (see listing above) offers a limited bar menu at dinner and lunch in a cozy 18th-century setting. You're probably better off heading to Salem if you want a fancier meal, but I prefer picnicking. You can stock up at a number of places in Old Town. **Crosby's Marketplace,** 118 Washington St. (© **781/631-1741;** www.crosbysmarkets. com), is a full-service market with a large prepared-food section. **Shubie's,** 32 Atlantic Ave. (© **781/631-0149;** www.shubies.com), carries a good selection of specialty foods. Another excellent option is to hit the road early and have breakfast near the harbor.

Driftwood Restaurant ★ ◢ DINER/SEAFOOD At the foot of State Street, next to Clark Landing (the town pier), is an honest-to-goodness local hangout that serves excellent food. Join the crowd at a table or the counter for a mug of strong coffee and breakfast (served all day) or lunch. Try pancakes or hash, chowder or a seafood roll—a hot dog bun filled with, say, fried clams or lobster salad. The house specialty, served on weekends and holidays, is fried dough, which is sort of a solid doughnut, as crispy as a good New Orleans beignet. At busy times, you may have to wait outside for a while.

63 Front St. © **781/631-1145.** Main courses $3–$12; breakfast items less than $7. No credit cards. Daily 5:30am–2pm.

Salem ★★

17 miles NE of Boston, 4 miles NW of Marblehead

Settled in 1626, 4 years before Boston, Salem later enjoyed international renown as a center of merchant shipping. Today it's famous around the world because of a 7-month episode in 1692. The **witchcraft trial** hysteria led to 20 deaths, 3-plus centuries of notoriety, countless lessons on the evils of prejudice, and innumerable bad puns ("Stop by for a spell" is a favorite slogan). But there's much more to the city, which embraces its history as a thriving seaport, a literary inspiration, and a vital partner in the post–Revolutionary War China trade.

The city abounds with witch-associated attractions, plus nearly as many reminders of Salem's seagoing legacy. Historic sites associated with **Nathaniel Hawthorne** complement the sorceresses and sailors. And one of the finest cultural institutions in New England, the **Peabody Essex Museum,** is a must-see for lovers of art and artifacts. Salem is a family-friendly destination that's worth at least a half-day visit (perhaps after a stop in Marblehead) and can easily fill a day.

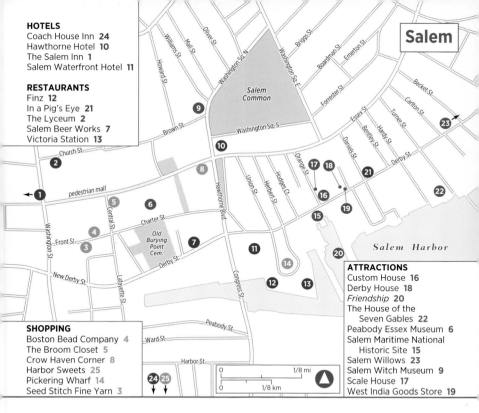

ESSENTIALS

GETTING THERE By car from Marblehead, follow Route 114 west. From Boston, take Route 1A north to Salem, being careful in Lynn, where the road turns left and immediately right. You can also take I-93 or Route 1 to Route 128 and then Route 114 into downtown Salem. There's metered street parking and a reasonably priced municipal garage across the street from the National Park Service Regional Visitor Center.

From Boston, the **MBTA** (✆ **617/222-3200**; www.mbta.com) operates commuter trains from North Station and bus no. 450 from Haymarket (Orange or Green Line). The train is more comfortable than the bus but runs less frequently and is more expensive. It takes 30 to 35 minutes; the round-trip fare is $11. The station is about 5 blocks from the downtown area. The one-way fare for the 35- to 55-minute bus trip is $2.80 with a CharlieCard, $3.50 with a CharlieTicket.

The **Salem Ferry** (✆ **978/741-0220**; www.salemferry.com) operates daily from Memorial Day weekend through October. The 50-minute catamaran trip connects Central Wharf, next to Boston's New England Aquarium (T: Blue Line to Aquarium) to the Blaney Street Wharf, off Derby Street, a 15-minute walk or quick hop on the Salem Trolley (see below) from downtown Salem. The peak adult fare (late June to early Sept) is $13

305

one-way, $24 round-trip, with discounts for seniors, children, and families. The one-way off-season fare is $9.50 for adults.

VISITOR INFORMATION A good place to start your visit is the **National Park Service Regional Visitor Center,** 2 New Liberty St. (✆ **978/740-1650;** www.nps.gov/sama), open daily from 9am to 5pm. Exhibits highlight early settlement, maritime history, and the leather and textiles industries in all of Essex County, not just Salem. The center also distributes brochures and pamphlets, including one that describes a **walking tour** of the historic district, and has an auditorium where a free film provides an overview of the region's history.

The city's Office of Tourism, **Destination Salem** (✆ **877/725-3662** or 978/744-3663; www.salem.org), produces and distributes a free visitor guide that includes an excellent map. Visit the website to see the calendar of events. The **Salem Chamber of Commerce,** 265 Essex St., Ste. 101, Salem, MA 01970 (✆ **978/744-0004;** www.salem-chamber.org), maintains a large rack of brochures and pamphlets, and the staff is up on the latest events. It's open weekdays from 9am to 5pm.

The city website (www.salem.com) and an excellent community site (www.salemweb.com) offer information for out-of-towners.

GETTING AROUND In the congested downtown area, **walking** is the way to go, but you might not want to hoof it to all the sights, especially if it's hot. At the Essex Street side of the visitor center, you can board the **Salem Trolley** ★ (✆ **978/744-5469;** www.salemtrolley.com) for a 1-hour narrated tour, and reboard as often as you like at any of the 13 stops. It's a good idea if you're spending the day and don't want to keep moving the car or carrying kids. The trolley operates daily April through October from 10am to 5pm (last tour at 4pm); check ahead for off-season hours and special tours. Tickets ($15 adults, $14 seniors, $5 children 6–14, free for children 5 and under) are good all day; they're available onboard; from the Trolley Depot, 191 Essex St. (at Central St.), on the pedestrian mall; at the office, 8 Central St. (at Charter St.); and at other locations around town.

SPECIAL EVENTS The city's month-long Halloween celebration, **Haunted Happenings** ★★ (www.hauntedhappenings.org), includes parades, parties, tours, and a ceremony on the big day. In August, the 2-day **Salem Maritime Festival** fills the area around the Salem Maritime National Historic Site (see listing below) with live music, food, and demonstrations of nautical crafts. The festival kicks off **Heritage Days,** a weeklong event when the city celebrates its multicultural history with musical and theatrical performances, a parade, and fireworks. Contact Destination Salem (see "Visitor Information," above) or Escapes North (www.escapesnorth.com) for details.

EXPLORING THE TOWN

The historic district extends well inland from the waterfront. Many 18th-century houses, some with original furnishings, still stand. Ship captains lived near the water at the east end of downtown, in relatively small houses crowded close together. The captains' employers, the shipping company owners, built their homes away from the water (and the accompanying aromas). Many of them lived on **Chestnut Street** ★★, now a National Historic Landmark. Residents along the grand thoroughfare must, by legal agreement, adhere to colonial style in their

The House of the Seven Gables and its period gardens.

decorating and furnishings. Ask at the visitor center for the pamphlet that describes a walking tour of the historic district.

By car or trolley, the **Salem Willows** (℗ **978/745-0251;** www.salem willows.com) amusements are 5 minutes away; many signs point the way. The strip of carnival-style diversions and snack bars has a retro honky-tonk air, and the waterfront park is a good place to bring a picnic and wander along the shore. There's no admission fee; meter parking is available. To enjoy the great view without the arcades and rides, have lunch one peninsula over at **Winter Island Park.**

The House of the Seven Gables ★ ☺ Nathaniel Hawthorne's cousin lived here, and stories and legends of the house—formally the Turner-Ingersoll Mansion—and its inhabitants inspired the author's 1851 novel. If you don't know the eerie tale, don't let that keep you away; begin your visit with the audiovisual program, which tells the story. The house, built by Capt. John Turner in 1668, contains six rooms of period furniture, including pieces referred to in the book, and a secret staircase. Tours include a visit to Hawthorne's birthplace (built before 1750 and moved to the grounds) and describe what life was like for the house's 18th-century inhabitants. The costumed guides are well versed in the history of the buildings and artifacts, and eager to answer questions. The site, a National Historic Landmark District overlooking Salem Harbor, also holds period gardens, the **Retire Beckett House** (1655), and a **counting house** (1830) where children and families find hands-on activities related to Salem's maritime legacy.

115 Derby St. ℗ **978/744-0991.** www.7gables.org. Guided tour of house and grounds $13 adults, $12 seniors and AAA members, $7.50 children 5–12, free for children 4 and under. Surcharges may apply for special exhibitions. July–Oct daily 10am–7pm; Nov–June daily 10am–5pm. Check ahead for extended Oct hours. Closed 1st 2 weeks of Jan, Thanksgiving, and Dec 25. From downtown, follow Derby St. east 3 blocks past Derby Wharf.

Peabody Essex Museum ★★★ ☺ Now in its third century, the Peabody Essex Museum has grown into a national presence. All by itself, this captivating museum is reason enough to visit Salem.

Impressive collections of art from New England and around the world are the Peabody Essex's calling card, but they're just part of the story. The museum owns 22 historic residences, including a well-preserved 18th-century Qing dynasty house, **Yin Yu Tang ★**, that was shipped to Salem from China and reassembled. The only example of Chinese domestic architecture outside that country, the house captures 2 centuries of rural life. It's part of a huge wing designed by Moshe Safdie that opened in 2003.

The 854,000 items in the museum's permanent collections blend contemporary acquisitions with "the natural and artificial curiosities" that Salem's sea captains and merchants brought back from around the world to the Peabody Museum (1799) and the local and domestic objects collected by the Essex Institute (1821), the county historical society. The displays help visitors understand the significance of each object, and interpretive materials (including interactive and hands-on activities) let children get involved. You might see objects related to the history of the port of Salem (including gorgeous furniture) or to the whaling trade (such as amazing scrimshaw). Other noteworthy collections include American, African, Indian, Asian, and East Asian art and objects; photography; and the practical arts and crafts of East Asian, Pacific Island, and Native American peoples. Portraits of area residents include Charles Osgood's omnipresent rendering of Nathaniel Hawthorne.

Special exhibitions during the period covered by this book include *Faces of Devotion: Indian Sculpture from the Figiel Collection* (through Jan 16, 2012), *Shapeshifting: Transformations in Native American Art* (Jan 14 to Apr 1, 2012), and *Written on the Waves: Shipboard Logs and Journals* (through Oct 1, 2012).

To explore the museum, take a guided or self-guided gallery tour. The cafe in the atrium closes 30 minutes before the rest of the museum.

East India Sq., 161 Essex St. ✆ **866/745-1876** or 978/745-9500. www.pem.org. Admission $15 adults, $13 seniors, $11 students, free for children 16 and under. Yin Yu Tang admission $5 with museum admission. Tues–Sun and Mon holidays 10am–5pm. Take Hawthorne Blvd. to Essex St., following signs for visitor center. Enter on Essex St. or New Liberty St.

Salem Maritime National Historic Site ★ ☺

An entertaining introduction to Salem's seagoing history, this complex includes an exciting attraction: a real ship. The *Friendship* ★★ is a full-size replica of a 1797 East Indiaman merchant vessel, a three-masted 171-footer that disappeared during the War of 1812. The tall ship is a faithful replica with some concessions to the modern era, such as diesel engines. The **guided ranger tour** includes a tour of the ship. You can also download one or more of the five available audio tours and set your own schedule.

With the decline of merchant shipping in the early 19th century, Salem's wharves fell into disrepair. In 1938, the National Park Service took over a small piece of the waterfront, **Derby Wharf.** It's now a finger of parkland extending into the harbor, part of the 9 acres that make up the historic site. On adjacent **Central Wharf** is a warehouse, built around 1800, that houses the orientation center. Tours, which vary seasonally, explore Salem's maritime history. Yours might include the **Derby House** (1762), a wedding gift to shipping magnate Elias Hasket Derby from his father, and the **Custom House** (1819). Legend—myth, really—has it that Nathaniel Hawthorne was working here when he found an embroidered scarlet "A." If you prefer to explore on your own, you can see a free film and wander around **Derby Wharf,** the **West India Goods Store,**

The Salem Witch Museum doesn't shy away from showing the gruesome reality of the witch trials.

the **Bonded Warehouse,** the **Scale House,** and Central Wharf. Check ahead for lectures and other special events that focus on topics related to Salem's seagoing legacy.

193 Derby St. ℂ **978/740-1660.** www.nps. gov/sama. Free admission. Guided tours $5 adults, $3 seniors and children 6–16. Daily 9am–5pm. Closed Jan 1, Thanksgiving, and Dec 25. Take Derby St. east; just past Pickering Wharf, Derby Wharf is on the right.

Salem Witch Museum ★★ ☺ This is one of the most memorable attractions in eastern Massachusetts—it's both interesting and scary. The main draw of the museum (a former church) is a three-dimensional audiovisual presentation with life-size figures. The show takes place in a huge room lined with displays that are lighted in sequence. The 30-minute narration tells the tale of the witchcraft trials and the accompanying hysteria. The well-researched presentation recounts the story accurately, with an enjoyable dash of drama. One of the victims was crushed to death by rocks piled on a board on his chest—smaller kids might need a reminder that he's not real. The narration is available translated into Cantonese, French, German, Italian, Japanese, Mandarin, Russian, and Spanish. There's also a small exhibit that traces the history of witches, witchcraft, and witch hunts.

19½ Washington Sq., on Rte. 1A. ℂ **978/744-1692.** www.salemwitchmuseum.com. Admission $8.50 adults, $7 seniors, $5.50 children 6–14. July–Aug daily 10am–7pm; Sept–June daily 10am–5pm; check ahead for extended Oct hours. Closed Jan 1, Thanksgiving, and Dec 25. Follow Hawthorne Blvd. to the northwest corner of Salem Common.

SHOPPING

Pickering Wharf (ℂ **978/740-6990;** www.pickeringwharf.com), at the corner of Derby and Congress streets, is a waterfront complex of shops, boutiques, restaurants, and condos. It's popular for strolling, snacking, and shopping, and the central location makes it a local landmark. Tiny Front Street, a block from the retail-rich **Essex Street pedestrian mall,** is home to several shops that cater to needlecrafters. I especially like **Seed Stitch Fine Yarn,** 21 Front St. (ℂ **978/744-5557;** www.seedstitchfineyarn.com), which is across the street from the **Boston Bead Company,** 10 Front St. (ℂ **978/741-2323;** www.boston beadcompany.com; p. 248).

You can't go more than a couple of blocks downtown without passing a fortune-telling parlor, and several shops specialize in witchcraft accessories. Bear in mind that Salem is home to many practicing witches, mystics, and others who take their beliefs very seriously. **Crow Haven Corner,**

 A Face in the Crowd

On the traffic island across from the entrance to the **Salem Witch Museum** is a statue that's easily mistaken for a witch. It's really **Roger Conant,** who founded Salem in 1626.

Confection Connection

Shops throughout New England sell the high-end chocolate creations of **Harbor Sweets ★★**, Palmer Cove, 85 Leavitt St., off Lafayette Street (*☎* **800/243-2115** or 978/745-7648; www.harbor sweets.com). The retail store overlooks the floor of the factory; tours begin Tuesday and Thursday at 11am (call ahead to confirm). The deliriously good sweets are expensive, but candy bars and small assortments are available. Closed Sunday except before candy-intensive holidays.

125 Essex St. (*☎* **978/745-8763;** www.crowhavencorner.net), and the **Broom Closet,** 3 Central St. (*☎* **978/741-3669;** www.broomcloset.com), stock everything from crystals to clothing.

WHERE TO STAY

The busiest and most expensive time of year is Halloween week, followed closely by the rest of October; it's not unusual for the whole city to be sold out months in advance. The **Salem Waterfront Hotel,** 225 Derby St., at Pickering Wharf (*☎* **888/337-2536** or 978/740-8788; www.salemwaterfronthotel.com), is a large, modern establishment with an indoor pool. Double rates in high season start at $179, which includes Wi-Fi and parking.

Coach House Inn Far enough from downtown to feel like a getaway, this welcoming inn is in a historic district 2 blocks from the harbor and just 9 blocks from the major attractions—an easy walk in fine weather. The three-story mansion, set back from the street behind a well-kept lawn, is elegantly furnished in just-frilly-enough style. All of the good-size rooms have high ceilings, period antiques, four-poster beds, and Oriental rugs, and most have (nonworking) fireplaces. Breakfast arrives at your door in a basket—a nice perk if dining-room chitchat isn't your thing. Built in 1879 for a ship's captain, the Coach House Inn is 20 minutes on foot or 5 minutes by car from the center of town, and just up the street from Salem State College.

284 Lafayette St. (Rtes. 1A and 114), Salem, MA 01970. www.coachhousesalem.com. *☎* **800/688-8689** or 978/744-4092. Fax 978/745-8031. 11 units, 9 with bathroom, 2 with shower only. $130–$195 double; $198–$250 2-room suite. Rates include continental breakfast. Rates are higher in late Oct. Minimum 2- or 3-night stay weekends and holidays. AE, DISC, MC, V. Free parking. *In room:* A/C, TV, fridge, Wi-Fi (free).

Hawthorne Hotel ★ ☺ This historic hotel, built in 1925 in the heart of downtown, is both convenient and comfortable. It books business travelers as well as vacationers, and it's popular for functions. The six-story building holds well-kept guest rooms that vary in size from snug to spacious. All are attractively furnished with reproduction Federal-style pieces, but bathrooms can be small. The best units, on the Salem Common (north) side of the building, have better views than rooms that overlook the street. Whatever direction you face, ask to be as high up as possible, because the neighborhood is busy. If you're traveling with children, ask about "Family Fun" packages, which include discounted tickets to area museums.

18 Washington Sq. W. (at Salem Common), Salem, MA 01970. www.hawthornehotel.com. *☎* **800/729-7829** or 978/744-4080. Fax 978/745-9842. 89 units, 30 with shower only. $139–$220 double; $209–$344 suite. Extra person $12. Children 15 and under stay free in parent's

room. 2-night minimum stay May–Oct weekends. Off-season, AAA, and AARP discounts, and weekend and other packages available. AE, DC, DISC, MC, V. Limited self-parking. Pets accepted ($100 deposit; $10/day). **Amenities:** Restaurant (American); tavern; concierge; exercise room; access to nearby heath club w/pool; room service. *In room:* A/C, TV, hair dryer, MP3 docking station, Wi-Fi (free).

The Salem Inn ★★ The Salem Inn occupies the comfortable niche between too-big hotel and too-small B&B. Its clientele includes honeymooners as well as sightsers and families, and the variety of rooms lets the innkeepers match guests with the right accommodations. The inn consists of three properties. The 1834 West House and the 1854 Curwen House, former homes of ship captains, are listed on the National Register of Historic Places. The best units are the honeymoon and family suites (which have kitchenettes) in the 1874 Peabody House. Guest rooms are large and tastefully decorated; some have fireplaces, canopy beds, and whirlpool baths. The peaceful rose garden at the rear of the main building is open to all guests.

7 Summer St. (Rte. 114), Salem, MA 01970. www.saleminnma.com. 🕿 **800/446-2995** or 978/741-0680. Fax 978/744-8924. 40 units, some with shower only. Mid-Apr to Sept $139–$199 double, $199–$259 suite; Oct $190–$245 double, $260–$350 suite; Nov to mid-Apr $119–$169 double, $169–$229 suite. Rates include continental breakfast. Extra person $15–$25. 2- or 3-night minimum stay during special events and holidays. Winter and family packages available. AE, DC, DISC, MC, V. Free parking. Pets accepted by prior arrangement (Nov–Sept $15/night, Oct $25/night). *In room:* A/C, TV, hair dryer, Wi-Fi (free).

WHERE TO EAT

Pickering Wharf has a food court as well as several restaurants with outdoor seating overlooking the marina: **Victoria Station** (🕿 978/744-7644; www.victoriastationinc.com) emphasizes seafood and traditional American dishes and has a huge salad bar, and **Finz** (🕿 978/744-8485; www.hipfinz.com) is known for innovative seafood preparations and creative drinks. A couple of blocks away is **Salem Beer Works,** 278 Derby St. (🕿 978/745-BEER; www.beerworks.net), a sibling of Boston Beer Works (p. 276) that serves a similar variety of pub grub and house-made brews. The cafe at the **Peabody Essex Museum** (p. 307) serves lunch.

In a Pig's Eye ★ AMERICAN/MEXICAN This neighborhood tavern near the House of the Seven Gables has a secret—the food is fantastic. Lunch features sandwiches, salads, and bar fare that's a step up from basic, with several vegetarian and Mexican options. The dinner menu is mostly Mexican on Monday and Tuesday; Mexican pizzas (mounds of vegetables and salsa on flour tortillas) are terrific, as are the gigantic burritos. The regular dinner menu offers creative pasta dishes, beef, chicken, and at least half a dozen tasty seafood choices—my hyper-picky friend raved about the mussels. There's live music Wednesday through Monday; Sunday is jazz night.

148 Derby St. (at Daniels St.). 🕿 **978/741-4436.** www.inapigseye.com. Reservations recommended at dinner in summer. Main courses $5–$8 at lunch, $7–$13 at dinner Wed–Sat, $6–$9 at dinner Mon–Tues. AE, DC, DISC, MC, V. Mon–Sat 11:30am–3pm and 6–10pm; Sun brunch 11:30am–4pm.

The Lyceum ★★ NEW ENGLAND/MEDITERRANEAN The elegance of the Lyceum's high-ceilinged front rooms and glass-walled back rooms matches the sky-high quality of the food, which attracts local businesspeople as well as out-of-towners. The kitchen has an especially skillful hand with seafood, often from local waters; be sure to check out the raw bar options. Bounteous chicken salad with unusual slaw or an overstuffed sandwich makes a hearty but not

A whale OF AN ADVENTURE

The depletion of New England's fishing grounds has led to the rise of another important seagoing industry, **whale-watching** ★★. The waters off the coast of Massachusetts are prime territory, and Gloucester is a center of whale-watching cruises. Stellwagen Bank, which runs from Gloucester to Provincetown about 27 miles east of Boston, is a rich feeding ground for the magnificent mammals. Species spotted in the area are mainly humpback, finback, and minke whales, which dine on sand eels and other fish that gather along the ridge. The whales often perform for their audience by jumping out of the water, and dolphins occasionally join the show. Naturalists onboard narrate the trip for the companies listed here, pointing out the whales—many of which they recognize and call by name—and describing birds and fish that cross your path.

Whale-watching is not particularly time- or cost-effective, especially if restless children are along, but it's so popular for a reason: The payoff is, literally and figuratively, huge. This is an "only in New England" experience that kids (and adults) will remember for a long time.

The season runs from April or May through October. Bundle up, even in the middle of summer—it's much cooler at sea than on land. Wear a hat and rubber-soled shoes, and take sunglasses, sunscreen, and a camera. If you're prone to motion sickness, take precautions, because you'll be at sea for 3 to 5 hours. If you plan to take Dramamine, allow some time for it to kick in.

The North Shore whale-watch operators are for-profit businesses, and they're extremely competitive—they'd probably deny it, but the companies are virtually indistinguishable. Most guarantee sightings, offer a morning and an afternoon cruise as well as deep-sea fishing excursions and charters, honor other firms' coupons, and offer AAA and AARP discounts. Check ahead for sailing times, prices (at least $45 for adults, slightly less for seniors and children),

and reservations, which are strongly recommended. If you're on a tight budget, ask whether the company imposes a fuel surcharge, and double-check the cut-off ages for kids and seniors.

If your schedule allows, plan to visit the **Whale Center of New England,** in the Gloucester Maritime Heritage Center, 24 Harbor Loop (© **978/271-6351;** www.whalecenter.org), before or after your trip, to see the humpback whale skeleton and explore the informative displays. It's open Monday through Saturday 9am to 5pm (call for winter hours), and admission is free.

In downtown Gloucester, **Cape Ann Whale Watch** (© **800/877-5110** or 978/283-5110; www.seethewhales.com) is the best-known operation. Also downtown are **Capt. Bill & Sons Whale Watch** (© **800/339-4253** or 978/283-6995; www.captbillandsons.com) and **Seven Seas Whale Watch** (© **888/283-1776** or 978/283-1776; www.7seaswhalewatch.com). At the Cape Ann Marina, off Route 133, is **Yankee Whale Watch** (© **800/942-5464** or 978/283-0313; www.yankeefleet.com).

incapacitating lunch in the middle of sightseeing. Sunday brunch here is an unexpected treat, with superb egg dishes and a good range of entrees for the breakfast-averse. At dinner, the menu takes a turn toward bistro style, with the

Party Line

Alexander Graham Bell made the first long-distance telephone call from the building that now holds the Lyceum Bar & Grill.

likes of delectable grilled beef tenderloin and roasted cod with saffron-tomato broth. Try to save room for a traditional yet sophisticated dessert—the brownie sundae is out of this world.

43 Church St. (at Washington St.). © **978/745-7665.** www.thelyceum.com. Reservations recommended. Main courses $8–$16 at lunch, $16–$27 at dinner. AE, DISC, MC, V. Mon–Fri 11:30am–2:30pm; daily 5:30–9:30pm; Sun brunch 11am–3pm. Validated parking available.

A DETOUR TO ESSEX

If you approach or leave Cape Ann on Route 128, head west on Route 133 to **Essex.** It's a beautiful little town known for Essex clams, salt marshes, a long tradition of shipbuilding, an incredible number of antiques shops, and one celebrated restaurant.

Legend has it that **Woodman's of Essex** ★★★, 121 Main St. (© **800/649-1773** or 978/768-6057; www.woodmans.com), was the birthplace of the fried clam in 1916. Today, the thriving family-owned eatery is a great spot to join legions of locals and visitors for lobster "in the rough," chowder, steamers, corn on the cob, onion rings, and (you guessed it) superb fried clams. In warm weather, people from all over the world flock here, especially on the way back from the beach. In the winter, the crowd is mostly locals desperate for a taste of summer (pass me a moist towelette, please). The line is long, but it moves quickly and offers a good view of the regimented commotion in the food-prep area. Eat inside, upstairs on the deck, or out back at a picnic table. You'll want to be well fed before you set off to explore the numerous antiques shops along Main Street. The restaurant accepts credit cards, opens daily at 11am year-round, and adjusts closing time seasonally; check the website or call ahead.

As with most cult-favorite foods, the fashion is to be contrarian and say that Woodman's is too crowded and too many people know about it. I disagree, but if you're interested in comparison shopping—in the interest of science, of course—two other excellent destinations are open in the summer only. **J. T. Farnham's,** 88 Eastern Ave., Essex (© **978768-6643**), lies about a mile east of Woodman's; the **Clam Box,** 246 High St., Ipswich (© **978/356-9707;** www.ipswichma.com/clambox), is a little over 7 miles northwest of Woodman's. Both are cash only.

Gloucester ★★

33 miles NE of Boston, 16 miles NE of Salem

The ocean has been Gloucester's lifeblood since long before the first European settlement in 1623. The French explorer Samuel de Champlain called the harbor "Le Beauport" when he came across it in 1606, some 600 years after the Vikings. The harbor's configuration and proximity to good fishing helped Gloucester earn the reputation it enjoys to this day. If you read or saw *The Perfect Storm,* you'll have a sense of what to expect here.

Gloucester (which rhymes with "roster") is a working city, not a cutesy tourist town. It's home to one of the last commercial fishing fleets in New England,

The North Shore & Cape Ann

Down by the Sea

On Stacy Boulevard west of downtown Gloucester is a reminder of the sea's danger. Leonard Craske's bronze statue of the **Gloucester Fisherman,** known as "the Man at the Wheel," bears the inscription "They That Go Down to the Sea in Ships, 1623–1923" (the phrase is from the 107th Psalm). A few hundred feet west is a memorial to the women and children who waited at home. As you take in the glorious view, consider this: More than 10,000 fishermen lost their lives during the city's first 300 years.

an internationally celebrated artists' colony, a large Portuguese-American community, and just enough historic attractions. Allow at least half a day, perhaps combined with a visit to the tourist magnet of Rockport; a full day would be better, especially if you plan a cruise or whale watch.

ESSENTIALS

GETTING THERE From Salem, follow Route 1A across the bridge to Beverly, pick up Route 127, and take it through Manchester-by-the-Sea (near, not on, the water) to Gloucester. From Boston, the quickest path is I-93 or Route 1 to Route 128, which runs directly to Gloucester. Use exit 14 and follow Route 133 east to go straight to the Stage Fort Park visitor center. Route 128 is mostly inland; to take in more scenery, leave Route 128 at Manchester and continue to Gloucester on Route 127. There's street parking (metered and not), and a free lot on the causeway to Rocky Neck.

The **commuter rail** (✆ 617/222-3200; www.mbta.com) runs from Boston's North Station. The trip takes about an hour; the round-trip fare is $15. The station is about 8 blocks from the waterfront area. The **Cape Ann Transportation Authority,** or CATA (✆ 978/283-7916; www.canntran. com), runs buses from town to town on Cape Ann and operates special routes during the summer (except Sun).

VISITOR INFORMATION The city's **Visitors Welcoming Center** (✆ 800/649-6839 or 978/281-8865; www.gloucesterma.com) is at Stage Fort Park, off Route 127 at Route 133. It's open during the summer daily from 9am to 5pm; closed in winter. The **Cape Ann Chamber of Commerce,** 33 Commercial St., Gloucester, MA 01930 (✆ 978/283-1601; www.cape annvacations.com), is open year-round (summer Mon–Fri 9am–5pm, Sat 10am–5pm, Sun 10am–4pm; winter Mon–Fri 9am–5pm). At either place, the helpful staff can offer insider tips and advice; be sure to grab a free copy of the annual *Cape Ann Guide.* For an entertaining look at the city through the eyes of a lobster dealer, visit **www.goodmorninggloucester. com**.

SPECIAL EVENTS Gloucester holds festivals and street fairs on weekends throughout the summer. Check in advance to find out what's up when you'll

Gloucester

ATTRACTIONS
Beauport (Sleeper-
  McCann House) **18**
Cape Ann Museum **10**
Gloucester Stage
  Company **15**
The Man at the Wheel **3**
North Shore Arts
  Association **13**
Rocky Neck Art Colony **14**

HOTELS
Atlantis Oceanfront Inn **17**
Bass Rocks Ocean Inn **16**

RESTAURANTS
Crow's Nest **12**
Cupboard **2**
Franklin Cape Ann **7**
Halibut Point Restaurant &
  Bar **11**
Latitude 43 Restaurant &
  Bar **6**
Lobsta Land **1**

SHOPPING
Cape Pond Ice **4**
Dogtown Book Shop **8**
Ménage Gallery **9**
Mystery Train **5**

315

Long after the release of the blockbuster movie, Sebastian Junger's bestselling book *The Perfect Storm* remains a popular reason to visit Gloucester. The thrilling but tragic true account of the "no-name" hurricane of 1991 centers on the ocean and a neighborhood tavern. The **Crow's Nest**, 334 Main St. (© 978/281-2965; www.crowsnest gloucester.com), a bit east of downtown, is a no-frills place with a horseshoe-shaped bar and a crowd of regulars who seem amused that their hangout is a tourist attraction. The Crow's Nest plays a major role in Junger's story, but its ceilings weren't high enough to accommodate a movie set, so the film crew built an exact replica nearby. If you admired the movie's wardrobe design, check out the shirts and caps at **Cape Pond Ice ★**, 104 Commercial St., near the chamber of commerce (© 978/283-0174; www.capepondice.com). "The Coolest Guys Around" have provisioned Gloucester's fishing fleet since 1848. The company offers 40-minute tours of its industrial facility, which is famous for its ice sculptures; bring (or buy) a sweatshirt. The price is $10 for adults, $6 for seniors and children 7 to 11; reservations are recommended.

be in town. The best-known event is **St. Peter's Fiesta,** a colorful 4-day celebration at the end of June. The Italian-American fishing colony's festival has more in common with a carnival midway than a religious observation, but it's great fun. There are parades, games, music, food, sporting events, and, on Sunday, the blessing of the fleet. The **Schooner Festival,** a floating party with plenty of land-based revelry, including fireworks, takes place over Labor Day weekend.

EXPLORING THE TOWN

Business isn't nearly what it once was, but fishing remains Gloucester's leading industry. Tourism is a very close second, and the city is an exceptionally welcoming destination—residents seem genuinely happy to see out-of-towners and to offer directions and insider info.

Stage Fort Park, off Route 127 at Route 133, offers a superb view of the harbor and has a busy snack bar (summer only) and a playground. It's a good spot for picnicking, barbecuing, swimming, or playing on the cannons in the Revolutionary War fort.

To reach **East Gloucester,** follow signs as you leave downtown or go directly from Route 128, exit 9. On East Main Street, you'll see signs for the world-famous **Rocky Neck Art Colony ★★**, headquartered in the Rocky Neck Gallery, 53 Rocky Neck Ave. (© 978/282-0917; www.rockyneckartcolony.org), the oldest continuously operating art colony in the country. Park in the lot on the tiny causeway and head west along Rocky Neck Avenue, which abounds with studios, galleries, restaurants, and people. The draw is the presence of working artists, not just shops that happen to sell art. Most galleries are open daily in the summer 10am to 10pm.

The prestigious **North Shore Arts Association,** 11 Pirates Lane, off East Main Street (© 978/283-1857; www.northshoreartsassoc.org), was founded in 1922 and now numbers more than 300 painters, sculptors, and other artists among its members. The exhibits are worth a visit before or after your excursion across the causeway; check ahead for the schedule of workshops, concerts, and other events. The building is open May through October, Monday through Saturday from 10am to 5pm, Sunday noon to 5pm. Admission is free.

Also in East Gloucester, the **Gloucester Stage Company ★**, 267 E. Main St. (📞 **978/281-4099;** www.gloucesterstage.org), is one of the best repertory troupes in New England. It schedules six plays a season (late May–early Sept); tickets cost $37.

NARRATED CRUISES For information on whale watches, see the box "A Whale of an Adventure," earlier.

The schooner ***Thomas E. Lannon ★*** (📞 **978/281-6634;** www.schooner.org) is a gorgeous reproduction of a Gloucester fishing vessel. The 65-foot tall ship sails from Seven Seas Wharf downtown, off Rogers Street; 2-hour excursions ($40 for adults, $35 for seniors, $28 for children 16 and under) leave about four times daily from mid-June to mid-September, less often on weekends from mid-May to mid-June and mid-September to mid-October. On Saturday morning in July and August, kids (one per parent) sail free. The company also offers music and dining cruises, including sunset lobster bakes. Reservations are recommended for all excursions.

The two-masted schooner ***Adventure ★*** (📞 **978/281-8079;** www.schooner-adventure.org) is a 122-foot fishing vessel built in Essex in 1926. It's being restored—a fascinating process—at Gloucester Marine Railways at Rocky Neck, on the tip of the peninsula that's home to the artists' colony. *Adventure* will eventually resume regularly scheduled public sailing; meanwhile, the staff of the "living museum," a National Historic Landmark, offers dockside educational programs. Check ahead for details and schedules, open days and hours, and prices.

Beauport, Sleeper-McCann House ★★ The rough-and-tumble fishing port of Gloucester has another face: exclusive summer community. Aficionados of house tours will want to build their schedules around a visit to this magnificent property on the stylish Back Shore, the product of a uniquely creative mind. Pioneering interior designer and antiquarian Henry Davis Sleeper created Beauport, transforming it into a repository for his vast collection of American and European decorative arts and antiques. From 1907 to 1934, he built and expanded the house, which has more than 40 rooms, and decorated many of the chambers to illustrate literary and historical themes. The entertaining tour concentrates more on the gorgeous house and rooms in general than on the countless objects on display, which remain virtually as Sleeper left them. You'll see architectural details rescued from other buildings, magnificent arrangements of colored glassware, secret staircases, the "Red Indian Room" (with a majestic view of the harbor), the "Master Mariner's Room" (overflowing with nautical items), and even the kitchen and servants' quarters. Explore the restored grounds, which look the way they did in the 1930s. Beauport, a National Historic Landmark, also schedules events such as afternoon tea, wine tastings, and specialty tours throughout the season.

75 Eastern Point Blvd. 📞 **978/283-0800.** www.historicnewengland.org. Guided tour $10 adults, $9 seniors, $5 students and children 6–12. Tours on the hour June to mid-Oct Tues–Sat 10am–4pm. Closed July 4, mid-Oct to May, and Sun–Mon year-round. Take E. Main St. to Eastern Point Blvd. (a private road), continue ½ mile to house, park on left.

Beauport's treasure-trove of antiques and beautifully restored grounds make it a popular stop for Gloucester visitors.

Cape Ann Museum ★ This meticulously curated museum makes an excellent introduction to Cape Ann's history and artists. If you're visiting on a weekend, a guided tour of the highlights of the collection (Fri–Sat 11am, Sun 2pm) will help you get your bearings. An entire gallery holds extraordinary works by **Fitz Henry Lane** ★★★ (formerly known as Fitz Hugh Lane), the Luminist painter whose light-flooded canvases show off the best of his native Gloucester. The nation's largest collection of his paintings and drawings is here. Other galleries feature works on paper by 20th-century artists such as Maurice Prendergast, Milton Avery, and Stuart Davis; work by other contemporary artists; and granite-quarrying tools and equipment. There's also an outdoor sculpture court. On display in the maritime and fisheries galleries are entire vessels (including one about the size of a minivan that crossed the Atlantic), exhibits on the fishing industry, ship models, and historic photographs and models of the Gloucester waterfront. Check ahead for information about touring the museum's two historic houses: The adjacent **Capt. Elias Davis House** (1804), decorated and furnished in Federal style with furniture, silver, and porcelains; and the 1710 **White-Ellery House,** a rare example of First Period architecture about a mile away at 244 Washington St.

27 Pleasant St. (℃ **978/283-0455.** www.capeannmuseum.org. Admission $8 adults, $6 seniors and students, free for children 11 and under. Mar–Jan Tues–Sat 10am–5pm, Sun 1–4pm. Closed Feb. Follow Main St. west through downtown and turn right onto Pleasant St.; museum is 1 block up on right. Metered parking on street or in lot across street.

SHOPPING

Rocky Neck (see "Exploring the Town," above) offers great browsing. Downtown, **Main Street** between Pleasant and Washington streets is a good destination. Agreeable stops include **Mystery Train,** 21 Main St. (℃ **978/281-8911;** www.mysterytrainrecords.com), which carries a huge variety of used music and films; the **Ménage Gallery,** 134 Main St. (℃ **877/283-6030** or 978/283-6030; www.

A guided tour of the Cape Ann Museum will help you make the most of your visit.

menagegallery.com), which shows varied works by artists and artisans, including gorgeous furniture; and the **Dogtown Book Shop,** 132 Main St. (*©* **978/281-5599;** www.dogtownbooks.com), noted for its used and antiquarian selection. **Cape Pond Ice** (see box, *"The Perfect Storm"*) sells T-shirts, sweatshirts, and other merchandise bearing the company's distinctive logo.

WHERE TO STAY

Gloucester abounds with B&Bs; for guidance, check with the Cape Ann Chamber of Commerce (*©* **978/283-1601**) or consult one of the agencies listed on p. 97.

Atlantis Oceanfront Inn Across the street from the water, the Atlantis enjoys stunning views from every window. The property has an outdoor pool, a helpful staff, and good-size guest rooms that were renovated in 2009. Decorated in comfortable, contemporary style, each has a terrace or balcony with a small table and chairs. Second-floor accommodations are slightly preferable because the view is a little better. The Atlantis doesn't have the resort feel of its more expensive neighbor, the Bass Rocks Ocean Inn, but the million-dollar views are the same.

125 Atlantic Rd., Gloucester, MA 01930. www.atlantisoceanfrontinn.com. *©* **800/732-6313** or 978/283-0014. Fax 978/281-8994. 40 units, 7 with shower only. Late June to Labor Day $180–$230 double; spring and fall $145–$195 double. Extra person $10. Rollaway or crib $15. Children 12 and under stay free in parent's room. Minimum stay may be required. Off-season midweek discounts available. AE, MC, V. Closed Nov to late Apr. Take Rte. 128 to the end (exit 9, East Gloucester), turn left onto Bass Ave. (Rte. 127A), and follow it ½ mile. Turn right and follow Atlantic Rd. **Amenities:** Cafe (breakfast only); heated outdoor pool. *In room:* A/C, TV, fridge, hair dryer, Wi-Fi.

Bass Rocks Ocean Inn This inviting property offers gorgeous ocean views, an outdoor pool, and modern accommodations. Across the road from the rocky shore, the Bass Rocks feels like an old-fashioned resort, which distinguishes it from the neighboring Atlantis. Each room in the 1960s-era motel, most recently

NORTH SHORE beaches

North of Boston, sandy beaches complement the predominantly rocky coastline. The water is *cold*—optimistic locals say "refreshing"—but typically not too rough. Parking can be scarce, especially on weekends, and lots often fill up despite costing as much as $25 per car. If you can't set out early, wait until midafternoon and hope that the people who arrived in the morning have had their fill. During the summer, lifeguards are on duty from 9am to 5pm at larger public beaches. Surfing is generally permitted outside of those hours. The beaches listed here all have bathhouses and snack bars. Swimming or not, watch out for greenhead flies in July and August. They don't sting—they take little bites of flesh. Bring or buy insect repellent.

The best-known North Shore beach is **Singing Beach ★★**, off Masconomo Street in Manchester-by-the-Sea. Because it's easily accessible by public transportation, it attracts the most diverse crowd—carless singles, local families, and other beach bunnies of all ages. They walk ½ mile on Beach Street from the train station to find sparkling sand and lively surf. Take the commuter rail (*✆* **617/222-3200;** www.mbta.com) from Boston's North Station.

Nearly as famous and popular is **Crane Beach ★**, off Argilla Road in Ipswich, part of a 1,400-acre barrier beach reservation. Fragile dunes and a white-sand beach lead down to Ipswich Bay. The surf is calmer than that at less sheltered Singing Beach, and quite chilly. Pick up Argilla Road south of Ipswich Center near the intersection of Routes 1A and 133, or take the Cape Ann Transportation Authority's summer-only, weekend-and-holidays-only **Ipswich Essex Explorer** bus service (*✆* **978/283-7916** or 978/356-8540; www.ipswichessexexplorer.com) from the Ipswich train station. Also on Ipswich Bay is Gloucester's **Wingaersheek Beach ★**, on Atlantic Street off Route 133. It has its own exit (no. 13) off Route 128, about 15 minutes away on winding roads with low speed limits. When you finally arrive, you'll find beautiful white sand, a glorious view, and more dunes. Because these beaches are harder to get to, they attract more locals—but also lots of day-tripping families. At the east end of Route 133, the beaches and snack bar in Gloucester's easily accessible **Stage Fort Park** are popular local hangouts.

renovated in 2008, has sliding glass doors that open onto a balcony or patio, and a king bed or two double beds. Second-floor rooms have slightly better views. A colonial revival mansion built in 1899 and known as the "wedding-cake house" holds a handful of one-bedroom suites and the public areas, including a billiard room and a library. In the afternoon, the staff serves coffee, tea, lemonade, and chocolate-chip cookies.

107 Atlantic Rd., Gloucester, MA 01930. www.bassrocksoceaninn.com. *✆* **888/802-7666** or 978/283-7600. Fax 978/281-6489. 51 units. Summer $249–$350 double, $450 suite; spring and fall $169–$249 double, $300–$350 suite. Extra person $10. Children 12 and under stay free in parent's room. Rollaway or crib $12. Rates include continental breakfast, afternoon refreshments, and use of bikes. Minimum 3-night stay summer weekends, some spring and fall weekends. AAA and AARP discounts available. AE, DC, DISC, MC, V. Closed Nov–late Apr. Follow Rte. 128 to the end (exit 9, East Gloucester), turn left onto Bass Ave. (Rte. 127A), and follow it ½ mile. Turn right and follow Atlantic Rd. **Amenities:** Heated outdoor pool. *In room:* A/C, TV/DVD, fridge, hair dryer, Wi-Fi (free).

WHERE TO EAT

See "A Detour to Essex," on p. 313, for information about the celebrated **Woodman's of Essex,** which is about 20 minutes from downtown Gloucester. The Stage Fort Park snack bar, the **Cupboard,** 41 Hough Ave. (© **978/281-1908**), serves excellent fried seafood and blue-plate specials in the summer. **Lobsta Land,** 10 Causeway St., near exit 12 off Route 128 (© **978/281-0415**), is a summer-only destination for familiar and unusual seafood dishes deftly prepared and served in a friendly atmosphere that belies the location, just off the busy highway. If you're in town just for a day, consider sticking around for dinner at the **Franklin Cape Ann,** 118 Main St. (© **978/283-7888;** www. franklincafe.com). It serves excellent bistro cuisine daily from 5pm to midnight (but unfortunately not at lunch).

Halibut Point Restaurant & Bar ★ SEAFOOD/AMERICAN A local legend for its chowders and burgers, Halibut Point is a friendly tavern that serves generous portions of good food. The "Halibut Point Special"—a cup of chowder, a burger, and a beer—hits the high points. The clam chowder is terrific, and the spicy Italian fish chowder is so good that some people come to Gloucester just for that. There's also a raw bar. Main courses are simple (mostly sandwiches) at lunch and more elaborate at dinner. Be sure to check the specials board—you didn't come all this way to a fishing port not to have fresh fish, did you?

289 Main St. © **978/281-1900.** www.halibutpoint.com. Main courses $7–$14 at lunch, $11–$20 at dinner. AE, DISC, MC, V. Daily 11:30am–11pm.

Latitude 43 Restaurant & Bar ★ SEAFOOD/CREATIVE AMERICAN/ SUSHI A harborfront location is sometimes a red flag—a popular myth says water views make up for other deficiencies—but here the view just adds to the funky, laid-back atmosphere. Popular year-round (which means the picky locals eat here, too), "Lat 43" offers something for everyone. Clam and fish chowder, greaseless fried seafood, and tasty burgers and lobster rolls are terrific renditions of perennial favorites. More sophisticated dishes include salads overflowing with local produce, bistro favorites such as braised lamb shank, or excellent paella. You can even get sushi, an option inexplicably absent in many New England seaports. There's seating on the pleasant deck in good weather, and the staff can point out notable features of the certified-green building.

25 Rogers St. (½ block from Washington St.). © **978/281-0223.** www.latfortythree.com. Reservations recommended at dinner. Main courses $7–$16 at lunch, $17–$25 at dinner; lobster market price. AE, DISC, MC, V. Sun–Thurs 11:30am–9pm, Fri–Sat 11:30am–10pm. Pub open until 1am (food served until midnight) daily. From intersection of Rogers and Main sts. (just north of downtown), follow Main St. south ½ mile; Duncan St. is on left.

Rockport

40 miles NE of Boston, 7 miles N of Gloucester

This lovely little town at the tip of Cape Ann was settled in 1690. Over the years it has been an active fishing port, a center of granite excavation and cutting, and a thriving summer community whose specialty appears to be selling fudge and refrigerator magnets to out-of-towners. Rockport is an entertaining half-day trip, perhaps combined with a visit to Gloucester.

There's more to Rockport than just gift shops. It's home to a lovely state park, and it's popular with photographers, painters, jewelry designers, and

Motif No. 1 is the most frequently painted and photographed object in Rockport.

sculptors. Winslow Homer, Fitz Henry Lane, and Childe Hassam are among the famous artists who have captured the local color. At times, especially on summer weekends, you'll be hard-pressed to find much local color in this tourist-weary destination. But for every year-round resident who seems startled when legions of camera-wielding visitors descend on Rockport each June, there are dozens who are proud to show off their beautiful town.

Out of season, especially January through mid-April, Rockport is pretty but somewhat desolate. The year-round population is large enough that some businesses stay open, though many keep reduced hours.

ESSENTIALS

GETTING THERE Rockport is north of Gloucester along Route 127 or 127A. At the end of Route 128, turn left at the signs for Rockport to take Route 127, which is shorter but more commercial. To take Route 127A, which runs near the east coast of Cape Ann, continue on Route 128 until you see the sign for East Gloucester and turn left. Parking is tough, especially on summer Saturday afternoons, but metered spots are available throughout downtown. Make one loop around downtown and then head to the free parking lot on Upper Main Street (Rte. 127). The shuttle bus to or from downtown costs $1.

The **commuter rail** (© 617/222-3200; www.mbta.com) runs from Boston's North Station. The trip takes 60 to 70 minutes, and the round-trip fare is $16. The station is about 6 blocks from the downtown waterfront. The **Cape Ann Transportation Authority,** or CATA (© 978/283-7916; www.canntran.com), runs buses from town to town on Cape Ann Monday through Saturday.

ATTRACTIONS
Halibut Point State Park **2**
Motif No. 1 **14**
Paper House **4**
Rockport Art Association **10**

HOTELS
Captain's Bounty
  on the Beach **6**
Emerson Inn by the Sea **3**
Inn on Cove Hill (Caleb
  Norwood Jr. House) **15**

RESTAURANTS
Helmut's Strudel **13**
The Lobster Pool **1**
Roy Moore Lobster
  Company **12**

SHOPPING
Crackerjacks **5**
Tidal Edge Gallery **9**
Toad Hall Bookstore **7**
Tuck's Candy Factory **11**
Willoughby's **8**

ATLANTIC OCEAN

0   1/2 mi
0   1/2 km

Rockport

VISITOR INFORMATION The **Rockport Chamber of Commerce,** 170 Main St. (✆ **978/546-6575;** www.rockportusa.com), is a division of the Cape Ann Chamber of Commerce (✆ **978/283-1601;** www.capeannvacations. com; see "Gloucester," earlier in this chapter). The chamber operates an information booth on Upper Main Street (Rte. 127) daily from July 1 through Labor Day and on weekends from mid-May to June and early September through mid-October. It's about a mile from the town line and a mile from downtown—look for the WELCOME TO ROCKPORT sign on the right as you head north. Ask for the pamphlet *Rockport: A Walking Guide,* which contains a good map and descriptions of three short walking tours.

SPECIAL EVENTS Rockport Music organizes the **Rockport Chamber Music Festival** (✆ **978/546-7391;** www.rcmf.org), which takes place each June. It's a good excuse to see the town before the height of tourist season. In addition to performances by promising young musicians and family-oriented concerts (tickets $20–$35), events include free lectures and discussions. Performances take place in the lovely **Shalin Liu Performance Center,** 37 Main St., which opened in 2010 to great acclaim. Check ahead for the schedule of events in the 330-seat concert hall, noted for the 2-story window overlooking the water at the back of the stage.

The annual **Christmas pageant,** on Main Street in December, is a crowded, kid-friendly event with carol singing and live animals.

EXPLORING THE TOWN

The most famous sight in Rockport has something of an "Emperor's New Clothes" aura—it's a wooden fish warehouse on the town wharf, or T-Wharf, in the harbor. The barn-red shack known as **Motif No. 1** is the most frequently painted and photographed object in a town filled with lovely buildings and surrounded by breathtaking rocky coastline. The color certainly catches the eye against the neutrals of the seascape, but you might find yourself wondering what the big deal is. Originally constructed in 1884 and destroyed during the blizzard of 1978, Motif No. 1 was rebuilt using donations from residents and tourists. It stands on the same pier as the original, duplicated in every detail and reinforced to withstand storms.

Nearby is a phenomenon whose popularity is easier to explain. **Bearskin Neck,** named after an unfortunate ursine visitor who drowned and washed ashore in 1800, has perhaps the highest concentration of gift shops anywhere. It's a narrow peninsula with one main street (South Rd.) and several alleys crammed with galleries, snack bars, antiques shops, and ancient houses. The peninsula ends in a plaza with a magnificent water view.

Throughout the town, more than two dozen **art galleries ★** display the works of local and nationally known artists. The **Rockport Art Association,** 12 Main St. (© **978/546-6604;** www.rockportartassn.org), sponsors major exhibitions and special shows. It's open daily mid-morning to late afternoon in the summer (except on Sun, when it opens at noon); in the winter, it's open Wednesday through Saturday 10am to 4 or 5pm, and Sunday noon to 5pm.

To get a sense of the power of the sea, take Route 127 north of town to the tip of Cape Ann. Turn right on Gott Avenue to reach **Halibut Point State**

Nature lovers should set aside time for a visit to Halibut Point State Park.

Bearskin Neck is home to a number of fun and funky shops.

Park ★★ (☏ **978/546-2997**; www.mass.gov/dcr and www.thetrustees.org). The park is a great place to wander around and admire the gorgeous scenery. On a clear day, you can see Maine. It has a staffed visitor center, walking trails, and tidal pools. Swimming in the water-filled quarries is absolutely forbidden. You can climb around on giant boulders on the rocky beach or climb to the top of the World War II observation tower. To take a self-guided tour, pick up a brochure at the visitor center or the chamber of commerce. Check ahead for information about talks, tours, demonstrations, and other special programs; a good resource is the park **blog** (www.halibutpoint.wordpress.com). The park is open daily from Memorial Day to Labor Day 8am to 8pm, otherwise daily dawn to dusk; parking costs $2 from Memorial Day to Columbus Day.

A genuinely wacky attraction between downtown and Halibut Point is the **Paper House,** 52 Pigeon Hill St., Pigeon Cove (☏ **978/546-2629**; www.paper houserockport.com). It was built beginning in 1922 entirely out of 100,000 newspapers—walls, furniture, even a newspaper-covered piano. Creator Elis Stenman made every item from papers of a different period. The house is open April through October daily from 10am to 5pm (closed Nov–Mar). Admission is $1.50 for adults, $1 for children 6 to 14. Follow Route 127 north out of downtown about 1½ miles, watching carefully until you see signs at Curtis Street pointing to the left, then go left on Pigeon Hill Street.

SHOPPING

Bearskin Neck is the obvious place to start. Dozens of little shops stock clothes, gifts, toys, jewelry, souvenirs, inexpensive novelties, and expensive handmade crafts and paintings. Another enjoyable stroll is along **Main** and **Mount**

Pleasant streets. Good stops include the nonprofit **Toad Hall Bookstore,** 47 Main St. (☎ **978/546-7323;** www.toadhallbooks.org); **Tidal Edge Gallery,** 3 School St., off Main Street (☎ **978/546-3196;** www.tidaledgegallery.com); and **Willoughby's,** 20 Main St. (☎ **978/546-9820**), a women's clothing and accessories shop.

Two of my favorite stops are retro delights. Downtown, you can watch taffy being made at **Tuck's Candy Factory,** 7 Dock Sq. (☎ **800/569-2767** or 978/546-6352; www.tuckscandy.com), a local landmark that opened in 1929. There's a retail location at 15 Main St. Near the train station, **Crackerjacks,** 27 Whistlestop Mall, off Railroad Avenue (☎ **978/546-1616**), is an old-fashioned variety store with a great crafts department.

WHERE TO STAY

When Rockport is busy, it's very busy, and when it's not, it's practically empty. The town's dozens of B&Bs fill in good weather and empty or even close in the winter. Make summer reservations well in advance or cross your fingers and call the Chamber of Commerce (p. 323) to ask about availability.

Two miles from downtown, the **Emerson Inn by the Sea,** 1 Cathedral Ave. (☎ **800/964-5550** or 978/546-6321; www.emersoninnbythesea.com), is a miniresort with sweet views of the Atlantic and the rocky shore. Open year-round; rates for a double in high season run $159 to $379, which includes breakfast and Wi-Fi.

If you're traveling by train, call ahead to request pick-up at the Rockport station, which most lodgings in town offer at no charge.

Captain's Bounty on the Beach This modern, well-maintained motor inn occupies a great location right on the beach, and is nearly as close to the center of town as to the harbor. Each room in the three-story building overlooks the water and has its own balcony and sliding glass door. Rooms are spacious and soundproofed, with good cross-ventilation but no air-conditioning. Each has a microwave and fridge in case you want to eat some meals in; kitchenette units are available. The best rooms are on the adults-only top floor. Although it's hardly plush, the staff is welcoming and the location unbeatable. All rooms and decks are nonsmoking.

1 Beach St., Rockport, MA 01966. www.captainsbountymotorinn.com. ☎ **978/546-9557.** Fax 978/546-9993. 24 units. Mid-June to mid-Sept $170 double, $180 efficiency, $210 efficiency suite; spring and fall $1400 double, $145 efficiency, $160 efficiency suite. Extra adult $10; $5 for each child. 2-night minimum stay weekends, 3-night stay holiday weekends. MC, V. Closed Nov–Mar. Pets accepted ($10/night). *In room:* TV/DVD, fridge, Wi-Fi (free).

Inn on Cove Hill (Caleb Norwood Jr. House) ★ This attractive Federal-style inn is just 2 blocks from the town wharf, but the building is set back from the street and has a delightful hideaway feel. The 1771 home was built using the proceeds of pirates' gold found nearby. Innkeeper Betsy Eck overhauls one guest room each winter, decorating them in exquisite period style; most have colonial furnishings and handmade quilts, and some have canopy beds. Water views from the windows and good-size decks at the back of the house are worth the climb to the third floor. The generous breakfast is served in the dining room or, in good weather, in the pleasant garden. Guests have the use of a phone in the living room. A harbor-view apartment across the street is available for long-term (1 week or more) stays.

37 Mount Pleasant St., Rockport, MA 01966. www.innoncovehill.com. ℂ **888/546-2701** or 978/546-2701. Fax 978/546-1095. 6 units, some with shower only. $145–$165 double; $250 suite. Extra person $25. Rates include continental breakfast. 2-night minimum stay mid-May to mid-Oct and most weekends. MC, V. *In room:* A/C, TV, no phone.

WHERE TO EAT

Depending on seasonal business is challenging enough, but Rockport has another drawback: The town was "dry" until 2005. The dining scene, consequently, isn't nearly as varied or sophisticated as Gloucester's; if you're not ravenous, head there or to **Woodman's of Essex** (p. 313).

My top suggestion for food comes from the "would be an insider tip if it weren't so crowded" file. The **Roy Moore Lobster Company ★★**, 39 Bearskin Neck (ℂ **978/546-6696**), is a fish market that specializes in ultra-fresh lobster cooked in seawater and served with drawn butter and plenty of paper towels. The luscious crustaceans and a limited selection of other dishes (including clam chowder) are available to stay or go. Prices are exceptionally reasonable, thanks in part to the lack of atmosphere—the small dining area is outdoors, and drinks come from the soda machine—and the service at the counter is efficient and friendly. Roy Moore's is open daily from 11am until 6pm from late March through October.

Another seasonal favorite is the **Lobster Pool,** a classic clam shack at 329 Granite St. (ℂ **978/546-7808;** www.lobsterpoolrestaurant.com). Follow Route 127 north along the peninsula past Halibut Point State Park to this family-run self-service restaurant with picnic tables, spectacular water views, and huge weekend crowds. It serves seafood "in the rough" as well as soup, salads, sandwiches, and homemade desserts. It's open from April through November, daily from 11:30am to 8:30pm.

Helmut's Strudel, 49 Bearskin Neck (ℂ **978/546-2824**), is known for its apple and cherry strudels—served warm and a la mode if you like. Helmut's offers a variety of other pastries and a good selection of beverages, including apple cider, hot chocolate, and freshly squeezed orange juice. The outdoor seating area enjoys a great view of the harbor. No credit cards.

PLYMOUTH ★★

45 miles SE of Boston

Everyone educated in the United States knows at least a little of the story of Plymouth—about how the Pilgrims, fleeing religious persecution, left Europe on the *Mayflower* and landed at Plymouth Rock in December 1620. Many also know that the Pilgrims endured disease and privation, and that just 53 people from the original group of 102 celebrated what we now call "the first Thanksgiving" in 1621 with Squanto, a Pawtuxet Indian associated with the Wampanoag people, and his cohorts.

What you won't know until you visit is how small everything was. The *Mayflower* (a reproduction) seems perilously tiny, and when you contemplate how dangerous life was at the time, it's hard not to marvel at the settlers' accomplishments. One of their descendants' accomplishments is this: Plymouth is in many ways a model destination, where the 17th century coexists with the 21st, and most historic attractions are both educational and fun. Visitors jam the downtown area and waterfront in the summer, but the year-round population of

60,000 is large enough that Plymouth feels more like the working community it is than like a touristy day-trip destination. It's a manageable 1-day excursion from Boston, particularly enjoyable if you're traveling with children. It also makes a good stop between Boston and Cape Cod.

Essentials

GETTING THERE By car, follow the Southeast Expressway (I-93) south from Boston to Route 3. Take exit 6A and then Route 44 east and follow signs to the historic attractions. The trip from Boston takes 45 to 60 minutes if it's not rush hour. Take exit 5 to the **Regional Information Complex** for maps, brochures, and information. To go directly to **Plimoth Plantation,** take exit 4. There's metered parking throughout town.

The **commuter rail** (✆ 617/222-3200; www.mbta.com) serves Cordage Park, on Route 3A north of downtown, from Boston's South Station four times a day on weekdays and three times a day on weekends (at other times, service is to nearby Kingston). The round-trip fare is $16. Plymouth and Brockton **buses** (✆ 508/746-0378; www.p-b.com) take about an hour from South Station. They run more often than the train, but they cost more ($14 one-way, $25 round-trip) and drop off and pick up passengers at the park-and-ride lot at Route 3, exit 5. The **Plymouth Area Link** bus (✆ 800/483-2500 or 508/747-1819; www.gatra.org/pal.html) connects downtown with the train station and park-and-ride lot. The fare is $1, free for children under 7.

VISITOR INFORMATION If you haven't visited the Regional Information Complex (above), pick up a map at the **Visitor Information Center** (✆ 508/747-7525), open seasonally at 130 Water St., across from Town Pier. To plan ahead, contact **Destination Plymouth,** 134 Court St., Plymouth, MA 02360 (✆ 800/872-1620 or 508/747-7533; www.visit-plymouth.com), and request information. The **Plymouth County Convention & Visitors Bureau** (✆ 800/231-1620 or 508/747-0100; www.seeplymouth.com), at the same address, publishes a vacation planner and other brochures.

GETTING AROUND The downtown attractions are easily accessible on foot. A shallow hill slopes from the center of town to the waterfront.

THE Adams FAMILY

A worthwhile detour en route to Plymouth is the **Adams National Historical Park** in Quincy, about 10 miles south of Boston. The park preserves the birthplaces of presidents John Adams and John Quincy Adams, the house where four generations of the family lived, and other buildings associated with the political dynasty. A trolley connects the buildings, which are open for 2-hour guided tours—the only way to see the interiors—daily from 9am to 5pm in season (Apr 19–Nov 10). Admission is $5 for adults, free for children 15 and under. The grounds and the visitor center, 1250 Hancock St. (✆ 617/770-1175; www.nps.gov/adam), are open in the winter Wednesday through Friday 10am to 4pm. The center is across the street from the Quincy Center stop on the Red Line; call or surf ahead for driving directions.

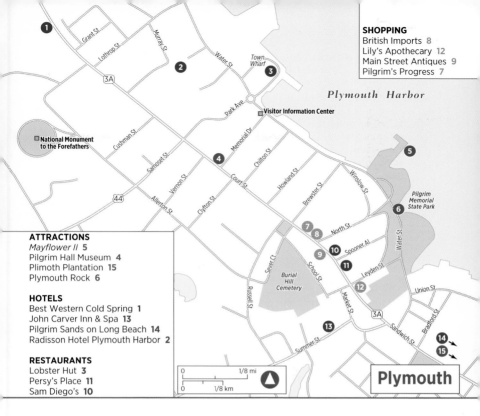

America's Hometown Shuttle (✆ 508/746-0378; www.p-b.com/ ahs.html) covers a loop throughout the town from late June through Labor Day weekend, daily from 10am to 5pm. The fare ($15 adults, $7.50 children 5–11) includes a narrated tour and unlimited reboarding. Check ahead for the schedule and route, which includes Plimoth Plantation.

Seeing the Sights

The logical place to begin (good luck talking children out of it) is where the Pilgrims first set foot—at **Plymouth Rock ★★**. The rock, accepted as the landing place of the *Mayflower* passengers, was originally 15 feet long and 3 feet wide. It was moved on the eve of the Revolution and several times thereafter. In 1867, it assumed its present permanent position at tide level. The rock itself isn't much to look at, but the accompanying descriptions are interesting, and the atmosphere is curiously inspiring.

The Colonial Dames of America commissioned the portico around the rock, designed by McKim, Mead & White and erected in 1920. This property's formal name is **Pilgrim Memorial State Park** (✆ 508/747-5360; www.mass.gov/ dcr); it's the smallest state park in Massachusetts.

The park just south of the Rock is **Brewster Gardens,** a lovely green space that traces Town Brook. This is a good shortcut to **Jenney Pond,** in Town Brook Park, across Summer Street from the John Carver Inn. A short distance from the bustle of the waterfront, the park has plenty of room to run around as well as a pond where ducks and geese live.

GUIDED TOURS To walk in the Pilgrims' footsteps, take a **Colonial Lantern Tour** ★ (✆ **774/454-8126;** www.lanterntours.com). Participants carry pierced-tin lanterns on a 90-minute walking tour of the original settlement, conducted by a knowledgeable guide. It might seem a bit hokey at first, but it's fascinating. Tours run nightly from April to Thanksgiving, rain or shine. The standard history tour begins at 7:30pm, the "Ghosts & Legends" tour at 8pm. Tickets are $12 for adults; $10 for seniors, AAA members, and children 6 to 16; free for children 5 and under. Check the meeting place when you make reservations. The company also offers special tours for Halloween and Thanksgiving.

Narrated cruises run from April through November from

Seeing Plymouth Rock in person is a moving experience.

Brewster Gardens is a lovely bit of greenery near the harbor.

State Pier and Town Wharf; check the departure point when you make reservations, which are always recommended and imperative at busy times. **Pilgrim Belle Cruises** (✆ **508/474-3434;** www.pilgrimbellecruises. com) offers 75-minute narrated **harbor tours** on a paddle wheeler ($17 adults, $15 seniors, $12 children 2–12) as well as sunset and dining cruises. **Lobster Tales** (✆ **508/746-5342;** www.lobstertalesinc.com) organizes **pirate cruises** ($18 per person), which allow kids aged 4 to 11 to don hats and face paint and "defend" the boat against marauding buccaneers, and **lobster excursions** ($16 adults, $14 seniors, $12 children 11 and under), which give passengers the chance to haul up traps and observe marine life. **Capt. John Boats** (✆ **800/242-2469** or 508/746-2643; www.captjohn. com) offers **whale watches** ($40 adults, $34 seniors, $28 children 4–12).

Mayflower II ★ ☺ Berthed a few steps from Plymouth Rock, the *Mayflower II* is a full-scale reproduction of the type of ship that brought the Pilgrims from England to America in 1620. Even at full scale, the 106½-foot vessel, constructed in England from 1955 to 1957, is remarkably small. Although little technical information about the original *Mayflower* survives, designer William A. Baker incorporated the few references in Governor Bradford's account of the voyage with other research to re-create the ship as authentically as possible.

Costumed guides provide interesting first-person narratives about the vessel and voyage, and other interpreters provide a contemporary perspective. Displays describe and illustrate the journey and the Pilgrims' experience, and include exhibits about 17th-century navigation techniques, stocking the ship with food and other provisions, and the history of the *Mayflower II.* Plimoth Plantation (below) owns and maintains the vessel and offers combined admission discounts. Alongside the ship are museum shops that replicate early Pilgrim dwellings.

Visitors are often surprised by just how small the Mayflower II is.

State Pier. ☏ **508/746-1622.** www.plimoth.org. Admission $10 adults, $9 seniors, $7 children 6–12. Plimoth Plantation (good for 2 consecutive days) and *Mayflower II* admission $30 adults, $26 seniors and students, $19 children 6–12, $110 families (2 adults and up to 4 children 6–17; not available online). Free for children under 6. Late Mar to late Nov daily 9am–5pm. Closed Dec to mid-Mar.

Pilgrim Hall Museum ★ ☺ This is a great place to get a sense of the day-to-day lives of Plymouth's first European residents. Many original possessions of the early Pilgrims and their descendants are on display, including one of Myles Standish's swords, Governor Bradford's Bible, and an uncomfortable chair (you can sit in a replica) that belonged to William Brewster. Regularly changing exhibits explore aspects of the settlers' lives, such as the immigrant experience or children's embroidery, and hands-on activities such as treasure hunts get families interested. Built in 1824, the Pilgrim Hall Museum is the oldest public museum in the United States.

75 Court St. ☏ **508/746-1620.** www.pilgrimhall.org. Admission $8 adults, $7 seniors, $6 AAA members, $5 children 6–15, $25 families. Feb–Dec daily 9:30am–4:30pm. Closed Jan, Dec 25. From Plymouth Rock, walk north on Water St. and up the hill on Chilton St.

Plimoth Plantation ★★ ☺ Allow at least half a day to explore this re-creation of the 1627 English village, which children and adults find equally interesting. Enter by the hilltop fort that protected the village and walk down to the farm area, visiting homes and gardens along the way. Although the experience can be a bit disorienting at first, talking to the "Pilgrims" is great fun. They're actors who, in speech, dress, and manner, assume the personalities of members of the original community. You can watch them framing a house, splitting wood, shearing sheep, preserving foodstuffs, or cooking a pot of fish stew over an open hearth, all

The Pilgrim Hall Museum contains numerous artifacts ranging from the mundane to the military.

Plimoth Plantation provides modern visitors with a glimpse into the lives of the early settlers.

as it was done in the 1600s and using only the tools and cookware available then. Sometimes you can join the activities—perhaps planting, harvesting, witnessing a trial, or visiting a wedding party. *Note:* Wear comfortable shoes, because you'll be walking a lot.

The plantation is as accurate as research can make it, constructed with careful attention to historical detail. The planners combined accounts of the original colony with archaeological research, old records, and the history written by the Pilgrims' leader, William Bradford (who often used the spelling "Plimoth"). There are daily militia drills with matchlock muskets that are fired to demonstrate the community's defense system. In fact, little defense was needed, because the Native Americans were friendly. Local tribes included the Wampanoags, who are represented near the village at a replica of a homesite (included in plantation admission), where staff members show off native foodstuffs, agricultural practices, and crafts.

At the main entrance are two modern buildings that house exhibits, a gift shop, a bookstore, a cafeteria, and an auditorium where visitors can view a film produced by the History Channel. There's also a picnic area. Call or surf ahead for information about the numerous special events, lectures, tours, workshops, theme dinners, and children's and family programs offered throughout the season.

137 Warren Ave. (Rte. 3). © **508/746-1622.** www.plimoth.org. Admission (good for 2 consecutive days) $26 adults, $22 seniors, $15 children 6–12. Plimoth Plantation and *Mayflower II* admission $30 adults, $26 seniors and students, $19 children 6–12, $110 families (2 adults and up to 4 children 6–17; not available online). Free for children 5 and under. Late Mar to late Nov daily 9am–5pm. Closed Dec to mid-Mar. From Rte. 3, take exit 4, Plimoth Plantation Hwy.

Shopping

Water Street, along the harbor, boasts an inexhaustible supply of souvenir shops. A less kitschy destination, just up the hill, is Route 3A, known as Court, Main, and Warren Street as it runs through town. **Lily's Apothecary,** 6 Main St. extension, in the old post office (© **508/747-7546;** www.lilysapothecary. com), stocks a big-city-style selection of skin- and hair-care products for women and men. Closed Sunday and Monday except by appointment. **Main Street Antiques,** 46 Main St. (© **508/747-8887**), is home to dozens of dealers, and **Pilgrim's Progress,** 13 Court St. (© **508/746-6033;** www.pilgrimsprogress clothing.com), carries stylish women's and men's clothing and accessories. After a stop in **British Imports,** 1 Court St. (© **877/264-8586** or 508/747-2972; www.britishsupplies.com), which attracts homesick Marmite fans from miles around, you'll be able to write your own English food joke.

Where to Stay

On busy summer weekends, it's not unusual for every room in town to sell out. Make reservations well in advance. Whenever you travel, don't book a room without checking for special packages and offers.

The **Radisson Hotel Plymouth Harbor,** 180 Water St. (© **800/395-7046** or 508/747-4900; www.radisson.com/plymouthma), is the only chain hotel downtown. The 175-unit hotel, on a hill across the street from the waterfront, offers all the usual chain amenities, including a swimming pool in the atrium lobby. Doubles in high season start at $159, which includes wireless Internet. The **Hilton Garden Inn,** 4 Home Depot Dr. (© **877/782-9444** or 508/830-0200; www.hiltongardeninn.com), is at Route 3 exit 5, about 10 minutes from downtown. The hotel has an exercise room, an indoor pool, and extensive business features; doubles in high season go for $135 and up, which includes wireless Internet.

Best Western Cold Spring ★★ ✒ The Cold Spring and its adjacent cottages surround landscaped lawns in a mostly residential neighborhood that makes a pleasant retreat from downtown's bustle. Rooms are attractively decorated and big enough for a family to spread out in; if the adults want some privacy, book a two-bedroom cottage. The fastidiously maintained property has a good-size outdoor pool. I especially like the location, which is both quiet and convenient. The tolerable distance from the water is what makes the Cold Spring a good deal. The two-story complex is 1 long block inland, set back from the street.

188 Court St. (Rte. 3A), Plymouth, MA 02360. www.bwcoldspring.com. © **800/678-8667** or 508/746-2222. Fax 508/746-2744. 58 units, 10 with shower only, 2 2-bedroom cottages. Mar–Nov $99–$169 double; $139–$199 suite; $109–$159 cottage. Extra person $10. Rollaway $10, crib $5. Children 11 and under stay free in parent's room. Rates include continental breakfast buffet. Packages and AAA and off-season discounts available. AE, DC, DISC, MC, V. Closed Dec–Feb. Pets accepted ($10 fee). **Amenities:** Outdoor pool. *In room:* A/C, TV, hair dryer, Wi-Fi.

John Carver Inn & Spa ☺ This centrally located hotel offers comfortable, modern accommodations and amenities, including a full-service spa, that appeal to both business and leisure travelers. The indoor "theme pool," a big hit with families, has a water slide and a Pilgrim ship model. The good-size guest rooms are regularly renovated and decorated in colonial style. The best units are lavishly appointed two-room suites, with fireplaces and private Jacuzzis; I like the "four-poster" rooms, which have king beds. A three-story colonial-style building with a landmark portico, the inn is on the edge of the downtown business district, within walking distance of the main attractions. Business features and meeting space make this hotel the Radisson's main competition for corporate business. Always check ahead for packages, which can be a great deal.

25 Summer St., Plymouth, MA 02360. www.johncarverinn.com. ✆ **800/274-1620** or 508/746-7100. Fax 508/746-8299. 80 units. Early Apr to mid-June and mid-Oct to Nov $119–$219 double, $259–$299 suite; mid-June to mid-Oct $159–$249 double, $299–$329 suite; Dec to early Apr $109–$199 double, $239–$279 suite. Extra person $20. Rollaway $20; cribs free. Children 18 and under stay free in parent's room. Packages and senior and AAA discounts available. AE, DC, DISC, MC, V. **Amenities:** Restaurant (American/seafood); concierge; fitness center; Jacuzzi; indoor pool; room service. *In room:* A/C, TV w/pay movies, hair dryer, Wi-Fi (free).

Pilgrim Sands on Long Beach ★★ ☺ This attractive motel sits directly on its own beach 3 miles south of town, within walking distance of Plimoth Plantation. An excellent choice if you want to avoid busy downtown area, the well-maintained, regularly updated property also has indoor and outdoor pools. The good-size guest rooms are tastefully furnished and well maintained; most have two double or queen beds. The helpful staff and amenities make the Pilgrim Sands popular with business travelers as well as vacationers. In the afternoon, the breakfast room becomes the lounge, a local hangout with indoor and outdoor seating. If you can swing it, book a beachfront room—the view is worth the money, especially when the surf is rough.

150 Warren Ave. (Rte. 3A), Plymouth, MA 02360. www.pilgrimsands.com. ✆ **800/729-7263** or 508/747-0900. Fax 508/746-8066. 64 units. Summer $155–$195 double; spring and early fall $114–$169 double; Apr and late fall $94–$134 double; Dec–Mar $84–$99 double. $159–$309 suite year-round. Extra person $6–$8 (suite $10–$15). Up to 2 children 6 and under stay free in parent's room. Rates include continental breakfast. Minimum 2-night stay holiday weekends. Rates may be higher on holiday weekends. AE, DC, DISC, MC, V. **Amenities:** Coffee shop and lounge (daily until 10pm); Jacuzzi; indoor and outdoor pools. *In room:* A/C, TV, fridge, hair dryer, Wi-Fi (free).

Where to Eat

Plimoth Plantation (p. 332) has a cafeteria and a picnic area, and occasionally schedules theme dinners. Should you happen to reach the "seafood again?" stage (it happens), a good destination downtown is **Sam Diego's,** 15 Main St. (✆ **508/747-0048;** www.samdiegos.com), a cheerful Tex-Mex restaurant and bar in a renovated firehouse. It serves tasty renditions of exactly what you'd expect and offers a kids' menu and seasonal outdoor seating. Hours are 11:30am to midnight daily. **Kiskadee Coffee Company,** 18 Main St. (✆ **508/830-1410;** www.kiskadeecoffee.com), is a wonderful place to start the day or to stop in for a snack and a caffeine boost.

Lobster Hut ★ SEAFOOD A busy self-service restaurant with a great view, the Lobster Hut is popular with both sightsers and, despite its touristy location, locals. Order and pick up at the counter, then head out onto the deck overlooking the bay (you can eat indoors, but the patio is nicer). This isn't an elegant place, but the food is ultra-fresh and expertly prepared. To start, try clam chowder or lobster bisque. The seafood rolls (hot dog buns with your choice of filling) are excellent. The many fried seafood options include clams, scallops, shrimp, and haddock. You can also opt for broiled fish and shellfish, burgers, chicken tenders—or lobster, of course. Beer and wine are served, but only with meals.

25 Town Wharf. ✆ **508/746-2270.** Reservations not accepted. Lunch specials (available Mon–Fri until 4pm) $8–$11, main courses $7–$19, sandwiches $3–$11 (most under $8), clams and lobster priced daily. MC, V. Summer daily 11am–9pm; winter daily 11am–7pm. Closed Jan.

Persy's Place AMERICAN Part of a small local chain, Persy's Place is known for its menu, reputedly the largest in New England. Among the breakfast selections, served all day, you'll find the usual suspects, including an extensive selection of pancakes—try Cape Cod style, with cranberries and walnuts, for a taste of local flavor. They're yummy, but the magic here is in throwback dishes like baked beans (yes, for breakfast) and finnan haddie (smoked haddock cooked in cream), and oddities like biscuits and gravy, served Southern-style with sausage gravy or Northern-style with turkey gravy. Oh, and giant omelets. And a dozen variations on eggs Benedict. And crepes. And quiches. And perfectly good lunch food, but that's not why this diner-style restaurant is packed, especially on weekends.

35A Main St. (at Middle St.). ✆ **508/732-9876.** www.persysplace.com. Breakfast items $4–$16, lunch items $6–$16. AE, MC, V. Daily 7am–3pm.

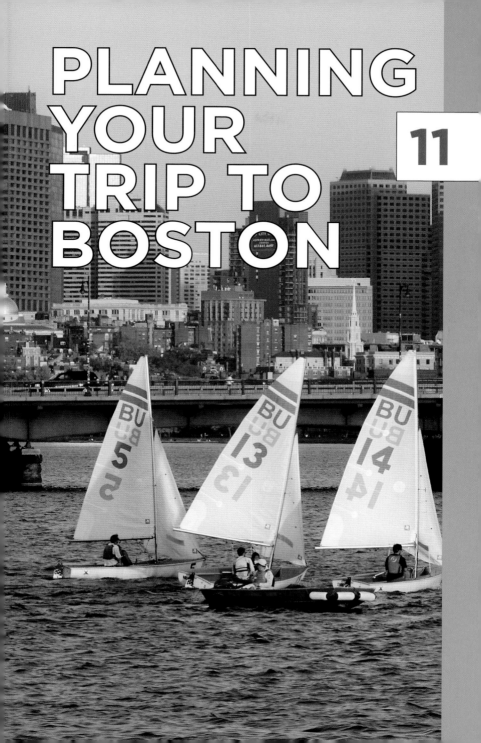

PLANNING YOUR TRIP TO BOSTON

11

A visit to Boston requires as much or as little forethought as you want, taking into account one important general rule: The later you plan, the more you'll pay. That isn't strictly true in the depths of winter, but for the other 44 or so weeks of the year, you'll most likely find yourself balancing spontaneity against thriftiness. This chapter provides a variety of planning tools, including information on how to get there and quick, on-the-ground resources.

GETTING THERE
By Plane

The major domestic airlines serve **Logan International Airport,** which the locals call "Logan" (© **800/235-6426;** www.massport.com/logan; airport code BOS).

Boston is an increasingly popular direct destination for international travelers, although many itineraries from overseas still go through another American or European city. Because of fluctuating demand, international routes and schedules are subject to change; double-check details (especially if you're traveling in the winter) well in advance.

Logan is in East Boston at the end of the Sumner, Callahan, and Ted Williams tunnels, 3 miles across the harbor from downtown. For a preview and real-time flight arrival and departure information, visit the website.

The airport has four terminals—A, B, C, and E (there's no D). Each has ATMs, Internet kiosks, free wireless Internet access, pay phones with dataports, fax machines, and an information booth (near baggage claim). Terminals C and E have bank branches that handle currency exchange. Terminals A and C have children's play spaces.

See the "Let's Make a Deal" box, below, for information on flying into Providence, Rhode Island, and Manchester, New Hampshire.

GETTING INTO TOWN FROM THE AIRPORT

The Massachusetts Port Authority, or **MassPort,** operates Logan Airport and coordinates ground transportation. The toll-free line (© **800/235-6426;** staffed daily 7am–11:55pm) provides information about getting to the city and to many nearby suburbs, and the website (**www.massport.com/logan**) has an application that lets you specify an origin point, destination, and mode or modes of travel, then returns suggestions for getting where you're going.

The trip into town takes 10 to 45 minutes, depending on traffic, your destination, and the time of day. Except at off hours, such as early on weekend mornings, driving is usually the slowest way to reach central Boston. If you must travel

PREVIOUS PAGE: **Boston's skyline viewed from the harbor.**

during rush hours or on Sunday afternoon, allow plenty of extra time or plan to take the subway or water taxi (and pack accordingly).

You can get into town by bus, subway, cab, van, or boat. If you're taking the Silver Line bus or the subway, look for MBTA fare kiosks near the exits closest to the public transit pick-up area in each terminal. Paying your fare before boarding speeds up the trip for everyone.

The Silver Line **bus** stops at each airport terminal and runs directly to South Station, where you can connect to the Red Line subway and the commuter rail to the southern suburbs. It takes about 20 minutes, not including waiting time, and costs just $1.70 (with a pass or CharlieCard) or $2 (with a CharlieTicket or cash)—a great deal if your final destination is near South Station or in Cambridge.

The **subway (the T)** takes just 10 minutes to reach downtown, but first you have to reach the subway. Free **shuttle buses** run from each terminal to the Airport station on the Blue Line of the T from 4am to 1am every day, year-round. The Blue Line stops at Aquarium, State Street, and Government Center, down-town points where you can exit or transfer to the other lines. The fare is $1.70 (with a pass or CharlieCard) or $2 (with a CharlieTicket or cash).

Just getting into a **cab** at the airport costs a whopping $10.10 (don't blame the driver—that's $7.50 in fees plus the initial $2.60 fare). The total fare to downtown or the Back Bay usually runs $20 to $35, and may be as high as $45 in bad traffic. Depending on traffic, the driver might use the Ted Williams Tunnel for destinations outside downtown, such as the Back Bay. On a map, this doesn't look like the fastest route, but often it is.

The Logan Airport website (www.massport.com/logan) lists numerous com-panies that operate **shuttle-van service** to local hotels. One-way prices start at $14 per person and are subject to fuel surcharges as gas prices fluctuate. Reservations are recommended.

The trip to the downtown waterfront in a weather-protected **boat** takes about 7 minutes and costs $10 one-way. Service is available from early morning through early evening, with reduced schedules on weekends; at press time, all four providers operate year-round. The free no. 66 shuttle bus connects the air-port terminals to the Logan ferry dock. Leaving the airport, ask the shuttle driver to radio ahead for water-taxi pickup; on the way back, call ahead for service.

Three on-call water-taxi services serve the downtown waterfront and other points around Boston Harbor: **Boston Harbor Water Taxi** (✆ 617/593-9168; www.bostonharborwatertaxi.com), **City Water Taxi** (✆ 617/422-0392; www.citywatertaxi.com), and **Rowes Wharf Water Transport** (✆ 617/406-8584; www.roweswharfwatertransport.com). The MBTA (✆ 800/392-6100 or 617/222-3200; www.mbta.com) contracts out scheduled ferry service to **Harbor Express** (✆ 617/222-6999; www.harborexpress.com), which runs to Long Wharf, behind the Marriott Long Wharf hotel.

Some hotels have their own **shuttles** or **limousines;** ask about them when you make your reservation. To arrange private limo service, call ahead for a reservation, especially at busy times. Your hotel can recommend a com-pany, or try **Boston Coach** (✆ 800/672-7676; www.bostoncoach.com), **Carey Limousine** (✆ 800/336-4646; www.carey.com), or **Commonwealth Limousine Service** (✆ 800/558-5466 or 617/787-1110; www.commonwealth limo.com). **PlanetTran** (✆ 888/756-8876; www.planettran.com) may be a bit more expensive, but all of its vehicles are hybrids.

LET'S MAKE A deal

Major national carriers serve two airports less than 2 hours from Boston. They're not nearly as convenient as Logan Airport, but fares to either one can be considerably cheaper. For budget-conscious travelers, a quick check can pay off handsomely.

T. F. Green Airport (☎ 888/268-7222; www.pvdairport.com; airport code PVD) is in the Providence, Rhode Island, suburb of Warwick, about 60 miles south of Boston. The **MBTA** commuter rail (☎ 800/392-6100 or 617/222-3200; www.mbta.com) connects the airport station to South Station in Boston; the one-way fare is $8.25. **Peter Pan/ Bonanza** (☎ 800/343-9999; www. peterpanbus.com) buses run to and from Boston; fares are $23 one-way, $42 round-trip. You can also take a cab or the local bus (☎ 401/781-9400; www. ripta.com) to downtown Providence and transfer to **Amtrak** (☎ 800/872-7245; www.amtrak.com). Allow at least 2 hours, and pack light.

Manchester–Boston Regional Airport (☎ 603/624-6556; www. flymanchester.com; airport code MHT) is in southern New Hampshire, about 51 miles north of Boston. **Greyhound** (☎ 800/231-2222; www.greyhound. com) runs buses to Boston's South Station and Logan Airport. The trip takes 60 to 90 minutes; fares start at $19 one-way, $37 round-trip. In addition, **Flight Line** (☎ 800/245-2525; www.flightlineinc.com) operates van service to and from destinations in Massachusetts, including the Sullivan Square Orange Line T stop and suburban Woburn; one-way fares start at $19.

Unless you need it right away, seriously consider waiting to pick up your **rental car** until you're starting a day trip or other excursion. You'll avoid airport fees, tunnel tolls, hotel parking charges, and, most important, Boston traffic.

By Car

Renting a car for a long trip will almost certainly be more expensive and less convenient than any other means of reaching Boston, and I can't recommend it. It's not that driving *to* Boston is difficult. But after you arrive, parking is scarce and wildly expensive, gasoline is pricey, traffic is terrible, and the drivers are famously reckless. If you're thinking of driving to Boston only because you want to use the car to get around town, think again.

If you have to drive, try to book a hotel or a special package that includes parking (see chapter 4). If you pay for parking, expect it to cost at least $30 a day downtown, and build that into your budget.

Three major highways converge in Boston. **I-90,** also known as the Massachusetts Turnpike ("Mass. Pike" to the locals), is an east-west toll road that originates at Logan Airport and links up with the New York State Thruway. **I-93/ U.S. 1** extends north to Canada. **I-93/Route 3,** the Southeast Expressway, connects Boston with the south, including Cape Cod. To avoid driving downtown, exit the Massachusetts Turnpike at Cambridge/Allston or at the Prudential Center in the Back Bay. **I-95** (Massachusetts Rte. 128) is a beltway about 11 miles from downtown that connects Boston to highways in Rhode Island, Connecticut, and New York to the south, and New Hampshire and Maine to the north.

Note: The Massachusetts Turnpike's **FastLane** toll-payment program is compatible with New York's **E-ZPass;** your regular transponder will work in designated lanes in all states that use these systems, including New Hampshire and Maine. If you have a prepaid device from another highway system, check before you leave home to see whether you too can zip (at the speed limit, 15 mph) through the special lanes.

The approaches to Cambridge are **Storrow Drive** and **Memorial Drive,** which run along either side of the Charles River. Storrow Drive has a Harvard Square exit that leads across the Anderson Bridge to John F. Kennedy Street and into the square. Memorial Drive intersects with Kennedy Street; turn away from the bridge to reach the square.

Boston is 218 miles from **New York City;** driving time is about 4½hours. The 992-mile drive from **Chicago** to Boston takes around 21 hours; from **Washington, D.C.,** plan on 8 to 9 hours to cover the 468 miles.

In an emergency, you can call the **State Police** on a cellphone by dialing ©**911.** The **American Automobile Association (AAA; © 800/AAA-HELP** [222-4357]; www.aaa.com) provides members with maps, itineraries, and other travel information, and arranges free towing if you break down. The Massachusetts Turnpike is a privately operated road that arranges its own towing. If you break down there, ask the AAA operator for advice.

It's impossible to say this often enough: When you reach your hotel, **leave your car in the garage** and walk or use public transportation. Use the car for day trips, and before you set out, ask at the front desk for a route that avoids construction (it's everywhere).

If you must drive, or if you decide to rent a car for day tripping, budget for gas, tolls, and parking. International visitors should note that quoted rental-car rates in the U.S. almost never include insurance and taxes. Be sure to ask your rental agency about those additional fees, which can significantly increase your total cost.

For information on car rentals and gasoline (petrol) in Boston, see the "By Car" section under "Getting Around," later in this section. For a map of Boston and the surrounding area, see p. 44.

By Train

Boston has three rail centers: **South Station,** 700 Atlantic Ave. (at Summer St.), near the Waterfront and the Financial District; **Back Bay Station,** 145 Dartmouth St. (btw. Huntington and Columbus aves.), across from the Copley Place mall; and **North Station,** on Causeway Street under the TD Garden arena. **Amtrak** (©**800/872-7245** or 617/482-3660; www.amtrak.com) serves all three, and each is also a stop on the MBTA **subway.** From South Station, you can take the Red Line to Cambridge or to Park Street, the system's hub, where you can make connections to the Green, Blue, and Orange lines. The Orange Line links Back Bay Station and Downtown Crossing, where there's a walkway to Park Street station. North Station is a Green and Orange Line stop.

Amtrak runs to South Station from New York and points south and in between, with stops at Route 128 and Back Bay. Its Downeaster service (www.amtrakdowneaster.com) connects North Station to Portland, Maine, with several stops en route. The MBTA **commuter rail** runs from North Station to Concord, Salem, Gloucester, and Rockport (see chapter 10), among other destinations, and from South Station to points south of Boston, including Plymouth (see chapter 10) and Providence, Rhode Island.

Especially on long trips, the train may not be cheaper than flying. Like the airlines, Amtrak adjusts fares depending on demand, so plan as far ahead as possible to get the lowest fares. Discounts are never available Friday or Sunday afternoon. Always remember to ask for the discounted rate.

Standard service from **New York** takes 4½ to just under 6 hours. High-speed Acela Express service is scheduled to take just over 3 hours. From **Washington, D.C.,** count on a grueling 7½ to 8½ hours for the slowest service, 6 hours for the Acela.

By Bus

The bus is the only way out of many small New England towns. If you're coming from almost anywhere else, consider long-distance bus travel a last resort. The exception is the **New York** route, which is so desirable that numerous operators, including Greyhound and Peter Pan, offer service. It's frequent and relatively fast (4–4½ hr.), and the price is about half the regular train fare.

For bargain-hunters, the trip from South Station to midtown Manhattan can cost as little as $1—if you book at exactly the right moment—on **BoltBus** (✆ 877/865-8287; www.boltbus.com) and **MegaBus** (✆ 877/462-6342; www.megabus.com). Fares top out around $25, subject to fuel-price adjustments, and include on-board Wi-Fi access. Another option is the so-called Chinatown buses; the highest-profile operator is **Fung Wah** (✆ 617/345-8000 or 212/925-8889; www.fungwahbus.com), which connects South Station to Canal Street in New York's Chinatown for about $15 each way.

The bus terminal, formally the **South Station Transportation Center** (✆ 617/737-8040; www.south-station.net), is on Atlantic Avenue next to the train station. The major lines are **Greyhound** (✆ 800/231-2222 or 617/526-1800; www.greyhound.com) and **Peter Pan** (✆ 800/343-9999; www.peterpanbus.com). Other operators include **C & J** (✆ 800/258-7111; www.ridecj.com), **Concord Coach Lines/Dartmouth Coach/Boston Express** (✆ 800/639-3317; www.concordcoachlines.com), and **Plymouth & Brockton** (✆ 508/746-0378; www.p-b.com).

Business-oriented **LimoLiner** (✆ 888/546-5469; www.limoliner.com) service connects the Back Bay Hilton, 40 Dalton St., to the Hilton New York, 1335 Ave. of the Americas (with an on-request stop in Framingham, MA). The luxury coach seats 28 and has Internet access, work tables, leather seats, and an on-board attendant. The one-way fare is $89, with occasional discounts for midweek, advance-purchase, and same-day round-trip travel.

World Wide Bus (✆ 888/457-9967; www.worldwidebus.reachlocal. net) steers clear of Boston traffic. From New York, it serves Riverside station in Newton, which is also a Green Line stop, and Alewife station in Cambridge, the northern terminus of the Red Line. One-way fares start at $15.

By Cruise Ship

Cruise ships arrive at the **Black Falcon Cruise Terminal,** 1 Black Falcon Ave., South Boston (✆ 617/330-1500; www.massport.com). Cabs are easy to find—the drivers know the cruise schedule—and a trolley shuttle operates when ships are in port. The terminal is about a mile from the nearest subway station, South

The T's Fare-Collection System

"Charlie," hero of the Kingston Trio song "Charlie on the MTA," is the face of the T's automated fare-collection system. Passengers store prepaid fares on one of two different reloadable passes: The **CharlieTicket** is heavy paper with a magnetic strip, and the **CharlieCard** is a plastic "smart card" with an embedded chip. What's the difference? (1) Fares are higher if you pay with a CharlieTicket than if you use a CharlieCard; and (2) the CharlieTicket goes into the front of the subway turnstile and pops out of the top (or in and out of the bus fare box), while the CharlieCard registers when you hold it in front of the rectangular reader on the turnstile or fare box.

CharlieTickets are available from the self-service kiosks at the entrance to each subway station and in each terminal at the airport. To get a CharlieCard, ask a T employee, order one in advance, or visit a retail location (check **www. mbta.com** for a list of convenience stores, newsstands, and other outlets). In addition to dispensing CharlieTickets, kiosks allow you to add value onto CharlieTickets and CharlieCards, using cash or a credit or debit card. Consider ordering CharlieCards or CharlieTickets online before you leave home; at press time, shipping is free, and you won't have to buy one immediately upon arriving.

Station; take the Silver Line SL2 bus from the Design Center Place stop if you don't feel like walking. Before heading out, make sure you have the number of a cab company programmed into your phone, and leave plenty of time for the trip back to the dock.

GETTING AROUND
On Foot

If you can manage a fair amount of walking, this is the way to go. You can best appreciate Boston at street level, and walking the narrow, picturesque streets takes you past many gridlocked cars.

Even more than in a typical large city, be alert. Look both ways before crossing, even on one-way streets, where many bicyclists and some drivers blithely go against the flow. The "walk" cycle of many downtown traffic signals lasts only 7 seconds, and a small but significant part of the driving population considers red lights optional anyway. Keep a close eye on the kids, especially in crosswalks. And you're all wearing comfortable shoes, right?

By Public Transportation

The **Massachusetts Bay Transportation Authority,** or MBTA (✆ **800/392-6100** or 617/222-3200; www.mbta.com), is known as "the T," and its logo is the letter T in a circle. It runs subways, trolleys, buses, and ferries in and around Boston and many suburbs, as well as the commuter rail, which extends as far as Providence, Rhode Island. The automated fare-collection system is a bit involved, but getting the hang of it is easy, and T employees who staff every station can answer questions.

For information on services and discounts for seniors and travelers with disabilities, see p. 356.

BY SUBWAY & TROLLEY

Subways and trolleys take you around Boston faster than any mode of transportation other than walking. The oldest system in the country, the T dates to 1897. Although it's generally reliable—the trolleys on the ancient Green Line are the most unpredictable—you should still leave extra time and carry cab fare if you're on the way to a vital appointment, because you may need to bail out and jump into a taxi. The system is generally safe, but always watch out for pickpockets, especially during the holiday shopping season. And remember, downtown stops are so close together that it's often faster to walk.

The Red, Green, Blue, and Orange lines make up the subway system. The commuter rail is purple on system maps and is sometimes called the Purple Line. The Silver Line is a fancy name for a bus line; route **SL1** runs from South Station to the airport via the South Boston waterfront, including the convention center and the Seaport Boston World Trade Center (the **SL2** stays on the downtown side of the harbor and serves the cruise ship terminal area). The fare on the subway and Silver Line routes SL1 and SL2 at press time is **$1.70** if you use a CharlieCard (transfers to local buses are free), **$2** with a CharlieTicket. Children 11 and under ride free with a paying adult. Route and fare information and timetables are available through the website (www.mbta. com) and at centrally located stations.

Service begins at around 5:15am and ends around 12:30am. (On New Year's Eve, or First Night, closing time is 2am and service is free after 8pm.) A sign in every station gives the time of the last train in either direction; if you're planning to be out late and don't see a sign, ask the attendant in the booth near the entrance.

BY BUS

The MBTA runs buses and "trackless trolleys" (buses with electric antennae) that provide service around town and to and around the suburbs. The local routes you're most likely to use are **no. 1,** along Massachusetts Avenue from Dudley Square in Roxbury through the Back Bay and Cambridge to Harvard Square; **no. 92** and **no. 93,** which connect Haymarket and Charlestown; and **no. 77,** along Mass. Ave. north of Harvard Square to Porter Square, North Cambridge, and Arlington. Two branches of the **Silver Line** run through the South End to Dudley Station in Roxbury and are part of the bus fare structure. Route **SL4** serves South Station (Essex St. at Atlantic Ave.), and Route **SL5** starts and ends on Temple Place, near Downtown Crossing between Washington and Tremont streets.

The fare on the local bus and Silver Line routes SL4 and SL5 at press time is **$1.25** with a CharlieCard (transferring to the subway costs 45¢), **$1.50** with a CharlieTicket or cash. Children 11 and under ride free with a paying adult. If you're paying cash, exact change is required.

BY FERRY

The MBTA Inner Harbor ferry connects **Long Wharf** (near the New England Aquarium) with the **Charlestown Navy Yard**—it's a good way to get back downtown from "Old Ironsides" and the Bunker Hill Monument. The fare is $1.70, or show your LinkPass. Call ✆ **617/227-4321** or visit www.mbta.com for more information, including schedules.

Ride & (Maybe) Save

The MBTA's 1-day and 7-day **LinkPasses** (☎ 888/844-0355 or 617/222-4545; www.mbta.com) can be a great deal—but only if you plan to use public transit enough. Passes cover unlimited travel on the subway and local buses, in commuter rail zone 1A, and on the Inner Harbor ferry. The cost is $9 for 24 hours, which translates to an awful lot of riding before you start to save money. The longer pass, which costs $15 for 7 consecutive days, is a more likely to pay off. At press time, passes must be loaded onto CharlieTickets. Check ahead to see whether you can put yours on a CharlieCard; that should be possible after the commuter rail and water transportation fare-collection systems are converted. You can order passes—long-term visitors may find one of the numerous commuter passes a better deal than a visitor-oriented LinkPass—in advance over the phone or the Web (minimum six; at press time, shipping is free), or buy them when you arrive at any kiosk or retailer that sells CharlieTickets and CharlieCards.

By Taxi

Taxis are expensive and not always easy to find—seek out a cabstand or call a dispatcher. Always ask for a receipt in case you have a complaint or lose something and need to call the company.

Cabs usually queue up near hotels. There are also busy cabstands at Faneuil Hall Marketplace (on North St. and in front of 60 State St.), South Station, and Back Bay Station, and on either side of Massachusetts Avenue in Harvard Square, near the Harvard Coop bookstore and Au Bon Pain.

To call ahead for a cab, try the **Independent Taxi Operators Association** (☎ 617/426-8700; www.itoataxi.com), **Boston Cab** (☎ 617/536-5010; www. bostoncab.us), **Top Cab/City Cab** (☎ 617/266-4800 or 617/536-5100; www.topcab.us), or **Metro Cab** (☎ 617/782-5500; www.boston-cab.com). In Cambridge, call **Ambassador Brattle/Yellow Cab** (☎ 617/492-1100 or 617/547-3000; www.brattlecourier.com) or **Checker Cab** (☎ 617/497-1500). Boston Cab will dispatch a wheelchair-accessible vehicle upon request; advance notice is recommended.

The Boston fare structure: The first $1/7$ mile (when the flag drops) costs $2.60, and each additional $1/7$ mile is 40¢. Wait time is extra, and the passenger pays all tolls. On trips leaving Logan Airport, you're on the hook for $10.10 in fare and fees, including the tunnel toll, before the cab goes an inch. Charging a flat rate is not allowed within the city; the police department (see below) publishes a list of flat rates for trips to the suburbs.

The city requires that Boston cabdrivers accept credit cards, and every vehicle has a card reader fastened to the divider. Drivers resisted the rule at first, and anecdotal evidence suggests that some "broken" card readers will suddenly come online if you say you don't have enough cash to pay up.

If you want to report a problem or have lost something in a Boston cab, contact the police department's **Hackney Unit** (☎ 617/343-4475; www.cityof boston.gov/police/hackney); visit the website for the list of suburban flat fares.

By Water Taxi

Three companies serve various stops around the waterfront, including the airport, in covered boats. They operate daily year-round, from 7am until at least 7pm (later in the summer). One-way fares start at $10. Reservations are recommended but not required; you can call from the dock for pick-up. The companies are **Boston Harbor Water Taxi** (☎ 617/593-9168; www.bostonharborwatertaxi.com), **City Water Taxi** (☎ 617/422-0392; www.citywatertaxi.com), and **Rowes Wharf Water Taxi** (☎ 617/406-8584; www.roweswharfwatertransport.com).

By Car

If you plan to visit only Boston and Cambridge, there's absolutely no reason to have a car. With its pricey parking and narrow, one-way streets, not to mention abundant construction, Boston in particular is a motorist's nightmare. If you arrive by car, park at the hotel and use the car for day trips. Drive from Boston to Cambridge only if you're feeling flush—you'll pay to park there, too. If you're not traveling to Boston by car and you decide to take a day trip (see chapter 10), you'll probably want to rent a vehicle. Here's the scoop:

RENTALS

Seriously consider waiting to pick up the car until you need it, to save yourself the hassle of driving and parking. The major car-rental firms have offices at Logan Airport and in Boston, and most have other area branches. Note that the Enterprise and Thrifty airport locations are nearby but not on the grounds, and allow time for the shuttle-bus ride. Rentals that originate in Boston carry a **$10 convention center surcharge**—you can get around it by picking up your car in Cambridge, Brookline, Somerville, or another suburb.

In general, Boston doesn't conform to the pattern of a big city that empties on weekends, when business travelers leave town and rental-car rates plummet. The parts of downtown Boston that aren't densely populated residential neighborhoods are near them, and at busy times—especially on summer weekends and during foliage season—you'll want to reserve a car well in advance or risk getting shut out.

Alamo, Avis, Budget, and Enterprise forbid smoking in their vehicles, as do corporate-owned Dollar and Thrifty branches. Hertz and National allow customers to request no-smoking vehicles. To rent from the major national chains, you must be at least 25 years old and have a valid driver's license and credit card. Some companies allow drivers aged 21 to 24 to rent, subject to a steep daily fee. And some chains enforce a maximum age; if you're over 70, check ahead to avoid an unpleasant surprise.

If you're visiting from abroad and plan to rent a car in the United States, keep in mind that foreign driver's licenses are usually recognized in the U.S., but you may want to consider obtaining an international driver's license.

Impressions

Boston's freeway system was insane. It was clearly designed by a person who had spent his childhood crashing toy trains. Every few hundred yards I would find my lane vanishing beneath me and other lanes merging with it from the right or left, or sometimes both. This wasn't a road system, it was mobile hysteria.

—**Bill Bryson**, *The Lost Continent*, 1989
(but it's still true)

Boston Drivers: Beware

The incredibly sappy movie *Love Story* includes one hilarious observation: "This is Boston—everybody drives like a maniac." And that was before cellphones. Boston drivers deserve their notoriety, and even though the truly reckless are a tiny minority, it pays to be careful. Never assume that another driver will behave as you might expect, especially when it comes to the rarely used turn signal. Watch out for cars that leave the curb and change lanes without signaling, double- and even triple-park, and travel the wrong way down one-way streets. And remember that most pedestrians and bicyclists are just drivers without their protective covering.

Money-saving tips: Rent the smallest car you're comfortable driving and you'll save on gas (petrol). The price per gallon at press time is more than $3; the posted price includes taxes. One U.S. gallon equals 3.8 liters or .85 imperial gallons.

If you belong to **Zipcar** or another car-sharing service at home, check ahead to see whether your membership is good in the Boston area. And if you don't mind taking a short T ride to (potentially) save a bundle, check rates at Enterprise and Hertz neighborhood locations. Most branches will pick you up at the nearest train station or bus stop if the office isn't close to public transit.

See the "By Car" section under "Getting There," earlier in this chapter, for information about driving (or not) to eastern Massachusetts.

Insurance

If you hold a private auto insurance policy, it probably covers you in the U.S. for loss of or damage to the rental car, and for liability in case a passenger is injured. The credit card you use to rent the car may also provide some coverage, but don't assume—check before you leave home.

International travelers should be aware that quoted rental car rates in the U.S. almost never include insurance and taxes. Be sure to ask your rental agency about these fees. They can add a significant cost to your car rental.

Car-rental insurance typically does not cover liability if you cause an accident. Check your own auto insurance policy, the rental company policy, and your credit card coverage for the extent of coverage: Is your destination covered? Are other drivers covered? How much liability is covered if a passenger is injured? If you rely on your credit card for coverage, you may want to bring a second card with you, because damages may be charged to your card, eating into your credit limit.

Car rental insurance from rental car companies starts at about $20 a day.

Package Deals

Many packages include airfare, accommodations, and a rental car with unlimited mileage. Compare these prices with the cost of booking airline tickets and renting a car separately. Don't saddle yourself with a car for a long period if you won't be using it, though. And don't forget to account for parking fees, which can quickly wipe out any savings a package might represent.

Booking Online

For booking rental cars online, the best deals are usually on rental-car company websites. *Tip:* Sign up for e-mail alerts before you book, and you may land a deal. You can always cancel the alerts after you return home.

Check out **www.bnm.com**, which offers domestic car-rental discounts. Also worth visiting are Orbitz.com, Hotwire.com, Travelocity.com, and Priceline. com, all of which offer competitive rates.

PARKING

It's difficult to find your way around Boston and practically impossible to find parking in some areas. Most spaces on the street are metered (and patrolled until at least 6pm Mon–Sat) or are open to nonresidents for 2 hours or less between 8am and 6pm. The penalty is a $45 ticket—the same as a full day at the most expensive garage. Read the sign or meter carefully. Some areas allow parking only at certain hours. Rates vary in different sections of the city (usually $1.25/hr. downtown); bring plenty of quarters. On some streets, you pay at a nearby machine and affix the receipt to the inside of the driver's-side window. Time limits range from 15 minutes to 2 hours.

If you blunder into a tow-away zone, retrieving the car will cost well over $100 and a lot of running around. The **city tow lot** (☎ 617/635-3900) is at 200 Frontage Rd. in South Boston. Take a taxi, or ride the Red Line to Andrew and flag a cab.

It's best to leave the car in a garage or lot and walk, but be aware that Boston's parking is the second-most expensive in the country (after Manhattan's). A full day at most garages costs no more than $30, but some downtown facilities charge as much as $45, and hourly rates typically are exorbitant. Many lots charge a lower flat rate if you enter and exit before certain times or if you park in the evening. Some restaurants offer reduced rates at nearby garages; ask when you call for reservations. Regardless of where you park, visit the attendant's booth as you exit on foot to ask whether any local businesses offer discounted parking with a purchase and validation; you may get lucky.

Enter the garage under **Boston Common** (☎ 617/954-2096; www. mccahome.com/bcg.html) from Charles Street between Boylston and Beacon streets. Access to the garage in the state **Transportation Building,** 8 Park Plaza (☎ 617/973-7054; www.pilgrimparking.com), is from Charles Street South. The **Prudential Center** garage (☎ 617/236-3060; www.prudentialcenter. com) has entrances on Boylston Street, Huntington Avenue, and Exeter Street, and at the Sheraton Boston Hotel. Parking is discounted if you buy something at the Shops at Prudential Center and have your ticket validated. The garage at **Copley Place** (☎ 617/375-4488; www.simon.com), off Huntington Avenue, offers a similar deal. Many businesses in Faneuil Hall Marketplace validate parking at the **75 State St. Garage** (☎ 617/742-7275; www.75statestreetgarage. com).

Good-size garage facilities downtown include the **Government Center Garage,** 50 New Sudbury St., off Congress Street (☎ 617/227-0385; www. governmentcentergarage.com); **Parcel 7 Garage,** 136 Blackstone St., entrance on New Sudbury Street off Congress Street (☎ 617/973-6954); and **Zero Post Office Square** in the Financial District (☎ 617/423-1500; www.posquare. com). In the Back Bay, there's a large facility near the Hynes Convention Center at **50 Dalton St.** (☎ 617/421-9484; www.pilgrimparking.com). The lots off **Northern Avenue** in the Seaport District are among the cheapest in town, but downtown proper is some distance away. Allow time for the walk or Silver Line bus ride.

DRIVING RULES

When traffic permits, drivers may turn right at a red light after stopping, unless a sign is posted saying otherwise (as it often is downtown). The speed limit on most city streets is 30mph.

Seat belts are mandatory for adults and children, children 11 and under may not ride in the front seat, and infants and children 7 and under must be strapped into car seats in the back seat. You can be stopped just for having an unbelted child in the car, though not for traveling with an unsecured adult. Text-messaging while behind the wheel is against the law for drivers of all ages, and cellphone use of any kind by motorists 17 and under is illegal except in an emergency.

And be aware of two other state laws, if only because drivers break them so frequently it'll take your breath away: Pedestrians in the crosswalk have the right of way (most suburbs actually enforce this one), and vehicles already in a rotary (traffic circle or roundabout) have the right of way.

By Bicycle

This is not a good option unless you're a real pro or plan to visit Cambridge, which has a decent network of bike lanes. Despite a recent push to improve traffic conditions for cyclists, the streets of downtown Boston, with their bloodthirsty drivers and oblivious pedestrians, are notoriously inhospitable to two-wheelers. Visit **www.cityofboston.gov/bikes** for information about the city's efforts to boost its bike friendliness, which includes a European-style bike-sharing system that was in the works at press time.

For information about renting a bike and about recreational biking, see "Biking" on p. 197. If you bring or rent a bike, be sure to lock it securely when leaving it unattended, even for a short time.

[FastFACTS] BOSTON

Area Codes Boston proper, **617** and **857;** immediate suburbs, **781** and **339;** northern and western suburbs, **978** and **351;** southern suburbs, **508** and **774.** *Note:* To make a local call, you must dial the 3-digit area code and the 7-digit number.

Business Hours Offices are usually open weekdays from 9am to 5 or 6pm. Banks are open weekdays from 9am to 4pm or later and sometimes on Saturday morning; most offer 24-hour access to automated teller machines (ATMs). Stores typically open between 9 and 10am and close between 6 (neighborhood shops) and 9pm (mall and shopping center locations) from Monday through Saturday. Sunday hours for shops that have them are usually 11am or noon to 5 or 6pm. Some drugstores and grocery stores are open 24 hours a day, 7 days a week.

Car Rental See the "By Car" section under "Getting There," earlier in this chapter.

Cellphones See "Mobile Phones," later in this section.

Crime See "Safety," later in this section.

Customs National customs agencies regulate what visitors to the United Stated may bring with them and what they may take home. For details regarding U.S. Customs and Border Protection, consult your nearest U.S. embassy or consulate, or visit **U.S. Customs** (www.customs.gov).

Doctors The front-desk staff at your hotel can often recommend a doctor, or you can use one of the referral services available through local hospitals. They include Massachusetts General Hospital (☎ **800/711-4644**) and Brigham and Women's Hospital (☎ **800/294-9999**). Also see "Hospitals," below.

Drinking Laws The legal age for purchase and consumption of alcoholic beverages is 21. Proof of age is required and often requested at bars, nightclubs, and restaurants, particularly near college campuses (in the Boston area, that's everywhere), so it's always a good idea to bring ID when you go out. At sporting events, everyone buying alcohol must show ID. Liquor stores and some supermarkets and convenience stores sell alcohol Monday though Saturday during regular business hours; in communities where selling alcohol on Sunday is legal, sales begin at noon. Happy hours with discounted drinks are illegal, but discounted food is permitted. Most restaurants have full liquor licenses, but some serve only beer, wine, and cordials. Last call typically is 30 minutes before closing time (1am in bars, 2am in clubs).

Do not carry open containers of alcohol in your car or any public area that isn't zoned for alcohol consumption. The police can fine you on the spot. Don't even think about driving while intoxicated.

Driving Rules See "Getting Around," earlier in this chapter.

Electricity Like Canada, the United States uses 110–120 volts AC (60 cycles), compared to 220–240 volts AC (50 cycles) in most of Europe, Australia, and New Zealand. Downward converters that change 220–240 volts to 110–120 volts are difficult to find in the United States, so bring one with you.

Embassies & Consulates All embassies are in the nation's capital, Washington, D.C. Some consulates are in major U.S. cities, and most nations have a mission to the United Nations in New York City. If your country isn't listed below, call directory assistance in Washington, D.C. (☎ **202/555-1212**) or check **www.embassy.org/embassies**.

The embassy of **Australia** is at 1601 Massachusetts Ave. NW, Washington, DC 20036 (☎ **202/797-3000;** www.usa.embassy.gov.au).

The embassy of **Canada** is at 501 Pennsylvania Ave. NW, Washington, DC 20001 (☎ **202/682-1740;** www.canadainternational.gc.ca/washington). The local Canadian consulate is at 3 Copley Place, Ste. 400, Boston, MA 02116 (☎ **617/262-3760;** www.boston.gc.ca).

The embassy of **Ireland** is at 2234 Massachusetts Ave. NW, Washington, DC 20008 (☎ **202/462-3939;** www.embassyofireland.org). The local Irish consulate is at 535 Boylston St., 5th floor, Boston, MA 02116 (☎ **617/267-9330;** www.consulategeneralofirelandboston.org).

The embassy of **New Zealand** is at 37 Observatory Circle NW, Washington, DC 20008 (☎ **202/328-4800;** www.nzembassy.com). Contact the **honorary consul** to the New England area at P.O. Box 1318, 57 N. Main St., Concord, NH 03302 (☎ **603/225-8228**).

The embassy of the **United Kingdom** is at 3100 Massachusetts Ave. NW, Washington, DC 20008 (☎ **202/588-6500;** http://ukinusa.fco.gov.uk). The Boston-area **British consulate** is at 1 Broadway, Cambridge, MA 02142 (☎ **617/245-4500**).

Emergencies Call ☎ **911** for fire, ambulance, or the police. This is a free call from pay phones. Dialing 911 on a cellphone connects you to a state police dispatcher, who transfers the call to the local authorities. The Boston police direct emergency number is ☎ **617/343-4911.**

Family Travel Boston is a top-notch family destination, with tons of activities that appeal to children and relatively few that don't. All area hotels, restaurants, and attractions have extensive experience meeting kids' needs.

The **Greater Boston Convention & Visitors Bureau** (✆ **888/733-2678;** www.bostonusa.com) sells a *Kids Love Boston* guide ($5) filled with travel information for families. The **Boston Parents Paper** website (http://boston.parenthood.com) lists activities and events.

To locate accommodations, restaurants, and attractions that are particularly kid-friendly, look for the "Kids" icon throughout this guide. Also consult the boxes on "Family-Friendly Hotels" (p. 80) and "Family-Friendly Restaurants" (p. 118), and the section "Especially for Kids" (p. 184).

Gasoline See the "By Car" section under "Getting There," earlier in this chapter.

Health Here's hoping you won't need to evaluate Boston's reputation for excellent medical care. The greatest threat to your health is the same as in most other North American cities: overexposure to the summer sun. Be sure to pack sunblock, sunglasses, and a hat, and don't forget to stay hydrated.

Hospitals The closest hospitals to downtown are **Massachusetts General Hospital,** 55 Fruit St. (✆ **617/726-2000;** www.massgeneral.org), and **Tufts Medical Center,** 800 Washington St. (✆ **617/636-5000;** www.tuftsmedicalcenter.org). At the Harvard Medical Area on the Boston-Brookline border are **Beth Israel Deaconess Medical Center,** 330 Brookline Ave. (✆ **617/667-7000;** www.bidmc.org); **Brigham and Women's Hospital,** 75 Francis St. (✆ **617/732-5500;** www.brighamandwomens.org); and **Children's Hospital Boston,** 300 Longwood Ave. (✆ **617/355-6000;** www.childrenshospital.org).

In Cambridge are **Mount Auburn Hospital,** 330 Mount Auburn St. (✆ **617/492-3500;** www.mountauburnhospital.org), and **Cambridge Hospital,** 1493 Cambridge St. (✆ **617/665-1000;** www.cha.harvard.edu/cambridge).

Nonemergency **MinuteClinics** (✆ **866/389-2727;** www.minuteclinic.com) deal with ear infections, strep throat, and such, but not with dire emergencies. At press time, the only one in the immediate Boston area is in the **CVS** at the Porter Square Shopping Center, 36 White St., off Mass. Ave., Cambridge (✆ **617/876-5519;** www.cvs.com).

Insurance Whether you choose to invest in travel insurance depends on numerous factors, including how far you're traveling, how much you're spending, how set your schedule is, and your physical condition. For domestic travelers, most reliable health-care plans provide coverage if you get sick away from home. International travelers should note that unlike many other countries, the United States does not usually offer free or low-cost medical care to visitors (or citizens).

For information on traveler's insurance, trip cancelation insurance, and medical insurance while traveling, please visit **www.frommers.com/planning**.

Internet & Wi-Fi Internet access is widely available in the Boston area, where a wireless connection can be easier to come by than a wired one, and Wi-Fi is often (but not always) free. Most hotels and many businesses offer Wi-Fi access. (Paradoxically, high-end hotels tend to charge guests a daily fee for access, while many cheaper lodgings include Wi-Fi in their room rates.) Many coffee shops and fast-food restaurants, some lines of the commuter rail, and numerous other businesses have free wireless access. Wi-Fi is free at Logan Airport, in and around the Quincy Market rotunda at Faneuil Hall Marketplace, and at Christopher Columbus Waterfront Park and Norman

B. Leventhal Park at Post Office Square. Most businesses on the upper end of Newbury Street provide free wireless thanks to **Tech Superpowers,** 252 Newbury St., 3rd floor (✆ **617/267-9716;** www.newburyopen.net), which also offers access by the hour with ($5/day) or without ($5/hr.; $3/15 min. minimum) your own computer or hand-held device. A good way to find public Wi-Fi hotspots is by searching **www.wififreespot.com.**

If you're traveling without a computer or hand-held device, Boston's Logan and most other major airports have **Internet kiosks** that provide basic Web access; the per-minute fee can be steep. **FedEx Office** (www.fedexoffice.com) offers free access at some locations if you have a hand-held device and charges about 25¢ a minute to use a computer. Locations include 2 Center Plaza, Government Center (✆ **617/973-9000**); 10 Post Office Sq., Financial District (✆ **617/482-4400**); 575 Boylston St. (✆ **617/536-2536**) and 187 Dartmouth St. (✆ **617/262-6188**), Back Bay; and in Cambridge at 1 Mifflin Place (Mount Auburn St. and University Rd.), Harvard Square (✆ **617/497-0125**).

Legal Aid While driving, if you are pulled over for a minor infraction (such as speeding), never attempt to pay the fine directly to a police officer; this could be construed as attempted bribery, a much more serious crime. Pay fines by mail, or directly into the hands of the clerk of the court. If accused of a more serious offense, say and do nothing before consulting a lawyer. In the U.S., the burden is on the state to prove a person's guilt beyond a reasonable doubt, and everyone has the right to remain silent, whether he or she is suspected of a crime or actually arrested. Once arrested, a person can make one telephone call to a party of his or her choice. The international visitor should call his or her embassy or consulate.

LGBT Travelers The capital of the first state to legalize same-sex marriage, Boston is overall a gay- and lesbian-friendly destination, with a live-and-let-live attitude that long ago replaced the city's legendary Puritanism. The South End, Jamaica Plain, and Cambridge's Porter Square are home to many LGBT residents—as are plenty of other neighborhoods and suburbs. **Pride Week** (www.bostonpride.org), in early June, is so popular that it's actually 10 days, ending with a festive parade.

The free weekly *Bay Windows* (✆ **617/266-6670;** www.baywindows.com) covers New England's LGBT community and features extensive entertainment listings. The alternative weekly *Boston Phoenix* publishes cultural and nightlife listings (www.bostonphoenix.com). A good online resource is **Edge Boston** (www.edgeboston.com).

An excellent guide to local gay- and lesbian-owned and -friendly businesses is the *Pink Pages* (www.pinkweb.com/boston.index.html). The website of the **Greater Boston Convention & Visitors Bureau** (www.bostonusa.com) has an LGBT Traveler section; click "Visit Boston," then "Boston Insider." The state tourism department has a separate website, **www.lgbtmassvacation.com,** devoted to information about activities and attractions across Massachusetts. Other useful resources include the **Gay, Lesbian, Bisexual and Transgender Helpline** (✆ **888/340-4528** or 617/267-9001) and the **Peer Listening Line,** for people 25 and under (✆ **800/399-7337** or 617/267-2535), both operated by Fenway Community Health (www.fenwayhealth.org); the **Boston Alliance of Gay and Lesbian Youth** (✆ **617/227-4313;** www.bagly.org), which holds a general meeting every Wednesday at 8pm; and the **Bisexual Resource Center** (✆ **617/424-9595;** www.biresource.net).

Mail At press time, domestic postage rates were 28¢ for a postcard and 44¢ for a letter. For international mail, a first-class letter of up to 1 ounce costs 98¢ (75¢ to Canada and 79¢ to Mexico); a first-class postcard costs the same as a letter. For more information, go to **www.usps.com.**

If you aren't sure what your address will be in the United States, mail can be sent to you, in your name, c/o General Delivery at the main post office of the city or region where you expect to be. (Call © **800/275-8777** for information on the nearest post office.) The addressee must pick up mail in person and must produce proof of identity (driver's license or passport). Most post offices will hold mail for up to 1 month, and are open Monday to Friday from 8am to 6pm, and Saturday from 9am to 3pm.

Always include zip codes when mailing items in the U.S. If you don't know your zip code, visit **www.usps.com/zip4**.

Medical Requirements Unless you're arriving from an area known to be suffering from an epidemic (particularly cholera or yellow fever), inoculations or vaccinations are not required for entry into the United States.

Mobile Phones Most Americans call mobile phones "cellphones." The major North American service providers all cover Boston; in the suburbs, you'll encounter some dead spots. Don't count on reliable service in rural areas, especially if your phone is on the GSM network, which most of the world uses. Among major U.S. carriers, AT&T and T-Mobile are compatible with GSM, and Sprint and Verizon use CDMA. To see where GSM phones work in the U.S., check out www.t-mobile.com/coverage.

If you're traveling from overseas and haven't used your phone internationally before, call your provider before you leave home to determine whether your phone will work where you're going, whether you'll be able to send and receive SMS (text messages), and how much everything will cost.

If you plan to call home frequently, the cheapest option in many cases is **Skype** (www. skype.com). Sign up before you leave home, and you can place calls from a computer or mobile device. Calls to other Skype users are free; add credit to your account to call non-members.

If you want a phone just for emergencies and don't have to know your number ahead of time, I suggest heading straight to one of the Boston area's numerous freestanding cellphone stores or to **Radio Shack** (© **800/843-7422;** www.radioshack.com) and buying a prepaid phone to use during your visit. Phones sell for as little as $15, but calling time can cost as much as 35¢/minute. Make sure you're choosing a provider that allows you to activate international calling immediately (try making an international call while you're still in the store). Most important, be sure you understand all fees and per-minute charges and have enough money loaded onto the phone to cover the calls you're likely to make and receive.

A reliable outlet for "unlocked" cellphones—which recognize any carrier's SIM card—is **Mega Mobile,** 278 Washington St., Downtown Crossing (© **617/573-0073;** www. megamobileboston.com). It also sells international SIM cards and does repairs. If you prefer to **rent** a phone, you can have it shipped to you before you leave from **InTouch Global** (© **800/872-7626** or 703/222-7161; www.intouchglobal.com). Rates start at $29 a week, plus a shipping charge.

WHAT THINGS COST IN BOSTON

	$
Taxi from airport to downtown or Back Bay	20.00–45.00
Water shuttle from airport to downtown	10.00
MBTA subway fare	1.70–2.00
Double at moderately priced hotel	159.00–259.00
Lunch for one at inexpensive restaurant	7.00–13.00
Three-course dinner for one, without wine, at moderately priced restaurant	20.00–29.00
Glass of beer	3.00–8.00
Cup of coffee	1.50 and up
Adult admission to the Museum of Fine Arts	20.00
Child (17 and under) admission to the Museum of Fine Arts	free

Money & Costs Frommer's lists exact prices in the local currency. The currency conversions quoted above were correct at press time. However, rates fluctuate, so before departing, consult a currency exchange website such as **www.oanda.com/convert/ classic** or **www.xe.com/ucc** to check up-to-the-minute rates.

Like other large American cities, Boston can be an expensive destination. At the high end, it's nearly as costly as New York. The average hotel room rate in Boston and Cambridge is about $190—down from $200 in 2008, before the recession set in—and that average includes deep off-season discounts. The area does offer numerous ways to offset the price of lodging. Some attractions offer free or discounted admission at certain times, and the performing arts provide options for every budget. Dining choices, from hole-in-the-wall noodle joints to acclaimed special-occasion restaurants, are equally diverse.

If you're visiting Boston from overseas, exchange enough petty cash to cover airport incidentals, tipping, and transportation to your hotel before you leave home, or withdraw money upon arrival at an airport ATM. Throughout eastern Massachusetts, you'll have little or no trouble finding ATMs (also known as "cash machines" or "cashpoints"); they're everywhere, even in some subway stations. **Cirrus** (✆ **800/4CIRRUS** [800/424-7787]; www.mastercard.com) and **PLUS** (✆ **800/THE-PLUS** [843-7587]; www.visa.com) are the major networks. The **NYCE** network (www.nyce.net) operates primarily in the eastern United States. NYCE administers the **SUM** network (www.sum-atm.com), which waives fees for customers of member banks using most ATMs belonging to other members. Look at the back of your bank card to see which network you're on, then call, check online, or download a smartphone app to find ATM locations in the Boston area.

Be sure you know your **personal identification number (PIN)** and your daily **withdrawal limit** before you depart. If you have a five- or six-digit PIN, ask your bank whether it will work; you may need to change it to a four-digit number. Also keep in mind that most banks impose a fee every time you use your card at a different bank's ATM, and the bank from which you withdraw cash may charge its own fee. At Massachusetts ATMs, a message should appear—onscreen or on a sticker near the keypad—specifying the amount of the charge.

US$	C$	£	€	A$	NZ$
1.00	.99	0.63	.74	1.01	1.32

Beware of hidden **credit card fees** while traveling. Check with your credit or debit card issuer to see what fees, if any, will be charged for overseas transactions. Recent reform legislation in the U.S., for example, has curbed some exploitative lending practices. But many banks have responded by increasing fees in other areas, including fees for customers who use credit and debit cards while out of the country—even if those charges were made in U.S. dollars. Fees can amount to 3% or more of the purchase price. Check with your bank before departing to avoid any surprise charges on your statement.

Stores and restaurants that accept credit cards generally accept **debit cards,** and some stores and most U.S. post offices enable you to receive "cash back" on your debit card purchases as well. If you don't keep a large checking balance, be aware that most banks "freeze" a portion of your account when you initiate a purchase without a definite total, such as a car rental or tank of gas.

Credit cards and debit cards are more often used, but **traveler's checks** are widely accepted in the U.S. In tourist-friendly Boston, you won't have much trouble using traveler's checks at any business. International visitors should make sure that they're denominated in U.S. dollars; foreign-currency checks are often difficult to exchange.

For help with currency conversions, tip calculations, and more, download the convenient Frommer's Travel Tools app for your mobile device. Go to **www.frommers.com/go/mobile** and click on the Travel Tools icon.

Newspapers & Magazines The daily *Boston Globe, Boston Herald, New York Times, USA Today,* and *Wall Street Journal* are available at convenience stores, newsstands, some supermarkets, and sidewalk newspaper boxes all over the Boston area. The *Boston Phoenix,* a free weekly with extensive entertainment and restaurant listings, comes out on Thursday and is available from newspaper boxes.

Where, a monthly magazine available free at most hotels, lists information about shopping, nightlife, attractions, and current shows at museums and art galleries. Newspaper boxes dispense free copies of *Stuff@Night,* a biweekly *Phoenix* offshoot with selective listings and arts coverage; the irreverent *Weekly Dig,* which covers news, entertainment, and dining; the biweekly *Improper Bostonian,* packed with event and restaurant listings; and the weekly *Tab,* which lists neighborhood-specific event information. Available on newsstands, *Boston* magazine is a lifestyle-oriented monthly with cultural and restaurant listings.

Most large bookstores, including the local branches of Barnes & Noble and Borders, have extensive periodicals sections. Newsstands with good selections of international periodicals include **Out of Town News,** Zero Harvard Sq. (© **617/354-1441**), and **Crimson Corner,** 1394 Massachusetts Ave. (© **617/864-0700**), across the street from each other in the heart of Harvard Square.

Passports Virtually every air traveler entering the U.S. is required to show a passport. All persons, including U.S. citizens, traveling by air between the United States and Canada, Mexico, Central and South America, the Caribbean, and Bermuda are required to present a valid passport. ***Note:*** U.S. and Canadian citizens entering the U.S. at land and seaports of entry from within the western hemisphere must now also present a passport or other documents compliant with the Western Hemisphere Travel Initiative (WHTI; see **www.getyouhome.gov** for details). Children 15 and under may continue entering with only a U.S. birth certificate, or other proof of U.S. citizenship.

Australia Australian Passport Information Service (✆ 131-232; www.passports.gov.au).

Canada Passport Office, Department of Foreign Affairs and International Trade, Ottawa, ON K1A 0G3 (✆ **800/567-6868;** www.ppt.gc.ca).

Ireland Passport Office, Setanta Centre, Molesworth Street, Dublin 2 (✆ **01/671-1633;** www.foreignaffairs.gov.ie).

New Zealand Passport Office, Department of Internal Affairs, 47 Boulcott St., Wellington 6011 (✆ 0800/225-050 in New Zealand or 04/474-8100; www.passports.govt.nz).

United Kingdom Visit your nearest passport office, major post office, or travel agency or contact the **Identity and Passport Service (IPS),** 89 Eccleston Sq., London SW1V 1PN (✆ **0300/222-0000;** www.ips.gov.uk).

United States To find your regional passport office, check the U.S. State Department website (travel.state.gov/passport) or call the **National Passport Information Center** (✆ **877/487-2778**) for automated information.

Petrol See the "By Car" section under "Getting Around," earlier in this chapter.

Police Call ✆ **911** for emergencies. This is a free call from pay phones. From a cellphone, 911 connects you to the state police. To call the Boston police emergency line directly from a cellphone, use ✆ **617/343-4911.** The non-emergency number is ✆ **617/343-4200.**

Safety Boston and Cambridge are generally safe, especially in the areas you're likely to visit. Nevertheless, you should take the same precautions you would in any other large North American city. Stash wallets and billfolds in your least accessible pocket, don't wave your expensive camera or biggest map around in a dicey-looking neighborhood, and take off your headphones (or at least turn the volume way down) when you're wandering around alone. In general, trust your instincts—a dark, deserted street is probably deserted for a reason.

As in any city, stay out of parks (including Boston Common, the Public Garden, the Esplanade, the Rose Kennedy Greenway, and Cambridge Common) at night unless you're in a crowd. Specific areas to avoid at night include Boylston Street between Tremont and Washington streets, and Tremont Street from Stuart to Boylston streets. Try not to walk alone late at night in the Theater District or on the side streets around North Station. Public transportation in the areas you're likely to visit is busy and safe, but service stops between 12:30 and 1am. If you're going to be out late, carry cab fare and a charged phone programmed with the number of at least one cab company.

Senior Travel Mention that you're a senior citizen when you make your travel reservations. Boston-area businesses offer many discounts to seniors with identification (a driver's license, passport, or other document that shows your date of birth). The cutoff age is usually 65, sometimes 62. Restaurants, museums, and movie theaters may offer special deals. Restaurants and theaters usually offer discounts only at off-peak times, but museums and other attractions offer reduced rates—usually the equivalent of the student price—at all times.

With a special photo ID card, seniors can ride the **MBTA** subways, local and express buses, commuter rail, and Inner Harbor ferries for at least half off the regular fare. You must have a Senior CharlieCard, available in person only from 8:30am to

5pm weekdays at Downtown Crossing and Back Bay stations. For more information, contact the Reduced Fare CharlieCard Office (✆ **800/543-8287** or 617/222-5976; TTY 617/222-5854; www.mbta.com; under "Fares & Passes," click "Reduced Fare Programs").

Smoking In a word, no. State law bans smoking in all workplaces, including restaurants, bars, and clubs, and the MBTA forbids smoking in subway stations. A growing number of hotel chains ban smoking in all guest rooms; in Boston, city law forbids smoking in hotels.

Student Travel Students don't actually rule Boston—it just feels that way sometimes. Many museums, theaters, concert halls, and other establishments offer discounts for college and high school students with valid identification. Some restaurants near college campuses offer student discounts or other deals. Visiting students can check schools' and student groups' Facebook pages, relevant Twitter streams, and old-school campus bulletin boards for information about events and activities, many of which are open to them. The weekly *Boston Phoenix* also lists activities for students.

Travelers with Disabilities Boston, like all other U.S. cities, has taken the required steps to provide access for people with disabilities. Hotels must provide accessible rooms, and museums and street curbs have ramps for wheelchairs. Some smaller accommodations, including most B&Bs, have not been retrofitted. In older neighborhoods (notably Beacon Hill and the North End), you'll find many narrow streets, cobbled thoroughfares, and brick sidewalks that can make getting around difficult. In the construction areas that dot the entire metropolitan area, especially in downtown Boston, you may have to negotiate uneven road surfaces and pedestrian detours.

Most stations on the Red, Blue, and Orange **subway** lines are wheelchair accessible. The Green Line, which uses trolleys, is problematic; some stops have ramps, lifts, or both; construction is under way or in the works at others; and some are inaccessible. Contact the **Massachusetts Bay Transportation Authority** (✆ **800/392-6100** or 617/222-3200; www.mbta.com) for details about the stations you need and possible work-arounds. For service updates on elevators, escalators, and lifts, call the toll-free number and press 6, call (✆ **617/222-2828,** or visit the "Rider Tools" area of the website. All MBTA **buses** have lifts or ramps. To learn more, contact the **Office for Transportation Access,** 10 Park Plaza, Room 5750, Boston, MA 02116 (✆ **800/533-6282** within MA or 617/222-5123; TTY 617/222-5415; www.mbta.com; under "Riding the T," click "Accessibility at the T").

One taxi company with wheelchair-accessible vehicles is **Boston Cab** (✆ **617/536-5010**); advance notice is recommended.

An excellent resource for out-of-towners with mobility issues is **VSA Arts Massachusetts,** 89 South St., Boston, MA 02111 (✆ **617/350-7713,** TTY 617/350-6536; www.vsamass.org).

Taxes The United States has no value-added tax (VAT) or other indirect tax at the national level. Every state, county, and city may levy its own local tax on all purchases, including hotel and restaurant checks and airline tickets. These taxes will *not* appear on price tags. The 6.25% Massachusetts sales tax does not apply to groceries, prescription drugs, newspapers, or clothing that costs less than $175. The tax on meals and takeout food varies by community; in Boston and Cambridge, it's 7%. The lodging tax is 14.45% in Boston and Cambridge.

Telephones See "Mobile Phones," earlier in this section, for information about staying in touch when you're on the road. If you can't use your mobile phone, you may be able to find a public pay phone. Pay phones are increasingly scarce on the street, but they remain available in most hotel lobbies and all airport terminals. Some hotels include local calls in the room rate, but most impose astronomical surcharges on both local and long-distance calls; a quick trip to the lobby can spare you an unpleasant surprise at checkout.

Many convenience stores, drugstores, and packaging services sell **prepaid calling cards** in denominations up to $50. Many public pay phones at airports accept American Express, MasterCard, and Visa. **Local calls** made from pay phones in most locales cost 25¢ or 35¢ (no pennies, please). Most long-distance and international calls can be dialed directly from any phone.

To make calls within the United States and to Canada, dial 1 followed by the area code and the seven-digit number. **For other international calls,** dial 011 followed by the country code, city code, and the number you are calling. The country code for Australia is **61;** for Ireland, **353;** for New Zealand, **64;** and for the U.K., **44.** To place **international calls to the United States,** dial your country's international code plus the country code (1), the area code, and the local number.

Calls to area codes **800, 888, 877,** and **866** are toll-free. However, calls to area codes **700** and **900** (chat lines, bulletin boards, "dating" services, and so on) can cost $3 or more per minute. Some numbers have minimum charges that can run $15 or more.

For **reversed-charge or collect calls,** and for person-to-person calls, dial the number 0, then the area code and number; an operator will come on the line, and you should specify whether you are calling collect, person-to-person, or both. If your operator-assisted call is international, ask for the overseas operator.

For **directory assistance** ("information"), dial 411 for local and national numbers in the U.S. and Canada. For dedicated long-distance information, dial 1, the appropriate area code, and 555-1212.

Time   Boston is in the Eastern time zone. The continental United States encompasses **four time zones:** Eastern Time (ET), Central Time (CT), Mountain Time (MT), and Pacific Time (PT). Alaska and Hawaii have their own zones. At noon in Boston and New York (ET), it's 7am in Honolulu (HT), 9am in Los Angeles (PT), 10am in Denver (MT), 11am in Chicago (CT), 5pm in London (GMT), and 2am the next day in Sydney.

Daylight saving time (summer time) is in effect from 1am on the second Sunday in March to 1am on the first Sunday in November, except in Arizona, Hawaii, the U.S. Virgin Islands, and Puerto Rico. Daylight saving time moves the clock 1 hour ahead of standard time.

For help with time translations and more, download our convenient Travel Tools app for your mobile device. Go to **www.frommers.com/go/mobile** and click on the Travel Tools icon.

Tipping   Tips are a very important part of some workers' income, and gratuities are the standard way of showing appreciation for services provided. (Tipping is certainly not compulsory if the service is poor!) In hotels, tip **bellhops** at least $1 per bag ($5 or more if you have a lot of luggage) and tip the **chamber staff** $2 per day (more if you've left a big mess). Tip the **doorman** or **concierge** only if he or she has provided you with some specific service (for example, calling a cab for you or obtaining difficult-to-get theater tickets). Tip the **valet-parking attendant** $1 or $2 every time you get your car.

In restaurants, bars, and nightclubs, tip **service staff** and **bartenders** 15% to 20% of the check, tip **checkroom attendants** $1 or $2 per garment, and tip **valet-parking attendants** $1 per vehicle.

Tip **cabdrivers** 15% to 20% of the fare; tip **skycaps** at airports at least $1 per bag ($5 or more if you have a lot of luggage); and tip **hairdressers** and **barbers** 15% to 20%.

For help with tip calculations, currency conversions, and more, download our convenient Travel Tools app for your mobile device. Go to **www.frommers.com/go/mobile** and click on the Travel Tools icon.

Toilets You won't find public toilets or "restrooms" on the streets in most U.S. cities; seek them out in hotel lobbies, bars, restaurants, museums, department stores, railway and bus stations, and service stations. The visitor center at 15 State St. has a public restroom, as do the CambridgeSide Galleria, Copley Place, Prudential Center, and Quincy Market shopping areas. The central branch of the Boston Public Library, in Copley Square, has toilets in the basement. Large hotels and fast-food restaurants are often the best bet for clean facilities. Restaurants and bars in heavily visited areas, including Boston and Cambridge, may reserve their restrooms for patrons.

You'll find freestanding, self-cleaning **pay toilets** (25¢) at locations around downtown. These include City Hall Plaza, Congress Street behind City Hall; the plaza in front of the New England Aquarium; Christopher Columbus Waterfront Park; and Commercial Street at Snowhill Street, off the Freedom Trail just before it heads from the North End to Charlestown. Check these facilities carefully before using them or sending a child in alone; despite regular patrols, IV-drug users have been known to take advantage of the generous time limits.

VAT See "Taxes," earlier in this section.

Visas The U.S. State Department has a **Visa Waiver Program (VWP)** allowing citizens of the following countries to enter the United States without a visa for stays of up to 90 days: Andorra, Australia, Austria, Belgium, Brunei, Czech Republic, Denmark, Estonia, Finland, France, Germany, Greece, Hungary, Iceland, Ireland, Italy, Japan, Latvia, Liechtenstein, Lithuania, Luxembourg, Malta, Monaco, the Netherlands, New Zealand, Norway, Portugal, San Marino, Singapore, Slovakia, Slovenia, South Korea, Spain, Sweden, Switzerland, and the United Kingdom. (**Note:** This list was accurate at press time; for the most up-to-date list of countries in the VWP, consult **http://travel.state.gov/visa**.) Even though a visa isn't necessary, in an effort to help U.S. officials check travelers against terror watch lists before they arrive at U.S. borders, visitors from VWP countries must register online through the Electronic System for Travel Authorization (ESTA) before boarding a plane or a boat to the U.S. Travelers must complete an electronic application providing basic personal and travel eligibility information. The Department of Homeland Security recommends filling out the form at least 3 days before traveling. Authorizations will be valid for up to 2 years or until the traveler's passport expires, whichever comes first. Currently, there is a US$14 fee for the online application. Existing ESTA registrations remain valid through their expiration dates. **Note:** Any passport issued on or after October 26, 2006, by a VWP country must be an **e-Passport** for VWP travelers to be eligible to enter the U.S. without a visa. Citizens of these nations also need to present a round-trip air or cruise ticket upon arrival. E-Passports contain computer chips capable of storing biometric information, such as the required digital photograph of the holder. If your passport doesn't have this feature, you can still travel without a visa if the valid passport was issued before October 26, 2005, and includes a machine-readable zone; or if the valid passport was issued between

October 26, 2005, and October 25, 2006, and includes a digital photograph. For more information, go to **http://travel.state.gov/visa**. Canadian citizens may enter the United States without visas, but they must show passports and proof of residence.

Citizens of all other countries must have (1) a valid passport that expires at least 6 months later than the scheduled end of their visit to the U.S.; and (2) a tourist visa.

For information about U.S. visas, go to **http://travel.state.gov** and click on "Visas." Or consult one of the following sources:

Australian citizens can obtain up-to-date visa information from the **U.S. Embassy Canberra,** Moonah Place, Yarralumla, ACT 2600 (✆ **02/6214-5600;** http://canberra.usembassy.gov/visas.html).

British subjects can obtain up-to-date visa information by calling the **U.S. Embassy Visa Information Line** (✆ **09042-450-100** from within the U.K. at £1.20 per minute; or ✆ **866/382-3589** from within the U.S. at a flat rate of $16 (payable by credit card only); or by visiting the "Visas to the U.S." section of the American Embassy London's website, **http://london.usembassy.gov/visas.html**.

Irish citizens can obtain up-to-date visa information through the **U.S. Embassy Dublin,** 42 Elgin Rd., Ballsbridge, Dublin 4 (✆ 1580-47-VISA [8472] from within the Republic of Ireland at €2.40 per minute; http://dublin.usembassy.gov).

Citizens of **New Zealand** can obtain up-to-date visa information by contacting the **U.S. Embassy New Zealand,** 29 Fitzherbert Terrace, Thorndon, Wellington (✆ **644/462-6000;** http://newzealand.usembassy.gov).

Visitor Information The **Greater Boston Convention & Visitors Bureau** (✆ **888/733-2678** or 617/536-4100; www.bostonusa.com) offers a comprehensive visitor information kit ($10 plus postage) that includes a travel planner, a guidebook, a map, pamphlets, and information about discounts on shopping, dining, attractions, and nightlife. The free BostonUSA iPhone app allows users to buy e-tickets for attractions and tours and enter by just showing the screen. The bureau also publishes a *Kids Love Boston* guide ($5) and free smaller guides to specific seasons and special events

The bureau operates the **Boston Common Information Center,** 148 Tremont St., on Boston Common, which is open Monday through Friday from 8:30am to 5pm, Saturday from 9am to 5pm; and the **Prudential Information Center,** on the main level of the Prudential Center, 800 Boylston St. It's open Monday through Friday from 9am to 5:30pm, Saturday and Sunday from 10am to 6pm.

For information about Cambridge, contact the **Cambridge Office for Tourism** (✆ **800/862-5678** or 617/441-2884; fax 617/441-7736; www.cambridge-usa.org).

The office's **information kiosk** is in the heart of Harvard Square, near the T entrance at the intersection of Massachusetts Avenue, John F. Kennedy Street, and Brattle Street. It's open Monday through Friday from 9am to 5pm, Saturday and Sunday from 9am to 1pm.

The **Massachusetts Office of Travel & Tourism** (✆ **800/227-6277** or 617/973-8500; fax 617/973-8525; www.massvacation.com) distributes information about the whole state. Its free *Getaway Guide* magazine includes information about attractions and lodgings, a map, and a calendar.

National Park Service rangers staff the **Boston National Historical Park Visitor Center,** 15 State St. (✆ **617/242-5642;** www.nps.gov/bost; T: Blue or Orange Line to State St.), across the street from the Old State House, and lead seasonal free tours of the

Freedom Trail. The center is open daily from 9am to 5pm. The ranger-staffed center at the Charlestown Navy Yard (© **617/242-5601**) keeps the same hours. A new Park Service visitor center on the first floor of **Faneuil Hall** was under construction at press time; check the website to see whether it's open during your visit.

There's a small information booth at **Faneuil Hall Marketplace** between Quincy Market and the South Market Building. It's outdoors and staffed in the spring, summer, and fall Monday through Saturday from 10am to 6pm, Sunday from noon to 6pm.

To surf around for information about Boston before and during your visit, check out the following websites:

Boston.com (www.boston.com): A comprehensive source that encompasses the on-line home of the *Boston Globe*.

National Park Service (www.nps.gov): An endlessly helpful resource for visitors to Boston and its history-rich suburbs.

MBTA (www.mbta.com): The go-to site for subway, trolley, bus, ferry, and commuter-rail schedules and route maps, plus fare and pass information and an interactive route planner.

HopStop (www.hopstop.com) and **Google Transit** (http://transit.google.com): These interactive sites are good backups to the MBTA route planner, which generally does a better job of accommodating local quirks.

Yelp (www.yelp.com/boston) and **Citysearch** (http://boston.citysearch.com): Exhaustive listings, including restaurants and clubs, accompanied by professional and hit-or-miss amateur reviews.

Bostonist (www.bostonist.com): A lively blog; features include original and rehashed news coverage and enjoyably random event listings.

Boston-to-English Dictionary (www.universalhub.com/glossary): Hilarious yet useful lingo and slang.

Twitter (www.twitter.com) and **Facebook** (www.facebook.com): Even social-networking novices can find plenty of useful information at these sites. If you're just getting your feet wet, pick out an appealing destination or two—museum, municipality, shop, whatever—to follow or friend. A good place to start is with the Greater Boston Convention & Visitors Bureau, **@BostonInsider**. To branch out, see what your chosen Twitterers recommend on "Follow Friday," and check out your Facebook friends' other friends.

iTunes App Store (http://itunes.apple.com): Hundreds of free iPhone apps deliver information about Boston. I'd start with the apps that put Frommer's and the Convention & Visitors Bureau in your hand, then check out the *Globe* and *Herald*, the MBTA, and at least a couple of local TV stations.

Wi-Fi See "Internet & Wi-Fi," earlier in this section.

INDEX

See also Accommodations and Restaurant indexes, below.

A

Abbot Hall (Marblehead),
302
Abiel Smith School, 169
Academic trips, 40
Accommodations, 61–98. *See
also* Accommodations
Index
at and near the airport,
94–96
the Back Bay, 77–86
bars and lounges, 277–278
Beacon Hill/North Station,
70–72
bed & breakfasts, 97–98
best, 3–5, 61–63
Cambridge, 89–94
Charlestown, 73
Chinatown/Theater District,
75–76
Downtown, 63–70
eco-friendly, 39
family-friendly, 80
Financial District and
Downtown Crossing,
68–70
Gloucester, 319–320
with gyms, 198
Marblehead, 303–304
outskirts and Brookline,
86–88
Plymouth, 334–335
practical information, 96–98
rates, 61, 62, 97
Rockport, 326–327
Salem, 310–311
smoking in, 63
South Boston Waterfront
(Seaport District), 73–75
South End, 77
Acme Fine Art and Design,
235
Adams National Historical
Park (Quincy), 328
Adventure (schooner), 317
Adventure trips, 40–41
African-American History
Month, 34
African Americans
African-American History
Month, 34

Black Heritage Trail, 172
Black Nativity, 38
Boston African American
National Historic Site, 172
Cambridge African
American Heritage Trail,
173
54th Massachusetts Colored
Regiment, 151
Martin Luther King, Jr.,
Birthday Celebration, 33
Museum of African
American History, 169
African Meeting House, 169,
180
Afternoon tea, 121
Agganis Arena at Boston
University, 257
Air travel, 338–340
Alcott, Louisa May, 295–296
Algiers Café & Restaurant,
281
Alpha Gallery, 235
AMC Loews Boston Common,
283
American Apparel, 241
American Automobile
Association (AAA), 341
American Repertory Theater
(ART; Cambridge), 266
American Revolution, 22–23
America's Hometown Shuttle
(Plymouth), 329
Amtrak, 340
Ancient and Honorable
Artillery Company of
Massachusetts, 159
An Evening with Champions,
35
Anne Fontaine, 241
Annenberg Hall (Cambridge),
225
Antiques and collectibles,
234
Main Street Antiques
(Plymouth), 334
Appalachian Mountain
Club, 41
Apple Store, 240
Aquarium, New England, 148,
193, 217

Architecture
books about, 28
Marblehead, 302
tours, 194
Area codes, 349
Arlington Street Church, 212
Arnold Arboretum, 174
Arnould Gallery & Framery
(Marblehead), 303
Art & Architecture Tours, 168
Art galleries, Rockport, 324
Arthur M. Sackler Museum
(Cambridge), 178, 224
Artists & Authors
(Marblehead), 303
August Moon Festival, 37
Aunt Sadie's, 245
Auto insurance, 347

B

The Back Bay, 49, 241
accommodations, 77–86
restaurants, 117–120
walking tour, 208–213
Back Bay Bicycles, 198
B&B Agency of Boston, 98
Bank of America Pavilion,
257
The Bar at Taj Boston, 277
Barbara Krakow Gallery,
235, 236
Barnes & Noble, 237
Barnes & Noble at Boston
University, 238
Barnes & Noble at Emerson
College, 238
Bars, 274–280
Baseball, 202–204
Basketball, 204
Battle of Bunker Hill
Museum, 166
Battle Road Trail (Lexington),
288
Bay State Cruise Company,
192
Beaches, 196, 320
Beacon Hill, 46, 169, 188
accommodations, 70–72
restaurants, 112
shopping, 232
sightseeing, 180–182

Beacon Hill Chocolates, 244
Beacon Hill Skate Shop, 201
Beantowne Coffee House, 281
Bearskin Neck (Rockport), 324, 325
Beauport, Sleeper-McCann House (Gloucester), 317–318
Bed and Breakfast Associates Bay Colony, 98
Bed & Breakfast Reservations North Shore/Greater Boston/Cape Cod, 98
The Beehive, 274
Benjamin Franklin Statue, 155–156
Berklee Beantown Jazz Festival, 271
Berklee Performance Center, 257
Berk's Shoes, 252
Big Apple Circus, 34
Biking, 197–198, 349
tours, 194
Bird by Bird, 244
Black Falcon Cruise Terminal, 342–343
Black Heritage Trail, 169, 172
Black Ink, 245
Black Nativity, 38
The Black Rose, 278
Bleacher Bar, 280
Blue Hills Trailside Museum, 185
Blue Man Group, 266
Boat tours and cruises, 190–192, 342–343
Boston Harbor Islands, 199
Gloucester, 317
Plymouth, 330–332
whale-watching, 193
Bobby From Boston, 253
Bodega, 241
BoltBus, 342
Books, recommended, 27–29
Bookstores, 237–239
Boomerangs, 183, 253–254
Borders, 237
BosTix, 257
Boston African American National Historic Site, 172
Boston Athenæum, 166–167
Boston Ballet, 265
Boston Baroque, 263
Boston Bead Company, 248
Salem, 309

Boston Beer Works, 276–277
Boston Blazers, 202
Boston Breakers, 202
Boston Bruins, 205
Boston By Foot, 185, 188
Boston Cannons, 202
Boston Celtics, 204
Boston Center for Adult Education, 193
Boston Center for the Arts, 257, 260
Boston Children's Museum, 186
Boston CityPass, 140
Boston Coach, 339
Boston College sports teams, 204, 205
Boston Common, 151, 173
garage, 348
Boston Common Coach, 243
Boston Common Coffee Co., 281
Boston Common Information Center, 360
Boston Duck Tours, 188–189
Boston Explorer Pass, 140
Boston Film Festival, 38
Boston Fire Department T-shirt, 245
Boston Folk Festival, 271
Boston Harbor Cruises, 185, 191–193
Boston Harborfest, 36–37
Boston Harbor Islands, 199
Boston Harbor Water Taxi, 339
Bostonian Society's Museum, 158
Boston International Comedy & Movie Festival, 268
Boston Irish Tourism Association, 194
Boston Landmarks Orchestra, 262
Boston Light, 191
Boston Lyric Opera, 263
Boston Marathon, 35, 205
Boston Massacre Site, 158, 214
Boston Movie Tours, 195
Boston Museum of Natural History, 212
Boston National Historical Park Visitor Center, 151, 360–361
Boston Opera House, 265

Boston Pops, 262
Boston Pops Concert & Fireworks Display, 37
Boston Pride Parade, 36
Boston Public Library, 167–168, 213, 218
Boston Public Market, 250
Boston Red Sox, 202–204
Boston's Best Cruises, 199
The Boston Shaker, 246
Boston Symphony Orchestra, 189, 262–263
Boston Tea Party, 157
Boston Tea Party Reenactment, 38
Boston Tea Party Ship & Museum, 136, 185
Boston Underfoot tour, 188
Boston University, 179
hockey, 205
Seminars in the Arts and Culinary Arts, 196
Boston Vegetarian Society, 196
Boston Wine Festival, 196
Boston Wine School, 196
Boutique Fabulous, 247
Bowling, 282
Brattle Book Shop, 237
Brattle Square (Cambridge), 228
Brattle Street (Cambridge), 175
Brattle Theatre (Cambridge), 227, 228, 282
Brewpubs, 276–277
Brewster Gardens (Plymouth), 329
Bridges, 190
"Brimstone Corner," 153–154
Bristol Lounge, 196
The Bristol Lounge, 277
British Imports (Plymouth), 334
Broadway Across America, 265
Bromfield Pen Shop, 234
Brookline
accommodations, 86–88
restaurants, 122–123
Brookline Booksmith, 237
Brooks Brothers, 241
Broom Closet (Salem), 310
Brown Paper Tickets, 256
Brush Hill Tours, 41, 243
Buckaroo's Mercantile, 245

Buckman Tavern (Lexington), 286, 289
Bulfinch, Charles, 152, 159, 163, 169, 171, 176, 180, 215, 220, 221
Bumpkin Island, 199
Bunch of Grapes Tavern, 214
Bunker Hill Monument, 165–166
The Burren, 278
Busch-Reisinger Museum (Cambridge), 178
Business hours, 349
Bus travel, 342, 344

C

Cafe 939, 269
Calendar of events, 33–39
Cambridge, 50
    accommodations, 89–94
    farmer's markets, 250
    restaurants, 124–132
        quick bites and picnic provisions, 120
    sightseeing, 174–179
Cambridge African American Heritage Trail, 173
Cambridge Antique Market, 234
Cambridge Artists' Cooperative Craft Gallery, 239
Cambridge Bicycle, 198
Cambridge Brewing Company, 274
Cambridge Carnival, 38
Cambridge Center for Adult Education, 193
Cambridge Common, 226
Cambridge Historical Commission, 173
Cambridge Multicultural Arts Center, 260
Cambridge Office for Tourism, 174, 360
Cambridge River Festival, 36
Cambridge School of Culinary Arts, 196
Cambridgeside Galleria, 249
C & J, 342
Cantab Lounge, 271
Cape Ann, 299–327
Cape Ann Museum (Gloucester), 318
Cape Ann Whale Watch (Gloucester), 312

Cape Pond Ice (Gloucester), 316
Capt. Bill & Sons Whale Watch (Gloucester), 312
Capt. Elias Davis House (Gloucester), 318
Capt. John Boats (Plymouth), 331
Carey Limousine, 339
Cargo Unlimited (Marblehead), 303
Carpenter Center for the Visual Arts (Cambridge), 223
Car rentals, 346–348
Car travel, 340–341, 346–349
Casablanca (Cambridge), 274
Cask 'n Flagon, 280
Catch a Falling Star (Lexington), 290
Catholic Mass, first, 17
Celebrity Series of Boston, 264, 265
Cellphones, 353
Cemeteries, 154, 155, 164, 176, 183, 296
Central Branch YMCA, 198
Central Burying Ground, 173
Central Wharf (Salem), 308
Chanel, 241
Charles Hayden Planetarium, 148
Charles Playhouse, 266
Charles Riverboat Company, 192
Charlestown, 46
    accommodations, 73
CharlieCard, 343
CharlieTicket, 343
Cheapo Records, 251
Cheers, 210
Cheers (Beacon Hill), 274
Cheers (Faneuil Hall Marketplace), 274
Cheese Shop of Concord, 298
Chefs Collaborative, 39
Chestnut Street (Salem), 306–307
Children. See Families with children
Children's Museum, 33–34
Chinatown, 37, 48
    accommodations, 75–76
    restaurants, 112–115
Chinatown Market Tour, 196

Chinese New Year, 33
Chinese stone lions (Cambridge), 225
Christ Church (Cambridge), 227
Christmas pageant (Rockport), 323
Christmas Revels (Cambridge), 38–39
Christmas Walk (Marblehead), 301
Christopher Columbus Waterfront Park, 160
Church of the Covenant, 211
Citi Wang Theatre, 260, 265
CityPass, Boston, 140
City Sports, 240
CityView Trolleys, 190
City Water Taxi, 339
Civil War, 24–25
Civil War Museum (Marblehead), 302
Clarendon Street, 182
Classical music, 262–264
Climate, 32–33
The Closet, 254
Club and music scene, 267–273
Club Café, 279
Club Oberon (Cambridge), 266
Club Passim (Cambridge), 271
Codzilla cruise, 185
Coffeehouses, 280–282
College merchandise, 238
Collette Vacations, 41
Colonial Drug, 251
Colonial Lantern Tour (Plymouth), 330
Colonial Theatre, 265
Colonnade Murals, 144
Comcast Center, 260
Comcast Town, 203
Comedy clubs, 268–269
The Comedy Studio, 268
Commonwealth Avenue Mall, 210
Commonwealth Limousine Service, 339
Commonwealth Shakespeare Company, 265
Community Boating, 201
Concord, 291–300
Concord Bookshop, 298
Concord Chamber of Commerce, 291

Concord Coach Lines, 342
Concord Museum, 294
Constitution, USS, 164–165, 191
Constitution, USS, Museum, 165, 184
Converse, 241
Coolidge Corner Movie Theater, 282–283
Copley Flair, 245–246
Copley Place, 249
garage at, 348
Copley Square, 212
Copp's Hill Burying Ground, 164
The Corner, 273
Counting house (Salem), 307
Crackerjacks (Rockport), 326
CraftBoston, 239
Crafts galleries and supplies, 239–240
Crafty Yankee (Lexington), 290
Crane Beach, 320
Crate & Barrel, 247
Credit cards, 354–355
Crocker Park (Marblehead), 301
Crosby's Marketplace (Marblehead), 304
Cross at the Pru, 246
Crow Haven Corner (Salem), 309–310
The Crow's Nest (Gloucester), 316
Crush Boutique, 242
Cuoio, 252
Curious George & Friends, 237
Custom House, 215
Custom House (Salem), 308
Customs regulations, 349
Cutler Majestic Theatre, 260
Cyclorama, 182

D

Dance clubs, 269
Dance performances, 265
Danish Country European and Asian Antiques, 234
Darwin's Ltd. (Cambridge), 120
Daylight saving time, 358
Debit cards, 355
DeCordova Sculpture Park and Museum (Lincoln), 297

Delux Cafe, 274–275
Department of Agricultural Resources, 250
Department of Conservation & Recreation, 196
Derby House (Salem), 308
Derby Wharf (Salem), 308
Destination Salem, 306
Deutsche Bank Championship, 205
Diane von Furstenberg, 241
Dim sum, 113
Disabilities, travelers with, 357
Discount shopping, 240
Discovering Justice, 194
Doctors, 350
Dogtown Book Shop (Gloucester), 319
Downtown, accommodations, 63–70
Downtown Crossing, 46
restaurants, 111
shopping, 232
Dragon Boat Festival, 36
Dress, 242
Dress codes, restaurants, 132
Drink, 278
Drinking laws, 350
Driving rules, 349
Dr. Paul Dudley White Charles River Bike Path, 197, 201
DSW Shoe Warehouse, 240
Duck Tours, Boston, 188–189

E

Eastern Standard, 277
East Gloucester, 316
Eating and drinking, 31. *See also* Food stores and markets; Restaurants
picnic provisions, 120
tours for foodies, 196
Eddie Bauer Outlet, 240
Electricity, 350
Elephant Walk, 196
1154 Lill studio, 242
Embassies and consulates, 350
Emerald Necklace, 173
Emergencies, 350
Emerson, Ralph Waldo, 291, 294, 295
House (Concord), 296
Emmanuel Church, 212

Emmanuel Music, 264
Equal Exchange Cafe, 281
Ermenegildo Zegna, 241
Escapes North, 300
Escorted tours, 41
Esplanade, 201
Essex, 313
Essex Street Pedestrian Mall (Salem), 309
The Estate, 269
Exeter Street Theater, 211

F

Families with children, 351
best activities for, 12–13
books for, 27
hotels, 80
restaurants, 118
School Vacation Week, 34
shopping, 244, 253
sightseeing, 184–187
theater, 266–267
Family Explorer Kit (Concord), 294
Faneuil Hall, 140, 151, 159, 214
Faneuil Hall Marketplace, 137, 160, 184, 249–250
accommodations near, 63–70
food court, 216
outdoor seating, 123
quick bites and picnic provisions, 120
restaurants, 109–110
shopping, 232
Farmer's markets, 250
Fashion (clothing), 240–244
vintage and secondhand, 253–254
The Fenway, 49–50
restaurants, 122–123
Fenway Park, 202–204
Ferries, 192, 344
Fiedler, Arthur, statue of, 210
54th Massachusetts Colored Regiment, 151
Filene's Basement, 231, 240
Films, 29–30, 36, 38
theaters, 282–283
The Financial District, 46
accommodations, 68–70
restaurants, 109–110
First Baptist Church, 211
First Friday Open Studios, 235
First Night, 39

First Public School, 155–156
Fitcorp, 198
Fitz Henry Lane (Gloucester), 318
Flat Top Johnny's, 282
Flight Line, 340
Fogg Museum (Cambridge), 178, 224
Folk music, 270–271
Food stores and markets, 120, 244
Football, 204
Forest Hills Cemetery, 183
Fort Sewall (Marblehead), 301
Foster's Rotunda, 169
The Fours, 280
Fourth of July concert at the Hatch Shell, 263
Franklin, Benjamin
  birthplace, 157
  Statue, 155
Franklin Park Zoo, 187
Freedom Trail, 150–166, 188
Freedom Trail Foundation, 151, 153, 172
Freedom Trail Players, 151
Freedom Trail Week, 35
Free Friday Flicks at the Hatch Shell, 282
Free or almost free activities, 7–8, 264
French, Daniel Chester, 168, 210, 213, 218, 221, 293
French Library Alliance Française, 194
Fresh Pond Golf Course, 198
Frette, 247
Fridays at Trinity, 264
Friendship (ship), 308
Friends of Mount Auburn Cemetery (Cambridge), 176
Friends of the Boston Harbor Islands, 199
Frog Pond, 173, 200
Fung Wah, 342

G
Galería Cubana, 236
Gallery Guide, 235
Gallery Naga, 236
Game On! Sports Cafe, 280
The Games People Play, 253
The Garment District, 254

Gays and lesbians, 352
  bars and clubs, 279–280
  Boston Pride Parade, 36
Georges Island, 199
Ghosts & Gravestones, 196
Gibson House Museum, 170
Gifts and souvenirs, 245–246
Glass Flowers (Cambridge), 177
Globe Corner Bookstore, 237
Globus and Cosmos, 41
Gloucester, 312–321
Gloucester Fisherman (statue), 314
Gloucester Stage Company, 317
Go Boston Card, 140
Golf, 198, 204–205
Government Center Garage, 348
Graduate School of Government (Cambridge), 229
Grafton Street, 275
Granary Burying Ground, 154
The Grand Canal, 278
Grape Island, 199
Grasshopper Shop (Concord), 298
Greater Boston Convention & Visitors Bureau, 39
Great Scott, 272
Green Street, 278
Greenward, 247
Grendel's Den, 275
Greyhound, 340, 342
Grolier Poetry Book Shop, 237
Gropius House (Concord), 297–298
Guerrilla Queer Bar, 279
Gyms, 198, 200

H
Habitat for Humanity, 41
Halibut Point State Park, 324–325
Hamilton, Alexander, statue, 211
Handel & Haydn Society, 263
H&M, 242
Harbor Express, 339
Harbor Sweets (Salem), 310
The Harborwalk, 149
Hard Rock Cafe, 273
Hart Nautical Galleries (Cambridge), 179

Harvard, John, statue of (Cambridge), 218, 221, 222
Harvard Art Museums (Cambridge), 178
Harvard Book Store (Cambridge), 238
Harvard College Observatory (Cambridge), 179
Harvard Coop (Cambridge), 219, 239
Harvard Film Archive (Cambridge), 283
Harvard Hall (Cambridge), 220
Harvard Lampoon Castle (Cambridge), 228
Harvard Museum of Natural History (Cambridge), 177–178, 225
Harvard Square (Cambridge), 174–175
  restaurants, 124–128
  shopping, 232
  walking tour, 219–229
Harvard University (Cambridge), 175–178
  football, 204
  hockey, 205
Harvard Yard (Cambridge), 220
Harvard-Yenching Library (Cambridge), 225
Hatch Shell, 210, 257
Haunted Happenings (Salem), 306
Havana Club, 269
Hawthorne, Nathaniel, 295, 304
  House of the Seven Gables (Salem), 307
  The Wayside (Concord), 296
Haymarket, 160
Head of the Charles Regatta (Boston and Cambridge), 38, 206
Health concerns, 351
Healthworks, 200
Heart of the Freedom Trail tour, 188
Helen's Leather Shop, 252
Henry Bear's Park, 253
Heritage Days (Salem), 306
Hermès of Paris, 241
High Gear Jewelry, 248
Hiking, 200

Hi-Rise at the Blacksmith House (Cambridge), 227
Historic houses, 169–172
  Lexington, 289–290
Historic New England, 170, 194
History of Boston, 17–28
  tours for history buffs, 194
Hockey, 205
Holden Chapel (Cambridge), 220
Holidays, 33
Hollis Hall (Cambridge), 220
Holyoke Center (Cambridge), 228
Home and garden products, 246–248
The Hong Kong, 275
Horse racing, 205
Hospitals, 351
Host Homes of Boston, 98
Hotels. *See* Accommodations
House of Blues, 271
The House of the Seven Gables (Salem), 307
Huntington Theatre Company, 265

I
Ice skating, 200
Improv Asylum, 268
ImprovBoston, 268
Independence Wharf, 169
Independent Designer's Market, 251
Independent Film Festival of Boston, 36
Injeanius, 242
InLine Club of Boston, 201
In-line skating, 200–201
Inn Boston Reservations, 98
Insight Vacations, 41
Institute of Contemporary Art, 140–141
Insurance, 351
  auto, 347
International Poster Gallery, 236
Internet and Wi-Fi, 351–352
In Your Ear Records, 251
Ipswich Essex Explorer, 320
Irish bars, 278–279
Isabella Stewart Gardner Museum, 141–142, 264, 272
Italian-American Feasts, 37
Itineraries, suggested, 50–59

J
Jacques Cabaret, 279
Jamaica Plain, 183
James Rego Square (Paul Revere Mall), 162
Jazz and blues clubs, 271–272
Jazz Club at the Multicultural Arts Center, 260, 271
Jazz Week, 271
Jenney Pond (Plymouth), 329
Jeremiah Lee Mansion/ Marblehead Museum & Historical Society, 302–303
Jerry Remy's Sports Bar & Grill, 280
Jewelry, 248
Jillian's Boston, 282
Jogging, 201
John Adams Courthouse, 195
John F. Kennedy National Historic Site, 170–171
John F. Kennedy Park (Cambridge), 229
John F. Kennedy Presidential Library and Museum, 142–144
John Harvard's Brew House, 277
John Joseph Moakley U.S. Courthouse, 194, 218
John Lewis, Inc., 248
Johnny Cupcakes, 242
Johnny D's Uptown Restaurant & Music Club, 270
Joie de Vivre, 246
JP Licks Homemade Ice Cream, 183

K
kate spade, 241
Kendall Square Cinema (Cambridge), 283
Kendall Square Community Skating (Cambridge), 200–201
Kenmore Square, 49
  restaurants, 122–123
Kennedy, John F.
  National Historic Site, 170–171
  statue of, 152
Kennedy, Rose Fitzgerald, 163

Kiehl's Since 1851, 251–252
King Hooper Mansion/ Marblehead Arts Association & Gallery, 303
Kings, 282
King's Chapel and Burying Ground, 155
King's Chapel Noon Hour Recitals, 264
Koo De Kir, 247
Kulturez, 254

L
L. A. Burdick Chocolates (Cambridge), 227
Lacrosse, 202
Lafayette House (Marblehead), 301–302
Landry's Bicycles, 198
La Perla, 241
Legal aid, 352
Legends Tour, 205
Le Grand David and His Own Spectacular Magic Company, 267
Lekker, 247
Lexington, 285–290
Lexington Historical Society, 289
Liberty Ride (Lexington), 288
Liberty Travel, 41
Life is Good, 242
Lilac Sunday, 36
Lily's Apothecary (Plymouth), 334
LimoLiner, 342
LinkPass, 140, 345
List Visual Arts Center (Cambridge), 179
Little Brewster Island, 191
The Littlest Bar, 278
Little Women (Alcott), 295–296
Lizard Lounge, 270
Lobster Tales (Plymouth), 331
Loeb Drama Center (Cambridge), 266
Logan Airport, accommodations at and near, 94–96
Logan International Airport, 338
Longfellow, Henry Wadsworth, 286

Longfellow Bridge, 190
Longfellow House–
  Washington's
  Headquarters
  National Historic Site
  (Cambridge), 175
Long Wharf, 190, 215, 217
Longy School of Music, 264
Looc Boutique, 243
Looks, 243
Lorem Ipsum Books, 238
Louis Boston, 243
Louisburg Square, 181
Lovells Island, 199
Lush, 252
Lux Bond & Green, 248
Lyric Stage, 266

M

Machine, 279
Magic Beans, 253
Mail, 352–353
Main Street Antiques
  (Plymouth), 334
Make Way for Ducklings, 209
Malls and shopping centers,
  249–250
Manchester-Boston Regional
  Airport, 340
Mapparium, 168–169
Marathon, Boston, 205
Marblehead, 300–304
Marblehead Arts Association
  & Gallery, 303
Marblehead Museum &
  Historical Society,
  302–303
Marblehead Neck Wildlife
  Sanctuary, 302
Marc by Marc Jacobs, 241
Marimekko Concept Store,
  247
Markets, 250–251. *See also*
  Food stores and markets
Martha Richardson Fine Art,
  236
Martin Luther King, Jr.,
  Birthday Celebration, 33
Mary Baker Eddy Library,
  168–169
Mascio-Ricci (Concord), 298
Massachusetts Audubon
  Society, 40, 41
Massachusetts Avenue (Mass.
  Ave), 49

Massachusetts Bay
  Transportation Authority
  (MBTA), 343–344
Massachusetts Golf
  Association, 198
Massachusetts Hall
  (Cambridge), 220
Massachusetts Institute
  of Technology (MIT;
  Cambridge), 179
Massachusetts Office of
  Travel & Tourism, 360
Massachusetts State House,
  152–153
MassBike, 198
MassPort, 338
Mather family, 181
Mayflower, 329
Mayflower II, 331–332
M Bar and Lounge, 277
MBTA (Massachusetts
  Bay Transportation
  Authority), 343–344
Media Lab (Cambridge), 179
Medical requirements for
  entry, 353
MegaBus, 342
Memorial Church
  (Cambridge), 223
Memorial Drive, in-line
  skating, 201
Memorial Drive (Cambridge),
  197
Memorial Hall (Cambridge),
  225
Ménage Gallery (Gloucester),
  318–319
The Middle East, 272–273
Minuteman Bikeway, 197
Minute Man National
  Historical Park, 285, 288,
  292–293
Minuteman statue
  (Lexington), 288–289
Minute Man Visitor Center
  (Lexington), 288
Miracle of Science Bar +
  Grill, 275
MIT (Massachusetts
  Institute of Technology;
  Cambridge), 179
MIT Coop (Cambridge), 238
MIT Museum (Cambridge),
  179
Mobile phones, 353
Modern Pastry, 107

Modern Theatre, 260
Money and costs, 354–355
Monument Square
  (Concord), 298
Motif No. 1 (Rockport), 324
Mottley's Comedy Club,
  268–269
Mount Auburn Cemetery
  (Cambridge), 175, 176
Movies
  theaters, 282–283
  tours for movie fans, 195–196
Moxie, 252
Mr. Dooley's Boston Tavern,
  278–279
Mud Puddle Toys
  (Marblehead), 303
Mugar Omni Theater, 147–148
Museum of African American
  History, 169
Museum of Fine Arts, 144–
  145, 184, 246, 276
Museum of Science, 146–148,
  184
Museums, best, 10–12
Museums on Us, 140
Music, 30
  classical, 262–264
  folk, 270–271
  jazz and blues, 271–272
Music stores, 251
Mystery Train (Gloucester),
  318

N

Nameless Coffeehouse
  (Cambridge), 270
Nanette Lepore, 241
Nashoba Brook Bakery
  (Concord), 298
National Heritage Museum,
  290
National Offshore One
  Design (NOOD) Regatta
  (Marblehead), 301
Navy Yard Visitor Center, 165
NCAA Men's Basketball
  Tournament East
  Regional, 34
Neighborhoods
  in brief, 43–50
  exploring, 180–183
Newbury Comics, 251
Newbury Street, 211, 241
  art galleries, 235
Newbury Yarns, 239

New England Aquarium, 148–150, 184, 217
whale watches, 193
New England Conservatory of Music, 264
The New England Holocaust Memorial, 160–161
New England Patriots, 204
New England Revolution, 202
Newspapers and magazines, 355
Newton Commonwealth Golf Course, 198
New Yard (Cambridge), 221
Nichols House Museum, 171
Nightlife, 256–283
bars, 274–280
clubs and music, 267–273
coffeehouses, 280–282
comedy clubs, 268–269
current listings, 256
films, 282–283
lectures and readings, 283
performing arts, 257–267
pool and bowling, 282
tickets, 256
Norman B. Leventhal Walk to the Sea, 149
North Bridge Visitor Center (Concord), 292
Northeastern University, hockey team, 205
Northeastern University Bookstore, 238
The North End, 43, 188
accommodations, 63–70
exploring, 181–182
restaurants, 104–108
shopping, 232
North End Market Tours, 196
Northern Avenue Bridge, 217
North Market building, 137
The North Shore, 299–327
North Shore Arts Association (Gloucester), 316
North Station, 46
accommodations near, 70–72
The Nutcracker, 38

O

Oak Bar, 277–278
Observatories, 179
Oktoberfest (Cambridge), 38
Old Burying Ground (Cambridge), 227

Old City Hall, 156
Old Corner Bookstore Building, 156
Old Ironsides. See USS Constitution
The Old Manse (Concord), 295
Old North Church, 35, 162–164
Old South Church, music program, 265
Old South Meeting House, 156–157
Old State House Museum, 157–158, 214
Old Town House (Marblehead), 302
Old Town (Marblehead), 300
Old Town Trolley Tours, 190
Old Yard (Cambridge), 220
Olmsted, Frederick Law, 173, 174
Oona's Experienced Clothing, 254
Open studio days, 235
Opera Boston, 263
Operation Sail, 37
Orchard House (Concord), 295–296
Orpheum Theater, 260
Otis House Museum, 171–172
Outdoor activities, 8–10, 196–201
Out of Town News (Cambridge), 219

P

Paper House (Rockport), 325
Paper Source, 239
Paradise, 280
Paradise Rock Club, 273
Paramount Center, 260
Parcel 7 Garage, 348
Parking, 348
Parks and gardens, 173–174
Park Street Church, 153
Passports, 355–356
Patriots' Day, 35
Paul Revere House, 161–162
Paul Revere Mall (James Rego Square), 162
"Paul Revere's Ride" (Longfellow), 286
Peabody Essex Museum (Salem), 304, 307

Peabody Museum of Archaeology & Ethnology (Cambridge), 177–178, 225
Peddocks Island, 199
Penzeys, 244
The Perfect Storm (Junger), 316
Performing arts, 257–267
Perfume and cosmetics, 251–252
Peter Pan/Bonanza, 340, 342
PhotoWalks, 194
Pickering Wharf (Salem), 309, 311
Picnic provisions, 120
Pierce/Hichborn House, 161
Pierre Lallement Bike Path, 197
Pilgrim Belle Cruises (Plymouth), 331
Pilgrim Hall Museum (Plymouth), 332
Pilgrim Memorial State Park (Plymouth), 329
Pilgrim's Progress (Plymouth), 334
The Place, 275
Planetarium, Charles Hayden, 148
PlanetTran, 339
Planning your trip, 338–361
Plimoth Plantation (Plymouth), 332–334
The Plough & Stars, 279
Plymouth, 327–336
Plymouth & Brockton, 342
Plymouth Rock, 329
Polcari's Coffee, 244
Police, 356
Pool, 282
Popular culture, 27–30
Porter Exchange Mall (Cambridge), food court, 131
Porter Square Books (Cambridge), 238
Provincetown, day trips to, 192
Provincetown II, 192
Provincetown III, 192
Prudential Center
garage, 348
The Shops at, 250
Prudential Information Center, 360

Public Garden, 173, 208–209
Pucker Gallery, 236
Puerto Rican Festival &
  Parade, 37
Puppet Showplace Theatre,
  267
The Purple Shamrock, 275

Q

Quincy Market, 137, 160

R

Radcliffe Yard (Cambridge),
  227
Radius, 275
Rainfall, average, 39
Ralph Waldo Emerson House
  (Concord), 296
Ramrod, 279–280
Raven Used Books, 238
Red Sox Opening Day, 34–35
The Red Wagon, 244
Regattabar, 271–272
Reservations, restaurants,
  132
Responsible travel, 39–40
Restaurants, 100–134. *See
  also* Restaurant Index
  afternoon tea, 121
  alfresco, 123
  the Back Bay, 117–120
  Beacon Hill, 112
  best, 6–7, 100
  breakfast and brunch, 109
  Cambridge, 124–132
  Chinatown/Theater District,
    112–115
  by cuisine, 133–134
  dim sum, 113
  Downtown Crossing, 111
  eco-friendly, 39–40
  family-friendly, 118
  Faneuil Hall Marketplace
    and Financial District,
    109–110
  Gloucester, 321
  gluten-free, 114
  Kenmore Square, the
    Fenway and Brookline,
    122–123
  late-night, 283
  Lexington, 290
  Marblehead, 304
  the North End, 104–108
  Plymouth, 335–336

practical information,
  132–133
price categories, 101
quick bites and picnic
  provisions, 120
Rockport, 327
Salem, 311–312
the South End, 115–117
steakhouse chains, 117
the Waterfront, 101–104
Restaurant Week, 111
Retire Beckett House
  (Salem), 307
Revere, Paul, 285–286
  grave of, 154
  House, 161–162
Richardson, H. H., 211, 212,
  223
Road Scholar, 40
Robert Gould Shaw
  Memorial, 172
Robert Klein Gallery, 235,
  236
Rockport, 321–327
Rockport Art Association,
  324
Rockport Chamber Music
  Festival, 323
Rocky Neck Art Colony
  (Gloucester), 316–317
Rose Fitzgerald Kennedy
  Greenway, 216
Rose Kennedy Greenway
  Boston Harbor Islands
  Visitor Center Pavilion,
  199
Rowes Wharf, 217
Rowes Wharf Water
  Transport, 339
Rowing, 206
Royale Boston, 269
Rumor, 279
Ruth and Carl J. Shapiro
  Rotunda, 144
Ryles Jazz Club, 272

S

Sacred Cod, 152
Sacred Heart Church, 162
Safety concerns, 356
Sailing, 201
St. Francis Gift & Book Store,
  246
St. Michael's Thrift Shop
  (Marblehead), 303

St. Patrick's Day
  Celebrations, 34
St. Peter's Fiesta
  (Gloucester), 316
St. Stephen's Church, 163
Salem, 304–313
Salem Chamber of
  Commerce, 306
Salem Haunted Happenings,
  38
Salem Maritime Festival, 306
Salem Maritime National
  Historic Site, 308–309
Salem Trolley, 306
Salem Willows, 307
Salem Witch Museum, 309
Sales tax, 231
Salumeria Italiana, 244
Sanders Theatre
  (Cambridge), 225, 260
Sargent, John Singer, 144
Savenor's Market, 120
Schoenhof's Foreign Books,
  238–239
School Vacation Week, 34
Schooner Festival
  (Gloucester), 316
Science Center (Cambridge),
  225, 264
Scribe Paper & Gift
  (Marblehead), 303
Scullers Jazz Club, 272
Seasons, 32–33
Second Time Around, 254
Seed Stitch Fine Yarn
  (Salem), 309
Semitic Museum
  (Cambridge), 225
Senior travel, 356–357
Sephora, 252
Seven Seas Whale Watch
  (Gloucester), 312
75 State St. Garage, 348
Sever Hall (Cambridge), 223
Shake the Tree, 246
Shalin Liu Performance
  Center (Rockport), 323
Shoes and boots, 252–253
Shopping, 231–254
  antiques and collectibles,
    234
  art galleries, 234–237
  best, 13–15
  bookstores, 237–239
  college merchandise, 238
  crafts, 239–240

discount, 240
fashion (clothing), 240–244
food stores and markets, 244
home and garden, 246–248
jewelry, 248
Lexington, 290
malls and shopping centers, 249–250
markets, 250–251
music stores, 251
perfume and cosmetics, 251–252
sales tax, 231
shoes and boots, 252–253
toys and games, 253
The Shops at Prudential Center, 250
Shubert Theatre, 265
Shubie's (Marblehead), 304
Sights and attractions, 136–206
Cambridge, 174–179
Freedom Trail, 150–166
historic houses, 169–172
for kids, 184–187
neighborhoods to explore, 180–183
organized tours, 188–195
parks and gardens, 173–174
top attractions, 136–150
Signature Stationers (Lexington), 290
Silvertone Bar & Grill, 275
Simon Pearce, 248
Simons IMAX Theatre, 149
Singing Beach, 320
Skywalk Observatory at the Prudential Center, 146
Sleepy Hollow Cemetery (Concord), 296
Smoking, 63, 357
Soccer, 202
Society of Arts and Crafts, 239
Somerville Theater, 283
South Boston Waterfront/ Seaport District, 48
accommodations, 73–75
South Bridge Boathouse (Concord), 292
The South End, 48, 231
accommodations, 77
restaurants, 115–117
sights and attractions, 182
South End Buttery, 182

South Market building, 137
South Station Transportation Center, 342
SoWa Artists Guild, 235
SoWa district, 235
SoWa Open Market, 250–251
Spectacle Island, 199
Spectator sports, 202–206
Sports bars, 280
Sports Museum of New England, 202
Stage Fort Park (Gloucester), 316, 320
Stata Center (Cambridge), 179
State Street, 214
Stellabella Toys, 253
Stereo Jack's, 251
Stoughton Hall (Cambridge), 220
Street Performers Festival, 36
Stuart Street Playhouse, 283
Subway, 344
Sudo Shoes, 252–253
Suffolk Downs, 205
Suffolk University Bookstore, 238
Swan Boats, 173, 209
Swan Boats Return to the Public Garden, 35
Sweet Beads (Lexington), 290
Symphony Hall, 262

T

Tanglewood, 263
Tanner Rock Fountain (Cambridge), 225
Tauck World Discovery, 41
Taxes, 357
Taxis, 345
airport, 339
TD Garden, 202, 262
Telecharge, 256
Telephones, 357–358
Television shows, 30
Temperatures, average, 39
Tennis, 201
Tercentenary Theater (Cambridge), 221–222
T.F. Green Airport (Providence, Rhode Island), 340
Thanksgiving Celebration (Plymouth), 38

Theater, 265–267
Theater District
accommodations, 75–76
restaurants, 112–115
Thinking Cup, 281
1369 Coffee House, 281
Thomas E. Lannon (Gloucester), 317
Thomas Pink, 243
Thoreau, Henry David, 291, 294
Walden Pond State Reservation (Concord), 293
Ticketmaster, 256
Tidal Edge Gallery (Rockport), 326
Time zones, 358
Tipping, 358–359
TistiK, 239
Toad, 273
Toad Hall Bookstore (Rockport), 326
Toilets, 359
Topaz, 248
Top of the Hub, 276
The Tortoise & Hare, 213
"Tory Row" (Cambridge), 175
Tours, 40–41, 188–195. See also Walking tours
orientation, 188–190
Plymouth, 330–332
sightseeing cruises, 190–192
specialty, 193–195
trolley, 189–190
Townshend Acts (1767), 20, 22
Toys and games, 253
Toy Shop of Concord, 298
Trader Joe's, 120, 244
Trafalgar Tours, 41
Train travel, 341–342
Transportation, 343–349
eco-friendly, 40
Traveler's checks, 355
Traveling to Boston, 338–343
Trident Booksellers & Café, 281–282
Trinity Church, 212
Trolleys, 344
Trolley tours, 189–190
T.T. the Bear's Place, 270
Tuck's Candy Factory (Rockport), 326
21st Amendment, 276
Twilight, 242

U

Union Park Street, 182
University Hall (Cambridge),
    221
Unofficial Tours, 188
Upper Deck Trolley Tours,
    190
Upstairs Downstairs
    Antiques, 234
Urban Adventours, 194, 198
USS *Constitution* Museum,
    165, 184
USS *Constitution* (Old
    Ironsides), 164–165
    cruises, 191

V

The Velvet Fly, 254
Vendome Memorial, 211
Via Matta, 276
Victorian Back Bay, 188
Vintage and secondhand
    clothing, 253
Visas, 359–360
Visitor information, 360
    Concord, 291
    Gloucester, 314
    Lexington, 288
    Marblehead, 300–301
    Plymouth, 328
    Rockport, 323
Volunteer and working
    trips, 41
Vose Galleries of Boston,
    235, 236–237

W

Wadsworth House
    (Cambridge), 219
Walden Pond State
    Reservation (Concord),
    293
Walking, 343
Walking tours
    guided, 188–189
    self-guided, 208
    the Back Bay, 208–213
    Harvard Square
        (Cambridge), 219–229
    the Waterfront, 214–218
Walk to the Sea, Norman B.
    Leventhal, 149
Wally's Cafe, 272
Wang YMCA of Chinatown,
    198
WardMaps LLC, 246
Washington, George, statue
    of, 210
Washington's Headquarters
    National Historic Site
    (Cambridge), 175
The Waterfront, 43
    accommodations, 63–70
    restaurants, 101–104
    walking tour, 214–218
Water Street (Plymouth),
    334
Water taxis, 346
The Wayside (Concord), 296
Weather, 32–33
West Concord 5 & 10, 298

The Western Front, 270
WGBH LearningTours, 40
Whale Center of New
    England (Gloucester),
    312
Whale-watching, 312, 331
Wheelchair accessibility, 357
Wheelock Family Theatre,
    267
White-Ellery House
    (Gloucester), 318
Widener Library
    (Cambridge), 222–223
Wilbur Theatre, 262
William J. Devine Golf
    Course, 198
Willoughby's (Rockport),
    326
Windsor Button, 240
Wingaersheek Beach, 320
Wish, 243
Witchcraft trial (Salem), 304
World Music, 264
World Wide Bus, 342
Wrentham Village Premium
    Outlets, 243

Y

Yankee Whale Watch
    (Gloucester), 312

Z

Zero Post Office Square, 348
Zipcar, 40
ZuZu, 273

Accommodations

Ames, 68

Anthony's Town House, 88

Atlantis Oceanfront Inn (Gloucester), 319

The Back Bay Hotel, 81–82

Bass Rocks Ocean Inn (Gloucester), 319–320

Best Western Cold Spring (Plymouth), 334

Best Western Hotel Tria (Cambridge), 93

Best Western Plus Boston/ The Inn at Longwood Medical, 87–88

Boston Harbor Hotel, 63, 66, 271

Boston Marriott Copley Place, 82

Boston Marriott Long Wharf, 66

The Boston Park Plaza Hotel & Towers, 82

Bulfinch Hotel, 72

Captain's Bounty on the Beach (Rockport), 326

Chandler Inn Hotel, 77

The Charles Hotel (Cambridge), 89

Charlesmark Hotel, 84

Coach House Inn (Salem), 310

Colonnade Hotel Boston, 78

Comfort Inn & Suites Boston/ Airport, 95–96

Concord's Colonial inn, 298

Copley Square Hotel, 82–83

Courtyard Boston Brookline, 87

Courtyard Boston Cambridge, 93–94

Doubletree Guest Suites, 87

Doubletree Hotel Boston Downtown, 76

Eliot Hotel, 78

Embassy Suites Hotel Boston at Logan Airport, 95

Emerson Inn by the Sea (Rockport), 326

Fairmont Battery Wharf, 66

The Fairmont Copley Plaza, 78–79

Fenway Summer Hostel, 88

XV Beacon, 71

40 Berkeley, 77

Four Seasons Hotel, 79

Hampton Inn Boston/ Cambridge, 90

Hampton Inn Boston Logan Airport, 95

Harbor Light Inn (Marblehead), 303–304

Harborside Inn, 67

Harvard Square Hotel (Cambridge), 94

Hawthorne Hotel (Salem), 310–312

Hilton Boston Back Bay, 83

Hilton Boston Financial District, 68

Hilton Boston Logan Airport, 95

Hilton Garden Inn (Plymouth), 334

Holiday Inn Boston at Beacon Hill, 72

The Holiday Inn Boston Brookline, 87

Holiday Inn Express Hotel & Suites Boston Garden, 71

Holiday Inn Express Hotel & Suites (Cambridge), 93

Hostelling International- Boston, 86

Hotel Commonwealth, 86–87

Hotel Marlowe (Cambridge), 90

Hotel 140, 84

Hotel Veritas (Cambridge), 89

Hyatt Harborside, 94–95

Hyatt Regency Boston Financial District, 68–69

The Hyatt Regency Cambridge, 90, 92

The Inn at Harvard (Cambridge), 92

Inn on Cove Hill (Caleb Norwood Jr. House; Rockport), 326

Inn @ St. Botolph, 81

Intercontinental Boston, 66–67

John Carver Inn & Spa (Plymouth), 335

The John Hancock Hotel & Conference Center, 85

The Langham, Boston, 69

Le Méridien Cambridge, 92

The Lenox Hotel, 79

The Liberty Hotel, 71

Longwood Inn, 88

Mandarin Oriental, Boston, 80–81

The Midtown Hotel, 85

Millennium Bostonian Hotel, 67

Newbury Guest House, 85

Nine Zero, 69

Omni Parker House, 70

Onyx Hotel, 71–72

Pilgrim Sands on Long Beach (Plymouth), 335

Radisson Hotel Boston, 76

Radisson Hotel Plymouth Harbor, 334

Renaissance Boston Waterfront Hotel, 74

Residence Inn Boston Harbor on Tudor Wharf, 73

The Ritz-Carlton, Boston Common, 75

Royal Sonesta Hotel (Cambridge), 90

The Salem Inn, 311

Salem Waterfront Hotel, 310

Seaport Hotel, 74–75

Sheraton Boston Hotel, 83

Sheraton Commander Hotel (Cambridge), 93

Taj Boston, 81

W Boston, 75–76

The Westin Boston Waterfront, 74

The Westin Copley Place Boston, 84

Restaurants

Abe & Louie's, 117
ArtBar (Cambridge), 123
Artú, 106–107, 112
Bangkok City, 119–120
Baraka Café (Cambridge), 130
Barking Crab, 104
Bertucci's, 114
Bertucci's (Lexington), 290
Bond Restaurant & Lounge, 121
Border Café (Cambridge), 126–127
Brasserie Jo, 119
Bricco, 283
Bristol, 121
the Bristol Lounge, 119
Café Jaffa, 120
Cafe Mami (Cambridge), 131
Cafe Vanille, 210
Caffè dello Sport, 104
Caffè Pompei, 283
Caffè Vittoria, 104
Capital grille, 117
Centre Street Café, 109, 183
Chacarero, 111
Charlie's Sandwich Shoppe, 109
Chau Chow City, 113
Cheers, 210
China Pearl, 113
Citizen Public House & Oyster Bar, 122
Clam Box (Gloucester), 313
Clover Food Lab, 111
Clover Food Lab (Cambridge), 127
Clover Food Truck (Cambridge), 131
Courtyard, 120, 121
Cupboard (Gloucester), 321
Daily Catch, 106
Dalí (Cambridge), 129
Dante (Cambridge), 123
Davio's Northern Italian Steakhouse, 114, 117–118
Dogwood Café, 183
Driftwood Restaurant (Marblehead), 304
Durgin-Park, 110
East Coast Grill & Raw Bar (Cambridge), 128
Elephant Walk, 109, 114

The Elephant Walk, 122
Elephant Walk (Cambridge), 129
Fajitas & 'Ritas, 111
Figs, 120
Finale, 122, 266
Finale (Cambridge), 124
Finz (Salem), 311
Fleming's Prime Steakhouse & Wine Bar, 112, 117
Franklin Cape Ann (Gloucester), 321
Galleria Umberto Rosticceria, 108
Garden at the Cellar (Cambridge), 127
Giacomo's Ristorante, 107
GiGi, 104
Great Harvest Bread Co. (Lexington), 290
Great Taste Bakery & Restaurant, 113
Grill 23 & Bar, 117, 118
Grotto, 112
Halibut Point Restaurant & Bar (Gloucester), 321
Hamersley's Bistro, 109, 115
Hei La Moon, 113
The Helmand (Cambridge), 130
Henrietta's Table, 123
Henrietta's Table (Cambridge), 124, 126
Hungry Mother (Cambridge), 129
Il Panino Express, 120
India Pavilion (Cambridge), 131
International House of Pancakes, 283
Jacob Wirth Company, 114
Japonaise Bakery (Cambridge), 131
Jasper White's Summer Shack, 119
Jasper White's Summer Shack (Cambridge), 129–130
Johnny D's Uptown Restaurant & Music Club (Cambridge), 130
J. T. Farnham's (Essex), 313
Kiskadee Coffee Company (Plymouth), 335
La Summa, 107–108

Latitude 43 Restaurant & Bar (Gloucester), 321
La Verdad Taqueria Mexicana, 122–123
Legal Sea Foods, 101, 113, 114
Legal Sea Foods (Cambridge), 124, 129
Lobby, 121
Lobsta Land (Gloucester), 321
Lobster Pool (Rockport), 327
Lounge, 121
The Lyceum (Salem), 311–312
McCormick & Schmick's Seafood Restaurant, 109, 112
Maggiano's Little Italy, 112
Mamma Maria, 104–105
Map Room Café, 120
Market, 112–113
Miel, 123
Mike's Pastry, 104, 181
Milk Street Cafe, 110
Morton's of Chicago, 117
Mr. Bartley's Burger Cottage (Cambridge), 127–128
Nashoba Brook Bakery & Café (Concord), 299
Nebo, 114
Neptune Oyster, 106
Oak Room, 117
Oleana, 123
Oleana (Cambridge), 128–129
Orinoco, 115–116
Other Side Cafe, 114
Palm, 117
Panificio, 210
Paramount, 109
Parish Cafe and Bar, 123
Peach Farm, 114–115
Peet's Coffee & Tea (Lexington), 290
Persy's Place (Plymouth), 336
P. F. Chang's China Bistro, 112, 114, 119
Picco Restaurant, 117
In a Pig's Eye (Salem), 311
Pizzeria Regina, 108
Plymouth Lobster Hut, 336
Redbones, 131
Rockport Helmut's Strudel (Rockport), 327
Rowes Wharf Sea Grille, 121

Roy Moore Lobster Company (Rockport), 327
Russell House Tavern (Cambridge), 126
Ruth's Chris Steak House, 117
Salem Beer Works, 311
Sam Diego's (Plymouth), 335
S&S Restaurant (Cambridge), 109, 131–132
Sapporo Ramen (Cambridge), 131
Sel de la Terre, 101, 104
Shay's Pub & Wine Bar, 123
Smith & Wollensky, 117

South End Buttery, 116
South Street Diner, 283
Stephanie's on Newbury, 123
Sultan's Kitchen, 110
Swans, 121
Tampopo (Cambridge), 131
Taranta Cucina Meridionale, 105–106
Tealuxe (Cambridge), 121
Teranga, 116
Upper Crust (Lexington), 290
Upstairs on the Square (Cambridge), 121, 124

Veggie Planet (Cambridge), 128
Via Lago Café (Lexington), 290
Victoria Station (Salem), 311
Volle Nolle, 108, 120
Wagamama, 114
Winsor Dim Sum Cafe, 113
Woodman's of Essex, 313
Xinh Xinh, 115
Ye Olde Union Oyster House, 109
Zaftigs Delicatessen, 123

PHOTO CREDITS